Inequality in U.S. Social Policy

In the second edition of *Inequality in U.S. Social Policy: An Historic Analysis*, Bryan Warde illuminates the pervasive and powerful role that social inequality based on race and ethnicity, gender, immigration status, sexual orientation, class, and disability plays and has historically played in informing social policy.

Using critical race theory and other structural oppression theoretical frameworks, this book examines social inequalities as they relate to social welfare, education, housing, employment, health care, and child welfare, immigration, and criminal justice. With fully updated statistics throughout, and an examination of the impact of the COVID-19 pandemic on the United States, this new edition addresses the mammoth political and social changes that have affected inequality in the past few years.

Inequality in U.S. Social Policy will help social work students better understand the origins of the inequalities that their clients face, as well as provide an introduction for other social science students.

Bryan Warde is a professor at the City University of New York, Lehman College.

Inequality in U.S. Social Policy

An Historical Analysis

Second Edition

Bryan Warde

NEW YORK AND LONDON

Second edition published 2022
by Routledge
605 Third Avenue, New York, NY 10158

and by Routledge
2 Park Square, Milton Park, Abingdon, Oxon, OX14 4RN

Routledge is an imprint of the Taylor & Francis Group, an informa business

First edition published by Routledge 2017

Library of Congress Cataloging-in-Publication Data
Names: Warde, Bryan, author.
Title: Inequality in U.S. social policy : an historical analysis / Bryan Warde.
Description: Second edition. | New York, NY : Routledge Books, 2022. |
Includes bibliographical references and index.
Identifiers: LCCN 2021015609 (print) | LCCN 2021015610 (ebook) |
ISBN 9780367903114 (hbk) | ISBN 9780367903091 (pbk) |
ISBN 9781003023708 (ebk)
Subjects: LCSH: United States—Social policy. | United States—Social conditions. |
Equality—United States.
Classification: LCC HN59.2 .W365 2022 (print) | LCC HN59.2 (ebook) |
DDC 306.0973—dc23
LC record available at https://lccn.loc.gov/2021015609
LC ebook record available at https://lccn.loc.gov/2021015610

ISBN: 978-0-367-90311-4 (hbk)
ISBN: 978-0-367-90309-1 (pbk)
ISBN: 978-1-003-02370-8 (ebk)

DOI: 10.4324/9781003023708

Typeset in Joanna MT & Frutiger
by Apex CoVantage, LLC

Contents

Extended Table of Contents

Acknowledgments

Writing the second edition was surprisingly no less arduous than the first edition, even though I was updating information more than writing from scratch. As always, I could not have completed the second edition as a writing project without others' assistance. Primary among these others was my daughter Deanne Warde. My daughter and I had countless hours of conversation about the social issues proving tumultuous for the nation. These conversations helped me think about the social issues and how I could weave them into the narratives of each of the respective chapters in the book.

I also want to acknowledge my brothers Steven Warde and Richard Jones, my nephew Nadean Fosu, and my great friend from our undergraduate studies in the York College, CUNY, social work program, Felicia Brown. Each of them has believed in me and given me unconditional support in my writing and other endeavors to find my voice.

I want to acknowledge my parents, Ralph Warde and Doreen Jones, for the sacrifices they made as Guyanese immigrants to England in the 1960s to allow their English-born children to be all they could be.

And lastly, I want to thank Routledge for allowing me to write a second edition. It is very much appreciated.

Preface

When Routledge approached me about writing a second edition, I initially thought it was too early; not enough had changed socially to warrant updating the book. How wrong I was. The intervening years have arguably been among the most tumultuous in United States history. When the first edition was published, President Obama was coming to the end of his second term in office. And Donald Trump was one of several candidates vying to be the Republican presidential candidate. He was very much an outsider candidate who had name recognition but absolutely no political experience and seemingly little chance against a field of established and politically experienced challengers. However, Trump's Make America Great slogan and his not too veiled nativist call to build a southern border wall to keep undocumented Mexicans out of the United States struck a chord with millions of voting-age citizens. His election and four years in office were seismic in terms of influence on social policy, regardless of one's political persuasion. He passed more than 400 executive orders and proclamations that reshaped United States' immigration policies for both documented and undocumented immigrants. He ordered his administration to stop paying for critical race theory training in federal agencies, expanding the scope of this order to include the U.S. military, government contractors, and other federal grantees. In doing so, President Trump argued that critical race theory was an effort to indoctrinate government employees with divisive and harmful sex- and race-based ideology. There was also the rolling back of various protections for transgender people. Many of these protections were put in place by the Obama administration.

Even more influential, though, was the Coronavirus disease 2019 (COVID-19). This global pandemic reached the United States in January 2020, and, as of February 1, 2021, it had accounted for 26 million infections and 456,000 deaths. Although a global pandemic, Blacks, Hispanics, and Native Americans have been disproportionality impacted in terms of infections and fatalities. In turn, this disproportionality has shone a light on the preexisting residential, labor market, and health and health care inequalities, which in combination have made these populations more susceptible to infection and death.

The pandemic has also shattered the economy, as the shutdown necessary to slow the spread of COVID-19 ended up closing down hundreds of thousands of businesses. The consequence has been mass unemployment and economic suffering for millions of American citizens and residents, resulting in President Trump passing of the Coronavirus Aid, Relief, and Economic Security Act (the CARES Act) in March 2020. This $2.2 trillion economic stimulus bill went some way to cushion the economic fallout of the COVID-19 pandemic in the United States, but not nearly enough to aid a full economic recovery.

Race and racial tension also struck a profound chord with a series of police-involved deaths of Black men and women, the two most prominent being Breonna Taylor and George Floyd. The civil unrest that followed George Floyd's death led to a call in some quarters to defund the police.

And to close the tumultuous intervening years was the unprecedented U.S. Capitol Hill riot. It was an incident in which rioters, who believed the presidential election of Joe Biden was fraudulent, battled Capitol police, and broke into the U.S. Capitol building, forcing members of Congress, who were counting the Electoral College votes to confirm the presidential victory of Joe Biden, to flee. The riot concluded with five dead.

Notwithstanding all the turmoil of the intervening years, there have also been real policy and legal inroads into battling social inequality based on the intersecting and socially defined categories of race/ethnicity, gender, immigration status, sexual orientation/identity, class, and disability. These inroads and tumultuous backdrop warranted writing the second edition. A second edition that ends as Joe Biden begins his term as president with the promise to battle social inequality and expand opportunity for all.

In writing the second edition, I did not make any wholesale changes. The history remains the history. Instead, I provided updates to the contemporary discussions in the respective areas. I identified the new social policies and legal rulings that impact social inequality both in the timelines and in the chapter's body. Charts were also updated where necessary. Also, I replaced the term Native Indian with Native American in the way of changes. And I corrected some minor mistakes and omissions.

As with the first edition, the second edition uses critical race theory (CRT) and other structural oppression theoretical frameworks to analyze from an historical perspective how social inequality, intersecting or otherwise, has influenced the development of both human capital and social regulation policies. The human capital policies examined include social welfare benefits, housing, and labor, health care, education, and child welfare, while the social control policies examined include immigration and criminal justice. Also aiding in the examination are historical timelines, profiles, case studies, tables, photographs, and figures.

By reading this book, social work students, most particularly in a social policy introductory course, will develop the knowledge and skills needed to do the following:

1. Analyze and deconstruct the extent to which societal structures and values oppress, marginalize, alienate, create, or enhance privilege and power;
2. Confront the forms and mechanisms of oppression and discrimination, as well as countervailing systems of empowerment;
3. Critically analyze the sociopolitical factors shaping social policy and the delivery of services to marginalized populations; and
4. Critically examine the historical roots of current social inequalities experienced by particular groups.

The Organization of the Book

This book is divided into two parts. Part I, Chapters 1 through 4, provides the book's conceptual framework. To this end, Chapter 1 defines social policy and its associated concepts, as well as describes the social policy development process in the United States. Chapter 2 provides a brief historical overview of the development of social policy from the nation's colonial beginnings through to the end of the progressive era. Chapter 3 defines social inequality and its origins and contemporary manifestations in the United States as regards race/ethnicity, gender, social class, sexual orientation/identity, and disability. Chapter 4 describes the book's theoretical frameworks.

Part II, Chapters 5 through 12, is an historical and contemporary analysis of the relationship between social inequality and social policy across eight domains. These domains are immigration (Chapter 5), social welfare benefits (Chapter 6), housing (Chapter 7), labor market (Chapter 8), health and health care (Chapter 9), criminal justice (Chapter 10), education (Chapter 11), and child welfare (Chapter 12). Each chapter ends with retrieval and discussion questions for the students.

About the Author

Bryan Warde is a professor in the social work program at Lehman College of the City University of New York. He is a licensed clinical social worker and holds a PhD in social welfare. Before obtaining his doctorate in 2005, Dr. Warde's social work practice experience was in foster care, where he began as a casework assistant and then caseworker, supervisor, and eventually agency director. In his role as director, Dr. Warde was involved in formulating agency policy as well as participating in legislative advocacy for foster care reform. As a social work educator since 2005, Dr. Warde teaches in Lehman's BSW and MSW programs. In the BSW program, he regularly teaches the introductory social policy course, and in the MSW program, he teaches across the curriculum. Dr. Warde's research interests include the experiences of Black and Hispanic men in higher education, racial and ethnic disproportionality in the child welfare and criminal justice systems, and pedagogy in social work education. Dr. Warde has published two books: *Inequality in U.S. Social Policy: An Historical Analysis* and *We the People: Social Protest Movements and the Shaping of American Democracy*. He has also published articles in peer-reviewed journals and has presented at numerous social work conferences across the country.

CHAPTER 1
Social Policy

What Is Social Policy?

In the industrialized countries around the world, social policies are a major determinant of citizens' standard of living and general welfare (Gil, 1970). For example, most developed countries have social policies that provide its members with universal or nearly universal access to a host of social protections against changing life circumstances and the unpredictability of a market economy. These protections include health care across the life cycle (the United States being a notable exception), social assistance, and social insurance. In spite of its importance to the quality of life, there is no universally accepted definition of social policy; each country has a definition that reflects its political ideologies, values, history, cultural norms, economic system, and structural institutions.

In the United Kingdom, where the pioneering social researcher and professor Richard Titmuss is credited with establishing social policy as an academic discipline, social policy is the study of human well-being and the systems promoting it. Of particular interest for analysis are the policies that the government has adopted in relation to social security, housing, and social services (Titmuss, 1974). Also of interest are how these policies shape the nature of caring and maximize people's chances of a good life (Alcock & May, 2014; Dean, 2012).

Titmuss identified three models of social policy: the residual model, the industrial achievement-performance model, and the institutional redistributive model. The residual model is predicated on the belief that there are two channels through which individual needs are best met. These channels are the private market and the family; only when the private market breaks down should public social policy come into play and then only temporarily (Titmuss, 1974, p. 30). The industrial achievement-performance model posits that individual and social needs should be met on the basis of merit, work performance, and productivity, prompted by incentives and rewards (Titmuss, 1974, p. 31). The institutional redistributive model sees social policy as an integral part of society, providing universal access to resources outside of the market, based on need (Titmuss, 1974, p. 31).

In the United States, the *Social Work Dictionary* defines social policy as the activities and principles of a society that guide the way it intervenes in and regulates relationships between individuals, groups, communities, and social institutions. These principles and activities are shaped by society's values and customs and determine the distribution of resources and level of well-being for its people. Thus, social policies include plans and programs for education, health care, crime and corrections, economic security, and social welfare made by governments, voluntary organizations, and the people in general. It also includes social perspectives that result in society's rewards and constraints (Baker, 1991, p. 220).

Another perspective from within the United States views social policy as part of public policy and practice that deals with what Rittle and Weber (1973) describe as "wicked problems." These problems are perennial social or cultural problems that are difficult to resolve because of the number of people and contradictory opinions. Also making these problems difficult to resolve are the substantial economic burden of doing so, as well as the typically interconnected nature of the problem. In the United States, these problems include but are not limited to poverty, health and wellness, education, and social inequality.

DOI: 10.4324/9781003023708-1

Dissenting from the enhancement thesis, American sociologists and political activists Piven and Cloward (1971) define social policy as a mechanism for powerful elites to contain, manage, and regulate poor people. To contain, manage, and regulate the poor, social policies impose the cultural norms and mores of the powerful elites on them by way of policy rules of suitable behavior and sanctions for noncompliance. Conceptually informing these social policies have been religious doctrine and ideas such as predestination and Protestant values of hard work and self-reliance, racism, patriarchy, xenophobia, and the "survival of the fittest" mantra of Social Darwinism.

In a similar vein, Blau and Abramovitz (2004) suggest that social policy in the United States has not always contributed to the well-being of all of its citizens, especially those with less power. Examples include social policies that displaced Native Americans from their tribal homelands, legalized the enslavement and segregation of Blacks, excluded particular groups of immigrants, denied women basic civil rights, criminalized homosexuality, and penalized single motherhood (Blau & Abramovitz, 2004).

Broadly speaking, then, the common themes from these various definitions imply that social policy is a multidimensional construct. It includes the courses of actions that a society takes to enhance the well-being of its citizens or deal with wicked problems. It also has social control and discriminatory functions. These courses of actions cover a broad range of functioning, which include but are not limited to social welfare, health care, education, labor, criminal justice, and social inequality. It is a political and dynamic process, and through its resulting programs and institutions reflects a nation's ideologies, values, history, cultural norms, and economic system. It also tells us about who we are and how we relate to each other.

Political Ideologies and Social Policy

In the politically pluralistic United States, social policy choices do not derive from any one single source; rather, they are the product of the competing political ideologies of citizens, political parties, religious groups, special interest groups, think tanks, and monied interests. Political ideology, simply put, is a belief system (Sartori, 1969). It consists of a relatively coherent set of ideas about human nature, the proper role of government, and which types of social policies should be prioritized (Blau & Abramovitz, 2004). These ideas derive from a variety of sources, including personal and societal values, religious doctrine, traditions, myths, and principles.

In the United States, there are numerous political ideologies, including but not limited to conservatism, liberalism, libertarianism, radicalism, feminism, communism, socialism, Black nationalism, and fascism (Sargent, 2009). Despite the number of political ideologies, the traditional range of ideological debate in the United States has been limited to conservatism, liberalism, and to a lesser extent libertarianism (Sargent, 2009). The other political ideologies are considered outside of the mainstream of political debate, or, as in the case of libertarianism, radicalism, and feminism, are included on the continuum of conservatism or liberalism (Abramovitz, 2008; Blau & Abramovitz, 2004). Examples include libertarian conservatives, radical centrist, and liberal feminists.

As these examples indicate, then, while political ideologies are a relatively coherent set of ideas, one cannot always apply unitary definitions to them. Rather, they are best understood as being fluid, contested, and existing along a continuum of beliefs (Blau & Abramovitz, 2004). Within conservatism, for example, as well as libertarian conservatives, there are classic conservatives, social conservatives, and neoconservatives. Similarly, within liberalism, as well as liberal feminist and radical centrist, there are classic liberals, social liberals, and neoliberals (Harvey, 2005).

Political ideologies are identified not just by their ideas but also by their positions on a political spectrum. On the political spectrum, there is a left wing, center (moderates), and right wing (Jost et al., 2009). Left-wing ideologies view the proper role of government as active and progressive in developing social policies that promote equality. Left-wing activists have been instrumental in advancing many of the progressive social changes in recent United States history, which include labor rights, civil rights, gender equality, and so forth. Liberalism is identified as being on the left of the political spectrum (Jost et al., 2009).

Right-wing ideologies view the proper role of government as passive and in deference to strong state and individual rights. There is the promotion of unregulated capitalism, a strong military, and personal responsibility. Conservatism is identified as being on the right of the political spectrum (Jost et al., 2009).

Centrists (moderates) are arguably the least ideological on the political spectrum, preferring instead a more pragmatic blend of left- and right-wing ideologies to maintain the status quo (Heywood, 2012). Most voting-age Americans identify themselves as centrists.

Conservatism

VIEW OF HUMAN NATURE

Classic and social conservatives believe that human beings are essentially limited and security seeking, with an inclination toward the familiar and the tried and tested (i.e., tradition, status quo, etc.). If left to their own devices, human beings also have a strong tendency toward irrationality. Neo- and libertarian conservatives have a slightly different view of human nature, which they see as fixed and dual in terms of the capacity for good and bad (Sargent, 2009). In order to negate the capacity for irrationality, conservatives, in general, believe that human beings need strong moral guidance from traditional authorities. Ideally, these traditional authorities are the family, religious institutions, and the community. Social conservatives add the government to the list of traditional authorities as it relates to their law and order functions (Heywood, 2012; Sargent, 2009).

Across the conservative ideological continuum, there is a consensus about the need for liberty from oppressive and regulating forces if human beings are to live up to their fullest potential. These oppressive and regulating forces include the federal government and controlling social policies. It also includes philosophies that posit equality or seek to promote a social order to achieve a certain desired outcome without regard to the limitations of human nature. Only with liberty, which recognizes and embraces the individual talents and skills that set human beings apart from one another, can people and society fully thrive (Heywood, 2012; Sargent, 2009).

VIEW OF SOCIETY

In general, conservatives see society as a living organism that exists as an entity outside of the individual. What holds society together are bonds of tradition, mutual obligation, authority, and a common morality (Heywood, 2012).

VIEW OF GOVERNMENT

Across the conservative ideological continuum, there is a stated preference for small government, strong states' rights, and a noninterventionist approach to the economy. In particular, neoconservatives have championed state responsibility for social welfare programs. Relatedly, libertarian conservatives have been consistent in their opposition to big government as embodied in the numerous federal government programs (Heywood, 2012; Sargent, 2009). Yet, in actual practice, traditional and social conservative lawmakers in Congress have all helped to the grow the federal government rather than diminish its size and influence. It has been done through the passage of federal legislation such as the Medicare Prescription and Drug Improvement and Modernization Act of 2003 (P.L. 108–173). Signing it into law was President George W. Bush, a Republican and a traditional conservative (U.S. Government Printing Office, 2003). Moreover, there was the Troubled Asset Relief Program of 2008, bailing out private financial institutions, also signed into law by President George W. Bush (Webel, 2013). These are two of a number of examples of actual policy practice being significantly different from the ideological rhetoric of the small government. Indeed, this seeming contradiction has caused much infighting among conservatives across the ideological continuum.

SOCIAL POLICIES THAT SHOULD BE PRIORITIZED

Across the conservative continuum, there is general support for prioritizing social policies that reduce social welfare spending, decrease taxes for the wealthy, and support and stimulate private sector employment. There is also the prioritization of social policies bolstering national defense and border security (Heywood, 2012).

In addition to those positions, social conservatives and neoconservatives, in particular, prioritize social policies that maintain the cultural status quo as regard to abortion, same-sex marriage, law and order, and undocumented immigration (Sargent, 2009). Traditional conservatives depart some from a rigid adherence to the cultural status quo and can be described best as socially liberal on a broad slate of civil rights issues (Heywood, 2012).

Liberalism

VIEW OF HUMAN NATURE

Liberals stress that human nature is malleable and under the right circumstances can flourish. There is little focus on innate differences between humans and their ultimate capacity. Rather, there is a focus on the environmental barriers, poverty, oppression, and so forth that prevent humans from reaching their undoubted potential. If these barriers can be removed, there is a belief that individual potential can be reached (Heywood, 2012; Sargent, 2009).

VIEW OF SOCIETY

Liberals across the ideological continuum see society as a collection of individuals, as opposed to an entity in its own right. To the extent that there is a society, it can be best understood as a system of contractual agreements made by self-interested human beings. With this said, society does tend to have a general balance of interest for promoting harmony and equilibrium (Heywood, 2012; Sargent, 2009).

VIEW OF GOVERNMENT

Historically and today, liberals, other than neoliberals, have maintained the position that the federal government should play an active role in promoting a socially progressive agenda that achieves equality of opportunity and access to resources. Neoliberals, who came to prominence in the 1980s, however, have a view of government that is a departure from the traditional liberal perspective (Rothenberg, 1984). Neoliberals are typically more cautious about the role of government in resolving social issues or promoting a progressive social agenda. Instead, neoliberals are much more likely to support government interventions in collaboration with states and corporations (Heywood, 2012; Sargent, 2009).

SOCIAL POLICIES THAT SHOULD BE PRIORITIZED

Across the liberal ideological continuum, social policies that equalize access to resources are typically prioritized. However, this is not the general thinking of neoliberals, who are much less likely to embrace universal entitlement programs (Sargent, 2009). Indeed, it was President Bill Clinton, a Democrat and neoliberal, who signed the Personal Responsibility and Work Opportunity Reconciliation Act (P.L. 104–193) of 1996 into law. It is an act that eliminated welfare as a right and gave states the unprecedented power to administer the Temporary Assistance to Needy Families (TANF) provisions, with some federal government guidelines (Burke, 2003).

In addition to these positions, liberals across the continuum take social positions that challenge the social and cultural status quo. In general, these positions are pro-choice and in support of same-sex marriage and a pathway to citizenship for undocumented immigrants.

Why Ideologies Are Important

Ideologies, limited as they are in the mainstream political discourse in the United States, are critical to social policies for a number of reasons.

First, they facilitate an identification of social policy stances and priorities. Each of the political ideologies has distinguishable social policy stances and priorities, and they each provide stakeholders with an essential road map for understanding a respective ideology's social policy approach to a social problem. In turn, this allows stakeholders to choose the ideology that best matches their personal values, beliefs, traditions, and myths (Blau & Abramovitz, 2004).

Second, they help people to decide what existing social policies are right or wrong, good or bad, fair or unfair (Abramovitz, 2008). The most prominent present-day example of this is the Patient Protection and Affordable Care Act (PPACA). Enacted in 2010 as proposed by President Barack Obama, a Democrat and a liberal, the PPACA has been the subject of intense ideological scrutiny by conservatives in Congress and state government. Conservatives assert that the PPACA is a bad social policy that undermines individual choice. Equally opposed to the PPACA are libertarians who see the notion of mandated health insurance as inherently anti-libertarian and an affront to the libertarian principles of individual autonomy and free choice. Indeed, to date, there have been several lawsuits filed in federal court by conservative states and libertarian groups challenging the constitutionality of PPACA.

Third, they shape social policy discourse. In doing so, they provide a conceptual framework for thinking about and discussing social policy. Social policy discourse is ongoing and involves a myriad of stakeholders all vying to have their voices included (Abramovitz, 2008; Jost et al., 2009, p. 309; Walsh et al., 2000).

Fourth, they drive agenda setting, which is the part of the process of bringing social problems to the public and policy makers' attention. The news media use ideological frameworks and their underlying beliefs and values to help frame social problems for the public in terms that are easily digestible. In turn, this allows for the audience and public to see the particular social policy as important (Wolf et al., 2013).

Fifth, they inform the social policy strategies developed to address social problems. Consistent with the respective ideologies, these strategies consider a number of factors. For example, to name but a few factors, who is best able to intervene and address the problem? Will the public or private market best resolve the problem? Who should bear the cost, and who will be the beneficiaries (Abramovitz, 2008)?

The Economy and Social Policy

There is an indissoluble link between a nation's political economy and its social policies. Simply put, political economy is the interaction of political and economic theories in understanding society (Karger & Stoesz, 2009, p. 6). The political economy of the United States is best understood as democratic capitalism, in which a representative government coexists with a market economy. Central to this arrangement are social policies that stabilize society and protect workers by mitigating the vagaries of a market economy. These vagaries include but are not limited to recessions, economic depressions, downsizing, unemployment, and wage inequality. Over the past 80 years, in particular, social policies such as unemployment insurance, Social Security, tax credits, and health insurance have been integral to maintaining social stability (Karger & Stoesz, 2009).

Two political and economic schools of thought have informed these social policies: liberalism/Keynesian economics and conservative/free market economics, with some variations.

Keynesian Economics

Devised by English economist John Maynard Keynes in 1936, Keynesian economics rejected the free-market notion that a competitive economy automatically guaranteed full employment and that therefore government should not tamper with the process. Keynes posited, instead, that free markets were by nature recession prone and not readily able to self-correct or provide full employment. Primarily informing the frequent recessions that cause high unemployment, Keynes suggested, was instability in investment expenditures. Specifically, when businesses lose confidence in investments, they, like the general public, stop spending. Instead, they hoard cash, which in turn leads to a shortage of money in the economy, recession, and inflation (Dullard, 1948). Keynes, whose theory came out of an attempt to understand the nature of recessions, argued that government can avert this predicament by doing what the private sector will not do—spending money by investing in social welfare programs. In doing so, the general public can satisfy its general economic needs without cutting spending. Funding for these programs would come from an increase in taxation on the richest Americans (Dullard, 1948). Keynesian economics, which saw good government as active in economic matters, formed the economic basis for the modern American welfare state. In doing so, its principles became a staple of social welfare policy programs that did not just protect the poor but also expanded opportunities for the middle class. These programs include Social Security, Medicare, Medicaid, and federally insured student loans and home mortgages, to name a few (Karger & Stoesz, 2009).

Conservative Free-Market Economy

In contrast to Keynesian economics is conservative free-market economics. As argued by Milton Friedman, considered by many the father of modern conservative economics, using government policy and intervention to smooth business cycles is harmful to the overall economy. Milton Friedman posited that instead of the federal government pumping money into the economy by creating social service programs, they should just ensure that there is enough money circulating in the economy. Informing this perspective is Friedman's assertion that the cause of the Great Depression was not the hoarding of money but rather the lack of money in circulation (Friedman, 1992, 2002). As such, Friedman, who favored a nonactive government in economic affairs, called for economic policies to be replaced by monetary rules (i.e., monetarism).

Most closely associated with Friedman, monetarism, simply put, is a school of economic thought that believes that the money supply is the main determinant of economic activity. From the monetarist perspective, if the money supply is growing, the economy will grow. Thus, Friedman argued, there was a need for monetary rules that keep the supply and demand for money commensurate with a rate consistent with stable prices and long-term economic growth. He further posited that social welfare spending was much more an altruistic process than it was an economic one (Friedman, 2002).

Supply-Side Economics

Very much a product of the 1980s and outside of the traditional economic theories is supply-side economics (SSE). Developed by neoconservative journalists, economists, and policy makers, SSE argued that both the demand side and monetary policies of Keynesian economics and monetarism were ineffective (Ettlinger & Linden, 2012; Karger & Stoesz, 2009; Lucas, 1990). SSE contended that the key to economic growth and a vibrant economy was the reduction of taxes, particularly for corporations and the wealthy. By reducing taxes, SSE posits that there is a trickle-down effect, which is characterized by a dramatic increase in economic activity, as well as a significant increase in the labor supply and business investment. As a consequence, there is an expansion in economic output. In the 1980s, SSE and neoconservatism became the dominant economic perspective among conservatives. Indeed, it became the economic basis for President Reagan's massive tax cuts, as well as justification for drastically cutting social programs (Ettlinger & Linden, 2012). In practice, SSE did not yield the expected trickle-down effects regarding the creation of new jobs and industries. Rather, corporations and the wealthy either hoarded or spent their tax savings on personal items (Ettlinger & Linden, 2012).

Although the term SSE was no longer in the lexicon of conservative economic thinking by the late 1980s, its principles are very much a feature of contemporary conservative economic thought. Indeed, President G.W. Bush's administration passed tax cuts, the Economic Growth Tax Relief Reconciliation Act of 2003, and the Jobs and Growth Tax Relief Reconciliation Act of 2003, which were consistent with SSE (Ettlinger

& Linden, 2012). However, it is estimated that these tax cuts, among other factors, lost the nation nearly a trillion dollars in revenue and contributed significantly to the deficit (Congressional Budget Office, 2012).

Neoconservative economists maintain that social welfare programs are an unnecessary drain on the economy and encourage dependency and run contrary to the entrepreneurial spirit. They further maintain that only through the market can we reach our full potential; thus, social welfare programs hold back rather than aid in this process. It is an economic position that underpinned the welfare reforms of 1996 and its many residual and social control features.

Social Work and Social Policy

The nation's approximately 713,000 social workers with BSW and MSW degrees are employed across a myriad of organizational settings, including policy-making institutions such as the U.S. Congress (U.S. Department of Labor, 2021). However, the majority of social workers are primarily engaged in some form of direct practice work with clients in a social service agency setting (U.S. Department of Labor, 2021). The predominance of direct practice with its focus on interactional skills, knowledge of human behavior in the environment, and service delivery cannot surprisingly seem remote from social policy and its intricacies. Indeed, ostensibly it might appear that social policy has little to do with the realities of day-to-day practice, which more often than not is concerned with meeting the immediate needs of clients. Yet, in reality, social policies do in fact pervade every aspect of social work practice (Blau & Abramovitz, 2004). Indeed, it would be true to say that social policy and social work are inextricably linked both at the macro and micro level of practice.

The link has its origin in the early years of preprofessional social work with the reform-oriented settlement house leaders and their pivotal role in the progressive movement of the late 19th century (Karger & Stoesz, 2009). It was a role that saw settlement house leaders and other progressives advocate for the federal government to enact wide-ranging social service policies. The purpose of these proposed policies was to protect vulnerable and oppressed populations against changing life circumstances and the unpredictability of a market-based economy. In their success at having progressive policies enacted, albeit at the state rather than the federal level, the settlement house leaders created a policy advocacy legacy. It is a legacy that remains one of the organizing principles of social work practice today.

In the early 20th century, the policy link was deepened as a result of two factors. The first was the establishment of social work as a fully-fledged profession. In becoming a profession, social work concentrated its practice focus on casework with individuals and families (micro) and de-emphasized concern with institutional causes and social reform (macro) (Popple & Leighninger, 2011). The second was President Franklin D. Roosevelt's New Deal programs and the enactment of the Social Security Act of 1935. The New Deal programs, which were Roosevelt's initial policy response for stimulating the economy during the height of the Great Depression, created thousands of new rank and file social work jobs (Marx, 2011). These numbers increased with the enactment of the Social Security Act of 1935 and its 11 initial titles, which created a broad range of social service provisions. These provisions included grants for state old-age assistance, unemployment compensation, aid to dependent children, and aid for maternal and child welfare.

Such was the breadth of the social service provisions that a rapid expansion and creation of existing and new social service agencies employing social workers was required. By the end of the 1930s, the number of employed social workers doubled from 30,000 to 60,000 (Marx, 2011). The social service provisions also required social service agencies and the social workers that staffed them to adhere to strict legislative guidelines as a condition of federal funding. These legislative guidelines not only bureaucratized social service provisions, but they also became the organizing framework for social work practice within the context of agency-based social service delivery (Popple & Leighninger, 2011).

Then, as it does today, the legislative guidelines of social policy, among other things, determine who is eligible for services, what the scope of services will be, and what service options clients will have. As such, while day-to-day social work within social service agencies remains overwhelmingly direct practice and service oriented, the truth is that social work is and has been for some time a policy-based profession (Popple & Leighninger, 2011).

Vignette 1 Social Policy and Client Service Eligibility

Nancy, a social worker in a multiservice drop-in center, is meeting for the first time with 26-year-old Carla, who is seven months pregnant with her first child. Carla reported to Nancy that because of a lack of money she has not eaten regularly in the past two months. Carla further reported that when she does eat, it is most often food from McDonalds or Burger King. Carla tells Nancy that she has heard about a program—the Women, Infants and Children program (WIC)—that helps pregnant women with food. However, Carla does not know if she is eligible and wants Nancy to help her find out. Nancy goes to her computer and pulls up the local WIC web page, which has a WIC prescreening tool that helps potential WIC applicants such as Carla determine if they are likely to be eligible for WIC benefits. After completing the prescreening tool with Nancy, it is determined that Carla is eligible to apply. With this determination, Nancy telephones the local WIC office and has Carla make an appointment with them to complete the application form.

Vignette 2 Social Policy and Scope of Services

Carlos is a social worker in a mental health clinic serving young people (ages 14 to 18). Administrators at the clinic have informed Carlos that as a result of the Affordable Care Act stipulation extending insurance coverage, the scope of his practice will be broadened. His practice will now include a young adult cohort (ages 19 to 26). The stipulation that allowed for this change was the expansion of coverage to allow young people ages 19 to 26 to be covered as dependents under their parents' health insurance policies.

Vignette 3 Social Policy and Service Options for Clients

Julie is a social worker with a child welfare agency. She is working with parents who have had their six-year-old son removed and placed in kinship foster care with paternal grandparents because of an allegation of educational neglect. In a planning meeting with the parents and kinship foster parents, the parents stated that they are overwhelmed and do not believe that they are in a position to care for their son adequately. However, they do not want their rights to be terminated or have their child adopted. The kinship foster parents expressed a desire and willingness to raise their grandson but do not want to see their son and daughter-in-law have their parental rights terminated, nor do they want to adopt. Given the Adoption and Safe Families Act's stipulation that permanency be achieved within 22 months, the parents and kinship foster parents want to know what options they have other than termination of parental rights and adoption. Julie explains that the one other option available is the Title IV-E Guardianship Assistance Program. This program is a federal grant that provides guardianship assistance payments for the care of children by relatives whom they previously cared for in foster care (Children's Bureau, 2013). The kinship foster parents agree that they would be willing to take legal guardianship of their grandson under the auspices of the Title IV-E Guardianship Assistance Program. The parents are also happy with this arrangement as a permanency option.

In recognition of the relationship between social policy and social work, the Council on Social Work Education (CSWE) has made policy practice one of the nine core competencies that social work students must master (CSWE, 2015). Relatedly, the National Association of Social Workers (NASW) and the International Federation of Social Workers (IFSW) have enshrined social and political action into their respective code of ethics. In the NASW code of ethics, for example, political action is one of a social worker's ethical responsibilities to the broader society (para 6.04). To this end, social workers should be aware of the effect of the political arena on practice. They should also, when necessary, advocate for changes in policy and legislation to improve social conditions in order to meet basic human needs and promote social justice. Furthermore, social workers should promote policies and practices that demonstrate respect for difference and support the expansion of cultural knowledge and resources. They should also promote policies that safeguard the rights of and confirm equity and social justice for all people (NASW, 2017). In the International Federation of Social Workers (IFSW) code of ethics, principle 3, Promoting Social Justice (para 3.4), social workers must challenge unjust policies and practices. Toward this end, social workers have a duty to bring to the attention of their employers, policy makers, politicians, and the general public situations where policies are oppressive, unfair, or harmful (International Federation of Social Workers, 2018).

The Social Policy Development Process

As defined earlier in this chapter, the function of social policy is to enhance the well-being of citizens and resolve social problems. However, in a contemporary America of competing and conflicting ideologies, values, special interests, and experiences, there is rarely a consensus on the issues or problems that require remedying through social policy. Emblematic of this is that in a typical year, more than 5,000 bills are introduced in Congress. Of this number, though, only 150 (3%) will become law and social policy (Govtrack.US, 2014).

Given social workers' ethical responsibility to be policy practitioners, a fundamental understanding of intricacies of the social policy development process is essential. Among the intricacies that need to be understood are the various stages of development and the institutional and noninstitutional policy actors who seek to influence or block social policy formulation (Popple & Leighninger, 2011; Theodoulou & Cahn, 2012).

The stages of development can be summarized as follows.

Problem Identification

In a diverse and complex society of contrasting experiences and competing interests, there is no universal or absolute definition of what constitutes a problem worthy of recognition as a public issue (Leon-Guerreor, 2013; Mooney et al., 2000). Instead, problems (or private troubles, as sociologist C. Wright Mills refers to them) are socially constructed and become recognized as a public concern or issue. There are several ways in which this can occur. One is that it is part of a trend affecting large numbers of persons in society, like increased food insecurity because of a nationwide recession or increased foreclosures as the result of a banking crisis. Another is the resurfacing of a problem that has been dormant. Examples include a spike in HIV/AIDS infection rates after a number of years of stability or a spike in poverty rates because of increased food costs. It could also be the result of growing dissatisfaction with the status quo and social exclusion. Examples in the past 50 years include LGBTQ rights, women's rights, civil rights, and disability rights. Another is demographic changes that put a strain on existing resources, such as increased immigration. Lastly, there are unforeseen circumstances or events, such as the COVID-19 pandemic.

Legitimization

The legitimization stage of social policy development validates that an identified problem is one that is indeed worthy of being placed on the public and policy makers' agenda (Blumer, 1971; Reisch, 2014). Critical to this validation is the work of a broad range of noninstitutional political actors, so called because they do not possess the legal authority to make binding policy decisions. These actors include the mass media, special interest groups, think tanks, activists, and political groups. These policy actors help shape and define the problem at hand. In doing so, the public and policy makers are made fully aware of the problem's dimensions, legitimacy, and need for placement on the public and policy agenda (Theodoulou & Cahn, 2012).

MASS MEDIA

Mass media exerts considerable influence on public opinion (see Ryan White Case Study). In its editorial decisions, newspapers and television decide what is newsworthy (DiNitto & Johnson, 2011). In the modern era of 24-hour news coverage, mass media can bring nationwide attention to a social problem and its components, as was the case after the Sandy Hook Elementary School shooting, when mass media not only highlighted the tragedy but also brought attention to the ongoing debate about gun control. The coverage was extensive and helped to alert the public nationwide as well as policy makers to the different views on whether gun control is a social problem. Without mass media coverage, it is very likely that a problem, regardless of legitimacy, will remain obscure and not get a public hearing nor the attention of policy makers (DiNitto & Johnson, 2011; Gilbert & Terrell, 2013).

Case Study: The Ryan White Comprehensive AIDS Resources Emergency Act of 1990

Ryan White was a teenager from Indiana who as a hemophiliac required regular clotting factor replacement treatment to prevent bleeding. The procedure required a weekly transfusion of a blood product created from the pooled plasma of non-hemophiliacs who donated their blood plasma. Donated blood plasma was not screened as it is today, however, and Ryan was infected with HIV from a contaminated blood treatment. He was diagnosed in 1984 and was given six months to live (Encyclopedia of World Biography, 2010). Despite his diagnosis and prognosis, Ryan wanted to return to school, and doctors assured school officials and parents that he posed no casual contact risk to other students. But even with this assurance, parents and teachers rallied against his return to school, and a lengthy legal battle with the school system followed. The legal battle went all the way to the Circuit Court, where Judge Jack R. O'Neil dissolved the restraining order of the lower court and allowed Ryan to return to school (Encyclopedia of World Biography, 2010).

Ryan's long-running legal battle was national headline news and brought much-needed attention to the stigmatization and discrimination experienced by people infected with HIV/AIDS. Ryan presented a sympathetic figure that the public and media could gravitate to and soon became the acceptable face of the AIDS crisis. He was courted by celebrities and involved in numerous public benefits for children with AIDS and campaigns to heighten public awareness about HIV/AIDS. In 1988, he also appeared before the President's Commission on the HIV epidemic and testified about the discrimination he faced when he first tried to return to school (Encyclopedia of World Biography, 2010).

Ryan's experiences and advocacy were not the deciding factors in bringing the HIV/AIDS epidemic to the attention of policy makers in Washington. Activist groups such as the AIDS Coalition to Unleash Power (ACT UP) were already bringing public and political attention to the HIV/AIDS crisis. What Ryan did, however, was raise public awareness of the fact that HIV/AIDS was not the problem of any one group but rather a social problem that affected all of society. This identification and acknowledgment of the problem as not just personal were crucial initial steps in the policy-making process at the federal level (Epstein, 1996).

Shortly after the death of Ryan White in 1990 at the age of 18, Senator Edward Kennedy (D-MA) introduced a bill in the Senate on March 6, 1990 (S.2240). The bill would eventually be known as the Ryan White Comprehensive AIDS Resources Emergency (CARE) Act. It would provide federal grants to improve care for individuals and families affected by HIV and AIDS. The bill had 66 co-sponsors. After introduction, the bill was received and considered by the U.S. Senate committee on Labor and Human Resources. The Senate passed the bill on May 16 by a vote of 95–4, with one senator not voting. On June 13, the bill was passed in the House of Representatives. The joint conference committee reported the bill, and it was agreed upon by the House on August 4, 1990, and the Senate on August 4, 1990. President George H.W. Bush signed the bill into law on August 18, 1990 (Hoffman, 2003).

In addition to the traditional forms of mass media (i.e., television, radio, newspapers), social media sites are also an essential means for making the public aware of the problem at hand. Indeed, social media sites such as Twitter, Facebook, Snapchat, Instagram, YouTube, TikTok, and so on, are more immediate in getting the problem out in real-time than mass media.

SPECIAL INTEREST GROUPS

Special interest groups, which include labor unions, professional associations, intergovernmental organizations, business associations, and political action committees (PACS), play an essential role in legitimizing a problem. Central to this essential role is lobbying. Lobbying, simply put, is the process of trying to influence the passage or defeat of policy (National Conference of State Legislators, 2015). It involves a paid representative of the special interest group (lobbyist) meeting with policy makers to try to persuade or dissuade them regarding the legitimacy of a problem and the need for or choice of a policy response (Grossman & Helpman, 2000). In 2019, there were 11,893 lobbyists in Washington, D.C., representing special interest groups. The net spent for lobbying was $3.51 billion, an amount that was on par with the previous six years (Center for Responsive Politics, 2020). Not unexpectedly then, studies indicate that special interest groups are particularly influential in the policy-making process (Berry, 1999; Baumgartner & Jones, 1993; Burstein & Linton, 2002; Grossman, 2012). The areas in which special interest groups have the biggest influence is support for a policy and lobbying. The influence is across all branches of the government and includes helping to set the policy agenda, drafting legislation and policy initiatives, and directing implementation (Baumgartner & Jones, 1993; Berry, 1999; Burstein & Linton, 2002; Grossman, 2012, p. 172).

Notably excluded in this process are the poor and other socially disadvantaged groups, whose problems rarely become legitimized because of the lack of access to lobbyists. Instead, powerful and wealthy individuals such as the libertarian Koch brothers and others have been able to use their wealth to lobby policy makers for policies that favor corporations and big business.

THINK TANKS

Think tanks, many of which have an ideological perspective on the problem at hand, use research and analysis to interpret the problem for the electronic and print media. Such is the influence of think tanks, whose numbers have grown dramatically over the past 30 years, that policy makers increasingly use their often ideologically driven research and analysis to justify a particular response to a problem or issue. In the 1980s and 1990s, neoconservative think tanks such as the Heritage Foundation and the Manhattan Institute were particularly influential in helping to shape and frame the policy debate for welfare reform (McGann, 2007).

ACTIVISTS

Activists bring attention to a problem in the most dramatic of ways, which include sit-ins, demonstrations, getting arrested, and interrupting public meetings. The strategic purpose of activism is to alert the public, the media, and policy makers to the urgency and gravity of the problem at hand. Activism has proved particularly effective for problems that emerge from dissatisfaction with the status quo and social exclusion (Theodoulou & Cahn, 2012).

Agenda Setting

Before a social policy can be formulated and adopted, the problem has to compete for a place on policy makers' already crowded agenda. For this to happen, the issue or problem must make it through several levels, which include the broad political system agenda, the congressional and presidential agenda, and the bureaucratic agenda. The key policy actors in this step are think tanks, interest groups, lobbyists, ordinary citizens, the media, political candidates, political parties, and government officials. All of these policy actors are seeking to maximize political pressure so their issue or policy can make it onto the policy maker's agenda (DiNitto & Johnson, 2011). However, in a political environment of conflicting ideologies, even if an issue or problem is well publicized and/or has plenty of public support, it is not guaranteed placement on a policy maker's agenda. Agenda setting, therefore, is an extremely political process that involves significant political jockeying and careful navigation and consideration of political ideology, values, and special interests (DiNitto & Johnson, 2011).

Nondecisions

As important as the problems that make the policy maker's agenda are the nondecisions. These nondecisions are social problems and issues that are kept off the policy agenda because of the influence of powerful interests, as well as those that make the agenda but do not survive the political process. Influenced by powerful interests using their access to the political agenda, nondecisions prevent certain challenges from developing into calls for policies that might disrupt the status quo (Blau & Abramovitz, 2004, p. 28). For example, the National Rifle Association has been particularly effective in keeping the problem of gun control off the policy agenda despite a number of highly publicized mass shootings. Indeed, it has been so effective that policy makers, regardless of ideological perspective, political party, or public opinion, have largely avoided the problem altogether for fear of political backlash.

The Legislative Process

For the social issue or problem that does make it onto the policy maker's agenda, it then has to go through the legislative process in the two houses of the U.S. Congress. These two houses are the Senate and the House of Representatives, both of whose primary function is to pass laws. Central to this process are the committees of both houses and its members, who are the official actors in the social policy-making process. These committee members are considered official policy actors because they possess the legal authority, as granted by the Constitution, to make binding policy decisions (Theodoulou & Cahn, 2012). In the 117th Congress (2021–2022), the Senate has 16 standing committees; five special, select, and other committees; and four joint committees with the House of Representatives. The House of Representatives has 20 standing committees; four special, select, and other committees; and four joint committees with the Senate (Congress.Gov, n.d.).

Following is a description of the legislative process for passing a bill into law and a social policy.

BEGINNING OF A BILL

An idea for a bill is formulated. In the process of formulating the bill, a decision must be made about what kind of bill it will be; specifically, whether it will be a private bill, affecting a particular person or group, or a public bill, affecting the general public (Sullivan, 2007; Theodoulou & Cahn, 2012).

PROPOSAL FOR A BILL

After the idea for the bill is developed and its content written, a member of Congress becomes its sponsor and officially introduces it in Congress. Although anybody can write a bill, only a member of Congress can introduce it to the House or the Senate (Sullivan, 2007; Theodoulou & Cahn, 2012).

Standing Committees

Agriculture, Nutrition, and Forestry
Appropriations
Armed Services
Banking, Housing, and Urban Affairs
Budget
Commerce, Science, and Transportation
Energy and Natural Resources
Environment and Public Works
Finance
Foreign Relations
Health, Education, Labor, and Pensions
Homeland Security and Governmental Affairs
Judiciary
Rules and Administration
Small Business and Entrepreneurship
Veterans' Affairs

Special, Select, and other Committees

Aging (Special)
Caucus on International Narcotics Control
Ethics (Select)
Indian Affairs
Intelligence (Select)

Joint Committees

Joint Committee on Printing
Joint Committee on Taxation
Joint Committee on the Library
Joint Economic Committee

Figure 1.1 U.S. Senate Committees

U.S. House of Representatives Committees
Standing Committees

Agriculture
Appropriations
Armed Services
Budget
Education and Labor
Energy and Commerce
Ethics
Financial Services
Foreign Affairs

Figure 1.2 U.S. House of Representatives Committees

Homeland Security
House Administration
Judiciary
Natural Resources
Oversight and Government Reform
Rules
Science, Space, and Technology
Small Business
Transportation and Infrastructure
Veterans Affairs
Ways and Means

Special, Select, and other Committees

House Permanent Select Committee on Intelligence
Select Committee on Economic Disparity and Fairness in Growth
Select Committee on the Climate Crisis
Select Committee on the Modernization of Congress

Joint Committees

Joint Committee on Printing
Joint Committee on Taxation
Joint Committee on the Library
Joint Economic Committee

Figure 1.2 (Continued)

INTRODUCTION OF THE BILL

The bill is introduced in the House by placing it in a box known as the hopper. In the Senate, the bill is introduced formally on the Senate floor.

After the introduction, a bill clerk in the House assigns the bill a number. House bills begin with "H.R." and Senate bills with "S." After a bill number is assigned, the bill's title is read on the House floor. It is the bill's first reading, after which it is referred to a committee for markup (Theodoulou & Cahn, 2012). After referral to the appropriate committee, the Library of Congress then receives an electronic copy of the bill and posts the bill and its status on the public website, at http://thomas.loc.gov/home/thomas.php.

COMMITTEE ACTION

The referred bill is placed on the committee's calendar. After placement, the committee members debate on the markup of the proposed bill, when they may or may not make changes. If changes are made to the bill, committee members vote to accept or reject the changes. After changes are made or not made and if committee members deem the bill unnecessary, the committee stops action and tables the bill. If the bill is tabled, it will die in committee and go no farther. However, if the bill is deemed necessary, it will be sent to the subcommittee for intensive study, or reported back to the House floor (Sullivan, 2007; Theodoulou & Cahn, 2012).

SUBCOMMITTEE ACTION

Once referred to a subcommittee, the bill is calendared. After the bill is calendared, hearings may be held to obtain the views of expert supporters and opponents. After these hearings, if the bill is deemed unnecessary, it will be tabled and die at subcommittee. If not, and changes are needed, the subcommittee will meet to mark up the bill. Subcommittee members will then vote to accept or reject the changes. If the subcommittee accepts the bill and its amendments, the bill is sent back to the full committee for approval or rejection (Sullivan, 2007; Theodoulou & Cahn, 2012).

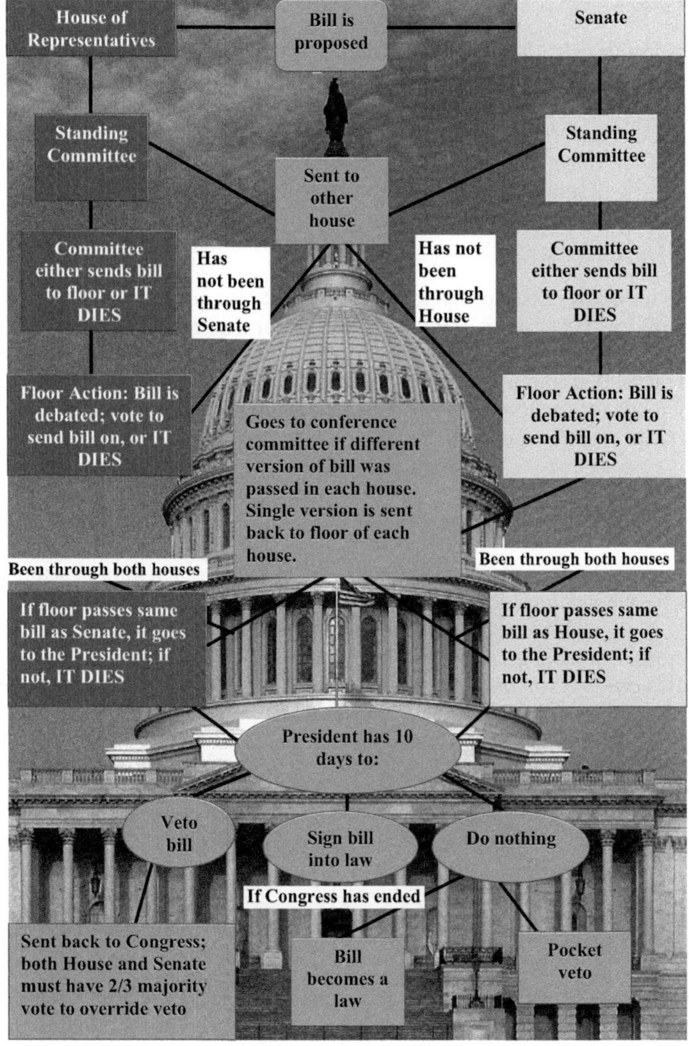

Figure 1.3 How a Bill Becomes Law in the U.S. Congress

REPORTING THE BILL

When the bill is released from the committee, along with a report explaining the provisions of the bill, the bill is ordered reported. The reported bill is put on one of the House calendars. The bill is then sent to the House floor for consideration (Sullivan, 2007).

CONSIDERING THE BILL ON THE HOUSE FLOOR

A bill can come to the House floor for consideration in a number of ways. One of the most common ways is through the parliamentary device known as the Committee of the Whole, which is a mechanism that permits faster consideration. Floor actions begin, and members debate the bill. The debate is typically dictated by the rules of the House. It may also be governed by a special rule granted specifically for the bill under consideration. Following the debate, the second reading of the bill begins in a section-by-section manner, during which amendments may be offered. At the end of the amendment debate, the bill is read a third time. After that, the House is ready to vote on the bill (Sullivan, 2007; Theodoulou & Cahn, 2012).

PUTTING THE BILL TO A VOTE

The bill is read by its title only. After the bill is read, it is put to a vote. Members in attendance will vote to pass or not pass the bill. Roll call votes cast by the U.S House of Representatives are recorded in the *Congressional Record*, the House journal, and posted on the website of the Clerk of the House. Members may vote "yea" for approval, "nay" for the disapproval, or "present" to record that they were in attendance but chose not to vote. If two-thirds of the House votes to pass the bill, the bill is then referred to the Senate, after which it undergoes a similar process of approval (Sullivan, 2007; Theodoulou & Cahn, 2012).

REFERRING THE BILL TO THE SENATE

When a bill passes the House, it is also required to pass in the Senate in order to become law. Once the bill and amendments have been passed by the house and are certified by the Clerk, the bill is considered "engrossed." In the Senate, the bill again may be sent to a committee for study or markup. Members may choose to ignore the bill and continue to work on their legislation. Members may vote to pass or not to pass the bill. If the bill passes with a different language, it must be sent for review to a joint committee, which is a committee made up of members of both the House and the Senate. Any difference must be agreed upon before the bill is sent to the president for signature (Sullivan, 2007; Theodoulou & Cahn, 2012).

SENDING THE BILL TO THE PRESIDENT

After passing in both the House and Senate, the bill is sent to the president for a signature. If the president approves the bill, he will sign it, and it becomes law. Conversely, if he disapproves the bill, he vetoes the bill by refusing to sign it and sending it back to the House of origin. The reasons for the veto are read and debated, after which roll call is taken. If the bill receives less than a two-thirds vote, it is defeated and goes no farther. However, if it receives a two-thirds vote or more, it is sent to the other House for a vote. If it receives a two-thirds vote or more in the other House, the president's veto is overridden, and the bill becomes law and social policy (Sullivan, 2007; Theodoulou & Cahn, 2012).

Implementation of the Policy

In this step of the social policy-making process, rulemaking becomes the central focus. As defined by the Federal Administrative Procedure Act, rulemaking is an agency process for formulating, amending, or repealing a rule. The act defines a rule as a whole or a part of an agency statement designed to implement, interpret, or prescribe law or policy or describing the organization, procedure, or practice requirements of an agency (USLegal, 2015).

The rulemaking process begins with Congress or, in some cases, the president selecting an existing executive agency, or passing legislation creating an agency, to issue regulations from the enacted law/ statutes (Office of the Federal Register, 2015).

For example, in the case of the Patient Protection and Affordable Care Act (PPACA) of 2010 and the Health Care and Education Reconciliation Act of 2010, various existing agencies were charged with implementing the specific rules and regulations of the policies. These agencies are located in the Department of Health and Human Services, the Department of Labor, and the Internal Revenue Services (Federal Register/Health Care Reform, 2014).

Selected or created agencies get their authority to issue rules and regulations from laws (statutes) enacted by Congress or delegated by presidential authority. At no point can an agency or agencies take actions that go beyond their statutory authority or that violate the Constitution. Moreover, agencies are bound to follow an open public process when they issue rules and regulations. Included in this process is the publishing of a statement of rulemaking authority in the Federal Register for all proposed and final rules (Office of the Federal Register, 2015).

HOW DOES AN AGENCY DECIDE TO BEGIN RULEMAKING?

Rulemaking for an agency may begin with Congress passing a law directing them to take action on a subject and set a schedule to follow in issuing rules. More commonly, however, the agency examines its areas of legal responsibilities, and then decides which issues and goals have priority for rulemaking (Office of the Federal Register, 2015, p. 2). In making the decision, the agency considers a number of factors. These factors include but are certainly not limited to some of the following:

- Recommendations from congressional committees or federal advisory committees;
- Directives issued by the president;
- New technologies or new data related to an existing issue;
- Petitions or lawsuits filed by interests groups, corporations, states, and other stakeholders;
- Prompt letter from the Office of Management and Budget.

(OMB, *Office of the Federal Register*, 2015)

ALERTING THE PUBLIC THAT AN AGENCY PLANS TO START RULEMAKING

By law, agencies are required to publish a Regulatory Plan once a year in the fall and an Agenda of Regulatory and Deregulatory Actions in both the spring and fall (Office of the Federal Register, 2015). Together, the Regulatory Plan and the Regulatory Agenda are commonly referred to as the Unified Agenda. The Unified Agenda is how agencies announce to the public their future rulemaking activities. It is also how the agencies update the public on any pending or completed regulatory actions (Office of the Federal Register, 2015). The Unified Agenda is posted on several sites. These sites include Reginfo.gov, and Regulations.gov, and the Federal Register. The Federal Register version of the Unified Agenda is available on the Government Printing Office's (GPO) Federal Digital system (FDsys.gov, Office of the Federal Register, 2015).

INVOLVING THE PUBLIC IN DEVELOPING A PROPOSED RULE

Before an agency issues a proposed rule, the public has a number of opportunities to help develop or refine the proposed rule. The opportunities come from both agency and public actions. Agency actions include gathering information through informal conversations with people and organizations interested in the issues. Agencies may also publish an Advance Notice of Proposed Rulemaking in the Federal Register. The Advance Notice is a formal invitation to the public to participate in shaping the proposed rule and begins the notice-and-comment process. Any interested parties from the public may respond to the Advance Notice by submitting comments with suggestions for developing and improving the draft proposal, or conversely recommending against issuing a rule (Office of the Federal Register, 2015). Agencies may also invite members of interested groups who they seek to develop proposed rules with through negotiated rulemaking. In this process, the agency and interested groups seek to reach a consensus on the terms of a proposed rule. If consensus is reached, the agency may endorse their ideas and use them as the basis for the proposed rule (Office of the Federal Register, 2015).

Publicly driven actions in the development of a proposed rule include the Petition for Rulemaking. The petition is generated by a member or members of the public and is issued to the agency, who may decide to announce the petition in the Federal Register and accept public comments on the proposed rule (Office of the Federal Register, 2015).

THE PRESIDENT AND DEVELOPING A PROPOSED RULE

Before a proposed rule is published in the Federal Register for public comment, the president may take the opportunity to review the rule. Assisting the president with this review is the Office of Information and Regulatory Affairs (OIRA), which analyzes the draft for the proposed rule, most particularly when the rules are significant because of economic effects or they raise important policy issues. For rules that are significant, the agency must consider the rule's economic costs/benefits and look at alternative solutions. If the proposed rule requires the public to provide information to the government, the agency is charged with the responsibility of estimating the administrative (paperwork) burden on the public and obtain permission to proceed from the OIRA. Moreover, the agency may be required to analyze the potential impact of the proposed rule on small businesses; state, local, and tribal governments; families; and federalism. Lastly, the agency may also need to examine issues such as just compensation and unfunded matters (Office of the Federal Register, 2015).

THE NOTICE OF PROPOSED RULEMAKING

The Notice of Proposed Rulemaking is the official document that explains the agency's plan to address a problem or accomplish the goals. The proposed rules must be, and are, published in the Federal Register to notify the public, and to give them an opportunity to submit comments. The proposed rule and the public comments received form the basis for the final rule (Office of the Federal Register, 2015).

THE STRUCTURE OF THE PROPOSED RULE

The proposed rules have preambles containing a summary, date and contact information, and supplementary information. A proposed rule starts with a summary of the issues and actions under consideration. Also stated is why the rule is necessary. Under the dates and addresses captions, the agency invites everyone to comment on the proposed rule, sets a comments submission date, and specifies methods for sharing comments. In the supplementary information section, the merits of the proposed solutions are discussed, as well as identifying the legal authority for issuing the rule. Following the preamble, the agency publishes the regulatory text of the proposal in full. The regulatory text sets out amendments to the standing body of law in the Code of Federal Regulations (Office of the Federal Register, 2015).

TIME PERIOD FOR PUBLIC TO SUBMIT COMMENTS

Typically, agencies specify a comment period ranging from 30 to 60 days in the Dates section of the Federal Register. However, for complex rulemaking, the comments period may be extended. Members may also request more time to allow comments, although agencies are not legally required to consider comments submitted after a deadline date. During the comments period, agencies also have the option of holding public meetings to collect more information or help affected groups get a better understanding of the proposed rule (Office of the Federal Register, 2015).

BEFORE THE FINAL RULE

At the end of the notice-and-comment process, the agency is not permitted to base its final rule on the number of comments in support of the rule over those in opposition to it. Rather, the final rule must be based on the rulemaking record, consisting of scientific data, expert opinions, and facts gathered during the pre-rule and proposed rule stages. In moving forward with the final rule, the agency must arrive at a judgment that its proposed solution will help accomplish the goals or resolve the problems identified. Also to be considered are whether alternative solutions are more effective or less costly. Once done, the agency may proceed with a final rule (Office of the Federal Register, 2015).

As with the draft proposed rule, the president and the OIRA may review the final rule before its publication in the Federal Register, particularly if it has a potentially significant economic effect or raises important policy issues. In some cases, interagency review of the final rule is mandatory (Office of the Federal Register, 2015).

THE FINAL RULE AND ITS STRUCTURE

Final rules have preambles, including the summary, effective date, and supplementary information. The final rule published in the Federal Register starts with a summary of the societal problems and regulatory goals and explains why the rule is necessary (Office of the Federal Register, 2015). Every final rule must have an effective date. In the supplementary information of the preamble, the agency must state the basis and purpose of the rule, describe the facts and data that the agency relied on to respond to major criticism, and explain why the agency did not choose other alternatives. The agency must also state its legal authority for issuing the rule and publish the regulatory text. The text sets out the amendments to the Code of Federal Regulations (CFR, Office of the Federal Register, 2015).

WHEN DO FINAL RULES GO INTO EFFECT?

When an agency publishes the final rule, the rule must be in effective no fewer than 30 days after the date of publication in the Federal Register. Significant rules, as defined by Executive Order 12866, and major rules, as defined by the Small Business Regulatory Enforcement Act, require a 60-day delayed effective date (Office of the Federal Register, 2015).

CONGRESS AND FINAL RULES

As a result of the Small Business Regulatory Enforcement Fairness Act (also known as the Congressional Review Act), a new rule must be sent to Congress and the Government Accountability Office for review before it can take final effect. If the House and Senate pass a resolution of disapproval, and the president signs it, the rule becomes void and cannot be republished by an agency in the same form without congressional approval. This is also the case if both houses override a presidential veto of a rule. Since this process began in 1996, Congress has disapproved only one rule (Office of the Federal Register, 2015).

Congress can exercise oversight of the rule by holding hearings and posing questions to agency heads. Congress may also enact new legislation or impose funding restrictions (Office of the Federal Register, 2015).

THE COURTS AND RULEMAKING

Individuals and corporations may go to court and file a lawsuit claiming that they have been or will be adversely affected by a rule or regulations. The reviewing court will consider factors such as the constitutionality of the rule/regulations, whether the rule/regulations go beyond the agency's legal authority, and was the notice-and-comment process adhered to as set out by the Administration Procedure Act. The court might also consider whether the rule/regulations are arbitrary, capricious, or an abuse of discretion (Office of the Federal Register, 2015).

If the court vacates all or part of a rule, it will usually send the rule back to the agency to correct the deficiencies. In doing so, the agency might have to reopen the comment period, publish a new statement of basis and purpose in the Federal Register to explain its decisions, or restart the rulemaking process by issuing a new proposed rule (Office of the Federal Register, 2015).

The Budget

At the core of all public policy is the federal government's budget. The budget consists of an expenditure side, which finances public programs, and a revenue side, which raises funds to pay for those programs. The budgetary process is the medium used for reviewing government programs, assessing their costs and relating them to financial resources, and making choices among expenditures (Office of Management and Budget, 2015).

THE OFFICE OF MANAGEMENT AND BUDGET

Located in the Executive Office of the President, the Office of Management and Budget (OMB) plays a pivotal role in developing and supporting the president's management budget and legislative agenda. To this end, the OMB assists the president in the preparation of the annual federal budget, which by law must be submitted to Congress on the first Monday of February for the next fiscal year (beginning in October). In meeting this responsibility, OMB, whose authority derives from Title 31 of the U.S. Code originally enacted in the Budget and Accounting Act of 1921, as amended, has a number of tasks. These tasks include the following:

- Reviewing agency budgets;
- Examining the effectiveness of agency programs, policies, and procedures;
- Assessing competing funding demands among agencies;
- Recommending funding priorities;
- Assuring that all budget proposals are consistent with relevant statutes and presidential objectives;
- Providing short- and long-range analysis and advice to government officials;
- Developing government-wide programs.

(*Office of Management and Budget*, 2015)

As well as these tasks, OBM develops the president's budget proposal and submits it to Congress and supports its enactment and oversees the Executive Branch's implementation of the enacted appropriations (Office of Management and Budget, 2015).

CONGRESS AND THE PRESIDENT'S FEDERAL BUDGET PROPOSAL

As mentioned earlier, the president is required to submit his federal budget proposal to Congress on the first Monday of February for the next fiscal year beginning in October. Upon the OBM's submission of the president's proposal, it is sent to the House and Senate Budget Committees and the Congressional Budget Office (CBO) for review. Once submitted, the president may, as need dictates, recommend further amendments (Office of Management and Budget, 2015).

THE HOUSE AND SENATE BUDGET RESOLUTIONS

After submission, both the House and Senate budget committees each write and vote on their budget resolutions. The budget resolution is not a binding document. Rather, it provides a framework for Congress for making budget decisions about spending and taxes. Furthermore, it sets annual spending limits for federal agencies. However, it does not set specific spending amounts for particular programs (Saturno, 2011).

After the passing of the budget resolutions, selected members of the House and Senate budget committees come together in a joint conference to resolve any differences between the two versions, with the resulting reconciled version being voted on again by each chamber (Saturno, 2011).

THE HOUSE AND SENATE SUBCOMMITTEES "MARKUP" APPROPRIATIONS BILLS

In the next step, the Appropriations Committees in both the House and Senate determine the precise levels of budget authority and/or allowed spending for all discretionary programs. In both the House and Senate, the Appropriations Committees are broken down into ten fairly independent subcommittees covering different areas of federal spending. For example, there is a subcommittee for defense spending and another for social security spending. Each subcommittee conducts hearings with agency leaders, posing questions to them about the requested budget. Based on all the information gathered, the chair of each subcommittee writes a draft of the subcommittees' appropriations bill abiding by the budget resolution spending limits. All subcommittee members then consider, amend, and then vote on the bill. Once passed, the bill is returned to the full Appropriations Committees. The full committees review it and then send it to the full House or Senate (Saturno, 2011).

THE HOUSE AND SENATE VOTE ON APPROPRIATIONS BILLS AND RECONCILE DIFFERENCES

After both the House and Senate pass their versions of the appropriations bill, a joint conference committee meets to resolve any differences between the two versions. After the conference committee produces a reconciled version of the bill, the House and Senate vote again on a now identical bill in both chambers. After passing, both the House and Senate appropriation bills are sent to the president (Saturno, 2011).

THE FEDERAL BUDGET BECOMES LAW

After each appropriations bill has passed Congress and is sent to the president, the federal budget only becomes law when the president signs each of the 12 appropriations bills. When done, the budget process is complete (Saturno, 2011).

THE BUDGET AND PARTISAN POLITICS

For all of the budget process, a near two-thirds of the budget (60%) falls into a mandatory spending category, which is spending that is controlled by laws other than appropriation acts. Included in the mandatory spending category are programs such as Social Security and Medicare, which take up the bulk of mandatory spending (Levit et al., 2015). Other programs in this category are Temporary Assistant to Needy Families (TANF), Supplemental Security Income (SSI), unemployment insurance, federal employee retirement, some veterans' benefits, and the Supplementary Nutrition Assistance Program (SNAP, Levit et al., 2015).

Nevertheless, because government spending is big business involving trillions of dollars, the budget-making process is highly political and increasingly partisan in recent years. At the heart of this contention is the size of government spending. Liberal democrats argue for a more expansive government with higher taxes and many more social programs for lower- and middle-income families. Conversely, conservative Republicans, Tea Party members, libertarians, and some neoliberals argue for leaner government, less social programs, and lower taxes. Of particular concern for conservatives is the continued growth in mandatory spending, which, in 1962, before the creation of Medicaid and Medicare, accounted for less than 30% of mandatory spending (Levit et al., 2015). Conservatives suggest that without some retrenchment or reworking of such programs, the government will spend itself into oblivion. Notably missing in this argument, however, is the state of discretionary spending, where, in 2015, the military accounted for 54% of spending, at nearly $600 billion (Office of Management and Budget, 2015).

Evaluating the Policy

Numerous policy actors, stakeholders, and interested parties are continuously evaluating the effectiveness of the policy to see if it is accomplishing its goals and indeed solving the issue or problem identified. Also of interest in the evaluation of the policy is its cost/benefits ratio and indirect and unintended consequences. Congress will also use its oversight function and the General Accounting Office for evaluation, and agencies will also evaluate policy performance (Sullivan, 2007; Theodoulou & Cahn, 2012).

Academics, social scientists, think tanks, and social workers, on the other hand, organize their analysis around a series of four questions:

1. What kinds of benefits are offered by the policy? Benefits include cash, in-kind benefits, services, vouchers, and/or increased opportunity.
2. What is the basis of social allocation? That is, who is entitled to the benefits and under what conditions?
3. How are the policy's benefits delivered? In other words, what structures and institutions administer the policy, and at what level of government is this done?
4. How are the benefits financed? Specifically, who pays for the benefits and how? For example, are they financed through taxes, charitable contributions, fees, or a mixture of the three?

(Gilbert & Terrell, 2013; Reisch, 2014; Sullivan, 2007)

In addition to these questions, social workers evaluate the social justice implications of the policy for beneficiaries. In other words, is the policy fair; what are the potential intended or unintended consequences of the policy; does the policy enhance or decrease autonomy? Also of interest for social workers is the ideological and/or value framework undergirding the policy. Is the ideological framework liberal, conservative, neoliberal, neoconservative, or some kind of hybrid?

Donald Chambers (2000) formulated a policy analysis framework that is particularly useful for social workers (Figure 1.4).

POLICY ELEMENTS					
1. Mission, Goals and Objectives	2. Forms of Benefits or Services Delivered	3. Entitlement (eligibility) Rules	4. Administrative Structure for Service Delivery	5. Financing Method	6. Interactions among the Foregoing Elements
EVALUATION CRITERIA	EVALUATION CRITERIA	EVALUATION CRITERIA	EVALUATION CRITERIA	EVALUATION CRITERIA	EVALUATION CRITERIA
***Adequacy*:** Are goals and objectives of the policy adequate to their task? ***Equity*:** *Proportional equity*—Are benefits or services in proportion to relative need for them? *Absolute* equity—citizens receive benefits or services in absolutely equal amounts regardless of their need. **Efficiency:** Was there a better means to achieve policy's given outcome? **Clarity:** Are goals and objectives well defined? **Measurability:** Are goals and objectives capable of being measured? **Manipulability:** Are objectives open to change or influence? **Concerns with outcomes, not services provided:** Is there greater concern with outcomes than services provided?	**Fit of the Benefit/ Service Type to the Social Problem Analysis:** Do provided benefits/ services fit social problem analysis? **Fit of the Benefit/ Service with Program Design:** Do provided benefits/services fit program design? **Benefits** a. Stigmatization: Are negative attributes assigned to consumers of benefits? b. Cost Effectiveness: How cost effective is the benefit? c. Substitutability d. Target Efficiency e. Trade-Offs **Services** a. Consumer Sovereignty: the degree to which the choice can be exercised with regard to services delivered. b. Coercion and Intrusiveness: degree to which public intrusion into the private life of consumer is mandated as a condition of service.	**Fit with Social Problems Analysis:** Correspondence between eligibility rules and the target specifications of the social problem analysis. Correspondence between eligibility rules and the ideology of the social problem. **Eligibility Rules:** a. Stigmatization. b. Off-targeted benefits—Are benefits directed to population groups who are not main object of the program? c. Overwhelming Costs d. Overutilization Underutilization. e. Political Interference. f. Negative Incentives and Disincentives (work, procreation, marriage, etc.)	Are services and benefits integrated and continuous? Are services and benefits easily accessible? Are organizations accountable for their actions and decisions, i.e., fair hearings and appeals procedure? Do citizens and consumers participate in organizational decision making? Are organizations and their staff able to relate to racial, gender and ethnic diversity?	Where is funding from? What is the amount of funding? What approaches are used to fund programs?	Coentitlement Disentitlement Contrary Effects Duplication Governmental-Level Interaction

Figure 1.4 Chambers' Policy Analysis Model: Value-Criteria

THEORIES OF SOCIAL POLICY DEVELOPMENT

Who gets to influence social policy development is increasingly the subject of debate in the contemporary United States. That this is a debate is hardly surprising given the substantial sums of money needed for political participation. Indeed, it has become even more of a debate since the *Citizens United v. Federal Election Commission* Supreme Court ruling in 2010 striking down by 5–4 the limits on the total amount that corporations can contribute to candidates and political committees. In its ruling, the majority maintained that political speech is indispensable to a democracy, which is no less true because the speech comes from a corporation (Oyez, 2015).

Social scientists have offered various theories to explain which individuals and groups have the power to meet their policy goals. The following are the most commonly used of these theories.

Pluralism Theory

Pluralism is the theory that most closely corresponds to what the mass media and mainstream political commentators present as the democratic political process of a free-market United States. As posited by the pluralism theory, a variety of organizations, not people as a whole, govern in the United States. These organizations, which include but are not limited to particular interest groups, civil rights activists, grassroots groups, political parties, and formal and informal coalitions, represent the interest of the American people. In doing so, they vie to influence the making of laws and policy. Despite often competing interests, all organizations ultimately strive for compromise in the system (Domhoff, 2014). Within the pluralism framework, no one organization, regardless of wealth or influence, is powerful enough to dictate the political process; rather, power emerges from the grass roots. Examples of pluralism include the passage of the Civil Rights Act of 1964. The act was passed despite strong opposition from influential southern political and business leaders, who saw it as destabilizing to local economies and the traditional social order.

Elite Theory

According to the power elite theory, change and policy are not the results of the work of a multiplicity of competing groups or organizations; rather, policy and change are dictated and dominated by an elite group of individuals that C.W. Mills described as the power elite. This power elite represents the interests of wealthy citizens and the leaders of corporations. In this model, those outside the elite class are viewed as powerless and, therefore, irrelevant. Even if not irrelevant, they rarely have the resources to organize as interest groups. In this model, power flows downward from the elite to the masses; they do not arise from mass demands (Gilbert & Terrell, 2013).

Conflict Theory

Conflict theory derived from the ideas of Karl Marx, who believed that society is a dynamic entity always undergoing change driven by class conflict. At the heart of this conflict is the push from the working class for greater access to societal resources. The conflict that comes from this push, which might include labor disputes, strikes, protest, or activism, brings about social change as society makes the necessary adjustments to allow greater access. An example in recent years of the use of conflict was the activism efforts of the AIDS Coalition to Unleash Power (ACT UP) in the 1990s.

Incrementalism Theory

The American political scientist Charles E. Lindbolm first developed incrementalism in the 1950s. According to Lindbolm, one of the consequences of a pluralistic society where power is shared is that it values compromise and stability over large-scale change. As such, policy makers "muddle through" by making incremental adjustments to a policy that maintains the status quo, rather than engaging in comprehensive policy changes. With small incremental changes, all groups and organizations can strategically influence policy making without upsetting the balance of power (Lindbolm & Woodhouse, 1993).

Rational Choice Theory

In this theoretical framework, policy making is a rational and objective exercise in which the benefits and costs of the policy options are examined, and the results are used to inform policy decisions. All political actors (lobbyists, voters, legislators, taxpayers, candidates) do this as part of the policy-making process (Gilbert & Terrell, 2013).

Chapter Summary

This chapter has identified the various dimensions of social policy and the social policy-making process, as well as established a working definition of social policy for the rest of the book.

Retrieval Questions

1. What are some of the common themes from the various definitions of social policy?
2. What is the institutional redistributive model of social welfare?
3. What is the residual model of social policy?
4. What are some of the conservative views on human nature?
5. What are some of the liberal views on human nature?
6. What are the stages of development in the social policy-making process?
7. Name three nonofficial policy actors in the stages of policy development.
8. Name two of the official policy actors in the stages of policy development.
9. Name two of the theories of policy development.
10. Give two reasons why social policy is important to social work.

Discussion Questions

1. Identify and discuss the role you think social policy knowledge has in developing a professional social work identity.
2. What is the relationship between social policy and ethical social work practice?
3. What role does social policy play in achieving human rights and social justice?
4. What are some of the dimensions of policy practice?
5. How does social policy affect the practice context?

References

Abramovitz, M. (2008). *Political ideology and social welfare: Encyclopedia of social work.* Washington, DC: National Association of Social Workers Press.

Alcock, P., & May, M. (2014). *Social policy in Britain* (4th ed.). London, England: Palgrave Macmillan.

Baker, R. (1991). *The social work dictionary* (2nd ed.). Silver Spring, MD: NASW Press.

Baumgartner, F. R., & Jones, B. D. (1993). *Agendas and stability in American politics*. Chicago, IL: University of Chicago Press.

Berry, J. (1999). *The new liberalism: The rising power of citizen groups*. Washington, DC: Brookings Institution Press.

Blau, J., & Abramovitz, M. (2004). *The dynamics of social welfare policy*. Oxford, England: Oxford University Press.

Blumer, H. (1971). Social problems as collective behavior. *Social Problems*, *18*(3), 298–306.

Burke, V. (2003). The 1996 welfare reform law. *Congressional Research Service*. Retrieved from http://royce.house.gov/uploadedfiles/the%201996%20welfare%20reform%20law.pdf

Burstein, P., & Linton, A. (2002). The impact of political parties, interest groups, and social movement organizations on public policy: Some recent evidence and theoretical concerns. *Social Forces*, *81*(2), 380–408.

Center for Responsive Politics. (2020). *Lobbying data summary database*. Retrieved from www.opensecrets.org/federal-lobbying

Chambers, D. E. (2000). *Social policy and social programs: A method of the practical public policy analyst* (3rd ed.). Boston, MA: Allyn & Bacon.

Children's Bureau. (2013). *Title IV-E Guardianship Assistance*. Retrieved from www.acf.hhs.gov/programs/cb/resource/title-iv-e-guardianship-assistance

Congress.Gov. (n.d.). *Committees of the U.S. Congress*. Retrieved from www.congress.gov/committees

Congressional Budget Office. (2012). *An update to the budget and economic outlook: Fiscal years 2012–2022*. Retrieved from www.cbo.gov/sites/default/files/08-22-2012-Update_to_Outlook.pdf

Council on Social Work Education. (2015). *Educational policy and accreditation standards for baccalaureate and master's social work programs*. Alexandria, VA: Author.

Dean, H. (2012). *Social policy* (2nd ed.). West Sussex, UK: Wiley-Blackwell.

DiNitto, D. M., & Johnson, D. H. (2011). *Essentials of social welfare: Politics and public policy*. Columbus, OH: Pearson Education.

Domhoff, G. W. (2014). *Theories of power: Who rules America?* Retrieved from www2.ucsc.edu/whorulesamerica/theory/alternative_theories.html

Dullard, D. (1948). *The economics of John Maynard Keynes: The theory of a monetary economy*. New York, NY: Prentice-Hall.

Encyclopedia of World Biography. (2010). *Ryan White facts*. Retrieved from http://biography.yourdictionary.com/ryan-white

Epstein, S. (1996). *Impure science: AIDS activism and politics of knowledge*. Berkeley: University of California Press.

Ettlinger, M., & Linden, M. (2012). The failure of supply side economics: Three decades of empirical economic data shows that supply-side economics does not work. *Center for American Progress*. Retrieved from www.americanprogress.org/issues/economy/news/2012/08/01/11998/the-failure-of-supply-side-economics/

Federal Register/Health Care Reform. (2014). *The daily journal of the United States government*. Retrieved from www.federalregister.gov/health-care-reform

Friedman, M. (1992). *Money mischief: Episodes in monetary history*. New York, NY: Harcourt Brace.

Friedman, M. (2002). *Capitalism and freedom: Fortieth anniversary edition*. Chicago, IL: University of Chicago Press.

Gil, D. G. (1970). A systematic approach to social policy analysis. *Social Service Review*, *44*, 411–426.

Gilbert, N., & Terrell, P. (2013). *Dimensions of social welfare policy* (8th ed.). Columbus, OH: Pearson.

Govtrack.US. (2014). *Bills and resolutions*. Retrieved from www.govtrack.us/congress/bills/

Grossman, G. M., & Helpman, E. (2000, Summer). Special interest groups and economic policy. *National Bureau of Economic Research*. Retrieved from www.nber.org/reporter/summer00/grosshelp.html

Grossman, M. (2012). Interest group influence on US policy change: An assessment based on policy history. *Interest Groups and Advocacy*, *1*, 171–192.

Harvey, D. (2005). *Neoliberalism: A brief history*. New York, NY: Oxford University Press.

Heywood, A. (2012). *Political ideologies: An introduction* (5th ed.). New York, NY: Palgrave Macmillan.

Hoffman, B. (2003). Health care reform and social movements in the United States: Public health then and now. *American Journal of Public Health*, *93*(1), 75–85.

International Federation of Social Workers. (2018). *Statement of ethical principles*. Retrieved from www.ifsw.org/global-social-work-statement-of-ethical-principles/

Jost, J. T., Federico, C. M., & Napier, J. L. (2009). Political ideology: Its structure, function and elective affinities. *Annual Review of Psychology*, *60*, 307–337.

Karger, H. J., & Stoesz, D. (2009). *American social welfare policy: A pluralist approach* (6th ed.). Columbus, OH: Pearson Publishing.

Leon-Guerreor, A. L. (2013). *Social problems: Community, policy and social action* (4th ed.). Thousand Oaks, CA: Sage.

Levit, M. R., Austin, D. A., & Stupak, J. M. (2015). Mandatory spending since 1962. *Congressional Research Service*. Retrieved from www.fas.org/sgp/crs/misc/RL33074.pdf

Lindbolm, C. E., & Woodhouse, E. J. (1993). *The policy-making process*. Upper Saddle River, NJ: Prentice Hall.

Lucas, R. E., Jr. (1990). Supply side economics: An analytical review. *Oxford Economic Papers*, 42(4), 293–316.

Marx, J. D. (2011). American social policy in the Great Depression and World War II. *The Social Welfare Project*. Retrieved from www.socialwelfarehistory.com/eras/american-social-policy-in-the-great-depression-and-wwii/

McGann, J. G. (2007). *Think tanks and policy advice in the United States: Academics, advisors, and advocates*. London, England: Routledge.

Mooney, L. A., Knox, D., & Schacht, C. (2000). *Understanding social problems* (2nd ed.). Cincinnati, OH: Wadsworth.

National Association of Social Workers. (2017). *NASW code of ethics*. Washington, DC: Author.

National Conference of State Legislators. (2015). *How states define lobbying and lobbyist*. Retrieved from www.ncsl.org/research/ethics/50-state-chart-lobby-definitions.aspx

Office of the Federal Register. (2015). *A guide to the rulemaking process*. Retrieved from www.federalregister.gov/uploads/2011/01/the_rulemaking_process.pdf

Office of Management and Budget. (2015). *Fiscal year 2015 budget*. Retrieved from www.whitehouse.gov/sites/default/files/omb/assets/organization/fy2015_omb_budget.pdf

Oyez. (2015). *Citizens United v. Federal Election Commission*. II Chicago-Kent College of Law. Retrieved from www.oyez.org/cases/2008/08-205

Piven, F. F., & Cloward, R. A. (1971). *Regulating the poor: The functions of public welfare*. New York, NY: Vintage Books.

Popple, R. P., & Leighninger, L. (2011). *The policy-based profession: An introduction to social welfare policy analysis for social workers* (5th ed.). Columbus, OH: Pearson.

Reisch, M. (2014). *Social policy and social justice*. Washington, DC & Thousand Oaks, CA: Sage.

Rittle, H., & Weber, B. (1973). Dilemmas in a general theory of planning. *Policy Science*, 4, 155–169.

Rothenberg, R. (1984). *The neoliberals*. New York, NY: Simon & Schuster.

Sargent, L. (2009). *Competing political ideologies: A comparative analysis* (14th ed.). Belmont, CA: Wadsworth Cengage Learning.

Sartori, G. (1969). Politics, ideology and belief systems. *American Political Science Review*, 63(2), 398–411.

Saturno, J. V. (2011). The Congressional budget process: A brief overview. *Congressional Research Service*. Retrieved from http://democrats.budget.house.gov/sites/democrats.budget.house.gov/files/documents/crs%20budget%20overview.pdf

Sullivan, J. V. (2007). How our laws are made. *U.S. Government Printing Office*. Retrieved from www.gpo.gov/fdsys/pkg/CDOC-110hdoc49/pdf/CDOC-110hdoc49.pdf

Theodoulou, S. Z., & Cahn, M. A. (2012). *Public policy: The essential reading* (2nd ed.). Saddle River, NJ: Pearson.

Titmuss, R. (1974). *Social policy*. London, England: Allen & Unwin.

U.S. Department of Labor, Bureau of Labor Statistics. (2021). *Occupational outlook handbook, social workers*. Retrived from https://www.bls.gov/ooh/community-and-social-service/social-workers.htm

U.S. Government Printing Office. (2003). *Medicare prescription drug improvement and modernization act of 2003*. Retrieved from www.gpo.gov/fdsys/pkg/PLAW-108publ173/pdf/PLAW-108publ173.pdf

USLegal. (2015). *Rulemaking defined under the federal Administrative Procedure Act*. Retrieved from http://administrativelaw.uslegal.com/administrative-agency-rulemaking/rulemaking-defined-under-the-federal-apa/

Walsh, M., Stephens, P., & Moore, S. (2000). *Social policy & welfare*. Cheltenham, UK: Stanley Thornes.

Webel, B. (2013). Troubled Asset Relief Program (TARP): Implementation and status. *Congressional Research Service*. Retrieved from www.fas.org/sgp/crs/misc/R41427.pdf

Wolf, M., Jones, B. D., & Baumgartner, F. R. (2013). A failure to communicate: Agenda setting in the media and policy studies. *Political Communication*, 30(2), 175–192.

CHAPTER 2
A Brief Historical Overview of Social Policy Development in the United States

Conflicting tendencies have powerfully shaped the development of social policy in the United States. On the one hand, there is an acceptance of a collective obligation to assist those in need and enthusiasm for developing policies that enhance opportunities (Jansson, 2009). On the other hand, there is a barely concealed antipathy toward certain categories of the needy, most specifically those perceived as the "unworthy" poor (Jansson, 2009; Segal, 2010). These include the able-bodied and voluntary jobless, people with substance abuse issues, unmarried single mothers, and the formerly incarcerated, particularly if for drug offenses. It also includes particular subordinated racial, ethnic, and social groups. Informed by religious doctrine, various ideological movements, and societal values, this antipathy is reflected in social policy, which among other things, makes various negative assumptions about its beneficiaries and the causes of the problems they experience (Martin, 2010). Perennially, these assumptions characterize the unworthy poor as morally bereft, shiftless, irresponsible, and lazy.

Certainly in the contemporary United States, the manifestation of these negative assumptions is a two-tier social policy system, one occupied by the so-called unworthy poor and one occupied by the worthy poor. For the unworthy poor, this system includes programs such as Temporary Assistance for Needy Families (TANF), the Supplemental Nutrition Aid Program (SNAP), and Medicaid. These programs are highly stigmatized and are closely associated with dependency (Stuber & Kronebusch, 2004). They are means-tested and, in the case of TANF, have lifetime eligibility limits, work requirements, and numerous stipulations and sanctions for noncompliance. Moreover, they are administered at the discretion of the states. Thus, they vary in terms of eligibility from state to state. In some states, for example, a drug felony conviction disqualifies TANF eligibility for life. Conversely, for the perceived worthy poor, the elderly, war veterans, and widows, programs include social security, social security survivors' benefits, Veterans Administration benefits, and Medicare. The federal government, not the states, administers these programs. Lastly, these programs are not means-tested and do not have the stigma of dependency attached to them (Stuber & Kronebusch, 2004).

The antipathy toward the perceived unworthy poor and its manifestation in social policy is not a new phenomenon. It is as old as the United States itself and has its origins in the colonial era with the adoption of the Elizabethan Poor Laws (Day, 2008). The following narrative highlights some examples of how this antipathy has been manifested in American history, as well as challenges to the perspective in the progressive era.

Colonial Period, 1601–1776

The culture, institutions, and social arrangements in the English-speaking colonies of the new world in most respects resembled those of England, where most of the earliest settlers were born (Jansson, 2009; Trattner, 1999). Not unexpectedly, then, when the colonial assemblies sought to install a formalized system of poor relief to address poverty in the colonies, they looked to the motherland and the Elizabethan Poor Laws of 1601.

DOI: 10.4324/9781003023708-2

Established by the British Monarchy and Parliament, the Elizabethan Poor Laws were a response to a severe economic depression in Britain, which among other things, caused large-scale unemployment and widespread hunger. The twin purposes of the laws were to regulate labor and the migration of people from one community to another and contribute to the general well-being of the destitute. Remaining as the principal form of poor relief in Britain for some 250 years after enactment, the laws had several features. These features included the following:

1. *Relative responsibility*. A needy person's family is primarily responsible for the care and welfare of that person. Moreover, the elderly should live with their children and dependent children should reside with grandparents. Public relief is only available if relatives cannot provide it themselves.
(Quigley, 1997)

2. *Local administration*. The administration of the poor laws was the responsibility of the smallest unit of government, which had the power to raise taxes for poor relief.
(Trattner, 1999)

3. *Residence requirements*. A local relief system is not responsible for those who are not members of the local community. Hence, residency requirements must be established to determine eligibility for relief.
(Trattner, 1999)

4. *Classification of poor*. The poor/dependent were classified into three major categories: the impotent poor, the able-bodied poor, and dependent children.
(Quigley, 1997)

5. *Poverty distinction*. A distinction was made between the "worthy" and "unworthy" poor. The worthy poor should receive a kinder and more benevolent relief, while the unworthy would get little if any relief. Related to this there were two kinds of relief: indoor relief in the form of placement in a house of correction or poorhouse; and outdoor relief, which subsidized people out of the poorhouse, usually with neighbors.
(Quigley, 1997)

6. *Less eligibility*. Relief should never be higher than the lowest available wage.

Beginning with Plymouth in 1642, Virginia in 1646, Connecticut in 1673, and Massachusetts in 1692, the colonies adopted poor laws fashioned almost entirely on the 1601 Elizabethan Poor Laws (Axinn & Stern, 2001; Hansan, 2011a; Trattner, 1999). Reinforcing the colonial poor laws, most particularly in the New England colonies, were Calvinist ideas about the virtues of hard work, the sins of idleness, and the sanctity of patriarchal family arrangements. Coined the Protestant work ethic by German sociologist Max Weber, hard work, frugality, and diligence were thought of within the Calvinist religious doctrine as necessary for a person's salvation in the Christian faith (Hall, 2008; Martin, 2010). Moreover, idleness was seen as the pathway toward temptation and sin, and patriarchal family arrangements were seen as critical to retaining moral and social order (Martin, 2010).

Although the Calvinist religious doctrine of predetermination certainly supported the notion of a collective obligation to assist those in need, the colonial poor laws nevertheless made a clear distinction between the worthy and the unworthy poor (Hansan, 2011a; Jansson, 2009; Martin, 2010; Trattner, 1999). The worthy poor were the elderly, infirmed, widows, dependent children, and injured war veterans. At least initially, relief for the worthy poor might be the delivery of food or the provision of a service. Much more typical, however, was placement with a family at the town's expense. Dependent children would be apprenticed. Although ostensibly generous, even for the worthy poor, relief was never so generous as to be more comfortable than work. The ethos here is that relief was a hand up, not a handout (Quigley, 1997).

The unworthy poor were individuals who were perceived as not having the requisite work ethic, or they had in some way demonstrated poor moral conduct. In the parlance of the day, these people included able-bodied men who refused to work, beggars, vagrants, idlers, and unmarried mothers (Quigley, 1997). For the unworthy poor, if not banished or placed in a house of detention, relief was indoors. It included placement in an almshouse or being auctioned to a farmer or other employer as labor for upkeep (Day, 2008). In this work, the unworthy poor were expected to take the opportunity to reflect on their moral failings (Quigley, 1997).

Notably excluded from the colonial poor laws, worthy or unworthy, were Native Americans and Blacks, free, indentured, or enslaved. Both groups were considered inferior to their White counterparts and existed outside of the colonial compact and obligation to help those in need (Jansson, 2009).

Although the colonial poor laws were the public response to need, they were not the only source of poor relief. Based on Protestant religious values and later nationality, a tradition of private philanthropy developed in the colonies, and in many instances led to jointly funded public and private donor relief efforts (Jansson, 2009). It also led to the creation, beginning with the Scots Charitable Society in 1657, of a number of nationality-based, private charity organizations, which were much less moralistic and punitive in their relief giving to fellow nationals than the colonial poor laws.

In its moralistic and punitive orientation toward those perceived as the unworthy poor, the colonial poor laws and the Calvinist values that underpinned them set a number of precedents that influence United States social welfare today. As will be discussed in the benefits chapter of the book (Chapter 6), these precedents, among other things, make an arbitrary distinction between worthy and unworthy at the expense of actually assessing need. They also disproportionally affect women and particularly subordinated racial, ethnic, and social groups.

The New Nation, 1776–1860

Having thrown of the shackles of the motherland to become a new nation, there were great hopes for the United States, including the hope of banishing the social ills of the past, such as poverty and discrimination. Certainly, the Enlightenment movement and the Great Awakening had allowed the nation and its residents to be optimistic about what they could achieve in this land of abundance (Day, 2008; Jansson, 2009; Trattner, 1999). They were no longer restricted by the notion of predetermination, as the Calvinist doctrine had asserted. People had potential, and if they worked hard enough, they could fulfill it. Moreover, poverty could be banished. It was a belief that was embraced with great enthusiasm, as numerous charities were founded with the express aim of eliminating poverty (Jansson, 2009; Hansan, 2011a).

Yet this very enthusiasm would also prove to be the catalyst for a shift back to the colonial era's more moralistic view of the poor and the notion of the unworthy poor. Prompting this return was the continued rise of poverty at the turn of the 19th century despite the efforts of the public relief and private charities. Much of this poverty could be attributed to the mass immigration of primarily impoverished German and Irish people to already overcrowded northeastern cities between 1800 and 1860.

Between 1785 and 1862, the federal government was active in social policy development. In 1785, it set aside land for public education. In 1789, it took responsibility for providing pensions for disabled veterans of the Revolutionary War. Relatedly, and also in 1789, it established a system of health insurance for merchant seaman. Lastly, in 1862, the Homestead Act offered settlers free land in exchange for five years of residency on the land and the promise to make improvements to it. Yet, for all these policies, the federal government played no role in providing relief for the poor.

Leaders of the public and private welfare organizations soon began to question how, in this land of abundance where new frontiers were opening up in the West and people could choose their own path, could people remain poor? Clearly, it was not the lack of opportunity but rather the poor's personal failings (Day, 2009).

This sentiment was echoed in the Second Annual Report of the Managers of the Society for the Prevention of Pauperism in New York. Read and accepted on December 29, 1819, the report listed a litany of reasons why poverty persisted. Among them was intemperance in the use of ardent spirits (p. 6). These spirits, it was suggested, "consumed every virtue of the poor and banished industry, honesty, and self-regard." It was also the nursery, the managers believed, for crime. Other causes of persistent poverty identified were lottery tickets, which it was believed encouraged the poor to gamble, leading to indigence and other vices. Also of particular concern for the managers was the poor's ignorance and illiteracy, which they described as being rife. The managers posited that charitable institutions were compounding the issue of persistent poverty. In extending charitable relief to the poor, the managers believed that idleness was encouraged, and the responsibility to be industrious and frugal was diminished (Second Annual Report of the Managers of the Society for the Prevention of Pauperism in the City of New York, 1819).

Concerned about the potential for social unrest in the wake of the growing number of poor, authorities grudgingly accepted that poverty was a problem that society needed to solve. To this end, local governments began to commission survey reports about their poor relief recipients. The intent of these reports was to identify the problems of poor relief and come up with recommendations for reform. Two of the most influential reports of the day were the Quincy Report, which was commissioned by the Massachusetts General Court in 1820, and the Yates Report, which was commissioned by the New York state legislature in 1824.

The Quincy Report

The author of the Quincy Report, Josiah Quincy, was a well-known politician and social reformer. Based on the report findings, taken from completed questionnaires sent to all of the towns in Massachusetts asking them to describe their poor relief systems and problems encountered, Quincy identified several concerns. Primary among these concerns was that while there were undoubtedly small pockets of those deserving of poor relief, for example, the elderly and absolutely impotent, there were much larger numbers that were undeserving. Quincy described these undeserving recipients as treating poor relief as a right to be relied upon as a wage (Quincy, 1821). Quincy suggested that relief in these cases was excessive, misplaced, and a disincentive to industry. More importantly, Quincy posited, "the pride of independence, so honorable to a man, in every condition, is thus corrupted by the certainty of public provision" (Quincy, 1821, p. 6). Quincy concluded his report with the following principles:

1. Providing for the poor is wasteful, expensive, and injurious to their morals and motivation to supply their own family.
2. The most economical mode of relief is that of the alms house, where the poor can provide for their families.
3. Of all modes of employment, agriculture affords the best and most healthy way for poor to be profitable by raising their own provisions.
4. The success of establishments is contingent upon being placed under the supervision of a Board of Overseers.
5. Of all causes of pauperism, nothing is more injurious as is spirituous liquors.

Yates Report

John Yates was the Secretary of State of New York. In 1824, he was commissioned by the legislature to conduct the first survey of public poor relief throughout New York state. The survey findings indicated that New York had no single method of poor relief; rather, it was divided between several public assistance methods (institutional relief, home relief, the contract system, and the auction system). Yates concluded that this method of poor relief was chaotic, wasteful, inefficient, and cruel, particularly in the areas of contract and auctioning of people. He also believed that the children whose parents were utilizing poor relief services suffered both educationally and morally and in terms of neglect. Finally, Yates concluded that home relief encouraged idleness, vice, and drunkenness.

As a result of the Yates Report, in 1824, the New York legislature enacted the County Poorhouse Act. The act mandated the following:

1. The building of poorhouses in each county to which all public relief recipients were to be sent unless sick or infirmed.

2. All expenses for the poorhouses were to be paid for by the county through taxes.
3. The appointment of Superintendents of the Poor officials.

The Quincy Report was instrumental in the termination of outdoor relief and the wholesale move toward institutional relief and almshouses in Massachusetts. Similarly, the New York State Poor Law of 1824 implemented the Yates' Report's recommendations, requiring every county in the state to build a poorhouse (Katz, 1987; Mohl, 1971). Following this trend, other northeastern states also turned to indoor relief. More importantly, though, the sentiments expressed in the reports perpetuated a belief that the poor were somehow morally defective, who, if not given the spur of work, would lapse into vice and bad behavior. It was a sentiment that would endure throughout the 19th century and inform almost all poor relief efforts.

Although the wholesale shift to indoor relief was supposed to cure the supposedly morally defective poor, in actuality the almshouses did no such thing. Rather, they better represented the intolerance for the poor and soon became institutions that simply warehoused them, often described as places of routine abuse and despair (Katz, 1987; Mohl, 1971). Moreover, there was little effort to separate residents by gender, age, or marital status. Thus, children were exposed and subjected to all kinds of abuse.

In addition to institutional poor relief, the mid-1800s saw the emergence of several new organizations whose specific purpose was to address the poor's so-called moral failings. One such organization was the New York Association for Improving the Conditions of the Poor. Robert Hartley, who believed poverty was caused by moral failings and the degrading conditions in which the poor were forced to live, founded the association in 1843 (Burrows & Wallace, 1999; Jackson, 2010). Disturbed by what Hartley saw as the lax oversight of charity distribution, the association represented a new, private, and systematic attempt to rectify the poor's so-called moral failing and their living conditions (Jackson, 2010). To this end, the association, which was funded by some of the richest individuals in the country, provided the poor with modest financial assistance, as well as encouraged them to adopt Protestant middle-class values.

To do this, the association hired middle-class visitors (all male). These visitors had a threefold responsibility. First, they had to identify and visit poor families in a designated section of the city. Second, they had to determine whether or not families fit the criteria for assistance, and, if not, refer them to the appropriate public or private institution. Third, if it were determined that families were eligible for services, the visitor would provide limited material support as well as friendly intercourse with the specific aim of reforming character and providing moral uplift (Burrows & Wallace, 1999; Jackson, 2010). In providing its relief, the association kept case records, coordinated services, and made referrals. In its use of scientific philanthropy and visitors, the association was a precursor to the scientific charity that would emerge in the last decades of the 19th century.

The Civil War and Social Welfare, 1860–1880

The Civil War, which lasted from 1861 to 1865, was the most bloody and destructive conflict of its day. The unprecedented level of poverty created during the conflict and its aftermath necessitated a significant involvement of the federal government in social welfare. Beginning in 1861, and as a response to the numerous reports of poor sanitary conditions and the lack of medical attention in the army camps and hospitals, the U.S. Sanitary Commission was created by federal legislation. Run by volunteers and private citizens, its purpose was to supplement government agencies in supporting sick and wounded soldiers, as well as attending to their spiritual needs. In a model of efficiency, the U.S. Sanitary Commission not only raised significant private funds for its operations, it also enlisted thousands of volunteers and united numerous local voluntary agencies into a coherent national relief organization. Going beyond its charge, the commission took on responsibilities that included recruiting and supplying nurses; setting up communication channels between soldiers on the front lines and their families at home; and distributing clean bandages, food, and clothing (Trattner, 1999, p. 78). So successful was the U.S. Sanitary Commission that it was credited with saving thousands of lives. Moreover, it stimulated the public health reform that would emerge some 20 years after the Civil War conclusion (Trattner, 1999).

In the aftermath of the war, thousands of permanently injured and often destitute soldiers needed ongoing medical attention and financial support. There was also the matter of what to do with the millions of newly emancipated slaves who were without support or resources. Moreover, there were thousands of widows and orphans due to the war's high rate of mortality. In response, Congress enacted a series of pensions acts for injured veterans. These pensions started in 1861 and culminated in the Dependent and Disability Act of 1890 (Trattner, 1999). Also established by Congress was the Freedman's Bureau under the direction of General Oliver Howard. In its six years of existence (1865–1871), the Freedman's Bureau provided newly emancipated slaves with social welfare, as well as economic, legal, health, educational, and land assistance (Trattner, 1999). Despite the continued need for the Freedman's Bureau's services, when it came up for renewal in 1871, President Andrew Johnson vetoed its continuation. In vetoing the Freedman's Bureau, President Johnson declared that the indigent's government support was never contemplated by the authors of the Constitution (Trattner, 1999).

Johnson's assertion, however, was not a new one. As far back as 1794, James Madison remarked that charity was no part of the government's legislative duty; rather, it was better located in the states whose powers are more general. It was the position that President Franklin Pierce would also take in 1854 when vetoing Dorothea Dix's bill for the Benefit of the Indigent Insane. In doing so, President Pierce opined that if the federal government assumed responsibility for the care of the indigent insane, the care of all impoverished Americans would then become its responsibility. This, Pierce suggested, was a development that the founders would never have accepted (Trattner, 1999).

Scientific Charity, 1877–1879

In the decade following the Civil War, there was a renewed focus on the plight of the poor, whose numbers had continued to swell despite the presence of almshouses and numerous private charity organizations. The Reverend Stephen Gurteen was one who saw the problem of persistent poverty as indiscriminate relief giving, which he suggested was wasteful and prone to fraud because of the duplication of services (Hansan, 2011b). Ultimately, this situation made private charity organizations ineffective in ameliorating poverty (Hansan, 2011b). In an attempt to reverse the ineffectiveness and make charitable organizations more efficient and direct in treating and decreasing poverty, Reverend Gurteen turned to scientific charity, which he had witnessed being practiced very effectively by the London Charity Organization Society (LCOS) in England (Hansan, 2011b; Trattner, 1999).

The Charity Organization Societies (COS)

Modeled along the lines of the LCOS, Gurteen established the first charity organization society in the United States in Buffalo, New York, in 1877. The Buffalo Charity Organization Society brought the disparate local charity organizations together as a systematically coordinated single charitable society employing a rational system of scientific, charitable administration. Methods of operation included a detailed investigation of each applicant for relief. Furthermore, there was the maintenance of a centralized register of relief applicants and the services and referrals rendered to them. In the field there was the use of trained volunteers known as "friendly visitors," who worked face-to-face with relief applicants in the field. Finally, there was the employment of a paid agent who would make the final decision on whether or not services were tendered to an applicant (Zastro, 2009). In short order, there were numerous COSs in the major cities employing scientific charity methods.

Much like most of the 19th-century voluntary charities, conceptually underpinning the COS movement's relief efforts was a philosophy that was predicated on a series of middle-class preconceived moral judgments about the poor (Hansan, 2011b). Unlike the views of the poor before the Civil War, these judgments were very much steeped in the self-help cult of the Gilded Age. They were also to a large degree influenced by the Social Darwinism perspective that had gained popularity among wealthy and middle-class elites in the late 1800s (Hansan, 2011b; Trattner, 1999). Popularized by the English philosopher Herbert Spencer, Social Darwinism located the causes of poverty within the person who was poor. The thinking was that if people were poor, it was a function of their actions and, as such, a personal flaw or defect. After all, it was reasoned, the United States was the land of opportunity. If people were not successful, it must be because of some personal flaw. More specifically, they were lazy, immoral, or lacked the initiative to take advantage of the country's many opportunities to progress (Day, 2009; Hansan, 2011b; Trattner, 1999). Added to this was a somewhat pessimistic view of human nature that suggested that the poor would not help themselves if they felt a sense of security. Thus, if the poor were to rise above their condition, they had to endure deprivation as a spur to keep them working and off the dole (Trattner, 1999).

As if not patronizing enough, among the remedies the COS movement proposed for relieving poverty was the use of friendly visitors, female volunteers from a middle-class or wealthy background, as role models for the poor. In this role, the no doubt well-intentioned friendly visitors not only investigated relief applicants but also determined who was "worthy" or "unworthy" of assistance. They also provided friendship and dispensed advice. The advice was typically about the virtue of hard work and initiative. The rationale and assumption for this kind of intervention were twofold. One, the poor wanted and would benefit from moral guidance rather than a living wage and decent housing. And two, proximity to and friendship with the middle class and wealthy would act as a spur for betterment (Hansan, 2011b).

In terms of actual relief, the COSs were remarkably reticent to recommend outdoor relief even to mothers with children. The rationale for this position being that material aid demoralized the poor and kept them from the moral salvation they really needed (Day, 2009). As such, the COSs only provided relief to women and children if a male breadwinner had died. If that was not the case, the mother would be sent to the poorhouse and the children to an orphanage to provide for their moral salvation and turn them away from pauperism. Likewise, unemployed nondisabled men were denied relief and instead encouraged to find work, even if none was available. Moreover, even if proved eligible for relief, one would have to provide evidence that they had exhausted all other avenues of support. These avenues of support were the family, then the church, or local relief organizations (Hansan, 2011b). Only in the event that the residual process had been followed could an eligible person or family receive relief. No surprise, then, that those individuals who were deemed to have contravened decent behavior—alcoholics, vagrants, so-called wayward husbands—were denied any relief. Instead, they were reported to the police and sent to a house of correction and then a house of rehabilitation (Day, 2009). All in all, then, when relief was given, it was nearly always institutional (Day, 2009; Trattner, 1999).

Though they did not significantly change their approach to poor relief, the COSs eventually realized that poverty was much more complicated than individual culpability or moral failings. As the data they had collected on poor relief applicants revealed, poverty was much more a function of environmental factors, among them unemployment (Day, 2009; Zastrow, 2009). The COSs would remain relevant into the early 20th century, but would continue to place greater emphasis on the individual. Importantly, though, they would transition from volunteers to professionals by the early years of the 20th century. They offered training and education and developed casework as a discipline. They also brought a focus to personal and social diagnoses, which were prototypes for the person-in-situation focus of social work today (Day, 2009, p. 228).

The Progressive Movement, 1880–1920

In the last decades of the 19th century, the United States experienced a second industrial revolution. Unlike the first industrial revolution in the 1830s, which was textile based, the second industrial revolution was technology based. It was characterized by railroads, large-scale iron and steel production, and the widespread uses of machinery in manufacturing, all of which were fueled by steam power, oil, and later electricity. In short order, the second industrial revolution ushered in an unprecedented period of social change and economic growth. Among the social changes was the transformation of the country from an agrarian society in which most adult workers were farmers living in rural communities to an urban society where most adult workers were waged factory employees living in industrialized cities (Foner, 2011). Indeed, so rapid was this transformation that within the lifetime of a single generation, the top ten largest industrialized cities in the United States grew from a population of 3.7 million in 1870 to 15.3 million in 1920 (U.S. Bureau of the Census, 1998). Furthermore, by 1870, eight of the ten largest industrialized cities were located in the northeastern and midwestern regions of the country: New York City, Philadelphia, Brooklyn, Chicago, Boston, St. Louis, Baltimore, and Cincinnati (Gibson, 1998).

During this period, which Mark Twain called the Gilded Age, wages, wealth, capital, and GDP all increased at the fastest rate in the nation's history. Moreover, the hundreds of factories in the industrialized cities churned out an array of consumer and industrial goods, which elevated the country to among the most powerful industrial nations globally, on par with England and Germany. In its elevation, a new class of super-wealthy industrialists embodying the capitalist ideal emerged. These wealthy industrialists, including John Jacob Astor, Andrew Carnegie, Jay Gould, J.P. Morgan, Charles Schwab, and Charles Yerks, to name a few, had a monopoly on the industry, all of whom were supported and encouraged by the federal government. In addition to these wealthy industrialists, was the emergence of a prosperous, educated, and well-to-do middle class.

Yet, for all the wealth created, the industrialized cities, the nation's cultural and economic lifeline, were also the hubs of unprecedented economic and social inequality. It was an economic and social inequality that saw the majority laboring class toiled in the factories and mines essentially as exploited labor (Ehrenreich, 1985). The exploitation of the laboring class had men, women, and children, mostly immigrants from Europe or rural migrants, working long hours for relatively low pay. Additionally, the working conditions under which these men, women, and children toiled were often hazardous with little in the way or regulation and/or insurance against injury or unemployment (Ehrenreich, 1985; Yarrow, 2009).

Figure 2.1 Conditions in the Meat Packing Plant: Chicago 1900

Figure 2.2 Breaker Boys, Woodward Cola Mines, Kingston, Pennsylvania

Figure 2.3 Glass Factory Workers

Living conditions for the laboring class were little better than their working conditions. Most typically it was in an overcrowded, subdivided, dilapidated tenement building located in an ethnic ghetto. Their living situation was often the result of property owners and landlords seeking to maximize rental profits because of the premium on housing and space. Toward this end, they would squeeze as many potential renters into a tenement building as possible (Ehrenreich, 1985).

Compounding the problem of overcrowding in the tenement buildings was the absence of essential municipal services such as clean water, refuse collection, and a sewage system. This lack was a symptom of a larger problem that the local municipalities of industrialized cities wrestled within the face of the population growth brought on by rapid urbanization—the needs of a rapidly growing population outpaced local municipalities' ability to respond effectively or appropriately. It was not surprising, then, that the overcrowded urban ghettos where the laboring classes resided were not only unsanitary but also host to a raft of infectious diseases. These diseases, including tuberculosis, smallpox, measles, and diphtheria, were little understood. Infant mortality rates were exceptionally high in these urban ghettos, with one in four children dying before the age of five in 1900 (Fogel et al., 2000; Yarrow, 2009).

In addition to inferior living conditions, the laboring class was also at the behest of corrupt city government officials. Specifically, these corrupt officials courted their votes and their unconditional support, typically along ethnic lines, in exchange for patronage.

So dire was the plight of the laboring class that industrialized cities such as New York, Chicago, Philadelphia, Baltimore, and Boston were as synonymous with urban blight as they were with wealth and

Figure 2.4 Tenement in Roosevelt Street, New York

Figure 2.5 In the Poverty Gap, West 28th Street, New York: An English Coal Heavers Home

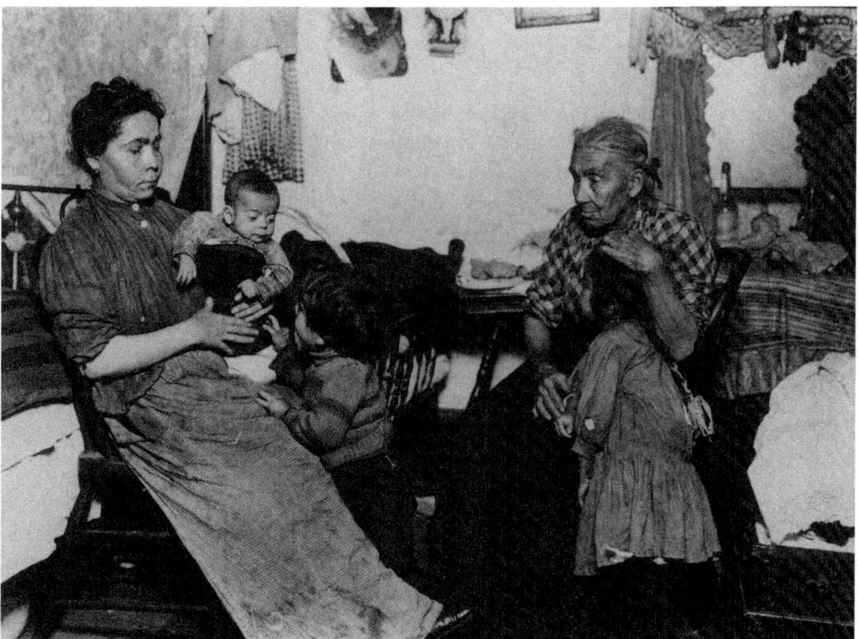

Figure 2.6 Three Generations in a New York Tenement

culture. This urban blight was characterized by poverty, periodic large-scale unemployment, overcrowding, unsanitary living conditions, high crime, family dislocation, corruption, and child and labor exploitation.

The Progressives

In response to the plight of the laboring class and the extreme levels of social, economic, and political inequality, progressives from across a broad spectrum of disciplines made a concerted push for social reform. The push, almost exclusively composed of middle-class elites, became the progressive movement. The movement would profoundly impact social policy, politics, and social science and would set in motion much of the social welfare agenda of the 20th century (Ehrenreich, 1985). Unlike the public and private poor relief efforts that went before them, the progressives did not see the poor as morally defective or the cause of their own suffering; they saw society's social structures and rampant capitalism as the real cause of poverty. For the progressives, the only way to eliminate poverty was to reform society so that, at the very least, it would provide citizens with basic protections against the laissez-faire economics of the day.

The Muckrakers

One representation of this push was the work of reform-oriented investigative journalists, writers, and photographers who used their medium to bring the plight of the laboring class to the attention of the American public. So effective were they at doing this that they were given the moniker "muckrakers." For example, Jacob Riis's hauntingly illustrated *How the Other Half Lives: Studies Among the Tenements of New York*, published in 1890, exposed the poor living conditions of the laboring class. Jacob Riis's work resulted in significant tenement reforms.

In 1904, Robert Hunter's book *Poverty* was the first to use extensive research to identify poverty's widespread prevalence. According to Hunter's research, at least ten million Americans, or one out of every eight, were poor in the early 1900s (Trattner, 1999, p. 101). In 1904, Lincoln Steffens's series of investigative articles, "The Shame of the Cities," revealed the full extent of the political corruption in Chicago and New York's party machines. And most famously, Upton Sinclair's *The Jungle*, which was published in 1906, vividly illustrated the abuses in Chicago's meatpacking industry. *The Jungle* was so well received that it led to two crucial labor reform policies: the Federal Meat Inspection Act of 1906 and the Pure Food and Drug Act of 1906.

These and the many other muckraking newspaper articles, books, and investigative photography by reformers such as Ida B. Wells, Lewis Hines, Ida Tarbell, and Frank Norris proved to be powerful tools of reform. They seared into the public consciousness the social issues of the day in a way that had not been done previously. In turn, this helped to create a groundswell of much-need public support for social reform and social justice for the laboring class.

The Settlement House Movement

Paralleling the muckraking journalists' work, novelists and photographers were the front line and policy advocacy efforts of the settlement house movement and influential progressives from academia and politics. Fashioned after the Toynbee Hall Settlement House in London, the first settlement house in the United States was the Neighborhood Guild, opened in 1866 by co-founders Stanton Coit, Charles B. Stover, and Edward King (Carson, 1990).

The settlement house movement had twin purposes: to address the immediate needs of neighborhood residents through a daily program of direct services and to bring about social reform to end pauperism. Unlike its English counterpart, the settlement house method in the United States made a point of locating the settlement house within the community. Furthermore, settlement workers moved into the settlements and lived in the community on a full-time basis. In doing so, settlement workers gained firsthand experience and insight into the plight of the disadvantaged, adding weight and legitimacy to their call for social reform.

In a country grappling with the social problems related to rapid industrialization, urbanization, and mass immigration/migration, the settlement house idea spread rapidly. By 1897, 74 settlement houses had been established, which increased to 100 by 1900, and 400 by 1910 (Carson, 1990; Hansan, 2011c). Most of the

Figure 2.7 The Muckrakers

settlements were located in large, urbanized cities, with 40% in Boston, Chicago, and New York. These settlements were typically located in immigrant neighborhoods. The settlement workers helped ease the residents' transition to the United States by providing English and civic lessons and daycare services and establishing penny-saving banks. No distinction was made between "unworthy" and "worthy." Moreover, every effort was made to empower residents through education and recognition of their inherent strengths and qualities.

The Black Settlement House Movement

For all its work in urban centers, the settlement house movement was not purely an urban phenomenon, nor work that was just with immigrants. For example, many small cities and rural communities had at least one settlement house (Hansan, 2011c). Moreover, because of racism and social exclusion, the settlement house movement remained a largely racially segregated endeavor. This segregation was maintained primarily because, although settlements had no problem believing that they could assimilate immigrants into middle-class American society, this was not the case for Black Americans (Carson, 1990). Consequently, Black female activists and reformers of the day, including Lugenia Burns Hope, Victoria Earl Matthews, and Gertrude Brown, to name but a few, involved themselves in establishing a separate Black settlement house movement. Black settlement houses proliferated in response to the increasingly needy population of Black southern migrants to midwestern and northeastern cities (Hounmenou, 2012). Indeed, Black settlement houses soon outnumbered their mainstream counterparts (Lasch-Quinn, 1993). As suggested by Hounmenou (2012), Black settlement houses were not just safe havens for poor Blacks, they were also an appropriate and free space for activism (p. 651). Much like their mainstream counterparts, the leaders of the Black settlement houses were educated women from the Black middle class (Hounmenou, 2012). They were progressive and used their platform to aid disadvantaged Blacks and address problems in the Black community (Hounmenou, 2012). However, because a substantial part of the resources for at least half the Black settlement houses came from White donors and reformers, leaders of these settlement houses had to be adept at straddling the line between confrontation and the call for equal rights and the less threatening call for racial uplift (Carlton-LeNey, 2001). However, for those Black settlement houses with full autonomy by virtue of having all Black funders and board members, activism was much more overtly confrontational and involved building networks with local politicians and lobbying for essential services, including improved schools and public facilitates, police protection, and equality (Neverdon-Morton, 1982).

So important was the Black settlement house movement in its activism that Hounmenou posits that it provided an environment for culturally based empowerment that contributed to the development of oppositional consciousness in the Black community. This oppositional consciousness, which simply put is the attitudes and disposition of members of a dominant community to challenge injustice and oppression, would be necessary to all future movements for racial equality (Mansbridge & Morris, 2001).

Settlement House Movement Activism

Notwithstanding racial segregation, between 1870 and 1920, the mainstream settlement house movement was a driving force in the progressive era. Much of this was the direct result of the social justice reform agenda of the female leaders and influential figures in the settlement house movement. These women included social workers and avid social reformers such as Jane Addams and Ellen Gates Starr, who co-founded Hull House in Chicago. There was also Lilian Wald and Mary Simkhovitch, founders of the Henry Street Settlement House and Greenwich Houses, respectively. Likewise, there was Helena Dudley, Florence Kelly, Alice Hamilton, and Edith Abbot (Carson, 1990). Their ambitious social justice reform agenda called on the federal government to create social policies that, as a matter of social justice, would address the issues of the day and bring about a more equitable society. Among the policies championed were child labor practices, workplace safety, widows' pensions, labor union rights, juvenile justice, unemployment compensation, maternal health care, social security, and universal health care (Abramovitz, 2008; Carson, 1990; Popple & Leighninger, 2011).

Inherent in this demand for governmental social policies offering all citizens a level of protection against the vagaries of life in a complex, modern industrialized city was a challenge to the American values of rugged individualism and self-reliance. It also called into question the viability in a complex modern society of the residual model of social welfare. Except for a couple of occasions in American history, the residential model had up until that point been the dominant social welfare model.

The Federal Government

Until the progressive movement, the notion that the federal government had a responsibility to formulate policies that addressed social inequality issues would likely have been anathema to most American presidents. However, this was to change in 1901 when Vice President Theodore Roosevelt assumed the United States' presidency after the assassination of President William McKinley (Gould, 2001). Roosevelt, a Republican, a product of privilege, and on the face of it a seemingly unlikely supporter of progressive ideals, believed very much in capitalism's ethos. However, he also believed in the notion that the government should use its resources to help achieve economic and social justice for all citizens, regardless of class. Indeed, the term "square deal" was to become synonymous with Roosevelt's domestic program (Gould, 2001). In his two terms in office, Roosevelt, among other things, took on the big corporations that had become monopolies and was successful, via Supreme Court rulings, in having them dismantled. He also pushed, after reading Upton Sinclair's *The Jungle*, for the passing of the Federal Meat Inspection Act and the Pure Food and Drugs Act of 1906 (Gould, 2001).

A New Era of Liberalism

The confluence of the muckraking journalism, social progressive policy advocacy on the part of the settlement house movement, and a strong and supportive voice in the White House achieved some impressive social policy outcomes in the progressive era, albeit mostly at the state level.

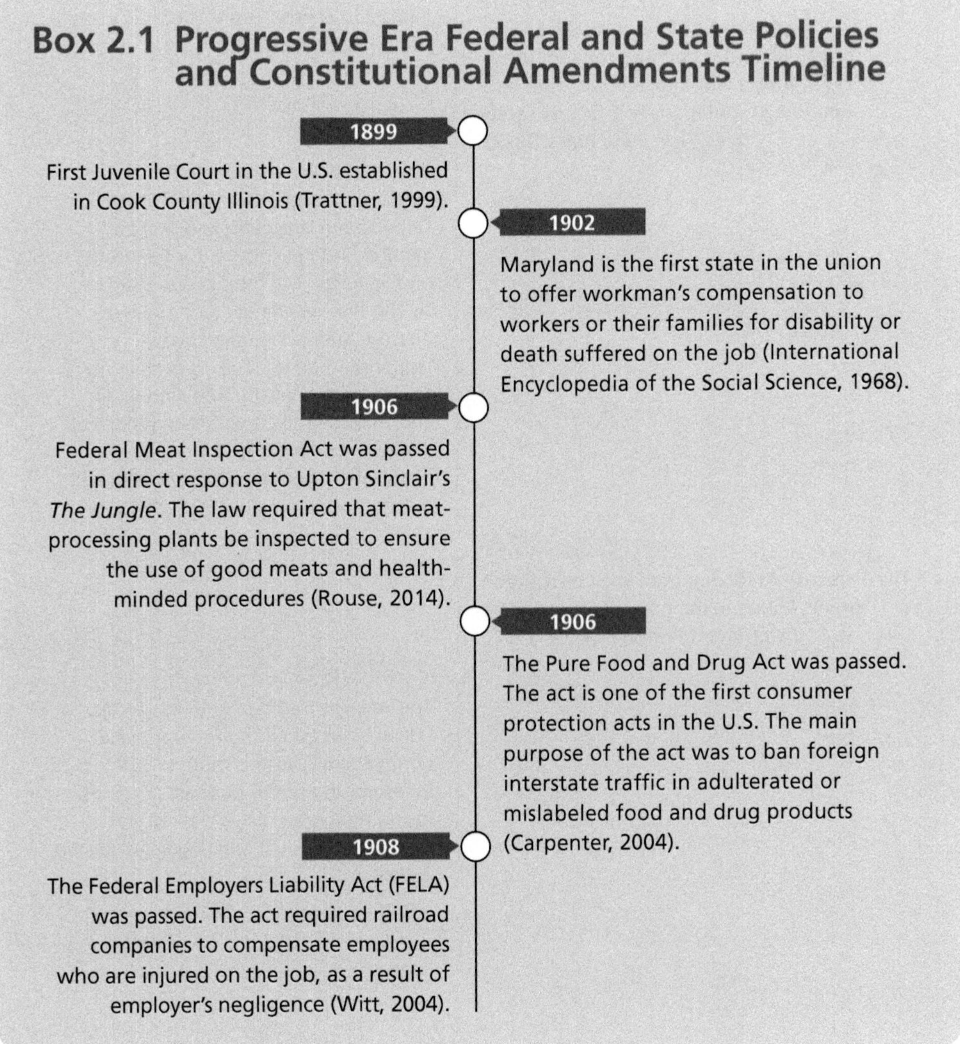

Box 2.1 Progressive Era Federal and State Policies and Constitutional Amendments Timeline

1899

First Juvenile Court in the U.S. established in Cook County Illinois (Trattner, 1999).

1902

Maryland is the first state in the union to offer workman's compensation to workers or their families for disability or death suffered on the job (International Encyclopedia of the Social Science, 1968).

1906

Federal Meat Inspection Act was passed in direct response to Upton Sinclair's *The Jungle*. The law required that meat-processing plants be inspected to ensure the use of good meats and health-minded procedures (Rouse, 2014).

1906

The Pure Food and Drug Act was passed. The act is one of the first consumer protection acts in the U.S. The main purpose of the act was to ban foreign interstate traffic in adulterated or mislabeled food and drug products (Carpenter, 2004).

1908

The Federal Employers Liability Act (FELA) was passed. The act required railroad companies to compensate employees who are injured on the job, as a result of employer's negligence (Witt, 2004).

1908

The Supreme Court ruling in *Muller v. Oregon* upheld a state law that limited women laundry workers to no more than ten-hour working days (Vogel, 1993).

1911

The first workman's compensation law to be upheld was enacted in Wisconsin. By 1920, workman's compensation laws are in effect in 43 states and in Alaska and Hawaii (Trattner, 1999).

1911

The first statewide mother's pension law was enacted in Illinois in 1911. By 1920, 39 states had enacted such laws. With few exceptions, assistance was limited to children up to 14 or 16 years of age (Trattner, 1999).

1912

The New York State legislature established a 54-hour workweek for women and prohibited children under 14 from working, and imposed new building regulations and factory safety rules (New York Times, 1912).

1912

The United States Children Bureau is established under the United States Department of Health and Human Services' Administration for Children and Families. The bureau was headed by the first female head of a federal agency, Julia Lathrop, and was responsible for all matters pertaining to the welfare of children among all classes of people. It was also responsible for investigating infant mortality, the birth rate, juvenile courts, and diseases affecting children (Trattner, 1999).

1913

The Sixteenth Amendment of the Constitution grants Congress the power to tax income (U.S. Government Printing Office, 1992).

1914

The Federal Trading Commission Act (1914) established the Federal Trade Commission, which is charged with investigating unfair business practices, including monopolistic activity and inaccurate product labeling (Hovenkamp, 2004a).

1914

The Clayton Antitrust Act was passed. The act outlawed the creation of a monopoly through any means. Also stated is that labor unions were not subject to anti-trust legislation (Hovenkamp, 2004b).

1916

Federal Employees' Compensation Act was passed. The act established compensation to federal civil service employees for wages lost due to job-related injuries. The act set the precedent for disability insurance across the country and was the forerunner to broad coverage health insurance (Nordlund, 1991).

1916

The Keating-Owen Child Labor Act was passed. The act limited the number of hours children were allowed to work and banned the interstate transport of goods produced by child labor. The Supreme Court invalidated the act in 1918 as a restraint on trade (Ross, 2004).

1916

The Adamson Act was passed. The act established an eight-hour day workday for railroad workers (Kaps, 1997).

1920

The Nineteenth Amendment to the U.S. Constitution was ratified prohibiting any U.S. citizen from being denied the right to vote based on sex (Trattner, 1999).

More importantly, though, it established a new "liberalism" for a new century (Halpin & Williams, 2010). In doing so, it updated the American liberal tradition from its Jeffersonian, small-government, republican roots (Halpin & Williams, 2010). These roots were well suited to the nation's founding era's agrarian economy but not to more democratic and modern liberalism (Halpin & Williams, 2010). This more democratic and modern liberalism demanded that the federal government have a central role in devising and using social policy to help citizens fulfill their human potential in an age of inequality.

In the decades following the progressive era, the institutional model and social policy as we know it today has become a permanent structural feature of the United States. Correspondingly, the policies produced have profoundly shaped almost every aspect of everyday life in the United States. These policies include the National Housing Act of 1934, the Social Security Act of 1935, the Servicemen's Readjustment Act of 1944, the Civil Rights Act of 1964, the Patriot Act of 2001, and the Patient Protection and Affordable Health Care Act of 2010. Later in this book, you will see just how much these and the many other post-progressive era social policies have shaped life in the United States.

Chapter Summary

To help provide context for the rest of the book, this chapter provided a truncated examination of the development of social policy from the colonial era to the end of the progressive era in 1920.

Retrieval Questions

1. What conflicting tendencies have shaped the development of social policy in the United States?
2. What role did muckraking journalism play in the progressive era?
3. What role did the settlement house movement play in the progressive era?
4. Why was a Black settlement house movement established?
5. What was President Theodore Roosevelt's view on the role that the federal government should play in helping to achieve economic and social justice for all citizens?

Discussion Questions

1. Does history have an important role to play in social work practice today?
2. As policy practitioners, what can today's social workers learn from the progressive movement?

References

Abramovitz, M. (2008). *Political ideology and social welfare: Encyclopedia of social work*. Washington, DC: National Association of Social Workers Press.

Axinn, J., & Stern, M. (2001). *Social welfare: A history of the American response to need* (5th ed.). Boston, MA: Allyn and Bacon.

Burrows, E. G., & Wallace, M. (1999). *Gotham: A history of New York City to 1898*. New York, NY: Oxford University Press.

Carlton-LeNey, I. B. (2001). Birdie Henrietta Haynes: A pioneer settlement house worker. In I. B. Carlton-LaNey (Ed.), *African American leadership: An empowerment tradition in social welfare history* (pp. 35–53). Washington, DC: NASW Press.

Carson, M. (1990). *Settlement folk: Social thought and the American settlement movement*. Chicago, IL: University of Chicago Press.

Day, P. J. (2008). *Social policy: History (Colonial times to 1900): Encyclopedia of social work*. Washington, DC: National Association of Social Workers Press.

Day, P. J. (2009). *A new history of social welfare* (6th ed.). New York, NY: Allyn and Bacon.

Ehrenreich, J. (1985). *The altruistic imagination: A history of social work and social policy in the U.S.* Ithaca, NY: Cornell University Press.

Fogel, R. W., Ferrie, J., Costa, D., & Karlan, D. S. (2000). *United States census of mortality: 1850, 1860, and 1870*. ICPSR02526-v1. Ann Arbor, MI: Inter-university Consortium for Political and Social Research [distributor]. http://doi.org/10.3886/ICPSR02526.v1

Foner, E. (2011). *Give me liberty: An American history* (4th ed.). New York, NY: W. W. Norton.

Gibson, C. (1998). *Population of the 100 largest cities and other urban places in the United States: 1790–1900*. Population Division Working Paper No. 27. United States Census Bureau. Retrieved from www.census.gov/population/www/documentation/twps0027/twps0027.html

Gould, L. (2001). *America in the progressive era: 1890–1914*. New York, NY: Taylor & Francis.

Hall, D. (2008). *The legacy of John Calvin: His influence in the modern world*. Phillipsburg, NJ: P&R Publishing.

Halpin, J., & Williams, C. P. (2010). The progressive intellectual tradition in America. *Center for American Progress*. Retrieved from http://cdn.americanprogress.org/wpcontent/uploads/issues/2010/04/pdf/progressiveintellectualism.pdf

Hansan, J. E. (2011a). Poor relief in early America. *The Social Welfare History Project*. Retrieved from www.socialwelfarehistory.com/programs/poor-relief-early-amer/

Hansan, J. E. (2011b). Charity organization societies: 1873–1893. *The Social Welfare History Project*. Retrieved from www.socialwelfarehistory.com/organizations/charity-organization-societies-1877-1893/

Hansan, J. E. (2011c). Settlement houses: An introduction. *The Social Welfare History Project*. Retrieved from www.socialwelfarehistory.com/programs/settlement-houses/

Hounmenou, C. (2012). Black settlement houses and oppositional consciousness. *Journal of Black Studies*, *43*(6), 646–666.

Jackson, K. T. (2010). *The encyclopedia of New York City*. New Haven, CT: Yale University Press.

Jansson, B. S. (2009). *The reluctant welfare state: Engaging history to advance social work practice in contemporary society* (6th ed.). Belmont, CA: Brooks/Cole.

Katz, M. B. (1987). *In the shadow of the poorhouse: Social history of welfare America*. New York, NY: Basic Books.

Lasch-Quinn, E. (1993). *Black neighbors: Race and the limits of reform in the American settlement house movement, 1890–1945*. Chapel Hill, NC: The University of North Carolina Press.

Mansbridge, J., & Morris, A. (Eds.). (2001). *Oppositional consciousness: The subjective roots of social protest*. Chicago, IL: University of Chicago Press.

Martin, M. E. (2010). Philosophical and religious influences on social welfare policy in the United States: The ongoing effect of reformed theology and social Darwinism on attitudes toward the poor and social welfare policy and practice. *Journal of Social Work*, *12*(1), 51–64.

Mohl, R. A. (1971). *Poverty in New York, 1783–1825*. New York, NY: Oxford University Press.

Neverdon-Morton, C. (1982). Self-help programs as educative activities of Black women in the South, 1985–1925: Focus on four key areas. *Journal of Negro Education*, *51*(3), 207–221.

Popple, R. P., & Leighninger, L. (2011). *The policy-based profession: An introduction to social welfare policy analysis for social workers* (5th ed.). Columbus, OH: Pearson.

Quigley, W. P. (1997). Reluctant charity: Poor laws in the original thirteen states. *University of Richmond Law Review*, 1–52.

Quincy, J. (1821). *Massachusetts general court committee on pauper laws*. Boston, MA: Russell and Gardner.

Second Annual Report of the Managers of the Society for the Prevention of Pauperism in the City of New York. (1819). *The subject of pauperism*. Retrieved from http://babel.hathitrust.org/cgi/pt?id=hvd.32044100870971;view=1up;seq=1

Segal, E. A. (2010). *Social welfare policy and social programs: A values perspective* (2nd ed.). Pacific Grove, CA: Brooks/Cole.

Stuber, J., & Kronebusch, K. (2004). Stigma and the other determinants of participation in TANF and Medicaid. *Journal of Policy Analysis and Management*, *23*(3), 509–530.

Trattner, W. I. (1999). *From poor law to welfare state: A history of social welfare in America* (6th ed.). New York, NY: The Free Press.

U.S. Bureau of the Census. (1998). *Census data: 1870–1920*. Retrieved from www.census.gov/population/www/documentation/twps0027/tab10.txt

Yarrow, A. L. (2009). History of U.S. children's policy, 1900: Present. *First Focus*. Retrieved from http://publicagendaarchives.org/articles/history-us-childrens-policy-1900-present

Zastrow, C. (2009). *Introduction to social work and social welfare: Empowering people* (10th ed.). Belmont, CA: Brooks/Cole.

CHAPTER 3
Social Inequality

What Is Social Inequality?

Social inequality is complex and multidimensional. It involves the unequal allocation or denial of society's resources, rights, goods, privileges, and services across socially defined and stratified categories (Massey, 2007; Ridgeway, 2014; Warwick-Booth, 2013). Socially defined and stratified categories include factors such as one's race/ethnicity, gender, social class, immigration status, sexual orientation/identity, and disability status. Society's resources, rights, goods, privileges, and services include but are not limited to education; health care; employment; income; wealth; housing; and social, political, and economic justice. Social inequality affects the quality of life of individuals, groups, and populations, as well as the cohesion of society as a whole.

Social Inequality and Social Work

A defining feature of contemporary social work is its concern with those who suffer from the adverse effects of social inequality. Whether it is direct practice with the economically disadvantaged or advocacy for policies to mitigate the deleterious effect of the social exclusion of clients, social work is at the forefront of ongoing efforts to end social inequality. Indeed, social work's commitment to challenging social inequality is enshrined in the National Associations of Social Workers' (NASW) core value of social justice and its accompanying ethical principle that *social workers challenge social injustice*. That is, among other things, social workers strive to ensure clients' access to equality of opportunity (National Association of Social Workers, 2017). This commitment is similarly reflected in the Council on Social Work Education's (CSWE) core competency: *advance human rights and social and economic justice*. This competency requires social work students to be able to confront the forms and mechanisms of oppression and discrimination, as well as participate in practices that advance human rights and social and economic justice (Council on Social Work Education, 2006).

United States Social Inequality

The ideals of meritocracy and equality for all regardless of individual circumstances are very much imbued in American lore. Yet, despite these ideals, the reality is that social inequality is a deeply embedded structural feature of American society and has been since its colonial beginnings. Powerfully shaping social inequality in the United States are social policies, laws, social institutions, and the prevailing ideologies and values of the day (Glenn, 2002; Hochschild & Weaver, 2007; Massey, 2007). As will be demonstrated in this book, social policy has been central not only to the creation and maintenance of social inequality but also to the many efforts to mitigate its wide-ranging deleterious effects. For these reasons, social inequality and social policy are inextricably entwined.

In the relatively short history of the United States, the most enduring social inequalities have always been those based on one's race, ethnicity, gender, class, and immigration status. Less visible historically but of contemporary importance and relevance are social inequalities based on one's sexual orientation/identity and disability.

DOI: 10.4324/9781003023708-3

Social Inequality and Intersectionality

Though the various experiences of social inequality are often treated as distinct and separate, in actuality, there is significant intersection between them (Crenshaw, 1991; Nash, 2008; Women's Rights and Economic Change, 2004). One cannot, for example, examine social inequality and race/ethnicity without also considering the effect of gender, class, sexual orientation/identity, and when applicable, immigration status and disability. While these intersections might not necessarily additively increase one's social inequality, it does produce substantively different experiences of it (Women's Rights and Economic Change, 2004, p. 2). Therefore, an intersectionality framework is a necessary tool for analysis, advocacy, and policy development. Not only does it reveal meaningful distinctions and similarities in social inequality, but it can also help social workers to understand how different sets of affiliations/identities affect one's access to society's resources, rights, goods, privileges, and services.

The rest of this chapter provides a context by discussing and highlighting the most persistent and enduring categorical bases for social inequality in the United States, focusing particularly on their historical origins.

The Origins of Race and Racial and Ethnic Inequality in the United States

Geneticists and anthropologists agree that race and the notion of demarcated, biologically distinct groups of people are devoid of scientific validity (American Anthropological Association, 1998; Fredrickson, 2002). More accurate is the concept that race is a socially, culturally, and politically constructed classification of people who share a common phenotype (James, 2008). Though a scientific myth, one's racial classification in the United States had and still has a profound impact on access to society's resources, rewards, and privileges (Massey, 2007). Similarly significant from the late 19th century onward was the social construction of people, specifically immigrants from eastern and southern Europe, as well as Mexico, into ethnic groups on the grounds of shared language and cultural heritage.

Race

The concept of race emerged relatively early in American history as a result of the intersection of three seminal developments. The first of these developments was colonial land encroachment, followed by American expansionism, which from the mid-1600s to the late 1800s forcibly displaced indigenous tribes while appropriating their homelands (Salisbury, 1996). The second development was the forcible lifetime enslavement of Africans and their American-born offspring and descendants (Horton & Horton, 2006). The third development was America's embrace in the 18th century of the pseudoscientific theories of Swedish botanist Carolus Linnaeus and German Professor of Medicine Johann Friedrich Blumebach. These pseudoscientific theories classified individuals of different phenotypes into discrete races with distinct and discernible characteristics—skin color and behavioral traits (Smedley & Smedley, 2012). Linnaeus posited that there were four races, which he classified as Americanus (Native Americans), Asiaticus (Chinese), Africanus (Blacks), and Europeanus (Whites). Europeanus was white, muscular, inventive, rational, and ruled by law. Americanus was reddish, stubborn, easily angered, and regulated by customs. Africanus was black, lazy, devious, and negligent. Asiaticus was shallow, greedy, and easily distracted (Smedley & Smedley, 2012).

Blumebach further refined the notion of racial classification and differences by coining the term "Caucasians" to describe Whites and splitting Asians into two groups: Mongoloid and Malay. Like Linnaeus, Blumebach believed that Caucasians most resembled the ideal human being. Blumebach posited that other races degenerated physically and morally as a consequence of moving away from their places of origin and having to adapt to new environments (Mukhopadhyay et al., 2013, p. 122; Smedley & Smedley, 2012).

The net result of these developments was the social, cultural, and political extension of racial meaning and classification to previously racially unclassified groups of people. These classifications were not based on shared culture, language, or affinity, but rather on a common phenotype (Rothenberg, 2013). Thus, by the early 18th century, Americans or migrants of European descent, regardless of differences in language and/ or culture, became "White." Indigenous natives, who were from distinct tribes with a myriad of languages, social structures, and values, became Indians. Africans, who had different tribal identities, including Ibo, Yoruba, and Fulani, became, in the parlance of the day, Negro/Black (Rothenberg, 2013).

Then, as now, these racial classifications were not merely benign descriptors; rather, they were the basis for the creation of an American racial hierarchy. In this hierarchy, Whites at the top and Native Americans and Blacks at the bottom were differently positioned in their access to society's resources, rewards, and privileges, thus, as Foner and Fredrickson (2004) suggest, creating a society in which privilege and pigmentation became closely correlated (p. 1).

Underpinning racial classifications were socially constructed myths and stereotypes. These myths and stereotypes, grounded in British and European cultural norms, rendered Native American and Black people and their cultures inferior to those of Whites (Allen, 1994), thus providing a moral justification for the racial subordination of Native Americans and Blacks on the grounds of their otherness and social and cultural inferiority (Allen, 1994).

For example, colonists saw Native Americans' belief in the land as a shared resource for the common good and not private ownership as antithetical to a rational and civilized society. Indeed, the colonists believed that in a rational and civilized society, private land ownership for profit was an essential social arrangement. Similarly opposite to colonists' understanding of a rational and civilized society were Native Americans' religious beliefs, which, though spiritual, were not at all consistent with Christianity (Allen, 1994).

As a consequence of these cultural differences and the frequent violent altercations at times of land encroachment, over time White colonists began to socially construct Native Americans as uncivilized, savage heathens. Indeed, the term "savage" as a descriptor of Native Americans became embedded in the Declaration of Independence, where Jefferson wrote that the King had "endeavored to bring on the inhabitants of our frontier, the merciless Indian Savages, whose warfare is an undistinguished destruction, of all ages, sexes, and conditions" (Declaration of Independence, 1776; Foner & Fredrickson, 2004; Sheehan, 1973).

The social construction of Blacks as "the other" and inferior to Whites took a more circuitous route than it did for Native Americans. At least initially, Blacks in the colonies had a range of experiences. Some were slaves, who had opportunities to become free, with legal rights and a degree of control over their day-to-day lives. Other Blacks were indentured servants, whose lives were for the most part not discernibly different from those of White indentured servants. Indeed, in the Virginia colony, indentured Black and White servants worked, fraternized, and lived together (Allen, 1994; Vaughn, 1989). They also shared a common bond of enmity toward the wealthy landowners and planters whose model of servitude kept them oppressed. Moreover, interracial marriages and relationships between servants were not uncommon, with a significant number of births in the Virginia colony being of mixed-race parentage. Lastly, others were freed persons who owned homes and land and had business dealings with White colonists that were on an equal footing (Allen, 1994; Morgan, 1975; Parent, 2003).

Socioeconomic forces, however, changed the trajectory of the Black experience in the colonies and eventually in an independent United States. Primary among the socioeconomic forces was the worldwide demand for the tobacco, cotton, rice, and sugar grown in the southern colonies, a demand that required a large and preferably permanent labor force (Allen, 1994; Vaughn, 1989). In response to the demand, the southern colonies turned to the importation and lifetime enslavement of Africans and their American-born offspring and descendants.

Paving the way for this enslavement was the Virginia Slave Code of 1705. The code served as a template for other colonies and would seal the fate for all Blacks for generations to come. It declared that all servants imported and brought into the country who were not Christians in their native country would be counted as slaves. As such, they would be deemed to be real estate and the property of their masters, with no legal rights. Children born to African slaves would also be considered real estate and the property of their masters. Slaves were prohibited from owning property, bearing arms (unless to fight Native Americans), moving or assembling without permission, or fraternizing with Whites. The code also established harsh physical punishment for slaves who were found to be offending in any way. For example, committing a robbery would result in a slave receiving 60 lashes and being placed in stocks. More tellingly, for associating with a White person, a slave could be whipped, branded, or maimed. Finally, if a slave resisted his master's correction and was killed in the process, the master was free of all punishment as if the incident did not happen (Allen, 1994; Vaughn, 1989).

From 1705 to 1770, approximately 300,000 enslaved Africans were imported primarily to the southern colonies. As non-Christians who were culturally diverse with different languages and customs, the imported Africans were very different from the Blacks who had preceded them (Horton & Horton, 2006). The difference, as well as their unfamiliarity with European culture and sensibilities, quickly saw imported African slaves socially constructed as a nearly subhuman species. They were perceived as being physically strong and imposing but lacking in intellect. Words commonly used to describe the African slaves included childlike, docile, primitive, backward, and sexually promiscuous (Allen, 1994; Horton & Horton, 2006). These social constructions linked dark skin color with moral and mental inferiority. They also stripped the African slave, and later their American-born offspring, of their humanity. The stripping of humanity allowed for slave masters to see African slaves and their American-born offspring as the "other," discernibly different from and inferior to Whites. It was a sentiment that was articulated by no less than Thomas Jefferson in his *Notes on the States of Virginia* in 1785. In the notes, Jefferson wrote "Blacks, whether originally a distinct race, or made distinct by time and circumstances, are inferior to Whites in the endowments both of body and mind" (Jefferson, 1785, p. 150; Smith, 1995, p. 21).

The social construction of Native Americans and Blacks as "the other" would, as suggested earlier, provide the justification for their racial subordination and exclusion from access to society's resources, rights, and privileges (Massey, 2007). This subordination and exclusion were codified and institutionalized—both explicitly and implicitly—through laws, treaties, social policies, and social institutions. In its effect, the codification and institutionalization of racial subordination and exclusion protected and promoted the political, economic, and cultural interests of Whites to the detriment of non-Whites (Vera & Feagin, 2007).

The 1790 Naturalization Act, for example, reserved naturalized citizenship for free Whites only (H.R.40, Naturalization Bill, 1790). Without citizenship, Native Americans and Blacks were denied the right to vote, own property, bring suit, or testify in court. Moreover, throughout the 19th century, a series of treaties and social policies would be used by the United States government to displace Native Americans from their tribal homelands in order to accommodate American expansionism and provide White settlers with land (Prucha, 2000).

The process of displacement was deliberate and ruthlessly efficient. In 1814, after the Battle of Horseshoe Bend (in present day Alabama near the Georgia border), where Major General Andrew Jackson routed and destroyed the military power of the Creeks, a treaty was forced upon the Creek compelling them to surrender to the United States over 20 million acres of their tribal homeland. Today, this land represents half the state of Alabama and one-fifth of the state of Georgia (Saltz, 2002; Sturgis, 2006).

In the decade after the Battle of Horseshoe Bend, Jackson led the Native American displacement campaign, negotiating nine of the 11 major treaties to remove Native Americans from their tribal homelands. These treaties culminated in the passage of the Indian Removal Act of 1830. The act authorized the recently elected President Andrew Jackson to grant unsettled lands west of Mississippi to Native Americans in exchange for the tribal homelands within the existing borders of the United States as they existed at the time. While some tribes relocated peacefully, many more were removed forcibly, one such example being the infamous "Trail of Tears," which saw approximately 4,000 Cherokee die on the march west (Saltz, 2002; Sturgis, 2006).

The Homestead Act of 1862 parceled out millions of acres of Native American land to eligible United States citizens upon the condition that they pledged to settle and farm the land for at least five years (Potter & Schamel, 1997). Similarly, the Dawes Act of 1887 dissolved Native American tribal homelands and explicitly prohibited communal land ownership. The result was a significant loss of Native American land and a further undermining of Native American culture (Nagel, 2012; Webster, 1992; P.L. 49–105)

The net impact of these and other discriminatory policies was that, by 1900, the United States government held almost total power over the Native American population, most of which was located on geographically and socially isolated reservations. They were governed not by ordinary American law but by treaties and statutes.

Blacks fared little better in the 19th century, as Congress passed laws such as the Fugitive Slave Act of 1850, which compelled free states to return fugitive slaves to their masters at the risk of fines, thus strengthening the institution of slavery (Campbell, 1970). Further confirming the second-class citizenship of Blacks was the Dred Scott decision of 1857. In that decision, the United States Supreme Court ruled that all people of African ancestry—slaves as well as free persons—could never become citizens and therefore could never sue in federal court (Finkelman, 2007). The decision further ruled that the federal government did not have the power to prohibit slavery in the territories. It also approved the Missouri Compromise of 1820, which restricted slavery in certain territories as unconstitutional (Finkelman, 2007).

Even with the Emancipation Proclamation and the end of slavery in America some six years after the Dred Scott decision, the institution would be replaced by something arguably more insidious: Jim Crow laws (see Chapter 8). The Jim Crow laws, which were in effect in the former southern slaveholding states from 1877 to 1964, were unabashed in their articulation of White superiority and Black inferiority (Foner & Fredrickson, 2004; Vann, 1974). Toward this end, Jim Crow laws segregated not only public venues but also restaurants, restrooms, hospitals, churches, libraries, schoolbooks, waiting rooms, housing, prisons, cemeteries, and asylums. The laws also regulated social relationships, with most states barring interracial relationships, and adopted the one-drop rule, which decreed that any person with even a trace of Black heritage, regardless of outward appearance, was considered Black (Vann, 1974).

Explicit support was given to Jim Crow with the *Plessey v. Ferguson* Supreme Court decision in 1896. The decision ruled that the segregation of Blacks and Whites (i.e., separate but equal) was fair and did not violate the Fourteenth Amendment, which recognized Blacks as citizens for the first time and gave Black men, but not women, the right to vote (Elliot, 2006).

Ethnicity

In a parallel development, mass immigration from eastern and southern Europe, Asia, and Mexico from the 1860s onward would force what Hochschild and Powell (2008) describe as a "profound process of racial restructuring" (p. 3). Informing the racial restructuring was the passionately debated question of who among the new immigrants belonged and did not belong in the racial classification of White. As will be described in Chapter 5, the groups that would not belong were the Chinese, southern Asians, and Pacific Rim Asians. All would be socially constructed as the other, racialized and placed alongside Native Americans and Blacks at the bottom of the racial hierarchy (Van Nuys, 2002). Conversely, the eastern and southern Europeans and Mexicans would be White but inhabit a new classification: ethnic (Hochschild & Powell, 2008). It was a classification that would not, at least initially, grant them unbridled access to society's resources, rights, and privileges, but it would ensure that they were afforded rights and privileges denied to Native Americans, Blacks, and Asians.

Box 3.1 U.S. Race Timeline, 1705–Present

1705: Virginia became the first of the colonies to establish a comprehensive slave code. The code declared that all servants imported and brought into the country that were not Christians in their native lands (i.e., Africans) shall be counted as slaves. Within this designation, all Negro, mulatto, and Indians were deemed to be real estate with no legal rights. They were prohibited from bearing arms, moving without permission, or fraternizing with Whites. If any slave was found to be offending in anyway, he or she was to be given 20 lashes on a bare back. Moreover, if any slave resisted their master and was killed in the process of correction, the master was free of all punishment, as if the incident had not happened (Allen, 1994; Morgan, 1975).

1705: Virginia defined any child, grandchild, or great-grandchild of a Black person a mulatto (Allen, 1994).

1705–1865: The permanent enslavement of Blacks and their offspring. This arrangement stripped Blacks and their offspring of all legal rights and power to determine their life course (Allen, 1994).

1790: The Naturalization Act of 1790 restricted citizenship to free Whites (Schultz, 2002).

1819: U.S. Congress passed the Civilization Fund Act. The primary goal of the act was to stimulate the "civilization process" of Native Americans. Toward this end, the act authorized federal funding for schools to educate Native American children. The education was provided by way of Indian boarding schools run by benevolent societies and Christian missions (Prucha, 2000).

1831: President Andrew signs the Indian Removal Act into law. The law authorized the president to grant unsettled lands west of the Mississippi to Native Americans in exchange for Native American lands within existing state boarders. Although some tribes agreed and went peacefully, many more resisted the relocation policy. Over the course of fall and winter of 1838 and 1839, the Cherokees were forcibly moved west by the U.S. government. An estimated 4,000 Cherokee died in the process of the forced move west, which became known as the "Trail of Tears" (Saltz, 2002).

1853: In ***People v. Hall***, the California Supreme Court ruling established that the Chinese had no rights to testify against White citizens. The ruling extended to the Chinese a ban already in place prohibiting Blacks and Native Americans from testifying for or against White people. In handing down the opinion, Justice Hugh Murray argued that the Chinese are a race of people whom nature has marked as inferior. Thus the consequences of allowing Chinese to testify "would admit them to all the equal rights of citizenship, and we might soon see them at the polls, in the jury box, upon the bench, and in our legislative halls" (Cheng, 1972; McClain, 1994).

1857: ***Dred Scott v. Sanford***, the landmark U.S. Supreme Court ruling that Blacks, enslaved or free, could not be American citizens and therefore had no legal standing to sue in federal court. It further argued that the federal government had no power to regulate slavery in the territories gained after the creation of the United States (Finkelman, 2007).

1862: President Lincoln signed the Homestead Act. The act allocated 160 acres of Native American land in what is now the West Coast to "anyone" who could pay $1.25 and cultivate it for five years. European immigrants and land speculators bought 50 million acres. The U.S. Congress gave another 100 million acres of Indian land free to the railroads. Because the act applied only to U.S. citizens, Native Americans, Blacks, and non-European immigrants were excluded (Potter & Schamel, 1997).

1864: The Thirteenth Amendment to the U.S. Constitution abolished slavery (Wormser, 2003).

1865–1866: After the Civil War and the end of slavery, southern states of the former Confederacy enacted a set of laws known as the Black Codes. The intent of the codes was to restrict the freedom of Blacks and compel them to work in a labor economy based on low wage or debt. One of the centerpieces of the codes was the vagrancy law, which permitted the authorities to arrest freed men who were congregating and commit them to involuntary labor (Wormser, 2003).

1866: The Civil Rights Act of 1866 was enacted despite a veto from President Andrew Johnson. The act granted Blacks citizenship and equal protection under the law (Foner, 2002).

1866: Virginia decreed that every person having one-fourth or more Black blood would be deemed a colored person (Allen, 1994).

1876–1965: Jim Crow laws were enacted, enforcing ***de jure*** racial segregation between Blacks and Whites in all public facilities in the southern states of the former Confederacy. The segregation led to conditions for Blacks that were not just inferior, but also provided southern Whites with nearly a hundred years of economic, educational, and social advantages. Segregation was enforced, when needed, with local or state violence. In the years between 1882 and 1990, there were 3,011 recorded lynchings of Blacks. The majority of these lynchings were in the southern states of the former Confederacy (Wormser, 2003).

1880: In ***Strauder v. West Virginia***, the U.S. Supreme Court ruled that the exclusion of Blacks from juries for no other reason that race violates the Equal Protection Clause (Foner, 2009).

1883: The U.S. Supreme Court struck down 1875 Civil Rights Act, which after Reconstruction guaranteed Blacks equal treatment in public accommodations and public transportation, and prohibited exclusion from jury service. In striking down the 1875 Civil Rights Act, the U.S. Supreme Court stated that the federal government cannot regulate behavior of private individuals in matters of race relations. This in turn allowed railroads, theaters, and other businesses to legally practice racial segregation (Blackmon, 2009).

1887: The U.S. Congress passed the Dawes Act. The stated purpose of the act was to stimulate Native American assimilation. Toward this end the act dissolved tribal lands, granting land allotments to individual families. The act also explicitly prohibited communal land ownership. As a result of the law, millions of acres of Mexican and Indian land in New Mexico was granted to White corporations (Nagel, 2012).

1896: ***Plessy v. Ferguson***, a landmark U.S. Supreme Court ruling that upheld the constitutionality of state laws mandating racial segregation in public facilities under the doctrine of "separate but equal" (Brook, 1997).

1897: ***In re Ricardo Rodriguez***, a federal district court in Texas upheld the right of Mexicans to naturalized citizenship of the U.S. under the Treaty of Guadalupe Hidalgo. In doing so, Mexicans were held to be White for purposes of naturalization (Rodriguez-Dominguez, 2005).

1923: ***Takao Ozawa v. U.S.***, a U.S. Supreme Court ruling denied Japanese businessman Takao Ozawa citizenship because he was not "White" within the meaning of the statute. As argued by the court, under the best-known science of the time, Ozawa was defined as being of the Mongolian race. In bringing the case to the U.S. Supreme Court, Ozawa argued that his skin is as white, if not whiter, than any so-called Caucasian (Chang, 2001).

1923: In ***U.S. v. Bhagat Singh Thind***, a U.S. Supreme Court ruling recognized that Indians from India were "scientifically" classified as Caucasians but concluded that they are not White in popular (White) understanding. As a result of the decision, no person of Indian origin could become a naturalized citizen, and those who were already citizens had their citizenship revoked (Garcia, 2013).

1924: The Virginia Racial Purity Act defined Black persons as having any trace of African ancestry. This act is also known as the one-drop rule (Allen, 1994).

1924: The Indian Citizenship Act granted Native Americans U.S. citizenship (Bruyneel, 2004).

1930–1940: The U.S. forcibly deported up to 500,000 Mexicans, many of whom were U.S. citizens (Rodriguez-Dominguez, 2005).

1942: President Franklin Delano Roosevelt signed Executive Order 9066, ordering the evacuation and mass incarceration of 120,000 persons of Japanese ancestry living on the West Coast, most of whom were U.S. citizens or documented immigrants (Kashima, 2011).

1944: ***Korematsu v. United States***, a landmark U.S. Supreme Court case, ruled that the exclusion order leading to Japanese American internment was not unconstitutional (Kashima, 2011).

1946: U.S. Court of Appeals for the Ninth Circuit ended ***de jure*** segregation in California in ***Mendez v. Westminster***. The court found that Mexican American children were segregated based on their "Latinized" appearance and district boundaries manipulated to ensure that Mexican American children attended separate schools (Strum, 2010).

1954: ***Brown v. Board of Education***, a landmark Supreme Court ruling, unanimously decided that segregation in education is inherently unequal (Foner, 2009).

1964: President Lyndon Johnson signed the Civil Rights Act of 1964 into law. The act outlawed discrimination in jobs and public accommodations based on race, color, religion, or national origin. By doing so, it provided the federal government with the power to enforce desegregation (Foner, 2009).

1968: In ***Loving v. Virginia*** the Supreme Court ruled that barring interracial marriage is unconstitutional. The ruling forced the 16 states that still banned interracial marriage in 1968 to change their laws (Newbeck & Wolfe, 2014).

1977: Directive No. 15, creating race and ethnic standards for federal statistical and administrative reporting, was adopted in response to civil rights legislation. The basic racial and ethnic categories for federal statistics and program administrative reporting were defined as follows:

a. ***American Indian or Alaskan Native***. A person having origins in any of the original peoples of North America, and who maintains cultural identification through tribal affiliation or community recognition.
b. ***Asian or Pacific Islander***. A person having origins in any of the original peoples of the Far East, Southeast Asia, the Indian subcontinent, or the Pacific Islands. This area includes, for example, China, India, Japan, Korea, the Philippine Islands, and Samoa.
c. ***Black***. A person having origins in any of the black racial groups of Africa.
d. ***Hispanic***. A person of Mexican, Puerto Rican, Cuban, Central or South American, or other Spanish culture or origin, regardless of race.
e. ***White***. A person having origins in any of the original peoples of Europe, North Africa, or the Middle East (U.S Census Bureau, 1977).

2001: The U.S. Congress passes the Patriot Act. The act gives the federal government the power to detain suspected "terrorists" indefinitely without access to legal representation. As a consequence of the act, Arab, Muslim, and South Asian men have been detained in secret locations, often without evidence (American Civil Liberties Union, 2009).

2017: President Trump signs Executive Order 13769, entitled Protecting the Nation from Foreign Terrorists Entry into the United States (also known as the Refugee and Muslim travel ban). The order lowered the number of refugees to be admitted into the United States in 2017 to 50,000. It also suspended the U.S. Refugee Admissions Program for 120 days and suspended entry of Syrian refugees indefinitely. Furthermore, it suspended for 90 days the entry into the U.S. of specific individuals from Iran, Iraq, Libya, Somalia, Sudan, Syria, and Yemen (Trump, 2017).

Racial and Ethnic Inequality in the United States and Its Contemporary Impact

During the last third of the 20th century, activism, laws, social policies, and Supreme Court rulings sought to alleviate the deleterious effects of decades of racial and ethnic inequality (see Box 3.1, U.S. Race Timeline). Ostensibly, at least, these efforts proved successful in providing unprecedented opportunities in all spheres of society for so-called racial and ethnic minorities. Indeed, for some, President Obama's election and reelection is seen as proof that the specter of racial and ethnic inequality is now a thing of the distant past.

Yet, while there is no denying the inroads made into banishing racial and ethnic inequality, it nevertheless remains a structural feature of contemporary American society. For the most part, however, it has none of the overt racial and ethnic hostility of the past, nor does it necessarily emanate from individual hate (Weinberg, 1996). Rather, it is reflected much more subtly in institutional policies and practices, as well as economic, political, and legal structures. As will be discussed in the book, these policies and structures assert color blindness and objectivity. However, in practice these policies and structures place certain racial and ethnic groups at a disadvantage in access to resources, rewards, and privileges in relation to the majority population. Thus, even with the inroads that have been made, significant disparities between Native Americans, Blacks, certain Hispanic groups, and the majority White population remain constant. These disparities are particularly telling in the areas of household income and wealth (Chapter 7), health outcomes (Chapter 9), employment (Chapter 8), educational attainment (Chapter 11) and poverty (Akee & Taylor, 2014; Indian Health Service, 2015; Hoyert & Xu, 2012; Kochhar et al., 2011; McCartney et al., 2013; National Center for Health Statistics, 2013). In short, Whites, in general, continue to enjoy considerable advantages over Native Americans, Blacks, and certain Hispanic groups vis-à-vis greater access to a range of society's resources and opportunities. Indeed, it is an advantage that has grown in the last decade and a half as a result of the housing crisis of 2008.

Not everyone, however, believes that the continued racial disparities between Native Americans, Blacks, certain Hispanic groups, and Whites have anything to do with institutional racism. Indeed, in the last 30 plus years, both neoconservatives and neoliberals have refuted the institutional racism thesis. They argue instead that what is to blame is a lack of individual responsibility and drive on the part of Blacks, in particular. Moreover, they posit that the social policies devised to alleviate the effects of racial and ethnic inequality over the years, which include benefits programs and affirmative action initiatives, have done more harm than good. No surprise, then, that in the contemporary United States, such policies and programs have been under attack by neoconservatives and neoliberals both (see Chapter 6).

What Social Workers Can Learn From the Historical and Contemporary Impact of Racial and Ethnic Inequality in the United States

1. The central role of social construction in determining the "other." Using myths and stereotypes to socially construct the other allows the majority to see the other's exclusion from access to society's resources, rewards, and privileges as justified and, in many cases, right for society. The social construction of the other was a central feature of the welfare reform movement of the 1980s and 1990s, which socially constructed Black mothers who were recipients of Aid to Families with Dependent Children (AFDC) as the undeserving poor who were bilking the system and hardworking Americans. It was a social construction that allowed the general public to view Black female welfare recipients as pariahs, thus justifying welfare reform that would be coercive as opposed to compassionate.
2. The instrumental role of policy in creating a racial and to a lesser extent ethnic hierarchy in which Whites, in general, enjoy greater access than other groups to society's resources, rewards, and privileges. Over time, this greater access has been and still is reflected in racial and ethnic disparities in most quality of life indicators, such as household income and wealth, health, employment, and education.
3. The inherent weakness of the personal responsibility argument to explain continued racial and ethnic disparities and inequality in contemporary America. It is an argument partly informed by stereotypes and myths, which fail to properly acknowledge the powerful role that policy and social structures and institutions such as the courts, banks, hospitals, and criminal justice system play in conferring access to resources.
4. The importance of activism as a counternarrative to racial and ethnic inequality and exclusion. Despite ongoing subjection, racial and ethnic groups have not simply acquiesced to their circumstances; they have challenged them through activism and legal challenges. Both activism and the legal challenges have brought forward a counternarrative in the call for humane treatment and inclusion.
5. The importance of advocating for policies that challenge racial and ethnic inequality.

6. The importance of the courts, specifically the U.S. Supreme Court, in bringing about policy and law changes.
7. How to pull from the history of race and racial and ethnic inequality to contextualize the current ideological debates about racial and ethnic inequality in the United States. By doing so, social workers, as a matter of social justice, are in a much better position to advocate and champion social policy that seeks to eliminate racial and ethnic inequality.

Box 3.2 Gender Timeline, 1776–Present

1776: Only White males who owned land could vote during the colonial and revolutionary period (Richter, 2013).

1839: Beginning in 1839, individual states in the United States enacted the Married Women's Property Act. The act enabled women to own and control personal property, inherit independently of their husbands, work for a salary of their own, write wills, and participate in contracts and lawsuits (Norton, 1999).

1848: Activists for women's rights and ending slavery joined together at the Women's rights convention in Seneca Falls, New York. The convention marked the beginning of the first-wave feminist movement. From 1848 to 1920, the first-wave feminist movement worked toward achieving suffrage for women (Wellman, 1991).

1851: Sojourner Truth delivered her famous "Ain't I a Woman" speech at the Women's Convention in Akron, Ohio (Orleck, 2015).

1861: ***Cole v. Van Ripper***, an Illinois Supreme Court ruling, gave a married woman exclusive control of her property as though she was single or unmarried. The ruling also exempted the married woman's property from attachment to her husband's debt (McCurdy, 1957).

1866: Elizabeth Cady Stanton and Susan B. Anthony came together to form an organization for White and Black women and men committed to the goal of universal voting groups. The organization splintered and reorganized over disputes about the best strategies to gain the vote for women and for Blacks (Gordon, 2000).

1867: The Fifteenth Amendment passed Congress and was ratified by the states in 1870. The amendment gave Black men, but not women, the right to vote (U.S. Government Printing Office, 1992).

1869: Arabella Mansfield became the first female lawyer in the United States (Encyclopedia Britannica, 2014).

1872: Susan B. Anthony was arrested and brought to trial in Rochester, New York, for attempting to vote in the presidential election. At the same time in Battle Creek, Michigan, Sojourner Truth, a former slave and social justice advocate, was turned away from a polling both when she attempted to vote (Gordon, 2000).

1872: Charlotte Ray became the first Black female lawyer in the United States (Smith, 1998).

1873: The U.S. Supreme Court decision in ***Bradwell v. State of Illinois*** ruled that states may statutorily deny women the right to practice law (Rierson, 1994).

1875: In ***Minor v. Happersett***, the U.S. Supreme Court upheld the Missouri State Court decision that refused to register women to vote because state laws allowed only men to vote (Basch, 1992).

1879: Belva Ann Bennett became the first female lawyer to practice before the U.S. Supreme Court (Norgren, 2007).

1890: Wyoming was admitted to statehood and became the first state to legislate voting for women in its constitution (McConnaughy, 2013).

1914: Margret Sanger was indicted on obscenity charges for sending birth control information through the mail (Sanger, 2004).

1917: Representative Jeannette Rankin of Montana became the first woman to serve in Congress (United States House of Representatives: History Art & Archives, 2014).

1920: The Nineteenth Amendment passed, giving women the right to vote in both the state and federal elections (McConnaughy, 2013).

1920: The "Ladies Agreement" immigration law ended the arrival of Japanese and Korean "picture brides." European women were also banned from entry if they could not show that either a man or a job was available for them (Loue, 2002).

1924: The right to vote was extended to Native Americans of both sexes by an act of Congress (Sabato & Ernst, 2007).

1928: Women in Puerto Rico won the right to vote (Clark, 1975).

1933: Francis Perkins became the first female Cabinet member. She was selected by President Franklin Delano Roosevelt to be Secretary of Labor (Downey, 2009).

1961: In ***Hoyt v. Florida***, the U.S. Supreme Court ruled that it is not unconstitutional to have an all-male jury (Grossman, 1994).

1963: Congress passed the Equal Pay Act, requiring wage equality for men and women doing the same work (U.S. Government Printing Office, 1963).

1963: The beginning of the second-wave feminist movement. The movement was involved in activism for women's rights and full inclusion. The second-wave feminist movement was at the forefront of all the major women's rights legislation throughout the 1960s and 1970s (Offen, 1988).

1964: The Civil Rights Act of 1964 was enacted. The act included Title VII, which guaranteed equal gender opportunity in employment (U.S. Equal Employment Opportunities Commission, 2015).

1972: Title XI of the Educational Amendments prohibited the exclusion of any person from participation in an educational program or the denial of benefits based on one's gender. More specifically, Title XI required that both genders have equal opportunities to participate in sports and enjoy the benefits of competitive athletics (National Women's Law Center, 2012).

1972: The Women's Rights Project of the Center for Law and Social Policy was established (O'Connor, 2010).

1972: Shirley Chisholm became the first woman and Black person to run for a place on the presidential ticket (Smith, 2013).

1973: In ***Roe v. Wade***, a landmark case, the U.S. Supreme Court ruled that the due process clause of the Fourteenth Amendment extended to a woman's right to an abortion (Garrow, 1994).

1974: ***Corning Glass Works v. Brennan*** was the U.S. Supreme Court's first ruling under the Equal Pay Act of 1973. The Court ruled that employers cannot justify paying women lower wages because that was what they had traditionally received as the going rate (Baird, 1975).

1975: ***Taylor v. Louisiana***, a significant U.S. Supreme Court decision, overturned ***Hoyt v. Florida*** by ruling that women could not be excluded from a jury (Grossman, 1994).

1978: The Pregnancy Discrimination Act prohibited sex discrimination on the basis of pregnancy (U.S. Equal Opportunity Commission, 2014).

1981: Sandra Day O' Connor becomes the first woman to serve on the U.S. Supreme Court. She was appointed to the Supreme Court by President Ronald Reagan. She served on the Court from 1981 until 2006 (Sandra Day O'Connor, n.d.).

1981: In ***Rostker v. Goldberg***, the U.S. Supreme Court upheld as constitutional the practice of requiring only men to register for the military service draft (MacDwyer, 1982).

1986: In ***Meritor Saving Bank v. Vinson***, the U.S. Supreme Court ruled that sexual harassment creates a hostile working environment and was covered by Title VII of the Civil Rights Act of 1964 (The Oyez Project, 2014a).

1991: In ***UAW v. Johnson Controls***, the U.S. Supreme Court ruled that mandatory sterilization for women or exclusion from certain jobs were gender-based discrimination and were prohibited under Title VII of the Civil Rights Act (The Oyez Project, 2014b).

1993: The Family and Medical Leave Act required covered employers to provide 12 weeks of unpaid protected leave to eligible employees for several reasons. Among those reasons were pregnancies, prenatal medical care, and child birth (U.S. Department of Labor, 2013).

1996: In ***United States v. Virginia***, the Supreme Court ruled that the all-male Virginia Military School had to lift its ban on women if it were to continue to receive public funding (Legal Information Institute, 1996).

2003: The lawsuit ***Gonzalez et al. v. Abercrombie & Fitch Stores, Inc., et al.*** was filed on the grounds that the retailer Abercrombie & Fitch violated Title VII of the Civil Rights Act of 1962. The lawsuit alleged that the nationwide retailer Abercrombie & Fitch maintained hiring practices that excluded women and racial and ethnic minorities by means of a restrictive marketing image and other policies. These alleged policies included not hiring strongly qualified female, Asian, Latino, and Black applicants, and/or placing them in positions of non-visibility. In 2005, the lawsuit was settled with Abercrombie & Fitch agreeing to pay $50 million to the class of female, Asian, Latino, and Black applicants and employees (U.S. Equal Opportunity Commission, 2004).

2003: U.S. Rep. Nancy Pelosi (D-CA) becomes the first female leader of a party in Congress—serving twice as House minority leader (2003–2007 and 2011–2019) (History.com).

2007: U.S. Rep. Nancy Pelosi (D-CA) becomes the first female speaker of the House (2007–2011 and 2019–2021) (History.com). She was selected again as the speaker of the House for 2021–2023 in December 2020.

2009: The Lily Ledbetter Fair Pay Restoration Act amended the Civil Rights Act of 1964 and stated that the 180-day statute of limitations for the filing of an equal-pay lawsuit resets with each new paycheck affected by the discriminatory action (Govtrack.US, 2011).

2009: On August 8, Sonia Sotomayor becomes the first Latina and Hispanic to serve on the Supreme Court (Sonia Sotomayor, n.d.).

2013: U.S. Defense Secretary Leon Panetta announced that the ban on women serving in combat roles would be lifted (Namarck, 2015).

2014: Senate Republicans blocked the Paycheck Fairness Act for the second time. Among other things, the act would have punished employers for retaliating against employees who shared wage information. It would allow workers to sue for punitive damages for wage discrimination. It would also require the Department of Labor to train employees to eliminate pay inequality and to continue to collect wage information based on gender. Lastly, the bill would create a grant program to train women on wage negotiation skills. Senate Republicans stated opposition to the bill on the grounds that it would remove caps on punitive damages against businesses found guilty of discrimination. The Chambers of Commerce urged a no vote on the bill, arguing it would erode employer defenses for legitimate pay disputes (Govtrack.US, 2011).

2016: Hilary Clinton becomes the first woman to receive a presidential nomination from a major political party (History.com, 2020).

2020: Kamala Harris becomes the first woman and woman of color to be elected vice president of the United States (History.com).

2021: On January 20, Kamala Harris is sworn in as vice president of the United States. Justice Sonia Sotomayor, the first Latina and Hispanic to serve on the Supreme Court, administers the swearing-in oath (Nadworny, 2021).

The Origins of Gender Inequality in the United States

That origins of gender inequality in the United States are deeply rooted in the nation's colonial beginnings and the patriarchy that came to dominate social arrangements. Patriarchy, brought to the new world from Europe by the colonists, predated the social construction of race. It was not, however, an initial feature of social arrangements in one of the first regions to be colonized, the Chesapeake, where in its earliest days a number of factors dictated that men and women work together as equals as a matter of survival. These factors included particularly high mortality rates, an imbalanced sex/gender ratio, and the scattered nature of settlement (Richter, 2013; Skinner, 2011). All of these factors, at least in the early 17th century, conspired to prevent the traditional patriarchal family arrangements of Europe from taking hold in Chesapeake. Planters' wives, indentured servants, and slaves labored alongside one another in the tobacco fields. Moreover, an unmarried women with land could engage in business on the same footing as her male counterpart (Richter, 2013).

As new colonies were established, however, many more people from Europe migrated to the new world. In doing so, the ratio of women significantly increased, as did the number of families, particularly among the Puritans fleeing religious persecution (Mintz & Kellogg, 1988). Colonists began to envision the new world as their permanent home and sought to establish a society that had many of the structural features they had known in their motherland, among them patriarchy.

Historians are not clear exactly when, but certainly sometime in the mid-17th century, the all-too-brief time of gender equality began to give way to patriarchal social arrangements (Richter, 2013). For example, the Puritans in New England organized their families, which they saw as the foundational unit of a godly society, around the unquestioned principle of biblical patriarchy (Mintz & Kellogg, 1988). In the Chesapeake colonies of Virginia and Maryland, the colony lawmakers used social constructs about gender, race, and class to codify two distinct roles for women in Virginia. One role was for free White women who were married. In this role, the "good" wife performed domestic labor in the home and reared children. The other role was for indentured servants and slaves who performed agricultural labor.

Within the patriarchal social arrangement in the colonies, men held ultimate authority over their wives, children, and other dependents. Beginning first with her father and then her husband, a woman's subordination to a man was a lifetime social arrangement, both in the home and in public life. Undergirding this subordination was the *doctrine of coverture*, which affirmed that a woman, once married, was entirely subsumed under her husband's person (Richter, 2013). Consequently, a married woman had no legal status and could not control property, even if she brought it to the marriage. Additionally, under the doctrine, a wife ceded to her husband full rights to all income or wages she earned (Richter, 2013).

Adult women who were unmarried or widowed were considered *feme sole*. As a consequence, they fared much better than their married counterparts in that they could buy and sell property and engage in other business and legal transactions (Richter, 2013). That said, women who did not marry were by the standards of the day deemed unnatural and called "spinsters" or "thornbacks."

Generally speaking, women were thought of in the patriarchal social arrangement of the colonies as the weaker vessel, that is, morally and mentally deficient and physically inferior. Thus, they were expected, most notably as wives, to be dutiful, demure, and obedient caretakers of children and the home (Skinner, 2011, p. 1). Women who did not conform to these gender norms and their constraints were seen, most particularly in the Puritan colony, as a threat to the collective social order and risked censure and banishment. Indeed, of great concern was controlling any expression of woman as a sexual being. Unmarried mothers not with the fathers of the children were, therefore marginalized and deemed immoral, a theme that would be all too present throughout the United States' development (Norton, 1999).

Though all women were victimized by patriarchal social arrangements of the colonial era, the effect was not uniform. How the patriarchal social arrangements affected women depended on the woman's race and class, as it still does today. For example, in most Native American tribes, gender roles were differentiated, but both sexes had power over decision making in the tribes, including such matters as when wars started and ended (Glenn, 2002). Moreover, unlike the practice of the colonists, some tribes had matrilineal systems, in which hereditary leadership and property were controlled and passed through the maternal line (Speck, 1938). In the matrilineal tribes such as the Cherokee, wives owned the family property, and children were considered to belong to their mother's clan. Furthermore, husbands had no standing in their wife or children's clan, as they were seen to belong to their mother's clan (Perdue, 1998).

Even in patrilineal systems, Native American women still had gender roles that were complementary with those of men rather than dichotomous and subservient. They often undertook hard labor and held powerful positions as farmers as well as cultivators of the land and food processers. These were all roles that were outside those of the gendered-role expectations of the colonists, particularly in the English-speaking colonies (Glenn, 2002).

Despite their standing in the tribes, in the larger colonial society, racism and the patriarchal social arrangements rendered Native American women very much at the mercy of the gendered and racial biases of White men and the colonial institutions they ran. Thus, they were not entitled to any of the legal protections available to "free" White women, such as they were. Moreover, regardless of need they were left outside the provision of the social welfare that colonies provided by way of a system of poor laws (Trattner, 1999).

Enslaved Black women had absolutely no rights within the patriarchal social arrangements of the colonial era by the mid-17th century. Not only were they in lifelong servitude, but also they had no legal rights that their master had to acknowledge. Their children became the property of the slave master or mistress and could be sold at his or her whim. As property, they could be forced into a nonconsensual sexual relationship with their masters with no recourse. They were not permitted to be married, educated, or form anything that resembled a permanent family structure that was recognized in law. Moreover, they were compelled to work the same long, backbreaking hours as the men, even when pregnant or ill (Glenn, 2002). Unlike their male counterparts, however, enslaved Black women had a dual value to their master, both as productive and reproductive labor. Thus, their value was seen strictly as labor. They would not have the luxury of work responsibilities that were entirely domestic and thus would not enjoy the respect that was afforded to White women (Abramovitz, 1996). Both enslaved and freed, Black women would be expected to work.

Indentured White women suffered the same indignities as their male counterparts. For instance, they were not paid a wage while in service for any of their long and backbreaking hours of work. Additionally, they were not allowed to marry while in service, nor could they leave the house or travel without permission. In addition, if they became pregnant, years were added to their service and they could be physically punished. Finally, they could not buy or sell anything, and had none of the few legal rights afforded to "free" unmarried or widowed White women (Morgan, 2001).

One notable exception in the 17th century to the patriarchal social arrangements was the Religious Society of Friends (Quakers). The Quakers rejected the gender restrictions of British and Colonial society and embraced the Testimony of Equality (Hawes & Shores, 2002). It evolved from the belief that all people were created equal, regardless of gender, race, creed, or color. To this end, as part of their testimony of equality, Quakers participated in actions to promote equality, which included equal rights for women. As George Fox, the founder of the Quakers, wrote in 1674:

> And some men say, "Men must have the Power and superiority over the woman, because God says, 'The man must rule over his wife, and that man is not of woman, but the woman is of the man'" (Gen 3:16). Indeed, after man fell, that command was. But before man fell, there was no such command. For they were both meet-helps. They were both to have dominion over all that God made. And as man and woman are restored again by Christ, up into the image of God, they both have dominion again in Righteousness and Holiness, and are helps-meet, as before they fell.
>
> *(Hallvworthington.com, 2016, p. 831)*

Within the Quaker organization, women served as preachers, and within the Quaker families, husbands did not occupy a hierarchical position over their wives. Rather, they followed the helps-meet model, which stressed equality and mutual companionship (Wulf, 2005).

At least for White women, going into the 18th century, changing social conditions challenged the traditional family patriarch. These social conditions included a population explosion in the 13 colonies, which increased from an estimated 250,000 in 1700 to 2.5 million in 1775 (Lemon, 1990). In their growth, the colonies, particularly on the eastern seaboard, became more heterogeneous, bringing in the Dutch and the Germans in Pennsylvania colony. Both groups brought with them a more egalitarian and relaxed view on gender roles than their British counterparts. Indeed, Dutch and German women labored in the fields and stables just as a man would. Moreover, they had more control of property than was allowed by English colonial law. They also owned their own clothes and other items and were permitted to write wills and dispose of the property brought into marriage, and could also own property in their own right (Kitch, 2009). Lastly, many served as deputy husbands and dependents when their husbands were away.

In the spirit of a revolutionary time when the 13 colonies were looking for freedom and independence from Britain and the crown, there was a growing call from upper-class women for equality. To be sure, while formal patriarchal laws and customs were in place empowering men, informally and in practice, women were finding ways to subvert patriarchy. They had a greater say about whom they married, rejecting suitors, engaging in or refusing premarital sex, and they founded and ran organizations that were beyond the grasp of men, such as charitable organizations. When men went to war, their mothers and wives stepped in and ran farms and shops, and protected them against all kinds of hazards (Kitch, 2009).

For all this, however, women in the 18th century did not gain any significant rights. They did not have the right to vote, as was the case initially for everybody other than White male landowners. Furthermore, the primary domestic labor of women was socially constructed as less valuable and subordinated to men's work outside of the home. Similarly subordinated was the labor of Native American and Black women. Consequently, women, regardless of their status, remained distanced from society's rewards and privileges. The degree to which women were distanced from these rewards and privileges was contingent on race, class, and immigration status (Glenn, 2002).

But in the 19th century, immigration, industrialization, migration, expansionism, civil war, emancipation, and a first-wave feminist movement would challenge the very foundation of patriarchy. Immigrants introduced even more diversity to the United States; most of them were from eastern and southern Europe, as well as Asia and Mexico. The migrant women, as a condition of survival, became workers in the mills of New England, which characterized the United States' first industrial revolution. Although they were valuable labor, they would still be exploited labor (see Chapter 8). Native American women would find themselves victimized by American expansionism that would tear them from their tribal homelands and undermine their culture and their traditional standing in their tribes. The Civil War and its high mortality and injury rates focused the responsibility for family well-being on women. Emancipation promised former slaves inclusion for the brief period of the Reconstruction, but ultimately was undone by racism and an unwillingness of President Andrew Johnson to see Reconstruction through to its rightful conclusion. The effect on Blacks in general and women in particular was devastating, as they were forced to rejoin the work force as necessary but nevertheless exploited labor under the shadow of Jim Crow. The second industrial revolution would move the United States from an agrarian to a fully industrialized nation by the end of the century. Immigrant women would feel keenly the implications of industrialization, as they were now compelled to make a living in the factories and mills, again as exploited labor.

The first-wave feminist movement, led by primarily White middle-class women, wanted equality and the franchise, which had been granted to former male slaves in the Fifteenth Amendment, but inexplicably not to women of any color. Black women were equally as vociferous in their call for liberation and equality, sometimes joining with White women in the struggle. It was a struggle that also saw the call for a progressive agenda that would reform the United States into a more just and equal society. Although women were not successful in getting the vote until the 20th century, a number of notable changes were gained regarding legal standards (see Box 3.2, Gender Timeline). However, Native American, Black women, and immigrant women from China continued to be denied some of the basic rights of citizenship, such as the ability to testify in court and access to fair pay and treatment, leaving them perpetually on the margins of society. Immigrant women from eastern and southern Europe and Mexico faired only slightly better, often subject to the xenophobic rants of nativist and Social Darwinists, who saw all groups other than Anglo-Saxon or Nordic Whites as culturally and intellectually inferior.

Gender Inequality in the United States and Its Contemporary Impact

As a result of the second wave of the feminist movement in the 1960s (see Box 3.2, Gender Timeline), the past 50 years has seen significant strides toward gender equality. In November 2020, Kamala Harris was the first woman and women of color to be elected vice president of the United States. Moreover, Joe Biden's first Cabinet as president has 11 women, ten of whom were confirmed between January and March 2021, and one, Shalanda Young, who, as of June 2021, is the serving Director of the Office of Management and Budget. It is a record-breaking Cabinet as regards the number of women, beating former President Clinton's second term of nine women serving concurrently (Center for American Women and Politics, 2021; Conroy et al., 2020; Times Staff, 2021, June 2). Three women are U.S. Supreme Court justices. A record number 126 women hold seats in the 116th Congress (23.6% of the 535 seats). Ninety women held statewide executive positions (28.9% of 311 available positions). There were 1,789 female state legislators (24.2% of 7,383 seats). Furthermore, as of June 2020, 378 women were mayors in cities with a population of at least 30,000 (23.3%), and 27 women were mayors of cities included in the nation's 100 largest cities (27%) (Center for American Women and Politics, 2020).

Yet, despite the recent unprecedented strides in political equality for women, gender remains stubbornly entrenched as a basis for social inequality in the United States. Women, regardless of race/ethnicity, class, immigration status, sexual orientation, or disability status still continue to experience significant wage disparities relative to their male counterparts (Payscale.com, 2020). As will be discussed in detail in Chapter 8, the wage disparity has significant implications for lifetime earnings loss. Also problematic and to be discussed in Chapter 8 is continued gender workforce segregation, which continues to find so-called women's work, primarily in the service sector, undervalued in comparison to so-called men's work.

Furthermore, across all racial, ethnic, and age groups, women are poorer than men (DeNavas-Walt & Proctor, 2014).

Relatedly, the intersection of gender, class, and race continues to find Native American/Alaskan Native, Black/Black American and Hispanic women facing particularly high levels of poverty (Payscale.com, 2020). Women also continue to bear the cost of raising children disproportionately, they are more likely to be victimized by domestic violence, and they spend more time than men providing unpaid caregiving (Cawthorne, 2008).

Finally, there has been an ongoing attempt by primarily conservative legislators both at the state and federal level to deny women full rights to their sexual and reproductive health. Among the rights are the right to autonomy and privacy in making sexual and reproductive decisions, as well as the right to family planning resources (Center for Reproductive Rights, 2011). Indeed, since the Supreme Court handed down its 1973

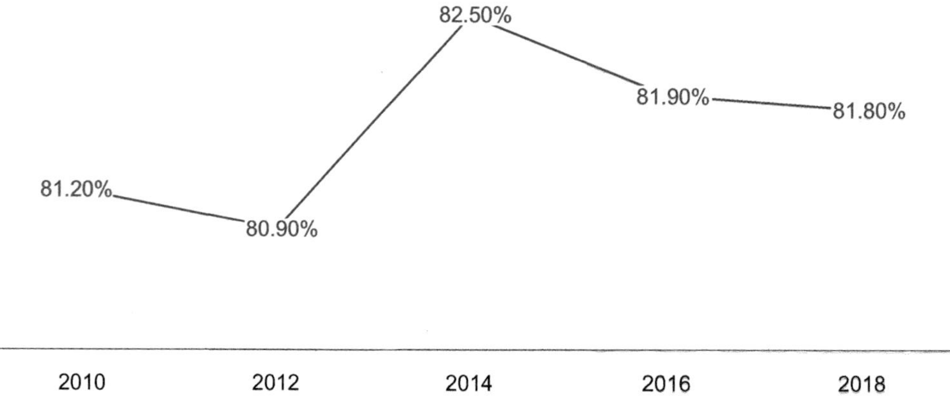

Figure 3.1 Women's Earnings as a Percentage of Men's for Full-time Wage and Salary Workers, 2010–2018 Annual Averages

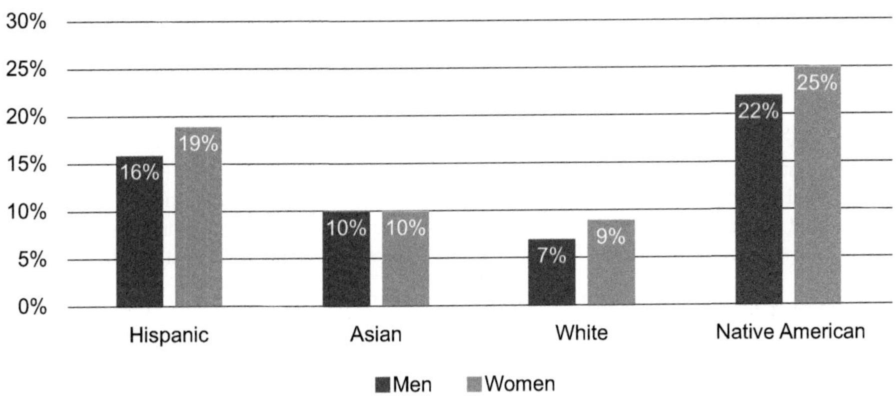

Figure 3.2 Percentage of Men and Women in Poverty by Race and Ethnicity, 2018

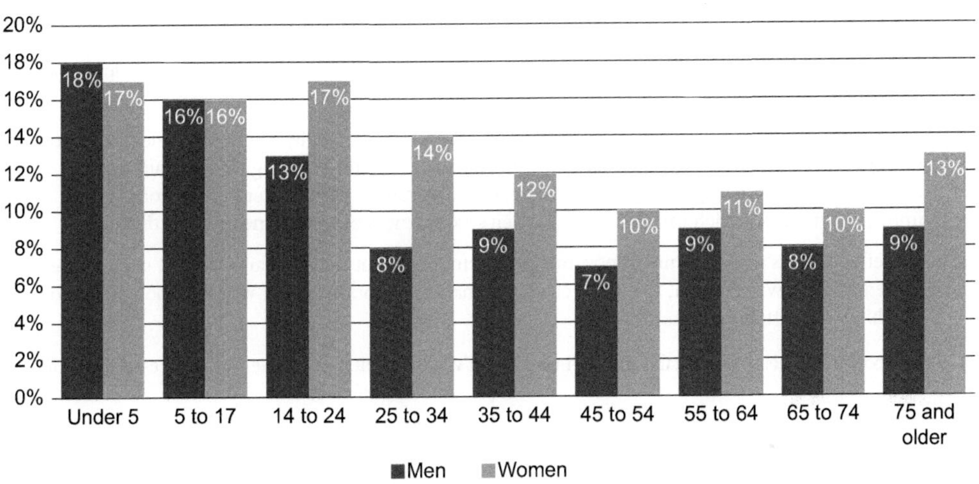

Figure 3.3 Poverty Rates by Age and Gender, 2018

landmark ruling in *Roe v. Wade* and *Doe v. Bolton*, states across the nation have constructed an intricate web of abortion law, codifying, regulating, and limiting whether, when, and under what circumstances women may obtain an abortion (Guttmacher Institute, 2020). Illustrative of this, as of December 2020, 25 states require women seeking an abortion to wait a specified period between when she receives counseling and the procedure. Fourteen of these states have laws that require women to make two separate trips to the clinic to obtain the procedure (Guttmacher Institute, 2020). Moreover, 33 states and the District of Columbia prohibit state funds for an abortion unless the women's life is in danger or the pregnancy is the result of rape or incest. South Dakota goes one step further in defiance of the federal requirement by only funding abortions in cases of life endangerment (Guttmacher Institute, 2020).

At the federal level, in 2015, conservative legislators were feverish in their attempts to defund health groups that perform abortions. In fact, in 2015, conservative legislators passed a bill in the House that would allow states to withhold Medicaid funding to health groups that perform abortions, and in doing so essentially strip Planned Parenthood of government funding (Guttmacher Institute, 2020).

Whatever one's opinions are on abortion, the state and federal policies represent an unprecedented intrusion on the rights of women to control their bodies in a way that has never been the case for most free men.

For social workers, the most pressing social policy issues related to gender inequality is the need for an equal pay bill to ensure equality of pay for women. As it is, the Lilly Ledbetter Fair Pay Act, which extends the time period in which claimants can bring pay discrimination claims, goes only part way to addressing the issue of pay inequality.

The other policy issue is related to lifting mothers out of poverty. Currently, benefits programs such as Temporary Assistance to Needy Families (TANF) and Supplement Nutrition Assistance Program (SNAP) are not universal or centralized. Rather, they are means tested and give states the discretion to decide who participates, and as a result, millions of working poor mothers are ineligible for these programs. To date, policy makers on both sides of the aisle are reluctant to challenge the austere nature of current benefits programs.

The final policy issue is giving women full rights to their sexual and reproductive health.

What Social Workers Can Learn From the Historical and Contemporary Impact of Gender Inequality in the United States

1. The long-standing social construction of women's work, domestic or otherwise, as less valuable and meaningful than men's work. This social construction has endured from the nation's colonial era and is manifested both explicitly and explicitly in the workplace in wage disparities, occupational segregation, and a lack of recognition or compensation for domestic labor.
2. The racial and ethnic differences in the experiences of gender inequality. These differences find women from racial and ethnic backgrounds, Asians being a notable exception, being differentially affected than their White counterparts in the workplace. One also cannot forget other designations such as immigration status, which can also affect women's experiences of gender inequality differently.
3. The effectiveness of the feminist movements in bringing about policy change that in some respects helped to empower women, as well as challenge male assumptions about women's potential and suitability for certain occupations.
4. The continued need for social policy to bring about wage equality for women of all races and ethnicities.

The Origins of Social Class Inequality in the United States

Unlike the European countries from which the United States emerged, social class as a concept is and has been a contentious issue in America. One of the reasons for this is that the United States has no history with monarchy, feudalism, or any of the other conditions that so clearly marked social class lines in the European monarchies (Trattner, 1999). Absent these clearly defined markers, the myth of a classless America has emerged and been bulwarked by the founding precept of meritocracy and America exceptionalism.

In actuality, social class has been an enduring contributor to social inequality in the United States since its colonial beginnings (Wood, 1993). In the English-speaking southern colonies, a small class of White, Anglo-Saxon, male, wealthy planters and landowners were all powerful (Vaughn, 1989). This power derived in part from their wealth and landholdings and in part from their role as representatives of the private investors who funded the growing and exporting of tobacco, rice, and sugar. They formed and ran the government, framed laws under the auspices of the British crown, and used indentured servants and slaves to tend to their land without compensation. Just as importantly, at the birth of the nation, they as a class (although less than 20% of the nation) were the only group eligible to vote (Wood, 1993).

Distinct from the elite class of wealthy planters and landowners were artisans, small farmers, religious leaders, and common laborers. Typically, they made a marginal living and would be considered middle class by today's standard. They had legal rights and opportunities for advancement (Wood, 1993). At the bottom of the social class hierarchy were slaves and indentured servants whose survival and living were completely dependent on their masters. They had little or nothing in the way of legal rights or opportunity for advancement (Wood, 1993). Paradoxically, recent studies indicate that despite the power differential between the classes in colonial America, income disparity was among the lowest in American history.

The years between 1760 and 1900 saw profound changes in American society and thinking about social class. The enlightenment philosophy of John Locke posited that an individual had natural rights, including the right of self-government. Moreover, John Locke argued that the character of individuals and societies were not fixed but could be changed through education, rational thinking, and purposeful action.

This philosophy would be one of the catalysts for the American Revolution and the founding of the United States as an independent nation (Wood, 1993). It would also challenge the notion of a society where social class bound one to a particular fate. In the years between 1776 and 1850, the idea of social mobility was embraced and evidenced by the millions who sought to make their fortunes free of the shackles of social class.

Though inspirational in theory and true for certain sections of the population, this philosophy did not hold true for everyone. In reality, race, ethnicity, gender, and immigration status obfuscated class and bound large swaths of the population to a set of experiences that did not allow for social mobility. For example, while the Gilded Age of the mid-1800s saw a small number of elite entrepreneurs, some from humble backgrounds, become fabulously wealthy, this was not the case for most people. Nor did it demonstrate that merit, not class, was the key to American success (Halpin & Williams, 2010). Even with a sizable educated middle class that emerged from the Gilded Age, most Americans remained within the laboring class, many of them being first-generation immigrants lured to the United States for a chance at the American dream (Halpin & Williams, 2010).

These conditions did not change for the vast majority of Americans until the progressive era and the call for government to become part of addressing the unfair nature of capitalism (Halpin & Williams, 2010). As will be discussed, 20th-century progressive social policies have contributed to the creation of a sizable middle class. They also challenged large-scale income and social and economic mobility disparities.

Social Class Inequality in the United States and Its Contemporary Impact

Despite the social policy efforts of the past 100 years, there has been a slow but gradual reemergence of class as one of the primary sources of inequality in the United States. With it, the United States has fallen behind other developed countries in intergenerational income mobility. Furthermore, the wealth disparity between the wealthiest 1% and the rest of the population is now at a level unprecedented in American history (Stone et al., 2014). For example, in 1980, the 90/10 ratio in the United States stood at 9.1. Simply put, this means that households at the top of the earnings chart had incomes about nine times the incomes of those at the bottom. Since 1980, the ratio has increased, reaching 12.6 in 2018, an increase of 39% (Horowitz et al., 2020).

Finally, a growing body of recent research indicates that one's current social class and its related circumstances are more predictive of one's opportunity for intergenerational income mobility than any other factor (Stone et al., 2014).

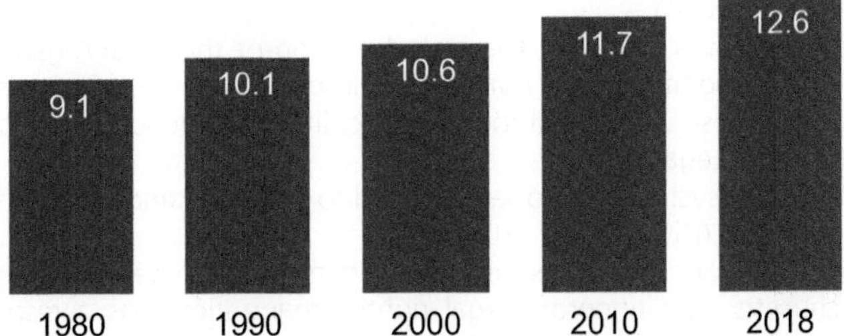

Figure 3.4 Ratio of Income at the 90th Percentile to Income at the 10th Percentile (90/10 ratio), 1980–2018

What Social Workers Can Learn From the Historical and Contemporary Impact of Social Class Inequality in the United States

1. Contrary to popular opinion, social class does exist in the United States.
2. The fallacy of the narrative that anyone can make it with hard work, which is at odds with the reality of the current income and wealth disparities.
3. The important role that progressive social policy played in creating an American middle class, which in the history of the United States is a relatively recent occurrence.
4. The need for redistributive social policies to lessen wealth and income disparities.

Box 3.3 Sexual Orientation/Identity Timeline, 1609–Present

1609–2003: All of the colonies and then states enacted some form of a sodomy law criminalizing homosexuality (Bronski, 2011).

1917: The Immigration Act of 1917, also known as the Asiatic Barred Zone Act, prohibited individuals considered to be psychopathically inferior, including LGBT individuals, from entering the United States (Campi, 2005).

1950: Harry Hay established America's first national gay rights organization, the Mattachine Society. The express purpose of the society was to eliminate discrimination, prejudice, and bigotry against homosexuals (Hay, 1996).

1952: The American Psychiatric Association listed homosexuality as a sociopathic personality disturbance (American Experience, n.d.).

1953: President Dwight Eisenhower signed into law Executive Order 10450 banning homosexuals from working for the federal government or any of its private contractors (American Experience, n.d.).

1958: *One, Inc. v. Olsen,* a landmark U.S. Supreme Court decision, ruled in favor of the First Amendment rights of the LGBT magazine *One*. In doing so, it rejected the U.S. Postal Service and FBI argument that the content of *One* was obscene material (Diversity Inc., 2014).

1962: Illinois became the first U.S. state to decriminalize homosexuality when it repealed its sodomy laws (Diversity Inc., 2014).

1969: After a long history of regular, city-sanctioned harassment by the New York City Police Department, patrons of the Stonewall Inn rebelled by physically defending themselves against the police. The Stonewall uprising, which occurred on June 28, 1969, is credited with being the catalyst for the modern Gay Rights movement (Diversity Inc., 2014).

1973: Lambda Legal was founded. The stated mission of this legal organization was to achieve full recognition of the civil rights of lesbians, gay men, bisexuals, transgender people, and those with HIV, through impact litigation, education, and public policy work (Lambda Legal, n.d).

1973: The American Psychiatric Association voted to remove homosexuality from its list of mental illnesses (Diversity Inc., 2014).

1978: Gay and Lesbian Advocates and Defenders (GLAD) was founded in Boston, Massachusetts. The nonprofit legal rights organization was a response to sting operations conducted by the Boston Police Department to entrap gay men in the men's room of the main building of Boston Library. The goal of the organization was to end discrimination based on sexual orientation, HIV status, and gender identity and expression (GLAD, n.d).

1980: The Democratic party became the first political party to endorse a homosexual rights platform (American Experience, n.d.).

1982: Wisconsin became the first state to outlaw discrimination on the basis of sexual orientation (Diversity Inc., 2014).

1987: The AIDS Coalition to Unleash Power (ACT UP) advocacy group was formed in response to the devastating impact of HIV/AIDS on the gay community in New York. ACT UP became a major activist and advocacy force for affordable medication and services for people living with HIV/AIDS (Epstein, 1996).

1989: The first U.S. case of asylum was granted on the grounds of persecution because of homosexuality. The subject of the case was a Cuban immigrant named Fidel Armando Toboso-Alfonso (Justice.gov, 1990).

1990: The Immigration Act of 1990 (P.L. 101–649) removed homosexuality as a ground for exclusion from immigrating to the United States (U.S. Government Printing Office, 1990).

1990: The Ryan White Comprehensive AIDS Resource Emergency Act (P.L. 101-381) is passed (Hoffman, 2003).

1993: The policy of Don't Ask, Don't Tell was adopted by the U.S. military. The policy directed military personal not to pursue or harass homosexual service members. Though ostensibly a lifting of a ban on homosexual service that been in effect since World War II, in effect it remained a ban on any overt expression of one's sexuality (Diversity Inc., 2014).

1996: In *Romer v. Evans*, the U.S. Supreme Court ruled that Colorado's 2nd amendment denying gays and lesbians protections against discrimination was unconstitutional (Diversity Inc., 2014).

1996: President Clinton signed the Defense of Marriage Act. The act defined marriage as the union between one man and one woman. As such, no state was bound to recognize same-sex marriage from out of state (Diversity Inc., 2014).

2000: Vermont became the first state in the United States to legalize civil unions and register partnerships between same-sex couples (Diversity Inc., 2014).

2003: In *Lawrence v. Texas*, a landmark case, the U.S. Supreme Court struck down state sodomy laws as unconstitutional (Diversity Inc., 2014).

2004: Massachusetts became the first state to legalize same-sex marriage (Diversity Inc., 2014).

2008: California voters approved Proposition 8, which made same-sex marriage in California illegal (American Experience, n.d.).

2009: The Mathew Sheppard Act was passed by Congress and signed into law by President Obama. The act expanded the 1996 U.S. Federal Hate Crime Law to include crimes motivated by a victim's actual or perceived gender or sexual orientation (Diversity Inc., 2014).

2010: The U.S. Senate voted 65–31 to repeal the Don't Ask, Don't Tell policy, thus allowing gay and lesbians to serve openly in the armed forces (Diversity Inc., 2014).

2011: President Obama stated that his administration would no longer defend the Defense of Marriage Act (Diversity Inc., 2014).

2011: New York state became the largest state to date to legalize gay marriage (American Experience, n.d.).

2015: The U.S Supreme Court ruled by a 5-to-4 vote that the Constitution guarantees a right to same-sex marriage (Supreme Court of the United States, 2015).

2015: Defense Secretary Ashton B. Carter's announced that in 2016 transgender troops will be allowed to serve openly in the military, ending a long-standing ban of transgender individuals. In his announcement, Defense Secretary Ashton B. Carter called the long-standing ban outdated and called for all who were willing to serve their country to be treated with respect and dignity (Gray, 2015).

2017: In the Smith V. Avanti case, Judge Raymond P. Moore of the United States District Court of Colorado ruled that the Federal Housing Act protects LGBT couples from housing discrimination (Lambda Legal, n.d.).

2017: President Trump issued a Presidential Memorandum for the Secretary of the Defense and the Secretary of Homeland Security prohibiting transgender individuals from serving in the military (UC San Diego, n.d.).

2018: President Trump revokes his 2017 Presidential Memorandum prohibiting transgender individuals from serving in the military. However, transgender persons with a history or diagnosis of gender dysphoria who may require substantial medical treatment, including medications and surgery, are still disqualified from military service except under certain limited circumstances (Federal Register, 2018)

2018: In the Masterpiece Cakeshop, Ltd v. Colorado Civil Rights Commission U.S. case , the U.S. Supreme Court rules in favor of a baker who refused to bake a cake for a same-sex couple because of religious objection (UC San Diego, n.d.).

2020: In the Bostock v. Clayton County, Georgia case, the U.S. Supreme Court rule that firing individuals because of their sexual orientation or transgender status violates Title VII of the 1964 Civil Rights Act prohibition on discrimination because of sex. The ruling provides LGBT persons with the same federal protections against discrimination that have been afforded to other groups of people since 1964 (Bostock v. Clayton County, n.d.).

2021: President Joe Biden signs an executive order revoking former President Trump's 2017 and 2018 memorandums prohibiting transgender persons serving in the military. In doing so, Transgender persons can now serve in the military unconditionally (Joe Biden, 2021).

References

American Experience. (n.d.). Timeline: Milestones in the American gay rights movement. Retrieved from http://www.pbs.org/wgbh/americanexperience/features/timeline/stonewall/.

Bostock V. Clayton County. (n.d.). Oyez. Retrieved from https://www.oyez.org/cases/2019/17-1618

Bronski, M. (2011). *A queer history of the United States*. Boston, MA: Beacon Press.

Campi, A. J. (2005). *Closed borders and mass deportations: The lessons of the Barred Zone Act*. Immigration Policy Center. Retrieved from http://icirr.org/sites/default/files/IPC%20 Barred%20Zone.pdf

Diversity Inc. (2014). *LGBT Pride Month: Timeline*. Retrieved from http://www.diversityinc.com/wp-content/uploads/2014/05/LGBT-Pride-Month-Timeline.pdf.

Epstein, S. (1996). *Impure science: AIDS activism and politics of knowledge*. Berkeley: University of California Press.

Federal Register.(2018). Military service by transgender individuals: Memorandum for the Secretary of Defense and the Secretary of Homeland Security. Retrieved from https://www.federalregister.gov/documents/2018/03/28/2018-06426/military-service-by-transgender-individuals

GLAD. (n.d). Mission and values. Retrieved from http://www.glad.org/about/mission.

Gray, E. (2015). Transgender solders are helpful but still in limbo. Time. Retrieved from http://time.com/3958502/transgender-soldiers-limbo/

Hay, H. (1996). *Radically gay: Gay liberation in the words of its founder*. Boston, MA: Beacon.

Hoffman, B. (2003). Health care reform and social movements in the United States: Public health then and now. *American Journal of Public Health, 93*(1), 75–85.

Joe Biden. (2021). *Executive order on Enabling All Qualified Americans to Serve Their Country in Uniform*. The White House. Retrieved from https://www.whitehouse.gov/briefing-room/

presidential-actions/2021/01/25/executive-order-on-enabling-all-qualified-americans-to-serve-their-country-in-uniform/
Justice.gov. (1990). *Matter of Toboso–Alfonso in exclusion proceedings*, A–23220644. Retrieved from http://www.justice.gov/sites/default/files/eoir/legacy/2012/08/14/3222.pdf
Lambda Legal. (n.d). *Lambda Legal history*. Retrieved from http://www.lambdalegal.org/about-us/history.
Supreme Court of the United States. (2015). *Obergefell et al. v. Hodges, Director, Ohio Department of Health, et al*. Retrieved from http://www.supremecourt.gov/opinions/14pdf/14-556_3204.pdf
UC San Diego. (n.d.). LGBTQ history in government documents: Timeline of documents. The Library. Retrieved from https://ucsd.libguides.com/lgbtdocs/timeline
U.S. Government Printing Office. (1990). *Public Law 101–649*. Retrieved from https://www.gpo.gov/fdsys/pkg/STATUTE-104/pdf/STATUTE-104-Pg4978.pdf.

The Origins of Sexual Orientation/Identity Inequality in the United States

Since the first sodomy laws were enacted in colonial America, sexual orientation has been the basis for social inequality. Although the first sodomy laws were not initially enacted with same-sex couples in mind, they would eventually be used to criminalize them. In some colonies, the sodomy laws applied to both men and women. For the ultra-religious Puritans, sodomy laws, as well as laws against fornication, fellatio, and masturbation, were enacted to ensure that its members did not fall prey to the temptations of the flesh. They were very much in keeping with the rigid European perspective of gender and sexuality (Bronski, 2011). They were also a response to the revulsion colonists felt when they became familiar with the sexual practices of the various Native American tribes. These practices, which had a much more fluid understanding of gender roles and sexual expression that included men in certain tribes dressing as women and specializing in women's work, were accepted and honored. In some tribes, women led men into battle, and in other tribes, men and women took on the dress and tribal duties of the opposite sex. Other tribes had young boys who served as a sexual resource for other boys in the tribe. In the eyes of the colonists, these practices marked Native Americans as less than human, morally derelict, and a threat to social order. To nullify the perceived threat of Native Americans' more fluid approach to gender roles and sexual expression, all of the colonies enacted laws that sought to enforce monogamous, same-race, heterosexual marriage as the mandatory institution (Bronski, 2011). Anything that fell outside of this arrangement was deemed an "abomination" or an "unspeakable act" against nature (Bronski, 2011). Punishment for infractions against these acts, most particularly sodomy, could be execution, as was the case with Richard Cornish, who was hanged in 1642 in the Virginia colony for sodomy (Goodbear, 2002).

The template set out by the colonies would be used for the next 300 years to marginalize and force individuals from the LGBTQ community underground. Gay men and lesbians would be socially constructed as sexual deviants whose sexual practices were an abomination and unspeakable acts against nature. Indeed, in 1953, the American Psychiatric Associations' first edition of the *Diagnostic Statistical Manual* (*DSM*) listed homosexuality as a sociopathic personality disturbance. In 1968, homosexuality was upgraded to a mere sexual deviation in the *DSM-II*, before being eliminated as a mental illness altogether in 1973.

In the 1950s, President Harry Truman signed into law the Uniform Code of Military Justice, which set up discharge rules for homosexual members. In the late 1970s and early 1980s, the HIV/AIDS crisis would see gay men stigmatized, blamed, and initially denied the resources needed to combat the disease. In the 1990s, the Don't Ask, Don't Tell military service policy directed military personal not to pursue or harass homosexual service members. Though ostensibly a lifting of a ban on homosexual service that had been in force since World War II, in effect it remained a ban on any overt expression of one's sexuality.

In 1996, the Defense of Marriage Act (DOMA) was enacted to allow states to refuse to recognize same-sex marriages granted under the laws of other states. In conjunction with other statutes, it barred same-sex couples from being recognized as spouses for the purpose of federal laws, thus preventing same-sex couples from receiving federal benefits.

In each of these examples, activism by the LGBTQ community forced a restructuring of the deviant narrative about individuals from the LGBTQ community. It also forced the repeal of policies such as DADT and DOMA.

LGBTQ activism was also successful in gaining marriage equality when on June 26, 2015, a 5–4 Supreme Court ruling in *Obergefell v. Hodges* legalized same-sex marriage (Supreme Court of the United States, 2015). In a dissent, Justice Antonin Scalia blasted the Court's ruling as a threat to American democracy, stating that "The substance of today's decree is not of immense personal importance to me, but what really astounds is the hubris reflected in today's judicial Putsch" (Supreme Court of the United States, 2015, p. 6).

Also significant was the 2017 *Smith v. Avanti* case in which Judge Raymond P. Moore of the U.S. District Court of Colorado ruled that the Federal Housing Act protects LGBTQ couples from housing discrimination (Lambda Legal, n.d.). It is a ruling that was critical because although 21 states had, up until 2017, passed laws prohibiting housing discrimination based on sexual orientation and gender identity, LGBTQ persons were not protected under the federal Fair Housing Act. Consequently, LGBTQ individuals remained the only federally unprotected class of people under the Fair Housing Act, a significant social inequality source (Grant et al., 2011; Freidman et al., 2013).

As seminal as the 2017 *Smith v. Avanti* ruling is the 2020 *Bostock v. Clayton County*, Georgia U.S. Supreme Court decision. The decision held that firing individuals because of their sexual orientation or transgender status violates Title VII of the 1964 Civil Rights Act prohibition on discrimination because of sex (*Bostock v. Clayton County*, n.d.). And as such, LGBTQ persons now finally have the federal protections against workplace discrimination that all other groups in the United States enjoy.

Sexual Orientation/Identity Inequality in the United States and Its Contemporary Impact

Some strides have been made in lessening sexual orientation/identity inequity; however, significant inequality remains. For example, despite the U.S. Supreme Court's ruling in 2003 that sodomy laws are unconstitutional, as of 2019, 12 states still have sodomy laws on the books (Villarreal, 2019). Similarly problematic is the *Masterpiece Cakeshop, Ltd v. Colorado Civil Rights Commission* U.S. Supreme Court decision in 2018, which ruled in favor of a baker who refused to bake a cake for a same-sex couple because of religious objection (UC San Diego, n.d.). The ruling opens the door for continued discrimination against LGBTQ persons based on religious objection.

Also problematic are continued health care disparities (Chapter 9) and disproportionality in criminal justice system involvement (Chapter 10) linked to societal stigma and discrimination.

What Social Workers Can Learn From the Historical and Contemporary Impact of Sexual Orientation/Identity Inequality in the United States

1. The historical use of heterosexual norms and social constructions to justify the exclusion and vilification of LGBTQ individuals.
2. The historical context that has forced LGBTQ people to hide their identify.
3. The need for federal social policy that provides LGBTQ individuals with the same protections against discrimination as is offered to every other class of people in the United States.

Box 3.4 Disability Timeline, 1600–Present

1600–1700s: Settlement laws prevented people with disabilities from settling in the colonies. For people with disabilities, the policy of care was indoor relief with either family, relatives, or other households (Trattner, 1999).

1636: Plymouth Colony passed a law that disabled solders would be supported by the colony (U.S. Department of Veterans Affairs, 2014).

1776: The Continental Congress provided pensions to disabled soldiers (U.S. Department of Veterans Affairs, 2014).

1800s: The primary policy of care for people with disabilities at the start of the 19th century was outdoor relief in the form of almshouses. There is also a growing policy movement toward education for people with disabilities (Trattner, 1999).

1811: The federal government authorized the first domiciliary and medical facilities for disabled veterans (U.S. Department of Veterans Affairs, 2014).

1817: The American School for the Deaf was established in Hartford, Connecticut. The school is the first for disabled children anywhere in the Western Hemisphere (American School for the Deaf, 2014).

1829: The Perkins School for the Blind is founded in Boston (Perkins School for the Blind, 2016).

1841: Dorothy Dix began her advocacy on behalf of people with disabilities incarcerated in jails and poorhouses (Trattner, 1999).

1848: The first residential institution for people with mental retardation was established at the Perkins Institution in Boston. Over the next hundred years, thousands of developmentally delayed children and adults spent their entire lives institutionalized (Disability Law Center, Inc., n.d.).

1854: President Franklin Pierce vetoed the Dorothy Dix-inspired Land Grant Bill for the Indigent Insane. The bill would have secured federal land and funds for the treatment of people with disabilities (Trattner, 1999).

1865: The National Home for Disabled Volunteer Soldiers, first known as the National Soldiers and Sailors Asylum, was established. It was the first federal government institution created for honorably discharged volunteer soldiers (U.S. Department of Veterans Affairs, 2014).

1883: The term "eugenics" was coined by Sir Francis Galton in England. This term and its concepts was the catalyst for the Eugenics movement in the United States. The stated goals of the movement were to improve the gene pool of the country. In doing so, among other things, the movement called for people with disabilities to be sterilized and eventually eliminated (Shapiro, 1993; U.S. Department of Transportation, 2014).

1901: The National Fraternal Society of the Deaf was founded. From 1901 to 1950, the Society advocated for the rights of deaf people to purchase insurance and obtain driver's licenses (Disability Law Center, Inc., n.d.).

1907: Indiana became the first of 29 states to pass compulsory sterilization laws for people with genetic illness or conditions (Reilly, 1991).

1912: Henry H. Goddard published *The Kadikak Family*. The book, which became a best seller, linked disability with immorality and genetics. In doing so, it further advanced the Eugenics agenda of sterilizing people with disabilities (Disability Law Center, Inc., n.d.).

1918: The Smith-Sears Veterans Vocational Act was passed. The Act established federal vocational rehabilitation programs for disabled veterans (Disability Law Center, Inc., n.d.).

1922: Harry Laughlin, a member of the Eugenics movement, devised a sterilization law, which served as a model for state legislators (Longmore & Unmansky, 2001).

1924: Virginia passed a state law that allowed unconsented sterilization of people found to be feeble minded, insane, depressed, mentally handicapped, or epileptic. It also included alcoholics, criminals, and drug addicts (Reilly, 1991)

1927: *Buck v. Bell*, a landmark U.S. Supreme Court case, ruled that forced sterilization of people with disabilities was not a violation of their constitutional rights. This ruling gave carte blanch to states to sterilize people with disabilities. By 1970, an estimated 60,000 people were sterilized without their consent (Disability Law Center, Inc., n.d.).

1935: The Social Security Act established benefits and grants to the states for assistance to blind individuals and disabled children (Disability Law Center, Inc., n.d.).

1940: The National Federation for the Blind is formed by Jacobus and other blind advocates in Wilkes-Barre, Pennsylvania. The federation advocated for white cane laws, as well the input from blind people for program design for blind centers (Disability Law Center, Inc., n.d.).

1940: The American Federation of the Physically Handicapped is founded by Paul Strachan. The federation advocated for an end to job discrimination against the physically handicapped (Disability Law Center, Inc., n.d.).

1943: Congress passed the Vocational Rehabilitation Amendments, also known as the Lafollette-Barden Act. The act authorized federal grants to the states for construction of hospitals, public health centers, and health facilities for the rehabilitation of people with disabilities (Disability Law Center, Inc., n.d.).

1948: The National Paraplegia Foundation was established. The foundation took a leading role in advocating for disability rights (Disability Law Center, Inc., n.d.).

1948: Advisory Council on Social Security proposed extending social security to cover total and permanent disability (Social Security, 2015).

1950: Social Security Amendments established a federal-state program to aid the permanently and totally disabled (Disability Law Center, Inc., n.d.).

1963: Congress passed the Mental Retardation Facilities and Community Health Centers Construction Act. The act authorized federal grants for the construction of public and private nonprofit community mental health centers (Trattner, 1999).

1964: The Urban Mass Transportation Act (P.L. 88–365) mandates that transportation systems accepting federal monies make those systems accessible to elderly and handicapped persons (Morrow, Jr., 2004).

1965: Medicare and Medicaid were established. The programs provided federal funding for subsidized health care to disabled and elderly citizens covered by the Social Security program (Trattner, 1999).

1968: The Architectural Barriers Act was passed. The act mandated that federally constructed buildings and facilities be accessible to people with physical disabilities (Disability Law Center, Inc., n.d.).

1972: The Social Security Amendments of 1972 created the Supplemental Security Income (SSI) program (U.S. Department of Transportation, 2014).

1973: Congress passes the Rehabilitation Act (P.L. 93–112). This landmark act prohibited programs receiving federal funds from discriminating against otherwise qualified disabled persons. It also mandated employers to make reasonable accommodations for employees with disabilities (Disability Law Center, Inc., n.d.).

1975: The Education for All Handicapped Children Act passed. The act provided states with funding to establish school programs for students with disabilities. It established the right to free and appropriate education for children with disabilities (Disability Law Center, Inc., n.d.).

1978: Rehabilitation Comprehensive Services and Developmental Disability Legislation (P.L. 95–602) authorized funding by Congress for independent living services for people with disabilities (Disability Law Center, Inc., n.d.).

1980: Congress passes the Civil Rights of Institutionalized Persons Act. The act authorized the U.S. Justice Department to file civil suits on behalf of residents of institutions whose civil rights have been violated (Disability Law Center, Inc., n.d.).

1980: Social Security Amendments of 1980 placed a cap on family benefits to disabled workers. The amendments also required periodic continuing disability reviews and creates work incentives (Social Security, 2014).

1981– 84: The Reagan administration terminated Social Security benefits for disabled recipients (Disability Law Center, Inc., n.d.).

1982: The Telecommunications for the Disabled Act was introduced in the House but was not enacted. The Act proposed telephone access for the deaf and hard-of-hearing people at all public places (Paglin, Rosenbloom & Hobson, 1999).

1984: The Voting Accessibility for the Elderly and Handicapped Act was passed. The act required that registration and polling places for federal elections be accessible to people with disabilities (Disability Law Center, Inc., n.d.).

1986: The Air Carrier Access Act was passed. The act prohibited airlines from refusing to serve people based on a disability (Disability Law Center, Inc., n.d.).

1988: Fair Housing Amendments mandated protections to people with disabilities in housing (Disability Law Center, Inc., n.d.).

1990: The Ryan White Comprehensive AIDS Resource Emergency Act was passed. The act was passed to help cope with the HIV/AIDS epidemic (Disability Law Center, Inc., n.d.).

1990: The American with Disabilities Act (ADA) is signed into law. The ADA, a civil rights law, prohibits discrimination against individuals with disabilities in all areas of public life and private places, including jobs, school, transportation, and other areas open to the general public (ADA National Network, 2021) .

1993: The American Indian Disability Legislation Project was established (ERIC, 1995).

1999: The Ticket to Work and Work Incentives Improvement Act of 1999 was enacted, enabling disability beneficiaries to seek employment services and other supports services needed to help them reduce their dependence on cash benefits (Social Security, 2014).

2001: The Commonwealth of Virginia House of Delegates approved a resolution stating its regret for its eugenics practices between 1924 and 1979 (Encyclopedia Virginia, 2013).

2002: In *Atkins v. Virginia* decision, the United States Supreme Court ruled that executing the mentally retarded violates the Eighth Amendment of cruel and inhumane treatment (Oyez Project, 2015).

2008: The ADA Amendments Act of 2008 makes significant change to the definition of disability as presented in the Americans with Disability Act. The changes favor a broad and inclusive interpretation. These changes make it easier for a person seeking protection under the laws to establish eligibility (Trainer, 2020)

References

ADA National Network. (2021). An overview of the American with Disabilities Act. Retrieved from https://adata.org/factsheet/ADA-overview

American School for the Deaf. (2014). *History of deaf history.* Retrieved from: http://www.asd-1817.org/uploaded/pdf/hartford_history.pdf

Disability Law Center, Inc. (n.d.). *A chronology of the disability rights movement*. Retrieved from http://www.dlc-ma.org/resources/General/chronology.htm

Encyclopedia Virginia. (2013). House Joint Resolution No. 607 (2001). Retrieved from http://www.encyclopediavirginia.org/House_Joint_Resolution_No_607_2001

ERIC. (1995). *American Indian Disability Project: Findings of a national survey of tribal governments.* Retrieved from http://eric.ed.gov/?id=ED399122

Longmore, P. K., & Umansky, L. (2001) *The new disability history: American perspectives*. New York: New York University Press.

Morrow, Jr. W.S.(2004). *Urban Mass Transportation Acts*. Retrieved from http://www.encyclopedia.com/doc/1G2-3407400292.html

Oyez Project. (2015). *Atkins v. Virginia*. Retrieved from http://www.oyez.org/cases/2000-2009/2001/2001_00_8452/#chicago

Paglin, M. D., Rosenbloom, J., & Hobson, J. R. (1999). *The Communications Act: A legislative history of the major amendments 1934–1996*. Silver Spring, MD: Pike & Fischer.

Perkins School for the Blind. (2016). *Perkins history museum*. Retrieved from http://www.perkins.org/history

Pfeiffer, D. (1993). Overview of the disability movement: History legislative record, and political implications. *Policy Study Journal*, 21(4), 724–734.

Reilly, P. (1991). *The surgical solution: A history of involuntary sterilization in the United States*. Baltimore, MD: Johns Hopkins University Press.

Shapiro, J. P. (1993). *No pity: People with disability forging a new civil rights movement*. New York, NY: Times Book.

Social Security. (2015). *1948 Advisory Council*. Retrieved from http://www.ssa.gov/history/reports/48advisegen.html

Social Security. (2014). *Social Security: Summary of major changes in the cash benefits programs*. Retrieved from https://www.socialsecurity.gov/history/reports/crsleghist2.html

Trainer, M. (2020). Equality for people with disabilities: A timeline. Share America. Retrieved from https://share.america.gov/equality-for-americans-with-disabilities-a-timeline/

Trattner, W. I. (1999). *From poor law to welfare state: A history of social welfare in America* (6th ed.). New York, NY: The Free Press.

U.S. Department of Transportation. (2014). *Disability rights movement timeline*. Retrieved from http://www.fta.dot.gov/12325_4064.html

U.S. Department of Veterans Affairs. (2014). *VA history*. Retrieved from http://www.va.gov/about_va/vahistory.asp

Vaugh-Switzer, J. (2003). *Disabled rights: American policy and the fight for equality*. Washington, DC : Georgetown University Press.

The Origins of Disability Inequality in the United States

Disability as a source of inequality is as old as the United States itself. The colonies enacted settlement laws whose restrictions included people with disabilities. Moreover, the commonly held belief of the day was that a physical or mental disability was a sign that one had either fallen from spiritual favor or evidence of possession by the devil or evil spirits. Thus, rather than being seen or treated as part of the larger colonial society, people with disabilities were cast as a dependent class of people. As such, they had to be segregated from the rest of society and their able-bodied contemporaries (Grzesiak & Hicok, 1994). They were also labeled in very pejorative terms; idiot, distracted, impotent, lunatic, feebleminded, and retarded were all part of the American lexicon.

As the colonies increased, the segregation of people with disabilities, specifically if poor, took the form of incarceration if suffering from severe mental disability or placement in almshouses. Funded by local councils or religious organizations such as the Quakers, almshouses provided "outdoor relief" in exchange for work. Just as was the case with jails, though, the almshouses left a lot to be desired in terms of its treatment of people with disabilities, most particularly if they had a mental disability (Trattner, 1999).

As documented by the renowned 19th-century mental health advocate Dorothea Dix in her two years of touring jails, almshouses, and private homes in Massachusetts, people with a mental disability were housed in horrid conditions. These conditions included having no heat, light, little in the way of clothing or furniture, and being without sanitary facilities. Dorothea Dix's response to these findings was to compile a detailed report and submit it first to the Massachusetts legislature and then the United States Congress in 1848 (Trattner, 1999). In each instance, Dix's report proposed the passing of a bill to address the plight of people with a mental disability. The main provision of the proposed bill (Land Grant Bill for the Indigent Insane) was for the federal government to set aside 12,225,000 acres of land. From this land 10,000,000 acres would be used for the benefit of people with a mental disability. The rest of the land would be sold for the benefit of the blind, deaf, and dumb, with the profits being used by states to build and maintain asylums. Though the bill passed the United States Senate, it initially failed the House. After three years of being sent back and forth, the bill eventually passed both the Senate and the House, but was vetoed by President Pierce in 1854. In vetoing the bill, President Pierce argued that social welfare was not a federal but a state responsibility (Herstek, 2001; Trattner, 1999).

Dorothy's Dix's efforts were not the first to address the issue of building institutions that would address the specific issues of people with disabilities in a humane way. Indeed, in the 19th century there was a proliferation of such institutions. In 1817, for example, the first school for the deaf, the American Asylum for the Deaf and Dumb, was established in Hartford, Connecticut (American School for the Deaf, 2014).

An important development that moved disabilities out of the society-imposed shadow and into the public's consciousness was the end of the American Civil War in 1865. The war had not only been responsible for the most American casualties in any war to date, it also left hundreds of thousands of soldiers with a physical disability. The most common disability was the result of an amputation (Kenzer, 2012). In fact, there were some estimated 30,000 amputations among the Union soldiers alone. There were also thousands of soldiers with what in the parlance of the day was called "nervous disorders." In response to the widespread suffering caused by the injuries sustained in the war, the federal government enacted the Dependent and Disability Act of 1890. The act provided a pension for eligible Union soldiers who had served in the Civil War. Specific eligibility requirements included at least 90-day service in the Union military or naval force, an honorable discharge, and an inability to perform manual labor, regardless of financial situation or when the disability was suffered (Blanck & Millender, 2000).

Though physically disabled veterans of all of America's previous conflicts going back to 1636 in the Plymouth colony had been similarly recognized with pensions, this was by far the biggest and most costly.

The suffering of the Civil War veteran did not, however, change the perceptions of people with disabilities who were seen as less worthy. Indeed, the mid to late 1800s through to the early 1900s were to see some disturbing trends. Two of the most notable of these trends was the use of disability to justify inequality, and the rise of the eugenics movement and the justification of use of sterilization to prevent people with disabilities from procreating.

As posited by Baynton (Longmore & Umansky, 2001), disability has functioned historically to justify inequality not just for disabled people, but also for other similarly marginalized groups. These marginalized groups included racial and ethnic minorities, women, and members of the LGBTQ community. As evidence of this, disability arguments were among the most often used to justify slavery. The common disability argument promulgated by medical journals of the day was that Black people lacked sufficient intelligence to participate or compete with Whites on equal terms. This lack of intelligence was attributed to, among other factors, deficiency in cerebral matter in the cranium and an excess of nervous matter. It was also argued that under conditions of freedom, Black people were prone to disability, a disability that was supposedly not evident when enslaved. Along the same lines, arguments were made that Black slaves who ran away from their masters suffered from a curious form of mental illness: drapetomania (Longmore & Umansky, 2001).

As for women, particularly during their quest for suffrage in the 19th and early 20th centuries, opponents argued that women had physical, intellectual, and psychological flaws. As a result, not only were they frail but also prone to irrationality and emotional excesses. These flaws were inherent and were disabilities that would prevent them from the rational thought and behavior needed for voting and political leadership, thus rendering them inferior to men with their rational thoughts and behavior. Physically, arguments were made that women's constitutions made them weak and prone to injury (Baynton, 2008; Longmore & Umansky, 2001).

After the mass immigration from Asia and eastern and southern Europe, the disability argument was used to label the Chinese, Indian, Jews, Italians, Slavs, Hungarians, Greeks, and so forth, the primary argument being that these groups were both mentally and physically inferior to White Anglo-Saxon males. Terms such as feebleminded, idiot, lunatic, and imbecile were commonly used to describe these immigrant groups. The argument posited was that their skulls and mental development were retarded and lower functioning than White Anglo-Saxon males. This argument got significant traction because of the pseudo-science of the eugenics movement, which claimed that there was a racial and ethnic hierarchy of intelligence and higher-order functioning among different racial groups. Therefore, society, as a matter of optimal functioning, needed to rid itself of its inferior groups, one of the most often suggested ways of doing this being through sterilization (Baynton, 2008).

It is no surprise then that in crafting the immigration laws of the late 19th and early 20th centuries, lunatics and idiots were specifically prohibited from entry to the United States. Added to this were immigrants who had suffered two or more attacks of insanity any time in their lives, imbecilic, feeble-minded people, and persons with abnormal sexual instincts, that is, gay or lesbian (Longmore & Umansky, 2001).

During the early 20th century, with mass immigration, the women's suffrage movement, and the first great Black migration north, the eugenic movement's push for the sterilization of people with disabilities got significant traction. Most notably in 1922, Harry Laughlin (part of the eugenics movement) devised a model sterilization law. This model served as a template for numerous state legislators. It required the sterilization of the following defective classes: the feeble-minded, the insane, criminals, epileptics, substance abusers, lepers, the blind, the deaf, the deformed, and paupers (Longmore & Umansky, 2001).

In 1924, Virginia enacted a law that allowed for the sterilization (without consent) of individuals found to be feeble-minded, insane, depressed, mentally handicapped, or drug addicted. Virginia and other states' use of sterilization of people with disabilities survived a legal challenge in the 1927 *Buck v. Bell* Supreme Court ruling. The ruling stated that the forced sterilization of people with disabilities was not a violation of their constitutional rights. In doing so, Justice Oliver Wendell Holmes likened sterilization to a vaccination. Nationwide, 27 states sterilized people with disabilities. By the 1970s some 60,000 people with disabilities had been sterilized (Baynton, 2008).

The advocacy efforts of people with disabilities from the 1970s onward have yielded significant social policy changes (see Box 3.4, Disability Timeline). These changes have not only ensured civil rights, full inclusion, and public accommodation, they have also challenged the pejorative language that has so contributed to the marginalization of people with disabilities.

Disability Inequality in the United States and Its Contemporary Impact

According to the latest available United States disability statistics, in 2018, an estimated 26.9% (five million) (plus or minus 0.31 percentage points) of noninstitutionalized persons aged 21 to 64 with a disability were living below the poverty line, compared with 12.2% of Americans without a disability (Elflein, 2020). Indeed, persons with disabilities are much more likely than citizens without a disability not only to be living below the poverty line, but also to be unemployed and highly reliant on public benefits programs. In 2019, persons with disabilities had a work force participation of 19.3%, compared with 66.3% for persons without a disability. They are also unemployed at twice the rate of persons without a disability, at 10% and 4%, respectively (U.S Bureau of Labor Statistics, 2020).

By far the largest groups of Americans with disabilities are Blacks and non-Hispanic Whites, at 14% and 11%, respectively (Goodman et al., 2019). The current challenge for disabled individuals is workforce participation, which is as much a function of employer perceptions as it is educational levels and disability. Among the six types of disabilities in 2014 with the highest rates of unemployment was a cognitive disability at 22.5%, and the lowest was people with a hearing disability (Mourssi-Alfash, 2016).

Without greater workforce participation, individuals with a disability will continue to be on the margins and locked out of opportunities in the workplace. The social policy challenge, therefore, is to find ways to integrate persons with all manner of disabilities into the workforce.

What Social Workers Can Learn From the Historical and Contemporary Impact of Disability Inequality in the United States

1. The historic and contemporary inability of society to be properly inclusive of individuals with disabilities in the larger society.
2. The differing treatment of a person with a disability. For example, provisions for the care of veterans with a disability have always been prioritized.
3. The types of disabilities most affected by unemployment.
4. Who composes the population of people with a disability.
5. Examples of past policies that have been successful in addressing the needs of people with disabilities.
6. Examples of past policies that have not been successful in addressing the needs of people with disabilities.

Chapter Summary

This chapter presented an historical overview of the origins and early development of the various bases for social inequality in the United States. As the chapter has shown, these bases for social inequality are as old as the country itself and are a deeply entrenched structural feature of American society. Thus, despite significant strides in lessening the effects of social inequity, most particularly over the past 50 years, social inequality still remains remarkably resilient and present in society. Social inequality can be banished, but for this to happen there will have to be continued advocacy efforts for policies that afford everyone equal access to society's rewards and privileges. In addition, society must challenge the social constructions, social policies, and social institutions that seek to deny people, groups, and populations equal access to society's resources, rights, goods, privileges, and services.

Retrieval Questions

1. The unequal allocation of society's resources, rights, goods, privileges, and services is a definition of what concept?
2. What is the relationship between social inequality and intersectionality?
3. What is race?
4. What three seminal events in American history were responsible for the emergence of race as a basis for social inequality?
5. In what areas are there still significant disparities between women and men?
6. Why is a definitive understanding of social class hard to come by in the United States?
7. How did the first ***Diagnostic Statistical Manuel*** (***DSM***) list homosexuality?
8. How was disability used against marginalized groups?
9. Why is Harry Laughlin notable?

Discussion Questions

1. Identify and discuss the role you think social inequality knowledge has in developing a professional social work identity.
2. What is the relationship between social inequality and ethical social work practice?
3. What responsibility do social workers have to eliminate social inequality?
4. What are some of the dimensions of social inequality?
5. How does social inequality affect the practice context?

References

Abramovitz, M. (1996). *Regulating the lives of women: Social welfare*. Boston, MA: South End Press.

Akee, R. K. Q., & Taylor, J. B. (2014). *Social and economic change on American Indian reservations: A databook of United States censuses and American community survey, 1990–2010*. Sarasota, FL: Taylor Policy Group. Retrieved from http://taylorpolicy.com/us-databook

Allen, T. W. (1994). *The invention of the white race, Vol. 1: Racial oppression and social control*. London, England: Verso.

American Anthropological Association. (1998). *American Anthropological Association statement on race*. Retrieved from www.aaanet.org/stmts/racepp.htm

American Civil Liberties Union. (2009). *Reclaiming patriotism: A call to reconsider the Patriot Act*. Retrieved from www.aclu.org/files/pdfs/safefree/patriot_report_20090310.pdf

American School for the Deaf. (2014). *History of deaf history*. Retrieved from www.asd-1817.org/uploaded/pdf/hartford_history.pdf

Baird, B. D. (1975). Interpreting the Equal Pay Act: Corning Glass v. Brennan. *Tulsa Law Review*, *10*(4), 681–689.

Basch, N. (1992). Reconstructing female citizenship: Minor v. Happersett. In D. G. Nieman (Ed.), *The constitution, law, and American life: Critical aspects of the nineteenth-century experience* (pp. 52–66). Athens: University of Georgia Press.

Baynton, D. C. (2008). Disability in history. *Disability Studies Quarterly*, *28*(3).

Blackmon, D. A. (2009). *Slavery by another name: The re-enslavement of Black Americans from the Civil War to World War II*. New York, NY: Anchor Books.

Blanck, P., & Millender, M. (2000). Before disability civil rights: Civil War pensions and the politics of disability in America. *Alabama Law Review*, *52*(1), 1–50.

Bostock V. Clayton County. (n.d.). *Oyez*. Retrieved from www.oyez.org/cases/2019/17-1618

Bronski, M. (2011). *A queer history of the United States*. Boston, MA: Beacon Press.

Brook, T. (1997). *Plessy v. Ferguson: A brief history with documents*. Boston, MA: Bedford Books.

Bruyneel, K. (2004). Challenging American boundaries: Indigenous people and the "gift" of U.S. citizenship. *Studies in American Political Development*, *18*(1), 30–43.

Campbell, S. W. (1970). *The slave catchers: Enforcement of the Fugitive Slave Law, 1850–1860*. Chapel Hill: University of North Carolina Press.

Cawthorne, A. (2008). The straight facts on women in poverty. *Center for American Progress*. Retrieved from www.in.gov/icw/files/women_poverty.pdf

Center for American Women and Politics. (2020). Women in elected office 2020. *Rutgers Eagleton Institute of Politics*. Retrieved from https://cawp.rutgers.edu/women-elective-office-2020

Center for American Women and Politics. (2021). Record number of women to serve in the presidential cabinet. *Rutgers Eagleton Institute of Politics*. Retrieved from https://cawp.rutgers.edu/sites/default/files/resources/press-release-pesidential-cabinet.pdf

Center for Reproductive Rights. (2011). Safe and legal abortion is a woman's right. *Briefing Paper*. Retrieved from www.reproductiverights.org/sites/crr.civicactions.net/files/documents/Safe%20and%20Legal%20Abortion%20is%20a%20Womans%20Human%20Right.pdf

Chang, G. H. (2001). *Asian Americans and politics: Perspectives, experiences, prospects*. Washington, DC: Woodrow Wilson Center Press.

Cheng, T. W. (1972). *Chink: A documentary history of anti-Chinese prejudice in America*. New York, NY: World Publishing Company.

Clark, T. R. (1975). *Puerto Rico and the United States, 1917–1933*. Pittsburg, PA: University of Pittsburg Press.

Conroy, M., Wiederkehr, A., & Rakich, N. (2020). Updated: A record breaking number of *women could be in Biden's cabinet. Five Thirty Eight*. Retrieved from https://fivethirtyeight.com/features/a-record-breaking-number-of-women-will-be-in-bidens-cabinet/

Council on Social Work Education. (2006). *Council on social work education commission on accreditation handbook on accreditation standards and procedures* (5th ed.). Arlington, VA: Author.

Crenshaw, K. (1991). Mapping the margins: Intersectionality, identity politics and violence against women of color. *Stanford Law Review*, 43(6), 1241–1299.

Declaration of Independence. (1776). Action of second continental congress, July 4, 1776. *The Unanimous Declaration of the Thirteen United States of America*. Retrieved from www.constitutionfacts.com/us-declaration-of-independence/read-the-declaration/

DeNavas-Walt, C., & Proctor, B. D. (2014). Income and poverty in the United States: 2013: Current population reports. *United States Census Bureau*. Retrieved from www.census.gov/content/dam/Census/library/publications/2014/demo/p60-249.pdf

Downey, K. (2009). *The women behind the new deal: The life of Frances Perkins, FDR's secretary of labor and his moral conscience*. New York, NY: Nan A. Talese.

Elflein, J. (2020). Poverty rate among people with and without disabilities from 2008 to 2018. *Statistia*. Retrieved from www.statista.com/statistics/979003/disability-poverty-rate-us/

Elliott, M. (2006). *Color-blind justice: Albion Tourgée and the quest for racial equality from the Civil War to Plessy v. Ferguson*. New York, NY: Oxford University Press. Retrieved from www.fhcmichigan.org/images/Arcus_web1.pdf

Encyclopedia Britannica. (2014). *Three hundred women that changed the world*. Retrieved from http://search.eb.com/women/article-9050613

Finkelman, P. (2007). Scott v. Sandford: The court's most dreadful case and how it changed history. *Chicago-Kent Law Review*, 82(1), 1–48.

Foner, E. (2002). *Reconstruction: America's unfinished business: 1863–1877*. New York, NY: Harper Collins.

Foner, E. (2009). *Give me liberty: An American history*. New York, NY: W.W. Norton.

Foner, N., & Fredrickson, G. M. (2004). *Not just black and white: Historical and contemporary perspectives on immigration, race, and ethnicity in the United States*. New York, NY: Russell Sage Foundation.

Fredrickson, G. (2002). *Racism: A short history*. Princeton, NJ: Princeton University Press.

Freidman, S., Reynolds, A., Scovill, S., Brassier, F. R., Campbell, R., & Ballou, M. (2013). An estimate of housing discrimination against same-sex couples. *United States of Housing and Urban Development/Office of Policy Development and Research*. Retrieved from http://big.assets.huffingtonpost.com/hud.pdf

Garcia, J. (2013). *United States v. Bhagat Singh Thind* (1923). In C. Cortés (Ed.), *Multicultural America: A multimedia encyclopedia* (pp. 2122–2124). Thousand Oaks, CA: Sage.

Garrow, D. J. (1994). *Liberty and sexuality: The right to privacy and the making of Roe v. Wade*. New York, NY: Macmillan.

Glenn, E. N. (2002). *Unequal freedom: How race and gender shaped American citizenship and labor*. Cambridge, MA: Harvard University Press.

Goodbear, R. (2002). *Sexual revolution in early America*. Baltimore, MD: John Hopkins University Press.

Goodman, N., Morris, M., & Boston, K. (2019). Financial inequality: Disability, race and poverty in America. *National Disability Institute*. Retrieved from www.nationaldisabilityinstitute.org/wp-content/uploads/2019/02/disability-race-poverty-in-america.pdf

Gordon, A. D. (2000). *Against an aristocracy of sex, 1866–1873, Volume 2 of the selected papers of Elizabeth Cady Stanton and Susan B. Anthony*. New Brunswick, NJ: Rutgers University Press.

Govtrack.US. (2011). *S.182 (111th): Paycheck Fairness Act*. Retrieved from www.govtrack.us/congress/bills/111/s182

Grant, J. M., Mottet, L. A., Tanis, J., Harrison, J., Herman, J. L., & Keisling, M. (2011). *Injustice at every turn: A report of the National Transgender Discrimination Survey*. Washington, DC: National Center for Transgendered Equality and National Gay and Lesbian Task Force. Retrieved from www.endtransdiscrimination.org/PDFs/NTDS_Report.pdf

Grossman, J. L. (1994). Women's jury service: Right of citizenship or privilege of difference? *Stanford Law Review*, 46(5), 1115–1160.

Grzesiak, R. C., & Hicok, D. A. (1994). A brief history of psychotherapy and physical disability. *American Journal of Psychotherapy*, 48(2), 240–250.

Guttmacher Institute. (2020). *An overview of abortion laws*. Retrieved from www.guttmacher.org/state-policy/explore/overview-abortion-laws

Hallvworthington.com. (2016). *The letters of George Fox*. Retrieved from www.hallvworthington.com/Letters/gfsection1.html

Halpin, J., & Williams, C. P. (2010). The progressive intellectual tradition in America. *Center for American Progress*. Retrieved from http://cdn.americanprogress.org/wpcontent/uploads/issues/2010/04/pdf/progressiveintellectualism.pdf

Hawes, J. M., & Shores, E. F. (2002). *The family in America: An encyclopedia* (Vol. 1). Santa Barbara, CA: ABC-CLIO, Inc.

Herstek, A. P. (2001). *Dorothea Dix: Crusader for the mentally ill*. Berkeley Heights, NJ: Enslow Publishers.

History.com. (2020). *Women's history milestones: A timeline*. Retrieved from www.history.com/topics/womens-history/womens-history-us-timeline

Hochschild, J. L., & Powell, B. M. (2008). Racial reorganization and the United States Census 1850–1930: Mulattoes, half-breeds, mixed parentage, Hindoos, and the Mexican race. *Studies in American Political Development*, 22(1), 59–96.

Hochschild, J. L., & Weaver, V. (2007). The skin color paradox and the American racial order. *Social Problems*, 86(2), 643–670.

Horowitz, J. M., Igielnik, R., & Kochhar, K. (2020). Most Americans say there is too much economic inequality in the U.S., but fewer than half call it a top priority. *Pew Research Center*. Retrieved from www.pewsocialtrends.org/2020/01/09/trends-in-income-and-wealth-inequality/

Horton, J. O., & Horton, L. E. (2006). *Slavery and the making of America*. Oxford, UK: Oxford University Press.

Hoyert, D. L., & Xu, J. (2012). *Deaths: Preliminary data for 2011: National vital statistics reports* (Vol. 61(6)). Hyattsville, MD: National Center for Health Statistics. Retrieved from www.cdc.gov/nchs/data/nvsr/nvsr61/nvsr61_06.pdf

H.R.40, Naturalization Bill. (1790, March 4). *A bill to establish a uniform rule of naturalization*. Retrieved from www.visitthecapitol.gov/exhibitions/artifact/h-r-40-naturalization-bill-march-4-1790

Indian Health Service. (2015). *Indian health disparities*. Retrieved from www.ihs.gov/newsroom/includes/themes/newihstheme/display_objects/documents/factsheets/Disparities.pdf

James, A. (2008). Making sense of race and racial classification. In T. Zuberi & E. Bonilla-Silva (Eds.), *White logic, white methods: Racism and methodology*. Lanham, MD: Rowan & Littlefield.

Jefferson, T. (1785). Notes on the state of Virginia. *Goggle Books*. Retrieved from www.google.com/books/edition/Notes_on_the_State_of_Virginia/NgKidsPa_QoC?hl=en&gbpv=1&printsec=frontcover

Kashima, T., & U.S. Commission on Wartime Relocation and Internment of Civilians. (2011). *Personal justice denied: Report of the commission on wartime relocation and internment of civilians*. Seattle: University of Washington Press.

Kenzer, R. C. (2012). Civil War pensions. *Encyclopedia Virginia*. Retrieved from www.EncyclopediaVirginia.org/Civil_War_Pensions

Kitch, S. L. (2009). *The specter of sex: Gendered foundation of racial formulation in the United States*. Albany: State University of New York Press.

Kochhar, R., Fry, R., & Taylor, P. (2011). Twenty-to-one: Wealth gaps rise between Whites, Blacks and Hispanics. *Pew Research Center: Social and Economic Trends*. Retrieved from www.pewsocialtrends.org/2011/07/26/wealth-gaps-rise-to-record-highs-between-whites-blacks-hispanics/

Lambda Legal. (n.d.). *Smith v. Avanti*. Retrieved from www.lambdalegal.org/in-court/cases/co_smith-v-avanti

Legal Information Institute. (1996). *United States v. Virginia et al. (94–1941), 518 U.S. 515 (1996)*. Retrieved from www.law.cornell.edu/supct/html/94-1941.ZD.html

Lemon, J. T. (1990). Colonial America in the eighteenth century. In R. D. Mitchell & P. A. Groves (Eds.), *North America: The historical geography of a changing continent* (pp. 121–146). Savage, MD & Lanham, MD: Rowman and Littlefield.

Longmore, P. K., & Umansky, L. (2001). *The new disability history: American perspectives*. New York: New York University Press.

Loue, S. (2002). *Gender, ethnicity, and health research*. New York, NY: Kluwer Academic Publishers.

MacDwyer, S. (1982). Rostkar v. Goldberg: The unequal development of the equal protection doctrine in military affairs. *Golden Gate University Law Review*, 12(3), 661–690.

Massey, D. S. (2007). *Categorically unequal: The American stratification system*. New York, NY: Russell Sage Foundation.

McCartney, S., & Bishaw, A., & Fontenot, K. (2013). Poverty rates for selected detailed race and Hispanic groups by state and place: 2007–2011. *U.S. Census Bureau*. Retrieved from www.census.gov/prod/2013pubs/acsbr11-17.pdf

McClain, C. J. (1994). *In search of equality: The Chinese struggle against discrimination in nineteenth century America*. Berkeley: University of California Press.

McConnaughy, C. M. (2013). *The women's suffrage movement in America: A reassessment*. New York, NY: Cambridge University Press.

McCurdy, W. E. (1957). Property torts between spouses and use during marriage of the matrimonial home owned by the other. *Villanova Law Review*, 2(24), 447–473. Retrieved from http://digitalcommons.law.villanova.edu/vlr/vol2/iss4/1

Mintz, S., & Kellogg, S. (1988). *Domestic revolutions: A social history of American life*. New York, NY: Free Press.

Morgan, E. (1975). *American slavery, American freedom: The ordeal of colonial Virginia*. New York, NY: W.W. Norton.

Morgan, K. (2001). *Slavery and servitude in colonial North America*. New York: New York University Press.

Mourssi-Alfash, M. (2016). The disability employment gap, by type of disability. *MN Employment and Economic Development*. Retrieved from https://mn.gov/deed/newscenter/publications/trends/december-2016/disability-employment-gap.jsp

Mukhopadhyay, C. C., Henze, R., & Moses, Y. (2013). *How real is race? A sourcebook on race, culture, and biology* (2nd ed.). Lanham, MD: Rowman & Littlefield.

Nadworny, E. (2021). Kamala Harris sworn as vice president. *NPR*. Retrieved from www.npr.org/sections/inauguration-day-live-updates/2021/01/20/958749751/vice-president-kamala-harris-takes-the-oath-of-office

Nagel, M. K. (2012). Nothing to trust: The unconstitutional origins of the post-Dawes Act trust doctrine. *Tulsa Law Review*, 48(1), 63–92.

Namarck, K. N. (2015). *Women in combat: Issues for congress*. Congressional Research Service. Washington, DC. Retrieved from https://fas.org/sgp/crs/natsec/R42075.pdf

Nash, C. (2008). Re-thinking intersectionality. *Feminist Review*, 89, 1–15.

National Association of Social Workers. (2017). *NASW code of ethics (Guide to the everyday professional conduct of social workers)*. Washington, DC: NASW.

National Center for Health Statistics. (2013). *Health, United States, 2013: With special feature on prescription drugs*. Hyattsville, MD. Retrieved from www.cdc.gov/nchs/data/hus/hus13.pdf#025

National Women's Law Center. (2012). *Title XI 40 years and counting: Fact sheet*. Retrieved from www.nwlc.org/sites/default/files/pdfs/nwlcathletics_titleixfactsheet.pdf

Newbeck, P., & Wolfe, B. (2014). Loving v. Virginia. *Encyclopedia Virginia*. University of Virginia. Retrieved from www.EncyclopediaVirginia.org/Loving_v_Virginia_1967

Norgren, J. (2007). *Belva Lockwood: The woman who would be president*. New York: New York University Press.

Norton, M. B. (1999). Either married or to be married: Women's legal equality in early America. In C. G. Pestana & S. V. Salinger (Eds.), *Inequality in early America* (pp. 25–45). Hanover and London: University Press of New England.

O'Connor, K. (2010). *Gender and women's leadership: A reference handbook*. Thousand Oaks, CA: Sage.

Offen, K. (1988). Defining feminism: A comparative historical approach. *Signs*, 14(1), 119–157.

Orleck, A. (2015). *Rethinking American women's activism*. New York, NY: Routledge.

The Oyez Project. (2014a). Meritor savings bank v. Vinson. *The Oyez Project at IIT*. Chicago-Kent College of Law. Retrieved from www.oyez.org/cases/1980-1989/1985/1985_84_1979

The Oyez Project. (2014b). Automobile workers v. Johnson Controls, Inc. *The Oyez Project at IIT*. Chicago-Kent College of Law. Retrieved from www.oyez.org/cases/1990-1999/1990/1990_89_1215

Parent, A. S., Jr. (2003). *Foul means: The formation of slave society in Virginia, 1660–1740*. Chapel Hill: University of North Carolina Press.

Payscale.com. (2020). *The state of the gender pay gap 2020*. Retrieved from www.payscale.com/data/gender-pay-gap

Perdue, T. (1998). *The Cherokee women: Gender and culture change 1700–1835*. Lincoln: University of Nebraska Press.

Potter, L. A., & Schamel, W. (1997). Teaching with documents: The Homestead Act of 1862. *National Archives*. Retrieved from www.archives.gov/education/lessons/homestead-act/

Prucha, F. P. (2000). *Documents of United States Indian policy* (3rd ed.). Lincoln: University of Nebraska Press.

P.L.49–105. (1887). *Dawes Act*. Retrieved from www.ourdocuments.gov/doc.php?flash=false&doc=50#

Richter, J. (2013). Women in colonial Virginia. *Encyclopedia Virginia*. Retrieved from www.EncyclopediaVirginia.org/Women_in_Colonial_Virginia

Ridgeway, C. L. (2014). Why status matters for inequality. *American Sociological Review*, 79(1), 1–16.

Rierson, S. L. (1994). Race and gender discrimination: A historical case for equal treatment under the fourteenth amendment. *Duke Journal of Gender and Law*, 1(89), 89–116.

Rodriguez-Dominguez, V. M. (2005). The racialization of Mexican Americans and Puerto Ricans-1890s–1930s. *Centro Journal*, 17(1), 71–105.

Rothenberg, P. S. (2013). *Race, class and gender in the United States: An integrated study* (6th ed.). New York, NY: Worth Publishers.

Sabato, L. J., & Ernst, H. R. (2007). *Encyclopedia of American political parties and elections*. New York, NY: Facts on File, Inc.

Salisbury, N. (1996). The Indians' old world: Native Americans and the coming of Europeans. *The William and Mary Quarterly*, 53(3), 435–458.

Saltz, R. N. (2002). *American Indian policy in the Jacksonian era*. Norman: University of Oklahoma Press. Retrieved from www.loc.gov/rr/program/bib/ourdocs/Indian.html

Sandra Day O'Connor. (n.d.). *Oyez*. Retrieved from www.oyez.org/justices/sandra_day_oconnor

Sanger, M. (2004). *The autobiography of Margaret Sanger*. Mineola, NY: Dover Printing Publications.

Schultz, J. D. (2002). *Encyclopedia of minorities in American politics: African Americans and Asians Americans*. Phoenix, AR: Oryx.

Sheehan, B. W. (1973). *Seeds of extinction: Jeffersonian philanthropy and the American Indian*. Chapel Hill: University of North Carolina Press.

Skinner, E. (2011). *Women and the national experience: Sources in American history, combined volume* (3rd ed.). New York, NY: Pearson.

Smedley, A., & Smedley, B. D. (2012). *Race in North America: Origin and evolution of a worldview*. San Francisco, CA: Westview Press.

Smith, J. C. (1998). *Rebels in law: Voices in history of Black women lawyers*. Ann Arbor: The University of Michigan Press.

Smith, J. C. (2013). *Black firsts: 4000 ground breaking and pioneering historical events* (3rd ed.). Detroit, MI: Visible Ink Press.

Smith, J. M. (1995). *The republic of letters: The correspondence between Thomas Jefferson and James Madison, 1776–1826*. New York, NY: W.W. Norton & Company.

Sonia Sotomayor. (n.d.). *Oyez*. Retrieved from www.oyez.org/justices/sonia_sotomayor

Speck, F. G. (1938). The question of matrilineal descent in the southeastern Siouan Area. *American Anthropologist*, 40(1), 1–12.

Stone, C., Trisi, D., Sherman, A., & Chen, W. (2014). A guide to historical trends in income inequality. *Center on Budget and Policy Priorities*. Retrieved from www.cbpp.org/files/11-28-11pov.pdf

Strum, P. (2010). *Mendez v. Westminster: School desegregation and Mexican-American rights*. Lawrence: University of Kansas Press.

Sturgis, A. H. (2006). *Trail of tears and Indian removal*. Santa Barbara, CA: Greenwood Press.

Supreme Court of the United States. (2015). *Obergefell et al. v. Hodges, director, Ohio Department of Health, et al*. Retrieved from www.supremecourt.gov/opinions/14pdf/14-556_3204.pdf

Times Staff. (2021, June 2) Who are president Biden's cabinet members? *LA Times*. Retrieved from https://www.latimes.com/politics/story/2021-03-08/bidens-cabinet-nominees

Trattner, W. I. (1999). *From poor law to welfare state: A history of social welfare in America* (6th ed.). New York, NY: The Free Press.

Trump, D. J. (2017). *Executive order 13769: Protecting the nation from foreign terrorists entry into the United States*. Retrieved from www.whitehouse.gov/presidential-actions/executive-order-protecting-nation-foreign-terrorist-entry-united-states/

UC San Diego. (n.d.). LGBTQ history in government documents: Timeline of documents. *The Library*. Retrieved from https://ucsd.libguides.com/lgbtdocs/timeline

United States House of Representatives: History Art & Archives. (2014). *Women in congress*. Retrieved from http://history.house.gov/Exhibition-and-Publications/WIC/Women-in-Congress/

U.S. Bureau of Labor Statistics. (2020). *Persons with a disability: Labor force characteristics summary*. Retrieved from www.bls.gov/news.release/disabl.nr0.htm

U.S. Census Bureau. (1977). *Race and ethnic standards for federal statistics and administrative reporting*. Directive No. 15. Retrieved from http://wonder.cdc.gov/wonder/help/populations/bridged-race/directive15.html

U.S. Department of Labor. (2013). *Employees' rights and responsibilities under the Family and Medical Leave Act*. WHD Publications. Retrieved from www.dol.gov/whd/regs/compliance/posters/fmlaen.pdf

U.S. Equal Employment Opportunities Commission. (2015). *Title VII of the Civil Rights Act of 1964*. Retrieved from www.eeoc.gov/laws/statutes/titlevii.cfm

U.S. Equal Opportunity Commission. (2004). EEOC agrees to landmark resolution of discrimination case against Abercrombie & Fitch. *Press Release*. Retrieved from www.eeoc.gov/eeoc/newsroom/release/11-18-04.cfm

U.S. Equal Opportunity Commission. (2014). *The Pregnancy Discrimination Act of 1978*. Retrieved from www.eeoc.gov/laws/statutes/pregnancy.cfm

U.S. Government Printing Office. (1963). *Pub. L. 88–38: Equal Pay Act of 1963*. Washington, DC. Retrieved from www.gpo.gov/fdsys/pkg/STATUTE-77/pdf/STATUTE-77-Pg56.pdf

U.S. Government Printing Office. (1992). *Fifteenth amendment: Right of citizens to vote*. Washington, DC. Retrieved from www.gpo.gov/fdsys/pkg/GPO-CONAN-1992/pdf/GPO-CONAN-1992-10-16.pdf.

Vann, W. C. (1974). *The strange career of Jim Crow* (3rd rev. ed.). New York, NY: Oxford University Press.

Van Nuys, F. (2002). *Americanizing the West: Race, immigrants and citizenship, 1890–1930*. Lawrence: University of Kansas Press.

Vaughn, A. T. (1989). The origins debate: Slavery and racism in seventeenth-century Virginia. *The Virginia Magazine of History and Biography*, 97(3), 311–354.

Vera, H., & Feagin, J. R. (2007). *Handbook of the sociology of racial and ethnic relations*. New York, NY: Springer.

Villarreal, D. (2019). Sodomy laws are still being used to harass LGBTQ people. *LGBTQ Nation*. Retrieved from www.lgbtqnation.com/2019/09/sodomy-laws-still-used-harass-lgbtq-people/

Warwick-Booth, L. (2013). *Social inequality: A student's guide*. Thousand Oaks, CA: Sage.

Webster, Y. O. (1992). *The racialization of America*. New York, NY: St. Martin's Press.

Weinberg, M. (1996). *Racism in contemporary America*. Westport, CT: Greenwood Publishing Group.

Wellman, J. (1991). The Seneca Falls women's right convention: A study of social networks. *Journal of Women's History*, 3(1), 9–37.

Women's Rights and Economic Change. (2004). Intersectionality: A tool for gender and economic justice. *Association for Women's Rights in Development*. Retrieved from https://lgbtq.unc.edu/sites/lgbtq.unc.edu/files/documents/intersectionality_en.pdf

Wood, G. S. (1993). *Radicalism of the American revolution*. New York, NY: Vintage Books.

Wormser, R. (2003). *The rise and fall of Jim Crow*. New York, NY: Macmillan.

Wulf, K. (2005). *Not all wives: Women of colonial Philadelphia*. Philadelphia, PA: University of Pennsylvania Press.Box 3.1 U.S. Race Timeline, 1705–Present

CHAPTER 4
Theoretical Frameworks

What Is Theory?

The social work dictionary defines theory as amongst other things explanations of the etiology/causes of social problems, such as inequality, poverty, discrimination, and so on. These explanations help social workers understand the development and causes of social problems as the basis for potential intervention that addresses those problems effectively (Baker, 2013).

Why Theories Are Important to Social Work

There are several reasons why theories are essential to social work. First, they provide a framework and order for practice. Even with the skills necessary for practice, social workers have to ground these in theoretical perspectives to help reflect on what they are doing and why they are doing it (Beder, 2000). Second, theories help social workers to identify, describe, explain, predict, control, and cope with various aspects of the worker–client relationship (Beer, 2000). Third, they inform specific practice interventions and strategies developed to address a vast array of human behavior. Fourth, they orientate/tell social workers about what is considered normative and abnormal development along a particular trajectory and supposed predictable life stages (Baker, 2013). Fifth, they explain how individuals, families, groups, organizations, communities, societies, and social movements develop and function (Baker, 2013). Sixth, and as indicated in the social work dictionary definition, they provide a conceptual framework for understanding the development of social problems and their impact on client populations, as well as possible solutions for addressing these issues (Baker, 2013).

This chapter introduces the three theories that provide the book's conceptual frameworks for examining social inequality and its pervasive and powerful influence on social policy. These theories are critical race theory (CRT), intersectionality theory (IT), and conflict theory (CT). Also introduced as a way of understanding the essence of social inequality is the capability approach.

Critical Race Theory

Though not initially conceived for social policy analysis, critical race theory (CRT) offers a framework for understanding why racial and to a lesser extent ethnic inequality have such a pervasive influence on social policies. It also provides a framework for understanding why some racial/ethnic groups are perennially disadvantaged by social policies while others have been disadvantaged for just a generation or two.

Conceived in the 1980s by Derrick Bell, an African American professor at Harvard Law School; Alan Freeman, a White scholar teaching at SUNY-Buffalo Law School; and later Richard Delgado, a Hispanic civil rights professor at the University of Alabama School of Law, CRT has its origins in legal scholarship (Bell, 1995; Delgado & Stefancic, 2012). As initially conceived, CRT was both a criticism of and an heir to the Critical Legal Studies Movement (CLSM), which sought to reform the legal system. It was a reform that the

DOI: 10.4324/9781003023708-4

CLMS perceived as necessary because of what they saw as a legal system that existed to protect the interests of the wealthy and the powerful (Unger, 1986).

While agreeing with the overall sentiments of the CLMS, Bell and Freeman and other legal scholars were nevertheless critical of its failure to incorporate race and racism in its analysis of the legal system (Bell, 1995; Delgado & Stefancic, 1998). It was an analysis, they argued, that should be in the foreground and central to any discussion of the legal system (Bell, 1995). Indeed, Bell, Freeman, and later Delgado and others suggested that by not listening to the lived experiences and histories of those oppressed by institutional racism, the CLSM was limited: It did not offer the strategies needed for transforming the legal system (Bell, 1995; Crenshaw et al., 1995; Delgado & Stefancic, 2000, 2012;Yosso, 2005).

In the early 1980s, Bell, Freeman, and the other legal scholars who wanted to put race and racism at the forefront of their analysis of racial injustice pulled away from the CLSM (Crenshaw et al., 1995; Delgado, 1988). After their departure, they began to produce legal scholarship that did put race and racism at the forefront. In a conceptual sense, then, CRT was a movement of a sort from the early 1980s. However, it was not until 1989 at a conference in Madison, Wisconsin, that it got the name CRT. From that point forward, CRT coalesced into a loosely defined organization with annual workshops, occasional conferences, and a certain degree of thematic agreement on what is important in racial politics and analysis (Delgado & Stefancic, 2000, p. 470).

In the past 30 years, CRT has become a dynamic and growing movement in law, and is taught in law schools across the country, and hundreds of legal and academic scholars consider themselves CR theorists (Delgado & Stefancic, 2012). Moreover, CRT has been incorporated into other disciplines, including education, social work, psychology, and public health (Constance-Huggins, 2012; Ford & Airhihenbuwa, 2010; Lynn & Dixon, 2013; Salter & Adams, 2013). It has also expanded beyond the Black/White racial binary to include the experiences of Native Americans (TribalCrit), Hispanics (Lat/Crit), and Asians (Asian/Crit) (Chang, 1993; Haynes, 2008; Museus & Ifikar, 2013;Valdez, 1996;Yosso, 2005). There is an intersection with theories such as Queer Critical Theory and Intersectionality Theory (Crenshaw et al., 1995). And lastly, CRT is being used not just in the United States but also in Europe and countries as far flung as Australia and China.

As it is today, CRTs central tenets are as follows:

- Race is the primary, although by no means the only, form of oppression in the United States.
(Bell, 1995; Delgado & Stefancic, 2012)
- Race is a contrived system of categorizing people, according to observable physical attributes. It has no correspondence to genetic or biological reality.
(Bell, 1995; Delgado & Stefancic, 2012)
- Racism is ordinary, not aberrational. It is deeply embedded in the social and economic landscape of the United States and is the usual way society does business.
(Bell, 1995; Carbado & Roithmayr, 2014; Delgado & Stefancic, 2012)
- Dominant social discourse and people in power can racialize groups of people in different ways at different times, depending on historical, social, or economic need.
(Carbado & Roithmayr, 2014)
- Racial stereotypes are ubiquitous in society and limit the opportunities for people of color.
(Carbado & Roithmayr, 2014)
- Racism brings material and psychic advantage to the dominant group, and progressive change occurs when, and only when, the interest of the dominant group converges with those of the racially disadvantaged.
(Bell, 1995; Carbado & Roithmayr, 2014; Delgado & Stefancic, 2012)

- The dominant group's accounting of history routinely excludes racial and other minority perspectives to justify and legitimize its power.
(Bell, 1995; Delgado & Stefancic, 2012)

- The nation's racial past exerts contemporary effects.
(Carbado & Roithmayr, 2014)

- Though society's social institutions claim neutrality, impartiality, objectivity, and even-handed dealings with diverse groups, in fact, they work in the interest of the dominant racial group. As such, through policies and practice they promote a system of racial and ethnic subordination for particular racial and ethnic groups.
(Bell, 1995; Delgado & Stefancic, 2012)

- The success of various social policy initiatives often depends on whether the perceived beneficiaries are people of color.
(Carbado & Roithmayr, 2014)

- Supposed color blindness allows society to address only extremely egregious forms of racial harm that everyone would notice and not condone, as opposed to the less obvious and more frequent forms.
(Bell, 1995; Delgado & Stefancic, 2012)

- Though race is considered the primary form of oppression, one cannot think of racial and ethnic subordination without considering the intersectionality and interlocking oppressions of gender, sexual orientation, and class.
(Bell, 1995; Delgado & Stefancic, 2012)

- Counternarratives that challenge the dominant narrative of race and ethnic neutral policies, as well as give voice to the experiences and perspectives of the oppressed, are critical to the empowerment of oppressed racial and ethnic groups.
(Bell, 1995; Carbado & Roithmayr, 2014; Delgado & Stefancic, 2012)

INTERSECTIONALITY THEORY

Intersectionality theory (IT), first named by legal scholar Kimberle Crenshaw in 1989, is a feminist sociological theory (Crenshaw, 1989). Rooted in Black feminist writing and scholarship, IT evolved from antidiscrimination law, feminist theory, and antiracist politics treating race and gender as mutually exclusive categories of experiences and analysis (Crenshaw, 1989, p. 91). In this dichotomous treatment, the multidimensionality of Black women's experiences, which are broader than a discrete category, were marginalized. As such, analysis and action in the oppression discourse were limited, the limitation being the failure to acknowledge that the interlocking oppressions of race, class, and gender mean that Black women experience discrimination in ways discernibly different from White women and Black men (Crenshaw, 1991).

To give voice to Black women's experiences, Black feminist scholars Crenshaw and Collins built on the writings of 19th-century Black feminist Anne Julia Cooper and contemporaries Angela Davis, bell hooks, and Debora King (Cooper, 2005; Davis, 1983; hooks, 1981, 1984; King, 1988). In doing so, they conceptualized a paradigm shift that sought an integrative approach to theorizing oppression. The shift stressed the significance of seeing race, class, and gender not as separate categories of oppression but rather as interlocking systems. Although race, class, and gender were the fundamental oppressions affecting Black women, Collins (1990) argued that it could also certainly be the case for other groups. Collins (1990) further suggested that race, class, and gender are not exclusive as regarding oppressions. Other interlocking oppressions include ethnicity, immigration status, sexual orientation/identity, disability, and religion.

As suggested by Collins (1990), placing Black women and other excluded groups at the center of analysis opens up a whole new conceptual stance. In this stance, all groups can be seen as having varying amounts of penalty and privilege within an historically created system. In any given context, one might be an oppressor, a member of an oppressed group, or simultaneously oppressor and oppressed. Moreover, they experience oppression in varying ways and with varying degrees of intensity.

Since its conceptualization, IT has become the predominate conceptualization of how a woman's multiple identities are affected by oppression and social locations in hierarchies of power and privilege (Carastathis, 2014). Moreover, in addition to Black feminists, Latina, post-colonial, queer, and indigenous scholars have produced work that reveals the complex factors and processes that shape human lives (Bunjun, 2010, Collins, 1990; Crenshaw, 1991; Hankivsky, 2014, p. 2; Ven Herk et al., 2011). It has also extended beyond the academy to international human rights discourse (Hankivsky, 2014).

As it stands today, intersectionality theory's central tenets are as follows:

- People have multiple, socially defined and constructed identities (i.e., gender, race, sexual orientation, etc.) with meanings that are historically and contextually contingent. As a consequence of having multiple identities, which can evolve or be constrained by historical events or context, people are members of more than one community at the same time. Hence, people can simultaneously experience oppression and privilege. They can also simultaneously oppress and be oppressed.
- Because of people's multiple, layered identities, IT rejects the additive models of oppression, which are rooted in either/or dichotomous thinking. Instead, it takes a both/and stance to reveal how a person's multiple and interlocking identities produce substantively distinct experiences of oppression and discrimination, which are part of an overarching matrix of domination.
- The matrices of domination, which are composed of laws, social policies, and social institutions, serve as vectors of oppression and privileges. As such, they identify and rank people and groups within society on a hierarchy of privilege by way of power and social relations (Collins, 1990). These rankings influence degree of access to political power, resources, equality of opportunities, and the potential for social justice. In the United States, these rankings privilege Whiteness, wealth, patriarchy, nativism, heterosexism, and ability.
- IT is an important tool for analyzing social policy; it can help to identify the ways that particular social policies address or contribute to the inequalities experienced by various social groups. In social policy analysis, IT takes into account how these social groups multiple identities interact to form unique meanings and complex experiences within and between groups in society.

Conflict Theory

At the core of conflict theory (CT) is the premise that the different groups in society are in an ongoing struggle to maximize their share of the existing finite resources that are desirous for human beings. As resources are finite, the struggle for access to them invariably leads to intergroup and intragroup competition and conflict. The winners and losers in these conflicts are reflected in the power dynamics of a society, that is, which groups have control of political and economic power, which groups control the society's social structures and institutions, and which groups have the greatest access to the society's finite resources.

The roots of contemporary conflict theory can be traced back to the work of contemporaries and collaborators Karl Marx (1818–1883) and Friedrich Engels (1820–1895), and later Max Weber (1864–1920). Marx and Engels, who lived in the early stages of industrial capitalism in Europe, saw conflict as chiefly resulting from class conflict within the industrial and economic sectors of society. In this class conflict, played out in a capitalist society promising equality through a market economy and fair exchange, Marx and Engels argued that the capitalist bourgeoisie few exploit the proletariat many (Marx & Engels, 1848). The exploitation occurs by way of the unequal exchange in the market between the property—owning classes, among whom are the owners of the means of production (the bourgeoisie), and the industrial working class (the proletariat), whose labor they purchase by way of waged employment. In theory, at least, the market exchange between the owners of the means of production and the labor force it employs should be one of equivalent value, in which each party receives a value equivalent to what they contribute to the exchange. Marx and Engels argued, however, that in reality, the owners of the means of production use labor surpluses to keep wages artificially low (Marx & Engels, 1848; Moseley, 2002). Thus, they are able to create wealth for themselves while those who provide the labor upon which it is built receive nowhere near the value of their contribution to the exchange. Marx and Engels believed that more so than the previously exploitative socioeconomic arrangements such as feudalism and slavery, capitalism creates a *false consciousness* for both the owners of means of production and labor, neither of whom are aware that the system is exploitative (Marx & Engels, 1848). The owners of the means of production believe they are rewarding the laborers fairly, and initially, at least, the laborers believe they are receiving a fair day's pay. Marx and Engel suggested that laborers, more so than the owners of the means of production, do eventually gain *class consciousness* and recognize their exploitation, prompting class conflict in the demand for equality (Marx & Engels, 1848).

Although sharing many of the ideas of Marx and Engels, Weber saw social class, more than economics, as the most basic division in society. Weber posited that all societies are organized in hierarchical systems of domination and subordination (Weber, 1978, 2010). In doing so, socially stratified classes are created based on wealth, power, and prestige. Those with the most wealth, power, and prestige (upper classes) not only have prime access to society's resources, which include land, capital, social respect, and political influence, but they can also limit the access of others (middle and lower classes) to these resources. According to Weber, this structure of social stratification, which allows those in the upper classes to effectively retain power by way of control of society's social institutions, acts almost exclusively on the upper class's behalf (Weber, 1978, 2010). These social institutions represent politics, economics, and law and order, all of whose resulting social policies aim at either overtly or covertly controlling those in the lower strata of society. Thus a system of inequality is perpetuated, serving as the source of conflict and antagonism between the upper class and elites (propertied), and the other classes in society (Weber, 1978). These other classes include white-collar professionals (upper middle class), petty bourgeoisie (lower middle class), and the working class (lower class). The propertied class has economic power, social status, and political power. The professional class has high positions in the labor market and ownership of lesser forms of property such as stocks and shares. They also have relatively high social status and some political influence. The petty bourgeoisie have relatively little property ownership, social status, or ability to exert political influence. Lastly, the working class lack property ownership and political influence, and have a low position in the labor market (Weber, 1978, 2010).

Lewis Coser (1964) broadened the social class perspective of Weber by proposing a pluralistic theory of social conflict. In the pluralistic approach there is recognition that class is not the only conflict in society. Rather, there is more than one social conflict going on at all times because individuals hold multiple and interlocking memberships in status groups. Consequently, social conflicts of access to resources, social justice, and equality exist between economic groups, racial groups, ethnic groups, age, groups, gender groups, and so forth (Coser, 1964). Therefore, and consistent with intersectional theory, the pluralistic approach to conflict theory recognizes vectors of oppression and privilege, including not just social class but also race, ethnicity, gender, global location, sexual orientation, immigration status, ability, and age.

In its most recent articulation, CT is associated with a number of other social inequality perspectives, which including Feminist Theory, Queer Theory, and the Race-Conflict Theory. CT's central tenets are as follows:

- Society is defined by inequality that produces conflict.
- Human potential and the capacity for creativity are deliberately suppressed for all but the ruling class by conditions of exploitation and oppression, which is necessary for any society with an unequal division of labor.

- Genuine consensus is not achieved in a capitalist society such as the United States, because the most powerful in society are able to impose their ideology and values on others and make them accept their discourse.
- The state, in the form of its institutions, serves the interests of the most powerful while claiming to represent those of all. Indeed, while claiming to represent the interests of disadvantaged groups, in practice this is an illusion.

THE THEORIES AND SOCIAL WORK PRACTICE

Critical Race Theory and Social Work

Critical race theory, intersectionality theory, and conflict theory provide social workers with analytical frameworks and vocabulary for situating social work practice and social policy analysis within the broader context of societal power relations, where racism and the other forms of oppression that underpin societal inequalities are woven into the fabric of the socio-historical-political context. In doing so, the theories reposition the debate about social inequality away from a deficit perspective and the supposed dysfunction of marginalized groups. The theories instead highlight the ways in which unequal power relations maintain the race, class, gender, nativist, and hetero-normative hierarchies that are and have been at the heart of social inequality. Thus, for example, the central tenets of CRT, which Huggins (2012, p. 9) argues are highly compatible with social work, can help social workers to understand race as a culturally constructed label given by the dominant group. As a cultural construct, race imposes boundaries on membership of the dominant group and limits access to society's resources for non-dominant group members. CRT can further help social workers recognize how embedded race is in the social and structural fabric, where it manifests in policies and practices that are ostensibly color-blind, but in practice are steeped in racial biases that maintain existing racial hierarchies and social inequality for the benefit of the dominant group. With this recognition, social workers become racially conscious and are ideally placed to challenge race-neutral explanations for the persistent racial disparities and inequality across most all quality of life indicators, including housing, education, criminal justice, labor market participation, and health care, to name a few.

Intersectionality Theory and Social Work

Intersectionality theory is an extremely useful analytical tool for social workers to examine the interplay between different categories of oppression and inequality, most notably race, gender, class, sexual orientation, and immigration status. With an understanding of the interaction, Mattsson (2014) suggests social workers can capture dynamic power relations and oppression in a way that is sensitive to differences and oppression both within and among groups. Thus, for example, while all women experience oppression when compared to men, the interplay of gender, race, class, sexual orientation, marital status, immigration status, and ability ensures that the experience differs significantly among women depending on their race, class, immigration status, and sexual orientation. With a recognition of this, social workers can move beyond a single axis analysis of social problems to a more expansive perspective that includes incorporating an intersectionality lens when working with all clients.

Conflict Theory and Social Work

Conflict theory provides social workers with a lens for an historical and contemporary analysis of the sources of conflicts—that is, ideological positions, values, cultural norms, etc.—that have shaped social inequality and informed social policy response (Reisch & Staller, 2011). In doing so, social workers pay particular attention to reoccurring themes, as well as the influence of race, gender, class, sexual orientation, immigration status, and ability on the emergence and resolution of conflicts (Reisch & Staller, 2011). With a conflict theory perspective, social workers can challenge the narratives, myths, values, and propaganda that both historically and in the present day justify the monopolization of society's most precious resources by a select few. Present-day examples include the growing income and wealth gap between upper- and middle-income households, with upper-income households having a net worth 6.6

times that of middle-income households, double what the gap was in 1983 and the widest on record (Fry & Kochhar, 2014). The income and wealth gap is even greater for low-income and or Black, Hispanic, and Native American households (Fry & Kochhar, 2014).

Capability Approach

Unlike CRT, IT, and CL, the capability approach (CA) is a normative theory that does not seek to explain inequality but rather helps to conceptualize its essence. First articulated by Indian economist and philosopher Amartya Sen in 1979, the capability approach (CA) is a theoretical framework for the evaluation of individual well-being as it relates to one's ability to achieve the kind of life they have reason to value (Sen, 1999; Wells, 2012). Two assertions underpin the capability approach: first, the freedom to achieve well-being is of primary moral importance, and second, the freedom to achieve well-being must be understood in terms of people's capabilities (Wells, 2012). Capabilities are a person's real freedoms, that is, the choices and opportunities to achieve functionings that are valuable to them (Sen, 1999; Wells, 2012). Functionings include employment, education, health care, leisure, shelter, recognition, and so forth. Sen posited that achieved functionings, as defined by the choice to act upon freedoms, makes a life valuable (Sen, 1999; Wells, 2012). However, Sen resisted the notion that you could or should determine which functionings matter for a good life. In doing so, Sen posited that the only legitimate source of decisions about a good life are the people involved (Sen, 1999; Wells, 2012).

Philosopher Martha Nussbaum rejected Sen's position in determining which functionings matter for a good life by adding a social justice perspective to the capability approach. In doing so, Nussbaum placed a focus not on the individual but on society and its structures as the determinants of one's capabilities. If one does not, for example, have access to education, this does not represent choice, but deprivation and a failure of society (Nussbaum, 1988, 2011). Nussbaum argued for and created, as a matter of social justice based on human dignity, a list of central human capabilities that must be present for a good life. These capabilities are:

1. *Life*. Being able to live a life of normal length.
2. *Bodily health*. Being able to have good health, including reproductive health, adequate nourishment, and adequate shelter.
3. *Bodily integrity*. Having the autonomy to move from place to place, be secure against violence, opportunities for sexual satisfaction, and reproductive choice.
4. *Senses, imagination, and thought*. Being able to use senses to be intellectually expansive, as regard to education, religious choice, freedom of speech, and so on.
5. *Emotions*. Being able to have a full range of emotional attachments and expression.
6. *Practical reason*. Being able to engage in critical reflection about the planning of one's life.
7. *Affiliation*. Being able to live with and show concern for others, and to share in various forms of interaction. Also, having the social base for self-respect and non-humiliation as manifested by the racism, sexism, homophobia, classism, xenophobia, and so forth.
8. *Other species*. Being able to live in harmony with animals, plants, and the world of nature.
9. *Play*. Being able to play, laugh, and participate in and enjoy recreational activities.
10. *Control over one's environment*. Being able to participate fully and effectively in the political process, and having the fair and equal access to home ownership, employment, and freedom from unwarranted search and seizure.

(Nussbaum, 1988, 2011)

As regard to social policies, Sen argues that they should be formulated as to not place obstacles in the way of people having opportunities and choices to achieve functionings that are valuable to them (Sen, 1999).

Nussbaum proposed that the ten previously described determinations of a good life should be enshrined in all developed society's constitutions (Nussbaum, 1988, 2011).

Drawing from both Sen and Nussbaum, social inequalities and the policies that support them can be seen as primary obstacles to people's capabilities. The lack of access to quality education and residential segregation, for example, have wide-ranging implications for the kinds of choices people have, that is, employment opportunities, health care availability, and so forth. Thus, the essence of inequality can be thought of as the lack of choices and opportunities to achieve those things one values.

Chapter Summary

This chapter introduced three theories that will provide the conceptual frameworks for the book. These theories were selected because they address social inequality and speak specifically to those groups that have been perennially disadvantaged in access to society's resources because of socially constructed categorizations. All three theories indicate that social inequality and its effect is multidimensional and cuts across people's multiple identities and group affiliations. Also introduced as a theoretical framework for understanding the essence of social inequality was the capability approach.

Retrieval Questions

1. As initially conceived, what was CRT?
2. Why did Bell, Freeman, and other legal scholars pull away from the CLSM?
3. Where did Bell, Freeman, and other like-minded legal scholars think race and racism should be located in the discussion of the legal system?
4. What are some examples of CRT's broadening to include other perspectives?
5. What are some of the central tenants of CRT?
6. IT is rooted in what kind of writing and scholarship?
7. What was the paradigm shift that IT wanted to achieve?
8. By placing Black women and other excluded groups at the center of analysis, what did Collins suggest would happen?
9. What are some of the central tenants of IT?
10. What did Weber posit about how societies are organized?
11. According to Weber, those in society with the most wealth, power, and prestige have what?
12. What are some of the central tenets of CT?
13. What is the capability approach?

Discussion Questions

1. Discuss how CRT might manifest itself in social policy.
2. Discuss how IT might manifest itself in social policy.
3. Discuss how CT might manifest itself in social policy.
4. What role do you think theoretical frameworks play in social work practice?

REFERENCES

Baker, R. L. (2013). *The social work dictionary* (6th ed.). Washington, DC: NASW Press.

Beder, J. (2000). The integration of theory into practice: Suggestions for supervisors. *Professional Development: The International Journal of Continuing Social Work Education, 3*(2), 40–48.

Bell, D. (1995). Who's afraid of critical race theory? *University of Illinois Law Review*, 893–901.

Bunjun, B. (2010). Feminist organizations and intersectionality: Contesting hegemonic feminism. *Atlantis, 34*(2), 115–126.

Carastathis, A. (2014). The concept of intersectionality in feminist theory. *Philosophy Compass, 9*(5), 304–314.

Carbado, D. W., & Roithmayr, D. (2014). Critical race theory meets social science. *The Annual Review of Law and Social Science, 10*, 149–167.

Chang, R. S. (1993). Toward an Asian American legal scholarship: Critical race theory, post-structuralism, and narrative space. *California Law Review, 81*(5), 1241–1323.

Collins, P. H. (1990). *Black feminist thought: Knowledge, consciousness, and the politics of empowerment*. New York, NY: Routledge.

Constance-Huggins, M. (2012). Critical race theory in social work education: A framework for addressing racial disparity. *Critical Social Work, 13*(2), 1–16.

Cooper, A. J. (2005). *A voice from the South*. New York, NY: Oxford University Press.

Coser, L. A. (1964). *The functions of social conflict*. New York, NY: Free Press.

Crenshaw, K. (1989). Intersectionality: The double bind of race and gender. *Perspectives Magazine*. Retrieved from www.americanbar.org/content/dam/aba/publishing/perspectives_magazine/women_perspectives_Spring2004CrenshawPSP.authcheckdam.pdf

Crenshaw, K. (1991). Mapping the margins: Intersectionality, identity politics, and violence against women of color. *Stanford Review, 43*(6), 1241–1299.

Crenshaw, K., Gotanda, N., Peller, G., & Thomas, K. (1995). *Critical race theory: The key writings that formed a movement*. New York, NY: The New Press.

Davis, A. Y. (1983). *Women, race and class*. New York, NY: Vintage Books.

Delgado, R. (1988). Critical legal studies and the realities of race: Does the fundamental contradiction have a corollary? *Harvard Civil Rights: Civil Liberties Law Review, 23*, 407–413.

Delgado, R., & Stefancic, J. (1998). Critical race theory: Past, present, and future. In M. Freeman (Ed.), *Current legal problems 1998: Legal theory at the end of the millennium* (pp. 467–492). New York, NY: Oxford University Press.

Delgado, R., & Stefancic, J. (2000). *Critical race theory: The cutting edge* (2nd ed.). Philadelphia, PA: Temple University Press.

Delgado, R., & Stefancic, J. (2012). *Critical race theory: An introduction* (2nd ed.). New York: New York University Press.

Ford, C. L., & Airhihenbuwa, C. O. (2010). Critical race theory, race equity, and public health: Toward antiracism praxis. *American Journal of Public Health, 100*(1), 30–35.

Fry, R., & Kochhar, R. (2014). *America's wealth gap between middle-income and upper-income families widest on record*. Washington, DC: Pew Research Center. Retrieved from www.pewresearch.org/fact-tank/2014/12/17/wealth-gap-upper-middle-income/

Hankivsky, O. (2014). Intersectionality 101. *The Institute for Intersectionality Research & Policy, Simon Fraser University*. Retrieved from www.sfu.ca/iirp/documents/resources/101_Final.pdf

Haynes, J. (2008). Unmasking, exposing, and confronting: Critical race theory, tribal critical race theory and multicultural education. *International Journal of Multicultural Education, 10*(2), 1–15.

hooks, b. (1981). *Ain't I a woman: Black women and feminism*. Boston, MA: South End Press.

hooks, b. (1984). *Feminist theory from margin to center*. Boston, MA: South End Press.

Huggins, M. C. (2012). Critical race theory in social work education: A framework for addressing racial disparities. *Critical Social Work, 13*(2), 2–6.

King, D. B. (1988). Multiple jeopardy, multiple consciousness: The context of a Black feminist ideology. *Signs: Journal of Women in Culture and Society, 14*(1), 42–72.

Lynn, M., & Dixon, A. D. (2013). *Handbook of critical race theory in education*. New York, NY: Routledge.

Marx, K., & Engels, F. (1848). *The manifesto of the communist*. London, England: International Publishing Company.

Mattsson, T. (2014). Intersectionality as a useful tool: Anti-oppressive social work and critical reflection. *Affillia: Journal of Women and Social Work, 29*(1), 8–17.

Moseley, F. (2002). *The heart and soul of Marx's critique of capitalism: Exploitation or social form: Or both? A reply to Murray*. Mount Holyoake College. Retrieved from www.mtholyoke.edu/~fmoseley/working%20papers/MURRAY.pdf

Museus, S. D., & Ifikar, J. (2013). *An Asian critical theory (AsianCrit) framework: Asian students in higher education*. New York, NY: Routledge.

Nussbaum, M. (1988). Nature, functioning and capability: Aristotle on political distribution. *Oxford Studies in Ancient Philosophy*, 6(Suppl.), 145–184.

Nussbaum, M. (2011). *Creating capabilities: The human development approach*. Cambridge, MA: Harvard University Press.

Reisch, M., & Staller, K. M. (2011). Teaching social welfare policy from a conflict perspective. *Journal of Teaching in Social Work*, 31, 131–144.

Salter, P., & Adams, G. (2013). Toward a critical race psychology. *Social & Personality Psychology Compass*, 7(11), 781–793.

Sen, A. (1999). *Development as freedom* (1st ed.). New York: Oxford University Press.

Unger, R. M. (1986). *The critical legal studies movement*. Cambridge, MA: Harvard University Press.

Valdez, F. (1996). Latina/o ethnicities, critical race theory, and post-identity politics in post-modern legal culture: From practice to possibilities. *Berkeley La Raza Law Journal*, 9(1), 1–31.

Ven Herk, K. A., Smith, D., & Andrew, C. (2011). Identity matters: Aboriginal mothers' experiences of accessing health care. *Contemporary Nurse*, 37(1), 57–68.

Weber, M. (1978). *Economy and society*. Berkeley: University of California Press.

Weber, M. (2010). *The distribution of power within the community: Classes, status, party*. Trans. by Dagmar. Friedrichshafen, Germany: Zeppelin University.

Well, T. (2012). Sen's capability approach. *Internet Encyclopedia of Philosophy*. Retrieved from www.iep.utm.edu/sen-cap/

Yosso, T. J. (2005). Whose culture has capital? A critical race theory discussion of community cultural wealth. *Race, Ethnicity and Education*, 8(1), 69–91.

CHAPTER 5
Immigration

Box 5.1 Immigration Laws Time Line, 1790–Present

1790: The Naturalization Act of 1790 established America's first uniform rule for naturalization. The law stipulated that "free White persons" who have resided in the U.S. for at least 2 years may be granted citizenship as long as they are of good moral character and swear allegiance to the constitution. The law also provided that children (21 and under) of naturalized citizens shall also become American citizens (Migration Policy Institute, 2013).

1868: The Burlingame Treaty was signed. The Treaty was an international agreement granting China most-favored-nation status. As part of the agreement, the U.S. and China granted certain privileges to citizens of each country to reside in the other country. These privileges did not, however, include the right of naturalization, which was specifically withheld. The treaty was credited with encouraging Chinese immigration to the U.S. (Higham, 1956).

1880: The Burlingame Treaty was amended after opposition from Congress to Chinese immigration. The treaty was amended to suspend Chinese immigration while protecting the rights of those Chinese immigrants already in the U.S. (Higham, 1956).

1882: The U.S. Congress passes the Chinese Exclusion Act. The act was the first federal law restricting free immigration into the U.S. based on race. The act provided a 10-year moratorium on unskilled Chinese labor immigration to the U.S. (Lee, 2003).

1892: The U.S. Congress passes the Geary Act. The act extended the Chinese Exclusion Act for 10 more years. In doing so, the law required Chinese residents to carry a resident permit. Failure to do so resulted in deportation or 1 year of hard labor. Furthermore, the Chinese could not testify in court or receive bail. In *Fong Yue Ting v. the U.S.*, the U.S. Supreme Court ruled that the Geary Act was not unconstitutional (Campi, 2004).

1902 – The Geary Act, and by extension the Chinese Exclusion Act, was extended indefinitely (Campi, 2004).

1907: The Gentleman's Agreement between the U.S. and Japan was enacted. This informal agreement, which was never signed into law by Congress, was entered into by Japan in order to change the perception of the day that Japanese immigrants were overrunning the west coast, most notably San Francisco. In this agreement, Japan would no longer issue passports to Japanese emigrants and the U.S. would allow immigration only for the wives, children, and parents of Japanese immigrants already residing in the United States (Van Nuys, 2002).

1907: The Expatriation Act, Section 3, ruled that an American women who married a foreigner loses her American citizenship and takes the citizenship of her husband (Bredbenner, 1998).

DOI: 10.4324/9781003023708-5

1911: The Dillingham Commission, established in 1907, published a 42-volume report warning that the new wave of immigration from eastern and southern Europe threatens to subvert American society (Kitty, 1984; LaMay & Elliot, 1999).

1917: The U.S. Congress passed the Immigration Act of 1917. One of the key provisions of the act was the ban on people from countries in the Asiatic Barred Zone Act entering the U.S.as immigrants. The countries in the Asiatic Barred Zone included Japan, China, India, Turkey, Ceylon (Sri Lanka), Burma (Myanmar), Siam (Thailand), Laos, Cambodia, Vietnam, Singapore, Indonesia, Malaysia, Korea, Saudi Arabia, the Philippines, and the Polynesian Islands (Campi, 2005).

1921: President Warren Harding signed into law, with almost total support from the Congress, the Emergency Quota Act of 1821. The act, also known as the Emergency Immigration Act of 1921, placed numerical limits on European immigration (Ngai, 1999).

1922: The Cable Act, also known as the Married Women's Independent Nationality Act, reversed Section 3 of the Expatriation Act. Section 3 had ruled that an American women who married a foreigner loses her American citizenship and takes the citizenship of her husband (Bredbenner, 1998).

1924: The U.S. Immigration Act of 1924, also known as the Johnson-Reed Act, superseded the Emergency Quota Act. This seminal social policy created the country's first permanent immigration quota system (Ngai, 1999).

1929: The Registry Act of 1929 was signed into law. This amnesty policy allowed "law-abiding" aliens who may be in the country under some technical irregularity to register as permanent residents for a fee of $20. They also had to prove they had lived in the country since 1921 and were of good moral character (Immigration Policy Center, 2008).

1942: President Franklin D. Roosevelt signed into law The Emergency Farm Labor Agreement. The agreement, also known as the Bracero Program, allowed Mexican nationals to enter the United States to serve as temporary agricultural workers. In doing so American employers were responsible for paying the living and transportation expenses of Mexican laborers. They also had to pay them wages equal to those of American farm workers doing similar work. The program was extended in 1949 and 1951, and was not disbanded until 1964 (Migration Policy Institute, 2013)

1943: The U.S. Congress enacted the Magnuson Act. Also known as the Chinese Exclusion Repeal Act of 1943, the act discontinued the provisions of Chinese Exclusion Act of 1882 and its extensions. The act also re-established Chinese immigration at a quota of around 105 visas per year. Lastly, it allowed Chinese nationals to become U.S. citizens (Campi, 2005; Office of the Historian, 2014).

1946: The U.S. Congress enacted the Luce-Celler Act, which extended naturalization and limited immigration rights to Asian Indians and Filipinos (Campi, 2005).

1952: The Immigration and Nationality Act was signed into law. Also known as the McCarran-Walter Act, the act totally revoked all of the provisions of the Immigrant Act of 1917, i.e., the Asiatic Barred Zone Act. In doing so, the act permitted a relatively small annual quota of 2,000 for Asian Pacific immigration to the U.S. The law also established U.S. counselor offices to screen foreign nationals for admissibility to the U.S. (Campi, 2005).

1953: The Refugee Act was signed into law. The act authorized the admission of up to 205,000 non-quota immigrants, who are fleeing persecution or have been expelled from their homes in Europe (Migration Policy Institute, 2013, p. 3).

1962: The Migration and Refugee Assistance Act was signed into law. The Act authorized funds to assist foreign nationals from the Western Hemisphere who had been forced to flee their country of origin because of racial, religious, or political persecution (Migration Policy Institute, 2013).

1965: President Lyndon Johnson signed into law the Immigration and Nationality Act. Also known as the Hart-Cellar Act, this seminal immigration policy abolished the national origin quota system. In its place, a capped number of immigrants were admitted to the United States based on their relationship to a U.S. citizen or a lawful permanent resident family member or U.S. employer. The cap did not apply to the number of related family members who would be permitted to settle. The law provided a cap of 120,000 permanent residents who could be admitted each year from Western Hemisphere countries (Migration Policy Institute, 2013).

1966: President Lyndon Johnson signed into law the Cuban Readjustment Act. This act was only the second time in U.S. history that an immigration policy was directed at one immigration group in particular. Unlike, the Chinese Exclusion Act, though, the Cuban Readjustment Act offered Cuban natives and citizens and their accompanying spouse and children who arrived at open port-of-entry, or otherwise, haven in the U.S. as permanent residents. This haven was contingent on a variety of factors. These factors included approval by the Attorney General and 1-year physical residency in the U.S. after admission. The policy was a response to political persecution in Cuba and allowed for the victims of this and other forms of persecution to find a haven in the U.S. (Migration Policy Institute, 2013).

1975: The Indochina Migration and Refugee Assistance Act was signed into the law. The act expanded the definition of the term "refugee" to include an individual fleeing persecution in Cambodia and Vietnam (Migration Policy Institute, 2013).

1986: The Immigration Reform and Control Act was signed into law. The act offers two programs for undocumented immigrants to be legalized. The law also increased border patrol staffing, as well imposed sanctions on employers who knowingly hired or recruited undocumented immigrants (Migration Policy Institute, 2013).

1990: The Diversity Immigration Visa Program (also known as Diversity Lottery) was established by the Immigration Act of 1990. The program mades 50,000 immigrant visas available to nationals of countries where fewer than 50,000 immigrants came to the United States over the previous 5 years. The visas were distributed throughout six geographic regions: Africa, Asia, Europe, North America, Oceania, and South and Central America (Ballotpedia, n.d).

1996: President Bill Clinton signed into law the Illegal Immigration Reform and Immigrant Responsibility Act. The act added new grounds of inadmissibility and deportability, as well as expanded the list of crimes for deportation and expedited removal procedures (Migration Policy Institute, 2013).

1996: President Bill Clinton signed into law the Violent Crime Control and Law Enforcement Act. The act gave the U.S. Attorney General the power to bypass deportation proceedings for certain immigrant-aggravated felons (Migration Policy Institute, 2013).

2001: The Patriot Act of 2001 was signed into law. The act broadened the terrorism grounds for excluding immigrants from entering the United States. The act also allowed for the increased monitoring of foreign students (Migration Policy Institute, 2013).

2001: On 08/01/ 2001, Senator Orin Hatch (R-UT) introduced the S.1291-DREAM Act into the Senate. The Act provided a pathway for undocumented immigrants who meet specific requirements for conditional residency, leading to permanent residency, based on age and time of entry into the United States. Requirements include proof of entry into the United States before age 16 with 5 years of continuous residence. Furthermore, the applicant will need to have graduated from high school or obtained a GED in the United States; demonstrate good moral character; and pass a criminal background check. After establishing conditional residency and then a further 6 years of residency, the applicant can apply for permanent residency, and in turn, a pathway to citizenship. They must have attended a post-secondary educational institution, served in the United States armed forces for at least 2 years with an honorable discharge, passed additional background checks, and demonstrated good moral character (Georgetown Law Library, 2020; S.1291, 2001). The DREAM Act failed to pass despite numerous introductions (Georgetown Law Library, 2020).

2002: The Enhanced Border Security and Visa Entry Reform Act of 2002 mandated the development of an electronic data system to share information about foreign nationals relevant to immigrant admissibility and removability (Migration Policy Institute, 2013).

2002: The Homeland Security Act of 2002 created the Department of Homeland Security, which restructured the U.S. Immigration and Naturalization Service (INS) and the Department of Justice into three new agencies (Migration Policy Institute, 2013).

2005: The Real ID Act of 2005 established guidelines for immigration removal cases, and expanded the grounds for terrorism-related deportation (Migration Policy Institute, 2013).

2006: The Secure Fence Act of 2006 was signed into law. Among other things, the act mandated the construction of 700 miles of double-reinforced fence to be built along the boarder states with Mexico. These states included Arizona, New Mexico, and Texas (Migration Policy Institute, 2013).

2007: On October 18, Dick Durbin (D-IL), along with Republican co-sponsors Charles Hagel (R-NB) and Richard Lugar (R-IN) introduced the DREAM Act as S2205. Although 52 senators voted for the bill, it was eight short of the required 60 for consideration. Senate opponents labeled the act as an amnesty that would encourage chain migration and further undocumented immigration (Congress.gov, 2007).

2008: Initiated by President George W. Bush, the Secure Communities program, a Department of Homeland program was launched. The purpose of the program was to identify immigrants in U.S. jails who were deportable under immigration law. Toward this end, the program collaborated with the FBI, state, and local law enforcement agencies by way of an immigration database that allows Immigration and Customs Enforcement (ICE) to access information on individuals held in jails. With this information (i.e., fingerprints), ICE can check against the U.S. Visitor and Immigrant Status Indicator Technology Program (US-VISIT) and the Automated Biometric Identification System (IDENT) for an individual's criminal and immigration history (Waslin, 2011).

2010: A revised version of the DREAM Act was introduced and passed in the House (H.R 6497). However, the act failed to pass the Senate and died (Georgetown Law Library, 2020).

2011: A Dick Durbin (D-IL)-sponsored Dream Act was introduced into the Senate (S. 952). The act lost vital support from Congressional Republicans and was not passed (Georgetown Law Library, 2020).

2012: President Obama initiated the immigration policy, an executive branch memorandum known as the Deferred Action for Childhood Arrivals (DACA), in response to the failure of the Dream Act legislation to pass both Congressional houses. DACA provided a 3-year deferment from deportation actions and included eligibility for a work permit. To be eligible for the program, potential recipients must be under the age of 31 as of June 15, 2012. Additionally, she/he must have entered the United States by their 16th birthday; had continuous residence in the United States since June 15, 2007; and be physically present in the United States at the time of the request for consideration under DACA. They cannot have had lawful status on June 15, 2012. She/he must currently be in school, graduated or obtained a GED, or be an honorably discharged military veteran. Lastly, she/he cannot have been convicted of a felon, significant misdemeanor or three or more misdemeanors, and not pose a threat to national security or public safety. Unlike the DREAM Act, DACA did not offer a pathway to citizenship (Georgetown Law Library, 2020).

2014: President Obama discontinued the Secure Communities program due to mounting litigation and criticism from undocumented immigrant advocates. In doing so, the Obama administration's Secretary of Homeland Security, Jeh Charles Jonson, expressed a belief that while the program's overarching goals remain valid, a fresh start and a new program are needed (Johnson, 2014).

2014: President Obama announced that he will use Immigration Accountability Executive Action to take an important step toward fixing a broken immigration system (USCIS, 2014; Whitehouse Office of the Press Security, 2014). The express purpose of the executive action was to stem the flow of undocumented immigration at the border, prioritize deporting felons, not families, and require undocumented immigrants to pass a criminal background check and pay taxes to temporarily stay in the United States without fear of deportation (USCIS, 2014). To this end, the executive action expanded the population eligible for DACA and lengthened the program's work authorization period from two to three years. Additionally, it allowed undocumented parents of U.S. citizens and lawful permanent residents to request deferred action and employment authorization for 3 years in a new Deferred Action for Parents of American and Lawful Permanent Residents program (DAPA). To be eligible, they must have resided continuously since January 1, 2010, and passed background checks (U.S. Citizen and Immigration Service, 2014; Whitehouse Office of the Press Security, 2014).

2014: Twenty-six states, led by Texas, filed a lawsuit challenging the implementation of DAPA because it has not gone through the notice-and-comment process and, as such, was arbitrary and capricious. The states also argued that DAPA violated the Take-Care-Clause of the Constitution, clarifying the President's power (*United States v. Texas*, n.d.).

2016: On June 23, in a one-line *per Curiam* opinion, an equally divided Supreme Court of the United States (4–4) affirmed the judgment of the lower court injunction blocking DAPA. In doing so, it agreed with the lower court judgment that President Obama's initiation of DAPA violated the Take-Care-Clause of the Constitution, which clarifies the President's power (*United States v. Texas*, n.d.).

2016: Within the first 100 days of his presidency, Donald Trump outlined 10 policy actions to address immigration reform:

1. Constructing a wall along the southern border.
2. Ending catch-and-release programs.
3. Having a zero-tolerance for undocumented immigrants who have committed a crime or crimes while in the country.
4. Blocking funding for sanctuary cities.
5. Canceling "unconstitutional executive orders" (DACA) and enforcing immigration laws.
6. Suspending visas to individuals from countries where adequate screening cannot occur.
7. Ensuring that foreign countries keep citizens who are deported from the United States.
8. Completing the biometric entry-exit tracking system.
9. Ending employment and benefits for individuals residing in the country without legal permission.
10. Reforming immigration regulations to benefit the country and its labor force (Ballotpedia, 2020).

2017: On January 12, outgoing President Obama directs the Department of Homeland Security to end the so-called "wet-foot/dry-foot" policy for Cuban migrants who enter the country by sea without legal documentation. The policy, put in place twenty-years prior, allowed Cuban nationals who set foot on American soil from the ocean would be granted humanitarian relief and residency status (White House, 2017).

2017: President Trump signed Executive Order 13767, titled Border Security and Immigration Enforcement Improvements. A key component of Trump's presidential campaign platform, the order calls for the construction of a wall along the southern United States border. The order also calls for additional detention centers to be built near the border to house individuals entering the U.S. without legal permission (Trump, 2017a).

2017: President Trump signed Executive Order 13768, titled Enhancing Public Safety in the Interior of the United States, which introduced penalties against sanctuary cities that limit the enforcement and prosecution of federal immigration laws against undocumented immigrants. The order prioritized the deportation of undocumented individuals who pose a risk to public safety or national security, for example, she/he has been convicted of any criminal offense, or she/he has been charged but not convicted of a criminal offense, she/he had committed acts that constitute a chargeable criminal offense, she/he had engaged in fraud or willful misrepresentation in connection with any official matter or application before a governmental agency, she/he had abused any program related to receipt of public benefits. In addition to these conditions, if an immigration officer judges the individual poses a risk to public safety or national security, this is also a reason for deportation. Additionally, the Secure Communities deportation program was reactivated, a program that was discontinued under the Obama administration (Trump, 2017b).

2017: President Trump signed Executive Order 13769, entitled Protecting the Nation from Foreign Terrorists Entry into the United States (also known as the Refugee and Muslim travel ban). The order lowered the number of refugees to be admitted into the United States in 2017 to 50,000. It also suspended the U.S. Refugee Admissions Program for 120 days and suspended entry of Syrian refugees indefinitely. Furthermore, it suspended for 90 days the entry into the U.S. of specific individuals from Iran, Iraq, Libya, Somalia, Sudan, Syria, and Yemen (Trump, 2017c).

2017: A federal judge in New York granted the American Civil Liberties Union's (ACLU) request for a nationwide temporary injunction blocking the deportation of all people stranded in U.S. airports under President Trump's new Muslim ban (American Civil Liberties Union-Washington, n.d.).

2017: U.S Federal District Judge James Robart in Seattle issued a restraining order halting Executive Order 13769 nationwide, allowing travel to proceed as it did before the executive order was enacted. The director of the ACLU's Immigrant's Rights Project, Omar Jadwat, vowed that his organization will keep fighting to permanently dismantle this un-American executive order (American Civil Liberties Union- Washington, n.d.).

2017: On February 4, the Department of Justice filed an appeal to Judge Robart's restraining order with the Ninth Circuit Court of Appeals in San Francisco. The Trump administration argued that the President was acting within his authority and that Robart's restraining order "second-guesses the President's national security judgment" (Ballotpedia, n.d.).

2017: On February 7, the ACLU-WA filed a class-action lawsuit (*DOES v. Trump*) in federal court in the Western District of Washington, challenging President Trump's ban on travel by people from seven Muslim-majority nations. The suit argued that the President's Executive Order on immigration violates the Constitution and federal law (American Civil Liberties Union-Washington, n.d.).

2017: On February 7, the ACLU sued President Trump (*International Refugee Assistance v. Trump*) on behalf of organizations that settle refugees. The suit charged that President Trump's Muslim ban violates the First Amendment's prohibition of government establishment of religion and the Fifth Amendment's guarantee of equal treatment under the law (American Civil Liberties Union-Washington, n.d.).

2017: On February 9, a federal appeals panel unanimously rejected President Trump's bid to reinstate his travel ban to travel into the United States from seven mostly Muslim nations. In doing so, the three-judge panel suggested that the ban did not advance national security. More specifically, the administration did not provide evidence that anyone from the seven nations had committed terrorist acts in the United States (American Civil Liberties Union-Washington, n.d.).

2017: On March 6, President Trump signed Executive Order 13780, entitled Protecting the Nation from Foreign Terrorists Entry into the United States. The Order revoked and replaced Executive Order 13769 in response to court rulings prohibiting some of its key provisions. The new order banned entry into the U.S. by immigrants and visitors from six predominantly Muslim countries: Sudan, Syria, Iran, Libya, Somalia, and Yemen. The order exempted specific categories of people, including lawful permanent residents and dual nationals traveling on a passport from a country that is not one of the six designated countries. Furthermore, there was a suspension of refugee resettlement to the United States for 120 days. There is also a significant reduction in the number of refugees that the U.S. Refugee Assistance Program (USRAP) could resettle in the fiscal year 2017 from 110,000 to 50,000 (National Immigration Forum, 2017).

2017: On March 7, Hawaii Attorney General Doug Chin filed a lawsuit (*Trump v. Hawaii*) against Executive Order 13780. The lawsuit asked the judge to uphold the restraining order imposed on Executive Order 13769 and apply it to Executive Order 13780 (Ballotpedia, 2020).

2017: On March 15, the U.S District Court Judge Derrick Watson ordered a temporary nationwide restraining order on Executive Order 13780. On March 30, Watson granted Hawaii's request to convert the temporary restraining order into an indefinite preliminary injunction (Ballotpedia, 2020).

2017: On March 16, in *International Refugee Assistance Project (IRAP) v. Trump*, U.S. District Judge Theodore Chuang handed down a nationwide preliminary injunction on the part of Executive Order 13780. In doing so, Chuang argued the revised order was intended to discriminate against Muslims (Ballotpedia, 2020).

2017: On June 12, the Ninth Circuit upheld the preliminary injunction issued by Judge Watson. The three-judge panel found that President Trump exceeded his broad authority over immigration (Ballotpedia, 2020).

2017: On June 17, the U.S. Security of Homeland Security John Kelly rescinded Deferred Action for Parents of American and Lawful Permanent Residents (DAPA). DAPA was an Obama administration policy that suspended the removal of individuals residing in the country without legal permission who are parents of U.S. citizens. However, as DAPA was never implemented because of a lawsuit by the state of Texas, putting it on hold, rescinding it made the case moot (Ballotpedia, 2020).

2017: On June 26, in a 5–4 ruling, the U.S. Supreme Court (*Trump v. Hawaii*) allowed the implementation of Executive Order 13780's temporary ban on entry into the U.S. of citizens of six Muslim-majority nations, with an exception for persons who have any bona fide relationship with a person or entity in the United States (Supremecourt.gov, 2017).

2017: On September 5, the Attorney General Jeff Sessions announced that the Trump administration would be rescinding DACA. DACA, established by the Obama administration, provided temporary relief from deportation for individuals who had been brought to the United States as children without legal permission (Ballotpedia, 2020).

2017: On September 24, President Trump Proclamation 9645 (Enhancing Vetting Capabilities and Process for Detecting Attempted Entry Into the United States by Terrorists or Other Public-Threats) continued and expanded on the travel ban outlined in Executive Order 13780, issued on March 7, 2017. The Proclamation indefinitely suspended entry to the United States for specific individuals who are already out of the country and do not have a valid visa on the applicable effective date from eight countries: Iran, Libya, Somali, Syria, Yemen, Chad, North Korea, and Venezuela. The suspension did not apply to green card holders and dual nationals. Moreover, immigrant or nonimmigrant visas would not be issued to nationals of North Korea and Syria. Immigrant visas would be issued for nationals of Iran. Nationals of Chad, Libya, and Yemen were banned from obtaining immigrant, tourist or business visas. The Proclamation exempted lawful permanent residents and foreign nationals who had been granted asylum. It also provided case-by-case waivers when a foreign national demonstrated undue hardship, and that his entry is in the national interest and would not pose a threat to public safety (National Immigration Forum, 2017).

2017: On September 27, The Trump administration notified Congress that it would not allow more than 45,000 refugees into the United States during fiscal year 2018. This is the lowest cap ever for resettlement, a cap that had never been set below 67,000 and is allowed up to 210,000 as per the 1965 Immigration and Nationality Act (Ballotpedia, 2020; Migration Policy Institute, 2013). The reason given for the size of the cap was the need to ensure proper vetting so that no one would be allowed through who would endanger the safety of the American people (Ballotpedia, 2020).

2017: On October 17, Federal Judge Derrick K. Watson in Hawaii issued a nationwide order freezing most of President Trump's third travel ban, set forth in his September 24, 2017 proclamation, before it was to take place (Ballotpedia, 2020).

2017: On November 1, the Trump administration called on Congress to end the Diversity Lottery program after a terrorist attack in New York (Ballotpedia, 2020).

2017: On November 20, Elaine Duke, Acting Security of Homeland Security, announced the Temporary Protected Status (TPS) designation that allowed Haitians to live and work in the United States after the 2010 earthquake that devastated the island nation. Haitian nationals with TPS had until July 22, 2019, to return to Haiti or apply for lawful immigration status (Ballotpedia, 2020).

2017: On December 11, President Trump called for end of chain migration, i.e., immigration preference for family members of legal U.S residents, after a Bangladeshi immigrant's failed terror attack (Ballotpedia, 2020).

2018: On January 8, Kirstien Nielsen, Security of Homeland Security, announced the termination of the Temporary Protected Status (TPS) designation that allowed 262,500 El Salvadorians to live and work in the United States after the humanitarian crisis created by the 2001 earthquake. El Salvadorian nationals with TPS had until September 9, 2019, to return to El Salvador or apply for lawful immigration status (Ballotpedia, 2020).

2018: On January 9, 2018, U.S. District Court Judge William Alsup (San Francisco) ordered the Trump administration to continue to renew applications for individuals who had already been granted deferred status under the DACA program (Ballotpedia, 2020).

2018: On January 16, the U.S Department of Justice appealed the DACA ruling (Ballotpedia, 2020).

2018: On February 13, Judge Nicholas Garaufis issued a preliminary injunction temporarily blocking the Trump administration's order ending the DACA program (Ballotpedia, 2020).

2018: On February 15, the Senate rejected four immigration reform bills. These bills aimed to find a legislative fix for the DACA program and border security measures program (Ballotpedia, 2020).

2018: On April 10, President Trump issued Proclamation 9723 (Maintaining Enhanced Vetting Capabilities and Process for Detecting Attempted Entry into the United States by Terrorists or Other Public-Safety Threats), removing travel restrictions on nationals of the Republic of Chad (Trump, 2020a).

2018: On April 24, U.S. District Judge Barnes ruled that the Trump administration must continue to accept new applications for the DACA program (Ballotpedia, 2020).

2018: On May 7, Attorney General Jeff Sessions announced that the Trump administration would prosecute parents who cross the U.S. border illegally with their children (Ballotpedia, 2020).

2018: On June 20, President Trump signed an executive order directing DHS to keep detained families together (Ballotpedia, 2020).

2018: On June 26, in *Trump, President of the United States, et al. v. Hawaii et al.*, the United States Supreme Court ruled (5–4) that the President lawfully exercised the broad discretion granted to him under §1182(f) to suspend the entry of aliens into the United States. Writing for the conservative majority, Chief Justice Roberts said that the Proclamation was squarely within the scope of Presidential authority (Supremecourt.gov, 2018).

2018: On November 8, the United States Court of Appeals for the Ninth Circuit upheld the preliminary injunction against the Trump administration's attempt to rescind DACA (Ballotpedia, 2020).

2019: On January 24, the DHS implemented the Migrant Protection Protocol, also known as the Remain in Mexico program. The program allowed U.S. border officers to return non-Mexican asylum seekers to Mexico while their claims are adjudicated in the U.S. immigration courts. In Mexico, they were to be provided with all appropriate humanitarian protections during their stay (Department of Homeland Security, 2019).

2019: The DHSS finalized a rule that expanded the list of received benefits and other factors to be considered in determining whether an applicant for admission into the United States is likely to become a public charge, that is, will need to receive any form of government or state assistance. The Trump administration defined "public charge" to refer to noncitizens who receive various government benefits, such as health care, for more than 12 months over 3 years (Howe, 2020).

2019: The DHS and U.S. Department of Labor signed a series of immigration agreements with Guatemala, Honduras, and El Salvador in response to what they said was a humanitarian and security crisis at the southwest border because of historic levels of undocumented migration and human smuggling. Of the migrants apprehended at the southwest border, 72% were from Guatemala, Honduras, and El. Salvador (DHS.gov, n.d.). Among the items agreed to are biometric data sharing, border securities, and most controversially, critics argue, an asylum cooperative agreement (also known as a safe third-country agreement). In short, the asylum cooperative agreement obliges Guatemala, Honduras, and El Salvador, not the U.S., to examine and process asylum protection claims for the U.S. It also allows the U.S. to deport rejected asylum seekers back to any of the countries, even if she/he is not a national of that country (DHS.gov, n.d.).

2020: On January 27, the Supreme Court of the United States ruled 5–4 to lift the nationwide injunction on the DHS public charge expansion imposed by a federal judge in New York while the case played out in the appeals court (Howe, 2020). Critics of the expansion and the Supreme Court ruling argued that the public charge rule is nothing more than a wealth test. Moreover, it is a wealth test that will be used to deny eligible aliens a green card, visa, or admission into the United States (Immigration Legal Resource Center, n.d.).

2020: On January 31, President Trump issued Proclamation 9983, which added six countries to the ongoing travel restrictions of Presidential Proclamation 9645. These countries are Nigeria, Africa's largest country, Myanmar, Eritrea, Kyrgyzstan, Sudan, and Tanzania (Travel.State.gov, n.d.).

2020: On February 29, the U.S. Court of Appeals on the Ninth Circuit struck down the Migrant Protection Protocols (MPP). It also ruled against a rule severely limiting the number of migrants who were eligible for asylum (Fischer, 2020).

2020: On April 22, President Trump issued Proclamation 10014 (Suspension of Entry of Immigrants Who Present a Risk to the United States Labor Market During the Recovery Following the 2019 Novel Coronavirus Breakout). The proclamation suspended, for a period of 60 days, the entry of aliens as immigrants, subject to certain exceptions (Trump, 2020b).

2020: On June 18, the Supreme Court of the United States ruled in *The Department of Homeland Security v. Regents of the University of California* that the DHS failed to provide relevant factors associated with ending the DACA program. The majority opinion argued that the decision to end the program was arbitrary and capricious. The court remanded the issue back to DHS to provide a more thorough explanation for ending DACA (Supremecourt.gov, 2020).

2020: On June 22, President Trump issued a continuation of Proclamation 10014 (Suspension of Entry of Immigrants Who Present a Risk to the United States Labor Market During the Recovery Following the 2019 Novel Coronavirus Breakout) until December 31, 2020. In doing so, it suspended and/or limited H-1B or H-BS visas, J visas, L visas, and any alien accompanying or following such a visa holder. The suspension applied only to an alien outside of the United States on the effective date of the proclamation (Trump, 2020b).

2021: On January 20, newly elected President Biden sent a memorandum for the Attorney General and the Secretary of Homeland Security. The memorandum, Preserving and Fortifying Deferred Action for Childhood Arrivals (DACA), ordered that immigrants with a DACA status should not be a priority for removal based on humanitarian concerns and that work authorization will enable them to support themselves and their families and to contribute to the economy, while they remain (Whitehouse.gov, 2021a).

2021: On January 20, President Biden sent a memorandum for Secretary of Homeland Security, Reinstating Deferred Enforced Departure for Liberians. The memorandum states that it is in the foreign policy interest of the United States to defer the enforced departure of Liberian refugees through June 30, 2022 (Whitehouse.gov, 2021a).

2021: On January 20, President Biden issued Proclamation on the Termination of Emergency with Respect to the Southern Border of the United and Redirection of Funds Diverted to Border Wall Construction. The Proclamation declared that the national emergency that was used as the rationale for building the southern border wall between the United States and Mexico will no longer be used and that building it will be terminated (Whitehouse.gov, 2021a).

2021: On January 20, President Biden issued Executive Order on the Revision of Civil Immigration Enforcement Policies and Priorities (Whitehouse.gov, 2021a). The executive order revoked former President Donald Trump's Executive Order 13768 (Enhancing Public Safety in the Interior of the United States). In doing so, President Biden's executive order stated that enforcing civil immigration laws will be done so that it will adhere to due process and safeguard the dignity and well-being of families and communities (Whitehouse.gov, 2021a)

2021: On January 21, President Biden issued a Proclamation of Ending Discriminatory Bans on Entry to the United States (Whithouse.gov, 2021b). The proclamation revoked former President Trump's Executive Orders 13780 and Proclamations 9645, 9723, and 9983. It also directed embassies and consulates to resume visa processing and clear case backlogs (Whitehouse.gov, 2021b).

References

American Civil Liberties Union-Washington. (n.d.). *Timeline of the Muslim ban*. https://www.aclu-wa.org/pages/timeline-muslim-ban

Ballotpedia. (2020). *Timeline of federal policy on immigration, 2017–2020*. https://ballotpedia.org/Timeline_of_federal_policy_on_immigration,_2017-2020#cite_note-100DaysVideo-200

Ballotpedia. (n.d.). *Diversity lottery*. https://ballotpedia.org/Diversity_Lottery

Bredbenner, C. L. (1998). *A nationality of her own: Women, marriage, and the law of citizenship*. University of North Carolina Press.

Campi, A. J. (2004). *Remembering December 17: Repeal of the 1882 Chinese Exclusion Act*. Policy Brief. Immigration Policy Center. http://www.immigrationpolicy.org/sites/default/files/docs/Chinese%20Exclusion%20Act%2012-04.pdf

Campi, A. J. (2005). *Closed borders and mass deportations*: The lessons of the Barred Zone Act. Immigration Policy Center. http://icirr.org/sites/default/files/IPC%20Barred%20Zone.pdf

DHS.gov. (n.d.). *Fact sheet: DHS agreement with Guatemala, Honduras, and El Salvador*. U.S. Department of Homeland Security. https://www.dhs.gov/sites/default/files/publications/19_1028_opa_factsheet-northern-central-america-agreements_v2.pdf

Department of Homeland Security. (2019). *Migrant protection protocols*. https://www.dhs.gov/news/2019/01/24/migrant-protection-protocols

Fischer, M. (2020). Ninth Circuit court rules against Trump immigration policies. *Jurist*. https://www.jurist.org/news/2020/02/federal-appeals-court-rules-against-trump-administrations-immigration-policies/

Georgetown Law Library. (2020). *Deferred Action for Childhood Arrivals (DACA)*. https://guides.ll.georgetown.edu/c.php?g=592919&p=4170929

Congress.gov. (2007). S2205-DREAM Act of 2007. Retrieved from https://www.congress.gov/bill/110th-congress/senate-bill/2205

Higham, J. (1956). American immigration policy in historical perspective. *Law and Contemporary Problems, 21*(2), 213–235.

Howe, A. (2020). No pause from Supreme Court for "public charge" rule during the COVID-19 pandemic. SCOTUS Blog. https://www.scotusblog.com/2020/04/no-pause-from-supreme-court-for-public-charge-rule-during-covid-19-pandemic/

Immigration Legal Resource Center. (n.d). Public charge. https://www.ilrc.org/public-charge

Immigration Policy Center. (2008). *De-romanticizing our immigrant past: Why claiming my family came legally is often a myth*. http://www.immigrationpolicy.org/just-facts/de-romanticizing-our-immigrant-past-why-claiming-my-family-came-legally-often-myth

Johnson, J. C. (2014). *U.S Department of Homeland Security: Memorandum for Thomas S. Winkowski, Acting Director, U.S. Immigration and Customs Enforcement*.

Kitty, C. (1984). *United States immigration law and the control of labor:1820–1924*. Academic Press.

LeMay, M., & Elliot, R. B. (1999). *United States immigration and naturalization laws and issues: A documentary history*. Greenwod Press.

Lee, E. (2003). *At America's gate: Chinese immigration during the exclusion era, 1882–1943*. University of North Carolina Press.

Migration Policy Institute. (2013). *Major United States immigration laws, 1790–present*. http://ihei.migrationpolicy.org/research/timeline-1790

National Immigration Forum. (2017). *Summary of President Trump's new proclamation that bans certain foreign individuals from entering the U.S*. https://immigrationforum.org/wp-content/uploads/2017/09/Travel-Ban3_Summary_Final.pdf

Ngai, M. M. (1999). The architecture of race in American immigration law: A reexamination of the Immigration Act of 1924. *Journal of American History*, 86(1), 67–92.

Office of the Historian. (2014). Chinese immigration and exclusion acts. https://history.state.gov/milestones/1866-1898/chinese-immigration

Supremecourt.gov, (2020). *Syllabus: Department of Homeland Security et al.* v. Regents of The University of California et al. Retrieved from https://www.supremecourt.gov/opinions/19pdf/18-587_5ifl.pdf

Supremecourt.gov. (2017). *Trump, President of the United States, et al. v. Hawaii et al.* Retrieved from https://www.supremecourt.gov/opinions/17pdf/17-965_h315.pdf

Travel.State.gov. (n.d). Presidential Proclamation 9645 and Presidential Proclamation 9983. Retrieved from https://travel.state.gov/content/travel/en/us-visas/visa-information-resources/presidential-proclamation-archive/presidential-proclamation9645.html?wcmmode=disabled

Trump, D. J. (2017a). *Executive Order 13767: Border Security and Immigration Enforcement Improvements*. https://www.whitehouse.gov/presidential-actions/executive-order-border-security-immigration-enforcement-improvements/

Trump, D. J. (2017b). *Executive Order 13768: Enhancing Public Safety in the Interior of the United States*. https://www.whitehouse.gov/presidential-actions/executive-order-enhancing-public-safety-interior-united-states/

Trump, D. J. (2017c). *Executive Order 13769: Protecting the Nation from Foreign Terrorists Entry into the United States*. https://www.whitehouse.gov/presidential-actions/executive-order-protecting-nation-foreign-terrorist-entry-united-states/

Trump, D. J. (2020a). *Proclamation on Maintaining Enhanced Vetting Capabilities and Process for Detecting Attempted Entry into the United States by Terrorists or Other Public Safety Threats*. https://www.whitehouse.gov/presidential-actions/proclamation-improving-enhanced-vetting-capabilities-processes-detecting-attempted-entry/

Trump, D. J. (2020b). *Proclamation 10014: Suspension of Entry of Immigrants Who Present a Risk to the United States Labor Market During the Recovery Following the 2019 Novel Coronavirus Breakout*. https://www.whitehouse.gov/presidential-actions/proclamation-suspending-entry-aliens-present-risk-u-s-labor-market-following-coronavirus-outbreak/

U.S. Citizenship and Immigration Services. (2014). *2014 Executive Actions on Immigration*. https://www.uscis.gov/archive/2014-executive-actions-on-immigration

Unites States v. Texas. (2016). Oyez. https://www.oyez.org/cases/2015/15-674

Van Nuys, F. (2002). *Americanizing the west: Race, immigrants and citizenship, 1890–1930*. University of Kansas Press.

Waslin, M. (2011). *The Secure Communities program: Unanswered questions and continuing concerns, American Immigration Council: Immigration Policy Center special report*. https://www.americanimmigrationcouncil.org/sites/default/files/research/SComm_Exec_Summary_112911.pdf

Whitehouse. (2017). *Statement by the President on Cuban Immigration Policy*. Retrieved from https://obamawhitehouse.archives.gov/the-press-office/2017/01/12/statement-president-cuban-immigration-policy

Whitehouse.gov. (2020). *Immigration*. The White House. https://www.whitehouse.gov/issues/immigration/

Whitehouse.gov. (2021a). *Presidential actions*. The White House. https://www.whitehouse.gov/briefing-room/presidential-actions/

Whitehouse.gov. (2021b). *Proclamation on Ending Discriminatory Bans on Entry to the United States*. The White House. https://www.whitehouse.gov/briefing-room/presidential-actions/2021/01/20/proclamation-ending-discriminatory-bans-on-entry-to-the-united-states/

Whitehouse Office of the Press Security. (2014). *Fact Sheet: Immigration Accountability Executive Action*. https://obamawhitehouse.archives.gov/the-press-office/2014/11/20/fact-sheet-immigration-accountability-executive-action

Although immigrants and their United States-born descendants have been integral to the forging of the United States as a nation, immigration status is a significant social inequality in the contemporary United States, most specifically for undocumented immigrants (Ewing, 2012a). As of 2017, an estimated 10.5 million undocumented immigrants were living in the United States, the majority from Latin America, including Mexico, Central America, South America, and the Caribbean, and Asia, including China, the Philippians, India, Vietnam, and South Korea (Passel & Cohn, 2019). These immigrants' many social inequalities derive almost entirely from the currently unresolved and increasingly contentious policy debate in Congress regarding a pathway to citizenship for them. This unresolved policy debate has left undocumented immigrants, many of whom have United States-born children and have resided in the country for years, in a legal limbo (Passel & Cohn, 2015; Passel et al., 2018). In this limbo, undocumented immigrants have few legal rights, protections, or access to needed services afforded to documented immigrants or citizens (Passel & Cohn, 2019). Despite their importance to the workforce and the fact that their financial contributions to the economy exceed the cost of the services they use, they are among the most vulnerable and oppressed populations in the nation (American Immigration Council, 2020; Kamarck & Stenglein, 2019).

On one side of the pathway to citizenship debate, the argument is made that as a matter of law and order, undocumented immigrants should be deported immediately, and a wall built on the southern United States/Mexican border to stem the flow of future undocumented immigrants. Lastly, there is the rejection of any form of an amnesty program that would allow currently undocumented immigrants a pathway to citizenship.

On the other side of the pathway to citizenship debate, the argument is made that as a matter of practicality undocumented immigrants should be given the opportunity to come out of the shadows and become part of the American mainstream. Central to this is some form of a pathway to citizenship.

This current immigration policy debate about who does and does not belong in the United States and under what conditions is not a new one. What it reflects, although often couched in a "rule of law" rhetoric, is a return to America's historical preference for racial and cultural homogeneity when granting immigrants entry to the country (Foner & Fredrickson, 2004). That preference is for White, English-speaking immigrants, and for much of United States history, of the Protestant faith. The preference is as old as the nation and was legitimized by Congress with the Naturalization Act of 1790. The act limited citizenship rights to free White persons/immigrants of good moral character who had lived in the country two years prior to becoming naturalized (Foner & Fredrickson, 2004; H.R.40, Naturalization Bill, 1790). As a consequence of these preferred criteria, the immigration laws, policies, and politics of the United States have historically been entwined with racial and, to a lesser extent, ethnic animus toward non-White immigrants (Garcia, 1995; Johnson, 2009). This animus has been manifested in an exclusionary immigration policy toward particular groups of immigrants that separates immigrants into legal and illegal and immigration quotas based on race and ethnicity (Johnson, 2009; Sanchez & Romero, 2010).

Theoretical Framework

This chapter uses intersectionality as an aspect of critical race theory (CRT) to examine the development of the United States' immigration policies. Consistent with CRT, the emphasis is on viewing laws and lawmaking within an historical context to deconstruct the racialized content of the United States' immigration policies. From an intersectionality perspective, a particular focus is on how immigration policy has been used to subjugate and oppress particular immigrant groups across the intersection of race, ethnicity, gender, class, sexual orientation, and ability, and the social forces and debates that informed this subjugation and oppression.

Immigration and Social Work

Since the early days of the settlement house movement, social workers have had an ongoing commitment to work with and advocate for immigrants. Presently, this commitment is embodied in the NASW Code of Ethics. It is also articulated in the NASW's public and social policy statement in *Social Work Speaks*.

NASW Code of Ethics (Immigration)

1.05 Cultural Awareness and Social Diversity

(c) Social workers should obtain education about and seek to understand the nature of social diversity and oppression with respect to race, ethnicity, national origin, color, sex, sexual orientation, gender, identity of expression, age, marital status, political belief, religion, immigration status, and mental or physical ability.

4.02 Discrimination

Social workers should not practice, condone, facilitate, or collaborate with any form of discrimination on the basis of race, ethnicity, national origin, color, sex, sexual orientation, gender identity or expression, age, marital status, political belief, religion, immigration status, or mental or physical ability.

6.04 Social and Political Action

(d) Social workers should act to prevent and eliminate domination of, exploitation of, and discrimination against any person, group, or class on the basis of race, ethnicity, national origin, color, sex, sexual orientation, gender identity or expression, age, marital status, political belief, religion, immigration status, or mental or physical ability (Workers, 2017).

A Selection of the NASW's Specific Position on Immigration Policy From the Most Recent Edition of *Social Work Speaks*

1. Promoting social justice and avoiding racism, discrimination, profiling and visa and travel bans or otherwise preventing immigration opportunities on the basis of race, religion, country of origin, gender, sexual orientation, immigration status.
2. Supporting federal and state services and programs for immigrants establishing comprehensive refugee resettlement programs adequate in length and substance that include supports to help with integration into communities, trauma and mental health counseling, and job readiness and placement.
3. Ensuring due process and access to legal counsel to all immigrants and refugees in accordance with international human rights for all asylum seekers.
4. Opposing mandatory reporting of immigration status by health, mental health, social service, education, police and other public service providers, and allow jurisdiction the right to create sanctuary cities without any restrictions in funds.

(NASW, 2018)

For the rest of the NASW's specific position on immigration and refugee policy, please see the most recent issue of *Social Work Speaks* (NASW, 2018).

The Colonial Debate, 1720–1776

The immigration debate in America began in earnest in the mid-18th century with vehement opposition to German, Irish, and Scottish immigration in the predominately English colonies. Reasons for this opposition included fears about the demands on already scarce resources; the Scottish and Irish's supposed tendencies toward disorder and violence; and the characterization of Germans as stupid, clannish, and unsuitable for assimilation into the English-speaking colonies (Seller, 1982). Indeed, in 1751, no less than one of the nation's future founding fathers, Benjamin Franklin, alarmed by the influx of German immigrants to Pennsylvania, wrote about what he saw as the potential overrunning of the primarily English colony by German immigrants. Franklin noted in his essay "Observations, concerning the increase of mankind,"

> Why should the Palatine Boors be suffered to swarm into our settlements, and by herding together establish their language and manners to the exclusion of ours? Why should Pennsylvania, founded by the English, become a colony of aliens, who will be so numerous as to Germanize us, instead of us Anglicizing them, and will never adopt our language or customs, any more than they can acquire our complexion?
>
> (Franklin, 1751)

Franklin's anxiety about German immigration was also linked to his desire for America to be exclusively English, White, Anglo-Saxon, and Protestant. For Franklin, purely White people in the world were proportionately small. As such, they were under threat relative to the combined numbers of Indigenous people in the Americas, Blacks in Africa, Asians, and the Spaniards, Italians, French, Russian, Swedes, and Germans in Europe, all of whom he described as swarthy in complexion (Franklin, 1751). Franklin wished that the numbers of purely White people would increase and saw America as the place where this could happen if it would exclude Blacks and other tawnies (i.e., anyone other than those who are purely White; Franklin, 1751).

Thomas Jefferson was another of the founding fathers who expressed skepticism about immigrants, more specifically, in 1782, "Immigrants from foreign monarchies who 'will infuse American legislation with their spirit, warp and bias its direction, and render it a heterogeneous, incoherent, distracted mass'" (Jefferson, 1832).

The Antebellum Debate, 1830–1860

In the antebellum period of the early to mid-19th century, similar anti-immigrant sentiments resurfaced and were directed toward the second wave of German and Irish immigrants. In the 1850s, the anti-Catholic, pro-slavery, nativist group, the Know-Nothings, officially known as the National American Party, targeted these German and Irish immigrants. Though anti-foreign and anti-immigrant in general, the Know-Nothings saw the Irish and those German immigrants of the Catholic faith as a particular threat to predominately Protestant and republican America (Higham, 1956).

Like Benjamin Franklin's description of German immigrants overrunning the colonies some 80 years earlier, the Know-Nothings similarly argued that the nation was being overrun by immigrants in general and the Irish and German Catholic immigrants in particular. They warned that German and Irish Catholic immigrants were agents of the Pope, sent for a Catholic takeover of the United States. They were portrayed as potentially subversive and hostile to the nation's Protestant faith and republican values (Seller, 1982). The Know-Nothings' hostility to Catholic immigrants was not restrained to rhetoric. During the 1850s, there were several cases of violence in Irish communities in which Catholic churches and convents were destroyed and priests attacked by Protestant mobs (Daniels, 1991). A Daily Dispatch newspaper report in 1854 noted,

> One of the organs of the Know-Nothing Party in the city of New York, attacks the Irish population of the city with a degree of ferocity and malignantly which we have rarely seen equaled, and which bode no good for the future peace and quiet of New York.
>
> (*Daily Dispatch*, 1854)

For all the rhetoric and vitriol of those opposed to immigration in the colonial and antebellum period, they could not translate this opposition into restrictive immigration policy. Among the reasons for this inability was a laissez-fair open-door immigration policy; furthermore, neither the federal government nor the Crown before it wanted to restrict immigration (Seller, 1982). The federal government's hands-off approach to immigration allowed the states to dictate immigration levels based on their labor needs. In a country expanding west, still relatively underpopulated and resource abundant, immigrants and their labor were essential despite any call for their restriction. Also, importantly, despite the opposition, the immigrants were, for all intents and purposes, White (Higham, 1956; Seller, 1982). Thus, they could fit easily into the existing racial hierarchy and be granted relatively unfettered access to society's resources.

Mass Immigration, 1860–1920

The years between 1860 and 1920 saw a wave of immigration and migration from Asia, eastern and southern Europe, and Mexico that was unprecedented in terms of the number of people it brought to America. In just 60 years, the population of the United States increased from a relatively small 31.5 million in 1860 to 106 million in 1920 (Gibson & Lennon, 1999). In contrast to the earlier immigrants from northern Europe and Scandinavia, these new immigrants were significantly distinguishable from the United States-born White Anglo-Saxon, Protestant population. Not only did they have different languages, but they also had different physical features, skin pigmentation, religious beliefs, and customs. These immigrants, most of who came to the United States in search of work and opportunity in the booming industrial sector, would change the face of the nation. They would also be a catalyst for a dramatic change in the United States' previously open-door immigration policy. Never again would the United States be so open to immigration. Instead, it would adopt immigration policies that functioned as a gatekeeper. These gatekeeping policies would determine who would and would not be accepted as an immigrant to the United States. Some of these policies would explicitly use race/ethnicity, class, gender, sexual orientation, and disability status to keep particular immigrants out (Higham, 1956; Johnson, 2009; Lee, 2003).

The Chinese Experience and Exclusionary Immigration Policy, 1860–1882

At the epicenter of the dramatic change in America's open-door immigration policy were Chinese immigrants. The Chinese were the first Asian immigrant group to arrive in the United States in the 1840s. The first arrivals numbered fewer than a thousand people and were located on the East Coast, working in factories and selling goods. But a confluence of events significantly increased Chinese immigration between 1850 and 1880 (Higham, 1956).

The first event was the discovery of gold in California in 1848 (Higham, 1956). The second event was the Huang He River's flooding in the Shandong Peninsula, which led to a series of disastrous crop failures, famine, and disease in 1852 in southern China (Nijjar, 2020). The third event was the signing of the Burlingame Treaty in 1868, which granted China the most-favored-nation status and allowed its citizens to reside freely in the United States (Higham, 1956).

Between 1850 and 1880, the Chinese immigrant population in the United States went from less than 1,000 to 104,000 (Carter et al., 2006). The majority of these Chinese immigrants, who were from the southeast Guangdong or Canton Provinces, went west to California in two waves. The first wave went in the California gold rush as laborers or speculators in the gold mines. The second wave was recruited as laborers by the Central Pacific Railroad to lay track on the transcontinental railroad (Lee, 2003). Indeed, by 1867, Chinese immigrants composed anywhere from 75% to 90% of the Central Pacific Railroad's 13,000-man workforce (Kraus, 1969; Uschan, 2003).

Almost from the beginning of their arrival in California, however, there was a level of enmity toward Chinese immigrants that was unprecedented in its severity. This enmity was based on both economics and race. In the gold mines, the large influx of Chinese immigrant labor and speculators over a relatively short period of time caused significant discontent and resentment on the part of native-born and European immigrant mine workers. The primary cause of this discontent and resentment was the competition the Chinese immigrants posed in terms of access to valued resources. In fact, such was the level of resentment and potential for violence against them that the Chinese had to work at less desirable sites in the gold mines to avoid confrontation (Higham, 1956; Lee, 2003). Even with these efforts, robberies and the murder of Chinese mine workers was not uncommon. In 1852, for example, the Alta, California, newspaper reported that 200 Chinese miners were robbed and four murdered at Rich Gulch (Pickoff-White & Brekke, 2015). Similarly, in 1856 the newspaper *The Shasta Republican* reported, "Hundreds of Chinamen have been slaughtered in cold blood in the last five years by desperados that infest our state" (Zia, 2001). As well as violence, there were also discriminatory policies enacted by the California state legislature aimed specifically at Chinese gold mine laborers. One of these policies was the Foreign Miner's Tax of 1852. The tax required a payment of $3 each month at a time when Chinese miners were making $6 a month. If Chinese miners could not or would not pay, tax collectors could legally take and sell their property. Because of the tax, many Chinese miners were expelled or forced out of the mines (Takaki, 1989).

Work on the Central Pacific Railroad was little better for the Chinese. As had been the experience in the gold mines, the native-born and European immigrant railroad workers similarly resented Chinese laborers. Moreover, despite being recruited to fill a severe labor shortage, they were paid at a different rate than their White counterparts. For example, Chinese laborers received $26 to $35 a month for a 12-hour day, six-day work week and had to provide their own food and tents, while White workers received $35 a month and were furnished with food and shelter.

Though they did not suffer the same level of violence as the Chinese gold miners and speculators, Chinese railroad workers were nevertheless exposed to hazardous working conditions on a daily basis. Nevertheless, they were acknowledged as skilled layers of track and invaluable to the building of the railroads. In fact, so skilled were the Chinese that in 1869, a select crew of 848 Chinese workers laid more than ten miles of track in 12 hours, a world record (Uschan, 2003).

As discriminatory as the workplace was for the Chinese immigrant, much more discriminatory and harmful were the social policies and laws that were enacted in response to the growing anti-Chinese sentiment. The sources of this resentment were the labor unions, elected officials, politicians, and nativist groups.

Primary among the anti-Chinese legislation and rulings were the *People v. Hall* California Supreme Court ruling (*People v. Hall*, 1854). The ruling established that the Chinese had no rights to testify against White citizens. In doing so, it extended to the Chinese a ban already in place prohibiting Blacks and Native Americans from testifying for or against White people. In handing down the opinion, Justice Hugh Murray argued that the Chinese were a race of people whom nature has marked as inferior. Thus, the consequences of allowing Chinese to testify "would admit them to all the equal rights of citizenship, and we might soon see them at the polls, in the jury box, upon the bench, and in our legislative halls" (Cheng, 1972; McClain, 1994; *People v. Hall*, 1854).

The significance of this ruling is that it conferred on the Chinese second-class citizenship. It also racialized them as separate, distinct, and inferior to Whites, thus placing them at the bottom of the United States' racial hierarchy alongside Native Americans and Blacks. Other policies would confirm the second-class citizenship of the Chinese. These policies included but were certainly not limited to the exclusion of Chinese children from public school in 1863. In 1876, there was a requirement, specifically aimed at Chinese homes, mandating that living areas have 500 cubic feet of air for each resident. Finally, in 1878, Chinese individuals were barred from owning real estate (Cheng, 1972; McClain, 1994; Sandmeyer, 1991).

Informing these policies was not just long-simmering resentment against the Chinese, but also their social construction as socially and intellectually inferior, dirty, and willing to work for meager wages. By doing this, they were portrayed as undercutting honest White labor (Lee, 2003). This was overlaid with a moral characterization of them as mysterious and immoral purveyors of opium dens and prostitution. Consequently, they were anything but deserving of citizenship and should be driven from our shores. For practical reasons, this was never possible with Native Americans and Blacks, but from late 1860s onward it became a *cause cèlébre* for labor unions, elected officials, politicians, and nativist groups (Lee, 2003), prompted by the completion of the transcontinental railroad in 1869 and the emergence of both great corporate wealth and a large floating labor supply. The narrowing of opportunities in the West and the resulting recession and large-scale unemployment of both White and Chinese labor increased the complaints against Chinese immigrants to a fever pitch (Lee, 2003; Higham, 1956, p. 216).

In the mid-1870s, Denis Kearney, a recent Irish immigrant and the leader of the Workingmen's Party, pledged to get rid of the Chinese (Higham, 1956). Kearney portrayed the Chinese as the cause of the recession because of their willingness to work for inhumanely low wages (Watermark.Silverchaor.com, n.d.). His inflammatory rhetoric was at least in part responsible for a wave of violence against the Chinese that swept across the state in 1870s (Carlsson, 1995). No less culpable were nativist groups such as the Chinese Exclusion League of San Francisco, the American Protective Association, and the Native American Mutual Protection Association, which called for restrictions on further immigration from Asia.

Most influential, though, were the politicians and prominent citizens. In the 1876 race for the California governorship, the Chinese question was the primary issue confronting the candidates. Also, in 1876, the California State Senate special committee hearings on Chinese immigration saw San Francisco lawyer H.N. Clement argue passionately for a Chinese exclusion policy. In his argument, Clement opined,

> that the greatest fundamental right of every nation was self-preservation, and the Chinese question was nothing less than a battle for America's survival and future. You have the right to say that the half-civilized subject from Asia, you shall not come at all.
>
> (*Lee*, 2003, p. 43; *see Figure* 5.1)

Though 77% of the Chinese immigrants were in California, Clement framed the issue as a national and not a regional issue. National Democratic and Republican politicians eager to court the Californian vote soon took on the call for Chinese exclusion. So successful was the call in California that in 1880, the Burlingame Treaty was amended after opposition from Congress to Chinese immigration. The amendment suspended Chinese immigration while protecting the rights of those immigrants who had already arrived (Higham, 1956). Two years later the Chinese Exclusion Act of 1882 was passed by Congress and signed into law by President Chester A. Arthur (Public Law 47–126, 1882). In signing the act into law, the opinion of the federal government was that the immigration of Chinese labor to the country endangered the good of certain localities within the territory (Lee, 2003; see Figure 5.2).

The Chinese Exclusion Act of 1882 provided a ten-year moratorium on Chinese labor immigration. It further stipulated that nonlaborers in China who wanted to enter the United States had to obtain a certificate from the Chinese government declaring that they were qualified to immigrate, meaning they were skilled workers other than laborers. Moreover, for the Chinese already in the United States, if they left the country, they needed to obtain a reentry certificate. Congress also refused state and federal courts the right to grant citizenship to Chinese resident aliens, though they still had the legal right to deport Chinese from the United States. When the act expired in 1892, Congress extended it for another ten years through the Geary Act. The Geary Act added more stipulations to those already in the Chinese Exclusion Act. These stipulations required that Chinese residents carry a resident permit, and failure to do so could result in deportation or one-year hard labor. Furthermore, the Chinese could not testify in court or obtain bail (Kitty, 1984; LeMay & Elliot, 1999). The extension was made permanent by congressional action in 1902. The act was finally repealed in 1943. However, before its repeal, the Chinese Exclusion Act had driven large numbers of Chinese immigrants out of the country, with the population falling from 107,000 in 1890 to 61,000 in 1920. Moreover, those who remained were forced into segregated Chinatowns (Campi, 2004). Until its eventual repeal, the Chinese Exclusion Act survived two constitutional challenges as the U.S. Supreme Court upheld its discriminatory practices in the *Chae Chan Ping v. United States* (1889) and the *Fong Yue Ting v. United States* (1893) rulings (Campi, 2004; Kitty, 1984; LeMay & Elliot, 1999).

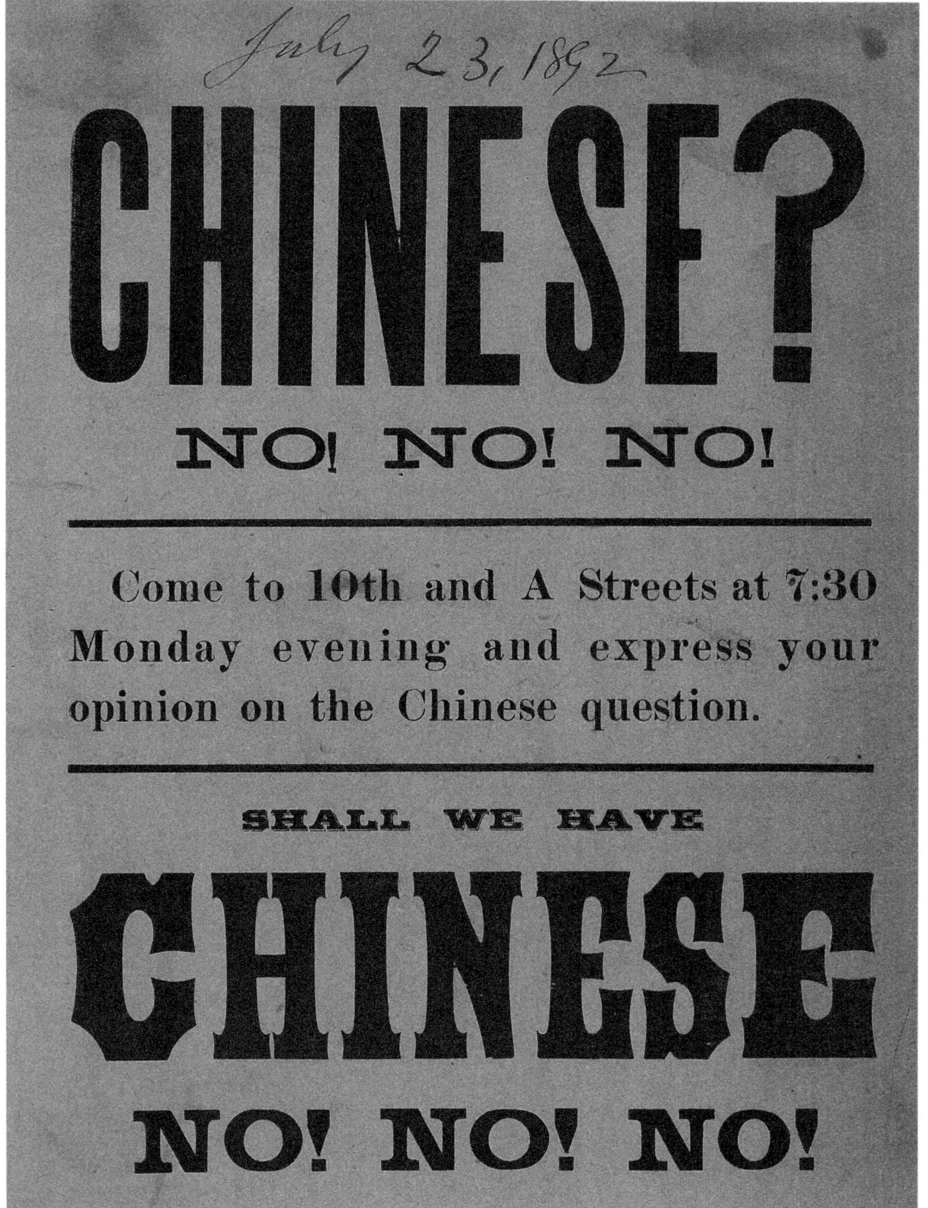

Figure 5.1 Say No to Chinese Poster

In the Chae Chan Ping ruling, refusing to strike down the Chinese Exclusion Act of 1882, U.S. Supreme Court Justice Field's opinion very much echoed the anti-Chinese sentiment of the day when he held:

> Notwithstanding the articles of the treaty of 1868, by which all the privileges, immunities, and exemptions were extended to subjects of China in the United States, they remained strangers in the land, residing apart by themselves, and adhering to the customs of their own country. It seemed impossible for them to assimilate with our people or to make any change in their habits or modes of living. As they grew in numbers each year, the people of the coast saw the great danger that portions of our country would be overrun by them unless prompt action was taken to restrict their immigration. (Odo & Pilk, 2002, p. 87)

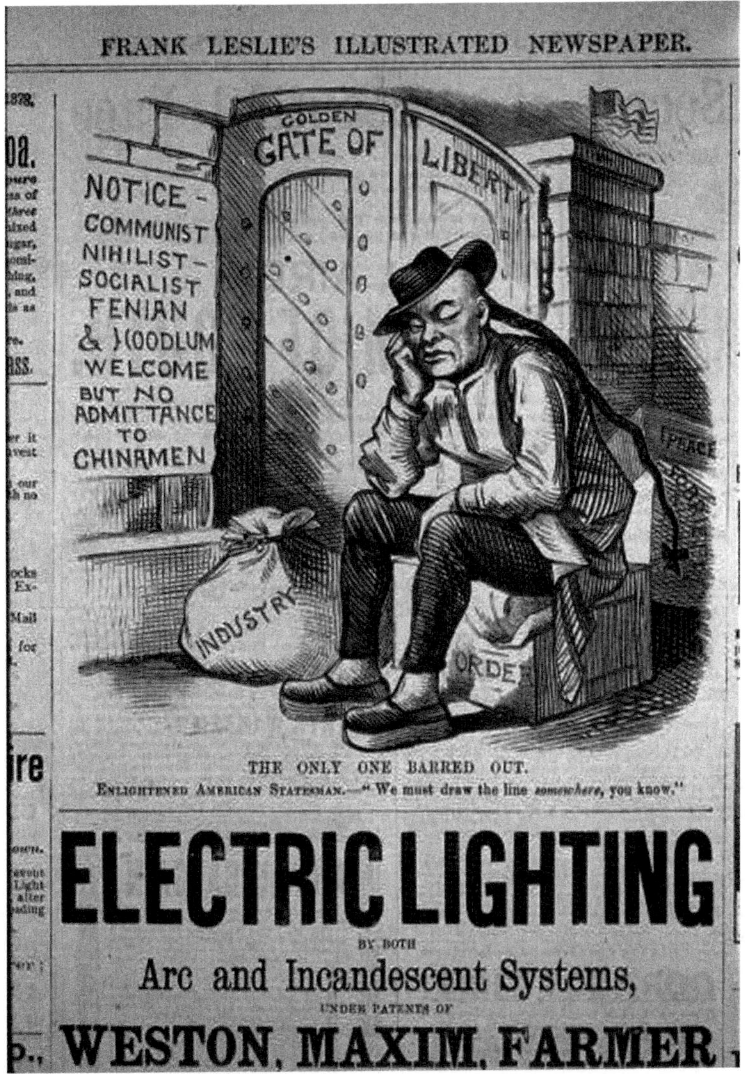

Figure 5.2 Chinese Exclusion Poster

As a piece of federal legislation, the Chinese Exclusion Act of 1882 was a seminal United States social policy. It was the first significant policy to restrict immigration to the United States based on race and class (Ourdocuments.gov, n.d.). Just as importantly, Lee (2003) posits that it set precedents for the admission, deportation, documentation, and surveillance of both new arrivals and immigrant communities within the United States (p. 37). By doing so, it introduced a gatekeeping ideology that through politics, policies, and culture transformed the ways in which Americans viewed and thought about race and immigration, that is, who belongs and does not belong in the United States based on race/ethnicity, nationality, and cultural identity. For those who do not belong, restriction, exclusion, and deportation are legalized in a way that was not present before the passing of the Chinese Exclusion Act. In this respect, Lee (2003) argues that the Chinese Exclusion Act and its accompanying government procedures and bureaucratic machinery were the precursors to the United States Immigration and Naturalization Services. The U.S. passport, green cards, illegal immigration, and deportation policies can all be traced back to the Chinese Exclusion Act of 1882 (Lee, 2003).

The Asian Experience and Exclusionary Immigration Policy, 1900–1917

The Chinese were not, however, the only Asian immigrant group to suffer the ignominy of being socially constructed and racialized as the other. In the late 19th and early 20th centuries, immigrants from Japan, Korea, and India, most of whom settled on the West Coast, were similarly seen as the polar opposite to Americans. Like the Chinese, these groups were portrayed as a threat to the jobs and employment prospects of the White native and immigrant laboring class. Additionally, they were thought of as dirty, diseased, and racially inferior to their White counterparts. Indeed, in San Francisco, the school board went as far as to approve separate schools for Japanese children. To meet the perceived threat of Asian immigrants as a collective, in 1905 nativist groups such as Asiatic Exclusion League of San Francisco and labor unions championed for restrictions on further immigration from Asia. The result of the calls for a restriction was the enactment of two policies that would indeed severely impede future Asian immigration (Campi, 2005).

The first policy was the Gentleman's Agreement of 1907. This agreement was between the United States and Japan and was informal in nature. As part of the agreement, Japan limited the number and types of citizens it would allow to migrate to the United States. The United States, in turn, would allow immigration for the wives, children, and parents of Japanese men who were already residing in the United States (Van Nuys, 2002).

The second policy was the Immigrant Act of 1917, also known as the Asiatic Barred Zone Act (Public Law 64–301, 1917). The stated purpose of the act was to regulate the immigration of aliens to, and the residence of aliens in, the United States. Among the many things the act stipulated was the restriction of undesirables from other countries. In the parlance of the day, these undesirables included idiots, imbeciles, epileptics, homosexuals, alcoholics, the poor, criminals, people with a physical disability, polygamists, and anarchists. Also included among undesirables were prostitutes or anyone involved in prostitution (Campi, 2005; Public Law 64–301, 1917).

The key provision of the act was the restriction of people entering the United States from what was called the Asiatic Barred Zone. This zone included people from Japan, China, India, Turkey, Ceylon (Sri Lanka), Burma (Myanmar), Siam (Thailand), Laos, Cambodia, Vietnam, Singapore, Indonesia, Malaysia, Korea, Saudi Arabia, the Philippines, and the Polynesian Islands (Campi, 2005).

Another important provision of the act was a literacy test that was imposed on all immigrants, unless entering because of religious persecution. The test required that those immigrants who were over the age of 16 and could read some language to read 30 to 40 words of English to show they were at least semi-literate in English (Campi, 2005).

Eastern and Southern European Immigration and the Call for Quotas, 1890–1924

Though the early federal immigration policies were directed to stemming the flow of immigration from Asia, the most significant flow to the United States during the period between 1860 and 1920 was from eastern and southern Europe. The largest number of eastern and southern European immigrants came to the United States in the decade from 1905 and 1914, at an average of more than a million a year (Higham, 1956). Unlike the immigration from Asia, however, the majority of eastern and southern European immigrants settled in the major industrialized midwestern and northeastern cities. In these cities they were heavily concentrated in the mining and manufacturing centers (Higham, 1956; Seller, 1982). Much smaller numbers settled in the south and far west of the country.

What fueled the massive wave of immigration from eastern and southern Europe was the enormous and rapid industrialization of the United States between the years of 1860 and 1920. This industrialization had turned the United States from a second-rate industrial nation in 1850 to a leading industrialized nation on par with England, France, and Germany by 1890. A key to this industrial success had been the ample supply of cheap, semiskilled, and unskilled foreign labor that had immigrated to the United States during this period. Yet, despite their undoubted contribution to making the United States a first-world industrialized nation, the public and political response toward these immigrants oscillated between ambivalence and hostility. Business leaders, for example, saw the tremendous benefits of immigrants from eastern and southern Europe, not least because they were a cheap labor force that could be used to thwart unionization. Toward this end, business owners routinely pitted immigrant labor against native-born labor, or immigrant labor against immigrant labor. No surprise, then, that business owners were in favor of an open-door immigration policy and opposed any call for restrictions or quotas on the number of eastern and southern European immigrants (Higham, 1956; Seller, 1982).

This was not a view, however, that was universally embraced, particularly in the late 1890s when recession saw immigrants being blamed for the lowering of wages, taking of American jobs, and diminishing union bargaining power. As a consequence, labor unions were by and large in the camp calling for immigration restrictions.

The unions were not the only part of public life that saw large-scale immigration as problematic. Charity organizations that provided relief to the indigent were also an unlikely source calling for immigration restrictions, primarily because the sheer level of need of the indigent immigrant population overwhelmed these charity organizations and their resources. Many of the indigent immigrant population were residing in dilapidated tenements without the most basic necessities. Moreover, many of the social ills associated with need were rampant among the indigent immigrant population.

Thus, the charity organizations called for restrictions on European immigration, or at the very least some federal assistance in helping to meet their needs (Higham, 1956). There were also nativist sentiments that among other things viewed the largely Catholic and Jewish immigrants as culturally incompatible with the Protestant and republican roots of the country (Higham, 1963; see Figure 5.3). Alongside the nativist sentiments were the perspectives of the eugenics movement that had come to prominence during the late 19th and early 20th centuries. The eugenics movement promulgated a scientific racism that called for improving the genetic quality of the human population. Within this framework, it is believed that some groups of people have more desirable traits than others, and those with less desirable traits are not just inferior but should be eliminated. From this perspective, White, Anglo-Saxon, and Nordic people have the most desirable traits. Among those groups with the least desirable traits were Slavs, Jews, Blacks, Native Americans, and Asians (Higham, 1956, 1963).

During the 1900s, this perspective was projected onto the eastern and southern European immigrants (see Figure 5.4). Both adherents to eugenics, who were mostly from the privileged elite, and nativist portrayed eastern and southern European immigrants as genetically inferior, diseased, and not fit to live in the United States. As evidence for this opinion, they pointed to their physical characteristics, as well as the living and social conditions of the overcrowded tenements. Along with eugenics, there was also the portrayal of these immigrants as a potential threat to the social order. This view was most notably illustrated in 1911 when the Dillingham Commission published a 42-volume report on immigrants from Europe. The report issued a warning that the new wave of immigration from eastern and southern Europe threatened to subvert American society (Kitty, 1984; LeMay & Elliot, 1999). Following the Dillingham Commission report, several other publications by wealthy conservatives supported the notion of White Anglo-Saxon and Nordic superiority and Jewish, Slavic, and Italian inferiority.

The racial and nationalist feelings stirred up by these publications and the anti-Semitic utterings of prominent citizens such as Henry Ford challenged the government to limit or better still close the immigration door. In doing so, it was argued, the United States could retain what was left of its White, Anglo-Saxon homogeneity. This sentiment, along with a high level of public support, was successful in influencing the enactment of the Immigration Act of 1917 (Kitty, 1984; LeMay & Elliot, 1999; Public Law 64–301, 1917).

It was also successful in influencing the enactment of the Emergency Quota Act of 1921. Signed into law by President Warren Harding with almost total support from Congress, the act, also known as the Emergency Immigration Act of 1921 (P.L. 67–5), proved to be another turning point in United States immigration policy. It became the first time in United States history that numerical limits were placed on European immigration. Toward this end, the act, which was intended to be temporary, restricted

Figure 5.3 Nativist Anti-Immigrant Poster

Figure 5.4 Anti-European Immigrant Poster

the number of immigrants from any country annually to 3% of the number of residents from the same country living in the United States based on the Census of 1910 (Higham, 1956). This quota system had the effect of decreasing the number of immigrants entering the United States from 805,000 in 1920 to 309,000 in 1921. Excluded from the act were temporary visitors, government officials, and nationals of Western Hemisphere countries: Canada and Mexico (Ngai, 1999).

Three years later, the even more restrictive United States Immigration Act of 1924, also known as the Johnson-Reed Act, superseded the Emergency Quota Act. This seminal social policy created the country's first permanent immigration quota system. The quota system reduced the number of total immigrants allowed in the country from 358,000 to 164,000. Furthermore, it reduced the immigration limit from 3% to 2% of each foreign-born group living in the United States in 1890 (Ngai, 1999; Public Law 68–139, 1924). By using the 1890 date rather than the 1910 date, it ensured that the eastern and southern European quotas would not be truly proportionate to their new numbers in the population. Finally, the act provided for a future reduction to 154,000 new immigrants annually. The new law cut the quota for northern and western countries by 29% but slashed the quota for eastern and southern Europe by 87% (Ngai, 1999). Notably excused from the quota were Mexicans.

The effect of the act on immigration was significant. Between 1924 and 1947, the United States welcomed a total of some 2.4 million immigrants. To put it into perspective, this was the number of immigrants who came to the United States in just two years between 1915 and 1920. Moreover, 1930 marked the first and only time in U.S. history that more people left than entered the United States (Immigration Policy Center, 2008).

Though the Immigration Act of 1924 did significantly affect the number of immigrants coming into the country, it was not particularly punitive toward eastern and southern European immigrants, certainly not anywhere near the way the Chinese Exclusion Act of 1882 and the Immigration Act of 1917 had been toward Asians or other immigrants not considered White. As such, while eastern and southern European immigrants might have been considered socially or culturally inferior to native White Americans, they were still entitled to the benefits of citizenship.

One important point to make about the Chinese Exclusion Act of 1882 and United States Immigration Act of 1924 is that in seeking to keep out less desirable immigrants, both acts had an unintended consequence: They became the catalyst for creating the first undocumented immigrant population (Immigration Policy Center, 2008). After the passing of the Chinese Exclusion Act of 1882, for example, large numbers of undocumented Chinese immigrants circumvented the law by crossing into the United States through either the Canadian or Mexican borders. Some also came to the United States by going to Cuba and hiring smugglers to bring them over by sea. Undocumented immigrants from Europe similarly circumvented the law by taking the same routes into the United States (Immigration Policy Center, 2008).

In 1925, the Immigration Service reported that there were some 1.4 million immigrants living illegally in the United States (Immigration Policy Center, 2008). In response, and in acknowledgment of the large number of undocumented immigrants, particularly from Europe, the federal government enacted the Registry Act of 1929. This amnesty policy allowed,

> law-abiding aliens who were in the country under some merely technical irregularity to register as permanent residents for a fee of $20. They also had to prove they had lived in the country since 1921 and were of good moral character (USCIS, n.d.). Between 1925 and 1965, some 200,000 undocumented European immigrants legalized their status through the Registry Act of 1929.
>
> (Immigration Policy Center, 2008, p. 2)

THE MEXICAN EXPERIENCE, 1882–1964

Aside from the 10,000 or so Mexican miners who entered California during the gold rush period from 1848 to 1855, Mexican migration to the United States was relatively small during most of the 19th century. Indeed, between 1850 and 1890 it averaged no more than 3,000 to 5,000 people per decade (Gutierrez, 2014). However, the need for labor created by the Chinese Exclusion Act of 1882 changed this dramatically when employers in western and southwestern cities began to look to Mexico for cheap, unskilled replacement labor (Gutierrez, 2014, p. 57). The industries in particular demand for this labor included agriculture, mining, construction, and railroad construction and maintenance (Gutierrez, 2014). In response to this demand, by 1900 some 100,000 Mexicans migrated to the United States. By 1910, this number doubled again to 200,000, and then again to 400,000 by 1920, after the Mexican civil war sparked an exodus of laborers to the Southwest (Romo, 1993).

Between 1900 and 1910, Mexican migrants had effectively replaced all of the Chinese labor on the railroads in the western divisions. Moreover, racially, Mexican laborers were more acceptable in California than had ever been the case for Asian labor, whether Chinese, Japanese, or Hindu, that is, South Asian Indians (Lee, 2003). Such was the value of Mexican labor that railroad and agricultural interests lobbied in Congress for the exception of new Mexican migrants from the literacy test of the Immigration Act of 1917. Furthermore, the railroad, agricultural, and mining companies employed a series of strategies to ensure public support for the continued availability of Mexican migrant labor. Among those strategies was warning the public that if there were no Mexican migrant laborers, there would be food shortages and/or a serious decline in food production (Lee, 2003). The advocacy was successful in allowing the Mexican migrants to be except from Section 3 of the Immigrant Act of 1917, which denied admission to aliens who could not read the English language (Lee, 2003).

Although the Mexican migrant labor was invaluable to the United States between 1900 and 1920 given the shortages caused by the restrictive immigration policy and World War I, their growing presence was not embraced by all sectors of society. As with Asian and European immigrants, among the strongest opposition to the seemingly open-door policy for Mexican migrants was organized labor. Ironically, though, this was not a position that organized labor first took. Initially, organized labor sought to bring all Mexican migrant labor into the organized labor fold, not least because they were often forced to work for wages below the standard, thereby lowering wages for all labor (Mellinger, 1992). However, this changed when World War I broke out in 1917 and thousands of Mexican workers were admitted to the United States to replace those workers who went to war. This need for labor saw Mexican migrants and the established Chicano population (i.e., Mexican Americans) fill labor positions in cities such as Chicago, Detroit, Gary, St. Louis, Kansas City, and Pittsburgh (Romo, 1993). This use of Mexican labor as a replacement for native White labor, albeit labor that was at war, led to organized labor became increasingly concerned about the growing presence of Mexican migrants (Romo, 1993). At this point organized labor began to see Mexican migrant labor much more as competitors for jobs held by native White laborers than potential union members. There was also the fear among organized labor that Mexican migrant labor would not always be content with unskilled low-wage jobs in agriculture and would at some point want to enter semiskilled and skilled trades (Romo, 1993). No surprise then, that by 1919 organized labor introduced resolutions advising that it would be bad for the country to allow Mexican migrant labor to do work other than what they had been recruited to do. There was also a call for the employment of red-blooded American citizens, who unlike the Mexican migrant labor, had an allegiance only to the United States (Romo, 1993). Finally, organized labor began to paint a picture of Mexican migrant labor as willing to work for starvation wages, and as a result, deflating wages and organized labor bargaining power. Consequently, organized labor argued for restrictions on the flow of Mexican migrant labor in order to protect the job prospects of White labor. The calls for Mexican migrant labor restrictions did not, however, gain the kind of traction it did for Asians and eastern and southern Europeans.

There were several reasons why the Mexican restriction movement got little to no traction at this point. One reason was that 90% of the Mexican population lived in just three states: Texas, Arizona, and California. None of these states were prominent in the call for restrictions on immigration. The second reason was that the Mexican migrant labor did indeed do the kind of work at a price that White labor balked at, thus rendering their labor invaluable (Romo, 1993).

This is not to say, however, that Mexican migrant labor did not face discrimination. Indeed, between 1920 and 1930, Mexicans would fall victim to the eugenics ideology of Anglo-Saxon and Nordic superiority thesis. This thesis placed Mexicans, whose racial designation in the United States had been White since the mid-1800s, as inferior to Anglo-Saxon and Nordic Whites. This view was notably played out in the California school system, where children of Mexican heritage were placed in schools segregated from White children (Menchaca & Valencia, 1990). Justification for this segregation was often around language differences and culture. Another justification was Mexican children's supposed lack of social etiquette when compared with their White counterparts (Donato, 1997). Indeed, the segregation of Mexican children in the school system in California was to become one of the early battlegrounds for school integration, namely, the *Roberto Alvarez v. the Board of Trustees of the Lemon Grove School District* court case (Patiño,

2020). In this 1931 case, the Court ruled that separate school facilities for Mexican or Chicano students were not conducive to their Americanization and prevented them from learning English (Donato, 1997; Patiño, 2020).

Adult Mexican migrants also had to contend with *de facto* social segregation that relegated them to the Mexican side of town when not at work. Consequently, while there were few official laws or policies that discriminated against Mexican migrants, they were nevertheless increasingly viewed and treated more as chattel labor than a valued part of wider American society. Good enough to provide labor, but not good enough to be fully socially integrated. Others in society, particularly at the onset of the Great Depression in 1929, began to see Mexican migrants with their Spanish language and Catholic faith as nonassimilable and undesirable as an ethnic group. Congressman Albert Johnson voiced a good example of this sentiment in 1929 when he noted that the time had come for Congress to save California for Californians by getting rid of Mexican migrant labor. Sociologist W. Garnett compared Mexican migrant labor to Black people as two groups that constituted nonassimilable populations (Romo, 1993). Journalist Kenneth L. Roberts of the *Saturday Evening Post* wrote that since the restriction of European immigration, "The brown flood of Mexican peon immigration had risen each year." In his investigative reporting, Roberts portrayed Mexican migrants as illiterate, living in shacks, constantly living on the edge of starvation, and producing progeny with reckless abandon (Romo, 1993, p. 130). Roberts concluded that they had little interest in community living.

In what was to symbolize the complicated and contradictory relationship between Mexican migrant labor and the United States, the onset of the worst depression in U.S. history in 1929 saw Mexican migrants and Chicanos suddenly become dispensable. More specifically, between 1929 and 1939, somewhere in the region of 250,000 to 500,00 Mexican immigrants and their children were coerced to return to Mexico in a mass repatriation campaign coordinated by western and southwestern local and state municipalities (Library of Congress, n.d.). During this period, Mexican immigrants and their families were rounded up, placed on a bus, and sent back across the border to Mexico. No distinction was made between migrant and/or naturalized citizens in this forced repatriation (Gutierrez, 2014). Though the anti-Mexican immigrant sentiment of the day certainly played some role in their mass repatriation, just as important was the lack of resources that local municipalities had to meet the relief needs of country that was enduring the worst recession in its history. As a consequence, the pressure was to prioritize relief to native-born Americans at the expense of immigrants, such as Mexicans (Hoffman, 1974).

As if to illustrate the value of Mexican labor to the United States, less than a decade after their forced repatriation, the U.S. and Mexican governments signed the Emergency Farm Labor Agreement in 1942. Prompted by labor shortages in the United States as the result of World War II, the act, also known as the Bracero Program, allowed Mexican nationals to enter the United States to serve as temporary agricultural workers. As a result, American employers were responsible for paying the living and transportation expenses of Mexican laborers. They also had to pay them wages equal to those of American farm workers doing similar work. The program was extended in 1949 and 1951 and was not disbanded until 1964 (Migration Policy Institute, 2013). Despite the efforts of the program to control the number of Mexican migrants flowing into the United States, as per the request of the Mexican government, it did have the unintended consequence of sparking a wave of undocumented migration to the United States. In response, an immigration law enforcement initiative named Operation Wetback was implemented (Gutierrez, 2014; Migration Policy Institute, 2013). Beginning in 1952, Operation Wetback used Border Patrol agents to locate, process, and deport Mexicans who had entered the United States without documentation. The operation was active in cities that included Los Angeles, San Francisco, and Chicago, although its primary targets were border areas in Texas and California. During its first year of operation, the patrols apprehended over a million Mexicans without documents (Migration Policy Institute, 2013). This number would fall precipitously, however, every year until Operation Wetback was discontinued in 1964. Moreover, Operation Wetback did little to curb the appetite of business for cheap labor. Operation Wetback resulted in the permanent strategic boarder control presence that is now in place to prevent crossing without documentation (Gutierrez, 2014; Migration Policy Institute, 2013).

Case Study: Puerto Rican Migration

The Puerto Rican migration experience occupies a unique chapter in United States' immigration and migration history. Located in the northeastern Caribbean with Spanish as the dominant language and a predominately Afro-Hispanic-Indian population, Puerto Rico has been an unincorporated territory of the United States since 1898 when it was acquired from Spain by way of the Treaty of Paris after the Spanish-American war (Duany, 2003). Relatedly, the people of Puerto Rico have been citizens of the United States since 1917, when President Woodrow Wilson signed into law the Jones–Shafroth Act of 1917 Act (P.L. 64–368). The act also created the Senate of Puerto Rico, established a bill of rights, and gave permission for the election of a Resident Commissioner (Duany, 2003). Despite citizenship of the United States, the fact that Puerto Rico has not been granted electors by way of a constitutional amendment, as in the case of District of Columbia, means that it does not have what states do – congressional representations. Additionally, they do not have a vote in the Electoral College (Hein, 2009). Thus, Puerto Rico finds itself in constitutional limbo where it belongs to but is not part of the United States (Duany, 2003).

Mirroring the island's marginalized political standing, the internal migration experiences of Puerto Ricans to the United States has historically been one of second-class citizenship. As migrants, Puerto Rican have resided in the United States since before the Spanish-American war (Duany, 2003). Their numbers, however, were in the low thousands, with the majority living in New York City. It was not until the 1900s, did sizeable numbers begin to migrate (Duany, 2003; Morris, 2015).

The firs wave of migration from Puerto Rico to the United States happened between 1900 and 1945. The numbers were not large in comparison to the European immigration between 1880 and 1920. It was nevertheless sizeable enough to have a significant Puerto Rican migrant population, the majority of who established themselves in various enclaves in New York City, which included Brooklyn, East Harlem, South Bronx, and upper and lower eastside Manhattan (Ayala, 1996). This first wave of Puerto Rican migrants are the pioneers (Ayala, 1996).

The second of wave of Puerto Rican migration happened between 1946 and 1964 and became known as the Great Migration. In 1945, for example, there were just 13,000 Puerto Ricans in New York; by 1946, the number had more than trebled to over 50,000. Over the next decade, an average of 25,000 Puerto Ricans a year would migrate to the United States, peaking at 69,000 in 1953. By the mid-1950s, 700,000 Puerto Ricans had migrated to the United States (Ayala, 1996).

Several push factors created the conditions for this Great Migration. Among these factors was Operation Boot Strap, an economic development program that had the United States government in Puerto Rico entice American corporations to do business on the island. In exchange for doing business on the island, American corporations were provided labor at costs below those of the United States, tax incentives, access to American markets without import duties, and transferable profits to the United States free from federal taxation (Ayala, 1996). As a consequence of Operation Boot Strap, between 1947 and 1951, Puerto Rico was transformed from an agricultural economy and workforce to a manufacturing and tourism economy and workforce. In the process, there was a shift in the rural population to the towns and cities and more troubling an absolute decline in the number of available jobs as a result of the rapidly growing population (Ayala, 1996; Morris, 2015).

In response to the economic woes caused by the resulting rise in unemployment and surplus labor, American factory owners and recruitment agencies looking for cheap labor, often with the support of the United States government, heavily recruited in Puerto Rico. Hugely helping the recruitment efforts was the availability for the first time of affordable air travel, a development that saw Puerto Rican migration between 1946 and 1964 being the first to the United States that was primarily by air and not boat or ship.

At least initially, Puerto Rican migrants were able to find employment and were a vital and active presence in the workforce. They worked in large numbers in the textile and garment industry in New York. Indeed, by the 1960s, Puerto Rican women made up 25 percent of the New York sewing machine operators. (Ruiz & Korrol, 2006). In Illinois, they were employed in large numbers in electronic factories. In Ohio, Indiana, and Pennsylvania, they worked in steel mills, as well as on farms in eastern and midwestern states (Morris, 2015).

Despite their presence in the workforce, and the fact that they were American citizens, Puerto Rican migrants faced intense discrimination and marginalization, in large part due to language, racism, perceived cultural differences, and ironically nativism (Morris, 2015). Never seen or treated as citizens, Puerto Rican migrants were residentially segregated in inadequate housing in poorly resourced communities, denied leadership positions in unions such as the International Ladies Garment Work Union because of discrimination from the fellow unionist, even as they made up a sizeable number of the workforce. Moreover, when economic restructuring in the 1960s reduced the need for low-skilled labor, Puerto Rican migrants found themselves displaced by a cheaper and more exploitable workforce: Newly arrived immigrants from other Caribbean islands (Morris, 2015). Also marginalized were the children of tPuerto Rican migrants who in school received nothing in the way of accommodation as regard English language instruction (Morris, 2015).

Alienated, discriminated against and without education and or employment opportunities, in the late 1950s, many children of Puerto Rican migrants drifted into delinquency and gang membership, immortalized in the Broadway play and film West Side Story. The result was the stereotyping of Puerto Rican youth as criminals (Morris, 2015). It was a stereotype hardened in 1959 with the high-profile murder of two White teenage gang members by a 16-year old Puerto Rican gang member, Salvador Agron, dubbed the Capeman (Jacoby, 2004). Within a fortnight of the Capeman murder, the killing of an Italian man in Chicago randomly targeted by two young Puerto Ricans sparked a public hysteria linking delinquency, criminal behavior and dangerousness with Puerto Rican youth (Morris, 2015). Indeed, this connection, as well as public and political concern about urban delinquency, in general, led to the passage of Juvenile Delinquency and Youth Offenses Control Act (P.L. 87–274) of 1961.

The reality, however, was that by the 1960s, most Puerto Rican children were living in households where poverty and insecurity outweighed opportunities. Much like Blacks, Puerto Rican migrants and their American-born children found themselves stuck in low-wage employment where they made 30 percent less in salary than their White counterparts if a male and 50 percent less if female. Moreover, mortgage lending discrimination and redlining excluded Puerto Rican migrant families from participating in the White flight to the suburbs in the 1950s and 1960s.

It is of little surprise, then, by the mid-1960s and spurred by the civil rights movement, many of the American-born children of Puerto Rican migrants rejected assimilation with the larger White society and instead embraced radicalization, community pride and the call for empowerment. Using classic social protest and advocacy strategies, grassroots groups as varied as the National Association of Puerto Rican Civil Rights, the Young Lords, and

ASPIRA emerged. These and other grassroots groups, often in collaboration with Black American grassroots and advocacy organizations, called for anti-poverty policies, an end to public housing exclusion, better schools, including bi-lingual education and an end to racial and ethnic segregation in school, and an end to employment discrimination and economic exploitation. There was also calls for an end to police brutality and the establishment of a civilian review board (Darien, 2013; Jennings & Rivera, 1984; Morris, 2015).

Some of the significant protests included a massive school boycott in New York City in1964, organized by the National Association of Puerto Rican Civil Rights and CORE. At the heart of the protest was the failure of the Board of Education to integrate New York City schools. It was a protest that crippled the New York City school system and was successful in bringing attention to BOE's neglect of Puerto Rican and Black children. Relatedly, there was the call for greater control and actual governance of schools by Puerto Rican and Black parents, a call that the DOE in New York acquiesced to when they set up several experiential community controlled schools. None of these schools, however, lasted more than a few years, but they nevertheless proved what could be done with community action (Song Ha Lee).

In Chicago, New York, and other cities, chapters of the Young Lords set up community organizations that fed poor children and offered cultural education. Furthermore, in New York, they championed the inclusion of Puerto Rican and Black studies on college campuses, where they were active in pushing the City University of New York (CUNY) to open up more educational opportunities for Puerto Ricans and Blacks.

All in all, there were some significant gains made from the advocacy efforts of the 1960s, including federal education policy (see Chapter 10) that introduced bilingual education, as well as the introduction of Puerto Rican and Black studies in college curriculums. Ultimately, however, ongoing discrimination continued to plague the Puerto Rican community, as did poverty. Moreover, at the end of the 1960s and going into the 1970s and 1980s, the conservative backlash against the civil rights gains would have a significant impact on the Puerto Rican community as social scientists would consider them, along with Blacks, a social underclass (Morris, 2015).

In 1991, President Reagan's former director of the U.S. Commission on Civil Rights Linda Chavez published the book *Out of the Barrio*. In the book, Chavez labeled Puerto Ricans a "tragic and curious exception" to the growing success of Latinos nationwide. Chavez argued that at the heart of the Puerto Rican problem was their dependence on benefits programs, which as citizens they were entitled to, but other Hispanics, as immigrants, were not. Missing in the argument, however, was a discussion of the structural barriers that had plagued Puerto Rican advancement.

Going into the new millennium, the descendants of both the pioneer and Great Migration generations have made significant strides. There are numerous notable American-born Puerto Rican descendants in law, journalism, art, politics, sport, finance, medicine and education, and in Bronx-born Sonia Sotomayer, there is a Supreme Court judge. Moreover, indicative of their permanent presence, as of 2013, there were more American and Puerto Rico-born individuals living in the United States (5.1 million) than there were inhabitants of Puerto Rico (3.6 million; Lopez & Patten, 2015). They reside in all 50 states in the union but are predominate in the Northeast (51%), with the majority in New York (21%). There is also a strong presence in the South (31%), mostly in Florida (19%; Lopez & Patten, 2015).

In comparison to the Hispanic population as a whole in the United States, Puerto Ricans are second only to Mexicans as the largest Hispanic population in the country at 9.5%, a number that was arrived at after 1980 with a new wave of migration from Puerto Rico. Contrary to the assertions of Chavez in 1991, Puerto Rican descendants have the highest levels of education within the Hispanic population of the United States, with 18% holding, at least, a bachelor's degree. They also have the highest median income among the Hispanic population in the United States (Lopez & Patten, 2015). Tempering this, however, is that Puerto Rican descendants are less likely to be married (36%) than Hispanics overall (46%; Lopez & Patten, 2015). They are also less liable to be homeowners (38%) than the general Hispanic population (45%). Moreover, the share of Puerto Ricans who live in poverty (27%) is higher than for all other Hispanic groups (25%) and the general population of the United States (16%; Lopez & Patten, 2015). They also have the highest infant mortality rates (8%) among the Hispanic population, second nationally only to Black Americans (Centers for Disease Control and Prevention, 2013). Just as troubling, however, is that when compared to Whites, there remains significant disparities in education attainment, median income, homeownership, and poverty (Lopez & Patten, 2015). This finding comes even as 57% of Puerto Rican descendants describe themselves as typical Americans, a number that is higher than for other Hispanic groups (49%; Lopez & Patten, 2015).

Much like the island from which they are descendants of, sections of the Puerto Rican population in America continue to face structural struggles that have been long in the making and deeply entrenched. Unlike other Hispanic groups who have immigrated to the United States, the American born citizens continue to be viewed and treated more as immigrants than the Americans they are, reflecting the unique second-class citizenship status that Puerto Rico has had with the United States for near one hundred years.

References

Ayala, C.J. (1996). The decline of the plantation economy and the Puerto Rican migration of the 1950s. *Latino Studies*, 7(1), 61–90.

Centers for Disease Control and Prevention. (2013). Infant death—United States, 2005–2008. *MMWR 2013*, *62*(Suppl. 3), 169–172. Retrieved from http://www.cdc.gov/mmwr/pdf/other/su6203.pdf

Darien, A.T. (2013). *Becoming New York's finest: Race, gender and the integration of the NYPD, 1935–1980*. New York, NY: Palgrave Macmillan

Duany, J. (2003). Nation, migration, identity: The case of Puerto Ricans. *Latino Studies*. 1, 424–444.

Fitzgerald, K.J. (2014). *Recognizing race and ethnicity: Power, privilege and inequality*. Boulder, CO: Westview Press

Hein, J.R. (2009). Born in the U.S.A., but not natural born: How Congressional territorial policy bars Native-born Puerto Ricans from the presidency. *Journal of Constitutional Law*, 11(2), 423–457.

Jacoby, R. (2004). *Conversation with the Capeman: The untold story of Salvador Agron*. Madison, WI: University of Wisconsin Press

Jennings, J., & Rivera, M. (Eds.). (1984). *Puerto Rican politics in urban America*. Westport, CT: Greenwood Press.

Lopez, G., & Patten, E. (2015). *Hispanics of Puerto Rican origin in the United States, 2013*. Washington D.C.: Pew Research Center. Retrieved from http://www.pewhispanic.org/files/2015/09/2015-09-15_puerto-rico-fact-sheet.pdf

Ruiz, L.V., & Korrol, V.S. (2006). *Latinas in the United States, set: A Historical Encyclopedia*. Bloomington, IN: Indiana University Press.

Song Ha Lee, S. (2014). Building a Latino civil rights movement: Puerto Rican, African American and the pursuit of racial justice in New York City. Chapel Hill, NC: University of North Carolina Press.

Thomas, L. (2015). Puerto Ricans in the United States. Oxford Research Encyclopedia's. Retrieved from http://americanhistory.oxfordre.com/view/10.1093/acrefore/9780199329175.001.0001/acrefore-9780199329175-e-32

Rethinking Immigration, 1942–1975

World War II and its aftermath saw the United States dramatically rethink its exclusionary and discriminatory immigration policies. Indeed, many of the immigration policies passed in the 25 years following the end of the war would more closely resemble the enlightenment principles the United States was founded on. The first of these policies was the Magnuson Act of 1943. Also known as the Chinese Exclusion Repeal Act of 1943, the act discontinued the provisions of the Chinese Exclusion Act of 1882 and its extensions. It also reestablished Chinese immigration, allowing for 105 new entry visas annually. Finally, it allowed Chinese nationals to become U.S. citizens (Campi, 2005).

In 1946, Congress enacted the Luce-Celler Act, which extended naturalization and limited immigration rights to Asian Indians and Filipinos (Campi, 2005).

In 1952, the Immigration and Nationality Act was signed into law. Also known as the McCarran-Walter Act, the act totally revoked all of the provisions of the Immigrant Act of 1917, that is, the Asiatic Barred Zone Act. The act permitted a relatively small annual quota of 2,000 for Asian Pacific immigration to the United States. The law also established consultant offices to screen foreign nationals for admissibility to the United States (Campi, 2005).

In 1953, the Refugee Act was enacted. The act authorized the admission of up to 205,000 nonquota immigrants who were fleeing persecution or had been expelled from their homes in Europe (Migration Policy Institute, 2013, p. 3).

In 1962, the Migration and Refugee Assistance Act authorized funds to assist foreign nationals from the Western Hemisphere who had been forced to flee their country of origin because of racial, religious, or political persecution (Migration Policy Institute, 2013).

In 1965, President Lyndon Johnson signed into law the Immigration and Nationality Act. Also known as the Hart-Cellar Act, this seminal immigration policy abolished the national origin quota system. In its place, a capped number of immigrants were admitted to the United States based on their relationship to a citizen or a lawful permanent resident family member or an American employer (Public Law 89–236, 1965). The cap did not apply to the number of related family members who would be permitted to settle. The law provided a cap of 120,000 permanent residents who could be admitted each year from Western Hemisphere countries (Public Law 89–236, 1965; Migration Policy Institute, 2013).

In 1966, President Lyndon Johnson signed into law the Cuban Readjustment Act. This act was only the second time in United States history that an immigration policy was directed at one immigration group in particular. Unlike the Chinese Exclusion Act, though, the Cuban Readjustment Act offered Cuban natives and citizens and their accompanying spouses and children who arrived at open port-of-entry haven in the United States as permanent residents. This haven was contingent on a variety of factors, including approval by the Attorney General and one-year physical residency in the United States after admission. The policy was a response to the political persecution in Cuba and allowed for the victims of this and other forms of persecution to find a haven in the United States (Migration Policy Institute, 2013).

In 1975, the Indochina Migration and Refugee Assistance Act expanded the definition of the term "refugee" to include individuals fleeing persecution in Cambodia and Vietnam (Migration Policy Institute, 2013).

If the immigration policies between the years of 1942 and 1975 reconnected the United States to its enlightened foundations, then the polices between the years of 1986 to the present more resemble immigration control and the limit of immigrants' rights. Several socio-geo-political events have been responsible for this immigration policy shift.

Immigration Control and Limits on Immigration Rights, 1986–2000

Beginning in the late 1970s and continuing through the 1980s and 1990s, there was a profound shift in the immigration patterns of the United States: There was a significant increase in immigration from Central America to the United States. The genesis of this increase was, in part economic, but was much more a function of the political upheaval and civil wars in the Central American nations of El Salvador, Guatemala, Honduras, and Nicaragua. These decades-long conflicts saw successive waves of nationals of these countries flee to Mexico, Canada, and the United States (Brick et al., 2011).

Added to the increase in Central American immigration was the growth in Mexican migration flow to the United States. This growth was in part a legacy of the Bracero Program, which was discontinued in 1964. More specifically, as suggested by Brick et al. (2011), the "Bracero program helped to foster a culture and economy of emigration in Mexican communities of origin by deepening dependence on low-wage labor on the part of United States agribusiness" (p. 3). The result of this mutual dependence, which still exists today, was a consistent flow of Mexican migration to the United States to work in agriculture in a handful of boarder states.

However, there were much more profound push/pull factors than the Bracero Program for significantly increasing the flow of Mexican migration to the United States in the 1980s and 1990s. These factors were changing labor markets, globalization, and industrial restructuring in both Mexico and the United States. These factors saw a dramatic decline in the home-based manufacturing industry, a decline in unions, deregulation, outsourcing, the mobility of goods and capital, and the rise of the service sector and the need for cheap migrant labor (Lee & Mather, 2008). This need, which was much more pronounced in the United States, increased the flow of Mexican migrants to work in the service sector (Brick et al., 2011).

The net result of the increased flow of immigration from Mexico and Central America is that over the past four decades the demographics of United States immigration has been transformed. Specifically, the Mexican and Central American immigrant population has doubled each decade between 1970 and 2000, reaching 20.4 million in 2010, a 20-fold increase since 1970 (Brick et al., 2011). The largest number of these immigrant populations came from Mexico.

Of the increased flow of immigrants from Mexico and Central America over the past four decades, a considerable number were undocumented because of changes in U.S. immigration policy and policy enforcement. These changes made it impossible for all of them to enter with the required documentation. Moreover, because of the difficulty entailed in leaving and returning to the country if undocumented, significant numbers of these undocumented immigrants made permanent homes in the United States and

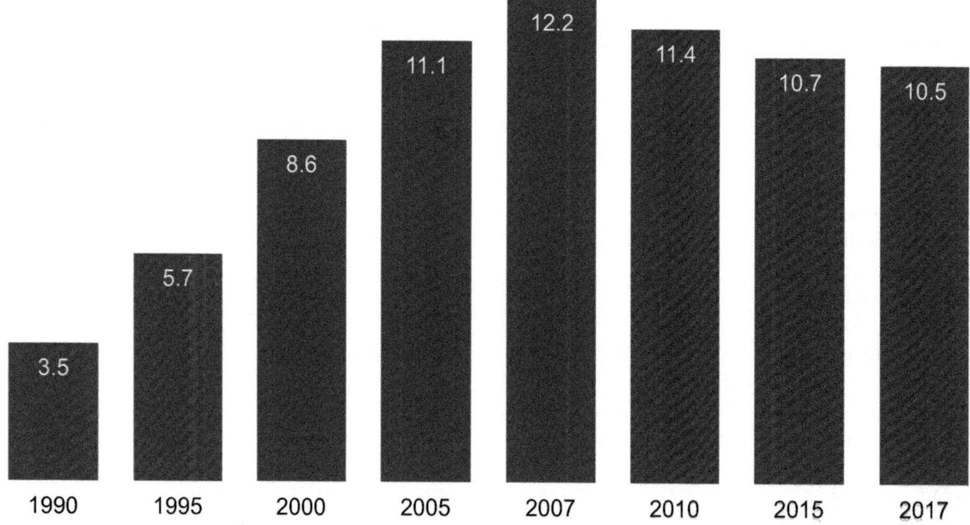

Figure 5.5 Estimates of the United States Undocumented Immigrant Population, 1990–2017

Source: Pew Research Center estimates based on augmented U.S. Census data. Retrieved from www.pewresearch.org/wp-content/uploads/2019/06/FT_19.06.12_5FactsIllegalImmigration_US-unauthorized-immigrant-total.png?w=64 had families. Hence, the current predicament for the 10.5 million estimated undocumented immigrants (Brick et al., 2011; Krogstad & Passel, 2014; Passel & Cohn, 2019; Figure 5.5).

Part of what created this predicament was the immigration policies of the United States from the mid-1980s. Beginning with the Immigration Reform Control Act of 1986 (Public Law 99–603, 1986), the first legislative attempt to address the issue of undocumented immigration comprehensively, United States immigration policy sought to control the flow of undocumented immigrants, as well as limit their rights (Cooper & O'Neil, 2005). The Immigration Reform Control Act of 1986, for example, used a carrot-and-stick approach toward undocumented immigration.

The carrot was the creation of two legalization programs that allowed undocumented immigrants to become legalized. One of the programs authorized undocumented immigrants who had worked in specific agricultural jobs for at least 90 days to apply for permanent residence (Cooper & O'Neil, 2005). The other program allowed undocumented immigrants who had been in the country since 1982 to legalize their status. The legalization program was responsible for some 2.7 million undocumented immigrants becoming documented and, therefore, legal residents (Migration Policy Institute, 2013). Conversely, the stick was a 50% increase in border patrol staffing and imposed sanctions on employers who knowingly hired or recruited undocumented immigrants. Thus, the successive waves of immigrants from Mexico and Central America who came after 1986 who were undocumented would not have an avenue for legal residence, nor would they have the opportunity to leave and return to the country because of increased border control (Cooper & O'Neil, 2005; Migration Policy Institute, 2013). As a consequence, they would be left in legal limbo: a resident with no chance of documentation.

The 1990s ushered in intense public and political debate about what to do about undocumented immigrants. This debate, though not as partisan as today, was in keeping with the law and order sentiments that were very much prevalent in the 1990s. This was reflected in immigration policy that sought more to punish and exclude rather than integrate. Emblematic of this sentiment was the enactment of the Illegal Immigration Reform and Immigrant Responsibility Act of 1996 (Public Law 104–208, 1996). Among the many things this act stipulated were the addition of new grounds of inadmissibility and deportability, an expansion the list of crimes for deportation, and expedited removal procedures. The act also allowed for the expansion of mandatory detention of immigrants in standard removal procedures if they had previously been convicted of certain crimes, as well as reduced the scope of judicial review for immigration decisions. Lastly, there was an increase in the number of border patrol agents, and new boarder control measures (Migration Policy Institute, 2013).

Equally punitive was the Violent Crime Control and Law Enforcement Act. Signed into law in 1994 by President Bill Clinton, the act gave the United States Attorney General the power to bypass deportation proceedings for certain immigrant-aggravated felons. Furthermore, it enhanced the penalties for immigrant smuggling and reentry after deportation (Migration Policy Institute, 2013).

Also, in 1996, the Personal Responsibility and Work Opportunity Reconciliation Act (PRWORA) tied the receipt of federal welfare benefits directly to citizenship. In doing so, undocumented immigrants were prohibited from receiving a range of benefits such as food stamps, Medicaid, and Supplemental Security Income. Moreover, new documented immigrants had to wait five years before they could be eligible for receiving any welfare benefits (Migration Policy Institute, 2013). The stipulations of the PRWORA recast the immigration question as not only between the undocumented and citizens but also between citizens and immigrants.

Immigration Control and National Security, 2001–Present

Following the September 11, 2001, terrorist attacks on the World Trade Center, U.S. immigration policy became even more punitive as it took on a national security responsibility. Furthermore, the public and political debate about undocumented immigrants became even more contentious with seemingly little ground for mutual agreement.

Informing this was a bipartisan national security stance that conflated terrorism and immigration. In doing so, Congress produced a slew of policies and significant fiscal backing that has put a legally sound, robust, and infinitely better-resourced immigration enforcement system in place than at any time in United States history (Chishti et al., 2017).

The Uniting and Strengthening America by Providing Appropriate Tools Required to Intercept and Obstruct Terrorism Act of 2001 (more commonly known as the USA Patriot Act), for example, permits indefinite detention of immigrants and other noncitizens (P.L. 107–56, 2001). Moreover, immigrants who are found not to be deportable for terrorism but have an immigration status violation of any kind (e.g., overstaying a student or tourist visa) could face indefinite detention if their home country refused to accept them (American Civil Liberty Union, 2001). The act also has stipulations that broaden the terrorism grounds for excluding immigrants from entering the United States and allows for increased monitoring of international students.

The Homeland Security Act of 2002 created the Department of Homeland Security (DHS), which restructured the United States Immigration and Naturalization Service (INS) and the Department of Justice into three new agencies. These agencies are United States Customs and Border Protection (CBP), United States Immigration and Customs Enforcement (ICE), and the United States Citizenship and Immigration Services (USCIS; Department of Homeland Security, 2002; P.L. 107–296, 2002).

The Enhanced Border Security and Visa Entry Reform Act of 2002 increased the number of Immigration and Naturalization Service (INS) investigators and inspectors by at least 200 employees over the amount authorized by the USA Patriot Act. It directed law enforcement agencies and intelligence entities to share deportation-related information about immigrants with the INS. It also prohibited the admission of a foreign national from a country the United States designated as a state sponsor of terrorism unless determined that such an individual does not pose a risk or security threat to the United States (P.L. 107–73, 2002).

The Real ID Act of 2005 established guidelines for immigration removal cases and expanded the grounds for terrorism-related deportation. It initially also had a requirement that states verify an applicant's legal status before issuing a driver's license or any other I.D. that might be accepted for federal purposes. States challenged this provision, which persuaded Congress to delay the implementation of this stipulation (H.R.418, 2005).

The DHS launched the Secure Communities program in 2008 (see Box 5.1, Immigration Timeline, for details of the program), prioritizing the removal of undocumented immigrants convicted of a crime, are repeat immigration violators, or pose a threat to public safety. Critics of the program, however, argue that after its discontinuation in 2014 and resurrection in 2017, it has broadened its focus to include those undocumented immigrants who have no criminal conviction (see the Box 5.1, Immigration Timeline, for details; Johnson, 2014; Trump, 2017a; Waslin, 2011).

The increased size of the ever-growing immigration enforcement bureaucracy is such that since the creation of DHS in 2002, the federal government has spent an estimated $381 billion on the agencies that carry out immigration enforcement, primarily for border security (CBP) and interior enforcement (ICE; American Immigration Council, 2020). Indeed, in fiscal year (FY) 2018, congressional appropriations for immigration enforcement were 34% higher than all of the other principal federal criminal law enforcement agencies combined: the Federal Bureau of Investigations (FBI); the Drug Enforcement Administration (DEA); Secret Service; U.S. Marshals Services; and the Bureau of Alcohol, Tobacco, Firearms, and Explosives (Meissner & Gelatt, 2019). As a result, the number of U.S. Border Patrol agents nearly doubled from FY2003 to FY2019. Similarly, the number of ICE agents devoted to Enforcement and Removal Operation (ERO) almost tripled in the same period (American Immigration Council, 2020).

Caught in the crosshairs of the immigration enforcement expansion are the estimated 10.5 million undocumented immigrants in the United States, not least because Congress has not passed any comprehensive immigration reform legislation since 1986 despite failed efforts such as the Dream Act (Georgetown Law Library, 2020). In the absence of comprehensive immigration reform legislation, successive presidents since 2001 have used their broad executive authority to take unilateral executive action to address gaps in immigration legislation that are in line with their ideological stance on immigration.

Although using this broad executive authority that bypasses Congress on a matter as necessary to a nation's well-being as immigration has its many critics, it is certainly not unprecedented. Indeed, since Congress first passed a comprehensive immigration law in the form of the 1952 Immigration and Nationality Act, every president from Dwight D. Eisenhower onward has used their broad executive authority to address gaps in immigration legislation (Farley, 2014; Masters, 2016; Wolgin, 2014).

During his two terms (2009–2017), President Obama, who came to office with the promise of immigration reform legislation that would provide a pathway to citizenship for undocumented immigrants, was every bit an adherent to the immigration and national security stance. Under his administration, most notably in the first term (2009–2013), there were record numbers of deportations, less than half on the grounds of a criminal conviction (see Figure 5.6), and included the practice of detaining families at the southern United States/Mexican border (Chishti et al., 2017).

Conversely, though, President Obama did use his broad executive authority to provide a level of protection to a specific demographic within the undocumented population—the Dreamers, young people brought to the country as children by their undocumented parents. The Dreamers had grown up as Americans, identified as American, and in most cases spoke only English. Still, under the current immigration system, they could not gain legal residency despite living most of their lives in the United States (ADL, 2020).

In 2012, after Congress failed to pass the DREAM Act, which offered a pathway to legal residency and citizenship for the Dreamers, President Obama initiated Deferred Action for Childhood Arrivals (DACA) by way of an executive branch memorandum (see Box 5.1, Immigration Timeline, for details; Georgetown Law Library, 2020). In Obama's words, DACA was a "temporary stopgap measure that lets us focus our resources wisely while giving a degree of relief and hope to talented, driven, patriotic young" (President Obama, 2012).

In 2014, President Obama again used his broad executive authority to expand DACA and create Deferred Action for Parents of Americans (DAPA) for eligible undocumented immigrant parents of citizens and lawful residents (see Box 5.1, Immigration Timeline, for details; USCIS, 2014). DAPA, however, did not survive the legal challenges from Texas and other states and was never initiated.

Upon President Obama leaving office, his executive actions had offered a degree of relief to the near 800,000 Dreamers who became DACA recipients (Roberts, 2018). However, in the continued absence of a congressional immigration reform bill, the Dreamers and the other 9.7 million undocumented immigrants

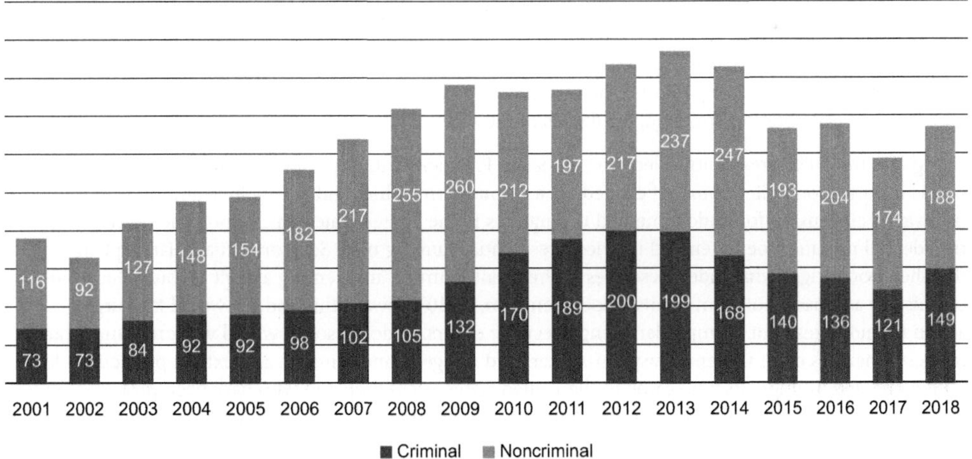

Figure 5.6 Deportations by the U.S. Department of Homeland Security, 2001–2018

Source: Pew Research Center: U.S deportations of immigrants slightly up in 2018. Retrieved from www.pewresearch.org/fact-tank/2020/08/20/key-findings-about-u-s-immigrants/ft_2020-08-20_immigrants_11/

remained in legal limbo. It was a legal limbo that would become even more precarious with Donald Trump's ascension as a presidential candidate in 2016.

Adopting the Make America Great Again campaign slogan first used by Ronald Reagan in his 1980 presidential campaign, Donald Trump promised bold action to reform what he called a broken immigration system. This reform's centerpiece was building a wall on the border between the United States and Mexico. Within the first 100 days of his presidency, President Trump outlined a ten-policy address for immigration reform (see Box 5.1, Immigration Timeline, for details; Ballotpedia, 2020).

Informing President Trump's immigration reform actions were nativist sentiments that were akin to the anti-immigrant sentiments discussed earlier in the chapter. It is a stance that saw President Trump utilize the existing immigration enforcement system and his broad executive authority to pass more than 400 executive orders that have dramatically reshaped the United States immigration system (Pierce & Bolter, 2020).

These executive actions were extensive in their scope. They included Muslim travel bans, more aggressive border and interior enforcement, paring down the refugee and asylum system, rescinding DACA, and seeking penalties against sanctuary cities who refuse to cooperate with ICE in the identification and removal of undocumented immigrants (see Box 5.1, Immigration Timeline, for details). Most controversial was the practice of not just detaining immigrant families that came across the southern border with Mexico without legal documents, which was also the case under the Obama administration, but also separating the parents from children, and then detaining the children away from their parents.

President Trump's immigration policies and executive actions were not without challenge, though. There were numerous legal challenges from immigrant advocates, states, and civil rights organizations to actions such as the Muslim travel ban and the rescinding of DACA, which the Supreme Court blocked. President Trump also had some significant wins as a result of the legal challenges (see Box 5.1, Immigration Timeline, for details). Moreover, President Trump was not deterred in his robust efforts to create an immigration system that, in his words, serves the national interest, restores the rule of law, constructs a border, swiftly removes unlawful entrants, and protects American workers (Whitehouse.gov, 2020). To this end, late in his term, President Trump widened his immigration reform scope to include aspects of legal immigration that he felt were not in the national interest. For example, he called for the end of chain migration, the Diversity Visa lottery program, limiting the number of migrants eligible for asylum, and reducing the number of H-1B visas (see Box 5.1, Immigration Timeline, for details of these actions).

With the arrival of the COVID-19 pandemic in early 2020 and the subsequent economic downturn and massive job losses, President Trump took the opportunity to chip away at various aspects of legal immigration. For example, in April 2020, he signed an executive order enacting a 60-day ban on legal entry into the United States for any foreign national who posed a risk to the United States labor market during the economic recovery efforts. The 60-day ban was extended to the end of 2020 in June of 2020 (see Box 5.1, Immigration Timeline, for details of these actions).

Going into the 2020 presidential election campaign, President Trump promised that he would stay on his immigration policy course if elected for a second term, which did not include any chance of a pathway to citizenship for undocumented immigrants in the United States. In contrast, the Democratic presidential nominee Joe Biden and his vice-presidential running mate Senator Kamala Harris pledged that they would right what Biden describes as President Trump's "unrelenting assault on our values and our history as a nation of immigrants" (Joebiden.com, 2020). Toward this end, he would take urgent action to undo President Trump's damaging executive orders. In doing so, he would welcome immigrants, reassert America's commitment to asylum-seekers and refugees, and reinstate and extend protections for undocumented immigrants who came to the United States as children and who have been protected under DACA (Joebiden.com, 2020). He also vowed to pursue comprehensive immigration legislation (Joebiden.com, 2020).

In the first two days of taking office after his election in November 2020, President Joe Biden signed his first round of immigration executives orders and memorandums, all of which are in keeping with his campaign promise to undo his predecessor Donald Trump's immigration policies. These executive orders and memorandums are:

1. Preserving and Fortifying Deferred Action for Childhood Arrivals (DACA);
   (Whitehouse.gov, 2021a)

2. Reinstating Deferred Enforced Departure for Liberians;
   (Whitehouse.gov, 2021a)

3. Proclamation on the Termination of Emergency with Respect to the Southern Border of the United and Redirection of Funds Diverted to Border Wall Construction;
   (Whitehouse.gov, 2021a)

4. Executive Order on the Revision of Civil Immigration Enforcement Policies and Priorities;
   (Whitehouse.gov, 2021a)

5. Proclamation of Ending Discriminatory Bans on Entry to the United States.
   (Whithouse.gov, 2021b; see Box 5.1, Immigration Timeline, for details of executive actions and memorandums)

Only time will tell if President Joe Biden, whose Democratic party has the majority in both houses of Congress, albeit a slim one in the Senate, can push through comprehensive immigration reform for the 10.5 million undocumented immigrants.

Chapter Summary

This chapter has examined some of the historical and contemporary debates and social forces that have informed U.S. immigration policies and thinking. What these policies illustrate is America's complicated history with immigration. In less than 200 years, the United States has moved from no numerical limitations and very little regulation of immigration and virtually no laws to the present where national security and immigration have been conflated and codified. In the interim, race, ethnicity, class, and country of origin have been consistently used to argue against the entry of new immigrant groups who do not fit the American ideal of the day. These immigrant groups, however, have been vital to the development of the United States we know today. Moreover, they have proceeded to disprove the arguments of nativists and become an integral part of the United States. Ironically, in some cases, they are now held up as model immigrants, such as the Chinese, Koreans, and Indians. This fact should be a primary source of consideration when debating the pathway to citizenship for the current 10.5 million undocumented immigrants. This is not a stretch, given the precedent for bringing undocumented immigrants out of the shadows and into the mainstream, such as the Registry Act of 1929 and the Immigration Reform Control Act of 1986.

Another reason to consider the pathway to citizenship is the changing demographic profile of the United States (Miller, 2017). The U.S. population is getting bigger, older, and more racially and ethnically diverse. Contributing factors to these developments are declining mortality rates (especially for the three most prevalent causes of death), fertility levels that are hovering around generational replacement levels, and trends in net international migration, where more people are migrating to the United States than are leaving (Shrestha & Heisler, 2011; Vespa, 2019). These demographic changes are particularly noteworthy as it relates to the aging of the United States. Largely because of the baby boom generation (Americans born between 1946 and 1964), by 2050, the population aged 65 or over is projected to be 83.7 million, almost double its estimated population of 43.1 million in 2012. By 2050, the surviving baby boomers will be over 85 (Ortman et al., 2014; Vespa, 2019).

The aging of the population will have wide-ranging implications and will present challenges to policy makers as it relates to a number of essential domains (Ortman et al., 2014, p. 1). These challenges include the significant slowing down of labor force growth in the next decade and the resulting need for new workers to take the place of those who retire. Relatedly, there will be an expanded need for categorical entitlement programs such as Social Security and Medicare, which as of 2015 already accounted for the bulk of the federal budget's mandatory spending (Levit et al., 2015). In short, there will be a growing demand within the United States economy for younger workers and taxpayers (Ewing, 2012b; Miller, 2017; Vespa, 2019).

For three demographic reasons, it is inevitable that more and more of these taxpayers will be immigrants and the United States-born children of immigrants, most particularly Hispanic immigrants, documented or undocumented. First, immigration fuels more than two-fifths of the United States population growth. Second, immigrants tend to be younger than the native population, as is currently the case in the United States. Third, although dropping, the birthrate among Hispanic immigrants is still larger than those of the native population. Thus, as suggested by Ewing (2012b), going forward, immigrants and the United States-born children of immigrants will play an increasingly critical role within the United States economy as workers and taxpayers for decades to come (p. 1).

Retrieval Questions

1. What is the current immigration debate about?
2. What were the immigration concerns of the colonial era?
3. What were the immigration concerns of the antebellum era?
4. How was the mass immigration between 1860 and 1920 different from immigration prior to 1860?
5. What was the significance of the Chinese Exclusion Act of 1882?
6. What was the Gentleman's Agreement of 1907?
7. What role did nativist sentiments play in restricting immigration to the United States?
8. What were some of the stipulations of the Immigration Act of 1917?
9. What is the significance of the United States Immigration Act of 1924?
10. What was the Bracero Program?
11. What did the Magnuson Act of 1943 do?
12. What social conditions contributed to the significantly increased immigration from Central America to the United States beginning in the late 1970s?
13. Identify some of the stipulations of the Illegal Immigration Reform and Immigrant Responsibility Act of 1996.
14. Identify some of the stipulations of the Secure Fence Act of 2006.
15. What changes did the Patriot Act of 2001 make to the immigration process?

Discussion Questions

1. Identify and discuss some of the social justice issues pertinent to the current immigration debate about a pathway to citizenship.
2. As policy practitioners, what responsibility do social workers have to advocate and support immigration reform?
3. What are social workers' ethical responsibilities when working with undocumented immigrants?
4. What is the relationship between immigration status and social inequality in the United States?
5. How might a client's immigration status affect the social work practice context?

References

ACLU. (2001). How the anti-terrorism bill permits indefinite detention of immigrants. *ACLU.org*. Retrieved from www.aclu.org/other/how-anti-terrorism-bill-permits-indefinite-detention-immigrants

ADL. (2020). What is DACA and who are the DREAMers? *The Current Events Classroom*. Retrieved from www.adl.org/education/resources/tools-and-strategies/table-talk/what-is-daca-and-who-are-the-dreamers

American Civil Liberties Union Washington. (n.d.). *Timeline of the Muslim ban*. Retrieved from www.aclu-wa.org/pages/timeline-muslim-ban

American Immigration Council. (2020). *Fact sheet: The cost of immigration enforcement and border security*. Retrieved from www.americanimmigrationcouncil.org/sites/default/files/research/the_cost_of_immigration_enforcement_and_border_security.pdf

Ballotpedia. (2020). *Timeline of federal policy on immigration, 2017–2020*. Retrieved from https://ballotpedia.org/Timeline_of_federal_policy_on_immigration_2017-2020#cite_note-100DaysVideo-200

Ballotpedia. (n.d.). *Diversity lottery*. Retrieved from https://ballotpedia.org/Diversity_Lottery

Bredbenner, C. L. (1998). *A nationality of her own: Women, marriage, and the law of citizenship*. Chapel Hill, NC: University of North Carolina Press.

Brick, K., Challinor, A. E., & Rosenblum, M. R. (2011). Mexican and Central American immigrants in the United States. *Migration Policy Institute*. Retrieved from www.migrationpolicy.org/pubs/MexCentAmimmigrants.pdf

Campi, A. J. (2004). Remembering December 17: Repeal of the 1882 Chinese Exclusion Act. *Policy Brief*. Immigration Policy Center. Retrieved from www.immigrationpolicy.org/sites/default/files/docs/Chinese%20Exclusion%20Act%2012-04.pdf

Campi, A. J. (2005). Closed borders and mass deportations: The lessons of the Barred Zone Act. *Immigration Policy Center*. Retrieved from http://icirr.org/sites/default/files/IPC%20Barred%20Zone.pdf

Carlsson, C. (1995). The Workingmen's party & the Denis Kearney agitation: Historical essay. *FoundSf*. Retrieved from www.foundsf.org/index.php?title=The_Workingmen's_Party_%26_The_Denis_Kearney_Agitation

Carter, S., Gartner, S. S., Haines, M., Olmsted, A., Sutch, R., & Wright, G. (2006). *Historical statistics of the United States: Millennial edition*. Cambridge: Cambridge University Press.

Cheng, T. W. (1972). *Chink: A documentary history of anti-Chinese prejudice in America*. New York, NY: World Publishing Company.

Chishti, M., Pierce, S., & Bolter, J. (2017). *The Obama record on deportations: Deporter in chief or not*. Migration Policy Institute. Retrieved from www.migrationpolicy.org/article/obama-record-deportations-deporter-chief-or-not

Congress.gov. (2007). *S2205-DREAM Act of 2007*. Retrieved from www.congress.gov/bill/110th-congress/senate-bill/2205

Cooper, B., & O'Neil, K. (2005). Policy briefs: Lessons from the Immigration Reform and Control Act of 1986. *Migration Policy Institute*. Retrieved from www.migrationpolicy.org/research/lessons-immigration-reform-and-control-act-1986

Daily Dispatch. (1854). War upon the Irish, April 3, 1854: Chronicling America: Historic American newspapers: Library of congress. Retrieved from https://chroniclingamerica.loc.gov/lccn/sn84024738/1854-04-03/ed-1/seq-2/

Daniels, R. (1991). *Coming to America: A history of immigration and ethnicity in American life*. New York, NY: Harper Perennial.

DHS.gov. (n.d.). Fact sheet: DHS agreement with Guatemala, Honduras, and El Salvador. *U.S. Department of Homeland Security*. Retrieved from www.dhs.gov/sites/default/files/publications/19_1028_opa_factsheet-northern-central-america-agreements_v2.pdf

Department of Homeland Security. (2002). Homeland Security Act of 2002. *Dhs.gov*. Retrieved from www.dhs.gov/homeland-security-act-2002

Department of Homeland Security. (2019). *Migrant protection protocols*. Retrieved from www.dhs.gov/news/2019/01/24/migrant-protection-protocols

Donato, R. (1997). *The other struggle for equal schools: Mexican Americans during the civil rights era*. New York: The State University of New York Press.

Ewing, W. A. (2012a). Opportunity and exclusion: A brief history of United States immigration policy. *Immigration Policy Center*. Retrieved from www.immigrationpolicy.org/sites/default/files/docs/opportunity_exclusion_011312.pdf

Ewing, W. A. (2012b). The future of a generation: How new Americans will help support retiring baby boomers. *Immigration Policy Center*. Retrieved from www.aarp.org/content/dam/aarp/livable-communities/learn/

demographics/the-future-of-a-generation-how-new-americans-will-help-support-retiring-baby-boomers-aarp.pdf

Farley, R. (2014). Obama's actions same as past presidents. *FactCheck.org*. Retrieved from www.factcheck.org/2014/11/obamas-actions-same-as-past-presidents/

Fischer, M. (2020). Ninth Circuit court rules against Trump immigration policies. *Jurist*. Retrieved from www.jurist.org/news/2020/02/federal-appeals-court-rules-against-trump-administrations-immigration-policies/

Foner, N., & Fredrickson, G. M. (2004). *Not just black and white: Historical and contemporary perspectives on immigration, race, and ethnicity in the United States*. New York, NY: Russell Sage Foundation.

Franklin, B. (1751). Observations concerning the increase of mankind, 1751. *Founders Online National Archives*. Retrieved from https://founders.archives.gov/documents/Franklin/01-04-02-0080

Garcia, R. (1995). *Critical race theory and proposition 187:The racial politics of immigration law*. Paper 662. University of Nevada School of Law. Retrieved from http://scholars.law.unlv.edu/cgi/viewcontent.cgi?article=1675&context=facpub

Georgetown Law Library. (2020). *Deferred Action for Childhood Arrivals (DACA)*. Retrieved from https://guides.ll.georgetown.edu/c.php?g=592919&p=4170929

Gibson, C. J., & Lennon, E. (1999). *Historical census statistics on the foreign-born population of the United States: 1850–1990*. Population Work Paper No. 29. United States Census Bureau. Retrieved from www.census.gov/population/www/documentation/twps0029/twps0029.html

Gutierrez, D. G. (2014). An historic overview of Latino immigration and the demographic transformation of the United States. *American Latino Theme Study*. National Park Service. Retrieved from www.nps.gov/history/heritageinitiatives/latino/latinothemestudy/immigration.htm

Higham, J. (1956). American immigration policy in historical perspective. *Law and Contemporary Problems*, *21*(2), 213–235.

Higham, J. (1963). *Strangers in the land: Patterns of American nativism, 1860–1925* (2nd ed.). New York, NY: Atheneum.

Hirschman, C. (2005). Immigration and the American century. *Demography*, *42*(4), 595–620.

Hoffman, A. (1974). *Unwanted Mexican Americans in the Great Depression: Repatriation pressures, 1929–1939*. Tucson, AZ: University of Arizona Press.

Howe, A. (2020). No pause from Supreme Court for "public charge" rule during the COVID-19 pandemic. *SCOTUS Blog*. Retrieved from www.scotusblog.com/2020/04/no-pause-from-supreme-court-for-public-charge-rule-during-covid-19-pandemic/

H.R.40, Naturalization Bill. (1790). *U.S. capital visitor center*. Retrieved from www.visitthecapitol.gov/exhibitions/artifact/h-r-40-naturalization-bill-march-4-1790

H.R.418. (2005). *Real ID Act of 2005*. Retrieved from www.congress.gov/109/bills/hr418/BILLS-109hr418rfs.pdf

Immigration Legal Resource Center. (n.d.). *Public charge*. Retrieved from www.ilrc.org/public-charge

Immigration Policy Center. (2008). *De-romanticizing our immigrant past:Why claiming my family came legally is often a myth*. Retrieved from www.immigrationpolicy.org/just-facts/de-romanticizing-our-immigrant-past-why-claiming-my-family-came-legally-often-myth

Jefferson, T. (1832). Notes on the state of Virginia. *Lilly and Wait, 1832*. Library of Congress. Retrieved from www.loc.gov/item/03004902/

JoeBiden.com. (2020). The Biden plan for securing our values as a nation of immigrants. *Biden Harris*. Retrieved from https://joebiden.com/immigration/

Johnson, J. C. (2014). *U.S department of homeland security: Memorandum for Thomas S. Winkowski, acting director, U.S. immigration and customs enforcement*. Retrieved from www.dhs.gov/sites/default/files/publications/14_1120_memo_secure_communities.pdf

Johnson, K. R. (2009). The intersection of race and class in U.S. immigration law and enforcement. *Law and Contemporary Problems*, *72*(1), 1–35.

Kamarck, E., & Stenglein, C. (2019). How many undocumented immigrants are in the United States and who are they? *Policy 2020 Brookings*. Retrieved from www.brookings.edu/policy2020/votervital/how-many-undocumented-immigrants-are-in-the-united-states-and-who-are-they/

Kitty, C. (1984). *United States immigration law and the control of labor:1820–1924*. London: Academic Press.

Kraus, G. (1969). Chinese laborers and the construction of the Central Pacific. *Utah Historical Quarterly*, *37*(1), 41–57.

Krogstad, J. M., & Passel, J. S. (2014). Five facts about illegal immigration in the United States. *Pew Research Center*. Retrieved from www.pewresearch.org/fact-tank/2014/11/18/5-facts-about-illegal-immigration-in-the-u-s/

Lee, E. (2003). *At America's gate: Chinese immigration during the exclusion era, 1882–1943*. Chapel Hill, NC: University of North Carolina Press.

Lee, M. A., & Mather, M. (2008). United States labor force trends. *Population Bulletin*, 63(2). Retrieved from www.prb.org/pdf08/63.2uslabor.pdf

LeMay, M., & Elliot, R. B. (1999). *United States immigration and naturalization laws and issues: A documentary history*. Westport, CT: Greenwood Press.

Levit, M. R., Austin, D. A., & Stupak, J. M. (2015). Mandatory spending since 1962. *Congressional Research Service*. Retrieved from www.fas.org/sgp/crs/misc/RL33074.pdf

Library of Congress. (n.d.). *Immigration and relocation in U.S. history: Depression and the struggle for survival*. Retrieved from www.loc.gov/classroom-materials/immigration/mexican/depression-and-the-struggle-for-survival/

Masters, J. (2016). The U.S. Supreme Court and Obama's immigration actions. *Council on Foreign Affairs*. Retrieved from www.cfr.org/backgrounder/us-supreme-court-and-obamas-immigration-actions

McClain, C. J. (1994). *In search of equality: The Chinese struggle against discrimination in nineteenth century America*. Berkeley: University of California Press.

Meissner, D., & Gelatt, J. (2019). Eight key U.S. immigration policy issues: State of play and unanswered questions. *Migration Policy Institute*. Retrieved from www.migrationpolicy.org/research/eight-key-us-immigration-policy-issues

Mellinger, P. (1992). The men have become organizers: Labor conflict and unionization in the Mexican mining communities of Arizona, 1900–1915. *Western Historical Quarterly*, 23(3), 323–347.

Menchaca, M., & Valencia, R. R. (1990). Anglo-Saxon ideologies in the 1920s–1930s: The impact of segregation on Mexican students in California. *Anthropology and Education Quarterly*, 21(3), 222–249.

Migration Policy Institute. (2013). *Major United States immigration laws, 1790: Present*. Retrieved from http://ihei.migrationpolicy.org/research/timeline-1790

Miller, M. (2017). Aging United States must get the economics right on immigration. *Reuters.com*. Retrieved from www.reuters.com/article/us-column-miller-immigration/aging-united-states-must-get-the-economics-right-on-immigration-idUSKCN1BP184

National Association of Social Workers. (2018). *Social work speaks* (11th ed.). NASW Policy Statements, 2018–2020. Washington, DC: NASW Press.

National Immigration Forum. (2017). *Summary of President Trump's new proclamation that bans certain foreign individuals from entering the U.S.* Retrieved from https://immigrationforum.org/wp-content/uploads/2017/09/Travel-Ban3_Summary_Final.pdf

Ngai, M. M. (1999). The architecture of race in American immigration law: A reexamination of the Immigration Act of 1924. *Journal of American History*, 86(1), 67–92.

Nijjar, C. (2020). China: Impacts of migration. *ArcGIS Story Maps*. Retrieved from https://storymaps.arcgis.com/stories/0fab6c336d2d4eaeb8e4d33097c4e5d6

Odo, F., & Pilk, F. (2002). *The Columbia documentary history of the Asian American history*. New York, NY: Colombia University Press.

Office of the Historian. (2014). *Chinese immigration and exclusion acts*. Retrieved from https://history.state.gov/milestones/1866-1898/chinese-immigration

Ortman, J. M., Velkoff, V. A., & Hogan, H. (2014). An aging nation: The older population in the United States: Population estimates and projections. *U.S. Department of Commerce*. Retrieved from www.census.gov/prod/2014pubs/p25-1140.pdf

Ourdocuments.gov. (n.d.). *Chinese Exclusion Act* (1882). Retrieved from www.ourdocuments.gov/doc.php?flash=false&doc=47

Passel, J. S., & Cohn, D. (2015). Number of babies born in U.S. to unauthorized immigrants declined in 2013. *Fact Tank*. Pew Research Center. Retrieved from www.pewresearch.org/fact-tank/2015/09/11/number-of-babies-born-in-u-s-to-unauthorized-immigrants-declines/

Passel, J. S., & Cohn, D. (2019). Mexicans decline to less than half the U.S. unauthorized immigrant population for the first time. *Fact Tank*. Pew Research Center. Retrieved from www.pewresearch.org/fact-tank/2019/06/12/us-unauthorized-immigrant-population-2017/

Passel, J. S., Cohn, D., & Gramlich, J. (2018). Number of U.S.-born babies with unauthorized immigrants' parents has fallen since 2007. *Fact Tank*. Pew Research Center. Retrieved from www.pewresearch.org/fact-tank/2018/11/01/the-number-of-u-s-born-babies-with-unauthorized-immigrant-parents-has-fallen-since-2007/

Patiño, J. (2020). You don't know exactly which country you have to belong to: Rethinking *Alvarez v. Lemon Grove* through deportation regime, 1924–1931. *Pacific Historical Review*, 89(3), 347–378.

People v. Hall, 4 Cal.399. (1854). *Oct. 1854: Supreme court of California*. Retrieved from https://cite.case.law/cal/4/399/

Pickoff-White, L., & Brekke, D. (2015). Picturing the first boom: Images of gold rush San Francisco. *KQED*. Retrieved from www.kqed.org/news/10398858/picturing-the-first-boom-images-of-gold-rush-san-francisco

Pierce, S., & Bolter, J. (2020). Dismantling and reconstructing the U.S. immigration system: A catalog of changes under the Trump presidency. *Migration Policy Institute*. Retrieved from www.migrationpolicy.org/research/us-immigration-system-changes-trump-presidency

President Obama. (2012). Remarks by the president on immigration. *The White House: Office of the Press Secretary*. Retrieved from https://obamawhitehouse.archives.gov/the-press-office/2012/06/15/remarks-president-immigration

Public Law 47–126. (1882). Chinese Exclusion Act of 1882. *Loc.gov*. Retrieved from www.loc.gov/law/help/statutes-at-large/47th-congress/session-1/c47s1ch126.pdf

Public Law 64–301. (1917). Asiatic Barred Zone Act of 1917. *Loc.gov*. Retrieved from www.loc.gov/law/help/statutes-at-large/64th-congress/session-2/c64s2ch29.pdf

Public Law 68–139. (1924). Immigration Act of 1924. *Loc.gov*. Retrieved from www.loc.gov/law/help/statutes-at-large/68th-congress/session-1/c68s1ch190.pdf

Public Law 89–236. (1965). Immigration and Nationality Act of 1965 (Also known as the Hart-Celler Act). *Govinfo.gov*. Retrieved from www.govinfo.gov/content/pkg/STATUTE-79/pdf/STATUTE-79-Pg911.pdf

Public Law 99–603. (1986). *Immigration and Nationality Act, also cited as the Immigration Reform and Control Act of 1986*. Retrieved from www.govinfo.gov/content/pkg/STATUTE-100/pdf/STATUTE-100-Pg3445.pdf

Public Law 104–208. (1996). *Omnibus Consolidated Appropriations Act, 1997*. Retrieved from www.govinfo.gov/content/pkg/PLAW-104publ208/pdf/PLAW-104publ208.pdf

Public Law 107–56. (2001). Uniting and strengthening America by providing appropriate tools required to Intercept and Obstruct Terrorism Act (USA *Patriot Act*). *Congress.gov*. Retrieved from www.congress.gov/107/plaws/publ56/PLAW-107publ56.pdf

Public Law 107–73. (2002). The Enhanced Border Security and Visa Entry Reform Act of 2002. *Congress.gov*. Retrieved from www.congress.gov/107/plaws/publ173/PLAW-107publ173.pdf

Public Law 107–296. (2002). Homeland Security Act of 2002. *Department of Homeland Security.gov*. Retrieved from www.dhs.gov/sites/default/files/publications/hr_5005_enr.pdf

Roberts, L. (2018). The facts on DACA. *Factcheck.org*. Retrieved from www.factcheck.org/2018/01/the-facts-on-daca/

Romo, R. (1993). Responses to Mexican immigration, 1910–1930. In M. R. Ornelas (Ed.), *Beyond 1848: Readings in the modern Chicano historical experience* (pp. 115–135). Dubuque, IA: Kendall/Hunt Publishing Company.

Sanchez, G., & Romero, M. (2010). Critical race theory in the United States sociology of immigration. *Sociology Compass*, 4(9), 799–788.

Sandmeyer, E. C. (1991). *The anti-Chinese movement in California*. Champaign, IL: University of Illinois Press.

Seller, M. S. (1982). Historical perspectives on American immigration policy: Case studies and current implications. *Law and Contemporary Problems*, 45(2), 137–162.

Shrestha, L. B., & Heisler, E. J. (2011). The changing demographic profile of the United States. *Congressional Research Service*. Retrieved from www.fas.org/sgp/crs/misc/RL32701.pdf

Supremecourt.gov. (2017). *Syllabus: Trump, president of the United States, et al. v. Hawaii et al.* Retrieved from www.supremecourt.gov/opinions/17pdf/17-965_h315.pdf

Supremecourt.gov. (2018). *Trump, president of the United States, et al. v. Hawaii et al.* Retrieved from www.supremecourt.gov/opinions/17pdf/17-965_h315.pdf

Supremecourt.gov. (2020). *Syllabus: Department of Homeland Security et al. v. Regents of the University of California et al.* Retrieved from www.supremecourt.gov/opinions/19pdf/18-587_5ifl.pdf

Takaki, R. (1989). *Strangers from a different shore: A history of Asian Americans*. Boston, MA: Little, Brown and Company.

Travel.State.gov. (n.d.). *Presidential proclamation 9645 and presidential proclamation 9983*. Retrieved

Trump, D. J. (2017a). *Executive order 13767: Border security and immigration enforcement improvements*. Retrieved from www.whitehouse.gov/presidential-actions/executive-order-border-security-immigration-enforcement-improvements/

Trump, D. J. (2017b). *Executive order 13768: Enhancing public safety in the interior of the United States*. Retrieved from www.whitehouse.gov/presidential-actions/executive-order-enhancing-public-safety-interior-united-states/

Trump, D. J. (2017c). *Executive order 13769: Protecting the Nation from Foreign terrorists entry into the United States*. Retrieved from www.whitehouse.gov/presidential-actions/executive-order-protecting-nation-foreign-terrorist-entry-united-states/

Trump, D. J. (2020a). *Proclamation on maintaining enhanced vetting capabilities and process for detecting attempted entry into the United States by terrorists or other public safety threats*. Retrieved from www.whitehouse.gov/presidential-actions/proclamation-improving-enhanced-vetting-capabilities-processes-detecting-attempted-entry/

Trump, D. J. (2020b). *Proclamation 10014: Suspension of entry of immigrants who present a risk to the United States labor market during the recovery following the 2019 novel coronavirus breakout*. Retrieved from www.whitehouse.gov/presidential-actions/proclamation-suspending-entry-aliens-present-risk-u-s-labor-market-following-coronavirus-outbreak/

Unites States v. Texas. (2016). *Oyez*. Retrieved from www.oyez.org/cases/2015/15-674

Uschan, M. V. (2003). *The transcontinental railroad: Landmark events in American history*. New York, NY: Gareth Stevens Publishing.

U.S. Citizens and Immigration Services. (n.d.). *Legislation from1901–1940*. Retrieved from www.schundler.net/Legislation%201901-1940.pdf

U.S. Citizenship and Immigration Services. (2014). *2014 executive actions on immigration*. Retrieved from www.uscis.gov/archive/2014-executive-actions-on-immigration

Van Nuys, F. (2002). *Americanizing the West: Race, immigrants and citizenship, 1890–1930*. Lawrence, KS: University of Kansas Press.

Vespa, J. (2019). The graying of America: More older adults than kids by 2035. *Census.gov*. Retrieved from www.census.gov/library/stories/2018/03/graying-america.html

Waslin, M. (2011). *The secure communities program: Unanswered questions and continuing concerns, American immigration council: Immigration policy center special report*. Retrieved from www.americanimmigrationcouncil.org/sites/default/files/research/SComm_Exec_Summary_112911.pdf

Watermark.Silverchaor.com. (n.d.). *The Workingmen's party of California, 1877–1882*. Retrieved from https://online.ucpress.edu/ch/article-abstract/55/1/58/30422/The-Workingmen-s-Party-of-California-1877-1882?redirectedFrom=PDF

Whitehouse. (2017). *Statement by the president on Cuban immigration policy*. Retrieved from https://obamawhitehouse.archives.gov/the-press-office/2017/01/12/statement-president-cuban-immigration-policy

Whitehouse.gov. (2020). Immigration. *The White House*. Retrieved from www.whitehouse.gov/issues/immigration/

Whitehouse.gov. (2021a). Presidential actions. *The White House*. Retrieved from www.whitehouse.gov/briefing-room/presidential-actions/

Whitehouse.gov. (2021b). Proclamation on ending discriminatory bans on entry to the United States. *The White House*. Retrieved from www.whitehouse.gov/briefing-room/presidential-actions/2021/01/20/proclamation-ending-discriminatory-bans-on-entry-to-the-united-states/

Whitehouse Office of the Press Security. (2014). *Fact sheet: Immigration accountability executive action*. Retrieved from https://obamawhitehouse.archives.gov/the-press-office/2014/11/20/fact-sheet-immigration-accountability-executive-action

Wolgin, P. E. (2014). By the numbers: Every president since Eisenhower has taken executive action on immigration. *Center for American Progress*. Retrieved from www.americanprogress.org/issues/immigration/news/2014/10/06/98321/by-the-numbers-every-president-since-eisenhower-has-taken-executive-action-on-immigration/

Workers, N. A. (2017). *NASW code of ethics (Guide to everyday professional conduct of social workers)*. Washington, DC: NASW Press.

Zia, H. (2001). *Asian American dreams: The emergence of an American people*. New York, NY: Farrar, Straus and Giroux.

CHAPTER 6
Social Welfare Benefits Programs and Social Control

What Is Social Welfare?

Social welfare, a subset of social policy, is a system of governmental laws, programs, benefits, and services that are designed to protect against the broadly distributed risks to income and general well-being inherent in a market economy (Hacker, 2002, p. 34; Richan, 1988). Examples of broadly distributed risks include economic downturns, employment downsizing, outsourcing of work to overseas labor markets, retirement, compromised and/or limited access to resources, ill-health, disability, and dependency (Baldwin, 2010; Blau & Abramovitz, 2009; Day, 2009; Hacker, 2002; Hout & Cumberworth, 2012). Protections include but certainly are not limited to unemployment insurance, social security, supplemental nutritional aid programs, supplemental security income, Medicare/Medicaid, and assistance programs for needy families. All of these protections come under the auspices of the United States social welfare system (Baldwin, 2010; Day, 2009; Hacker, 2002; Roberts, 1992, 1996).

Social Welfare and Social Work

As a profession whose primary mission is to enhance human well-being, with particular attention to those who are vulnerable, oppressed, and living in poverty, social work is inextricably linked to social welfare (Jansson, 2009). For instance, social workers were instrumental in the development of the United States social welfare system. Furthermore, the majority of social workers practice in the social service agencies that compose the United States social welfare system. In doing so, they help their clientele on several levels, including direct service work to help solve problems (micro), making referrals to suitable programs (micro), and engaging in case and policy/cause advocacy (micro/mezzo/macro) (Jansson, 2009; Kirst-Ashman & Hull, 2014).

The importance of the relationship between social welfare and social work is reflected in its presence in the National Association of Social Workers (NASW) Code of Ethics as one of a social worker's responsibilities to the broader responsibility. Listed as 6.01 (Social Welfare) of the NASW Code of Ethics, social workers are expected to promote the general welfare of society, from local to global levels, and the development of people, their communities, and their environments. Social workers should also advocate for living conditions conducive to the fulfillment of basic human needs and should promote social, economic, political, and cultural values and institutions that are compatible with the realization of social justice (National Association of Social Workers, 2018).

Social Welfare Ambivalence

Beginning with the English colonies' adoption of legislation patterned after the Elizabethan Poor Laws and the Law of Settlement and Removal, America has always had some provision for providing assistance for the needy (Jansson, 2009; Katz, 1983). Yet right from the very first colonial poor laws, there has been an enduring ambivalence toward providing assistance to particular categories of the needy (Jansson, 2009;

DOI: 10.4324/9781003023708-6

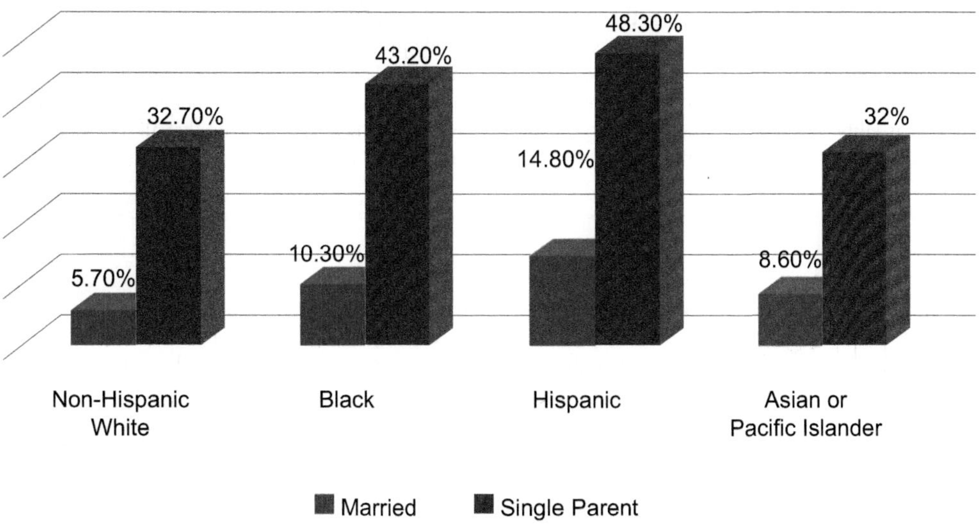

Figure 6.1 Percentage of Children in Poverty by Family Structure and Race/Ethnicity, 2017
Source: Child Trends: Children in Poverty 2017. Retrieved www.childtrends.org/indicators/children-in-poverty

Quigley, 1997). Perennially victimized by this ambivalence are unmarried single mothers with dependent children, whose poverty rates are among the highest of any group in the United States (Children's Defense Fund, 2018).

The historical and current ambivalence toward unmarried single mothers (as opposed to widows with children) is reflected in the structural characteristics of the social welfare benefits programs designed specifically for mothers and dependent children. These structural characteristics include a lack of universal access and comprehensiveness and the centrality of services, as well as coercive mechanisms for social control. Consequently, despite delivering many of the same benefits as other developed nations, the United States social welfare benefits programs for mothers and dependent children have not succeeded as well as those other nations in reducing poverty and inequality (Beland et al., 2014; Jansson, 2009).

The structural characteristics of the United States social welfare benefits programs for mothers and dependent children have not developed without thought. Rather, they have evolved slowly and deliberately from the colonial poor laws and the Protestant work ethic values and Puritan morality that underpinned them (Baldwin, 2010; Day, 2009; Katz, 1983; Trattner, 1999). These poor laws recognized a collective responsibility to aid the needy, particularly given the vagaries of colonial life. However, Protestant work ethic values, reinforced by Puritan morality, dictated that clear distinctions be made between those who were worthy and those who were unworthy of assistance (Handler & Hasenfeld, 1997).

In this subjective distinction, worthy or unworthy was not determined by one's economic conditions or need. Instead, it was the product of Puritan morality that bestowed worthiness on virtuous behavior as defined by compliance with dominant cultural norms and deviance on behavior that was noncompliant (Baldwin, 2010; Handler & Hasenfeld, 1997). In the prevalent patriarchal society that privileges White, middle, and upper class, with heterosexual family arrangements considered the ideal family structure, unmarried mothers have always been the epitome of the unworthy poor, particularly those of color.

How this perspective on unmarried mothers shaped and affected the three most important social welfare benefits programs serving mothers and dependent children in the past 100 plus years is examined in this chapter. These social welfare benefits programs are the Mothers' Pension (1911–1935); Aid to Dependent Children (ADC) Aid to Families with Dependent Children (/AFDC) (1935–1996), and Temporary Assistance to Needy Families (1996 to the present). The conceptual lenses for this chapter are intersectionality and critical race theory (see Chapter 4). As will be demonstrated, the intersection of race, gender, class, and immigration status are still powerfully present in the development and effect of the benefits programs on unmarried single mothers' lives. Race has also loomed large in the ubiquitous use of negative racial stereotyping to, among other things, limit Black women's access to benefits programs as well as vilify them as immoral and irresponsible. It was also the basis for ensuring that all the benefits programs had a social control mechanism for regulating recipients' behavior.

Mothers' Pension, 1911–1935

No single issue of the progressive era galvanized as much public and political support as the call for a mothers' pension (Skocpol, 1992). Prompted by the advocacy of politicized White middle-class female reformers in sympathy with poor women, the call was in response to the plight of families who had lost the financial support of a male breadwinner (Leff, 1973). Apropos the social conditions of the late 19th- and early 20th-century industrialized and urbanized United States, it was a concern that was indeed warranted. Men, women, and children worked long hours for relatively low wages with little protection against injury or unemployment in the nation's factories, mills, and mines. Also, as a result of death and other unforeseen circumstances it was all too common for families to lose the financial support of a male breadwinner. Without this financial support, mothers became the family's primary breadwinner and had few alternatives other than to work outside of the home to stave off destitution. In turn, children were left unsupervised for long periods, or they too joined the workforce, which happened in large numbers (Katz, 1983). Indeed, the 1900 census revealed that one out of every six children between 10 and 15 years old worked to support their families (Zelizer, 1994). Even with work, low wages and periodic recessions still resulted in thousands of mothers being forced into almshouses with their children, or their children being placed in orphanages, and in extreme cases being abandoned (Mink, 1996). Hence, family dislocation because of maternal poverty was a common feature of midwestern and northeastern industrialized cities (Skocpol, 1992).

Alarmed by the wide-ranging impact of maternal poverty on children, women's groups and progressives drew on maternalist and child-saving sentiments as a political platform to call for a solution to this predicament (Ward, 2005). With the military pension as a model, the proposed solution was a mothers' pension. The pension would be a publicly funded grant or payment to "deserving" single mothers who had lost the financial support of a male breadwinner, their husband. The pension would have a threefold purpose: It would help to stem the tide of family dislocation; it would reward mothers who stayed at home with their children; and it would improve the conditions for children by keeping them in a supervised home and thus out of the workplace, orphanage, or delinquency.

Informed by a 19th-century romanticized ideal of motherhood that all mothers were supposed to aspire to, the middle-class proponents of the mothers' pension posited that mothers and the home represented the highest form of civilization (Baldwin, 2010; Leff, 1973). It was mothers and home life that were at the heart of a child's healthy development. Indeed, mothers were akin to soldiers and nurses, serving the nation by raising children to be ideal and productive citizens (Marten, 2004; Reef, 2002). Thus, "worthy" mothers, specifically widows, were deserving of public support when they lacked a male breadwinner (Katz, 1983; Skocpol, 1992, p. 424). With this support, poor families, many of them in the late 19th- and early 20th-century first- or second-generation eastern and southern European immigrants, could aspire to middle-class respectability. Largely excluded from the discourse and organizational efforts surrounding the call for a mothers' pension were the voices of Black progressives (Baldwin, 2010; Constance-Huggins, 2011). This was an exclusion that came despite the fact that Black widows had by far the highest labor force participation of any group of widows (Kleinberg, 2006). In 1890, for example, four out of five Black widows between the ages of 24 and 44 were in the workforce (Kleinberg, 2006, p. 30). In addition, even by age 65 when there was almost no labor force participation for White widows, three-fifths of Black widows were still working (Kleinberg, 2006, p. 30). In constructing the mothers' pension along White middle- and upper-class standards and norms, Baldwin (2010) argues that women's groups ignored the reality of Black family life. It was a reality shaped by the legacy of slavery and Jim Crow legislation. Within this reality, Black women and men were equally expected to toil in the labor force in much the same way as they had in slavery, as exploited and low-wage agricultural or domestic labor (Baldwin, 2010; Constance-Huggins, 2011). Black women and men were the preferred labor force, and Black women, even if widowed, were compelled as a matter of course to remain in the workforce. They had neither the choice nor structural support to do otherwise (Baldwin, 2010).

The exclusion of Blacks aside, women's groups and the influential women's journal the *Delineator* were able to garner a tidal wave of public support for the mothers' pension (Hard, 1913). This support came from areas of the public as disparate as the trade union movement, newspapers, suffragettes, and the Women's Christian Temperance Union (Goodwin, 1997; Kleinberg, 2006).

Although it had widespread support, there were some dissenting voices against the idea of a mothers' pension. Among the dissenters were business owners afraid of losing labor, and more tellingly the influential Charity Organization Society (COS) and the county superintendents of the poor (Katz, 1983). The COS and county superintendents argued that the mothers' pension and the abolition of indoor relief would create unjust hardships for the worthy poor and foment social discontent (Katz, 1983, p. 191). The COS also believed that as an outdoor relief, the mothers' pension would encourage laziness and dependency. The dissent of COS was not entirely surprising given that indoor relief (institutionalization) and the Protestant work ethic values that underpinned it had been the dominant form of poor relief for more than 250 years. In keeping with Protestant work ethic values, the purpose of indoor relief was to encourage self-reliance and discourage laziness and dependency. Thus, poor relief recipients had to work for their benefits, which were purposely low to discourage dependency (Hansan, 2011). Given this, the mothers' pension and its payment for staying at home were antithetical to the Protestant work ethic values of indoor relief. Ironically, the COS would have a significant role to play in the administration of the mothers' pension (Hansan, 2011).

Despite the few sources of dissent, women's groups and other progressives pushed ahead to get political support for the nationwide enactment of the mothers' pension. To this end, groups such as the General Federation of Women's Clubs, the National Child Labor Committee, and the National Congress of Mothers waged an incredibly successful state-by-state legislative campaign (Kleinberg, 2006; Leff, 1973).

As a result of the campaign, the mothers' pension was one of the items on the agenda of the first-ever White House Conference on the Care of Dependent Children in 1909. Hosted by President Theodore Roosevelt, the theme of the conference was opposition to the institutionalization of dependent and neglected children. In the conference, statistical evidence of the extent of the plight of destitute mothers and dependent children without a male head or breadwinner were presented to President Roosevelt (Skocpol et al., 1993; Ward, 2005). The evidence submitted at the conference revealed that almost 100,000 dependent children were placed in orphanages and children's homes (Ward, 2005). Another 50,000 dependent children were in foster care, and 25,000 in the juvenile justice system (Ward, 2005). Shocked by the findings and swayed by the appeals of progressives such as Lillian Wald, Florence Kelly, and Jane Addams, Roosevelt resolved that no child should be made to leave home because of poverty alone. In doing so, he gave tacit support for the mothers' pension (Skocpol et al., 1993).

Implementation

Two years after White House Conference on the Care of Dependent Children, in 1911, the first statewide Mothers' Pension Law in the United States was passed by the state legislature of Illinois. By 1919, 39 of the 48 states in the union had passed similar laws. This number increased to 46 of the 48 states by 1931 (Skocpol, 1992).

While remarkable for the speed of its enactment across the nation and its national scope, in practice, the mothers' pension had no unifying national formula. As a result, most states did not assume direct responsibility for administering it. Instead, they passed legislation allowing but not mandating local counties to use public funds to implement mothers' pensions. When counties did implement the pension, as most did, administrative responsibility was in the hands of the Juvenile Court system, a locally appointed board, or the COSs that had so vehemently opposed it. In each case, the structural characteristics of the mothers' pension reflected local norms, values, and customs. Consequently, other than the understanding that the mothers' pension was a benefits program for widows, the conditions for access and continued eligibility varied from county to county, state to state, and region to region. For example, some counties and states expanded access to include divorced mothers, deserted mothers, and mothers whose husbands were institutionalized, as well as widows. In other cases, eligibility also included grandparents or legal guardians (Children's Bureau, 1922).

The category of motherhood, however, was only one part of the equation for access; county and states also wanted potential recipients of the mothers' pension to meet other criteria. Depending on the county or state, these criteria included having exhausted all other possible forms of assistance, having no personal items of worth, and not owning real estate. Paradoxically, given the purpose of the mothers' pension, five states—Illinois, Minnesota, Ohio, Oregon, and Washington—required that potential recipients be in the workforce (Children's Bureau, 1922; Goodwin, 1997).

Ethnicity, Citizenship, Race, and Social Control

In different regions of the country, ethnicity, citizenship status, and race all played a significant role in determining access to the mothers' pension. In the western states where most of the mothers' pension programs were administrated locally, Native Americans, Asians, and Mexicans were largely denied access because of existing ethnic discrimination (Ward, 2005). Conversely, in the midwestern and northeastern states, eastern and southern European immigrant mothers deemed worthy were granted access to the mothers' pension, but it came with significant social control. Primary among these controls was the requirement that they become citizens within a given period and assimilate fully into the American way of life, meaning they had to discontinue cultural practices that were seen as incongruent with the culture of the United States, including type of foods eaten and multigenerational living arrangements (Grossberg & Tomlins, 2011). Other social controls were the demand for adherence to moralistic codes of conduct, which included church attendance and being a teetotaler and celibate. Lastly, they had to acquiesce to the monitoring and directives of caseworkers and visiting nurses who enforced adherence to American standards (Grossberg & Tomlins, 2011).

In the Jim Crow southern states, where the majority of the nation's Black population was located, 90% of mothers' pension programs were administered locally, with 60% having no state supervision (Ward, 2005). Reproducing and reinforcing existing Jim Crow practices, southern localities had criterion for access that were so stringent that Black mothers in effect were systematically excluded from the mothers' pension program (Ward, 2005). Among these criteria was the suitable home provision, which was an arbitrary determination of whether a mother was of good moral standing and the home in a good state of repair. Good moral standing was a euphuism for whether or not the Black mother was single or a widow. If single, then she would be deemed of low moral character; thus, making her ineligible. Likewise, if a widow and her home were in a state of disrepair, she would be made similarly ineligible because of poor housekeeping standards (Ward, 2005).

Indeed, so proficient nationwide was the exclusion of Blacks that even with higher levels of need than their White counterparts, Black families composed only 3% of mothers' pension recipients nationwide in 1931. Of this 3%, half of the recipients were in just two states: Ohio and Pennsylvania (Ward, 2005).

Legacy

In evaluating the relative merits of the mothers' pension, it would be true to say that between 1921 and 1931, families receiving mothers' pension grants doubled from 46,000 to 94,0000, affecting some 250,000 children. As suggested by Skocpol (1992), prior to the mothers' pension, these children would have been placed in an orphanage or foster care.

That said, overall, the mothers' pension did not deliver on its promise. For example, inadequate funding and restrictive eligibility accelerated rather than decreased the number of mothers working outside of the home. In fact, the number of mothers in the workforce did not decline until the enactment of the New Deal initiatives in 1935 (Leff, 1973). Likewise, the number of children in institutions because of maternal poverty also continued to rise instead of decreasing during the years that the mothers' pension was active. The trend reversed only after the passing of the Social Security Act of 1935. Next, while addressing the needs of widows, some 80% were recipients; the mothers' pension's scope was small, reaching only 6% of all single-mother households. Notably absent from coverage were single or divorced mothers who because of local norms and cultural values were considered "unworthy" of aid. Likewise, in its local application, the mothers' pension reproduced and reinforced the existing racial and ethnic hierarchy, effectively barring Black, Mexican, and Asian mothers. Finally, in handing over administration to local relief agencies, many of the worst aspects of the COS were inculcated into the mothers' pension selection process, most notably, an application procedure that was intrusive and morally judgmental of mothers, essentially dividing them into worthy or unworthy.

Nevertheless, as one of the slates of social policies coming out of the progressive era advocacy, the mothers' pension was a seminal social welfare benefits program. Among the factors that made it so was its demand for government involvement, even if at the state level, in protecting families against the loss of a breadwinner. The demand, which transformed the public's understanding of public welfare, was a forerunner for more encompassing social welfare reforms. These reforms would ask the government to not only protect families against the loss of a breadwinner but also against the vagaries of a market economy. As such, the mothers' pension served as a prototype for the 1935 Social Security Act's Aid to Dependent Children (Goodwin, 1997). The mothers' pension also, as Roberts (1996) suggests, helped to illuminate and shape the terms of the debate about single motherhood that still governs social welfare policy discussion today. In this ongoing debate, middle- and upper-class perceptions of ideal motherhood is a reoccurring theme in determining which mothers in time of need are seen as "worthy" or "unworthy" of relief.

Aid to Dependent Children/Aid to Families With Dependent Children, 1935–1996

Following a decade of prosperity that saw the widespread availability of consumer goods, increased home ownership, and a public turning away from social problems, the stock market crashed in 1929. The crash ushered in an unprecedented depression. Although the United States had experienced several recessions subsequent to its rapid industrialization, the market had always been able to recover without government intervention in a relatively short period. The 1929 depression, however, was different in terms of scale, severity, and impact (Watkins, 2009). Not only was it the deepest and longest-lasting depression of the western industrialized world, but also the most significant, touching every financial institution and all Americans, regardless of demographics. By the time the depression reached its nadir in 1933, the national unemployment rate had climbed to its highest point, 25% (United States Bureau of the Census, 1949). More than half the banks had been closed by the Federal Reserve because of a lack of funds, reducing them from 27,000 to 14,000 (Federal Reserve Bulletin, 1937; Richardson, 2007). Asset values declined, businesses closed, and homes and savings were lost. In addition, soup kitchens, bread lines, and tent cities became commonplace across the nation as the sheer level of destitution overwhelmed the capacity of the public and charity organizations (Watkins, 2009).

At the outset of this Great Depression, there were calls for federal intervention to stem its wide-ranging impact, not least because the federal government was the only institution with the resources to do so. However, Herbert Hoover, the president at the time, resisted these calls, placing his faith instead on the free market to resolve the depression (Watkins, 2009).

Hoover's faith in the free market to resolve the crisis cost him his presidency in 1931 when the American people did not reelect him, but instead voted Franklin D. Roosevelt (FDR) into office. Roosevelt, a son of privilege, a former New York state senator, governor, and vice-presidential candidate, was a believer in progressive government (Leuchtenburg, 1963). Once in office, FDR signaled his intent to have a progressive government that as part of its responsibility would ensure the general welfare of all Americans. To this end, FDR proposed, and Congress passed legislation allowing for sweeping economic reforms, commonly known as the New Deal. Central to the New Deal was what Roosevelt called the 3R's: relief, recovery, and reform (Leuchtenburg, 1963).

The relief was the immediate policy and program action that FDR took to halt the economy's downward spiral. These policies included the Emergency Banking Act, which closed insolvent banks and kept opened only solvent banks. Another policy was the Federal Emergency Act, which gave immediate help in the form of cash payments to those in need. Finally, a series of programs were designed to provide temporary jobs to unemployed adults. These programs included the Civil Works Administration (CWA) and the Civilian Conservation Corps (CCC). Both programs provided employment opportunities for the long-term unemployed (Leuchtenburg, 1963).

The recovery was stimulated by the creation of temporary programs to stimulate consumer demand. The Agriculture Adjustment Act (AAA), for example, taxed food processors and then gave the proceeds to farmers as payment not to grow food, thus decreasing the supply and in turn increasing the price. Somewhat differently, the Tennessee Valley Authority (TVA) was created to build dams and provide cheap hydroelectric power. The Works Progress Administration (WPA) provided long-term government jobs building schools and other public works projects, and the Home Owners Loan Corporation (HOLC) prevented homelessness by providing loans to help homeowners who were in danger of foreclosure (Leuchtenburg, 1963). (See Chapter 7 for a more detailed discussion.)

The reform was the most profound of the R's in that it was the implementation of permanent programs to avoid another Great Depression and to protect citizens against economic disaster. By doing so, not only were the ideals of the progressives who had fought so hard for this moment realized, but also a seismic shift in the role of government occurred, a shift that would see the federal government permanently take on the responsibility for the welfare of citizens (Leuchtenburg, 1963). It is no surprise, then, that there was significant conservative opposition to the New Deal programs. Indeed, there were several legal challenges to the New Deal.

Despite these challenges, FDR was able to enact the heart of his reform policies, although often with a number of concessions. These concessions included the formation of the Securities and Exchange Commission (SEC), with the express purpose of monitoring stock market activity and ensuring that no fraud or insider trading takes place. Prior to the SEC, there was no such monitoring of the stock market. As well as the SEC, there was the establishment of the Federal Deposit Insurance Corporation (FDIC), which provided insurance for depositors' money in the banks, and the enactment of the National Labor Relations Act and National Labor Relations Board (NLRA/NLRB). The act and the board it created helped unions and enforced labor law and championed fair business practices (Leuchtenburg, 1963).

The centerpiece of the reform legislation, however, was the Social Security Act (SSA) of 1935. The stated purpose of the SSA was to provide for the general welfare by establishing a system of federal old-age benefits. Adequate state provisions were also established for various categories of the needy, including aged persons, blind persons, and dependent and crippled children. Likewise, administration was put in place for maternal and child welfare, public health, and unemployment compensation laws (Our Documents, 2015).

Implementation

In 1935, Title IV of the SSA created the Aid to Dependent Children (ADC) program. As stated by Congress, the purpose of the program was to furnish financial assistance to needy children who were living with relatives in family homes but were deprived of normal support or care (Alling & Leisy, 1950). Initially, ADC supplemented the existing state mothers' pension program, but eventually superseded it and became the primary assistance program for dependent children. Though ADC began as a relatively small benefits program within the context of the SSA, in its 60 years of existence, it became arguably the most controversial and demonized of the SSAs benefits programs. Its conservative critics accused ADC of encouraging dependency and single motherhood and undermining the moral fabric of society. Its liberal and radical critics accused ADC of perpetuating a system of White racial hegemony. These counter criticisms played themselves out in the court of public opinion in which race and carefully crafted narratives and images of ADC receipts would be used to repeal AFDC and replace it with TANF.

Yet when ADC began, there were few signs it would become the lightning rod for such vociferous criticism. The brainchild of social workers Grace Abbot and Katherine Lenroot, ADC was conceptualized as a program that would use the highest social work standards (Mink, 1996). In doing so, it would aid families and dependent children who were without the economic support of a male breadwinner because of death or other unforeseen circumstances. Proposed services would include personal casework, a sufficiently generous stipend to live a healthy life, and federal oversight to prevent state or local discrimination against applicants based on marital status or race. However, Abbot and Lenroot's plan, which they lobbied hard for inclusion in the SSA, was revised and significantly pared down by the Committee on Economic Security (CES). FDR charged the CES with proposing benefits programs that would decrease dependency and need for citizens. Congress would further revise the plan in committee, where provisions such as federal oversight of the program to prevent discrimination would be omitted at the request of the states.

Thus, the final version of ADC was a federal grant-aid program. Participation by the states was voluntary. If a state chose to participate, however, they had to submit a plan for approval of the federal government's Social Security Board. The plan had to outline the administrative structure that was in place to meet federal stipulations related to fair and proper access and due process for all ADC-eligible children (Neubeck & Cazenave, 2001). If the plan was approved, the state was given a federal grant for one-third (33%) of the cost of their ADC program on a quarterly basis (Ross, 1985). Importantly, other than the relatively few federal government stipulations, states were given considerable discretion to determine ADC eligibility and the grants level.

Although state participation in ADC was gradual, by 1941 all but eight states had an ADC program. Nationwide, these programs provided assistance to some 925,00 children, tripling the 250,000 of the mothers' pension program just a decade earlier in 1931 (Alling & Leisy, 1950). Yet, as suggested by Gordon and Batlan (2011), in practice, ADC operated much like a private charity; states used their considerable discretion to disqualify applicants deemed unworthy on grounds such as single parenthood and/or race. States did this by devising eligibility requirements that were either open to subjective interpretation like the suitable home requirement or would knowingly disqualify applicants based on work history. Indeed, in the southern states, the requirement that only children in a suitable home could receive assistance was used to deny Black children access to ADC. Having a mother who had not worked, which was not the case for Black mothers, was also used as a requirement to deny Black children access to ADC. As a consequence, in the early years of ADC, the question of racism was always present, particularly given the high rates of Black children living in poverty (Baldwin, 2010).

However, a number of social developments brought marked changes to the character, size, and composition of ADC from the late 1930s to the 1962 amendments renaming it Aid to Families with Dependent Children (AFDC). In doing so, ADC went from a program primarily serving children of White widowed mothers to a program primarily serving single-parent, female-headed households with dependent children. This shift saw the question of gender, race, and social welfare enter the lexicon of public discourse, first at the state level and then at the national level. Underpinning this discourse would be the familiar theme of the "worthy" and "unworthy" poor (Gilens, 1999).

The first social development occurred with the 1939 SSA amendment creating the Survivors Insurance Program for widows whose deceased husband's job was covered by the SSA (SIP). With the creation of the program, eligible widows and children in the ADC program were transferred to the SIP (DeWitt, 2010). Moreover, as a larger number of jobs came under the umbrella of SSA, the SIP and not ADC or ADFC would be the primary benefits program for widows and dependent children. As noted earlier, the result was that ADC went from being a program primarily serving the children of widows to one primarily serving children in single-parent households. An example of the distinction is that, unlike ADC, the SIP program was administered directly by the federal government and therefore not subject to state-level discretion on eligibility, benefits level, or rules of participation (Blank & Blum, 1997; DeWitt, 2010; Mink, 1996).

In addition to the SIP, the late 1940s saw a dramatic change in the nation's divorce rate and marriage patterns, resulting in all-time peaks in divorce rates and out-of-wedlock births. Furthermore, World War II causalities added to the existing number of half orphans and full orphans. Indeed, in 1948, approximately 3.9 million children under 18 were living with a single parent. Another 1.3 million were with relatives and half a million in an institution or with unrelated persons. No surprise, then, that in 1948, the number of ADC families in which the mother was divorced, separated, or single was significantly higher than those headed by widows (Alling & Leisy, 1950).

Also, in the 1940s, increasing numbers of women entered the workforce, a trend that continued in the 1950s and 1960s. With this trend, more and more children were placed in childcare. As a result, public assumptions about women's work, childcare, and the actual merits of assisting children of working mothers began to change (Spitzer, 2012a).

In addition, the SSA amendment in 1950 expanded benefits to include the mother as well as the children. Further amendments were passed in 1962. The primary purpose of these amendments was the rehabilitation of recipients by way of expanded services to promote work. The services emphasized vocational training, day care, and counseling. To assist states with the administration of services to promote work, the federal government provided financing for 75% of the cost (Spitzer, 2012a). As a result of the 1962 amendment, ADC was renamed Aid to Families with Dependent Children (AFDC) (Walker & Vatter, 1997, p. 206).

Compounding these social developments were significant demographic shifts. These shifts were the result of the second great migration of rural Black Americans from the Jim Crow South to major western, midwestern, and northeastern cities in the years between 1941 and 1970. Many of the families needed assistance, which was much more readily accessible in these cities than in the southern states they had left (Herrick & Stuart, 2005).

Collectively, the social developments and demographic changes contributed to a precipitous increase in both expenditures and the number of families receiving ADC and then AFDC (Blank & Blum, 1997; Herrick & Stuart, 2005; Spitzer, 2012a). There was also a significant change in the racial composition of the recipient population. For example, in 1938, 12 months before the SSA amendments created SIP, 13.8% of the children receiving ADC were Black. By 1961, 44% of all the ADC cases were Black families (Soule & Zylan, 1997, p. 736).

Displeased with increasing state expenditures and the changing demographic composition of its recipients, ADC drew the attention of state legislators. Determined to rein in costs, state legislators went about reforming the program's eligibility requirements to reduce the representation of Black, unmarried, divorced, and deserted women among the recipient population (Soule & Zylan, 1997, p. 737). Cost containment aside, underpinning the desire to reform ADC eligibility requirements was an emerging narrative that portrayed recipients, particularly Black single mothers, as sexually promiscuous, irresponsible, and lacking in morality (Baldwin, 2010; Neubeck & Cazenave, 2001). Thus, even in a time of need, they represented the epitome of the "unworthy" and "undeserving" poor. And so, it was that this narrative underwrote a spate of state legislation that among other things changed eligibility requirements to disqualify unmarried mothers, who nationwide were disproportionately Black (Soule & Zylan, 1997). Other legislation included the suitable home requirement, man-in-the house/substitute father stipulations, special investigative units, and residency and work requirements.

Suitable Home Requirement

Between 1952 and 1960 the suitable home requirement as a condition for ADC eligibility were strengthened or adopted in several states: Georgia, Mississippi, Virginia, Michigan, Arkansas, Texas, Florida, Tennessee, and Louisiana (Gooden, 2003). The suitable home requirement acted as a form of social control and moral policing and allowed caseworkers to visit the homes of ADC recipients at any time to question family, neighbors, and friends about the household. It also allowed for the disqualification of a recipient on grounds as arbitrary and subjective as moral suitability, that is, having a child out of wedlock. Of all the states that used the suitable homes laws, Louisiana, where Black single mothers composed 66%

of the approximately 100,000 ADC recipients, was particularly draconian in its use. Indeed, in 1960, Louisiana's Department of Public Welfare cut 5,991 families with some 22,000 thousand children from the state ADC program using the suitable home law. Ninety percent of these children were Black (Briggs, 2012).

Man-in-the-House/Substitute Father Stipulations

A number of states adopted the man-in-the-house/substitute father stipulation, which denied ADC to families where the mother was suspected of illicitly cohabiting or consorting with a man. To monitor families in which this was suspected, caseworkers were authorized to make unannounced visits and to question family, friends, and neighbors. They would also check the house for signs of male clothing or other items. Again, underpinning this stipulation was the narrative of promiscuity and moral unsuitability (Baldwin, 2010; Neubeck & Cazenave, 2001; Soule & Zylan, 1997).

Special Investigative Units

Critical to the man-in-the house/substitute father stipulations were special investigative units, which states and large cities established to root out the presence of a man in the home. By 1962, eight states and 18 large cities had established special investigative units (Soule & Zylan, 1997, p. 737). As with caseworkers, special investigative units could make unannounced visits to a recipient's home; conduct midnight raids; and question relatives, friends, and family to monitor and ensure compliance.

Residency Requirements

A residency requirement, which was commonly implemented across all states, denied ADC applicants who had not lived in the state for a stated amount of time. In the southern states, the residency requirement was used as a mechanism for denying poor families the ability to cross state lines for possibly improved conditions. For the states outside of the South, it also discouraged migration from the South (Soule & Zylan, 1997).

Work Requirements

Work requirements as a condition of ADC eligibility had been in place from the first ADC amendments in 1950. However, the 1962 amendment and the development of workfare in the mid-1960s saw a significant increase in the demand that ADC and then AFDC recipients work for their benefits in an effort to enhance self-reliance and lessen dependence. By 1967, 28 states had some form of work requirement for AFDC recipients (Soule & Zylan, 1997).

Fighting Back

The draconian actions of states across the nation did not, however, continue without political or legal challenge. Drawing inspiration from the Civil Rights Movement, the mid-1960s saw welfare recipients begin to organize themselves into grassroots advocacy groups (Jaynes, 2005). These welfare recipients were primarily Black women who were intent on challenging what they saw as unfair treatment and stigmatization. With the use of classic confrontational and advocacy methods, these grassroots welfare advocacy groups staged demonstrations, marches, and sit-ins to bring attention to the plight of welfare recipients (Bailis, 1974).

Local advocacy efforts soon grew into a national movement as a result of a couple of key developments. One of them was the Frances Fox Piven and Richard Cloward strategy. The strategy asked welfare recipients to overload the public welfare system. By overloading the system, Piven and Fox posited it would precipitate a crisis that would lead to a replacement of the welfare with a national system of a guaranteed income. In doing so, poverty would be ended. The second key development was the decision of civil rights activist Dr. George Wiley to join forces and support welfare recipients from Cleveland. These welfare recipients were marching to the state capital in Columbus, Ohio, in protest. So successful was the march that similar marches were planned in 20 other cities across the country (Jaynes, 2005).

The success of these marches precipitated the creation of a national movement, which resulted in the establishment of the National Welfare Rights Organization (NWRO) in 1967. Dr. Wiley was selected as its director, and in collaboration with civil rights organizations, churches, social work groups, and labor organizations, the NWRO became the national voice of welfare recipients' rights (Jaynes, 2005).

The NWRO's earliest strategy was organizing welfare recipients into pressure groups. These pressure groups would stage sit-ins and protests specifically aimed at welfare reform. The NWRO'S first major lobbying effort was against 1967 work incentive provisions that were written into the Social Security Amendments of 1967. The Work Incentive Program (WIP) was one of a number of new federal requirements looking to encourage self-sufficiency that included establishing paternity for AFDC children and allowing aid to go to unemployed male partners with a work history (Spitzer, 2012a). The Work Incentive Program (WIP) required states to establish employment and training programs for welfare recipients. Initially, the program was voluntary, but in 1971, it was made compulsory for welfare recipients with no special responsibilities in the home (Blank & Blum, 1997). In protest against the WIN program, the NWRO staged a number of high-profile sit-ins and demonstrations, the most notable being in the hearing room of the U.S Senate Committee on Finance in 1967. In the summer of 1968, the activities of the NWRO gained recognition when the leaders of the organization met with the United States Secretary of Health, Education and Welfare (Jaynes, 2005).

From 1969 through to 1973, the NWRO grew rapidly both in size and influence. They had an estimated 20,000 dues-paying members of the organization, serving the interests of approximately 75,000 families (West, 1981). The majority of members were poor Black women (Bailis, 1974). Politically, and with the support of 540 separate welfare rights organizations across the country, the NWRO expanded the push for welfare reform by adopting the Piven and Cloward strategy, which did indeed increase the welfare rolls significantly (Kornbluh, 1997). The NWRO leadership also had the ear of both President Lyndon Johnson's and President Richard Nixon's administrations. In fact, the NWRO received sizeable grants from

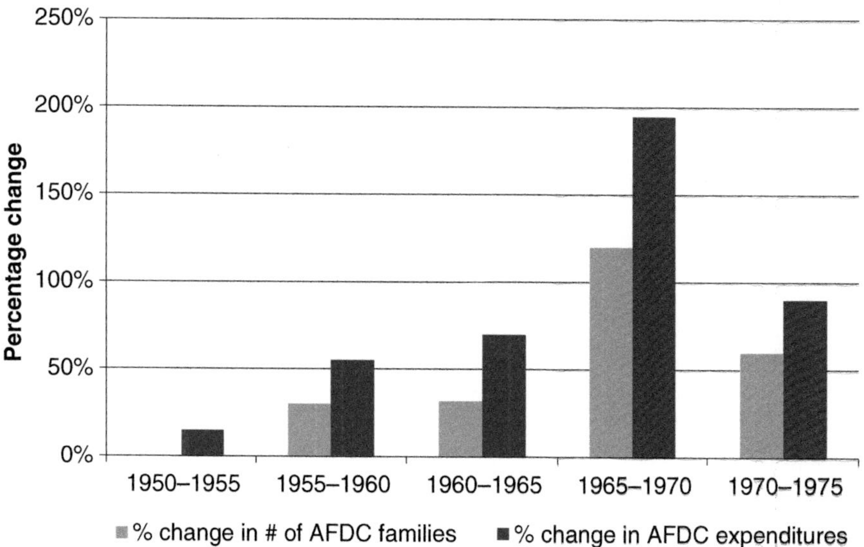

Figure 6.2 Change in AFDC 1950–1975

Source: Social Security Bulletin, Annual Statistical Supplement, various years the Johnson administration (Finkelman, 2009). Moreover, they negotiated with the Nixon administration on welfare reform, a negation that broke down over the question of a guaranteed minimum income (Finkelman, 2009). However, internal conflict that led to the resignation of Dr. Wiley, and the conservative and public backlash against welfare recipients began the road to the erosion of financial support and eventually bankruptcy (Finkelman, 2009). In its relatively short history, the NWROs accomplishments and legacy were substantial. They helped to get welfare benefits for tens of thousands of women who might not otherwise have received them. Moreover, they were influential in the improvement of public housing programs and the development nutrition and health program for mothers, children, and infants, programs such as Women's Infant and Children. Furthermore, they were the template for community organizations such as ACORN (Jaynes, 2005). Lastly, they in no small part influenced the legal challenges that were mounted against some of the draconian measures of ADFC.

Now firmly on the national stage, the question of AFDC became a contentious national concern because of its continued growth and spiraling costs, which reached its highest point in the years between 1965 and 1970.

A parallel development to the NWRO was the emergence of small-government conservatism in the Republican Party. The catalyst for this emergence was 1964 Republican presidential nominee Barry Goldwater. Goldwater, a senator from Arizona, was a fiscal conservative with libertarian leanings (Dallek, 1995; Goldberg, 1995). Though heavily defeated by Lyndon B. Johnson in the 1964 presidential election, Goldwater's best-selling book, *The Conscience of a Conservative*, expressed political ideals that served as the foundation for a conservative political revolution. It was a revolution that would have a direct bearing on AFDC some 30 years later with the election of Ronald Reagan as president in 1980 and the Republican capture in 1994 of the United States House of Representatives (Williams, 1997).

Among the conservative ideals expressed by Goldwater was a strong opposition to welfare provisions by the federal government. Goldwater opined that despite the strong appeal of welfare, conservatives had a duty to demonstrate the difference between being concerned with welfare problems and insisting that the federal government is the proper agent for their solution. Goldwater further believed that government policies that create dependent citizens inevitably rob a nation and its people of both moral and physical strength (Williams, 1997). Goldwater's musings served as a clarion call for a new breed of small-government conservative Republicans to wage war on welfare and big government in general.

To be sure, conservative opposition to federal government provision of welfare benefits was not a new sentiment. What was different in the 1960s were the seismic societal shifts that were being created by the civil rights movements and the federal government's war-on-poverty policies. These shifts saw not just a call for greater inclusion and equality for Blacks and other traditionally marginalized groups but also the exponential growth in social welfare. There was, for example, the passing of the Food Stamp Act in 1964. Even more importantly in the growth of social welfare in the 1960s were the Social Security Act Amendments of 1965 (P.L. 89–97, 79 STAT 286). These amendments created the Medicare and Medicaid programs and increased funding for the maternal and child health and the crippled children's program. It also increased funding for AFDC, old age, and disability insurance benefits (Walker & Vatter, 1997).

Although these programs were widely supported politically and served both urban and rural Americans across the racial and ethnic spectrum, they sparked vocal opposition to welfare programs and welfare recipients from small-government conservatives. Primarily intellectual, this opposition was manifested in magazine articles and social commentary. Publications such as *Human Events*, the *National Review*, and the *Wall Street Journal* regularly featured commentary that railed against the evils of big government as embodied in the bloated welfare system. Welfare was portrayed as robbing America of its republican soul and moving the country away from self-reliance and personal responsibility (Williams, 1997). By the late 1960s, Spiliakos (2012) suggests that conservative publications such as the *National Review* began to see and frame welfare as a class war. It was a war that the *National Review* argued pitted welfare recipients, such as those of AFDC, middle-class radicals, and welfare bureaucrats against the American taxpayers. Welfare recipients, who were exclusively viewed as Black, unemployed, single mothers living in an urban center as part of a Black underclass, were increasingly seen as the problem because of their supposed irresponsibility (Williams, 1997).

Ironically, it was a Democrat and sociologist, Daniel Patrick Moynihan, who gave traction to the notion of a Black underclass and Black single mothers' irresponsibility. He did this in his 1965 publication *The Negro Family: The Case for National Action*, commonly known as the Moynihan Report (United States Department of Labor, 1965). In the report, Moynihan posited that the rise of Black single-mother families was not due to the lack of jobs but rather to the ghetto culture that could be traced back to slavery. Moynihan argued that the structure of family life in the Black community represented a tangle of pathology that had little to do with the White world. It was a pathology in which the matriarchal structure of the Black family weakened the authority of Black men to function as breadwinners. The increased use of welfare by Black single mothers, Moynihan suggested, was an indication of the disintegration of the Black family (Baldwin, 2010; United States Department of Labor, 1965).

The Moynihan Report articulated a perspective that the media latched onto and used to sensationalize and distort the facts about welfare and welfare recipients. As found by Gilens in his 40-year analysis of news media coverage up until the mid-1960s, poverty was portrayed as an overwhelmingly White problem. In the mid-1960s, this changed dramatically, as coverage began to portray poverty as an overwhelmingly Black phenomenon, and more tellingly, a phenomenon in which the Black poor were undeserving because of immorality and bad life choices. Stories of AFDC recipients bilking the system by having multiple out-of-wedlock children and living on the dole became a staple in the media. Indeed, surveys of White attitudes found that they overwhelmingly associated poverty and welfare with Blacks (Gilens, 1999). By focusing on a program such AFDC and not on other widely used welfare programs such as Medicare, Medicaid, and old-age and disability benefits, welfare became synonymous with Black people, most particularly single Black mothers. Thus, Black people, who had been systematically excluded or marginalized from the provision of public or private welfare benefits for most of American history, became the unacceptable and unworthy face of welfare.

In 1969, with the United States reeling from social discord that deeply divided the nation, Richard Nixon, a Republican, was elected to the presidency. Though not a Goldwater adherent, Nixon did, among other things, articulate his opposition to social welfare, advocating instead for programs to help Blacks start their own business. Once in office, welfare reform rose to the top of Nixon's domestic policy agenda (Spitzer, 2012b). Ironically, Nixon's first welfare reform proposal would have increased both the size and cost of welfare, if enacted. The reform proposed in August of 1968 was the replacement of AFDC with a program called the Family Assistance Plan (FAP). The FAP was based on conservative economist Milton Friedman's negative income tax (NIT) innovation (Spitzer, 2012b). As proposed by Nixon, the FAP would offer a basic minimum income for all families, as well as expanded coverage for AFDC to cover the working poor and two-parent families. Also, FAP would include a work incentive for adult AFDC recipients by reducing their welfare payments by less than a dollar for every additional dollar earned (Spitzer, 2012b). However, estimates within the administration projected that FAP would double the number of welfare recipients and triple its costs, from $2.2 billion for AFDC in 1970 to approximately $5.8 billion.

Although seemingly a program supportive of welfare, in intent, FAP was no such thing. Rather, as posited by Spitzer (2012b), it was Nixon's attempt to garner the political support of the blue-collar, northern White ethnic. However, small-government conservative Republicans and publications such as *Human Events* railed against FAP as an extraordinary costly expansion of AFDC that would guarantee annual income for people who did not work (Williams, 1997). Relatedly, an American public that was increasingly identifying itself as conservative for the first time in decades had little appetite for any policy that could be seen as expanding welfare. Despite Nixon's push for the passage of a FAP bill in various forms until 1972, it failed to get any level of support in Congress and was never enacted.

The failure of FAP arguably marked a symbolic starting point for a small-government conservative revolution that would end with a monumental reform of welfare in 1996. Unlike the 1960s when small-government conservative welfare reform got more intellectual than actual political traction, the 1980s and 1990s ushered in a more aggressive political push. This push drew on the ideas of conservative commentators who were financially supported by think tanks such as the Manhattan Institute and the Heritage Foundation (Williams, 1997).

Embodying these ideas were three seminal books: *Losing Ground*, by Charles Murray; *Wealth and Poverty*, by George Gilder; and *Mandate for Leadership*, a Heritage Foundation publication series (Williams, 1997). With Blacks as the welfare protagonists, Charles Murray's *Losing Ground* argued that the social welfare programs of the 1960s "War on Poverty" hindered rather than helped its supposed beneficiaries, the poor and racial and ethnic minorities. At best, Murray opined, social welfare programs rewarded shortsighted irresponsible behavior, such as out-of-wedlock birth. Consequently, Murray claimed, social welfare programs were a failure and thus should be abolished (Murray, 1984). Gilder's *Wealth and Poverty* similarly argued that social welfare programs created by New Deal liberalism, most particularly AFDC, were a failure. For Gilder, though, the failure was a moral hazard, with family breakdown being the result. A decade after the publication of *Wealth and Poverty*, Gilder would suggest that the United States did not have a poverty problem but a moral problem, and what the poor needed was morals (Gilder, 1994). *Mandate for Leadership* offered no commentary on social welfare programs per se; rather, it provided guidelines for reducing the size and scope of government (Heatherly et al., 1981). All three books had a profound influence on the president, who would launch an attack on welfare and its conservative reform. The president was Ronald Reagan, who was elected in 1980.

Ronald Reagan, a former film actor, General Electric spokesperson, and governor of California, was an ardent small-government conservative Republican. In 1964 as co-chairman of Californians for Barry Goldwater, Reagan announced himself to the public as a small-government adherent when he made a nationally televised appeal for Goldwater, the GOP nominee. In the appeal, Reagan railed against President Lyndon Johnson's Great Society vision and the use of big government to achieve it. Reagan's message struck a chord, and Goldwater's campaign committee was soon inundated with calls pledging money to the tune of $8 million.

More significantly, seven years later as the governor of California, Reagan seized upon the spiraling AFDC costs in the state and called for significant welfare reform to hold back spending. Not unsympathetic to the plight of the truly needy as he perceived them, Reagan's particular focus was on welfare fraud and those AFDC recipients he viewed as not being the neediest. In framing his call for welfare reform, Reagan evoked the picture of suburban homeowners having to pay higher and higher taxes to support a welfare system that had run amok; in short, a system that was primarily serving those who could easily do for themselves. As suggested by Burbank (1991), in his framing of the need for welfare reform, "Reagan made himself the spokesperson of the earners and bungalow owners. By doing this, Reagan became an especially appealing figure to the skilled working people, the independent businessmen, and suburban professional classes" (p. 279). In doing so, he divided California along class, racial, and ethnic lines, with suburban Whites supporting reform, and Hispanic and Black grassroots advocacy groups opposing Reagan reform.

In his second term in office, Reagan pushed the Democratic-controlled California state legislature for a welfare reform bill that among other things would have a closed-ended welfare budget, with a trigger for ratable reductions. Considered to be too harsh by the Democratic members, this became the starting point for a long and contentious bipartisan battle for a workable and agreeable welfare reform bill. In 1971, an agreement was reached, and Reagan signed into law the Welfare Reform Act of 1971 (Burbank, 1991).

Arguably one of the most significant pieces of state welfare reform legislation, the Welfare Reform Act in actuality was not anywhere near as draconian as Reagan had initially proposed. Nevertheless, it did have provisions that tightened AFDC eligibility and lowered the AFDC grant for recipients who worked in part-time low-wage jobs. Paradoxically, the act also significantly increased the monthly welfare grants to those AFDC families who had no income and were unable to work (Keef, 1983).

In passing the Welfare Reform Act of 1971, Reagan's credentials as a small-government conservative Republican who was committed to welfare reform was solidified. No surprise, then, that once in the office of the presidency, welfare reform was one of his top priorities. Reagan's thinking about welfare while in office was monumentally influenced by the work of Murray, Gilder, and the Heritage Foundation. Gilder had argued that liberal social welfare benefits programs like AFDC induced dependency on the part of the poor, and what the poor needed was not more government, but the spur out of their poverty. As a result, the welfare system needed dismantling (Midgley & Livermore, 2008). This ideological perspective took hold and was disseminated across the nation by neoconservative think tanks, the most notable being the Heritage Foundation, the Manhattan Institute, the Cato Institute, and the Stanford Institute (Midgley & Livermore, 2008). Just as importantly, in Reagan there was a president who was not only totally committed to welfare reform but was also able to deliver the message effectively to the American public.

While Reagan did pass legislation reforming welfare, notably the Omnibus Budget and Reconciliation Act of 1981 and the Family Support Act of 1988, his biggest impact was as a communicator (Midgley & Livermore, 2008). Reagan was masterful in selling to the American people the need for welfare reform. In his 1986 radio address to the nation on welfare reform, for example, Reagan talked about what he described as the crisis of family breakdown, especially among the welfare poor in the inner cities. He made reference to the number of children born out of wedlock and generations of poverty. He contrasted this with the immigrants of the late 19th and 20th centuries, who despite the presence of poverty, nevertheless pulled together as families and achieved the American dream. Reagan ended the address by declaring that the welfare tragedy had gone on too long, and it was time to reshape the American welfare system (Reagan, 1986). In evoking the stereotypical and in many cases inaccurate observations about welfare and welfare recipients, Reagan gave traction to a construction of welfare recipients as the undeserving other. This was never more evident than in Reagan's repeated telling of the story of Linda Taylor. Taylor was a Black welfare recipient from Chicago, who in 1977 was convicted of fraud and perjury involving $8,000 in welfare checks. In Reagan's telling of the story, which he did on the campaign trail and to Congress, Linda Taylor was recast as a welfare recipient who had cleverly worked the system. In doing so, she had gained over a $100,000 (Gilens, 1999). She was able to do this by having multiple names, addresses, and telephone numbers. So compelling was the story that the term Welfare Queen entered the lexicon of the discourse on welfare reform and would be used endlessly as propaganda (Gilens, 1999).

Temporary Assistance to Needy Families, 1996–Present

In the 1990s, neoconservative Republicans, with the help of a like-minded neoliberal Democratic president, would finally reform welfare in their image. It began in 1994 during the congressional election campaign, when 300 Republican congressional candidates met on the steps of the United States Capitol to sign the Contract with America, co-authored by Newt Gingrich and Richard Armey (Gingrich, 1994). The contract pledged to enact ten specific bills within the first 100 days of the 104th Congress. It also laid out in precise detail the Republican party's plan to become the majority party in the House of Representatives for the first time in 40 years. The contract served as a manifesto for conservative Republicans, particularly those who agreed with shrinking government, welfare reform, and lower taxes to encourage increased entrepreneurial activity (Gingrich, 1994). It was a manifesto that clearly captured the American public's imagination.

Results of the 1994 congressional election saw the Republicans winning 54 House and nine Senate seats, thus gaining a majority in both houses. With this majority, the Republican party went about making good on their contract with America. The welfare reform intent of the Republican party had garnered substantial coverage and public support by way of a well-orchestrated media blitz by the likes of Charles Murray, William Bennett, Irving Kristol, and Robert Rector. All, in some way, talked about the runaway epidemic of illegitimacy in the Black community and the generations of families on welfare, thus again reinforcing the very picture of the unworthy and undeserving poor (DeParle, 2005; Midgley & Livermore, 2008). Thus, when the Republican party took control of Congress in 1994, the pressure was on to pass meaningful welfare reform legislation that would return America back to a moral order. Indeed, so important was welfare reform that it was number three of the ten items listed in the Republican party's Contract with America (Midgley & Livermore, 2008).

As well as having control of Congress, further propelling the Republican party's welfare reform agenda was the sitting president, Bill Clinton. Clinton had promised the American people on his campaign trail to reform welfare so it would be a second chance and not a way of life. Although a Democrat and a seemingly unlikely collaborator, Clinton had long been committed to welfare reform. In the 1980s as the governor of Arkansas, for example, Clinton experimented with a workfare program for AFDC recipients. Likewise, representing the National Governors Association, he worked with Congress and the Reagan administration to draft the Welfare Reform Act enacted in 1988. Furthermore, as president, he granted waivers to 45 states to institute their own welfare reforms (Clinton, 2006). After vetoing to two earlier versions of the Republican party's welfare reform bill, Clinton agreed to the third effort.

Implementation

On June 27, 1996, congressional Republicans made good on their promise to reform welfare in America. They did this with the introduction into the 104th Congress of the Personal Responsibility and Work Opportunity Reconciliation Act of 1996 (H.R. 3734): P.L. 104–193. Sponsored by Representative John Kasich (R-OH), PRWORA represented the most significant social welfare legislation since the Social Security Act of 1935, 60 years earlier. Informed by values privileging marriage, self-reliance, and personal responsibility, which it was believed AFDC undermined, PRWORA repealed AFDC as a categorical entitlement (Falk, 2013). In doing so, AFDC became the only program of the Social Security Act of 1935 to have been repealed. In its place, PRWORA created the aptly named Title 1 Temporary Assistance for Needy Families (TANF) Block Grant for states to provide time-limited cash assistance for needy families, with work requirements for most recipients. The four purposes of TANF were to:

1. Provide assistance to needy families so children can be cared for in their own homes.
2. Reduce the dependency of needy parents by promoting job preparation, work, and marriage.
3. Prevent and reduce the incidence of out-of-wedlock pregnancies.
4. Encourage the formation and maintenance of two-parent families.

To this end, the key provisions of TANF included elimination of cash welfare entitlement and established block grant funding, work requirements, sanctions, a 60-month life-time limit, family formulation, child-support enforcement, and restrictions of benefits (Falk, 2013).

Elimination of Cash Welfare Entitlement

Under the AFDC program, states were obligated by federal guidelines to provide aid to all eligible families under state income standards. Under TANF, however, recipients are no longer guaranteed welfare benefits based on eligibility. Instead, states, within broad federal requirements, are free to determine which families receive assistance and under what circumstances. Thus, after 60 years of welfare provisions as an entitlement, it is now a privilege. Notably unaffected by this entitlement change are Medicaid and food stamp eligibility (Falk, 2013).

Block Grant Funding

The federal government provides a fixed-sum block grant to states, which they use to operate their own TANF programs. For states to receive the grant, they are obligated to show maintenance of effort (MOE) by also contributing state dollars to programs for the needy. Failure to do so leads to severe fiscal penalties. States may use the block grant funding and MOE dollars to meet any of four purposes of TANF (Falk, 2013).

Work Requirements

With some exceptions, all adult TANF recipients are expected to participate in a work program. For a one-parent family, the expected minimal total hours of work per week is 30 hours. For a two-parent family, the expected minimum total hours of work per week are 35 hours, and in some circumstances 55 hours. Included as work is job skills training, education directly related to employment, or study leading to a high school diploma. Failure to comply with the work requirements will result in some form of sanction, which might include a reduction or loss of benefits (Falk, 2013).

Sanctions

As well as not meeting work requirements, a state may also sanction a recipient family with an adult aged 20 to 51 who does not have or is not working for a high school diploma or equivalent. Similarly, a state may also sanction TANF family recipients for failing to ensure minor children attend school (Falk, 2013).

Time Limit

TANF puts a 60-month lifetime limit on states assisting families, but states have the discretion to shorten the lifetime limit. Moreover, states can apply for exemptions to the 60-month lifetime limit for a percentage of its TANF cases (Falk, 2013).

Family Formulation

To encourage two-parent families and decrease out-of-wedlock births, particularly for teenagers, TANF gives states the flexibility to serve two-parent families. It also provides bonuses to states that lower their out-of-wedlock birth rates. Relatedly, it established federal funding for abstinence-only sex education. Lastly, it denies assistance to unmarried minor parents not in school or living with parents (Falk, 2013).

Child Support Enforcement

TANF requirements mandate that states operate a Child Support Enforcement Program (CES) with the express purpose of increasing the percentage of identified fathers. Toward this end, the state CES program must establish an integrated, automated network linking all states to information about the location and assets of parents. It also requires states to revise the rules governing the distribution of past due (arrearage) child support payments to former recipients of public assistance (Falk, 2013).

Restrictions of Benefits

Expressly prohibited from receiving TANF are undocumented immigrants and documented immigrants who have resided in the country for less than five years since 1996. Also prohibited are fugitive felons and probation and parole violators.

Such was the congressional support for PRWORA that the final bill was passed in both the House (328/101) and Senate (78/21) with large majorities. President Clinton signed the bill into law on August 22, 1996, less than two months after its introduction to Congress. In passing the law, both the Republican party and President Clinton, who had also promised to reform welfare on his presidential election campaign trail, kept their promises to the American people (Falk, 2013).

The Impact of TANF

In the 25 years since TANF's enactment, neither the fears nor the promises of the program have been fully realized (Tanner, 2016). Within the first decade of the program's implementation, the total number of TANF recipients went from 12.6 million in 1996 to 4.7 million in 2006, representing the most dramatic decline in U.S welfare history (see Figure 6.3) (U.S. Department of Health & Human Services, 2008).

For supporters of TANF, this early success was lauded as proof positive of the efficacy of welfare reform in moving single mothers out of poverty and dependency (Grogger, 2003). While certainly a factor, measuring TANF's initial success is not as easy as the numbers indicated. The primary reasons for this are because it occurred against the backdrop of a simultaneously booming economy and the substantial expansion of the Earned Income Tax Credit (EITC) in 1986, 1990, and 1993 (Greenstein & Shapiro, 1998; Grogger, 2003; Tanner, 2016).

It was a boom that began in the transition years from AFDC to TANF (1994–1996). During this time, AFDC recipients had already declined from an historic high 14.2 million in 1994 to 12.6 million in 1996 (see Figure 6.3). The decline would continue under TANF as the economic environment presented ample opportunities for single mothers, particularly those without a high school diploma, to leave the welfare rolls and enter the workforce, which they did in record numbers (Grogger, 2003; Marr et al., 2015). Also, critically, once in the workforce, the EITC boosted single mothers' income (Marr et al., 2015). For example, in 1996, more than 19 million low-and-moderate income households—a significant majority being single mothers with children—received the credit (Greenstein & Shapiro, 1998).

Indeed, noted economist Jeffery Grogger (2003) found that welfare reform accounted for just 13% of the rise in employment among single mothers in the 1990s. Much bigger factors were the strong

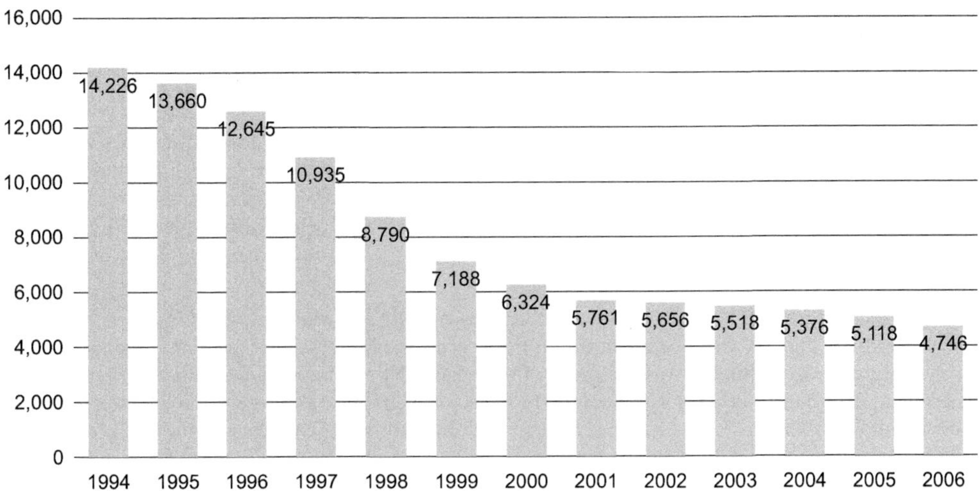

Figure 6.3 AFDC/TANF Recipients, 1994–2006

Source: U.S. Department of Health and Human Services. Indicators of Welfare Dependence: Annual Report to Congress, 2008. AFDC/TANF Program Data

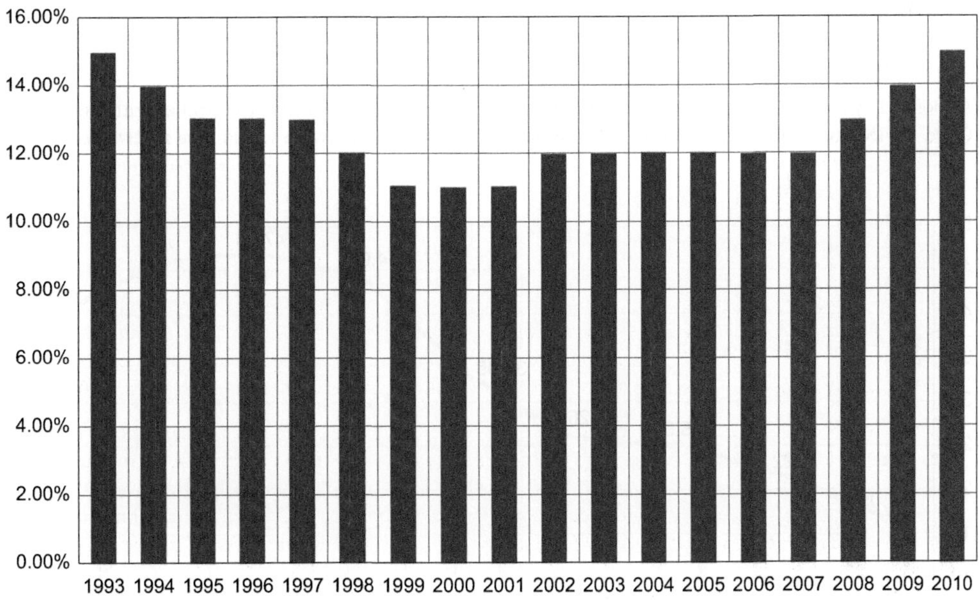

Figure 6.4 Poverty Rates in the United States, 1993–2010

Source: Statista: Poverty Rate in the United States 1990 to 2019. Retrieved from www.statista.com/statistics/204745/poverty-rate-for-families-in-the-us/

economy and the Earned Income Tax Credit, which accounted for 21% and 34% of the decline, respectively (Grogger, 2003).

Significant declines in the national poverty rates would accompany the booming economy and expansion of the EITC. They would see rates drop from 15.1% in 1993 to 13.7% in 1996 to 11.3% in 2000 (see Figure 6.4) (Duffin, 2020). However, the importance of a booming economy would never be more evident than during the early and mid-2000s. During this period, the economy experienced a slowdown and an eventual recession in 2008, which saw a six-year flattening and a decrease in single mothers' numbers without a high school diploma in the workforce. It also saw a gradual increase in poverty rates. These rates went from 11.3% in 2000 to 12.3% in 2006 to a high 15.1% in 2010 (see Figure 6.4) (Duffin, 2020).

Moreover, in 2008, participation in the Supplemental Nutrition Aid Program (SNAP), previously known as the Food Stamp Program, hit an historic high of 28.2 million people, following a significant decline in participation through the late 1990s. It was a participation that would continue to hit new record highs every year until it hit an historic peak in 2013 of 47.6 million recipients (see Figure 6.5) (U.S. Department of Agriculture Food and Nutrition Program, n.d.).

As suggested by Pavetti (2014), during the economic downtown, and when compared to its predecessor AFDC, TANF fell short of what one might expect from such a basic safety net program in response to tough economic times. One of the primary reasons for this is that TANF was not designed to provide relief in challenging economic times, not least because the block grant structure allows states broad discretion on how to fund cash assistance. As mentioned earlier, much more responsive to need during the recession and post-recession years was the SNAP program.

As the nation moved out of the recession and into better economic times from 2013 onward, the program's weaknesses have become even more evident. For example, over time, the reach of the program has dramatically diminished (see Figure 6.5). As an illustration, in 2018, for every 100 families in poverty nationally, less than a quarter, 22, received cash assistance from TANF (Center on Budget and Policy Priorities, 2020; Floyd, 2020). This number was down from 68 families when the program was first enacted in 1996 (Floyd, 2020). The result is that the TANF-to-poverty ratio (TPR) is at the lowest point in TANF's history (Center on Budget and Policy Priorities, 2020; Floyd, 2020). These numbers are starker in terms of reach, depending on the state of residence. For example, in 2018, 16 states had a TPR of 10 or less, compared to two in 2006 (see Figure 6.6).

As posited by Floyd (2020), if TANF had the same reach as its predecessor, Aid to Families with Dependent Child (AFDC) in 1995–1996, around 2.4 million more families nationwide would have received cash

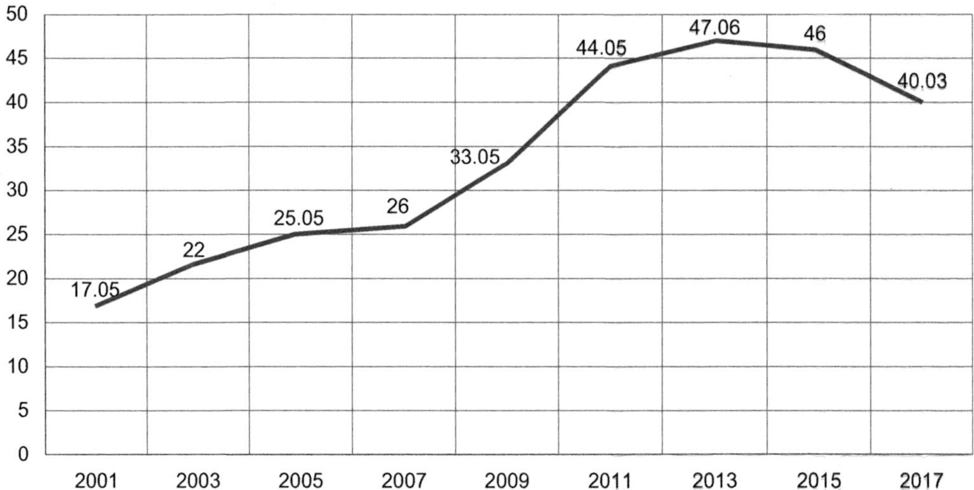

Figure 6.5 Individuals Receiving Food Stamps/SNAP, 2001–2017

Source: Matt Trivisonno from U.S. Department of Agriculture Food Stamp Chart. Data retrieved from www.trivisonno.com/food-stamps-charts

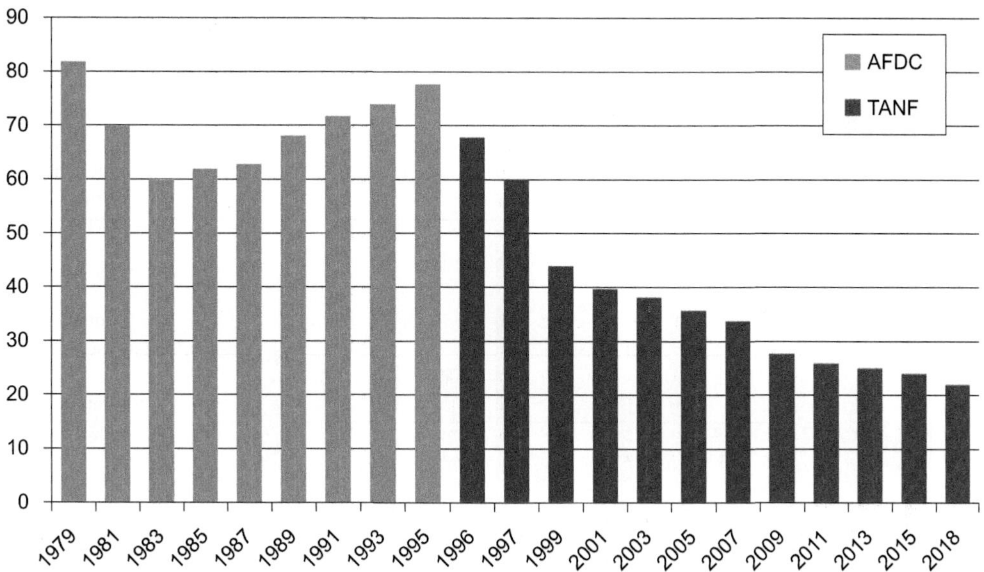

Figure 6.6 TANF's Reach Declined Dramatically Over Time

Source: CBPP analysis of poverty data from the Census' Current Population Survey and AFDC/TANF caseload data from the Department of Health and Human Services, and since 09/2006 onward caseload data collected by CBPP from state agencies.

assistance in 2018 than was the case (p. 1). In 2019, the number of families receiving cash assistance was 1.1 million, which is 4 million less than the historical peak of 5.4 million families in 1994 under the AFDC. Indeed, it is the lowest number of families receiving cash assistance in the United States since 1959 (Falk & Landers, 2020).

One of the reasons for the dramatically diminished reach of TANF is connected to the State Family Assistance Grant (SFAG) funding of TANF established by law for the states in 1996. The allocated amount for the SFAG was $16.5 billion paid to the states in the form of a block grant. The services funded by the block grant include cash assistance, childcare, work/education/training, refundable tax credits, pre-K/Head Start, child welfare, and emergency/short term benefits and administration (Falk & Landers, 2020).

From FY1997 to FY2016, this block grant amount was not adjusted for inflation or the poverty population changes. As a consequence, the cash value of the SFAG has declined an estimated 33.1%. Moreover, in FY2017, the SFAG was reduced by 0.33% to $16.5 billion, to finance TANF-related research and technical assistance (Falk & Landers, 2020). In FY2019, in real (inflation-adjusted) terms, the block grant's cash value was 37% below its value in FY1997 (Falk & Landers, 2020).

Criticism of TANF

Regardless of ideological perspective, there has been ongoing criticism of TANF. The libertarian/conservative Niskanen Center argues that while TANF may be a political success for some, it has failed the conservative vision of welfare reform and is deeply flawed. Among the reasons for this is that the work requirements do not and have not worked. More specifically, while successful in the early years when the economy was booming, when the economy was less robust, single mothers could not get the kinds of jobs

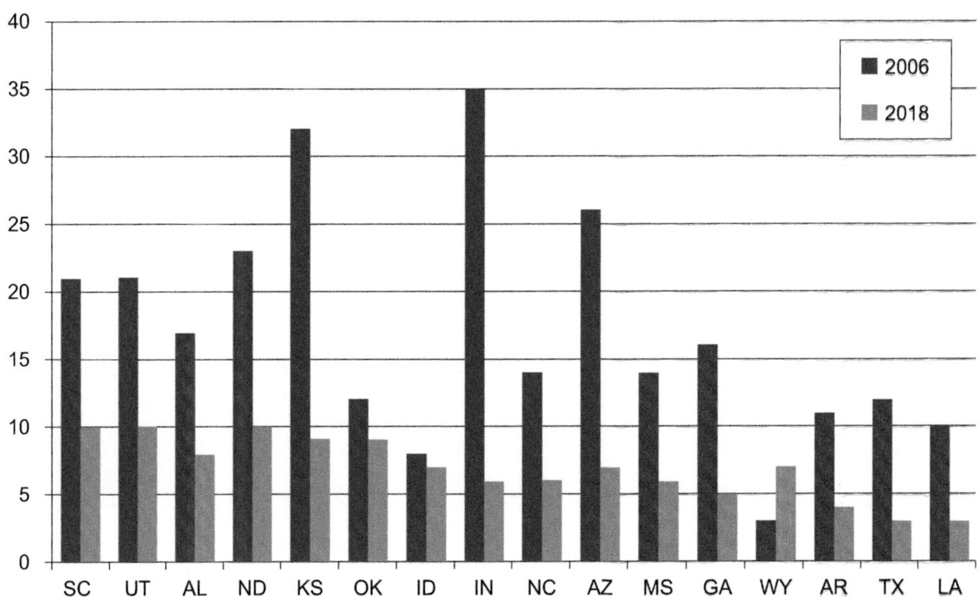

Figure 6.7 TANF-to-Poverty Ratio Comparison

Source: CBPP analysis of poverty data from the Current Population Survey and TANF caseload data from the Department of Health and Human Services, and since 09/2006 onward caseload data collected by CBPP from state agencies.

that would lift them out of poverty and dependency. Instead, they are concentrated in low-wage work with little chance of advancement and dependence on supplemental programs such as SNAP. Also problematic is the block grant structure, which Hammond (2016) describes as Pseudo-Federalism that allows states to use the funding for filling budget holes that have nothing to with workfare or poverty reduction. Lastly, having asset limits for recipients, while on the surface seems reasonable, in practice, encourages poor households to spend down their limited savings when it exceeds the value of welfare payments. In doing so, this runs counter to what a conservative welfare policy should do: setting the poor up with bank accounts and teaching the virtue of prudence (Hammond, 2016).

The independent nonpartisan Center for American Progress (CAP) argues that TANF is a poor example of an anti-poverty program. Among the reasons for this is that the diminishing value of block-grant funding means that in practice, as discussed earlier, TANF has grown significantly weaker as a tool to protect families with children living under the federal poverty line against destitution (see Figure 6.7) (Vallas & Boteach, 2015). Next, TANF is woefully unresponsive to recessions, as evidenced by the increased reliance on other supplemental programs such as SNAP in times of a recession. There is also a lack of accountability for results or how funds are spent. Moreover, despite all the rhetoric about family values, TANF does not effectively serve two-parent families. Lastly, CAP stress that TANF does a poor job of cutting poverty, not least because no state provides benefits at even half the federal poverty level (Vallas & Boteach, 2015).

Floyd notes that while TANF is touted as a color-blind program, it is troubling that access is mainly dependent on where a family lives, which can and appears to have exacerbated disparities among racial groups. Whether by design or not, Black children are likelier than their White counterparts to live in states with the lowest TPRs (Floyd, 2020), which is very much in keeping in the historical relationship between state politics, race, and welfare. In his study of state politics, race, and cash assistance spending under TANF, Fusaro (2020) found a prevalence of negative stereotyping of Blacks among Whites is related to TANF cash assistance efforts. However, how related it is to the decline in cash assistance is ambiguous.

Chapter Summary

For single mothers and their children, social welfare benefits programs have been a significant source of inequality. This inequality is manifested in the lack of universal access and stringent eligibility requirements, and the coercive measures are taken to control or punish the recipients' behavior. One would be hard-pressed to identify any other group who receives social welfare benefits that has been as stigmatized as single mothers. As shown in this chapter, the single mother as the "unworthy" and "undeserving" poor has been a consistent theme of the three major social welfare benefits programs discussed. Indeed, the very structural characteristics of TANF are predicated on this theme, with Puritan-laced language and goals that speak to promoting marriage, reducing the incidence of out-of-wedlock births, and encouraging the maintenance of two-parent families. Consequently, rather than assistance to needy mothers with children being determined by universal entitlement, we have benefits programs premised on moral character and cultural conformity. Thus, social welfare benefits programs for mothers and dependent children continue to be inferior to other similarly developed nations.

Box 6.1 Social Welfare Benefits Programs and Social Control Timeline

1642: Plymouth is the first colony to enact poor laws. The Plymouth poor laws are strongly influenced by and fashioned after the English Poor Laws and were ideologically informed by Calvinist ideas. More specifically, the virtues of hard work, the sin of idleness, and the sanctity of patriarchal family arrangements. The poor are divided into two distinct categories: "worthy" and "unworthy." The worthy poor are widows, children, and the aged. The unworthy include unmarried single mothers and the nondisabled who refuse to work. The poor laws have six essential features that will be present in the poor laws of other colonies. These features are:

1. Relative responsibility
2. Local administration
3. Residence requirements
4. Classification of the poor
5. Poverty distinction
6. Less eligibility (Quigley, 1997; see Chapter 6 for details of poor law features).

1646: The Virginia Colony enacts poor laws (Quigley, 1997).

1647: Rhode Island enacts poor laws (Quigley, 1997).

1657: The Scots Charitable Society is founded in Massachusetts. It is the first American private charitable society (Quigley, 1997).

1673: The Connecticut Colony enacts poor laws (Quigley, 1997).

1692: The Massachusetts Colony enacts poor laws (Quigley, 1997).

1771: Pennsylvania enacts poor laws (Quigley, 1997).

1773: New York enacts poor laws (Quigley, 1997).

1819: The ***Second Annual Report of the Managers of the Society for the Prevention of Pauperism in the City of New York*** is published. The report lists a litany of reasons why poverty persists despite the abundance of land and the new frontiers opening up in the West (Second Annual Report of the Managers of the Society for the Prevention of Pauperism in the City of New York, 1819; see the New Nation in Chapter 2 for details of the report).

1821: The Quincy Report is published. It will be instrumental in the termination of outdoor relief and the wholesale move toward institutional relief and almshouses in Massachusetts (Quincy, 1821; see the New Nation in Chapter 2 for details of the report).

1824: The Yates Report is published. The recommendations of the Yates Report will be the catalyst for every county in New York and other northeastern states to build poor houses and move toward institutional relief. The undergirding belief about the poor is that they are morally defective (Katz, 1987; see the New Nation in Chapter 2 for details of the report).

1843: Robert Hartley and associates organize the New York Association for Improving the Condition of the Poor. The association later merges with the Charity Organization Society of New York (Burrows & Wallace, 1999; Jackson, 2010).

1853: Charles Loring Brace founded the Children's Aid Society with the express purpose of saving the destitute children of New York by the end of the century. Central to this will be the Orphan Train movement (see Chapter 12, Child Welfare Inequality, for details). The actions of Charles Loring Brace are the catalyst for the child saving movement that will be present through to the early 20th century (McGowan, 2005).

1887: Reverend Gurteen established the first charity organization society in the United States in Buffalo, New York, in 1877. The Buffalo Charity Organization Society brought the disparate local charity organizations together as a systematically coordinated single charitable society employing a rational system of scientific, charitable administration (Zastro, 2009; see Scientific Charity in Chapter 2 for details).

1909: At the White House Conference on the Care of Dependent Children, initiated by President Theodore Roosevelt, it is agreed that children should not be deprived of home life. The conference resulted in developing the mother's pension movement (Skocpol et al., 1993; Ward, 2005).

1911: Illinois is the first state to enact a mother's pension program. By 1931, 46 of the 48 states had passed some form of a mother's pension program (Skocpol, 1992).

1935: Aid to Dependent Children (ADC) is created by Title IV of the Social Security Act of 1935 as part of the New Deal. The federal program, which superseded the state devised mothers' pension, was a means-tested entitlement program that subsidized the incomes of families where fathers were deceased, absent, or unable to work (Alling & Leisy, 1950).

1939: An amendment to the Social Security Act of 1935 creates survivor benefits and dependent benefits. Aged widows and those caring for dependent children are eligible for their deceased spouse's retirement benefits at a 75% rate. These benefits were not available to men until later in the program's history. Dependent children of retired or deceased workers received a 50% benefit. In its structure, the survivor benefit and dependent benefit privileged patriarchal family arrangements and allowed widowed mothers and their dependent children to migrate away from the state-administered ADC program to the federally administered survivor and dependent benefit programs (Martin & Weaver, 2005).

1950: A Social Security Administration (SSA) amendment to ADC expands benefits to include the mother as well as the child(ren) (Walker & Vatter, 1997).

1962: ADC is renamed Aid to Families and Dependent Children (Walker & Vatter, 1997).

1996: The Personal Responsibility and Work Opportunity Reconciliation Act (PRWORA) is signed into law by President Bill Clinton. The PRWORA and its Temporary Assistance for Needy Families (TANF) will be the most significant social welfare legislation since the Social Security Act of 1935 in its repeal of AFDC. In doing so, access to social welfare benefits for single mothers (and fathers who are the primary caretaker of the child(ren)), move from a lifetime right if needed, to a time-limited privilege (Clinton, 2006; Falk, 2013). In its design and ideological underpinnings, the act is unabashedly patriarchal and punitive toward single-parent motherhood, channeling the Calvinist ideas of the colonial poor laws.

Retrieval Questions

1. What value underpinned the colonial poor laws?
2. What group has been perennially victimized by the ambivalence toward providing assistance to particular categories of the needy?
3. In the prevalent patriarchal society, what family arrangement is considered ideal?
4. Name one of the dissenting voices against the mothers' pension.
5. Name one legacy of the mothers' pension.
6. Name one of the 3R's of the New Deal.
7. What was the purpose of ADC?
8. What was the role of the suitable home requirement in both the mothers' pension program and AFDC?
9. Who is Linda Taylor, and why is she significant?
10. What are the four purposes of TANF?

Discussion Questions

1. Identify and discuss the social justice issues related to TANF.
2. Identify and discuss two diversity issues presented in this chapter.
3. Identify and discuss the role that moral judgments played in the development of the three social welfare benefits programs discussed in this chapter.
4. What responsibility do social workers have to eliminate social inequality?
5. As a policy practitioner, discuss your thoughts about TANF.
6. Discuss how conflict theory and critical race theory would explain TANF and its role.

References

Alling, E., & Leisy, A. (1950). Aid to dependent children in a postwar year. *Social Security Bulletin*. Retrieved from www.ssa.gov/policy/docs/ssb/v13n8/v13n8p3.pdf

Bailis, L. N. (1974). *Bread or justice: Grassroots organizing in the welfare rights movement*. Lexington, MA: D.C. Heath.

Baldwin, B. (2010, Spring). Stratification of the welfare poor: Intersections of gender, race, and worthiness in poverty discourse and policy. *The Modern American*, 4–14.

Beland, D., Howard, C., & Morgan, K. (2014). *Oxford handbook of U.S. social policy*. New York, NY: Oxford University Press.

Blank, S. W., & Blum, B. B. (1997). A brief history of work expectations for welfare mothers. *The Future of Children*, 7(1), 28–38.

Blau, J., & Abramovitz, M. (2009). *The dynamics of social welfare policy* (2nd ed.). Oxford, England: Oxford University Press.

Briggs, L. (2012). *Somebody's children: The politics of transracial and transnational adoption*. Durham, NC: Duke University Press.

Burbank, G. (1991). Governor Reagan and California welfare reform: The grand compromise. *California History*, 70(3), 278–289.

Burrows, E. G., & Wallace, M. (1999). *Gotham: A history of New York City to 1898*. New York, NY: Oxford University Press.

Center on Budget and Policy Priorities. (2020). State facts sheets: Trends in state TANF-to-poverty ratios. *Cbpp.org*. Retrieved from www.cbpp.org/research/family-income-support/state-fact-sheets-trends-in-state-tanf-to-poverty-ratios

Children's Bureau. (1922). *Public aid to children in their own homes: A tabular summary of state laws in effect*. Bureau Publication, Legal Chart No. 3. Washington, DC: Government Printing Office.

Children's Defense Fund. (2018). *Child poverty in America 2017: National analysis*. Retrieved from www.childrensdefense.org/wp-content/uploads/2018/09/Child-Poverty-in-America-2017-National-Fact-Sheet.pdf

Clinton, B. (2006, August 22). How we ended welfare, together. Op-ed. *The New York Times*. Retrieved from www.nytimes.com/2006/08/22/opinion/22clinton.html?_r=0

Constance-Huggins, M. (2011). A review of the racial biases of social welfare policies. *Journal of Human Behavior in the Environment, 21*(8), 871–887.

Dallek, M. (1995). The conservative 1960s. *The Atlantic*. Retrieved from www.theatlantic.com/magazine/archive/1995/12/the-conservative-1960s/376506/

Day, P. (2009). *A new history of social welfare* (6th ed.). New York, NY: Pearson-Allyn and Bacon.

DeParle, J. (2005). *American dream: Three women, ten kinds, and a nation's drive to end welfare*. New York, NY: Penguin Books.

DeWitt, L. (2010). The decision to exclude agriculture and domestic workers from the 1935 Social Security Act. *Social Security Bulletin, 70*(4), 49–68.

Duffin, E. (2020). Poverty rates in the United States from 1990 to 2019. *Statista*. Retrieved from www.statista.com/statistics/200463/us-poverty-rate-since-1990/

Falk, G. (2013). The Temporary Assistance for Needy Families (TANF) block grant: A primer on TANF financing and federal requirements. *Congressional Research Services*. Retrieved from www.fas.org/sgp/crs/misc/RL32748.pdf

Falk, G., & Landers, P. A. (2020). The Temporary Assistance to Needy Families (TANF): Responses to frequently asked questions. *Congressional Research Service*. Retrieved from https://fas.org/sgp/crs/misc/RL32760.pdf

Federal Reserve Bulletin. (1937). *Board of governors of the Federal Reserve System*. Retrieved from https://fraser.stlouisfed.org/docs/publications/FRB/1930s/frb_091937.pdf

Finkelman, P. (2009). *Encyclopedia of African American history, 1986 to the present: From the age of segregation to the twenty-first century*. New York, NY: Oxford University Press.

Floyd, I. (2020). Cash assistance should reach millions more families. *Center on Budget and Policy Priorities*. Retrieved from www.cbpp.org/sites/default/files/atoms/files/6-16-15tanf.pdf

Fusaro, V. A. (2020). State politics, race, and "welfare" as a funding stream: Cash assistance spending under temporary assistance for needy families. *Policy Studies Journal*. Retrieved from https://onlinelibrary.wiley.com/doi/abs/10.1111/psj.12390

Gilder, G. (1994). Freedom from welfare dependency. *Religion & Liberty, 4*(2). Retrieved from www.acton.org/pub/religion-liberty/volume-4-number-2/freedom-welfare-dependency

Gilens, M. (1999). *Why Americans hate welfare: Race, media and the politics of antipoverty policy*. Chicago, IL: University of Chicago Press.

Gingrich, N. (1994). *A contract with America*. Evanston, IL: McDougal Littell.

Goldberg, R. A. (1995). *Barry Goldwater*. New Haven, CT: Yale University Press.

Gooden, S. T. (2003). Contemporary approaches to enduring challenges: Using performance measures to promote racial equality under TANF. In F. Sanford, J. S. Schram, & R. C. Fording (Eds.), *Race and the politics of welfare reform* (pp. 254–275). Ann Arbor, MI: The University of Michigan Press.

Goodwin, J. L. (1997). *Gender and the politics of welfare reform: Mothers' pension in Chicago, 1911–1929*. Chicago, IL: University of Chicago Press.

Gordon, L., & Batlan, F. (2011). *The legal history of the aid to dependent children program*. Retrieved from www.socialwelfarehistory.com/programs/aid-to-dependent-children-the-legal-history/

Greenstein, R., & Shapiro, I. (1998). New research findings on the effects of the earned income tax credit. *Center on Budget and Policy Priorities*. Retrieved from www.cbpp.org/archives/311eitc.htm

Grogger, J. (2003). The effects of time limits, the EITC, and other policy changes on welfare use, work, and income among female-headed families. *The Review of Economics and Statistics, 85*(2), 394–408.

Grossberg, M., & Tomlins, C. (2011). *The Cambridge history of law in America: Volume II: The long nineteenth century (1789–1920)*. Cambridge, UK: Cambridge University Press.

Hacker, J. S. (2002). *The divided welfare state: The battle over public and private social benefits in the United States*. Cambridge, UK: Cambridge University Press.

Hammond, S. (2016). Three ways welfare reform failed conservatives. *Niskanen Center*. Retrieved from www.niskanencenter.org/welfare-reform-failed-conservatives/

Handler, J. F., & Hasenfeld, Y. (1997). *We the poor people: Work, poverty and welfare*. New Haven, CT: Yale University Press.

Hansan, J. E. (2011). Charity organization societies: 1873–1893. *The Social Welfare History Project*. Retrieved from www.socialwelfarehistory.com/organizations/charity-organization-societies-1877-1893/

Hard, W. (1913). Watch the results. *The Delineator Journal, 81/82*, 172–173.

Heatherly, C. L., Feulner, E. J., & Heritage Foundation. (1981). *Mandate for leadership: Policy management in a conservative administration*. Washington, DC: Heritage Foundation.

Herrick, J. M., & Stuart, P. H. (2005). *Encyclopedia of social welfare history in North America*. Thousand Oaks, CA: Sage.

Hout, M., & Cumberworth, E. (2012). *The labor force and the Great Recession*. Stanford, CA: Stanford Center on Poverty and Inequality. Retrieved from https://web.stanford.edu/group/recessiontrends/cgi-bin/web/sites/all/themes/barron/pdf/LaborMarkets_fact_sheet.pdf

Jackson, K. T. (2010). *The encyclopedia of New York City*. New Haven, CT: Yale University Press.

Jansson, B. S. (2009). *The reluctant welfare state: Engaging history to advance social work practice in contemporary society* (6th ed.). Belmont, CA: Brooks/Cole.

Jaynes, G. D. (2005). *Encyclopedia of African American society*. Thousand Oaks, CA: Sage.

Katz, M. B. (1983). *Poverty and policy in American history*. New York, NY: Academia Press.

Katz, M. B. (1987). *In the shadow of the poorhouse: Social history of welfare America*. New York, NY: Basic Books.

Keef, D. E. (1983). Governor Reagan, welfare reform, and AFDC fertility. *Social Service Review, 57*(2), 234–253.

Kirst-Ashman, K., & Hull, G. H., Jr. (2014). *Generalist practice with organizations and communities* (6th ed.). Belmont, CA: Brooks/Cole.

Kleinberg, S. J. (2006). *Widows and orphans first: The family economy and social welfare policy, 1880–1939*. Urbana: University of Illinois Press.

Kornbluh, F. (1997). To fulfill their "rightly needs": Consumerism and the national welfare rights movement. *Radical History Review, 66*, 76–113.

Leff, M. (1973). Consensus for reform: The mothers' pension movement in the progressive era. *Social Service Review, 47*(3), 397–417.

Leuchtenburg, W. E. (1963). *Franklin D. Roosevelt and the new deal, 1932–1940*. New York, NY: Harper Collins.

Marr, C., Huang, C. C., Sherman, A., & Debot, B. (2015). EITC and child tax credit promote work, reduce poverty, and support children's development, research finds. *Center on Budget and Policy Priorities*. Retrieved from www.cbpp.org/research/federal-tax/eitc-and-child-tax-credit-promote-work-reduce-poverty-and-support-childrens

Marten, J. (2004). *Childhood and child welfare in the progressive era: A brief history with documents*. New York, NY: Bedford Books.

Martin, P. P., & Weaver, D. A. (2005). Social security: A program and policy history. *Social Security Office of Policy*. Retrieved from www.ssa.gov/policy/docs/ssb/v66n1/v66n1p1.html

McGowan, B. G. (2005). Historical evolution of child welfare services. In G. P. Mallon & P. M. Hess (Eds.), *Child welfare for the 21st century: A handbook for practices, policies, and programs* (pp. 10–46). New York, NY: Columbia University Press.

Midgley, J., & Livermore, M. M. (2008). *The handbook of social policy*. Thousand Oaks, CA: Sage.

Mink, G. (1996). *The wages of motherhood: Inequality in the welfare state, 1917–1942*. Ithaca, NY: Cornell University Press.

Murray, C. (1984). *Losing ground: American social policy, 1950–1980*. New York, NY: Basic Books.

National Association of Social Workers. (2018). *NASW code of ethics*. Retrieved from www.socialworkers.org/About/Ethics/Code-of-Ethics/Code-of-Ethics-English

Neubeck, K. J., & Cazenave, N. A. (2001). *Welfare racism: Playing the race card against America's poor*. New York, NY: Routledge.

Our Documents. (2015). *Transcript of Social Security Act* (1935). Retrieved from www.ourdocuments.gov/doc.php?doc=68&page=transcript

Pavetti, L. (2014). Data show that TANF didn't respond adequately to need during recession, contrary to new study's claims. *Center on Budget and Policy Priorities*. Retrieved from www.cbpp.org/blog/data-show-tanf-didnt-respond-adequately-to-need-during-recession-contrary-to-new-studys-claims

Quigley, W. P. (1997). Reluctant charity: Poor laws in the original thirteen states. *University of Richmond Law Review*, 1–52.

Quincy, J. (1821). *Massachusetts general court committee on pauper laws*. Boston, MA: Russell and Gardner.

Reagan, R. (1986). Radio address to the nation on welfare reform, February 15, 1986. *Gerhard Peters and John T. Woolley*. The American Presidency Project. Retrieved from www.presidency.ucsb.edu/ws/?pid=36875

Reef, C. (2002). *Childhood in America: An eyewitness history*. New York: Facts on File.

Richan, W. C. (1988). *Beyond altruism: Social policy in American society*. New York, NY: Haworth Press.

Richardson, G. (2007). The collapse of the United States banking system during the Great Depression, 1929 to 1933, archival evidence. *Australasian Accounting Business and Finance Journal*, *1*(1), 39–50.

Roberts, D. E. (1992). Racism and patriarchy in the meaning of motherhood. *American University Journal of Gender, Social Policy and Law*, *1*(1), 1–38.

Roberts, D. E. (1996). Welfare and the problem of Black citizenship. *Faculty Scholarship*. Paper 1283. Retrieved from http://scholarship.law.upenn.edu/faculty_scholarship/1283

Ross, J. A. B. (1985). 1935–1985: Fifty years of service to children and their families. *Social Bulletin*, *48*(10), 5–9.

Second Annual Report of the Managers of the Society for the Prevention of Pauperism in the City of New York. (1819). *The subject of pauperism*. Retrieved from http://babel.hathitrust.org/cgi/pt?id=hvd.32044100870971;view=1up;seq=1

Skocpol, T. (1992). *Protecting soldiers and mothers: The political origins of social policy in the United States*. Cambridge, MA: Harvard University Press.

Skocpol, T., Abend-Wein, M., Howard, C., & Goodrich-Lehmann, S. (1993). Women's associations and the enactment of mother's pensions in the United States. *The American Political Science Review*, *87*(3), 686–701.

Soule, S. A., & Zylan, Y. (1997). Runaway train: The diffusion of state-level reform in ADC/AFDC eligibility requirements, 1950–1967. *American Journal of Sociology*, *103*(3), 733–762.

Spiliakos, P. (2012). The roots of the conservative class war. *First Things*. Retrieved from www.firstthings.com/web-exclusives/2012/09/the-roots-of-conservative-class-war

Spitzer, S. J. (2012a). The emergence of race in national welfare politics: The 1962 and 1964 amendments to AFDC. *The Sixties: A Journal of History, Politics and Culture*, *5*(1), 75–112.

Spitzer, S. J. (2012b). Nixon's new deal: Welfare reform for the silent majority. *Presidential Studies Quarterly*, *42*(3), 455–481.

Tanner, M. D. (2016). Twenty years after welfare reform: The welfare system remains in place. *Cato Institute*. Retrieved from www.cato.org/publications/commentary/twenty-years-after-welfare-reform-welfare-system-remains-place

Trattner, W. I. (1999). *From poor law to welfare state: A history of social welfare in America* (6th ed.). New York, NY: The Free Press.

United States Bureau of the Census. (1949). *Historical statistics of the United States, 1789–1945: A supplement to the statistical abstract of the United States, Part I*. Washington, DC: U.S. Department of Commerce.

United States Department of Labor. (1965). *The negro family: The case for national action*. Retrieved from www.dol.gov/dol/aboutdol/history/webid-meynihan.htm

U.S. Department of Agriculture Food and Nutrition Program. (n.d.). *A short history of SNAP*. Retrieved from www.fns.usda.gov/snap/short-history-snap#1999

U.S. Department of Health & Human Services. (2008). *Office of the assistant security for planning and evaluation: Indicators of welfare dependence: Annual report to congress, 2008: AFDC/TANF program data*. Retrieved from https://aspe.hhs.gov/report/indicators-welfare-dependence-annual-report-congress-2008/afdctanf-program-data

Vallas, R., & Boteach, M. (2015). Top 5 reasons why TANF is not a model for other income assistance programs. *Center for American Progress*. Retrieved from www.americanprogress.org/issues/poverty/news/2015/04/29/112034/top-5-reasons-why-tanf-is-not-a-model-for-other-income-assistance-programs/

Walker, J. F., & Vatter, H. G. (1997). *The rise of big government in the United States*. New York, NY: M.E. Sharpe.

Ward, D. E. (2005). *The white welfare state: The racialization of the U.S. welfare state*. Ann Arbor: The University of Michigan Press.

Watkins, T. H. (2009). *The Great Depression: America in the 1930s*. New York, NY: Second Back Bay.

West, G. (1981). *The national welfare rights movement: The social protest of poor women*. New York, NY: Praeger.

Williams, L. A. (1997). Decades of distortion: The right's 30-year assault on welfare. *Political Research Associates*. Retrieved from www.politicalresearch.org/1997/12/06/decades-of-distortion-the-rights-30-year-assault-on-welfare/

Zastrow, C. (2009). *Introduction to social work and social welfare: Empowering people* (10th ed.). Belmont, CA: Brooks/Cole.

Zelizer, V. A. (1994). *Pricing the priceless child: The changing social value of children*. Princeton, NJ: Princeton University Press.

CHAPTER 7
Residential and Housing Segregation

Despite the passage of the Fair Housing Act in 1968, residential and housing segregation by race, and to a lesser extent ethnicity, remains stubbornly entrenched in the United States. For several reasons, residential segregation by race and ethnicity is a particularly vexing social inequality. Primary among those reasons is that place of residence and its related property values and tax base play such a critical role in determining the level of access and proximity to a number of society's rewards and privileges. As such, beneficiaries of residential segregation by race and ethnicity enjoy greater access and proximity than nonbeneficiaries to quality housing, education, health care, goods and services, and a range of fully functioning municipal services as well as the opportunity to build household wealth through home equity (Gotham, 2000; Ichiro & Berkman, 2003; Ludwig et al., 2012; Prakash, 2013; U.S. Housing Scholars and Research and Advocacy Organizations, 2008). This greater access and proximity to society's rewards and privileges over time allows for the perpetuation of inequality over generations between the beneficiaries and nonbeneficiaries of residential segregation by race and ethnicity.

This residential segregation and the disparities it causes in structural access to society's privileges and rewards has not happened by chance or personal choice (Seitles, 1996). Rather, it has developed slowly and deliberately and is the result of decades of racial and ethnic zoning ordinances, restrictive deed covenants, and local and federal policies, policies undergirded by a reoccurring narrative that applies racial and ethnic worth to real estate values (Gotham, 2000; Jackson, 1980; Seitles, 1996; Squires & Kubrin, 2006).

In this chapter, the social policies, forces, and institutions that helped produce and maintain residential segregation along racial and ethnic lines are examined and illustrated from an historical and contemporary perspective. The social policies and initiatives that have been enacted or proposed to eliminate residential segregation are also examined. The chapter is infused with figures and short profiles of some of the key actors in the creation of residential segregation.

Defining Residential Segregation

Residential segregation is the physical separation of a socially defined group within a spatial context, such that members of one group are disproportionally concentrated in a particular area, such as a neighborhood or community. The said group can be defined on the basis of characteristics such as race, ethnicity, sexual orientation, socioeconomic status, age, and religion (Massey & Denton, 1988).

Theories of Residential Segregation

A range of explanations for the phenomenon of residential segregation by race and ethnicity have been offered. The self-segregation hypothesis asserts that residential segregation is a matter of private action and consumer choice, with people, regardless of race, ethnicity, class, sexual orientation, and so on, wanting to live with others who are like them. Consequently, communities that are made up predominately of one

DOI: 10.4324/9781003023708-7

group are not a sign of exclusion or bigotry but rather a choice. Conflict theory, conversely, posits that residential segregation, most particularly when racial or ethnic, is a way to keep non-White groups from gaining access to the privilege and power of the neighborhood of the racial majority. Similarly, critical race theory views residential segregation by race and ethnicity, which is by far the most common and enduring form of residential segregation in the United States, as a structural construct that is designed to perpetuate inequality for the benefit of the White majority and to the detriment of the non-White population.

The Development of Residential Segregation

Residential segregation by race and ethnicity has long been a part of the American landscape. One of its earliest incarnations (1831–1842) was the forced displacement and relocation of Native Americans and Alaskan Natives from their homelands to reservations (Johansen, 2006). In 1835, there was the informal segregation of Mexicans in Texas following the Texas War of Independence (Manchaca, 2001). In 1876, there was the enactment of Jim Crow legislation that segregated Black and White residents in all spheres of daily life in the former slaving-holding southern states (Chafe, 2001; Deyle, 2006; Packard, 2002). And in 1884, in response to the growing and thriving Chinese population, there was California's adoption of anti-Chinese ordinances restricting the movement of Chinese immigrants to specific areas (Maltz, 1994).

These forms of residential segregation were largely policy driven and rooted in a racist ideology that articulated a view of Blacks as inferior, Native Americans and Alaskan Natives as in need of civilizing, Mexicans as interlopers, and the Chinese as a threat to the moral order of the country. The early forms of American residential segregation, although overtly racist, had a more specific purpose than just racial and ethnic animus. It was the mechanism by which inequality in structural access to the expanding nation's land and other resources could be maintained.

Racial Zoning Ordinances, 1910–1917

Despite the historical examples, until the start of the 20th century, residential segregation by race and ethnicity was not a national phenomenon but rather a regional issue. The Chinese, for example, were mainly located on the West Coast, Mexicans and Native Americans in the Southwest, Blacks in the rural South (Massey, 2001). However, a number of social forces changed this dynamic and ushered in the beginning of residential segregation by race and ethnicity as both a national phenomenon and permanent feature of social arrangements in the United States.

These social forces were the Industrial Revolution, which was at its height; the growth of northeastern and midwestern industrial cities in need of labor; and the first Great Migration of southern Blacks to northeastern and midwestern industrial cities in response to the call for labor. Between 1910 and 1930, this Great Migration of some 1.6 million southern Blacks saw the populations of northeastern and midwestern industrial cities such as New York, Philadelphia, Baltimore, Chicago, and Detroit grow exponentially (Gotham, 2000; Jackson, 1980; Seitles, 1996). In Chicago, for example, the Black population increased from 44,000 to 234,000 between 1910 and 1930. Over the same period, New York City's Black population tripled from 100,000 to 328, 000, Philadelphia's from 84,500 to 220,000, Detroit's from 6,000 to 120,000, and Cleveland's from 8,500 to 72,000 (Gotham, 2000).

The working-class native White and ethnic White immigrant residents (who themselves were victims of xenophobia, marginalization, and discrimination) of these cities greeted the influx of such large numbers of Blacks with both fear and disdain. Much of the source of these feelings came from the increased competition for employment, as well as the threat it posed to the bargaining power of the labor unions to negotiate rates of pay (Arnesen, 2002; Lemann, 1991). Indeed, companies regularly used Blacks as strikebreakers to undermine or prevent the unionization of the White working class (Arnesen, 2002).

Besides the competition for employment, there was also competition for living space. In contrast to the years before the Great Migration when northern Blacks were dispersed in small clusters in White

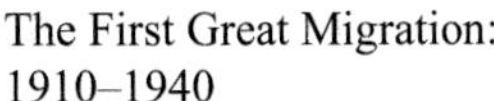

The Second Great Migration:
1940–1970

The change in share of Blacks in cities is based on the percentage point difference in the percent of population that was Black in the later time period compared to the earlier. For example, 18.3 percent of the population in Gary, IN was Black in 1940 but was just 2.3 in 1910, which represented a 16.0 percentage-point change in the share of Blacks in the city. It was the largest change in share during the First Great Migration. By the end of the Second Great Migration, Newark, NJ had realized the largest increase in Black population share, with the Black proportion of the city rising from 10.6 in 1940 to 54.2 in 1970.

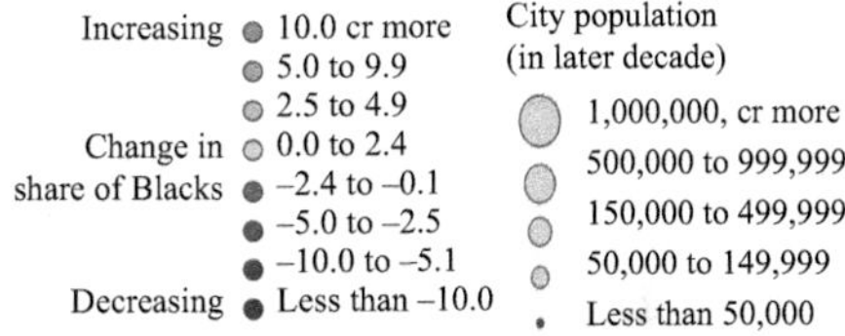

Figure 7.1 Great Migration Map, 1910–1970

NOTE: Data are from decennial censuses, 1910 through 1970. Population counts are based on unrevised numbers. Data for the Black population for cities in Alaska and Hawaii were not available in 1940 or earlier decades. Cities shown are those that were either in the top 100 cities in the country or top three of a state and had a Black population of at least 100 people. These criteria were placed on 1940 data for the First Great Migration and 1970 data for the Second Great Migration.

neighborhoods, living in relative obscurity, the large number of new southern Black migrants had no such luxury. Rather, they were in direct competition with newly or established ethnic White immigrants for the scarce supply of housing. This situation allowed landlords to charge prohibitively high rents to both ethnic White immigrants and Black migrants alike (Arnesen, 2002).

In response to the increased competition caused by the presence of such large numbers of Blacks, local municipalities racialized their public spaces and enacted racial zoning ordinances. Like those used in California to control the movement of Chinese immigrants in the late 19th century, the racial zoning ordinances in the northeastern urban cities restricted Blacks to residency in particular segregated enclaves. Most typically, these enclaves were in the least desirable parts of the city with housing stock that was dilapidated or in a state of disrepair. Over the course of time, these enclaves became identified as ghettos, rife with social problems and not worthy of investment (Florette, 1975; Massey & Denton, 1988).

What emerges from this erroneous and racially biased assessment of Black enclaves is a real estate ideology associating Blacks with declining property values and neighborhood instability (Gotham, 2000). This ideology was soon disseminated and amplified as incontrovertible truth in the numerous published textbooks, pamphlets, and periodicals of the powerful and influential National Association of Real Estate Boards (NAREB). Informing this ideology was the view that all-White racially homogenous neighborhoods were superior for both residential life and a requisite for protecting the homeowner's investment (Gotham, 2000). Ironically, this definition of all-White homogenous neighborhoods did not just mean non-Black. In many cases, it also meant a neighborhood free of Jewish, Irish, Italian, Mexican, and Asian immigrants, all groups who had their own enclaves and were often viewed as racially and ethnically undesirable as neighbors by White, American-born Protestants in the early part of the 20th century (Brodkin, 1998; Guglielmo, 2003; Jackson, 1980).

Racial zoning ordinances and the ideology informing them did not, however, exist without challenge. Indeed, the National Association of Colored People (NAACP) and its allies took the issue to the Supreme Court in 1917 (*Buchanan v. Warely*). The Supreme Court ruled that outright racial zoning ordinances were unconstitutional as they violated the Fourteenth Amendment (*Buchanan v. Warely*, 245 U.S. 60, 1917; Jones-Correa, 2001).

The Restricted Deed Covenant, 1918–1948

Although the *Buchanan v. Warely* Supreme Court ruling ended racial zoning ordinances, it did not put an end to racial and ethnic residential segregation by race and ethnicity. Instead, it prompted local municipalities and cities, at the behest of powerful institutional actors such as property owners, developers, and the National Association of Real Estate Boards (NAREB), to adopt a more insidious policy for racializing public space. This restricted deed covenant was an agreement that bound all involved not to sell, rent, or lease property to minority groups, most typically Blacks, but also, depending on the part of the country, Jews, Asians, Mexicans, and other groups considered non-White (Brooks, 2002; Jones-Correa, 2001; Silva, 2008). Undergirding this agreement was the sentiments of the NAREB, whose 1923 publication *Principles of Real Estate Practice* stated, "the purchase of property by certain racial types is very likely to diminish the value of other properties" (Fisher, 1923, p. 116). In later publications, the NAREB concluded that "foreigners were the most undesirable residents." In fact, as late as the 1950s, the NAREB's code of ethics urged realtors not to introduce into the neighborhood members of any race or nationality whose presence would be detrimental to property values (U.S. Commission on Civil Rights, 1973).

The restricted deed covenant proved to be a much more robust practice for residentially segregating people by race and ethnicity than racial zoning ordinances. Indeed, in the 1926 *Corrigan v. Buckley* legal challenge, the Supreme Court ruled that as a form of private contract, restricted deed covenants were legally enforceable (*Corrigan v. Buckley*, 271 U.S. 323, 1926; Jones-Correa, 2001). In their ruling, the judges stated:

> The constitutional right of a Negro to acquire, own, occupy property does not carry with it the constitutional power to compel sale and conveyance to him of any particular private property. The individual citizen, whether he is Black or White, may refuse to sell or lease his property to any particular individual or class of individuals.
>
> (*Corrigan v. Buckley*, 271 U.S. 323, 1926; *Jones-Correa*, 2001, p. 544)

From 1918 until 1948, when ruled unconstitutional by the Supreme Court, the restricted deed covenant or something similar to it was used by all of the northeastern and midwestern urban cities to restrict the ability of Blacks to reside in any place other than a Black enclave (Jones-Correa, 2001). The restricted deed covenant was also used in other parts of the country where the local White population felt threatened by the presence or influx of new racial and ethnic groups. In Seattle, a series of deed restrictions relegated the Chinese, Filipino, and Jewish communities to residency in the older parts of the Central District and Chinatown (Majumdar, 2007; Silva, 2008). In Baltimore, it prohibited Jewish occupancy in gentile suburbs (Power, 1996). In the Lakeshore district of Pennsylvania, it restricted residency for Mexicans and European immigrants from Hungary, Greece, and Italy to specific non-White enclaves (Fogelson, 2005). In Chicago and Los Angeles, it was responsible for restrictive codes barring not just Black families but also Mexican (Chicano) families from 80% of the city's property (U.S. Commission on Civil Rights, 1973).

Though the intent of the restricted deed covenant was to create residential segregation by race and ethnicity, it is important to note that absentee landlords regularly violated them. The principal reason for this was that landlords could earn more money by renting to Blacks or ethnic White immigrants at higher rates than they could native-born Whites (Brooks, 2002; Hirsch, 1983). Moreover, Hirsch (1983) suggests when neighbors sought judicial enforcement against violators, courts, at least in Chicago, were unresponsive. Indeed, Hirsch (1983) argues that residential segregation for Blacks was as much a function of a shortage of available housing and threats of violence as it was the restricted deed covenant.

There is certainly evidence to support Hirsh's view, given the threats and actual cases of violence that occurred when Blacks flouted the covenant deed and dared to move into the White community or challenge White supremacy. The most telling example of this violence came in the Red Summer of 1919, when White mobs in 38 cities across the nation, half of them in the Northeast, attacked and killed more than a hundred Blacks, injured hundreds more, and destroyed scores of Black homes and businesses (Tuttle, 1996). The result of such violence in support of the restricted deed covenant confirmed that Blacks would continue to be denied equal access to the rewards and privileges of residing in a racially and ethnically diverse community (Williams, 1972).

The Home Owners Loan Corporation and the Federal Housing Act, 1933–1943

If the first two decades of the 20th century can be seen as providing a foundation for establishing residential segregation by race and ethnicity as a permanent feature of social arrangements in the United States, the third decade can be seen as establishing and solidifying the process. The social force at the heart of this was the Wall Street crash of 1929. The Wall Street crash, which came after a decade of prosperity that saw the introduction of credit, consumerism, and the building of national highways, so devastated the economy that there was widespread destitution in all areas of American life. Moreover, the bank runs that followed the crash all but froze available credit. Such was the enormity of the task of preventing a complete collapse of the American economy that the federal government had to step in and turn around the floundering economy (Trattner, 1999).

The Home Owners' Loan Corporation (HOLC) was among the many federal initiatives put in place to turn around the economy. Signed into law by President Franklin D. Roosevelt (FDR) in 1933 as part of an overall plan to make homeownership a national policy, the HOLC had two primary responsibilities: (1) protect small homeowners from foreclosure, and (2) relieve them of part of the burden of excessive mortgage interest and principal payments (Jackson, 1980).

To do this, the HOLC refinanced tens of thousands of mortgages in danger of default or foreclosure. It also granted loans at low interest rates to permit owners to recover homes lost through forced sales. In its two years of granting loans, 1933–1935, the HOLC supplied over $3 billion in mortgage assistance or loans (Jackson, 1980).

As important as the financial support was, the real legacy of the HOLC was its introduction, perfecting, and proving in practice the feasibility of the long-term self-amortizing mortgage with uniform fixed-interest spread over the life of the debt, 20 to 25 years. Prior to this, in order to buy a home, there were a couple of things that made a mortgage prohibitively expensive. First, one had to have a down payment of 30% to 50% of the value of the home, and second, the mortgage was no more than five years in length and came with variable rate interest that would balloon after a fixed period (Jackson, 1980).

The HOLC's other legacy, and the one that would later significantly contribute to racial and ethnic residential segregation, was its initiation of the practice of redlining. The practice came out of the HOLC's appraisal method for predicting safe and risky mortgage loans. The HOLC had developed the appraisal method because it needed a mechanism for predicting who of all the small homeowners would be the best risk not to foreclose after receiving federal mortgage assistance or a loan (Jackson, 1980). Toward this end and with great attention to detail, the HOLC created security maps for 239 cities. Each city was divided into neighborhoods that were assessed by HOLC appraisers. Appraisers evaluated factors such as stability of the neighborhood, adequacy of transportation, marketability of the properties, conditions of sidewalk and street surfacing, connected utilities, racial and or ethnic homogeneity/heterogeneity of neighborhood residents, as well as their socioeconomic status, to name but a few items (Jackson, 1980). Based on the appraiser's determination, and with the support of local realtors and banks, each neighborhood would receive a grade determining level of risk for a loan. These grades, which ranged from A to D, came with an accompanying color (Figure 7.2). On the security map, neighborhoods given an A grade were considered the best risk—new homes, homogeneous population as represented by the presence of White American business and professional men, and in demand as a residential location. These neighborhoods were

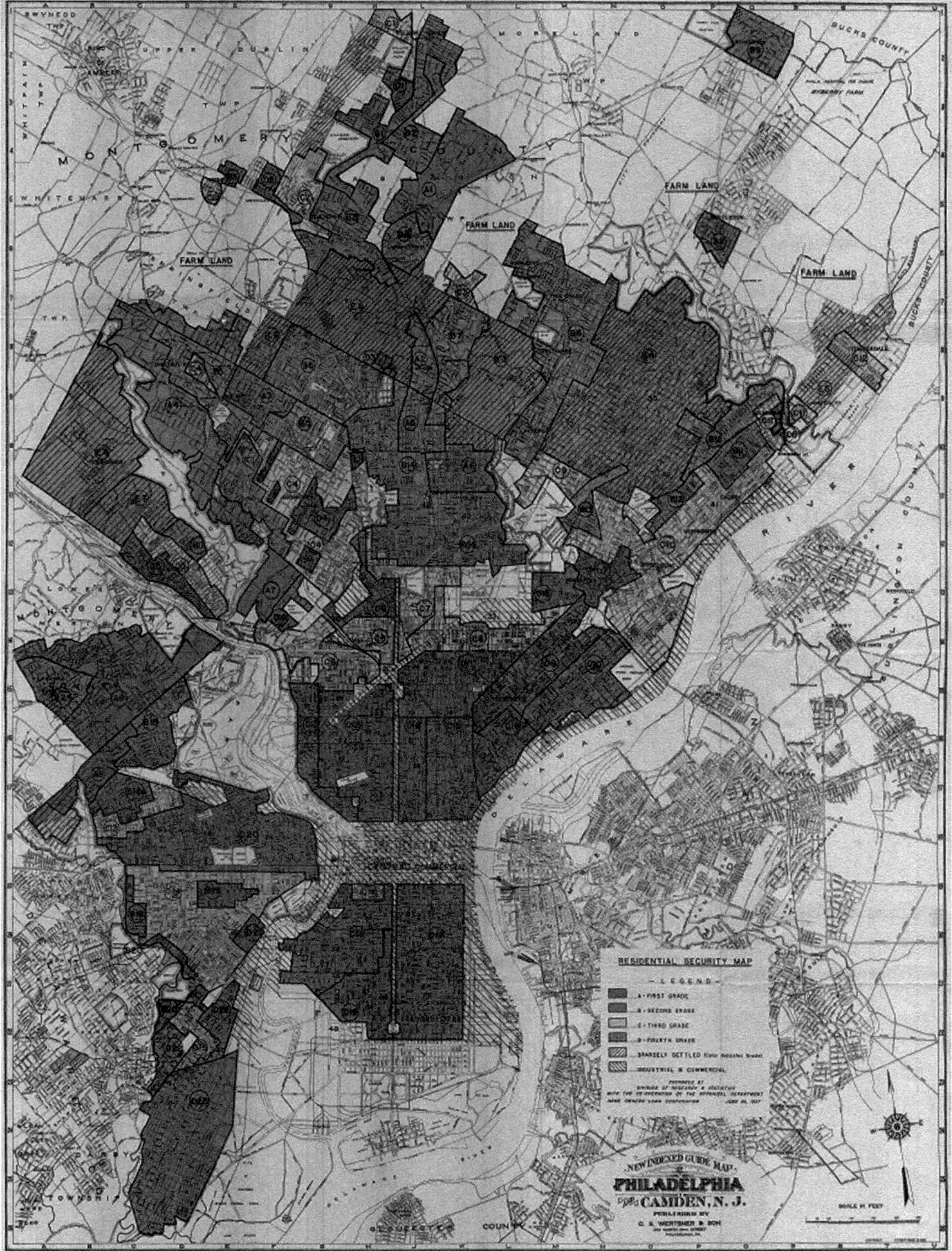

Figure 7.2 HOLC Security Map, Philadelphia, Showing Redlining

outlined in green. Neighborhoods given a B rating were considered the next best risk—desirable and stable, but not necessarily homogeneous as represented by professional and working people who were Jewish, Irish, Italian, and so on. These neighborhoods were outlined in blue. Neighborhoods given a C rating were considered a poor risk and in decline, and were outlined in yellow. Finally, neighborhoods given a D rating were considered the worst risk. These neighborhoods were older, in a state of disrepair, considered on the way down, poorly resourced, and characterized by social instability. Although not always the case because of restricted deed covenants, these neighborhoods were most typically primarily composed of Black or poor, foreign ethnic residents. These neighborhoods were outlined in red.

Hence the term "redlining," referring to a neighborhood and its residents being appraised as a poor risk for a loan or mortgage only because of where they live and without due consideration of their individual circumstances. All this said, there is no evidence that during its two years of granting loans that the HOLC discriminated racially or ethnically when granting assistance to homeowners in danger of foreclosure (Massey & Denton, 1993).

Although applying racial and ethnic worth to real estate appraisal had long been in practice, the HOLC's use of it as part of its appraisal method was significant because it marked the first time it was used at a federal or large-scale level. The impact of this was to be monumental, not least because the appraisal methods devised by the HOLC were praised by National Association of Real Estate Boards for improving the standard of real estate appraising in America (Jackson, 1980). Indeed, lenders and other federal agencies would use it, most especially redlining, for years to come as a template for assessing mortgage loan risk.

The Federal Housing Administration (FHA)

The National Housing Act of 1934 was a New Deal initiative signed into law by FDR. Also known as the Capehart Act, the National Housing Act created the Federal Housing Administration (FHA), the Federal Savings and Loan Insurance Corporation (FSLIC), and the U.S. Housing Authority (HUD). Of these programs, the FHA was by far the most prominent.

Although a federal program, the FHA in its earliest days was run mostly by representatives of the National Association of Real Estate Boards (NAREB) and the banking industry. Its principal responsibilities were to reduce the cost of mortgages and spur homebuilding. As suggested by Jackson (1980), between the years of 1934 and 1968, the FHA had a remarkable record of accomplishment in both these endeavors. It did so by providing federal insurance coverage for long-term mortgage loans made by private lenders for home construction and sale. To be able to do this, the FHA collected premiums, set up reserves for losses, and in the event of a mortgage default, indemnified the lender (Jackson, 1980).

With the full weight of the U.S. Treasury behind insuring private lenders against loss, the FHA profoundly changed the home finance business in a number of ways. First, it significantly lowered the down payment needed to purchase a home. Second, it instituted the practice originated by the HOLC and extended the self-amortizing mortgage repayment period to 25 or 30 years, thus reducing average monthly payments and the national rate of mortgage foreclosures. Third, it established minimum standards of home construction, standards that would become almost universal in the industry. Fourth, it lowered the mortgage interest rates (Jackson, 1980). The net result of these changes was that many more American families could reasonably expect to purchase a home (Jackson, 1980; Seitles, 1996).

Unfortunately, though, for all its good work, the FHA was not an equal opportunity insurer. Right from its beginnings, the FHA denied non-Whites, most notably Blacks, mortgage insurance. This denial was premised on the prevailing segregationist attitude of the NAREB and influential real estate figures Fredrick Babcock, who helped to craft the FHA's underwriting manual, and Homer Hoyt, who served as an advisor to the FHA. Babcock, for example, argued in his influential textbook *The Valuation of Real Estate* (1932) that more than any other factor, race had the biggest impact on real estate value. In the language of the day, Babcock posited that so different were the traits and characteristics of the White and Negro populations that if they were to live together, land values in White neighborhoods would decline dramatically. Consequently, the only way to maintain the land values of White neighborhoods was to segregate the two populations residentially (Babcock, 1932). Similarly, Hoyt argued that because of poverty and unique cultural values, Blacks, eastern European Jews, southern Italians, and Mexicans had lower standards of living. As such, they were unstable tenants as well as repugnant to native Whites and to northern European ethnic groups. Therefore, they must be kept separate from the White community if economic stability and property values were to be maintained (Hoyt, 1933).

Indeed, the FHA's underwriting manual explicitly stated these sentiments in its warning of inharmonious racial groups and the conclusion that if a neighborhood were to retain stability, it was necessary that properties continued to be occupied by the same social and racial class (Massey & Denton, 1993; Seitles, 1996). In explicitly stating these sentiments, the FHA's underwriting manual gave tacit approval to banks, private lenders, land developers, realtors, and community associations to use redlining, racial zoning ordinances, and racial and ethnic restrictive deed covenants to maintain all-White communities. The full impact of this would be realized in the years between 1944 and 1970.

The FHA, the G.I. Bill, and the Building of Suburbia, 1944–1960

The years between 1944 and 1960 witnessed an unprecedented transformation of the American homeownership landscape and completed the process by which residential segregation, primarily by race and to a lesser extent ethnicity, would become a permanent feature of social arrangements in America. A confluence of interrelated social forces and federal policy informed this transformation.

The first of these social forces was the end of World War II in 1945 and the passing of the Servicemen's Readjustment Act, signed into law by FDR in 1944. In keeping with FDR's promise to the returning troops of a new and prosperous America, the Servicemen's Readjustment Act, also known as the G.I. Bill, provided veterans of World War II and later the Korean War a range of benefits, among them a guaranteed low-interest mortgage for the purchase of a single-family or mobile home (Trattner, 1999). Consequently, hundreds of thousands of working-class men were in a position for the first time in their lives to become homeowners, which was particularly significant for the generation of men born between 1900 and 1920, many of whom served in either World War II or the Korean War (Mettler, 2005).

The second social force was the chronic shortage of housing in the now decaying urban cities, a shortage that was exacerbated by the Second Great Migration beginning in 1940 of five million southern Blacks to northeastern and western urban cities (Boustan, 2010). Many of these cities, New York in particular, had also experienced high levels of migration from Puerto Rico in the 1950s. Added to this were the Housing Act of 1949 and Title II of the Housing Act of 1954. Both of these acts promised to demolish urban slums and revitalize the economy of cities across the nation, as well as end de facto segregation. In actuality, however, they did little more than facilitate the razing of long-standing thriving and close-knit racial and ethnic enclaves and communities in cities as disparate as Camden, New York, Boston, Seattle, Stockton, Kansas City, Minnesota, Charlotte, Milwaukee, and San Francisco. In the process, master builders such as Robert Moses (see Profile) used eminent domain to construct expressways and buildings that were considered good for the cities if not necessarily for its residents.

Profiles

Robert Moses (1888–1981)

Born in Connecticut, raised in Manhattan, and educated at Yale, Oxford and Columbia, Dr. Robert Moses was one of America's leading builders and a major force behind the shaping of the modern American city. Moses' rise to prominence began in the 1920s as an assistant to the New York Governor, Al Smith. As an assistant to Al Smith, Moses earned the reputation as an excellent bill-drafter in the state capital. Moses' excellence as a bill-drafter not only allowed Al Smith to reorganize and consolidate many aspects of state government, but it also allowed him to implement a number of post-Great Depression reforms. Among these reforms, and the one that Robert Moses would make his life work once out of state government, was urban planning and renewal (Caro, 1974).

Although never holding an elected post, as the creator and leader of several public authorities, Moses was able to get New York State more New Deal financed public works corporations than any other state in the nation, thus allowing for massive infrastructure rebuilding in New York. It also gave Moses a powerbase second only to the governor. Form this powerbase, and with a clear vision for the urban renewal of New York, Moses had sole control of all income from his projects' revenue generation, such as tolls, as well as the ability to issue bonds so he could borrow vast sums of money to fund and initiate new construction projects. Indeed, such was his level of power that Moses was not bound by the power of purse (i.e., the ability of one group to control the actions of another by withholding or putting stipulations on funding), as typically is the case with public works, nor was he answerable to public comment on his projects (Caro, 1974).

In the years between 1930 and 1969, Moses used this unbridled power to reinvent the urban landscape of New York by way of numerous construction projects. These construction projects included the building of 10 public swimming pools, 13 bridges, 416 miles of parkways, 658 playgrounds, 150,000 housing units, zoos, civic centers, exhibition halls, and the 1964-65 New York World Fair, at a cost equivalent to $150 billion dollars in today's money (Caro, 1974).

Moses' influence was not contained to New York as urban planners in cities across the country hired him to design freeway networks in the 1940s and early 1950s. However, because of local opposition, and lack of funding many of the projects did not go past the planning phase (Caro, 1974).

For all of his achievements, Moses was a polarizing figure, not least because of his seeming disregard for the people displaced, some 250, 000 and neighborhoods destroyed by his building projects. When asked about this, Robert Moses responded with the following quote:

> "I raise my stein to the builder who can remove ghettos without removing people as I hail the chef who can make omelets without breaking eggs."

Reference

Caro, R.A. (1974). *The power broker: Robert Moses and the fall of New York*. New York, NY: Alfred A. Knopf.

The third social force was the mass building of single-family homes by developers such as William Levitt (see Profile) in the late 1940s. Spurred on by the housing shortage and the prompting of the FHA and Veterans Administration (VA), these homes were located in self-contained suburban communities far from the urban centers. They were also built to FHA and VA specifications, thus ensuring mortgage approval for eligible borrowers (Massey & Denton, 1993; Seitles, 1996).

The fourth social force was the active recruitment of urban city residents to take up the offer of a new home in the suburbs, a proposal that was made all the more attractive because of the Federal Highway Act, which was signed into law in 1956 by President D. Eisenhower. The act authorized the construction of 41,000 miles of the interstate highway system, and expanded roadway infrastructure, increased suburbanization, and made the commute between urban centers and the suburbs possible and relatively quick (Massey & Denton, 1993; Seitles, 1996).

Figure 7.3 Levittown Advertisement

Also making the move an attractive proposition was the relative affordability of the homes, the guarantee of a low-interest FHA or VA mortgage for nonveterans and veterans alike, and the opportunity to ascend into the middle class by becoming a homeowner. No surprise, then, that the years between 1950 and 1970 saw an unprecedented "White flight" from the urban centers to the suburbs; record numbers of Whites of various European ancestries, some of whom had not been considered desirable neighbors at the turn of the century (e.g., Italian, Irish, Jewish, etc.), left ethnically mixed urban neighborhoods to live in racially homogeneous, self-contained suburban communities (Roediger, 2006).

As a result, 18 of the nation's top 25 cities suffered a net loss of people, with the suburban population doubling from 37 to 74 million (Jackson, 1980).

Furthermore, in the years between 1960 and 2000, the suburban homeownership rate, which fluctuated between 70% and 73%, far exceeded those in the central city and metropolitan areas.

A corollary to this White flight to the suburbs was that the urban centers were stripped of long-standing residents, hastening the centers' decay (Jackson, 1980). Furthermore, Black and Hispanics, in particular, were denied anything like fair or equal access to the huge number of new homes constructed in the suburbs, as illustrated by the fact that between 1934 and 1969, only 2% of FHA loans went to non-Whites. Even when Blacks and Hispanics could get a loan, for instance G.I. Bill recipients, they still faced significant barriers to obtaining a home in the suburbs. These obstacles included the discriminatory practices of realtors, home associations, and homebuilders. Indeed, William Levitt had a clause in his homeownership agreement barring occupancy by any person other than members of the Caucasian race (Herbold, 1995). Even when the Supreme Court struck down this practice in 1948, de facto racial and ethnic segregation was still practiced.

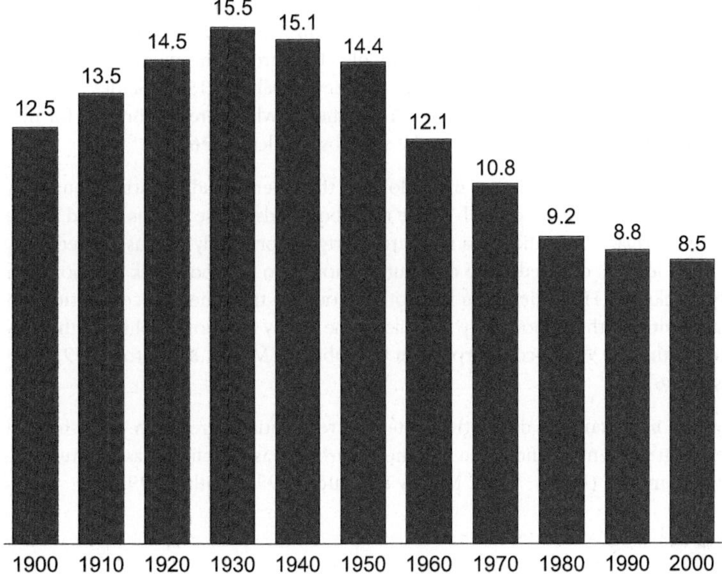

Figure 7.4 Percentage of Total Population Living in the Ten Largest Cities, 1900 to 2000

Source: U.S. Census Bureau, decennial census of housing, 1960 to 2000

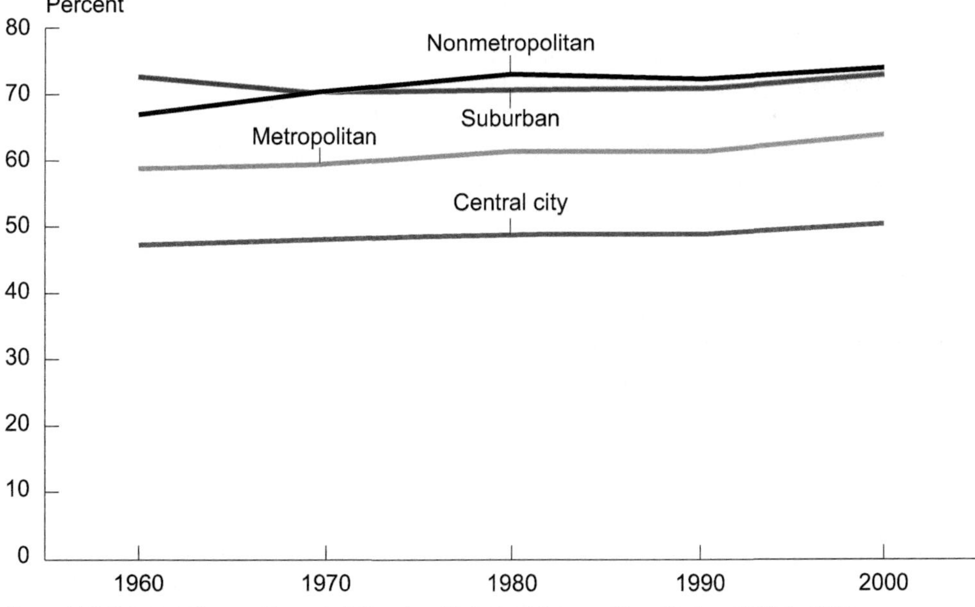

Figure 7.5 Percent Owner-Occupied Housing Units by Metropolitan Status, 1960 to 2000

Source: U.S. Census Bureau, decennial census of housing, 1960 to 2000

The net result of the discriminatory practices of the FHA, the VA, private lenders, real estate brokers, and homebuilders was the creation of a dual housing market in which millions of White working-class males and their families were able to ascend into the middle class through homeownership. In turn, they were able to build home equity and household wealth (Massey & Denton, 1993; Seitles, 1996). This process was almost completely underwritten by the FHA and the VA, who were responsible for three-fifths of the mortgages that facilitated the White flight to the suburbs (Seitles, 1996).

Conversely, Blacks and Hispanics had to make do with the older, already existing housing, previously occupied by Whites in what had been all-White neighborhoods. These homes would not, however, be eligible for FHA mortgage insurance or a standard mortgage, primarily because of redlining; the FHA, banks, and private lenders deemed these older urban homes to be a poor risk for mortgage insurance. Consequently, Blacks and Hispanics were left not only outside the sphere of conventional mortgage lending but also without the opportunity to build home equity and household wealth anywhere near commensurate with their White counterparts in the suburbs (Massey & Denton, 1993; Oliver & Shapiro, 1997; Seitles, 1996).

Finally, and just as importantly, a distinctive pattern of residential segregation—in which Blacks and Hispanics live in urban centers and Whites in the suburbs—was established as a feature of structural arrangements in America (Baylor, 1996; Massey & Denton, 1993; Seitles, 1996).

The Quest for Equality, 1960–2000

In the years between 1960 and 1977, several significant legislative actions were taken to remedy the entrenched racialized structures and discriminatory practices that so disadvantaged Black and Hispanics in the housing market (Jolly, 2006).

First, in 1968, against the backdrop of civil unrest and the findings of the National Advisory Commission on Civil Disorders, more commonly known as the Kerner Commission, President Lyndon Johnson signed into law Title VIII of the Civil Rights Act. More commonly known as the Fair Housing Act (FHA), Title VIII of the Civil Rights Act created the Office of Fair Housing and Equal Opportunity. The FHA made it illegal to discriminate in the sale, lease, or rental of housing or otherwise making housing unavailable because of race, color, religion, sex, handicap, familial status, or national origin (Trifun, 2009). Note that sex and handicap were added by way of amendments in 1974 and 1988, respectively. Also, note that in 2017, in the *Smith v. Avanti* case, Judge Raymond P. Moore of U.S. District Court of Colorado ruled that the FHA protects LGBTQ couples from housing discrimination, the first ruling of this kind (Lambda Legal, n.d.).

Second, in response to the severe shortage of credit available in low and middle-income Black and Hispanic urban communities, President Gerald Ford signed into law the Equal Credit Opportunity Act of 1974. The law made it unlawful for any creditor to discriminate against any applicant, with respect to any aspect of credit transaction, on the basis of race, color, religion, national origin, sex, marital status, or age (Trifun, 2009).

Third, as a result of concern that credit shortages were contributing to the structural decline of urban communities, not least because financial institutions were not providing home financing for qualified applicants, President Gerald Ford signed into law the Home Mortgage Disclosure Act (HMDA) of 1975. The law required financial institutions to maintain and annually disclose to the public and federal government data about home purchase, pre-approvals, home improvement, and refinance applications. In 1989, amendments to the law required the collection and disclosure of data about applicant and borrower demographics to help identify potential discriminatory lending patterns and enforcing antidiscriminatory statutes (Trifun, 2009).

Fourth, as a result of national pressure to address deteriorating conditions in low-income and minority urban communities, President Jimmy Carter signed into law the Community Reinvestment Act of 1977. The law addressed discrimination in loans made to individuals and businesses from low- and moderate-income urban neighborhoods. The law required all Federal Deposit Insurance Company (FDIC) chartered banks to end redlining and meet the credit needs of low- and middle-income urban communities (Trifun, 2009).

The cumulative impact of these policies was mixed. On one hand, residential segregation between 1980 and 2000 declined for all racial and ethnic groups, most particularly for Blacks. The declines were most concentrated in urban areas with small Black populations (Charles, 2003). In the urban areas with large Black populations and a tradition of residential segregation by race and ethnicity, such as New York, Chicago, Detroit, Atlanta, Houston, and Washington, the declines were minimal at best (Iceland et al., 2002). As a result, Blacks remained the most residentially segregated group and in many urban communities hyper-segregated. Hispanics remained the second most segregated group in urban areas, followed by Asians and Pacific Islanders, and then Native Americans not on reservations, and Alaskan Natives (Iceland et al., 2002).

Furthermore, the Fair Housing Act was not a watershed moment as predicted by President Lyndon Johnson, not least because it lacked a critical enforcement mechanism. Indeed, between 1968 and 1995, there were two million confirmed housing discrimination incidents, of which only 400 fair housing cases in the same period were settled (Powell & Cardwell, 2013). Similarly, despite laws on the book prohibiting redlining, the practice did not fully abate. Rather, it was replaced by the practice of steering, that is, real estate brokers maneuvering a client from a racial/ethnic minority group away from considering a home in a White neighborhood and vice versa (Trifun, 2009).

Moreover, none of the acts related to increasing access to credit with reasonable terms and conditions in residentially segregated communities proved as successful as was hoped, and as a result the residents of these communities became a natural market for predatory lending. Simply put, predatory lending involves a lender enticing, inducing, and/or assisting a borrower into taking a loan or mortgage that carries high fees and interest rate and strips the borrower of equity, all for the benefit of the lender and to the detriment of the borrower (Trifun, 2009).

Subprime Lending, 1999–2006

By far the most insidious and significant form of predatory lending in residentially segregated communities is the subprime mortgage, a class of mortgage offered to borrowers with a poor credit history. Because of a poor credit history and a default risk that is higher than for borrowers with a good credit history, lending agencies charge significantly higher fees and interest rates on subprime loans than prime loans. Although the subprime loan is a legal and valuable service for individuals with a poor credit history and very few avenues for borrowing, there is ample evidence that in residentially segregated urban communities, they were offered to Black and Hispanic borrowers even when they qualified for prime loans with much lower fees and interest rates (Smith, 2007).

Subprime mortgages emerged in residentially segregated urban communities in the late 1990s with the repeal of the Glass–Steagall Act of 1933, an act that had prohibited commercial banks from engaging in the investment banking following the collapse of nearly 5,000 banks during the Great Depression. With no Glass–Steagall Act in place, banks were allowed for the first time in decades to earn 25% of their revenue from investment banking (Rugh & Massey, 2010). One of the investment products designed because of the newly acquired ability of banks to make money from investment banking was the securitized mortgage. Simply put, the securitized mortgage involved banks originating, pooling, and then dividing mortgages into low- and high-risk tranches, known as collateralized debt obligations (CDOs), for sale to investors (Rugh & Massey, 2010). With the housing boom in the late 1990s and early 2000s, banks turned to the lucrative subprime mortgage market and began originating, pooling, and dividing subprime mortgages into their collateralized debt obligation. Because of the high fees charged for subprime mortgages, these CDOs offered huge profits and relatively low risk for banks and investors alike (Rugh & Massey, 2010). However, the banks, which were now no longer bound by their available deposits for the number of mortgages they could originate and offer, needed to expand their subprime borrowing pool if they and their investors were to profit from the housing boom (Rugh & Massey, 2010).

Given the hundreds of thousands of residents in racially and ethnically segregated urban communities who had been previously shunned by banks because of redlining, this was a population that suddenly became an attractive source of potential borrowers for those very same banks. What made them such an attractive source was that they were ideal candidates for subprime mortgages that as part of a collateralized debt obligation would make huge profits for the banks and their investors (Rugh & Massey, 2010).

Toward this end, from 1996 on, lending institutions systematically targeted and induced Black and to a lesser extent Hispanic residents of racially and ethnically segregated urban communities to take out subprime mortgages, regardless of suitability (Rugh & Massey, 2010; U.S. Department of Housing and Urban Development, 1998).

To induce borrowers, banks or their representative mortgage brokers offered gimmicks such as 0% down with teaser adjustable rate mortgages, which started out with a discounted (and affordable) fixed low-interest rate for a set number of years. Hidden, however, were the realities of a subprime mortgage (Rugh & Massey, 2010). These realities included balloon payments and interest rates that after a fixed period adjusted to higher rates, suddenly adding hundreds or thousands of dollars to a monthly mortgage repayment of a borrower who might already be leveraged to the maximum when paying at the initial rate of interest (Rugh & Massey, 2010).

So successful were banks and mortgage brokers in inducing new borrowers to the subprime mortgage market that from 1996 to 1998 the number of subprime mortgages went from 300,000 to 800,000, with a dollar volume increase of $20 billion to $150 billion.

By 2005, the dollar volume had increased again to a massive $625 billion (Gramlich, 2007). A disproportionate number of these subprime originations went to Blacks, among which single women were significantly overrepresented (Castro-Baker, 2014), and to a lesser extent Hispanic residents of racially and ethnically segregated urban communities, be they low, middle, or high income (Rugh & Massey, 2010). In fact, in Black residentially segregated communities, subprime lending accounted for 51% of all home loans in 1998, compared to only 9% in predominately White communities. Comparable 1993 figures were 8% for Black residentially segregated communities and 1% for predominately White communities.

Just as tellingly, though, is that even in high-income Black residentially segregated communities in 1998, 39% of the home loans were subprime, compared to 18% in low-income White communities (see

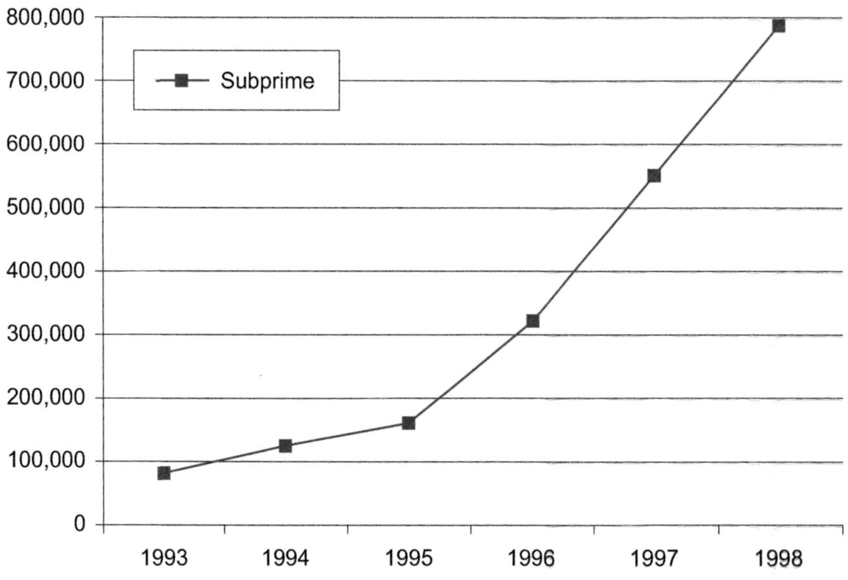

Figure 7.6 Growth in Subprime Refinance Lending

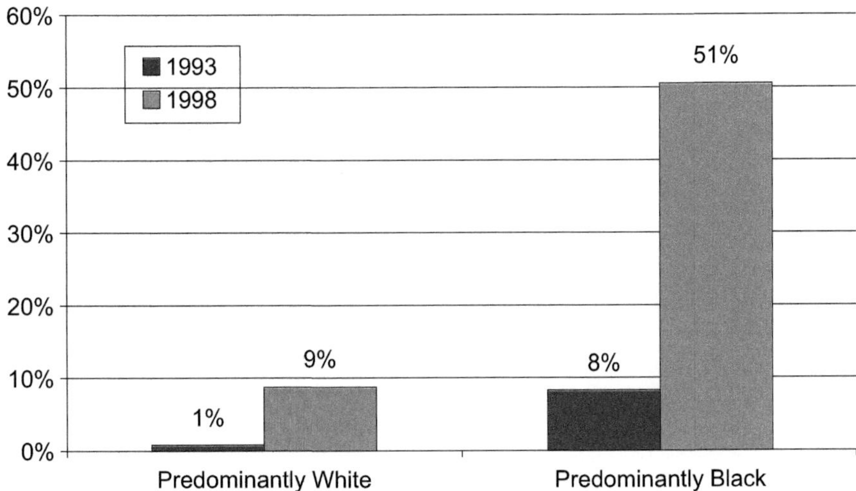

Figure 7.7 Subprime Share of Refinance Rates by Neighborhood Race

Figure 7.7). What this suggested was that discrimination in lending was based on race, even when the borrower might clearly qualify for a prime rather subprime loan (U.S. Department of Housing and Urban Development, 1998).

Indeed, this discrimination was to be confirmed a decade or so later in 2011 when Countrywide Financial Lending Corporation reached a $335 million settlement with the U.S. Justice Department resolving an allegation of racial and ethnic lending discrimination. Specifically, Countrywide and its subsidiaries were found to have steered 200,000 Black and Hispanic borrowers into subprime mortgages, when non-Hispanic Whites with the same credit history and income received prime loans. They were also found to have charged Black and Hispanic borrowers higher fees and interest because of their race/ethnicity and not creditworthiness (U.S. Department of Justice, 2011). Countrywide's actions were not an isolated incident among lending institutions. Another example was Wells Fargo, the largest mortgage providers in the nation. In 2012, Wells Fargo agreed to pay $175 million to resolve allegations that its mortgage brokers charged Black and Hispanic borrowers higher rates and fees than their White counterparts on mortgages, even when they qualified for prime mortgages (Rothacker & Ingram, 2012).

A product of the increased activity in the subprime market was the largest growth in U.S. homeownership since the 1950s and the White flight to the suburbs.

Between 1994 and 2004, the U.S. homeownership rate increased for all racial/ethnic groups with a dip after the 2008 recession (see Figure 7.8) (Zillow.com, n.d.).

Between 2006 and 2007, the U.S. subprime market imploded when record numbers of homeowners, many of whom were highly leveraged with little savings or home equity to cope with newly adjusted interest rates, defaulted on their mortgage obligations. What followed was a collapse of the securities that had been backed by these mortgages and pervaded the financial system. The collapse was to be one of the precipitating factors leading to America's great recession in 2008. This recession saw all but the wealthiest homes losing household wealth. Most affected, though, were Black and Hispanic subprime borrowers who experienced disproportionate numbers of foreclosures, as well significant declines in household wealth (Rugh & Massey, 2010). (See Figure 7.10 Median Net Worth of Households, 2005, 2009.)

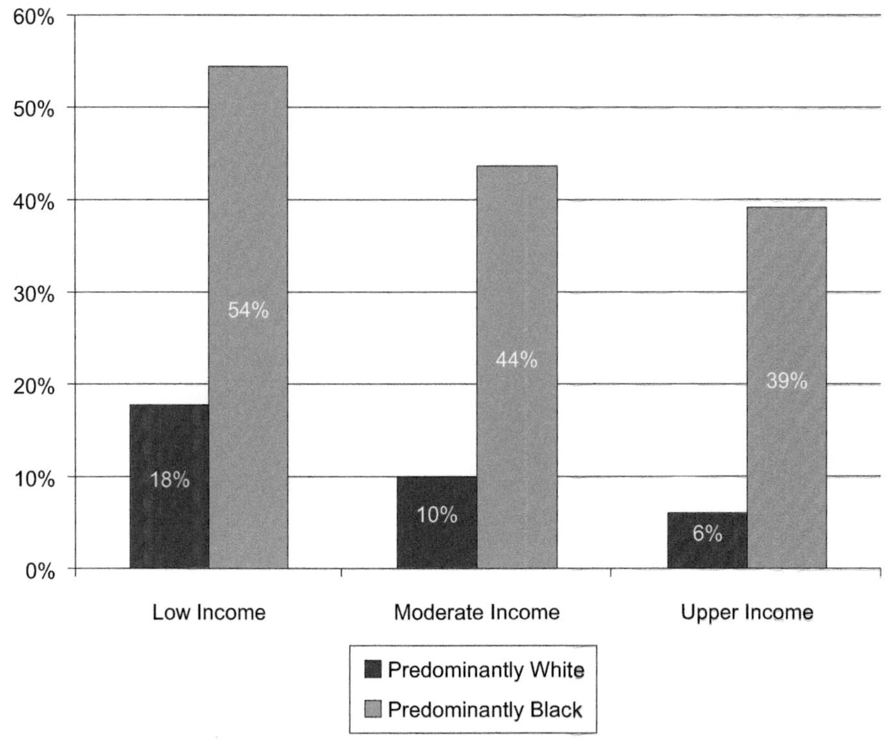

Figure 7.8 Subprime Share of 1998 Refinance Mortgages by Neighborhood Race and Income

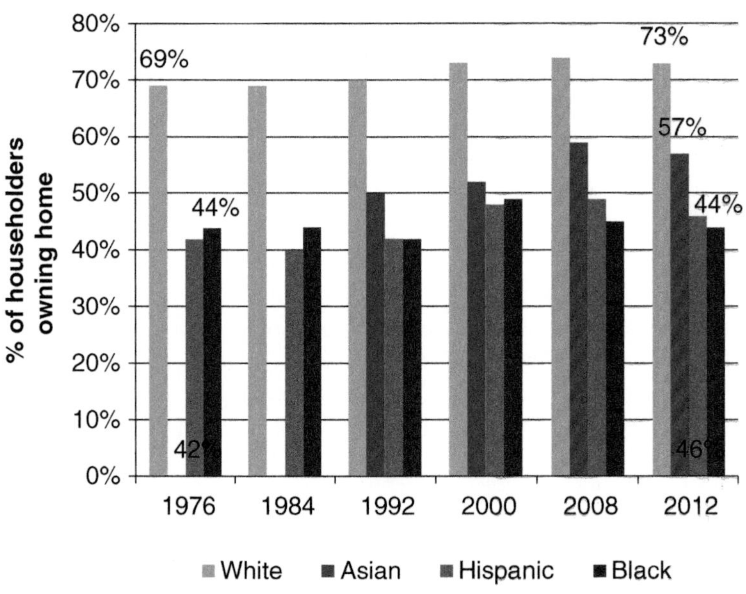

Figure 7.9 Homeownership Rates by Race/Ethnicity, 1994–2018

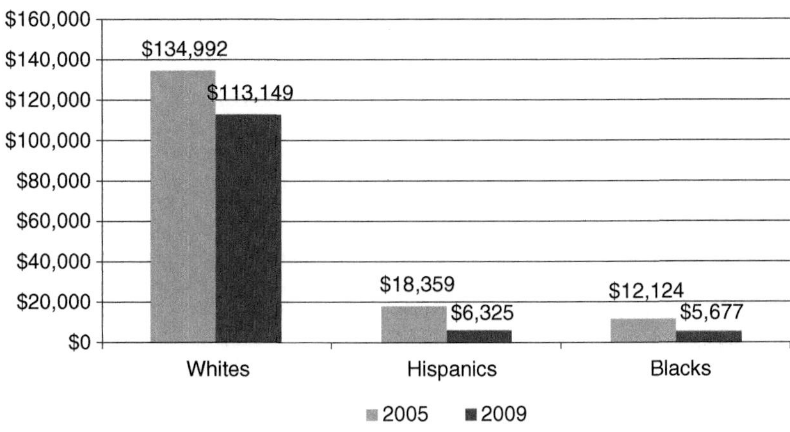

Figure 7.10 Median Net Worth of Household by Race, 2007–2016

Gentrification and Residentially Segregated Communities, 2000–Present

In the new millennium, residential segregation by race, most particularly for Blacks, remains stubbornly entrenched despite continued declines. However, many of the low-income residentially segregated urban communities across the nation have undergone significant changes in terms of look, population, and available resources. The primary reason for this is gentrification, a term coined by German-born sociologist Ruth Glass in 1964 to describe the process of renewal and rebuilding that accompanies the influx of middle-class or affluent people into an area that is perceived as deteriorating. This most recent gentrification, although not finished, began across the country in 2000 and peaked in 2007 with the influx of primarily young, White, middle-class professionals into what were racially and or ethnically hyper-segregated low-income urban communities (Goetz, 2011). Unlike the gentrification of the 1960s, 70s, 80s, and 90s, gentrification in the new millennium has been large scale and has dramatically changed the American housing landscape (Goetz, 2011; Smith & Williams, 1986).

Like the suburbanization of America some 50 years earlier, this reverse migration of young, White, middle-class professionals from the suburbs to urban centers has been driven by a complex set of social forces, local dynamics, and federal policies. Unlike suburbanization, though, there is the added element of a global dynamic (Hyra, 2012). In their coming together, they have created the conditions that made living in previously undesirable low-income urban centers an attractive proposition for young, White, middle-class professionals.

The policy seeds of this gentrification were planted against the backdrop of the urban decay and intense poverty of the 1970s and 1980s. Most associated with this decay were the high-rise public housing complexes that pervaded the urban centers across the country. Although not always the case, these high-rises and their residentially segregated surrounding areas were often strong, stable communities knit together in the context of their hyper-segregation (Glick, 2008). However, as resources and jobs moved away from the urban centers and employment opportunities decreased and unemployment and crime increased, public housing high-rises and their surrounding areas became synonymous with a hyper-segregated culture of concentrated poverty and urban blight (Glick, 2008).

In response to the urban decay, the U.S. Congress created the HOPE VI program, also called the Urban Revitalization Demonstration Program, which was introduced by the Department of Housing and Urban Development (HUD) in 1993. The purpose of the HOPE VI program was to assist local authorities to revitalize public housing projects, through their demolition and reconstruction into mixed-income developments (Fraser et al., 2012). Informed by the new urbanism philosophy and the notion of defensible space, the new mixed-income developments would encompass the principles of traditional neighborhood design with universally accessible public spaces and community institutions. It would also be pedestrian friendly, and transit accessible with a diverse population of residents, both in terms of income and class. For housing project residents, these new mixed-income developments would not just deconcentrate poverty and crime, but it would also offer them greater control and investment in their occupied space than was possible in high-rise public housing (Fraser et al., 2012).

Between 1993 and 2007, the HOPE VI program gave a little more than $6 billion in grants to local housing authorities to demolish distressed public housing units and replace them with mixed housing developments (Turner et al., 2009). During this period, housing authorities across the country took the opportunity to raze low-income public housing in their distressed districts. Cities such as New Orleans, Atlanta, and Chicago took the opportunity to either completely raze their entire public housing stock or significantly diminish it (Hyra, 2012). This in turn created the conditions for urban renewal that reimagined the urban space as a place that could be both prosperous and nice to live in (Hyra, 2012).

What helped to propel this renewal of the urban space was the Empowerment Zone program (EZ), along with the Enterprise Community (EC) and the Renewal Community initiatives (RC), which was launched by the Congress in 1993. As part of a holistic partnership between all stakeholders, the goal of the EZ program was to help EZ-designated impoverished urban, rural, and native reservations throughout the nation create self-sustaining, long-term developments. The key part in this development was revitalizing distressed areas by encouraging businesses to invest in these areas, the rationale for urban centers being that expanding business development and commerce would lead to greater job opportunities for residents and improved access to goods and services, which in turn would energize long-term revitalization (U.S. Department of Housing and Urban Development, 2001). As an incentive for businesses to invest in distressed urban centers, the EZ program offered a number of incentives, including wage credits (e.g., employment credit), deductions (e.g., commercial revitalization deductions), bond financing (e.g., enterprise zone facility bonds), capital gains (e.g., partial exclusion of gain from the sale of EZ assets), and low-income tax credit (U.S. Department of Housing and Urban Development, 2001). In Chicago, New York, Cleveland, Philadelphia, Los Angeles, and Baltimore, the EZ designation helped to stimulate private capital investment and a significant increase in businesses in urban areas (Hyra, 2012).

In addition to the HOPE VI and the EZ program, economic globalization in the 1990s and its creation and concentration of upper-income professionals in the downtowns of major cities such as New York, Chicago, and Washington, priced many middle-class professionals out of these communities. What this created, in turn, was a demand for more affordable housing in low-income neighboring or adjacent communities (Hyra, 2012).

Finally, and also related to economic globalization, were the government financial deregulation and the opening up of credit markets to compete in the worldwide credit market in the 1990s. As a result, credit for home purchases, both subprime and prime, became widely available, stimulating homebuilding across the nation, most particularly in the Sunbelt regions and in northeastern inner cities. This homebuilding in turn became an essential component of the revitalization of the urban centers. Although the subprime market crash and resulting recession of 2008 would have a devastating impact on the Sunbelt region of the country, as well as low-income Black and Hispanic subprime mortgage holders, it did not slow gentrification.

To date, there is very little consensus on whether gentrification has been a good thing for Black and Hispanic residents of previously hyper-segregated or just segregated urban communities. On one hand, there are those who argue with some justification and evidence that gentrification has increased the value of homes in the community. It has also attracted greater resources, decreased crime and other social ills, integrated the community, and made for favorable living conditions for all (Brummet & Reed, 2019). Indeed, Hyra (2012) argues that for middle-class Black and Hispanic residents this is almost certainly the case.

Conversely, there are those who suggest that programs such as HOPE VI and EZ did little to live up to their promise to make low-income Black and Hispanic public housing residents an integral part of the urban

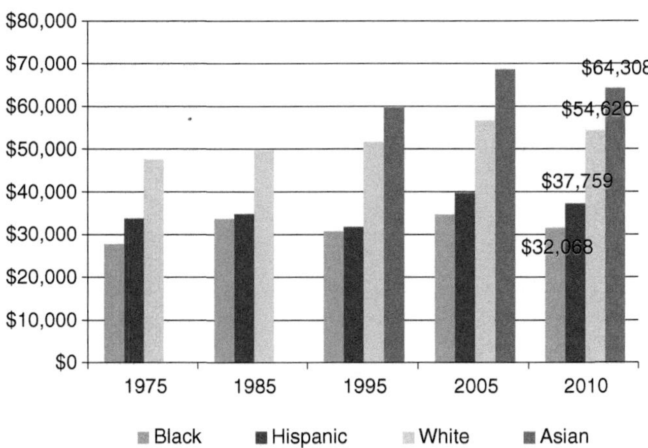

Figure 7.11 Real Median Household Income by Race, 1975–2017

redevelopment. Rather, the programs were simply a mechanism for clearing away long-term residents from desirable city space to make way for affluent Whites (Goetz, 2011; National Association to Restore Pride to American Cities, 2002). To be sure, there is clear evidence that many of the low-income residents were either shut out of the new mixed income developments because of cost or unavailability of low-income slots (Goetz, 2011). There is also evidence that displaced low-income residents were simply relocated into other hyper-segregated public housing, never to return (Fraser et al., 2012; Goetz, 2011). Finally, there is an argument made, though difficult to substantiate empirically, that though gentrification has created greater spatial proximity between Black and White residents in urban spaces, it has not diminished the social barriers between the two groups, most particularly for low-income residents.

The full story of gentrification is still to be played out. As of now, however, it and numerous policy efforts over the years have not managed to fully banish residential segregation by race and ethnicity, most particularly for low- and middle-income Blacks and to a lesser extent Hispanics. Moreover, the income and household wealth disparities that have resulted from residential segregation have persisted and even grown over the past few years, despite the gains made by Blacks and Hispanics. As such, residential segregation remains a vexing inequality still to be conquered.

Chapter Summary

As demonstrated throughout this chapter, nearly 100 years of discriminatory housing practices and policies on the part of local municipalities, homeowners, builders, banks, and federal agencies has created a social dynamic in which residential segregation by race and ethnicity have become a permanent feature of social arrangements in the United States. The beneficiaries of this social arrangement have been given a significant structural advantage in access to society's rewards and privileges, which include quality housing, education, health care, employment, and wealth-building opportunities. Moreover, beneficiaries have been able to accumulate home equity and household wealth for transfer through successive generations, an opportunity denied to nonbeneficiaries. Even with the policy efforts to remedy past discriminatory practices and policies, household income and wealth inequalities between the beneficiaries and nonbeneficiaries remain as wide, and in some cases, wider than 50 years ago.

In reality, "separate" translates to "unequal," even for the most successful nonbeneficiaries. As recent U.S. Census data show, on average, affluent Black and Hispanic households live in neighborhoods with more than one and a half times the poverty rates of neighborhoods where the average non-Hispanic White lives. Moreover, even Asians, who have a higher average income than Blacks, non-White Hispanics, and Hispanics, and are also less residentially segregated, live in poorer neighborhoods than the average low-income Whites (Logan, 2011).

The policy and social justice challenge for the coming years is to decrease and/or eliminate residential segregation by race and ethnicity and the disparities it causes. Only then can the United States reach the promise of an inclusive society.

Retrieval Questions

1. What were some of the earliest forms of residential segregation in the United States?
2. Name one of the social forces that contributed to residential segregation becoming a national rather than just a regional or county issue.
3. Name the initial practice used by local municipalities to create Black enclaves in the least desirable parts of their respective cities.
4. What was the significance of the 1917 *Buchanan v. Warely* Supreme Court ruling?
5. What was the name of the agreement between property owners, developers, and NAREB representatives not to lease, rent, or otherwise convey property to certain racial, ethnic, religious, or national groups?
6. What was the significance of the HOLC?
7. What were security maps?
8. What role did the FHA play in residential segregation?
9. Name one of the acts that was signed into law between 1960 and 2000 to remedy the discriminatory housing policies of the FHA, private lenders, banks, etc.
10. What is a subprime loan?
11. Name some of the factors that contributed to the gentrification of residential segregated urban communities in the years between 2000 and 2007.

Discussion Questions

1. Identify and discuss the diversity issues inherent in residential segregation by race and ethnicity.
2. What are the some of the human rights and social justice issues related to residential segregation by race and ethnicity?
3. How might the U.S. Census data identified in this chapter be used to inform your practice?
4. Identify and discuss how residential segregation by race and ethnicity might affect human behavior in the environment.
5. What policy practice strategies would you use to address residential segregation by race and ethnicity?
6. In day-to-day practice, how might the disparities caused by residential segregation by race and ethnicity be manifest?

Box 7.1 Residential and Housing Segregation Timeline

1908: Los Angeles City Council passes the first municipal zoning ordinance in the United States. The ordinance separates a portion of Los Angeles into residential and industrial communities to protect residential communities from nuisances and environmental hazards of certain industries. It also puts laundries, mostly run by Chinese entrepreneurs, into the industrial category to keep the Chinese out of White neighborhoods (Weiss, 1987).

1910: Baltimore, Maryland, adopts the first racial zoning code, which prevents Blacks from living in White neighborhoods (Rothstein, 2017).

1917: The U.S. Supreme Court rules in the *Buchanan v. Warely* case that outright racial zoning ordinances were unconstitutional as they violated the Fourteenth Amendment (*Buchanan v. Warely*, 245 U.S. 60, 1917).

1923: The National Association of Real Estate Boards publication *Principles of Real Estate Practice* stated, "the purchase of property by certain racial types is very likely to diminish the value of other properties" (Fisher, 1923, p. 116).

1926: In the *Corrigan v. Buckley* legal challenge to restricted deed covenants, the Supreme Court ruled that restricted deed covenants were legally enforceable as a form of private contract (*Corrigan v. Buckley*, 271 U.S. 323, 1926). The restricted deed covenant was an agreement binding all involved not to sell, rent, or lease property to minority groups. In the ruling, the Court argues that the Negro's constitutional right to acquire and own property does carry with it the constitutional power to compel sale to him of any particular private property (*Corrigan v. Buckley*, 271 U.S. 323, 1926).

1933: As part of the New Deal recovery aids, President Franklin D. Roosevelt (FDR) signed into law the Home Owners Loan Corporation (HOLC). One of the HOLC legacies was its initiation of the practice of redlining. The practice came out of the HOLC's appraisal method for predicting safe and risky mortgage loans (Jackson, 1980).

1934: The National Housing Act, a New Deal initiative, creates the Federal Housing Administration (FHA). Over the next 40 years, the FHA will become a remarkably successful program that transforms and greatly expands homeownership in the United States. However, its underwriting manual will give tacit approval to all banks, private lenders, land developers, realtors, and community associations to use redlining, racial zoning ordinances, and racial and ethnic restrictive deed covenants to maintain all-White communities (Massey & Denton, 1993).

1944: The Servicemen's Readjustment Act, better known as the G.I. Bill, is signed into law by President Franklin D. Roosevelt in 1944. The G.I. Bill provided veterans of World War II and later the Korean War a range of benefits, among them a guaranteed low-interest mortgage for the purchase of a single-family or mobile home (Trattner, 1999).

1947: Home building begins in Levittown, New York. Levittown was the first mass-produced, large-scale suburban development. It provided affordable housing to veterans. Financing for the development was underwritten by the FHA and Veterans Administration. Levittown was the catalyst for a homeownership boom as millions of urban, White families moved to the suburban developments. Notably excluded from this boom were Blacks who were victims of redlining, and racially restricted deed covenants written into lease agreements signed by White families (Herbold, 1995).

1948: In the landmark *Shelly v. Kraemer* ruling, the U.S Supreme Court struck down racially restrictive housing covenants (Shelly v. Kraemer, n.d.).

1968: President Lyndon Johnson signed into law Title VIII of the Civil Rights Act, more commonly known as the Fair Housing Act (FHA). The FHA made it illegal to discriminate in the sale, lease, or rental of housing or otherwise making housing unavailable because of race, color, religion, sex, handicap, familial status, or national origin (Trifun, 2009).

1974: President Gerald Ford signed into law the Equal Credit Opportunity Act of 1974. The law made it unlawful for any creditor to discriminate against any applicant, with respect to any aspect of credit transaction, on the basis of race, color, religion, national origin, sex, marital status, or age (Trifun, 2009).

1975: President Gerald Ford signed into law the Home Mortgage Disclosure Act (HMDA). The act required financial institutions to maintain and annually disclose to the public and federal government data about home purchase, pre-approvals, home improvement, and refinance applications. In 1989, amendments to the law required the collection and disclosure of data about applicant and borrower demographics to help identify potential discriminatory lending patterns and enforcing antidiscriminatory statutes (Trifun, 2009).

1977: President Jimmy Carter signed into law the Community Reinvestment Act. The act required all Federal Deposit Insurance Company (FDIC) chartered banks to end redlining and meet the credit needs of low- and middle-income urban communities (Trifun, 2009).

1988: Investigative reporter Bill Dedman wins the Pulitzer Prize for his series "The Color of Money," published in the *Atlanta Journal*. Using federal mortgage data, Dedman was able to show that lenders nationwide rejected Black loan applicants at twice the rate of White applicants, and that high-income Blacks were rejected at the same rate as low-income Whites. And that White middle-income neighborhoods got four times as many loans as middle-income Black areas (Dedman, 1988).

2017: In the landmark *Smith v. Avanti* case, Judge Raymond P. Moore of the U.S. District Court of Colorado ruled that the FHA protects LGBTQ couples from housing discrimination. It was the first ruling of this kind and gave federal protections against housing discrimination that had been in place for other groups, but not for the LGBTQ population (Lambda Legal, n.d.).

2019: Black homeownership hits a 50-year low (Coleman, 2019).

REFERENCES

Arnesen, E. (2002). *Black protest and the great migration: A brief history with documents*. Bedford, MA: St. Martins.

Babcock, F. M. (1932). *The valuation of real estate*. New York, NY: McGraw.

Baylor, R. H. (1996). *Race and the shaping of twentieth century Atlanta*. Chapel Hill: University of North Carolina Press.

Boustan, L. P. (2010). Was postwar suburbanization "white flight"? Evidence from the black migration. *The Quarterly Journal of Economics*, 125(1), 417–443.

Brodkin, K. (1998). *How Jews became white folks and what that says about race in America*. New Brunswick, NJ: Rutgers University Press.

Brooks, R. R. W. (2002). *Covenants and conventions*. Northwestern University Law and Economic Research Paper No. 02–8. Retrieved from SSRN: http://ssrn.com/abstract=353723 or http://dx.doi.org/10.2139/ssrn.353723

Brummet, Q., & Reed, D. (2019, July 16). *The effects of gentrification on the well-being and opportunity of resident adults and children*. FRB of Philadelphia Working Paper No. 19–30. Retrieved from www.philadelphiafed.org/-/media/frbp/assets/working-papers/2019/wp19-30.pdf

Buchanan v. Warely, 245.U.S. 60. (1917). *Justia: US supreme court*. Retrieved from https://supreme.justia.com/cases/federal/us/245/60/

Castro-Baker, A. (2014). Eroding the wealth of women: Gender and the subprime foreclosure crisis. *Social Service Review*, 88(1), 59–91.

Chafe, W. H. (2001). *Remembering Jim Crow: African Americans tell about life in the segregated south*. New York, NY: The New Press.

Charles, C. Z. (2003). The dynamics of racial residential segregation. *Annual Review of Sociology*, 29, 167–207.

Coleman, E. (2019). Black homeownership hits a 50-year low. *Route Fifty*. Retrieved from www.route-fifty.com/management/2019/07/black-homeownership-50-year-low/158467/

Corrigan v. Buckley, 271 U.S. 323. (1926). *Justia: US supreme court*. Retrieved from https://supreme.justia.com/cases/federal/us/271/323/

Dedman, B. (1988). Home mortgage lending practices discriminate blacks. *The Atlanta Journal*. Retrieved from http://powerreporting.com/color/color_of_money.pdf

Deyle, S. (2006). *Carry me back: The domestic slave trade in American life*. Oxford, England: Oxford University Press.

Fisher, E. M. (1923). *Principles of real estate practice*. New York: Macmillian Company.

Florette, H. (1975). *Black migration*. Garden City, NY: Doubleday.

Fogelson, R. M. (2005). *Bourgeois nightmares: Suburbia 1870–1930*. New Haven, CT: Yale University Press.

Fraser, J. C., Burns, A. B., Bazuin, J. T., & Oakley, D. A. (2012). HOPE VI, colonization and the production of difference. *Urban Affairs Review, 49*(4), 525–556.

Glick, J. (2008). Gentrification and the racialized geography of home equity. *Urban Affairs Review, 44*(2), 280–295.

Goetz, E. (2011). Gentrification in black and white: The racial impact of public housing demolition in American cities. *Urban Studies, 48*(8), 1581–1604.

Gotham, K. F. (2000). Urban space, restrictive covenants and the origins of racial residential segregation in a US city 1900–50. *International Journal of Urban and Regional Research, 24*(3), 616–633.

Gramlich, E. M. (2007). *Subprime mortgages: America's latest boom and bust*. Washington, DC: The Urban Institute Press.

Guglielmo, T. A. (2003). *White on arrival: Italians, race, color, and power in Chicago, 1890–1946*. New York, NY: Oxford University Press.

Herbold, H. (1995). Never a level playing field: Blacks and the G.I. bill. *The Journal of Blacks in Higher Education, 6*, 104–108.

Hirsch, A. R. (1983). *Making the second ghetto*. Cambridge, England: Cambridge University Press.

Hoyt, H. (1933). *One hundred years of land values in Chicago*. Chicago, IL: University of Chicago Press.

Hyra, D. S. (2012). Conceptualizing the new urban renewal: Comparing the past to the present. *Urban Affairs Review, 48*(4), 498–527.

Iceland, J., Weinberg, D. H., & Steinmetz, E. (2002). *Racial and ethnic residential segregation in the United States, 1980–2000*. U.S. Census Bureau Special Report Series, CENSR-3. Washington, DC: U.S. Government Printing Office. Retrieved from www.census.gov/hhes/www/housing/resseg/pdf/front_toc.pdf

Ichiro, K., & Berkman, L. F. (2003). *Neighborhoods and health*. Oxford, England: Oxford University Press.

Jackson, K. T. (1980). Race, ethnicity, and real appraisal: The Home Owners Loan Corporation and the Federal Housing Administration. *Journal of Urban History, 6*(4), 419–452.

Johansen, B. E. (2006). *The native peoples of North America*. New Brunswick, NJ: Rutgers University Press.

Jolly, K. S. (2006). Black liberation in the Midwest: The struggles in St. Louis, Missouri, 1964–1970. In G. Hodges (Ed.), *Studies in African American history and culture* (pp. 1–16). New York, NY: Taylor & Francis.

Jones-Correa, M. (2001). The origins and diffusion of racial restrictive covenants. *Political Science Quarterly, 115*(4), 541–568.

Lemann, N. (1991). *The promised land: The great black migration and how it changed America*. New York, NY: Vintage Books.

Lambda Legal. (n.d.). *Smith v. Avanti*. Retrieved from www.lambdalegal.org/in-court/cases/co_smith-v-avanti

Logan, J. R. (2011). Separate and unequal: The neighborhood gap for Blacks, Hispanics, and Asians in metropolitan America. *US 2010 Project: Discover America in the New Century*. Retrieved from www.s4.brown.edu/us2010/Data/Report/report0727.pdf

Ludwig, J., Duncan, G. J., Gennetian, L. A., Katz, L. F., Kessler, R. C., Kling, J. R., & Sanbonmatsu, L. (2012). Neighborhood effects on the long-term well being of low-income adults. *Science, 337*(6101), 1505–1510.

Majumdar, R. D. (2007). Racially restrictive covenants in the state of Washington: A primer for practitioners. *Seattle University Law Review, 30*(1095), 1095–1117.

Maltz, E. M. (1994). The federal government and the problem of Chinese rights in the era of the fourteenth amendment. *Harvard Journal of Law and Public Policy, 17*(1), 1–17.

Manchaca, M. (2001). *Recovering history, constructing race: The Indian, Black, and White roots of Mexican Americans*. The Joe R. & Teresa Lozano Long Series in Latin American and Latino Art and Culture. Austin: University of Texas Press.

Massey, D. S. (2001). Residential segregation and neighborhood conditions in U.S. metropolitan Areas. In N. J. Smelser, J. W. Williams, & F. Mitchell (Eds.), *America becoming: Racial trends and their consequences* (Vol. 1, pp. 1–31). Washington, DC: National Academy Press.

Massey, D. S., & Denton, N. A. (1988). The dimensions of residential segregation. *Social Forces, 67*(2), 281–315.

Massey, D. S., & Denton, N. A. (1993). *American apartheid*. Cambridge, MA: Harvard University Press.

Mettler, S. (2005). *Solders to citizens: The G.I. bill and the making of the greatest generation*. Oxford, England: Oxford University Press.

National Association to Restore Pride in American Cities. (2002). *False hope: A critical assessment of the HOPE IV public housing redevelopment program*. NARPAC, Inc. Retrieved from www.narpac.org/ITXFALSE.HTM

Oliver, M., & Shapiro, T. (1997). *Black wealth/white wealth*. New York, NY: Routledge.

Packard, J. M. (2002). *American nightmare: The history of Jim Crow*. New York, NY: St. Martin's Press.

Powell, J. A., & Cardwell, K. (2013). *Homeownership, wealth & the production of racialized space*. Paper resented at a National Symposium on April 1 and 2, at Harvard Business School. Retrieved from www.jchs.harvard.edu/sites/jchs.harvard.edu/files/hbtl-07.pdf

Power, G. (1996). The residential segregation of Baltimore's Jews: Restrictive covenants or gentleman's agreement? *Generations*, 5–7.

Prakash, S. (2013). Racial dimensions of property value protection under the fair housing act. *California Law Review*, *101*(5), 1437–1497.

Roediger, D. R. (2006). *Working toward whiteness: How America's immigrants became white: The strange journey from Ellis Island to the suburbs*. New York, NY: Basic Books.

Rothacker, R., & Ingram, D. (2012). Wells Fargo to pay $175 million in race discrimination probe. *Chicago Tribune Business*. Retrieved from www.reuters.com/article/2012/07/12/us-wells-lending-settlement-idUSBRE86B0V220120712

Rothstein, R. (2017). *The color of law: The forgotten history of how our government segregated America*. New York, NY: Liveright Publishing Corporation.

Rugh, J. S., & Massey, D. S. (2010). Racial segregation and the foreclosure crises. *American Sociological Review*, *75*(5), 629–651.

Seitles, M. (1996). The perpetuation of residential racial segregation in America: Historical discrimination, modern forms of exclusion, and inclusionary remedies. *Journal of Land Use and Environmental Law*, *14*(1), 1–30.

Shelly v. Kraemer. (n.d.). *Oyez*. Retrieved from www.oyez.org/cases/1940-1955/334us1

Silva, C. (2008). Racial restrictive covenants: Enforcing neighborhood segregation in Seattle. *Seattle Civil Rights and Labor History Project*. Retrieved from https://depts.washington.edu/civilr/covenants_report.htm

Smith, B. C. (2007). The subprime mortgage market: A review and compilation of research and commentary. *Prepared by Homer Hoye Institute*. Retrieved from www.kansascityfed.org/publicat/events/community/2009carc/Hyra.pdf

Smith, N., & Williams, P. (1986). *Gentrification of the city*. New York, NY: Harper Collins Publishers Ltd.

Squires, G. D., & Kubrin, C. E. (2006). Privileged places: Race, opportunity and uneven development in urban America. *National Housing Institute Shelterforce Online*, #147, Fall. Retrieved from nhi.org/online/issues/147/privilegedplaces.html

Trattner, W. I. (1999). *From poor law to welfare state: A history of social welfare in America* (6th ed.). New York, NY: The Free Press.

Trifun, N. M. (2009). Residential segregation after the fair housing act. *Human Rights Magazine*, *36*(4), 1–11.

Turner, M. A., Popkin, S. J., & Rawlings, L. (2009). *Public housing and the legacy of segregation*. Washington, DC: The Urban Institute Press.

Tuttle, W. M. (1996). *Race riot: Chicago in the red summer of 1919*. Urbana, IL: Illini Books.

U.S. Commission on Civil Rights. (1973). *Understanding fair housing*. Clearinghouse Publications. Retrieved from www.law.umaryland.edu/marshall/usccr/documents/cr11042.pdf

U.S. Department of Housing and Urban Development. (1998). *Unequal burden: Income & racial disparities in subprime lending in America*. Retrieved from www.huduser.org/Publications/pdf/unequal_full.pdf

U.S. Department of Housing and Urban Development. (2001). *Tax incentive guide for businesses in renewal communities, empowerment zones and enterprise communities*. Retrieved from http://portal.hud.gov/hudportal/HUD?src=/program_offices/comm_planning/economicdevelopment/programs/rc

U.S. Department of Justice. (2011). *DOJ/Countrywide settlement information*. Retrieved from www.justice.gov/usao/cac/countrywide.html

U.S. Housing Scholars and Research and Advocacy Organizations. (2008). *Racial segregation and housing discrimination in the United States*. A Report to the U.N. Committee on the Elimination of Racial Discrimination, January. Retrieved from www.prrac.org/pdf/FinalCERDHousingDiscriminationReport.pdf

Weiss, M. A. (1987). *The rise of the community builders: The American real estate industry and urban land planning*. New York, NY: Columbia University Press.

Williams, L. E. (1972). *Anatomy of four race riots: Racial conflict in Knoxville, Elaine (Arkansas), Tulsa, and Chicago, 1919–1921*. Hattiesburg, MS: University and College Press of Mississippi.

Zillow.com. (n.d.). *African Americans and the homeownership divide*. Retrieved from www.zillow.com/research/african-americans-homeownership/

CHAPTER 8
Labor Market Inequality

Defining Labor

Labor is the aggregate of all human physical and mental effort used in the creation of goods and services. It is a primary factor of production (BusinessDictionary.com, 2015a).

Defining the Labor Market

The labor market is the nominal market in which workers find paying work, employers find willing workers, and wage rates are determined. Labor markets may be local, national, or international in their scope and are composed of smaller, interacting labor markets for different qualifications, skills, and geographical locations. They depend on exchange of information between employers and job seekers about wage rates, conditions of employment, level of competition, and job creation (BusinessDictionary.com, 2015b).

Defining Labor Market Inequality

Labor market inequality simply put is the existence of unequal workplace opportunities and rewards for different social positions and groups based on race, ethnicity, social class, immigration status, nationality, disability status, sexual orientation, and gender identification. Labor market inequality manifests in a number of ways, including but not limited to the segregation of work, wage disparities, exclusion from consideration for employment, and preferential hiring.

Current Labor Market Inequality

In 1964, President Lyndon Johnson signed into law the Civil Rights Act of 1964 (P.L. 88–352). Title VII of the act made it unlawful for an employer to discriminate in the hiring or terminating of an individual on the basis of race, color, religion, sex, or national origin. Also made unlawful was the advertising of job positions in such a way as to deprive employment opportunities to individuals on the basis of race, color, religion, sex, or national origin (United States Equal Employment Opportunities Commission, 2015b). Along with wide-ranging affirmative action initiatives, Title VII and later the American with Disabilities Act of 1990 removed many of the long-standing formal barriers to an inclusive and equitable labor market (United States Department of Labor, 2015a). Consequently, over the past 50-plus years, perennially disadvantaged groups have gained unprecedented access to the higher professions and work in the major corporations (Hegewisch & Hartman, 2014; Masur, 1999; United States Department of Labor, 2015b). Most notably, there are now Black doctors, lawyers, civil engineers, Supreme Court justices, and Armed Forces generals. And women are similarly present in these occupations and professions (Hegewisch & Hartman, 2014; Masur, 1999; United States Department of Labor, 2015b).

DOI: 10.4324/9781003023708-8

For all the undoubted progress that has been made, labor market inequality remains a structural feature of the United States labor market. Reflecting preexisting societal inequalities, the most pressing of these inequalities are the gender wage gap, occupational segregation by gender, and racial and ethnic disparities in unemployment and earnings (Hegewisch & Hartman, 2014; Masur, 1999). Structurally, the inequalities have disadvantaged these groups in the labor market. The disadvantages are financial, through the loss of human capital and a compromised ability to maximize labor force potential.

The Gender Wage Gap

In 1963, John F. Kennedy signed into law the Equal Pay Act of 1963 (P.L. 88–38). Amending the Fair Labor Standards Act, the Equal Pay Act's purpose was to abolish wage disparity based on gender (United States Equal Opportunities Commission, 2015a). Although going some way to shrinking the gender wage gap, 57 years later, in 2020, the median salary for men and women still sees Asian and White women with at least a bachelor's degree earning 86 and 81 cents, respectively, for every $1 made by White men. The disparity is even more considerable for women who are Native American/Alaskan Natives, 75 cents; Black, 75 cents; Hispanic, 75 cents; and Native Hawaiian/other Pacific Islanders, 80 cents (Payscale.com, 2020).

The gender wage gap has proven remarkably robust and wide reaching. It knows no boundaries and is present in all industries and occupations to varying degrees and affects almost all women in the labor force regardless of educational attainment level.

For example, the Gender Pay Gap Report for 2020 estimated that when looking at a median salary for a 40-year career, and taking into account presumptive raises, women with at least a bachelor's degree stand to lose $900,000 on average, when compared to their male counterparts, over a lifetime (Payscale.com, 2020). When the median salary is compared for women and men with the same job and qualifications, the lifetime loss of earnings for women narrows to $80,000, which, while lower, is still significant if you consider the compound interest that would be gained if invested over 40 years (Payscale.com, 2020).

There are a number of residual effects for women and their families due to this loss (National Partnership for Women and Families, 2020). Among the possible residual effects are higher rates of poverty for women throughout their lifetimes. The higher poverty rates are particularly true for Native American/Alaskan Natives, Black, and Hispanic women (National Partnership for Women and Families, 2020; Payscale.com, 2020).

For female-headed households with children under 18, who make up half of all families with children under 18, the pay loss has implications for economic security and whether or not incomes fall below the poverty and children fall into poverty (Institute for Women's Policy Research, 2020; National Partnership for Women and Families, 2020; Payscale.com, 2020). The loss also contributes to women being less prepared for retirement (Institute for Women's Policy Research, 2020).

The National Partnership for Women and Families report on the wage gap (2020) puts this loss in some context with its highlighting that if there were no gender wage gap, working women in the United States would have enough money for approximately:

- More than 13 months of additional child care.
- One additional year of tuition and fees for a four-year public university, or the full cost of tuition and fees for a two-year college.
- Nearly 65 months of food.
- More than six months of mortgage and utilities payments.
- More than nine months of additional rent.
- Enough money to pay off student loan debt in under three years (p. 2).

Occupational Gender Segregation

Occupational gender segregation is another glaring element of gender inequality in the labor market. It is characterized by the majority of women, irrespective of race, ethnicity, or education, being significantly more likely to work in occupations with other women than with men. Consequently, they are concentrated primarily in what can be termed as caring or service occupations, such as health care, caregiving, and education (Hegewisch & Hartmann, 2014). Indeed, despite the significant educational gains women have made since the passage of the Title IX Education Amendment of 1972, occupational segregation remains high. Moreover, it did not substantially decline in the decade of the 2000s for the first time since the 1960s (United States Equal Opportunities Commission, 2015b). The substantial literature on the topic of occupational gender segregation is not definitive on why it happens or continues. The literature does seem to agree somewhat that this segregation incorporates a confluence of factors, including culturally defined choices by workers themselves, discrimination by employers, and differences in skill levels and qualities (Cohen, 2013; Weeden et al., 2018). Regardless of the reasons, research indicates that this segregation is an important dimension of gender inequality in earnings. It also contributes to other forms of inequality, as well as to the devaluation of women's labor (Cohen, 2013; Weeden et al., 2018).

Race and Ethnicity in the Labor Market

The unprecedented strides made by racial and ethnic groups in the labor market are undeniable. However, particularly for Black workers in the labor market and to a lesser extent Hispanic workers, the strides are tempered by ongoing structural inequalities when compared with Whites. These areas of inequalities are most telling in unemployment rates, salaries, and occupational segregation. In unemployment, for example, across all education levels, Blacks are on average twice as likely as their White counterparts to be unemployed (Macrotrends.net, 2020). They also stay unemployed for longer than their White counterparts.

While having lower rates of unemployment than Blacks, Hispanic workers in the labor force nevertheless still have a significantly higher rate of unemployment than Whites (Macrotrends.net, 2020). Indeed, the trend of higher rates of unemployment for Blacks and Hispanics compared with Whites has been consistent for the past 40 years (Macrotrends.net, 2020). Furthermore, for those in the labor market, even when controlling for education, Black and Hispanic men and women across all occupational spheres earn less than their White counterparts.

Finally, Blacks and Hispanics in the labor force are, like women in general, victims of occupational segregation. For example, Black and Hispanic men and women are underrepresented in the highest-paying

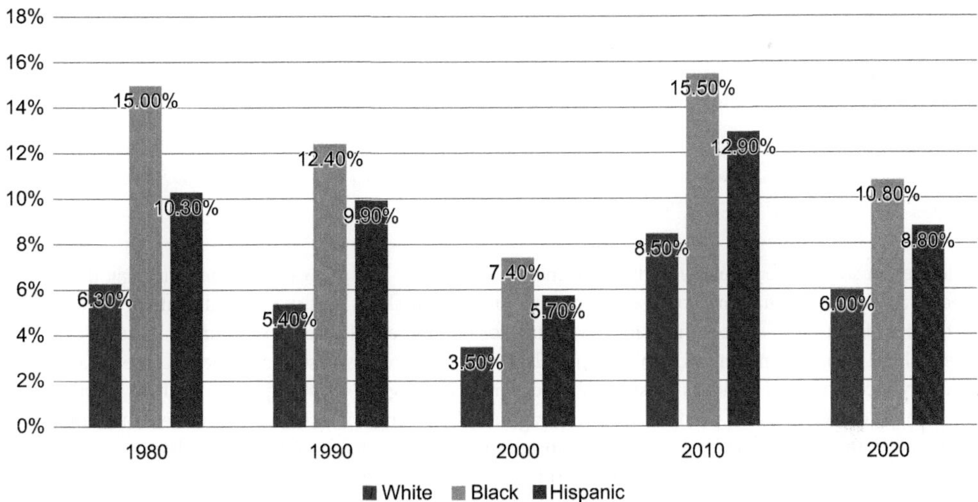

Figure 8.1 Unemployment Rate by Race and Ethnicity, 1980–2020

Source: Macrotrends: Unemployment rate by race 1980–2020. Retrieved from www.macrotrends.net/2508/unemployment-rate-by-race

occupations, for example, chief executives, legislators, lawyers, judges, physicians, and surgeons (Bahn & Sanchez-Cumming, 2020). Hispanic men, however, are a disproportionate share of construction occupations. Black men are a disproportionate share of driver/sales workers and truck drivers and cooks (Bahn & Sanchez-Cumming, 2020). Black and Hispanic women comprise a disproportionate share of nursing assistants, personal care aides, and cashier jobs (Bahn & Sanchez-Cumming, 2020). Asian American and Pacific Islander women are disproportionately represented in accounting and auditing and nursing (registered) (Bahn & Sanchez-Cumming, 2020).

Although occupational segregation has been offered as one explanation for the persistent wage disparities between Blacks and Hispanics and Whites, it does not tell the whole story. As in the case of gender inequality, the available research indicates a confluence of factors that include education, racial and ethnic and discrimination, and the lack of social capital better explain the disparities.

Advocacy and Policy Response

In response to the structural inequality they face in the labor market, women have been particularly active in pushing for federal legislation to redress these inequalities. In 2009, the Paycheck Fairness Act was introduced in the 111th Congress. Introduced as S.182 and H.R.12 in the Senate and the House, the purpose of the act was to expand the scope of the Equal Pay Act of 1963. It would also further amend the Fair Labor Standards Act of 1938 by providing remedies to victims of discriminatory practices regarding the payment of wages on the basis of gender. The House of Representatives approved the bill in January 2009; the Senate, however, failed to move the bill forward. With some urging from President Barack Obama, the bill was reintroduced in 2011 as S.797 and H.R.1519. The bill was rejected again by the Senate (Govtrack.US, 2011). In 2019, the bill was again reintroduced in the 116th Congress. It passed in the House. The bill was read in the Senate and placed on the Senate legislative calendar under general orders (Congress.gov, 2019).

One related act that was signed into law was the Lily Ledbetter Fair Pay Act of 2009. The act restored an antidiscrimination law that existed prior to the Supreme Court decision in *Ledbetter v. Goodyear Tire and Rubber Company* (Govtrack.US, 2009). In the decision, the Supreme Court ruled that an individual must file a complaint within 180 days of an employer committing pay discrimination if he or she wishes to be indemnified. The Lily Ledbetter Fair Pay Act of 2009 overrides the Supreme Court ruling and clarifies that each discriminatory paycheck is a new act of discrimination; it resets the 180-day limit to file a claim. Accordingly, the act states that plaintiffs still can recover back pay for a period of no more than two years before they challenge the discrimination (Govtrack.US, 2009).

Theoretical Perspective

The present struggle for equality in the labor market is not new. It is part of an ongoing struggle that has been waged since the nation's colonial beginnings. From a pluralistic theory of social conflict, the struggle is the manifestation of the conflict between groups for fair and equal access to resources. In America's hierarchical social arrangements, White upper-class men who are business and property owners have primary access to all of society's most valuable resources. Among the most important of these resources is the control of the means of production, labor, wages, and working conditions. From the nation's colonial beginnings, this control has been manifested in systems such as indentured servitude, slavery, and peonage, as well as practices such as strikebreaking, workforce exclusion, and the undermining of collective bargaining. Conflict occurs when victims of these systems and practices seek to have greater access to the profits of their labor. At the center of the conflict is the intersectionality between race, ethnicity, gender, class, immigration, sexual orientation, and so on. The remainder of this chapter examines the historical development of these conflicts.

Labor Force Inequality and Struggle: An Historical Perspective

Indentured Servitude

In the early years of the colonies, labor shortage was an ongoing concern for plantation owners and British investment companies wishing to profit from the multiple sources of cash crops. Initial efforts to secure a labor force, which included contracting and renting labor, proved unsuccessful for a myriad of reasons (Galenson, 1984). What did prove to be successful was the system of indentured servitude.

Indentured servants were men, women, and children who signed a contract (also known as a covenant) agreeing to work for a fixed number of years in exchange for transportation to Virginia. Once in Virginia they would also be furnished with food, clothing, and shelter. Adult contracts were between four to seven years in length while children's contracts were typically much longer. Most of the initial indentured servants worked in the tobacco fields in Virginia (Galenson, 1984).

Indentured servants came in three categories. The first category was people who could not afford the passage to Virginia but wanted to escape poverty and/or unemployment in England for the chance of a potentially better life in the new world.

The second category of indentured servants was people sponsored under the headright system. The headright system was a plan designed by the Virginia Company to encourage immigration to Virginia. It offered a legal grant of 50 acres of land to any person who paid his or her passage to settle in Virginia. Another 50 acres of land was given to the person for every other person they sponsored to come along with them as an indentured servant (Wolfe & McCartney, 2012). The sponsored indentured servant or servants were known as headrights. As there was no restriction of headrights, men, women, children, and families were all part of the system. The headright system not only encouraged a greater variety of people to immigrate to Virginia, but it also proved a substantial incentive for wealthy planters to sponsor and import indentured servants (Galenson, 1984; Wolfe & McCartney, 2012). As a result, not only did they get needed labor, they also significantly increased their land holdings. It was especially true of wealthy planters in the Virginia and Maryland colonies, whose labor was primarily recruited through the headright system.

The third category of indentured servants was involuntary. These were people who in England were deemed to be socially undesirable, such as criminals and drunkards. Most typically, they were given the Hobson's choice of indentured servitude in Virginia or prison or worse in England. They were transported to the colonies and sold or placed into servitude, as was the case with any servant who arrived without an indenture (Wolfe & McCartney, 2012).

The Virginia Company introduced the first indentured servants to the colonies in 1619. Within a remarkably short period, indentured servitude became a central institution in the colonial economy and society. Indeed, historian Abbot Emerson Smith (1971) estimated that between one-half and two-thirds of all White immigrants to the British colonies between the Puritan migration of 1630s and 1776 came under indentured servitude. Moreover, even with the presence of slaves, indentured servants as a labor force were of greater qualitative importance to the colonies than the slaves (Galenson, 1981).

On the Virginia and Maryland tobacco and wheat fields, they worked from dawn to dusk, six days a week, through a growing season from February to November. During the sweltering summer season, the combination of the backbreaking labor and disease killed the majority of unseasoned new arrivals, accounting for the exceptionally high mortality rates among indentured servants (Wolfe & McCartney, 2012). In a firsthand account, Dutchman David Peterson DeVries (1853), describing English indentured servants in Virginia who reported to him, said that the months of June, July, and August were very unhealthy for them. During these months, which they called the sickly season, the English indentured servants were described as dying like cats and dogs.

Although the work was backbreaking in the southern colonies for indentured servants, in the northern colonies, where the climate and soil did not support the growing of cash crops, the working life was much easier. Rather than plantations or fields, the dominant subsistence technology was independent farms with traditional crops and livestock. The growing seasons were short with much less need for indentured servants year round. Indentured servants who did labor in the northern colonies were often skilled craftsman (Galenson, 1984; Wolfe & McCartney, 2012).

However, regardless of where in the colonies indentured servants were, they were nevertheless seen and in many respects treated as commodities and second-class citizens. Even with the protection of a contract of service, indentured servants were at the mercy of the whims of their masters, who controlled much of their personhood (Galenson, 1984; Wolfe & McCartney, 2012). In most colonies, for example, indentured servants could not marry without the permission of their masters. They could not buy or sell goods, own property, or profit from their labor. Moreover, the terms of their servitude could be extended for infractions that ranged from stealing to running away, and everything in between. Furthermore, female indentured servants who became pregnant would not only have their term of service extended, but they could also be physically punished (Galenson, 1984; Wolfe & McCartney, 2012).

Indeed, in many respects, the life of an indentured servant, particularly in Virginia and Maryland, was not too different from that of the Black slaves with whom they worked and lived. In fact, there is ample evidence that they developed relationships with Black slaves because of the mutual antipathy toward their masters. This antipathy was the source of a number of uprisings that saw indentured servants and Black slaves come together against their masters. The last and most notable of the uprisings was the Bacon's Rebellion in 1676.

Ultimately, for all of the chattel-like experiences of indentured servants, they did enjoy significant advantages over slaves, particularly after the passing of the slave codes. Among the advantages indentured servants enjoyed was access to legal protections and the right to take their master to court in the case of a breach of contract or unreasonable physical punishment (Beverly, 1947). There was also the obvious advantage that the terms of their indenture were temporary, and one day they would be free of service, if they lived to see it. In fact, for many, the end of indenture came with a negotiated cash payment known as freedom dues. In Virginia, they were entitled to a year's worth of corn, two suits, and the right to take up 50 acres of unpatented land. Finally, the children of indentured servants did not, like slaves, inherit their parent's status of servitude. These significant differences allowed indentured servants to eventually become part of the mainstream society on their terms (Beverly, 1947).

Although the system of indentured servitude would remain in America until being outlawed in the early 19th century, its central role and influence would wane and be superseded by slavery in the late 17th century. The catalyst for this shift was the worldwide market's insatiable demand for the southern colonies' cash crops of tobacco, rice, indigo, and sugar. It was a demand that required a large, permanent, controlled, and geographically static workforce. These were requirements that for a couple of reasons could not be satisfied by an indentured workforce (Galenson, 1984): One, the indentured workforce was temporary, and two, as a result of improved conditions in England, the supply of indentured servants willing to come to the colonies was dwindling (Galenson, 1984).

Slavery

The system that could meet the requirements was slavery, organized around skin pigmentation and a lifetime of enslavement. To this end, the colonies, beginning with Virginia, entered into the transatlantic slave trade and the importation of Black slaves directly from Africa (Morgan, 2001; Vaughn, 1989). For the establishment figures of the southern colonies and their English backers nervous about the militancy of joint forces of indentured servants and Black slaves, importing slaves directly from Africa had a twofold benefit. One, it satisfied the all-important need for a large, permanent, controlled, and geographically static labor force, and two, it ensured by basing slavery around skin color that Black and White labor interests would never again converge as they did with the Bacon's Rebellion. In doing so, slavery in America around skin pigmentation, as well as a narrative and social construction of Black inferiority, created a template whereby skin color and race would trump the mutual labor interests of White and Black workers (Morgan, 2001). As will be discussed later in the chapter, it would be used as a wedge by employers to play one group against the other in labor conflicts for equality in the marketplace.

The colonies entered the African slave trade in 1682 when Virginia declared that all imported Black servants would be slaves for life. In 1702, Virginia became the first colony to enact a comprehensive slave code following this declaration. The slave code, which became the model for the other 12 colonies, asserted that slaves were real estate. It further declared 30 lashes as punishment for any slave or person of color who assaulted a White person. It also prohibited slaves from bearing arms without permission and absolved any master of punishment who killed a slave in the course of correction. The code also decreed that all children born to a slave also inherited their mother's slave status (Morgan, 2001; Vaughn, 1989).

Between the years of 1682 and 1806, an estimated 400,000 Black slaves were forcibly transported to the colonies from Africa (Thomas, 1997). Although primarily from West Africa, the slaves were from diverse cultures and spoke a myriad of languages. While present in all 13 colonies, they were overwhelmingly sold to plantation owners in the colonies of the upper South. The early slave imports worked on the tobacco plantations of Virginia and Maryland; the slaves imported in the 1700s worked on the rice and indigo plantations in South Carolina. Adopting African techniques, the slaves turned South Carolina into a rice empire. In fact, from 1770 to 1775, they were able to raise the annual production of rice from 100,000 pounds to 65 million pounds (Miller & Thompson, 2007, p. 91). The last arrival of imported slaves to America worked on the sugar and cotton plantations that were established in the 1800s. By this time, the invention of the cotton gin in 1793 had made cotton the cornerstone of the southern economy, superseding both tobacco and rice in world market importance (Miller & Thompson, 2007). Indeed, by 1860, the southern states were providing two-thirds of the world's cotton supply and, more crucially, 80% of the British market.

Slaves of course saw none of the profits of their considerable labor, which required men, women, and children to work in the plantation fields from sunup to sundown, six days a week, year round. The work was backbreaking and in many cases prematurely aged the slaves (Allen, 2012). Understanding well the potential for slaves to rebel against their treatment, which did happen on several occasions, colonies sought to preempt this possibility by enacting legislation that completely subjugated the slaves both economically and socially as well physically, when necessary. Virginia alone enacted more than 130 slave statutes between 1689 and 1865 (Vaughn, 1989). South Carolina enacted the Negro Act of 1740, which made it illegal for slaves to gather in groups, earn money, and learn to read or raise food. It also gave slave owners the right to kill rebellious slaves. New York and Connecticut also passed similar legislation curtailing the movement and autonomy of slaves (Morgan, 2001). Even Congress passed legislation that helped to keep slaves bound to their masters in the form of the Fugitive Slave Acts of 1793 and 1850. These acts provided the seizure and return of runaway slaves who escaped from one state into another or a federal territory (Morgan, 2001).

Although the total of subjugation of slaves was beneficial to slave and plantation owners, the fact is that relatively few Whites themselves held slaves or directly profited from their labor. Indeed, noted historian Theodore Allen (2012) argues that Whites, particularly poor White subsistence farmers, were more likely hurt economically by losing out to the free labor of slaves. Yes, laws did require plantation owners to employ one White person for every so many Blacks, the number depending on the size of the plantation, and the laws also urged slave owners to prohibit Blacks from trades in order to preserve these positions for White artisans (Allen, 2012). These marginal privileges and social advantages, however, did little for White workers in general, nor is there any evidence that the profits made by cash crops did anything but stay in the pockets of wealthy slave holders and plantation owners. What it did, though, which would have implications for the labor market for generations to come, was draw a distinct line between White work and the subjugated condition of Black labor. Within the context of slavery, it allowed southern White workers to accept the argument for the necessity for Black slavery, even though their economic status did not rise in any way nearly commensurate with that of the wealthy (Allen, 2012). Thus, the wealthy used race to maintain the economic status quo.

Industrialization and the Battle for Equality, 1860–Present

Beginning with the revolution and the founding of an independent America, technological and social developments profoundly changed the nation and its labor market. Technological innovations in the late 18th and the 19th centuries helped to harness water and steam as a source of power, create new machine tools and labor-saving devices, build and expand a nationwide transportation system, and move labor from the fields to the factories. Social developments included American expansionism, the opening up of the western frontier, a bloody civil war freeing the slaves, mass immigration and migration, and rapid urbanization.

Between 1860 and 1920, the technological and social developments were the catalysts for the nation's transition from a primarily nonwaged agrarian society to a waged industrialized society. Illustrative of this transition was the massive redistribution of labor out of agriculture into capital-intensive manufacturing, with machines replacing human labor (Healy, 2014). In contrast to the agrarian imperative to organize and control a large, involuntary, geographically immobile labor force, industrialization required a labor force that was geographically and socially mobile, skilled, and literate (Healy, 2014, p. 133). Within this framework, all groups in the labor market were freer than they had ever been in a paternalistic agrarian society to compete with each other for jobs and other commodities.

However, as suggested by Healy (2014), this freedom did not mean that the industrialized society's labor market competition was anything like a level playing field. From the 1830s to the present, it is more accurate to say that it reflects existing patterns of social inequality and is manifested in segments of the dominant groups seeking to minimize or eliminate competition from minority groups in the market place. As you might recall (see Chapter 5), the Chinese Exclusion Act of 1882 was passed in large part to satisfy calls to eliminate Chinese immigrants as competition to native-born White Americans and White immigrant groups in the labor market (Campi, 2004). The Gentleman's Agreement of 1907 and the Immigration Act of 1917 were similarly enacted with this purpose in mind as it related to other Asian groups (Campi, 2007). In the rest of this section, we consider how existing patterns of social inequality in the industrialized era manifested in labor market competition for jobs and other commodities.

Jim Crow, De-Facto Racial Segregation, and Black Americans in the Labor Market (1870–1940)

With the Emancipation Proclamation and Reconstruction from 1863 to 1887, following the end of the Civil War, newly freed slaves were given the opportunity to participate fully in the larger society. To this end, they sought employment of their own; in some cases, acquired land; participated in the political process, electing a number of Blacks to the highest political high office; and started educational institutions. Although the emancipation strengthened the hand of Black labor in the South, it did so against the backdrop of lingering inequality and racial animus from southern White landowners bitterly opposed to Black equal rights (Huq, 2001). White landowners willing to negotiate with former slaves did so with the express purpose of reestablishing plantation-like labor arrangements through contract labor. These contracts had unsuspecting signees agreeing to work for an undetermined amount of time for nothing but food, clothes, and board. Throughout the reconstructed South, Blacks who were contracted as labor under the plantation-like labor arrangements of slavery were little more than peons deprived of mobility or access to fair and proper compensation (Huq, 2001).

Concerned with their plight in the labor market and wishing to achieve collective representation, Black workers began to organize themselves into unions. This action was not just a phenomenon of the Reconstruction period. Prior to the Civil War, Blacks had successfully participated in labor actions, the most notable being a strike by Black caulkers at the Washington Navy Yard in 1835; caulking was the process of making the seams in wooden boats or ships watertight (Foner, 1982, p. 11). Reconstruction, however, brought a new urgency and need for organizing Black labor, not least because the formation of trade unions increased during this period. These newly formed trade unions were primarily for White workers of all skill levels, and except for the Knights of Labor, typically excluded Black workers. In 1869, a delegate of 214 Black labor union leaders attended the Colored National Labor Union (CNLU) convention in Washington, D.C. (Foner, 1982). Of particular importance for CNLU was the condition of Black workers in the southern states, many of whom were unemployed or toiling as exploited contract laborers. In response to this concern, the CNLU assembly sent a petition to Congress asking for direct intervention in attenuating the condition of Black workers in the southern states, that is, subdividing the public lands of the South into 40-acre farms and providing low-interest loans to Black farmers. After receiving no response from Congress, the petition was sent again in 1872. Once again, however, Congress showed no interest in the petition (Foner, 1982).

By 1877, Reconstruction and the nation's first attempt at an interracial democracy would come to a shuddering halt. The federal government relinquished their promise to protect the rights of Black citizens. Absent this protection, the former slave-holding southern states began in earnest to wrestle back political control and reinstate social and economic subordination of its Black citizens (Logan, 1997). Central to this effort were the Redeemers, conservative, pro-business Democrats who believed they could redeem the changes made in Reconstruction by replacing the pro-Black integration Republican politicians, many of who were Black, with White Democrats, also known as Bourbon Democrats. Using armed White paramilitary organizations such as the Ku Klux Klan, the White League, and the Red Shirts to commit violence and intimidation, the Redeemers and Bourbon Democrats were successful in wrestling back political power sometimes by gunpoint or at the end of a rope.

To solidify this power, the southern states instituted *de jure* segregation (meaning "by law"; Healy, 2014). More commonly known as Jim Crow, *de jure* segregation physically and socially separated Whites and Blacks, consigning Blacks to an inferior position in all aspects of daily life. Sanctioned and reinforced by law, Jim Crow resulted in separate facilities for Whites and Blacks, adherence to social codes such as riding at the back of the bus, stepping off the sidewalk if a White person was coming in the opposite direction, and deferring to Whites of any age in all situations. Blacks could not negotiate with Whites on equal terms, and they had no franchise or political power save that given to them by Whites. Jim Crow allowed Whites in the South to subjugate Blacks in ways every bit as dehumanizing as slavery (Healy, 2014).

Never was this more evident than in the labor market arrangements in the southern states, arrangements that were particularly advantageous to the plantation elite who retained ownership of large tracts of land, where even in a now industrialized country, cotton remained the cash crop of the South. Missing, however, was the labor needed to work the land. Moreover, because of the ravages of the Civil War, landowners had very little in the way of liquid cash needed to attract and hire workers (Harris, 1982). To resolve this issue, landowners developed a system of tenant farming known as sharecropping. In this system, the sharecropper worked the land in exchange for a place to live, food, and clothing, all of which were given on credit. At the end of the harvest, the landowner and tenant farmer would split the profits, minus the debt owed. As the landowner kept the accounts, it was easy and commonplace for them to inflate the indebtedness and claim the tenant as still in debt even after the profits were split (Huq, 2001). Because of Jim Crow, Black tenant farmers could not challenge the situation. As a consequence, Black tenant farmers were in many cases bound to the land, relentlessly trying to pay off a debt that could never be paid (Huq, 2001).

Just as troubling on the labor front, access to wage-paying industrial jobs in the South was off limits to Black workers because of Jim Crow. Therefore, Black male workers in particular were relegated to agriculture work on the land and Black women as domestic workers or maids for White families. An example of just how locked in Black workers were to the less lucrative areas of the labor market, by 1910, 50% of all Black workers, the majority still living in the South, worked in agriculture. Another 25% were working in domestic occupations such as maids and janitors (Healy & O'Brien, 2015).

In 1917, World War I began in Europe after the assassination of Archduke Ferdinand and the subsequent Austria-Hungary invasion of Serbia. Although happening thousands of miles away in Europe, World War I would be the catalyst for a series of events that would have a profound impact on the trajectory of Black labor. The first event was that the flow of immigrants from Europe, the primary source of additional labor fueling the industrial economy, slowed to a trickle. Indeed, many of these immigrants returned to Europe to fight in the war. The second event was the conscription of American men to fight in World War I. The third event was the soaring European demand for U.S. agriculture and industrial products to meet wartime needs. The consequence of these events was an enhanced demand for U.S. industrial products but a reduced supply of ready labor to meet these demands.

In the industrialized labor markets of the Midwest and Northeast, the untapped labor force was composed of Blacks in the South. Given their repressed circumstances in the southern labor market, it was a labor force that was all too ready to respond to the call for labor in the factories, mines, and mills in the industrialized urban cities of the Midwest and Northeast.

In what became known as the Great Migration, the years between 1915 and 1930 saw 1.6 million Black people leave the South and move to the industrialized cities of the Midwest and Northeast. As we have discussed (see Chapter 7), the migration dramatically changed the demographic makeup of cities such as Chicago, St. Louis, New York, and Philadelphia (Gotham, 2000; Jackson, 1980; Seitles, 1996). More than this, for the first time Black labor had the opportunity to compete in an open labor market for employment.

In the midwestern and northeastern industrialized cities, the Black male labor force doubled to nearly 500,000 as they found work in the factories, mills, and the automobile and the railroad industries, where they were hired as unskilled labor (Fuchs, 1995). In addition, because of labor union exclusion, they entered industries as strikebreakers, working on the docks in Baltimore and in the iron and steel industries of western Pennsylvania (Fuchs, 1995). There were also middle class, educated Blacks who secured employment in the Civil Service. These gains, however, were against the backdrop of racial attitudes and practices that while not sanctioned by any official Jim Crow-type legislation, nevertheless sought to marginalize Blacks as competition in the labor force. Complicit in this marginalization were the unions and a federal government that at best were indifferent to the plight of Black workers. Two notable examples of this indifference were President Woodrow Wilson's racial segregation of the Civil Service from 1913 onward and Black labor union leader A. Phillip Randolph's 12-year fight to have the Pullman Car Company, the American Federation of Labor (AFL), and the U.S. government recognize the all-Black Brotherhood of Sleeping Car Porters.

Woodrow Wilson and the Racial Segregation of the Civil Service

After the end of Reconstruction, there were few laws protecting Blacks against racial discrimination on the job or in the labor market, but the one place this was not true was in work for the federal government. Black Americans had gained entrance into the Civil Service after the passing of the Pendleton Act of 1883. Enacted after the assassination of President James A. Garfield and the scandal of Civil Service jobs being given on the basis of patronage and political support, the Pendleton Act mandated that federal government jobs be awarded on the basis of merit and that government employees be selected through competitive exams (Theriault, 2003). The act also made it unlawful to terminate or demote employees for political reasons. Finally, it forbade the requirement that employees give political service or contributions to a political party cause. To enforce these mandates, the Civil Service Commission was established (Theriault, 2003).

After the passing of the Pendleton Act, the merit system increased the number of Black civil servants from 620 in 1883 to 24,000 by 1917 (Smith, 2003). These Black men and women worked in every area of government service. They helped produced reports for the Census Bureau, managed appropriations in the Treasury Department, and sorted mail in the Post Office Department. Indeed, in 1912, every dollar printed by the Bureau of Engraving bore the signature of a Black man who served as the register of the Treasury (Yellin, 2013). Black men also served as auditor for the Navy Department; U.S. consul in Cognac, France; and the collector of the Port of New York. More than 400 mostly men worked as white-collar clerks in Washington, D.C., some in supervisory positions over Whites. Then, as now, work in the Civil Service allowed Blacks social and economic mobility and a solidly middle class life (Yellin, 2013).

However, the election of Woodrow Wilson in 1913 was to profoundly affect the circumstances of Black civil servants. Wilson, a progressive Southern Democrat, was the first southern-born president to hold office after the Civil War. During his 1912 presidential election, Wilson had courted Black support with the promise to be as progressive as the Republicans had been in appointing Blacks to patronage positions. Yet, once in office, Wilson needed the support of the strongly anti-Black Southern Democrats if his progressive economic reform for America were to be enacted. Prioritizing the need for this support, anti-Black forces soon gained a foothold in Washington and Jim Crow thinking began to hold sway. The promised Black patronage did not materialize, but rather declined significantly from those of previous administrations. Moreover, half way through his first term, Wilson allowed a total of 12 positions occupied by Blacks appointed by President Taft to lapse and be placed in White hands.

More egregiously, though, Wilson and his Cabinet, at least three of whom were supporters of racial segregation, acquiesced to calls from groups such as ironically named National Democratic Fair Play Association (NDFPA) to racially segregate the civil services. Unabashedly racist, the NDFPA posited that great harm would come to the country if the 24,500 Blacks employed by the federal government were allowed to continue to work in integrated settings among 450,000 White fellow employees (Fuchs, 1995, p. 99). It was a perspective that Wilson's newly appointed postmaster general, Albert S. Burleson, a former Texas congressman, fully endorsed. Indeed, in a 1913 cabinet meeting, Burleson called for the segregation to begin with the post office and the railway mail service. The call was not opposed and began with incredible speed and enthusiasm.

For example, post office window service to the public was segregated. Black postal workers were transferred to the dead letter office. Others were reassigned or demoted to janitorial or low-level clerical positions. Furthermore, the workspace was segregated, with Black employees relegated to segregated cubicles in poorly lit areas. Promotions were denied, and in many cases Black employees were purged as the result of bogus allegations of incompetence. Even on the railway mail service, where Blacks and Whites had worked together across the country, including in southern states, Black employees were reassigned and segregated (Smith, 2003). Moreover, in 1914, to get around the merit system for new applicants, the Wilson administration instituted a rule that all applicants submit photographs to accompany the results of their Civil Service exam. So effective was this rule that after its institution the Railway Mail Service hired almost no Blacks after 1914 (Smith, 2003).

Although fairly successful in racially segregating the post office service, not all departments embraced this action. The Department of Labor, for example, actively resisted racially segregating its workforce. Moreover, Black advocacy groups and postal workers did not accept racial segregation passively. The National Postal Alliance, formed by Black postal workers who had experienced discrimination on the job, confronted the Wilson Administration with reports on the discrimination. Supporting the reports were the campaigning efforts of the National Association for the Advancement of Colored People and luminaries such as W.E.B. Dubois. Indeed, the campaigning and the letter-writing efforts denouncing the treatment of Black civil service employees certainly took Wilson by surprise. But even with the campaigning and the threat of the loss of Black political support, Wilson still staunchly defended his segregation policy. Indeed, he told a Black delegation led by William Trotter, one of the founders of the Nigeria Movement, that segregation was necessary because of the friction between Black and White workers, echoing the sentiments of the NDFPA (Fuchs, 1995).

The actions of Wilson would in part be undone by the Roosevelt administration in the 1940s following the threats of massive protest from A. Phillip Randolph and the ACL-CIO unions. Among the actions the Roosevelt administration took was to end the photograph requirement. He also issued Executive Order 8802 banning discriminatory employment practices by federal agencies and all unions and companies engaged in war-related work. To enforce the policy, the order created the Fair Employment Practices Commission (Executive Order 8802, 1941).

A. Phillip Randolph and the Brotherhood of Sleeping Car Porters

In 1925, 500 disgruntled Black Pullman Company workers held an historic meeting in Harlem and agreed to form a union to bargain for better working conditions and pay. The company they were about to take on, however, was no ordinary corporation. Founded by George Pullman in the 1880s and headquartered in Chicago, the Pullman Company had pioneered the sleeping car trains that transported Americans across the country (Harris, 1982). They were also one of the largest single employers of Black workers in the United States, with approximately 12,000 on their payroll, the majority of them working on the sleeping cars as porters or maids. Moreover, the Pullman Company had long cultivated an image of itself as a friend to the

Black community, providing financial support to churches, newspapers, and other cultural organizations (Tye, 2005). Indeed, within the Black community, the Pullman Company not only enjoyed great support, but the Black porters and maids who worked for them were considered an elite class of worker because they had a steady job that allowed them to travel (Tye, 2005).

In actuality, work as a porter, commonly known as George because of the founder's first name, or a maid with the Pullman Company was much less glamorous than was portrayed. As well as catering to every travel need of their passengers in the sleeping cars, the porters and maids worked long hours and were responsible for unpaid preparatory and terminal set-up and cleanup duties. Moreover, they had to pay for their own food, lodging, and uniforms, which accounted for approximately half of their already meager average salary of two dollars a day. In addition, they were financially liable if their passengers stole Pullman Company property, such as a towel or water pitcher (Harris, 1982). Thus, porters and maids were heavily reliant on passengers' tips to supplement their salary. Maids, who were paid even less than the porters, received shorter rest periods and were not provided with sleeping space on long-distance trips, were more unlikely to earn tips. In addition to the poor working conditions and pay, the porters, all of whom were Black, had no opportunity for advancement to the next position up as a conductor because that was a job reserved for Whites (Harris, 1982).

These conditions proved too much for a growing number of porters and maids, hence the 1925 meeting in Harlem to form a union. This call for a union, however, was not the first by porters and maids; a decade earlier, Pullman porters and maids had made similar calls. However, that call was soon abandoned when the Pullman Company fired any porter or maid advocating for a union (Bates, 2001). Determined not to repeat the mistake of having a union president who was also a Pullman Company employee, the porters and maids approached noted civil rights activist and newspaper reporter A. Phillip Randolph to be their president. After initially declining the offer, Randolph relented and took on the position with his co-leader Milton Webster, who worked out of Chicago. In 1925, the Brotherhood of Sleeping Car Porters and Maids (BSCP) was born with the motto "Fight or Be Slaves" (Bates, 2001).

Right from its birth, the BSCP and A. Phillip Randolph faced long odds in their efforts to secure better working conditions and pay for porters and maids from the Pullman Company. To begin with, Randolph and his co-leaders, Pullman porters Milton Webster in Chicago, Ashley Totten in New York, and C.L. Dellums in Oakland, had no funds, office staff, organizational budget, telephone, or national chapters to rely on as strategic outposts. Moreover, they initially lacked a critical mass of support from the porters and maids in the Pullman Company. Furthermore, the Pullman Company responded to the forming of the BSCP by firing any porter or maid who was heard or seen to be supporting the union (Bynum, 2010). The Pullman Company also recruited respected Black leaders to denounce the BSCP and its leaders as communists and troublemakers (Smith et al., 2006). Finally, they asked the porters and maids to form a new, company-friendly union, the Pullman Porters Protective Union (Bynum, 2010).

Compounding the initial lack of resources and critical mass of support, the BSCP also had to wage battles on two fronts to be recognized as a legitimate union representative of the Pullman porters and maids. The first battle was with the federal government's National Mediation Board (NMB), who would not certify the BSCP as a legitimate union representative because of the presence of the Pullman Company-approved union. Without the certification, the NMB was not bound to hear any labor dispute between the BSCP and the Pullman Company. Relatedly, the BSCP was not an approved charter member of the American Federation of Labor (AFL), many of whose members were racist and opposed to Black membership, but the BSCP needed to be a AFL charter if they were ever to be able to sit at the table and participate in collective bargaining with the Pullman Company on an equal footing as White workers (Bynum, 2010; Smith et al., 2006).

But despite these odds, Randolph and his leadership team proved to be remarkably resourceful. They made dozens of membership recruitment visits across the country, spreading their message to the rank and file of the porters and maids. These efforts did not go unrewarded, as they were eventually able to recruit at least half the workforce, all of whom chose BSCP over the company union. Randolph also used his newspaper, the *Messenger*, to hammer home to the Black community the need to support the BSCP against the exploitative Pullman Company (Bates, 2001). Randolph's message did resonate with many

Blacks, and support in the Black community for the BSCP increased significantly. Nevertheless, it still took ten years of dogged determination, including threatened strikes, intimidation, and mass firings of union members, near bankruptcy, and falling membership for the BSCP to eventually prevail. In 1935, following the enactment of the Wagner-Connery Act of 1935 outlawing company unions, the BSCP defeated the Pullman Company union in a vote and was certified by the NMB. In the same year, the AFL granted the BSCP an international charter (Bates, 2001). In 1937, the BSCP became the first Black labor union to win collective bargaining rights from the Pullman Company or any other major America company. Porters won significantly higher wages, better working conditions, and shorter working days (Bates, 2001).

Although the BSCP's victory did not extinguish the labor market inequalities that plagued Black men and women in the labor force, who were less than a hundred years removed from chattel slavery and still in the midst of Jim Crow and de-facto segregation, it was a watershed moment in labor history. It was arguably also one of the catalysts for the civil rights movement of the 1960s.

Women and the Fight for Labor Market Equality (1880–1912)

The years between 1880 and 1912 were unprecedented in the degree of labor conflict experienced in the United States. These years pitted labor unions against managers and owners in a fight for fair pay, decent work conditions, and the right to collective bargaining. It was a battle fought on many fronts by many different groups across the country. Often lost or overlooked in the discussion of these battles is the role of female workers, who were at the forefront of many of the key labor conflicts of the late 19th and early 20th centuries. That women workers had such a key role in labor conflicts is not altogether surprising.

In the early stages of industrialization, pre-Civil War, women were the first industrial workers in the burgeoning and profitable textile mills in Lowell, Massachusetts. As such, they were the first group to bear the hardships of work in the new mechanized factories. Hired to tend the power looms, the mill girls worked 14-hour shifts, 5:00 am to 7:00 pm, in hot, noisy, and often dangerous conditions for what were relatively low wages (Larson, 2010). With little in the way of rights or collective bargaining powers, the mill girls were very much at the mercy of the mill owners. However, this changed in 1834 when the mill owners cut wages because of increased competition among the mills. For the mill girls, this proved to be a step too far, prompting a walkout and a strike that gained national attention (Larson, 2010). The strike also became the catalyst for political action and the call for shorter working hours, increased pay, and better working conditions. In their call to be delivered from what they described as tyranny and cruel oppression, the mill girls, who formed themselves into the Lowell Female Reform Association in 1845, argued for a 10-hour day. It was a battle that the women of Lowell won, and just as importantly it set a precedent for other women workers similarly oppressed in the work force or labor market (Larson, 2010).

The Atlanta Washerwomen and the Fight for Dignity and Respect

In 1880, Atlanta's nearly all-Black female laundresses provided commercial laundry services for the city. Indeed, Atlanta had more laundresses than common labors. Of all the domestic jobs, laundry work was the most difficult. The hours were long and the pay poor. Making it more difficult was that the laundresses had to make their own soap, starch, and washtubs (Greenfield, 1999). They also had to carry gallons of water from wells, pumps, and hydrants for washing, boiling, and rinsing the clothes. Moreover, because of the low pay for their services, if they wanted to make more money, they had to take on extra clients outside of their daily responsibility (Greenfield, 1999).

Dissatisfied with this arrangement and seeking higher pay, respect, and autonomy, 20 laundresses formed a trade union organization, the Washing Society, in 1881. With the support of Black ministers, they called a strike, which within three weeks grew to 3,000 workers and included White laundresses. Retaliation was swift, as strikers were arrested and fined and the city's politicians threatened levying heavy fees on businesses. The resolve of the strikers encouraged other domestic workers, maids, cooks, and nurses to begin demanding higher wages. Not sure that they could replace all of the domestic labor and aware of the magnitude of Black labor unrest, the city council relented to the demands of the Washing Society (Greenfield, 1999; Hunter, 1997).

In the 20th century, the second United States' industrial revolution saw mainly immigrant women in the workforce have particularly bloody and sometimes deadly labor conflicts with factory owners who thought nothing of using strikebreakers to intimidate strikers physically. By 1900, anywhere from 25% to 40% of the labor force were women. While a great majority of these women still worked in the agriculture sector in the southern and western regions of the country, in the midwestern and northeastern industrialized cities the majority of women worked in the mills and factories. Two labor conflicts in the first two decades of the 20th century were to have a profound impact on the labor movement: the Triangle Shirtwaist factory and the women of Lawrence, Massachusetts.

The Triangle Shirtwaist Factory Tragedy and Labor Law Change

The first conflict was the result of the now infamous Triangle Shirtwaist factory fire on March 25, 1911, in Manhattan, New York. The fire broke out on the top floor of the factory, and because the doors were locked and firefighters did not have ladders tall enough to reach the top of the building, 146 of the 500 mostly young immigrant women workers either jumped to their deaths or died from the smoke and flames. This was a shocking event because of the number of people who perished, but they certainly were not the first deaths in the United States' industrialized workforce, where an estimated 100 workers a day died as a result of accidents in the nation's mines, mills, factories, and shipyards (Von Drehle, 2004). What made the Triangle Shirtwaist factory so compelling in labor's history were the events leading up to the tragedy and the labor movement that emerged after it.

The shirtwaist was a women's blouse that at the time was the height of fashion. It was an accessory garment that crossed all class lines and was one of the top products in the booming clothing manufacturing industry. The factories that produced the shirtwaist blouses employed predominately young, Yiddish-speaking immigrant women from eastern Europe. As young as 15, these women and girls worked as seamstresses seven days a week, from 7:00 am to 8:00 pm, with a 30-minute lunch break. During the busy season, they could work nonstop (Von Drehle, 2004). Indeed, because the women had to leave the building to use the toilets, the factory owners took to locking the steel exit doors so work would not be interrupted. The workers were paid $6 per week, but were required to buy and use their own needles, thread, irons, and sometimes even their own sewing machines (Von Drehle, 2004).

Two years before the Triangle Shirtwaist fire, garment workers had pressed owners about the practice of locking the exit doors in the high-rise factory. Yet the only response they got was a demand for more work and less money. As a result, several hundred workers went on strike in 1909. Shortly after, Local 25 of the International Ladies Garment Workers' Union (ILGWU) convened to discuss a general strike for better working conditions and pay. Among the luminaries at the meeting was the American Federation of Labor leader Samuel Gompers. Yet it was 19-year-old Clara Lemlich, one of the founders of Local 25, who gave the most impassioned plea for the need to strike. In Yiddish, she told the convened audience, "I have no further patience for talk, as I am one of those who feels and suffers from the things pictured. I move we go on general strike now." The audience cheered and voted to strike (Von Drehle, 2004). Within 24 hours, more than 15,000 shirtwaist workers in New York walked out, demanding a 20% pay rise, a 52-hour week, and overtime pay. Just as importantly, they wanted a closed shop, which means that the factories could only hire union members. By the time picketing began, the work of the local union along with Women's Trade Union League saw 20,000 workers from 500 factories walk out. Fearing ruin, 70 smaller factories agreed to the union demands within 48 hours of the strike.

In contrast, the owners of the Triangle Shirtwaist factory met with owners of 20 of the largest factories and agreed to do whatever it took to defeat the union and quash their demands. The *whatever it took* included hiring strikebreakers to hurt or physically intimidate the strikers. It also included using the police and political influence to arrest strikers and having courts fine them. Yet the strikers were able to find support from wealthy suffragists who saw their cause as one aligned with that of women's suffrage (Von Drehle, 2004).

As the strike proceeded into its first month, the small and mid-sized factories acquiesced to the union's demands. Further, realizing they had the lost in the court of public opinion, the large factories agreed to negotiate. For their part, the large factories agreed to higher pay and shorter hours, but adamantly rejected a closed shop. The young women workers who wanted collective bargaining power rejected the offer. As more and more factories settled, the women of the Triangle Shirtwaist factory eventually returned to work; however, they did so without a union agreement. Moreover, they never addressed the concerns of the workers, most notably the demand to unlock the steel exit doors, which two years later resulted in tragedy (Von Drehle, 2004).

After the tragedy, people from across the social classes demanded action on fire safety in the factories. Three months after the funeral of Triangle Shirtwaist women and girls, which saw 350,000 people participate in a march, the New York governor created the Factory Investigating Commission. The commission investigated more than 2,000 factories across all industries. After the investigations, laws were passed addressing fire safety, factory inspections, and sanitation and employment rules for women and children. Furthermore, 12 months after the tragedy, New York State totally rewrote its labor laws, creating the Department of Labor to enforce them (Von Drehle, 2004).

The Bread and Roses Strike in Lawrence, Massachusetts

Just 12 months after the Triangle Shirtwaist factory tragedy, the second labor conflict that would have a profound impact on the labor movement was the Bread and Roses strike in Lawrence, Massachusetts, in 1912. It happened in the Everett Mill in Lawrence, which was known as immigrant city (Watson, 2005). On January 11, 1912, the women who worked in the mill opened their pay envelopes to find that their wages had been reduced by 32 cents. The reduction in the wages was a result of a new law enacted by the state of Massachusetts reducing the workweek for women and children from 56 to 54 hours. Unlike the past, however, the mill owners reduced the mill workers' wage commensurate with the reduction in the working hours. Incensed by the mill owners' action, the mill women put down their tools, refused to operate the power looms, and walked off the job (Watson, 2005). Although paltry by today's standards, for the immigrant women of Everett Mill, 32 cents was the difference between eating and not eating. In the small, interconnected tenements of Everett Mill, news of the strike spread quickly, and by morning women from the other mills went out on strike.

By the end of January, 10,000 mill workers from 51 nations with a myriad of languages were on strike marching through the streets and parading with banners outside of the mill demanding both a living wage and dignity. Clashes between the female mill workers who were on strike and the militiamen who were brought in to protect the mills at bayonet point were frequent and violent. So violent did clashes become that the strikers attacked a streetcar carrying workers who crossed the picket line, to which the police responded by battling with strikers. The result was a gunshot that killed striker Anna LoPizzo. Also killed was 18-year-old John Ramsey, who died after being stabbed by a soldier's bayonet (Watson, 2005).

Such was the level of tension and resolve of the strikers that American laborers from around the country helped the strikers by making food donations. Families from outside the state also took in the children of the strikers. Those who did not go with strangers were sent to stay with relatives to avoid the conflict that engulfed their neighborhoods. Indeed, what became known as the Children's Exodus was also a turning point in gaining national support, as the country reacted to reports of marshals trying to halt the exodus by force (Watson, 2005).

In response, President Taft ordered an inquiry into the strike in March 1912. Results of the inquiry found that children dropped out of school early to work in the factories, whose hot and humid conditions proved to be a long-term health risk to workers, to the extent that a third of the mill workers had a life expectancy of less than 40 years and died of respiratory health complications from breathing in dust and lint within ten years of taking the job. The inquiry also revealed, from the firsthand testimony of workers, the numerous dangers posed by the mill machines. These were dangers that included mill machines severing limbs and tearing scalps (Watson, 2005).

Subsequent to the inquiry and the testimony of the mill workers, the mill owners agreed to the demands of the strikers. These demands included a 15% wage increase, overtime compensation, and a promise not to retaliate against strikers. The deal was ratified nine weeks after the start of the strike on March 14, 2012, when 15,000 strikers shouted their agreement to accept the offer (Watson, 2005). As with labor agreement garnered by the BSCP 23 years later, the agreement signed by the Lawrence Mill workers was a seminal moment in American labor's fight for equality and dignity in the workforce. It was achieved at a time when only a fraction of American workers were unionized and thus set a platform for labor unions to come. It also again illustrated the critical role women played in the labor unions, a role just like that of the Lawrence Mill strike that was one of the foundations for Labor Day (Watson, 2005).

The New Deal

Starting in the 1930s, there were numerous unions in America, but only 8% of the workforce were actually union members, a decrease from 15% just a decade earlier (Mayer, 2004). These union members were predominately from the skilled craft unions that were in the main affiliated with the America Federation of Labor; there was almost no representation from the much larger labor pool in the mass production industries (Library of Congress, 2015), such as the steel, coal, automobile, and textile industries. Indeed, such was the dire state of the unions in the 1930s that their future as a collective bargaining force in the labor market looked bleak. However, in the throes of the Great Depression and with a near 25% unemployment rate, President Franklin D. Roosevelt signed into law the National Industry Recovery Act (NIRA) (P.L. 73–67) of 1933 as part of his "new deal with America" (Library of Congress, 2015). In addition to seeking to stimulate economic recovery, put people back to work through federal work programs, and regulate industry, the NIRA guaranteed trade union rights by protecting the collective bargaining rights of labor unions (True III, 2005). After a decade in which industry and business had all but quashed labor union rights, the NIRA emboldened labor unions to press for even more pro-union legislation, which just two years later came in form of the National Labor Relations Act (P.L. 74–198) of 1935 (also known as the Wagner Act). Now considered a foundational statute of United States labor law, the act guaranteed the basic rights of most private sector employees to organize into trade unions, participate in collective bargaining for better terms and conditions in the workplace, and if necessary take strike action (True III, 2005).

The act also created the National Labor Relations Board (NLRB), which facilitates elections that can require employers to engage in collective bargaining with labor unions (Library of Congress, 2015). Notably excluded from the act, and as a result weakening their bargaining potential in the years to come, were agricultural employees, supervisors, domestic employees, and independent contractors (Lehman & Phelps, 2005). The passing of the act, nevertheless, was a watershed moment that saw union membership pushed to nearly 40% of the labor force, which, as Gordon notes (2013), positioned the labor movement as a countervailing power at the bargaining table, and just as importantly, in local, state, and national politics. Not unexpectedly, the corporate community was vehemently opposed to the NLRB and in its aftermath continued to resist unionization. For example, there were legal challenges to the constitutionality of the NLRB, as well as numerous injunctions. Moreover, in the extreme, companies such as General Motors and Goodyear Tire and Rubber prepared for violent confrontations with labor organizations by stockpiling guns and dynamite, infuriating union membership with company spies, and hiring men to attack pro-union activists (Auerbach, 1966; Scheinberg, 1986). Despite the opposition to the NLRB, in the decade following its enactment, labor unions were at their strongest. They were able to win higher wages and improve working conditions for members, although they were reluctant to extend the benefits of union membership to Blacks and women (Gordon, 2013).

In the years following World War II, two pieces of federal legislation would significantly curtail the growing power of the unions. Enacted against the backdrop of ongoing industrial strife and emerging cold war sentiments and anti-communist and anti-union rhetoric, the first of these legislations was the Labor Management Relations Act of 1947 (P.L. 80–101), otherwise known as the Taft-Hartley Act after its two Republican co-sponsors (Gordon, 2013). The act, which remains in effect today, was the first major revision of the NLRB. It was sweeping in effect and placed significant restrictions on unions and their power. Among the many restrictions were a ban on closed shops in which only union members could be hired, a ban on unauthorized (wildcat) strikes by the rank-and-file on the shop floor, and a ban on unions contributing to political campaigns (Gross, 1995). Furthermore, states were allowed to enact right-to-work laws, making it illegal to set union membership as a condition of employment. The act also required union leaders to take an oath stating that they were not Communists. Other examples of the act's reach included a provision that gave the United States Attorney General the power to obtain an 80-day injunction when he or she believed a proposed or actual strike threatened national health or safety (Gross, 1995).

The second piece of legislation curtailing union power came with the enactment of the Labor Management Reporting and Disclosure Act of 1959, more commonly known as the Landrum-Griffin Act. Ostensibly, the act was a response to congressional concern with union corruption, racketeering, and other misconduct. In its provisions, however, it went further and addressed gaps in both the NLRB and Taft-Hartley legislation (Gross, 1995). The act mandated that unions hold secret elections reviewable by the Department of Labor (DOL), barred members of the Communist Party and convicted felons from holding union office (although this was ruled unconstitutional in 1965), and required unions to submit annual financial reports to the DOL (Gross, 1995).

The 1960s and the Fight for Labor Market Equality

For all of the attacks on organized labor, after World War II, collective bargaining was nevertheless successful in advancing its central purpose of improving the economic and job interests of union members. Impressively, between 1945 and 1970, collective bargaining helped triple weekly earnings in manufacturing (History.com, 2015). Just as impressively, it secured for union members unprecedented measures of security against unemployment, illness, and old age, as well as strengthening the right to fair treatment in the workplace (History.com, 2015). However, going into the 1960s, unions covered only a third of wage earners and had no involvement with the low-wage secondary labor market, most notably migrant farm workers and domestics. Just as tellingly, construction and industrial unions were largely a closed shop, excluding racial and ethnic minorities and women. Moreover, outside of union membership, racial and ethnic minorities and women had only limited access to the full range of available jobs and careers (History.com, 2015).

The 1960s, a time of great revolutionary ferment, saw the emergence of a plethora of civil rights and grassroots advocacy groups determined to challenge this status quo in the labor market. Among the most prominent of these groups were the Urban League, headed by Whitney Young Jr. (see Profile); the National Farm Workers Association (NFWA), later called the United Farm Workers (UFW), co-founded by Cesar Chavez (see profile) and Dolores Huerta; Radical Women; and the National Organization of Women (NOW). These groups' use of advocacy, protest, civil disobedience, and legislative actions all helped to bring attention to the labor force inequality experienced by Blacks, Latino, and Filipino farm workers; other ethnic minority groups; and women. They also, as in the case of the Urban League, were able to open employment opportunities in major corporations that had hitherto been closed to Blacks. In the same vein, the NFWA and UFW were able to win higher salaries and better working conditions for previously exploited migrant farm workers. The next three decades would see the passing of workplace legislation that would be far more inclusive of diverse groups and offer better workplace protections for most groups at the federal level (see Box 8.1 Timeline). Yet, as was noted in the beginning of this chapter, inequality still remains stubbornly entrenched in the labor market for the historically marginalized, even as their numbers have grown across all sectors and occupations.

Profiles

Whitney Young, Jr. (1921–1971)

Born in Lincoln Ridge, Kentucky, Whitney Young, Jr., was the middle child of a school president and schoolteacher. In his relatively short life, Young, a social worker and civil rights leader, served as the first dean of the Atlanta School of Social Work (1954), state president of the NAACP, executive director of the Urban League (1961–1971), and the national president of the National Association of Social Workers (1969–1971). Young was also consultant to both President John F. Kennedy and President Lyndon Johnson (Biography, 2015).

In a lifetime commitment, Young used all his considerable skills as a mediator and power broker to fight racial discrimination and exclusion in employment for Black Americans. Most notably, Young took the Urban League from a small, cautious, and moderate organization of just 38 employees in 1961 to a vibrant organization with 1,300 employees in only 4 years. Young's efforts thrust the Urban League on the forefront of American civil rights in the 1960s. In this role, Young positioned the Urban League to be social engineers rather than street-level activists. The goal was to change employment policy at the highest echelons of corporate America and local, city, state, and federal government. To accomplish this, Young cultivated relationships with major corporation heads and policy makers. He pushed corporate leaders to open employment opportunities for Black Americans. Moreover, he advocated politically to President Johnson for a domestic Marshall Plan, which would see the federal government invest funds to address America's racial and poverty issues. Indeed, this plan would become the framework for the War on Poverty policies of the 1960s (Biography, 2015).

Such was Young's influence that among many other things he is credited with almost single-handedly persuading corporate America to open employment opportunities to Black Americans. For his civil rights work, Young was recognized with America's highest civilian award in 1969—The Presidential Medal of Freedom. After Young's untimely death in 1971, President Nixon stated in his eulogy that Young knew how to accomplish what others could only talk about doing. Young's work was instrumental in breaking down barriers of segregation and inequality that held Black Americans back in both the work place and larger society (Biography, 2015).

References

Biography. (2015). *Whitney Young, Jr.* Retrieved from http://www.biography.com

Profiles

Cesar Chavez (1927–1993)

Born in Yuma, Arizona, to Mexican immigrant parents, Cesar Chavez rose to prominence as a nationally influential union leader and labor organizer. This rise was rooted in his early life experience as a migrant farmer worker, first working with his family picking peas and lettuce in the winter, beans in the spring, and cotton in the fall. Chavez dropped out of school in the seventh grade and worked full time as a migrant farm worker from 1942 to 1952, with a 2-year break when he joined the Navy in 1944 (Biography, 2015).

In 1952, Chavez began his life as an activist when he became an organizer for the Community Service Organization (CSO), a grassroots Latino civil rights organization. The express purpose of the CSO was to empower Mexican Americans in California who in their work in the fields, railroads, construction sites, and service jobs faced ongoing racism and discrimination. The CSO sought to change the status quo by empowering poor Mexican Americans to make demands of the political system and thereby move from the periphery to the mainstream of American society. Strategies included voter registration drives, citizenship classes, lawsuits, and legislative campaigns., Chavez was active in all these strategies in the CSO, as well as traveling through California making speeches and advocating for workers' rights (Biography, 2015)

In 1958, Chavez became the national leader of the CSO, but resigned his post in 1962 and with Dolores Huerta co-founded the National Farm Workers Association (NFWA), later called the United Farm Workers (UFW). It was with the NFWA that Chavez would gain national prominence when he supported Filipino American farm workers who initiated the Delano grape strike for higher wages in 1965. Using the advocacy skills learned with the CSO, Chavez and the NFWA supported and advocated for the Filipino American farm workers' strike for the full 5 years of its duration. During this time, the strike, marches, protest, and Chavez's speeches brought national attention and support from Robert F. Kennedy, then a member of the Subcommittee on Migratory Labor. The activities of NFWA were the catalyst for similar movements in southern Texas (1966), Wisconsin (1966), and Ohio (1967) (Biography, 2015).

Even after victory in the Delano grape strike, Chavez remained a tireless labor organizer and advocate for labor equality for agriculture workers throughout the 1970s. His Gandhi-inspired methods of protest included hunger strikes, fasts, and civil disobedience, all with an emphasis on nonviolence. A series of defeats between 1976 and 1988 saw the decline of the UFW and the diminishing influence of Chavez, but his legacy of Chavez of his work first with CSO and then the NFWA/UFW is undoubted. In recognition, he was nominated for the Noble Prize three times, had his portrait placed in the National Portrait Gallery in Washington, DC, was posthumously awarded the Presidential Medal of Freedom, and received the Jefferson Award for public service benefiting the disadvantaged. The U.S. Postal Service also honored Chavez with a postage stamp (Biography, 2015).

Most importantly, however, Chavez and the UFW succeeded in improving working conditions and raising salaries for farmworkers in California, Texas, Arizona, and Florida (Biography, 2015).

References

Biography. (2015). *Cesar Chavez biography*. Retrieved from http://www.ourdocuments.gov/doc.php?flash=true&doc=84

Chapter Summary

There has been tremendous progress in the opening up of opportunities for all people in the labor market. No occupation or career is out of reach for anyone with the necessary qualifications, at least on the surface. Moreover, a raft of federal social policies protects all groups from workforce discrimination, most recently the 2019 Supreme Court ruling that an employer who fires an individual merely for being gay or transgender defies the Title VII stipulation of the 1964 Civil Rights Act. Title VII prohibits employers from discriminating against employees and job applicants based on race, color, religion, sex, and national origin (*Bostock v. Clayton County*, Georgia, No.17–1618, 2020). The landmark ruling offers the same federal protections against workplace discrimination for LGBTQ workers that have been enjoyed by every other group of workers in the United States.

Despite these gains, however, inequality in the labor market remains alive and well for most historically marginalized groups. These inequalities exact a heavy toll on their victims, such as the substantial loss in lifetime earnings for women who still on average earn less than their male counterparts.

Retrieval Questions

1. What is labor market inequality?
2. What is the significance of Title VII of the Civil Rights Act of 1964?
3. What is the gender wage gap?
4. What was the third category of indentured servitude?
5. What did South Carolina's Negro Act of 1740 stipulate?
6. Who were the founders of the Brotherhood of Sleeping Car Porters?
7. What was one example of women's fight for labor market equality in the years from 1880 to 1912?
8. What was the significance of the National Labor Relations Act of 1935?
9. What was the significance of the Labor Management Relations Act of 1947?
10. What was the significance of the Labor Management Reporting and Disclosure Act of 1959?

Discussion Questions

1. Identify and discuss some of the social justice issues pertinent to labor force inequality.
2. As policy practitioners, identify and discuss how social workers might address labor force inequality.
3. Identify and discuss some of the potential practice challenges you might have when working with individuals who are the victims of workplace discrimination.

Box 8.1 Labor Market Key Events Timeline

1869: The Knights of Labor is formed by Uriah Stephens in Philadelphia, Pennsylvania. Beginning as a secret society, the Knights organize labor around the country without management's knowledge. The Knights are an important force in the early days of labor organizing (Shmoop Editorial Team, 2008).

1886: Labor organizer Samuel Gompers establishes the American Federation of Labor (AFL), a collection of trade unions that will play a significant role in the labor movement over the next hundred years (Shmoop Editorial Team, 2008).

1890: Congress passes the Sherman Anti-Trust Act. Although intended to prohibit business monopolies, in the decades to come employers attempt to use it against unions (Shmoop Editorial Team, 2008).

1892: An employer lockout at the Homestead Steel Works becomes a violent confrontation when 300 Pinkerton detectives hired by the company engage in a pitched battle with picketing workers. Seven detectives and 11 union members are killed as a result of the battle. Court injunctions help to nullify the union and as a consequence protect the steel industry from organized labor for the next five decades (Shmoop Editorial Team, 2008).

1909: The International Ladies' Garment Workers' Union (ILGWU) calls a strike in New York. The union demands a 20% pay raise and a 52-hour week. Within 48 hours

20,000 workers from 500 factories walk off the job. The ILGWUs action is the largest labor action by women in the nation's history (Shmoop Editorial Team, 2008).

1911: A fire in the Triangle Shirtwaist factory in New York kills nearly 150 workers (ACL-CIO, 2015).

1912: The Bread and Roses strike by immigrant women in Lawrence, Massachusetts, begins. At its height, 23,000 men, women, and children are on strike and as many as 20,000 on the picket line (ACL-CIO, 2015).

1912: The nation's first minimum wage law for women and children is established in Massachusetts (Shmoop Editorial Team, 2008).

1913: The United States Department of Labor is established (Shmoop Editorial Team, 2008).

1914: In Ludlow, Colorado, National Guardsman machine gun strikers and set fire to their tents. Their actions kill five striking miners, two women, and 12 children. Over the course of the strike, 75 people are killed (Shmoop Editorial Team, 2008).

1914: The Clayton Act is enacted, exempting unions from the provisions of the Sherman Act, (Shmoop Editorial Team, 2008).

1916: The Adamson Act is enacted. It establishes an eight-hour workday for employees of interstate railroads, with overtime for working additional hours (Shmoop Editorial Team, 2008).

1925: A. Philip Randolph and Milton Webster create the Brotherhood of Sleeping Car Porters (ACL-CIO, 2015).

1926: The Railway Labor Act of 1926 gives railroad and airline employees the right to unionize. It also allows some supervisors to be union members (Mayer, 2004).

1931: The Davis-Bacon Act stipulates that federal contractors pay their workers salaries and benefits that are consistent with local market rates when working on public works projects. It also prohibits employers from importing cheaper workers from outside the region (Shmoop Editorial Team, 2008).

1935: President Roosevelt signs into law the National Labor Relations Act, more commonly known as the Wagner Act. The act guarantees the basic rights of most private sector employees to organize into trade unions, participate in collective bargaining for better terms and conditions in the workplace, and if necessary take strike action (True III, 2005). The act also creates the National Labor Relations Board (NLRB), which facilitates elections that can require employers to engage in collective bargaining with labor unions (Library of Congress, 2015).

1938: The Fair Labor Standards Act establishes a 40-hour workweek with time-and-a-half for additional working hours. Also established by the act is a national minimum wage and restrictions on child labor (Shmoop Editorial Team, 2008).

1941: President Franklin D. Roosevelt signs Executive Order 8802, which requires federal agencies and departments involved with defense production to ensure vocational and training programs are administered without discrimination as it relates to race, creed, color, or national origin. Furthermore, all defense contracts are to include the same stipulation against discrimination (Executive Order 8802, 1941).

1947: The Labor Management Relations Act, otherwise known as Taft-Hartley Act, is signed into law. The act, which remains in effect today, is the first major revision of the NLRB. It is sweeping and places significant restrictions on unions and their power (Gross, 1995).

1948: The Women's Armed Service Integration Act (P.L. 625–80) is enacted. The act enables women to serve as permanent, regular members of the armed forces (Morden, 1978).

1948: President Harry Truman signs into law Executive Order 9981, which establishes equality of treatment in the armed forces, ending the practice of a racially segregated armed forces (Executive Order 9981: Desegregation of the Armed Forces, 1948).

1949: The Congress of Industrial Organizations (CIO) expels 11 unions with nearly one million members because of their association with Communism (Shmoop Editorial Team, 2008).

1955: The American Federation of Labor (AFL) and the Congress of Industrial Organizations (CIO) merge into the ACL-CIO (Shmoop Editorial Team, 2008).

1959: The Labor Management Reporting and Disclosure Act, more commonly known as the Landrum-Griffin Act, is signed into law. The act is a response to congressional concern with union corruption, racketeering, and other misconduct (Gross, 1995).

1962: President John F. Kennedy passes Executive Order 10988, which allows federal employees to bargain collectively with the government. The order does not, however, allow federal employees the right to strike (Shmoop Editorial Team, 2008).

1963: The Equal Pay Act is enacted. The act abolishes wage disparity based on gender (United States Equal Opportunity Committee, 2015a).

1964: Title VII of the Civil Rights Act makes it unlawful for an employer to discriminate in the hiring or terminating of an individual on the basis of race, color, religion, sex, or national origin. Also made unlawful is the advertising of job positions in such a way as to deprive employment opportunities to individuals on the basis of race, color, religion, sex, or national origin (United States Equal Employment Opportunities Commission, 2015b).

1965: The United Farm Workers Organizing Committee, later called the United Farm Workers (UFW), is co-founded by Cesar Chavez and Dolores Huerta (ACL-CIO, 2015).

1970: In the first national strike of public employees, more than 200,000 Post Office workers walk off the job. President Nixon calls on the Army and National Guard to keep the mail moving during the two-week strike (Shmoop Editorial Team, 2008).

1972: The Coalition of Black Trade Unionists is formed (ACL-CIO, 2015).

1974: The Coalition of Labor Union Women is formed (ACL-CIO, 2015).

1974: The Employee Retirement Income Security Act (P.L. 93–406) is enacted. The act establishes minimum standards for pension plans in private industry (Shmoop Editorial Team, 2008).

1978: Title VII of the Civil Service Reform Act of 1978 gives collective bargaining rights to federal employees. The law, however, only applies to executive branch agencies, the Library of Congress, and the Government Printing Office. Notably excluded are supervisors and members of the armed forces (Mayer, 2004).

1978: The Pregnancy Discrimination Act is enacted. The act amends Title VII of the Civil Rights Act of 1964 to prohibit sex discrimination on the basis of pregnancy (United States Equal Employment Opportunities Commission, 2015c).

1981: President Reagan fires 11,345 striking members of the Professional Air Traffic Controllers Organization (PATCO) and bans them from federal service for life (ACL-CIO, 2015). President Reagan's actions embolden employers around the country to take an even tougher stance against unions (Shmoop Editorial Team, 2008).

1997: Pride at Work, a national coalition of LGBTQ workers and their supporters, becomes an ACL-CIO constituency group (ACL-CIO, 2015).

2009: The Lily Ledbetter Fair Pay Act (P.L. 111–2) is enacted (Govtrack.US, 2009).

2020: On March 27, President Donald Trump signed into law the Coronavirus Aid, Relief, and Economic Security Act, also known as the CARES Act (P.L. 116–136). The act provides $2.2 trillion economic stimulus in response to the economic fallout of the COVID-19 pandemic (Public Law 116-136, 2020).

2020: In the *Bostock v. Clayton County,* Georgia case, the Supreme Court of the United States ruled 5–4 that an employer who terminates an individual merely for being gay or transgender defies Title VII of the Civil Rights Act of 1964. The landmark ruling establishes that LGBTQ workers are federally protected by Title VII of the Civil Rights Act of 1964, which prohibits employers from discriminating against employees and job applicants based on race, color, religion, sex, and national origin (*Bostock v. Clayton County*, Georgia, No.17–1618, 2020).

References

Allen, T. (2012). *The invention of the white race*. Vol. 1: Racial oppression and social control. New York, NY: Verso Books.

Auerbach, J. S. (1966). *Labor and liberty: The LaFollette Committee and the new deal*. Indianapolis, IN: Bobbs Merrill.

Bahn, K., & Sanchez-Cumming, C. (2020, July). *Four graphs on U.S. occupational segregation by race, ethnicity, and gender*. Washington Center for Equitable Growth. Retrieved from https://equitablegrowth.org/four-graphs-on-u-s-occupational-segregation-by-race-ethnicity-and-gender/

Bates, B. T. (2001). *Pullman porters and the rise of protest politics in Black America, 1925–1945*. Chapel Hill: University of North Carolina Press.

Beverly, R. (1947). *The history and present state of Virginia 1705*. Chapel Hill: The University of North Carolina Press. Retrieved from http://nationalhumanitiescenter.org/pds/amerbegin/power/text8/BeverlyServSlaves.pdf

Bostock v. Clayton County, Georgia, No.17–1618. (2020). *Supreme Court of the United States*. Retrieved from www.supremecourt.gov/opinions/19pdf/17-1618_hfci.pdf

BusinessDictionary.com. (2015a). *Labor*. Retrieved from www.businessdictionary.com/definition/labor.html

BusinessDictionary.com. (2015b). *Labor market*. Retrieved from www.businessdictionary.com/definition/labor-market.html

Bynum, L. C. (2010). *A Philip Randolph and the struggle for civil rights*. Urbana: University of Illinois Press.

Campi, A. J. (2004). *Remembering December 17: Repeal of the 1882 Chinese Exclusion Act*. Policy Brief. Immigration Policy Center. Retrieved from www.immigrationpolicy.org/sites/default/files/docs/Chinese%20Exclusion%20Act%2012-04.pdf

Campi, A. J. (2007). *Closed borders and mass deportations: The lessons of the Barred Zone Act*. Immigration Policy Center. Retrieved from http://icirr.org/sites/default/files/IPC%20Barred%20Zone.pdf

Cohen, P. N. (2013). The persistence of workplace gender segregation in the U.S. *Sociology Compass*, *7*(11), 889–899.

Congress.gov. (2019). *H.R.7: Paycheck Fairness Act: 116th Congress (2019–2020)*. Retrieved from www.congress.gov/bill/116th-congress/house-bill/7

DeVries, D. P. (1853). Arriving in Virginia: An excerpt from voyages from Holland to England, A.D. 1632 to 1644. Trans. Henry C. Murphy. *Encyclopedia Virginia*, 46, 51–54. Retrieved from www.encyclopediavirginia.org/Arriving_in_Virginia_an_excerpt_from_Voyages_from_Holland_to_America_A_D_1632_to_1644_1853

Executive Order 8802. (1941). *General records of the United States Government. Record Group 11: National Archives*. Retrieved from www.ourdocuments.gov/doc.php?flash=true&doc=72

Executive Order 9981: Desegregation of the Armed Forces (1948). *Ourdocuments.gov*, n.d. Retrieved from https://www.ourdocuments.gov/doc.php?flash=false&doc=84

Foner, P. S. (1982). *Organized labor and the black worker, 1619–1981*. New York, NY: International Publishers.

Fuchs, L. H. (1995). *The American kaleidoscope: Race, ethnicity and the civic culture*. Middletown, CT: Wesleyan University Press.

Galenson, D. W. (1981). *White servitude in colonial America: An economic analysis*. Cambridge, UK: Cambridge University Press.

Galenson, D. W. (1984). The rise and fall of indentured servitude in the Americas: An economic analysis. *The Journal of Economic History*, 44(1), 1–26.

Gordon, C. (2013). *Growing apart: A political history of American inequality*. Inequality.org. Retrieved from http://scalar.usc.edu/works/growing-apart-a-political-history-of-american-inequality/index

Gotham, K. F. (2000). Urban space, restrictive covenants and the origins of racial residential segregation in a US city 1900–50. *International Journal of Urban and Regional Research*, 24(3), 616–633.

Govtrack.US. (2009). *S.181 (111th): Lilly Ledbetter Fair Pay Act of 2009*. Retrieved from www.govtrack.us/congress/bills/111/s181

Govtrack.US. (2011). *S.182 (111th): Paycheck Fairness Act*. Retrieved from www.govtrack.us/congress/bills/111/s182

Greenfield, C. (1999, Spring). The identity of Black women in the post-bellum period, 1865–1885. *Binghamton Journal of History*. Retrieved from www.binghamton.edu/history/resources/journal-of-history/article1.html

Gross, J. A. 1995. *Broken promise: The subversion of U.S. labor relations' policy*. Philadelphia, PA: Temple University Press.

Harris, W. H. (1982). *The harder we run: Black workers since the Civil War*. New York, NY: Oxford University Press.

Healy, J. F. (2014). *Diversity and society: Race, ethnicity and gender* (4th ed.). Thousand Oaks, CA: Sage.

Healy, J. F., & O'Brien, E. (2015). *Race, ethnicity, gender & class: The sociology of group conflict and change* (7th ed.). Thousand Oaks, CA: Sage.

Hegewisch, A., & Hartmann, H. (2014). *Occupational segregation and the gender wage gap: A job half done*. Institute for Women's Policy Research. Retrieved from www.iwpr.org/publications/pubs/occupational-segregation-and-the-gender-wage-gap-a-job-half-done

History.com. (2015). *Labor*. Retrieved from www.history.com/topics/labor

Hunter, T. W. (1997). *To 'joy my freedom: Southern Black women's lives and labors after the Civil War*. Cambridge, MA: Harvard Press.

Huq, A. (2001). Peonage and contractual liberty. *Columbia Law Review*, 351. Retrieved from http://chicagounbound.uchicago.edu/cgi/viewcontent.cgi?article=2519&context=journal_articles

Institute for Women's Policy Research. (2020, April). *Breadwinner mothers by race/ethnicity: Quick figures*. Retrieved from http://iwpr.org/wp-content/uploads/2020/05/QF-Breadwinner-Mothers-by-Race-FINAL-46.pdf

Jackson, K. T. (1980). Race, ethnicity, and real appraisal: The Home Owners Loan Corporation and the Federal Housing Administration. *Journal of Urban History*, 6(4), 419–452.

Larson, J. L. (2010). *The market revolution in America: Liberty, ambition, and the eclipse of the common good*. Cambridge, England: Cambridge University Press.

Lehman, T. G., & Phelps, S. (2005). *West's encyclopedia of American law* (Vol. 1). Detroit, MI: Thomson/Gale.

Library of Congress. (2015). *Great depression and World War II, 1929–1945: Labor unions during the great depression and new deal*. Washington, DC: Library of Congress.

Logan, R. (1997). *The betrayal of the Negro: From Rutherford. B Hayes to Woodrow Wilson*. Cambridge, MA: Da Capo Press.

Macrotrends.net. (2020, October). *Unemployment rate by race*. Retrieved from www.macrotrends.net/2508/unemployment-rate-by-race

Masur, L. P. (1999). *The challenge of American history*. Baltimore, MD: The John Hopkins University Press.

Mayer, G. (2004). *Union membership trends in the United States*. Washington, DC: Congressional Research Service. Retrieved from http://digitalcommons.ilr.cornell.edu/cgi/viewcontent.cgi?article=1176&context=key_workplace

Miller, J., & Thompson, J. (2007). *National Geographic almanac of American history*. Washington, DC: National Geographic.

Morden, B. J. (1978). *The women's army corps, 1945–1978*. Washington, DC: Center of Military History, United States.

Morgan, K. (2001). *Slavery and servitude in colonial North America*. New York, NY: New York University Press.

National Partnership for Women and Families. (2020, September). *America's women and the wage gap: Fact sheet*. Retrieved from www.nationalpartnership.org/our-work/resources/economic-justice/fair-pay/americas-women-and-the-wage-gap.pdf

Payscale.com. (2020). *The state of the gender pay gap 2020*.

Public Law 74–198. (1935). *The National Archives catalog*. Retrieved from https://research.archives.gov/id/299843

Public Law 116–136. (2020). *Congress.Gov*. Retrieved from https://www.congress.gov/116/plaws/publ136/PLAW-116publ136.pdf

Scheinberg, S. (1986). *Employers and reformers: The development of corporation labor policy, 1900–1940*. New York, NY: Taylor & Francis.

Seitles, M. (1996). The perpetuation of residential racial segregation in America: Historical discrimination, modern forms of exclusion, and inclusionary remedies. *Journal of Land Use and Environmental Law*, 14(1). Retrieved from http://archive.law.fsu.edu/journals/landuse/Vol141/seit.htm?referer=www.clickfind.com.au

Shmoop Editorial Team. (2008). *History of labor unions timeline of important dates*. Retrieved from https://www.shmoop.com/study-guides/history/history-labor-unions/timeline

Smith, A. E. (1971). *Colonist in bondage: White servitude and convict labor in America 1607–1776*. New York, NY: W.W. Norton & Company.

Smith, J. C., Jackson, M. L., & Wynn, L. T. (2006). *Encyclopedia of African American business*. Westport, CT: Greenwood Press.

Smith, R. C. (2003). *Encyclopedia of African American politics*. New York, NY: Facts on File, Inc.

Theriault, S. M. (2003). Patronage, the Pendleton Act, and the power of the people. *The Journal of Politics*, 65(1), 50–68.

Thomas, H. (1997). *The slave trade: The story of the Atlantic slave trade: 1440–1870*. New York, NY: Simon and Schuster.

True III, J. M. (2005). The blue eagle at work: Reclaiming democratic rights in the American workplace. *Berkeley Journal of Employment and Labor Law*, 26(1), 182–203.

Tye, L. (2005). *Rising from the rails: Pullman porters and the making of the Black middle class*. New York, NY: Macmillan.

United States Department of Labor. (2015a). *American with Disabilities Act*. Retrieved from www.dol.gov/dol/topic/disability/ada.htm

United States Department of Labor. (2015b). *Title IX, Education Amendments*. Retrieved from www.dol.gov/oasam/regs/statutes/titleix.htm

United States Equal Employment Opportunities Commission. (2015a). *The Equal Pay Act of 1963*. Retrieved from www.eeoc.gov/laws/statutes/epa.cfm

United States Equal Employment Opportunities Commission. (2015b). *Title VII of the Civil Rights Act of 1964*. Retrieved from www.eeoc.gov/laws/statutes/titlevii.cfm

Vaughn, A. T. (1989). The origins debate: Slavery and racism in seventeenth-century Virginia. *The Virginia Magazine of History and Biography*, 97(3), 311–354.

Von Drehle, D. (2004). *Triangle: The fire that changed America*. New York, NY: Atlantic Monthly Press.

Watson, B. (2005). *Bread and roses: Migrants, and the struggle for the American dream*. New York, NY: Penguin Books.

Weeden, K. A., Newhart, M., & Gelbgiser, D. (2018). *State of the Union: Occupational segregation*. Stanford Center on Poverty and Inequality. Retrieved from https://inequality.stanford.edu/sites/default/files/Pathways_SOTU_2018_occupational-segregation.pdf

Wolfe, B., & McCartney, M. (2012). Indentured servants in colonial Virginia. *Encyclopedia Virginia*. Retrieved from www.encyclopediavirginia.org/Indentured_Servants_in_Colonial_Virginia#start_entry

Yellin, E. S. (2013). *Racism in the nation's service: Government workers and the color line in Woodrow Wilson's America*. Chapel Hill: The University of North Carolina Press.

CHAPTER 9
Health and Health Care Inequality

PRESENT-DAY HEALTH AND HEALTH CARE INEQUALITY

The United States is a global leader in medical innovations and amount of money spent on health care, but is one of the very few developed nations that does not guarantee its population universal access to health care across the lifespan (Fuchs, 2013; Peterson & Rachel, 2007). Thus, despite federal health care programs like the Children's Health Insurance Program (CHIP), Medicaid, Medicare, and the Patient Protection and Affordable Health Care Act (PPACA), health disparities and health care inequality are ever-present in the United States (Centers for Disease Control and Prevention, 2013a).

As determined by the director of the National Institute on Minority Health Disparities (NIMHD) in consultation with the director of the Agency for Health Care Research and Quality (AHCRQ), "health disparities" refers to the significant differences in the overall rate of disease incidence, prevalence, morbidity, mortality, or survival rates in vulnerable populations compared with the health status of the general population (National Institutes of Health, U.S. Department of Health and Human Services, n.d.). "Health care inequality" refers to avoidable and unnecessary inequalities in the distribution of health and medical care and its access, including inequalities relating to race/ethnicity, gender, socioeconomic status, sexual orientation, immigration status, geographic location, and disability (Kilbourne et al., 2006, p. 2114).

Together, health disparities and health care inequality generate a significant human and economic cost that is borne directly by the individuals involved and indirectly by the larger society, including families, communities, employers, social service agencies, health care and medical providers, and government programs (Russell, 2011, p. 6). Particularly telling examples of the human costs include notable differences in life expectancy and other metrics of mortality between vulnerable and less-vulnerable populations, and the disproportionate burden of preventable diseases, injuries, and other risk factors for ill health (Arias, 2014; Cullen et al., 2012; Ezzati et al., 2008; LaVeist et al., 2009; Murray et al., 2006). Examples of the economic costs are the direct expenses related to the provision of care as a result of elevated rates of chronic illness among vulnerable populations, as well as the indirect expenses incurred by the economy because of lost work productivity, lost wages, absenteeism, and lower quality of life (LaVeist et al., 2009). There is also the cost of premature death, which results in the loss of human potential, as well as tax revenue and lifetime productivity (LaVeist et al., 2009). Indeed, in their study *The Economic Burden of Health Inequalities in the United States* for the Joint Center for Political and Economic Studies, LaVeist et al. (2009) estimated that between 2003 and 2006 the combined direct and indirect cost of health inequalities and premature deaths in the United States was a staggering $1.24 trillion.

Underpinning health disparities and health care inequality in the United States is a confluence of interrelated and often intersecting social determinants. These social determinants are consistent with those that inform existing social inequalities related to race/ethnicity, gender, socioeconomic status, sexual orientation/identity, immigration status, and disability. They include institutional racism and bias, low levels of income and education, residential segregation, unemployment, residence in poorly resourced and environmentally hazardous communities, absence of health insurance coverage, and lack of access to healthy lifestyle options (Brondolo et al., 2011; Centers for Disease Control and Prevention, 2013a,

DOI: 10.4324/9781003023708-9

2013b, 2013c, 2013d, 2013e; Cullen et al., 2012; Hong et al., 2014; Olden & White, 2005; Russell, 2011; Smedley et al., 2003). It is no surprise, then, that the populations in the United States most negatively affected by health disparities and health care inequality are racial and ethnic minorities, the economically disadvantaged, the medically uninsured, and increasingly, members of the LGBTQ community, particularly if they are of color or lesbian or transgender (American College of Obstetricians and Gynecologists, 2011; Heck et al., 2006; Kaiser Family Foundation, 2012; McLaughlin et al., 2010; Kwok, 2013; Smedley et al., 2003; Xavier, 2000).

The following snapshot examples, which are consistent with ongoing trends, illustrate just some of the ways health disparities and health care inequality are manifest among these populations:

- Between 2017 and 2018, Black (49.6%) and Hispanic (44.8%) adults had the highest prevalence of obesity compared with all other racial and ethnic groups (Hales et al., 2020). In the same period, 13.8% of Black adults were severely obese, which was just over six and a half times that of the Asian adults at 2%, who had the lowest prevalence, followed by Hispanic (7.9%) and White adults (9.3%) (Hales et al., 2020). Obesity, severe or otherwise, is associated with serious health risks, including coronary heart disease, end-stage renal disease, diabetes, cancer, and high blood pressure (Hales et al., 2020).
- Between 2017 and 2018, the prevalence of diagnosed diabetes was highest among Native Americans/Alaska Natives (14.7%), followed by Hispanics (12.5%), Blacks (11.7%), and Whites (7.5%) (Centers for Disease Control and Prevention, 2020f). Risk factors associated with diabetes-related complications include obesity, physical inactivity, high blood pressure, and high cholesterol (Centers for Disease Control and Prevention, 2020f).
- In the 2020 American Association for Research cancer disparities progress report, several disparities were found. For example, Black men and women have a 111% and 39% higher risk of dying from prostate cancer and breast cancer, respectively, compared to their White counterparts. Hispanic children and Hispanic adolescents are 20% and 38% more likely to develop leukemia than White children and adolescents, respectively. Native American/Alaska Native adults are twice as likely to develop liver and bile duct cancer as White adults. And bisexual women are 70% more likely to be diagnosed with cancer than heterosexual women (Cancer Disparities Progress Report, 2020).
- In 2017, the likelihood of one or more emergency room (ER) visits was greater among Native American/Alaska Natives (32.1%) and Blacks (26.3%) compared to White adults (18.6%) (U.S. Department of Health and Human Services, 2020). Lesbian, gay, bisexual, and transgender individuals also had a higher likelihood of one or more ER visits. ER visits are associated with adults with fair/poor self-assessed health, activity limitation, obesity, smoking, or those who delayed or forwent needed medical care due to cost (U.S. Department of Health and Human Services, 2020).
- Between 2010 and 2018, the uninsured rate for all racial and ethnic groups declined. However, Native Americans/Alaska Natives (21.8%), Hispanic (19%), and Blacks (11.5%) are still uninsured at higher rates than their White (7.5%) and Asian counterparts (6.8%) (Aritga et al., 2020b).

As illustrative as these selected snapshots of health care inequality and disparities are, no event in modern history has done more to illuminate dire consequences than the COVID-19 pandemic, which is part of the worldwide coronavirus disease 2019, first detected in the United States in January 2020. Since the early stages of COVID-19 in the United States, multiple analyses of available federal, state, and local data show that Black, Hispanic, Native American, and Pacific Islander populations are experiencing a disproportionate burden of COVID cases, hospitalization, and deaths (APM Research Lab, 2020; Artiga et al., 2020a; Centers for Disease Control and Prevention, 2020a; Centers for Disease Control and Prevention, 2020b; Centers for Disease Control and Prevention, 2020c; Health Resources & Services Administration, 2020; Khazanchi et al., 2020; Substance Abuse and Mental Health Services Administration (SAMHSA), 2020; see Figures 9.1 and 9.2).

To put this in some context, by August 2020, the number of COVID cases for Black, Hispanic, and Native American/Alaska Natives were between 2.6% (Black) and 2.8% (Hispanic and Native American /Alaska Natives) higher than those of their White counterparts, who comprise a much larger size of the nation's population. Hospitalization rates were between 4.6% and 7% (Hispanic and Black) and 5.3% (Native

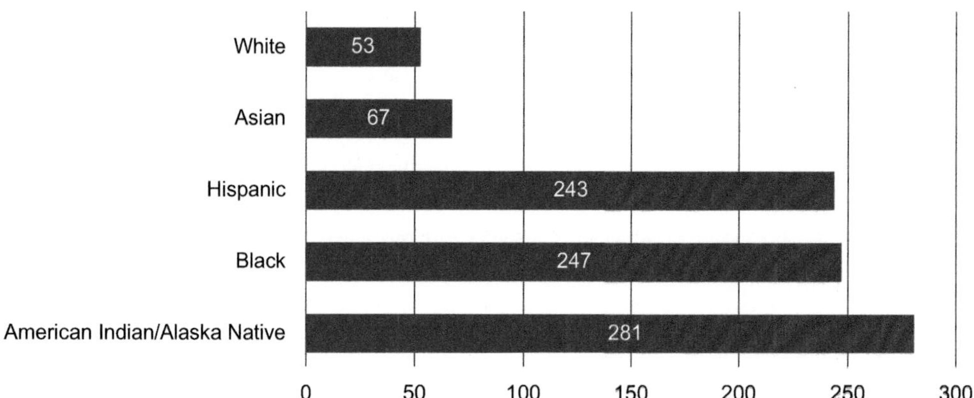

Figure 9.1 Age-Adjusted COVID-19 Associated Hospitalization by Race and Ethnicity
Source: CDC: www.cdc.gov/coronavirus/2019-ncov/covid-data/images/July-28_Race_Ethnicity_COVIDNet.jpg

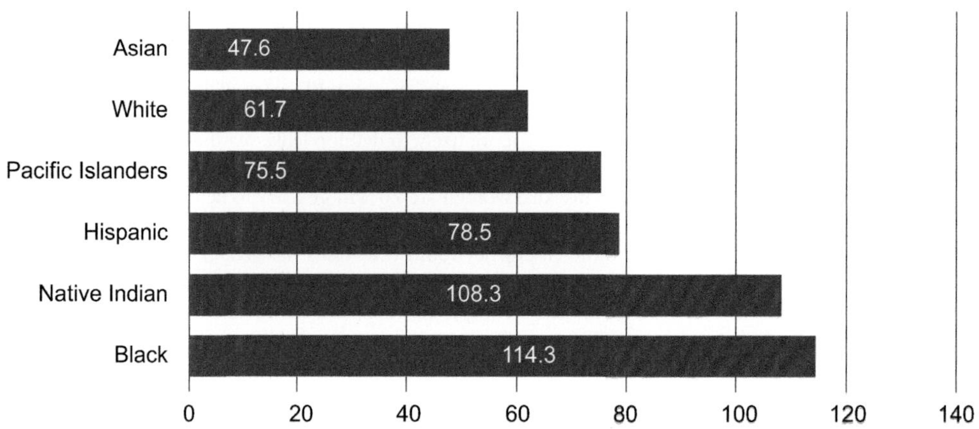

Figure 9.2 Coronavirus (COVID-19) Death Rate in the United States as of November 10, 2020, by Race
Source: Statista: www.statista.com/statistics/1122431/coronavirus-covid19-death-rate-by-race-us/

American/Alaska Natives) higher. And death rates were between 1.1% and 1.4% (Hispanic and Native American/Alaska Natives) and 2.1% (Black) higher [Centers for Disease Control and Prevention (2020a); see Figure 9.2].

That these disparities exist even amid a global pandemic that can affect anyone is not entirely surprising. As discussed earlier, Black, Hispanic, and Native American/Alaska Natives are much more likely than Whites to have low income levels. They are also more likely to live in underresourced and environmentally hazardous communities and have limited access to quality health care and healthy lifestyle options. Moreover, as described in some of the health care inequality and disparities snapshots, they are more likely to have comorbidities that put them at increased risk of severe illness from the virus that causes COVID-19 (Pirtle, 2020). These comorbidities include chronic kidney disease, cancer, heart conditions, obesity, sickle-cell, and Type II diabetes, all of which, to different degrees, Black, Hispanic, and Native American/Alaska Natives suffer at disproportionately high rates (American Cancer Society,

2019; American Diabetes Association, 2018; Centers for Disease Control and Prevention, 2020d; Centers for Disease Control and Prevention, 2020e; National Institute of Diabetes and Digestive and Kidney Diseases, 2014; WebMD, 2019).

Along with this, Black, Hispanic, and Native American/Alaska Natives are much more likely to live in crowded living conditions. Blacks and Hispanics are also more likely to be in essential work settings with more chance of exposure to the virus because of factors such as close contact with the public or inability to work from home or work virtually (Bureau of Labor Statistics, 2019). Indeed, there is a disproportionate representation of Black and Hispanics in essential work settings such as health care facilities, farms, factories, grocery stores, and public transportation (Bureau of Labor Statistics, 2020).

Although the described disparities and their manifestations are striking, more striking is that for Native Americans and Black Americans these disparities are perennial and have existed for more than 400 years. For other groups, the disparities are a more recent occurrence (Jones, 2006; Randall, 2006).

Theoretical Perspective

From a critical race theory perspective, the enduring nature of Native American and Black health disparities are rooted in centuries of social exclusion and marginalization. Be it tribal homelands displacement, forced residency on socially and resource-isolated reservations, slavery, Jim Crow, or residential segregation, social exclusion and marginalization have taken numerous forms over the past 400 years for Native Americans and Blacks. These forms of social exclusion and marginalization, which are the result of a deeply entrenched racial hierarchy that supposes White superiority and assumes Native American and Black inferiority, have had a deleterious and ongoing effect on Native American and Black health. Yet, despite the clear evidence of social exclusion and marginalization, until very recently the dominant group explanation of Native American and Black health disparities has been historically rooted in racist assumptions. Among these assumptions was a supposed physiological difference between the races, most notably between Blacks and Whites, as well as a perception that Native Americans and Blacks were indifferent to cleanliness and sanitary practices (Jones, 2006; Randall, 2006).

Consistent with critical race theory, properly understanding the perennial nature of Native American and Black health disparities requires examining its historical context and development. The following is such an examination.

Native American Health Disparities: An Historical Context

Health disparities between Native Americans and other groups, most notably Whites, have persisted since the first Europeans arrived in the Americas (Jones, 2006, p. 1). The genesis of these disparities can be traced to the years directly following Christopher Columbus's voyage to the Americas in 1492. In these years, which American historian Alfred W. Crosby Jr., refers to as the Columbian exchange, there was the widespread transfer of livestock, people, plants, ideas, and technologies between Europe and the Americas (Crosby, 2003; Nunn & Qian, 2010). Also inadvertently transferred to the Americas were communicable diseases. These diseases, all new to the Americas, included but were not limited to bubonic plague, chicken pox, typhoid, cholera, diphtheria, influenza, measles, scarlet fever, smallpox, typhus, tuberculosis, and whooping cough (Nunn & Qian, 2010). As a consequence of the lack of prior exposure, Native Americans had no internal immunities to European diseases.

This is not to say, however, that the Americas were a disease-free paradise before the arrival of Europeans. Indeed, anthropological evidence from the analysis of skeletal remains indicates the presence of a number of diseases in the pre-Columbus Americas, including tuberculosis and pneumonia (Jones, 2006). Moreover, although many Native Americans in different regions of the Americas enjoyed excellent health, this was certainly not the case for all. In what is now Mexico and Peru, for example, malnutrition, diseases, and violence kept life expectancy below 25 years of age (Jones, 2006, p. 2123). Further, there is evidence of periodic bouts of widespread malnutrition and disease across a number of regions in the Americas. None of this, however, proved as catastrophic to Native American health and mortality as did exposure to European diseases (Diamond, 1997; Francis, 2005). As evidence, from the 16th through to the 19th centuries, historians estimate 20 million Native Americans (95% of the Native American population in the Americas) perished, principally through diseases from Europe (Diamond, 1977). Also responsible, although arguably slightly less so, but always in tandem with European disease was warfare, enslavement, casual murder, and displacement by European colonists (Diamond, 1997).

The British colonization of North America in the 17th century was no less catastrophic for the health and mortality of the Native American population than in Central and South America (Diamond, 1997). Consequently, while the earliest British colonists did initially succumb in large numbers to endemic diseases such as malaria, an immune system made robust by generations of regular exposure to numerous pathogens allowed them to ward off many if not all of the diseases they brought with them to America (Merrens & Terry, 1984). Conversely, Native Americans lacking as robust an immunity to European diseases soon succumbed to them after coming into contact with British colonists. Indeed, as early as 1616, there were reports of local tribes in Maine being sorely afflicted with the plague (probably smallpox, chicken pox, or hepatitis), leaving Native American villages from the coast of Maine to Cape Cod abandoned (Gorges, 1658; Speiss & Speiss, 1987). As British colonists moved further into the North American interior, each initial encounter with Native Americans repeated a new wave of epidemic decimation. Smallpox, in particular, was virulent throughout the 17th, 18th, and 19th centuries, decimating Native American tribes in the Northwest Plains in the 1780s, the Pacific Northwest in 1802, and along the Missouri River and in the Central Plains in 1831 and 1832 (Boyd, 1999; Jones, 2006, p. 2126; Robertson, 2001; Rife & Dellapenna, 2009; Wood et al., 2011).

Such was the concern about the devastation smallpox caused among Native American tribes that by 1830 self-interested parties, which included fur traders and Christian missionaries, called upon the federal government to fund vaccination programs for Native Americans (Wood et al., 2011). The Reverend Isaac McCoy, an influential Baptist missionary among the Native American tribes and an advocate for a Native American state in what is now Kansas, Nebraska, and Oklahoma, was particularly vocal in this respect. He personally lobbied members of Congress and the Commissioner of Indian Affairs in Washington, D.C. (Pearson, 2003). In doing so, he spoke of the horrors of smallpox and its striking down of tribe after tribe located on the western frontier. Echoing the pleas of McCoy were Indian agents, the officials representing the United States government in dealing with Native American tribes. In 1830, these agents had been authorized by the acting Secretary of War Randolph to hire doctors on an ad hoc basis to vaccinate or treat Native Americans at their agencies (Cohen, 1982; Lawrence, 2000). Despite these efforts, Indian agents saw firsthand the futility of their individual regional responses, as smallpox spread across the Native American tribes along the Missouri River and on the Central Plains at a rapid rate between 1831 and 1832 (Pearson, 2003).

In 1832, the United States Congress responded to the calls for a vaccination program and enacted the first piece of federal legislation designed to deal with Native American health problems, specifically the smallpox epidemic (Pearson, 2003). Commonly known as the Indian Vaccination Act of 1832, the legislation authorized the appropriation of $12,000 for the purchase and administration of the smallpox vaccine (Lawrence, 2000). The act established no specific demographic parameters other than the provision that vaccinations were to be extended to those tribes on the American frontier. Frontier was not defined, but instead left to the War Department, whose leader and Secretary of War Lewis Cass had absolute authority over the vaccination program. As such, Cass alone determined what was meant by frontier, as well as which Native American nations were vaccinated and when and where they would be vaccinated (Pearson, 2003).

Although ostensibly seeking to protect Native Americans from smallpox, in reality and practice the program intent was not entirely humanitarian. Rather, it in large part served as a mechanism to remove perceived obstacles to the federal government's most pressing social agenda—Indian removal and relocation and the westward expansion of the United States (Rife & Dellapenna, 2009). Toward this end, Cass, a staunch supporter of President Andrew Jackson's Indian Removal Act of 1830, used the vaccination program to reward those Native American sovereign nations and tribes who had signed land cession treaties favorable to the westward expansion of the United States (Rife & Dellapenna, 2009). Also duly rewarded were Native American sovereign nations and tribes involved with the United States through treaties of peace, friendship, development or protection of trade, removal, or reservations (Pearson, 2003).

Excluded from the vaccination programs were Native American tribes or nations that had been branded as aggressor nations or who were regarded by Cass as beyond the concern of the United States. Notable in this regard were the Upper Missouri River tribes, who Cass loathed and described in an 1826 *North American Review* publication as being beyond the pale of civilization. The exclusion of these tribes was to have devastating consequences in 1837 when a smallpox outbreak in Upper Missouri laid waste to 90% of the afflicted tribes, killing some 10,000 to 15,000 Mandans, Blackfeet, Hidatsas, Arikaras, Crees, and Assiniboines (Duffy, 1951; Thornton, 1987). In turn, villages and hunting grounds were left desolate, and the demographic profile of Upper Missouri was significantly altered (Wood et al., 2011).

Despite its less than humanitarian intent, the Indian Vaccination Act of 1832 was the largest program of its kind. Moreover, by 1841, U.S. Army and contract physicians had managed to vaccinate between 38,000 and 55,000 Native Americans, which was a fraction of the total Native American population (Rife & Dellapenna, 2009). Overall, the program was generally inadequate in countering the threat of smallpox. Part of the problem was a failure to vaccinate Native Americans in remote western areas, as well as the lack of sufficient resources to act in a timely manner to ensure the vaccination of Native American tribes before removal and deportation (Pearson, 2003; Rife & Dellapenna, 2009). As a consequence, large numbers of Native Americans remained unprotected from smallpox despite the vaccination program (Rife & Dellapenna, 2009).

By the time the program was terminated in 1849 with its transfer from the War Department to the Bureau of the Interior, other federal initiatives to address Native American health issues had been established. By the mid 1850s, these initiatives were embedded in treaties made between Native American nations and the United States, and included federal vaccination benefits. However, these treaties offering health care came with a high price for Native Americans, including land cession and the demand for assimilation into the general population by way of promoting dependence on western medicine and the elimination of traditional Native American healers (Shelton, 2004).

Despite the presence of medical treatment, albeit situational and ad hoc, health disparities remained for Native Americans as disease continued to take a heavy toll on their population through the 1860s. Central to these disparities was the reservation system, which was imposed on Native Americans by the federal government between 1830 and 1880. The reservations housed Native Americans in damp, poorly ventilated log cabins with inadequate government rations (Jones, 2006). Not only did the reservations strip Native Americans of their independence, but they also severed their ties to traditional food sources and cultural practices. Reservations also transformed Native Americans' patterns of morbidity and mortality (Jones, 2006). Consequently, while smallpox, measles, cholera, malaria, venereal disease, and alcoholism remained common, vaccination, fumigation, and quarantine resulted in these acute diseases being superseded by chronic infections, most particularly tuberculosis. Indeed, tuberculosis soon became the leading cause of death among the Sioux (Jones, 2006).

In 1873, the federal government made the first sustained effort to address Native American health with the establishment of a Division of Medicine and Education within the Office of Indian Affairs. However, this effort was short lived and was ended in 1877 as a result of inadequate funding (Pearson, 2003).

It was not until the 1920s with Native American health on reservations in its most critical condition did the federal government pass comprehensive legislation that would seriously address Native American health issues. This legislation was the Indian Citizenship Act (P.L. 67–85), commonly known as the Snyder Act of 1921. The act authorized appropriate funds for the benefit, care, and assistance of the Native Americans throughout the United States, including conservation and preservation of health (U.S. Public Health Service, 1957). Despite congressional appropriations that continued to grow from $596,000 in 1925, to $2,980,000 in 1935, to $5,730,000 in 1945, and to $17,800,000 in 1955, health disparities persisted (Jones, 2006; U.S. Public Health Service, 1957). For example, tuberculosis infection and mortality rates for Native Americans, most particularly the Navajo in Arizona in the 1920s, 30s, 40s, and 50s was significantly higher than for the general population (Hadley, 1955). Similarly, this was also the case for pneumonia, trachoma, and infant mortality (Krug, 1948).

Numerous explanations were offered for the continued health disparities, most particularly for the Navajo. Some explanations, as was the case with smallpox in the early 1800s, blamed the behavior of the Navajo and their ignorance of all things medical and sanitary (Jones, 2006). More-reasoned explanations located the blame within the poor and isolated living conditions of the Navajo reservations. These reservations were without roads, water, sanitation, or the opportunity to earn a living (Jones, 2006).

In 1950, troubled by the continued disparities and the plight of the Navajo, the American Medical Association reported on the inadequacy of existing health services on reservations (Moorman, 1950). It was a sentiment echoed to Congress by Annie Wauneka, who led the Navajo tribal council. In her testimony to the Congress, Wauneka asserted that there were no real health programs on the reservations and the Navajo people were paying for it with their poor health (Shelton, 2004).

In 1954, frustrated by the continued health disparities, Congress enacted the Transfer Act, which moved responsibility for Native American health from the Bureau of Indian Affairs to the Public Health Service (PHS). Under the auspices of the PHS, the Indian Health Service (IHS) was established. Although never fully funded, the HIS did build hospitals and staff hospitals and health centers in or near Native American communities and reservations (Shelton, 2004).

In the 1960s and 70s, the American Indian Movement was successful in shifting health policy from a paternalistic stance in which Native Americans had little say in addressing their health needs to one of self-determination. Two such policies were the Indian Self-Determination and Educational Assistant Act of 1975 (P.L. 93–638) and the Indian Health Care Improvement Act of 1976 (P.L. 93–437) (Shelton, 2004).

Although greater autonomy and self-determination has gone some way in improving Native American health and decreasing health disparities with larger populations, health disparities nevertheless persist. Indeed, of all groups, the health disparities are most telling for Native Americans, which is not altogether surprising given the continued presence of a socially and resource-isolated reservation system that both historically and currently has proved to be bad for Native American health.

Black Health Disparities: An Historical Context

The origins of Black health disparities can be traced back to the system of lifetime enslavement, which in its practice in the United States weakened the physical and psychological health of enslaved Africans and their American-born offspring and descendants. Though there was some variation, slaves, most specifically field hands on the cash crop plantations of the southern colonies, carried out backbreaking labor from dusk to dawn, depending on the season, six days a week (Kolchin, 1993). In the summer months, which, depending on the crop, could be particularly arduous, field hands were exposed to searing heat, humidity, and numerous mosquito-borne diseases, including yellow fever and malaria (Lockley, 2012). Conversely, in the winter months, they often worked in bitterly cold conditions without the proper clothing needed to protect them against the elements.

Living conditions were little better than work conditions for slave health. Slaves typically lived in crowded cabins, known as quarters. With some variation, the cabins were poorly ventilated, had dirt floors, and were leaky as well as drafty, exposing the occupants to the elements (Stampp, 1956). Slaves had a limited clothing allowance, which they could wash and change only weekly, thus making their clothing a vector for disease. Further, the slave diet, which was generally composed of a weekly and fixed allowance of cornmeal, salted pork, molasses, and sometimes game or fish, was bulky but not nutritionally sound (Randall, 2006; Stampp, 1956). Thus, slaves were particularly susceptible to nutrition-related diseases, such as pellagra, beriberi, and scurvy, as well as malnutrition (Randall, 2006).

Despite the poor conditions under which slave owners made their slaves work and live, they did have a vested interest in their health. With doctors few and far between, southern slave plantation owners most typically turned to lay medicine in the absence of trained physicians to treat ill or injured slaves.

Administered by an overseer or other assigned person, lay treatment would be partly based on homespun herbal remedies (Covey, 2007). Plantation owners would also turn to domestic medical manuals written by medical practitioners offering a guide to diagnosing and treating slaves; one such manual was *Practical Rules for the Management and Treatment of Negro Slaves*, written in 1803 (Postell, 1951). Many of the larger southern plantation owners went much further than lay medicine and manuals in their attention to their slaves' health care needs. Some, for example, kept trained physicians on contract to provide medical care for slaves. Others established and operated plantation hospitals, infirmaries, and sick houses to care for sick slaves (Covey, 2007; Postell, 1951). As suggested by Postell (1951), these establishments, as well as health care to slaves in general, ranged in quality from good for the time to deplorable.

The level of health care provided to slaves was not simply the function of the benevolence or concern of plantation owners, but rather the notion of soundness. In short, soundness was the value of a slave to a plantation owner vis-à-vis her or his sound health, which on the auction block a doctor would have to attest. The better a slave's general health, the more value she or he was to the plantation owner. Thus, ailments such as rheumatism, arthritis, disabilities, and compromised childbearing capacity would reduce slaves' value and mark them as unsound and unworthy of medical attention. Conversely, good health would indicate soundness and worthiness regarding the investment for medical care (Covey, 2007).

Paralleling the health care provisions of slaveholders was the informal health care that slaves received from their own folk practitioners. As noted by Covey (2007, p. 42), these slave folk practitioners treated slaves with an eclectic mixture of strategies culled from European, Native American, Caribbean, and African medical folklore. When ill or injured, it was the slave medical folk practitioner that slaves wanted to treat them. Of course, familiarity was part of this preference, but just as important was a mistrust of White medical practices. This mistrust was well earned, as the White medical knowledge used to treat slaves was in large part informed by a racist ideology that perceived Blacks as biologically and physiologically different from and inferior to Whites (Covey, 2007; Fett, 2002).

Some common beliefs that came out of this racist ideology were that Blacks were able to endure more illness and were less tolerant of drugs, and they had more tolerance and capacity to feel pain than Whites (Fett, 2002). Also, it was believed that their brains were a ninth or tenth the size of other races (Covey, 2007), and slave women were more robust than White women and as such needed less treatment and attention during childbirth (Gates et al., 2002). Runaway slaves were considered to be mentally ill as a result of being inflicted with *Drapetomania*—runaway disease—and Black men were prone to raping White women because of a sexual disorder known as *Furor Sexualis* (Covey, 2007). Indeed, many southern physicians concluded that because of these so-called differences, Africans were nonhuman peculiarities that had to be medically managed differently (Covey, 2007; Savitt, 1982). The consequences of this perspective were medical practice on slaves that was often cruel, inhumane, and ultimately unsuccessful because of misdiagnosis, poor treatment, and in extreme cases death, a fact not lost on the slaves (Fontenot, 1994). Indeed, this would engender a mistrust of White doctors and medicine, a mistrust that would endure well into the 20th century and beyond (see Tuskegee experiment case study).

Also contributing to this mistrust was the routine use of slaves as research subjects by physicians, primarily in the Antebellum South. During the 19th century and long before the institution of procedures for the protection of subjects, slaves in the Antebellum South were treated and experimented on routinely by White physicians without consultation or right of refusal. They were put on display in medical school classrooms, amphitheaters, or public spaces to demonstrate their ailments (Covey, 2007, p. 30; Savitt, 1982, p. 331). In the hospitals and infirmaries that treated slaves, they were the subject of bedside demonstrations and consultation for medical students, as well as the subject of minor experiments (Covey, 2007; Savitt, 1982). Moreover, in a time when the common belief of Americans was that the dissection of a dead body was degrading and sacrilegious, as well as illegal, a disproportionate number of the cadavers of slaves or free blacks were dissected (Fett, 2002; Humphrey, 1973). In Baltimore, for example, Black bodies were exclusively taken for dissection. As remarked by Harriet Martineau (1838), in 1835, the situation in Baltimore prevailed because Whites did not like the idea of dissection and Black people were not in a postion to resist. The thought of the dissection of a loved one's body had a tremendously negative effect on Blacks, both free and enslaved. Indeed, it informed a prevailing rumor among slaves and free persons that Blacks were sometimes murdered solely for the use of their bodies for experimentation (Savitt, 1982).

Although this was not the case, so powerful and present was the narrative that it remained another reason not to trust the White medical establishment, a perspective that would linger well beyond the abolition of slavery (Savitt, 1982).

The fact is that the relationship between slaves—and to a lesser extent freed Blacks—and the medical profession in the 19th century was that Black bodies had a tremendous influence on the medical

Death Rates for Slaves and Whites, 1850
(Deaths per 1000 population)

Age Group	Slave Male	Slave Female	White Male	White Female
0	197.51	167.90	112.05	92.50
1–4	36.75	33.72	31.83	29.18
5–9	11.45	10.62	10.50	9.40
10–14	7.06	9.10	4.85	6.25
15–19	9.64	11.57	6.75	8.10
20–29	10.85	11.93	9.70	10.67
30–39	13.05	13.21	12.17	12.33
40–49	19.84	14.91	17.43	13.10
50–59	28.21	21.8	22.97	17.73
60–69	43.26	36.75	38.67	32.87
70–79	81.72	67.43	83.97	69.37

Figure 9.3 Death Rate for Slaves and Whites, 1850
Source: Jacobson, *An Estimate of the Length of Life* (1850, p. 9)

LIFE EXPECTATION IN THE UNITED STATES, 1850 (YEARS)

AGE	SLAVE MALE	SLAVE FEMALE	WHITE MALE	WHITE FEMALE
0	35.54	38.08	40.4	43.0
1	44.24	45.73	47.1	48.4
5	46.96	48.06	50.1	51.2
10	44.58	45.54	47.8	48.6
15	41.09	42.54	43.9	44.9
20	37.99	39.92	40.1	41.7
30	31.72	34.30	33.6	35.8
40	25.40	28.40	27.1	29.1
50	19.82	22.10	21.2	23.3
60	14.60	16.20	15.3	16.7
70	9.79	11.15	9.6	10.9

Figure 9.4 Life Expectation in the United States, 1850
Source: White figures from Jacobson, *An Estimate of the Length of Life* (1850, p. 198). Slave figures calculated from Greville's abridged life table (Dublin et al., 1949)

profession (Fisher, 1968). Even as White physicians argued that Blacks were distinctly different from Whites both physiologically and psychologically, White physicians would nevertheless experiment on slaves and paradoxically extrapolate their findings to Whites. The findings from Dr. James Marion Sims's experimental use of slave women from 1845 to 1849 to develop a cure for vesico-vaginal fistula, for example, would prove to be beneficial not just for slave women but also for all women who suffered from this most debilitating of ailments after childbirth (Covey, 2007; Savitt, 1982). Similarly, Dr. Francois Prevost's early use of slave women in operations and experiments in the 1830s to perfect cesarean sections would benefit all women, regardless of race.

However, despite the role of slaves and freed blacks in advancing the medical profession in the 19th century, albeit mostly involuntarily, little was done to specifically advance Black health. The reality was that due to the combination of poor living standards, poor nutritional diets, poor medical care, heavier labor demands, and greater exposure to environmental risks, slaves and freed Blacks had a shorter life expectancy and higher mortality rate than Whites (Stampp, 1956, p. 318). This was the case even as many Whites had only slightly better health care and access to hospitals, which especially in the Antebellum South were still few and far between (Stampp, 1956).

By the 19th century, the major causes of death for slaves were extensive but not dissimilar to those for the rest of the population. They included malaria, yellow fever, cholera, dysentery, typhoid, pneumonia, influenza, whooping cough, dengue, scrofula, scarlet fever, smallpox, diphtheria, and dropsy (Durant & Knottinerus, 1999).

Other common health problems but not quite as deadly to slaves were mumps, inflammation of the lungs, rheumatism, and effusions of the chest. All of these health issues among slaves were more acute for those in the lowlands of the South—Tennessee, Kentucky, and Virginia (Durant & Knottinerus, 1999). Slave children and expectant mothers were particularly vulnerable, with mortality rates for slave children being four times that of White children, and poor prenatal care and living conditions of slave women resulted in low infant birthrates. Indeed, expectant slave mothers lost half their pregnancies to stillbirth (Durant & Knottinerus, 1999).

Health Care and Health After Emancipation

With emancipation in 1865, plantation owners were released from the responsibility of providing health care for former slaves. In their stead, the federal government assumed responsibility for their health care for the first time. This responsibility came in the form of the Freedman's Bureau, which was established in 1865. Among the bureau's many services for former slaves and Whites displaced by the Civil War were health care facilities (Leavitt & Numbers, 1997; Trattner, 1999). These facilities were spread throughout the South and in the border states, but with all the best will in the world, a lack of funding undermined the effectiveness of the bureau's health care facilities. For example, the facilities could not attract the best doctors because pay was low and turnover was high. Moreover, instead of building new facilities, the bureau had to make do with locating their medical facilities in old hospitals or abandoned houses (Leavitt & Numbers, 1997; Trattner, 1999). Thus, at its peak in 1867, the Freedman's Bureau medical facilities numbered 45 hospitals with a capacity of 5,292 beds, which was grossly inadequate for the medical needs of some five million former slaves (Leavitt & Numbers, 1997).

When Congress failed to pass legislation in 1872 renewing the Freedman's Bureau on the grounds that it interfered with states' rights and contravened the U.S. Constitution, the health care of former slaves and Blacks in general came under the auspices of state governments (Leavitt & Numbers, 1997).

At the end of Reconstruction, in the South, where 90% of Blacks still lived, this meant decades of inadequate or nonexistent health care services. This was made worse by Jim Crow legislation that mandated segregation in all spheres of public and private life. Thus, while Whites were to have access to private hospitals and the best medical services as they existed, Blacks were relegated to separate but not necessarily equal medical services (Rice & Jones, 1994). These services were provided by segregated Black hospitals that emerged in the late 1800s as a result of donations from numerous private individuals and philanthropic organizations, both Black and White. From the late 1800s through the 1930s, these donations helped to build Black-controlled hospitals all over the country, the first of which was Provident Hospital and Training School in Chicago in 1891 (Brown & Stentiford, 2014). The next Black hospital established was the Frederick Douglas Memorial Hospital in Philadelphia (Rice & Jones, 1994). By 1900 there were 40 Black hospitals and 11 Black medical schools in the nation, Howard University Medical School being the first. In 1911, the Hubbard hospital was founded in Nashville, and the Tuskegee Institute Hospital was founded in 1913 (Rice & Jones, 1994). Hospitals were also established to serve White patients' health care needs, but with demographic changes, they evolved into Black-serving institutions. One such institution was New York City's Harlem Hospital, which first opened its doors in 1887 to serve the White community (Johnson & Daniels, 2002). Black settlement houses and churches were also vital in the provision of medical services in the wake of the discrimination by White medical facilities (Brown & Stentiford, 2014).

Informing the rise of health services by Black hospitals and settlement houses was the understanding that health was inextricably bound to the human condition. It was a point that W.E.B Dubois made in 1899 in his *Philadelphia Negro: A Social Study*. As posited by Dubois, it was racism and social exclusion and not any inferiority to Whites that explained the health issues that continued to plague Blacks well into the 20th century and beyond (Brown & Stentiford, 2014; Gamble & Stone, 2006).

While Dubois focused on the causes, the founder of Tuskegee Institute, Booker T. Washington, viewed the poor health status of Blacks as an obstacle to economic progress. In 1914, Washington and other Black leaders who recognized the link between health and social and economic well-being initiated the Negro Improvement Week, which grew into the National Negro Health Movement (Brown & Stentiford, 2014). As part of this movement, which included schools, churches, businesses, and local health departments, individual Black communities sought to develop local health services (Brown & Stentiford, 2014).

Despite the efforts of Black hospitals, settlement houses, and local health services, social exclusion, racism, and ongoing exposure to harsh environmental stressors continued to have a deleterious effect on Black health. Moreover, as a result of the Flexner Report in 1910 that concluded that there were too many medical schools in the United States, Black medical schools were significantly decreased (Savitt, 2006). Among the many observations and recommendations of the report, written by Abraham Flexner under the aegis of the Carnegie Foundation, was that only two of the existing Black medical schools were worthy of accreditation and the remainder should be closed. Flexner observed that Black medical education in general was deficient and lacking in equipment, laboratories, and clinical facilities (Savitt, 2006). Going far beyond just describing the lack of resources, Flexner suggested that Black physicians possessed less potential and ability than their White counterparts. He also noted that the medical care of the Negro race would never be left wholly to Negro physicians. For Flexner, Black physicians' usefulness was limited to teaching Blacks the fundamental principles of hygiene and preventing the spread of disease from Blacks to Whites (Savitt, 2006). As a consequence of the Flexner report, only two Black medical schools survived, Howard and Meharry (Savitt, 2006).

The closing of Black medical schools only compounded the lack of resources that Black hospitals had to contend with, illustrated by the fact that in 1932, there was only one hospital bed for every 1,000 Blacks. For Whites the number was significantly higher, with one hospital bed for every 110 Whites (Rice & Jones, 1994). In the wake of the Great Depression, the federal government sought to address that disparity as well as the continued health disparity with the establishment of the Office of Negro Health Work under the auspices of the Department of Health, Education and Welfare in 1932 (Centers for Disease Control and Prevention, 2015). Running until 1950, the office sought with varying levels of success to end discrimination in the delivery of health care services to Blacks. Some 50 years later in the report of the HHS Secretary's Task Force on Black and Minority Health in 1985, often referred to as the Heckler Report, there was acknowledgment of the continuing existence of disparities in health status of minority groups and the majority White population. These minority groups were Native Americans, Blacks, Latino/Hispanics, and Asians/Pacific Islanders. The report concluded that despite the unprecedented explosion of scientific knowledge and the outstanding ability of medicine to diagnose, treat, and cure disease, these ethnic groups had not benefited fully or equitably from these advances.

As a response to the Heckler report, the HHS Office of the Federal Office of Minority Health was established with the specific aim of improving minority health through health policies and programs (Centers for Disease Control and Prevention, 2015). While the policies instituted have in a number of respects reduced some health disparities for Blacks, disparities that began in slavery continue to be stubbornly entrenched. Moreover, Blacks remain underrepresented in the medical professions (Centers for Disease Control and Prevention, 2015).

The Road to Health Care Reform

Although perennial for Native Americans and Blacks, health status concerns and the call for access to health care have not historically been theirs alone. At different times in recent American history, it continues to be a concern for the economically disadvantaged, the working class, immigrants, persons with physical and mental disabilities, children, the elderly, expectant mothers, and the LGBTQ community.

A concern and a call to action emerged in the mid-19th century as a response to the serious public health problems of the urbanized cities of the antebellum United States. These urbanized cities were disorderly, foul-smelling places where animals roamed freely and streets were cluttered with accumulated garbage, including both human and animal waste. Indeed, such was the accumulation of garbage that in some cities it could reach as high as three feet (Shryock, 1937).

Housing in the poor sections of these cities, which in the mid-19th century was heavily populated by Irish and German immigrants, were rickety, overcrowded, and poorly ventilated tenements. The tenements had no running water, toilets, or sewage systems. These conditions, along with the absence of pure water, refrigeration, and pasteurization, were ideal for the spread of bacteria and infectious disease (Shryock, 1937). Illustrative of this spread were the recurrent yellow fever and cholera epidemics of 1832 and 1835 that plagued the poor sections of major cities from New Orleans to New York. Other infectious diseases, fevers, and influenzas that were all too common in the poor sections of the major cities included diphtheria, whooping cough, typhoid, and typhus (Shryock, 1937). As a consequence, at a time when the death rate in the nation was 20 per 1,000 inhabitants, in the poorest areas of the large cities the number was between 30 and 40 per 1,000 inhabitants and as many as 135 per 1,000 for children under the age of five (Trattner, 1999).

There were two dominant assumptions about disease in the mid-1800s, before anyone had a scientific understanding of the etiology of disease. One assumption was that it was an act of God in response to poor morals and behavior, and the other was that it was a consequence of environmental factors, such as dirt, or in some cases odors (Trattner, 1999). These assumptions were challenged in 1842 with the publication of the seminal *The Sanitary Condition of the Laboring Population of Great Britain*. Written by Edwin Chadwick for a British audience, its account of the squalid living conditions of the British laboring class and the effect on their health status paralleled what was happening to the poor and their health status in American cities. Just as importantly, in its suggestion that poor health was not caused by vice or immorality but rather by one's physical living and working environment, it alerted the public to the importance of sanitation and the environment. This conclusion influenced the passing of the Public Health Act of 1848 in Britain, which created the world's first modern board of health. In America, it inspired two similar reports. John Griscom's *Sanitary Conditions of the Laboring Population of New York* (1845) and Lemuel Shattuck's *Report of the Sanitary Commission of Massachusetts, 1850* (1948) echoed many of the sentiments of Chadwick's report, chief among them being the need for sanitary reform. Griscom (1845, p. 2), a physician with Quaker roots, argued that the poor were the victims and not the cause of the living conditions that caused their ill health. He further argued that poor people did not have the necessary resources to ensure a clean water supply, construct a sewage system, and regularly clean the streets. This, Griscom suggested, was the responsibility of the city through establishing permanent public health boards to ensure a clean water supply, the construction of a sewage system, and the establishment of systematic street cleaning and waste disposal. In doing so, Griscom posited that the heavy burden of sickness and mortality that oppressed the pauper class would be lifted. It would also demonstrate a measure of humanity, give justice to the poor, and protect society as a whole and its economy. In much the same vein and using statistical evidence as proof, Shattuck argued for the need to implement public health agencies and public health laws to promote public health through the collection of data. These were suggestions that were indeed enacted by the Massachusetts state legislature in 1866 and widely emulated by other states.

The sanitary movement that emerged, which the antebellum public health movement was most commonly referred to, spread across the states and cities of the United States after the reports of Shattuck and Griscom. Although well intentioned, in actual practice the sanitary movement was less than effective, partly because sanitary science was for the most part established by evangelical social reformers who were outside of the medical profession, Griscom being one of the notable exceptions. As such, their focus was much more on charitable reforms and not scientific concerns. Because of this focus and the paucity of exiting scientific evidence to justify preventive measures such as providing clean water and sewage systems, physicians took little interest in the sanitary movement (Trattner, 1999). Moreover, the unstable economic conditions of the mid-1800s made city officials and state legislators less than enthusiastic about the recommendations for sanitary reform that would be costly to implement and offered little in the way of guaranteed success (Trattner, 1999).

Because of these circumstances, it was not until the last quarter of the 19th century that the public health movement gained traction. Primarily responsible for this was science and the work of Louis Pasteur and Robert Koch, who discovered the true etiology of disease—germs. This discovery justified the need to invest in public health. In doing so it transformed public health in the United States (Trattner, 1999). In 1866, the N.Y. Metropolitan Health Law was enacted, creating the nation's first municipal board of health. Other major cities soon followed New York's lead. In 1872, the American Public Health Association (APHA) was founded by a group of physicians in Washington, D.C., with the mission of improving the health of the public and achieving equity in health status. In 1878 the federal government passed the National Quarantine Act and in 1879 created the National Board of Health (Trattner, 1999).

Additionally, the origins of the diseases that had been the scourge of American cities and how to prevent them were being discovered rapidly. Indeed, between 1880 and 1898, scientists discovered the origins of TB, cholera, diphtheria, tetanus, bubonic plague, and dysentery (Trattner, 1999). Just as importantly, the discovery of the personal factor in contagion in the late 19th century prompted municipal health boards to set up diagnostic laboratories to produce vaccines and antitoxins to control infectious diseases. Additionally, departments of health developed screening programs to identify bacterial contamination of milk and the water. They also designed public health education programs. These education programs were designed with an improved understanding of the relationship between poverty and ill health (Trattner, 1999).

By the early years of the 20th century, social workers began to take a central role in public health education through their work in the poor communities of the major cities and their shared common concerns with public health workers. In this role, social workers not only championed public health education for the poor but also, as part of a larger progressive agenda shared with trade unions, journalists, public health advocates, and like-minded public officials, called for some form of a universal government-funded health care system (Trattner, 1999). This system was deemed necessary because, despite the inroads made on controlling infectious diseases, high medical costs, and missed days because of sickness posed a real problem for American industry; not only did workers lose pay, factories also lost productivity. Sickness also cost the larger society, as it was one of leading causes of poverty and dependency.

From this time forward, conflict would characterize the call for health care reform. Consistent with conflict theory, the powerful players, which included the American Medical Association (AMA), business owners, and conservative ideologues, political and otherwise, battled to resist any reform that would redistribute that most precious of resources, health care. The following describes some of the ways these conflicts played out on the way to health care reform.

Theodore Roosevelt and the Call for a National Health Service and Health Insurance, 1912

In 1912, Theodore Roosevelt and his Progressive Party became the first political party in United States history to endorse social insurance, including health insurance. The party also endorsed a National Health Service. As part of what he called New Nationalism, Roosevelt argued that human welfare was more important than property rights, and consequently, a powerful federal government had the responsibility not to just regulate the economy but also to protect working men, women, and children against exploitation and sickness. The keys to this protection, as Roosevelt and the Progressive Party saw it, were social insurance, including health insurance, and a National Health Service (Woolley & Peters, 2015). Although Roosevelt and his Progressive Party did not win the presidential election in 1912, their endorsement of health insurance and a National Health Service set in motion the call for progressive health reform, be it government-funded health insurance, universal health care, or a National Health Service.

The American Association for Labor and the Campaign for Compulsory Health Insurance, 1915

In 1915, the American Association for Labor (AALL), a group of progressive academic reformers, published and promoted a draft bill for compulsory health insurance to protect workers against both lost wages and prohibitive medical costs during sickness. The bill was modeled on the social insurance programs that already existed in Europe. These programs first began in Germany in 1883, followed up to 1912 by Austria, Hungary, Norway, Britain, Russia, and the Netherlands (Hoffman, 2003).

The AALL promoted campaigns in several states in an effort to have the bill enacted. However, the bill was not universally popular, not least because it was drafted without input from the working people. Therefore, Samuel Gompers, the president of the American Federation of Labor (AFL), urged workers to win their own health care benefits through union organization and action, rather than government action (Hoffman, 2003). Also opposed to the AALL's bill were physicians who feared that it would jeopardize their incomes and compromise their independence. Other opponents included businesses, insurance companies, and conservative legislators, all of whom branded health insurance as Bolshevism.

This is not to say that the AALL had no support for their bill. Drawn by its inclusion of maternity benefits for women workers, women trade unionists and suffragettes threw their support behind the bill. Also throwing their support behind it was the New York State Federation of Labor. Another supporter, albeit surprisingly and for a very short time before opposing it, was the American Medical Association. Such was the strength of its support in New York, that in 1919 it was the only state in which the bill was introduced to the Senate, where it won a majority vote but died in committee after the powerful Speaker of the House Thaddeus Sweet denounced the bill as socialism (Hoffman, 2003).

The ideological attacks on the AALL's bill set a precedent for what to this day remains an ongoing ideological divide on health care reform through compulsory health insurance or government-funded universal health care. On the left of this debate, supporters see it as the most effective way to deliver effective health care and lessen health disparities and maximize health care access for all people. On the right of this debate, opponents see it as analogous to socialism and stripping away choice.

The Committee on the Cost of Medical Care, 1926–1932

In response to the rising cost of health care and concerns about its unequal distribution, a privately funded committee composed of economists, physicians, public health specialists, and major interest groups came together as the Committee on the Cost of Medical Care (CCMC) to discuss the cost of medical care in America (Gore, 2013).

From conducted research, published in research reports over a five-year period, the CCMC found that because of the lack of a system to organize care, health care costs, particularly those for physicians services, were prohibitively high for the lowest income groups (Gore, 2013). Consequently, despite much pro bono care by physicians, hospitals, and health departments, about half of low-income groups received no medical care at all (Gore, 2013; The Committee on the Costs of Medical Care, 1932). The CCMM concluded that that if medical care were organized economically, all the necessary health care for the entire population could be provided at a cost that was in reach for all people (Gore, 2013; The Committee on the Costs of Medical Care, 1932).

Although the majority of committee members opposed compulsory government health insurance, there was consensus on the need for additional national resources to be directed toward making health care accessible to all members of society. One of the ways the committee recommended to defray the cost of doing so was through voluntary health insurance. The AMA denounced the CCMM's final report and relatively modest proposals for making health care more accessible, stating that the proposals were radical and were advocating for socialized medicine (Gore, 2013; Hoffman, 2003). The conservative editor of the *Journal of American Medical Association (JAMA)*, Dr. Morris Fishbein, was even more vociferous in his denunciation, calling the CCMM's final report and proposals "an incitement to revolution," "socialist and communist" (Gore, 2013, p. 143).

In the midst of the Great Depression, President Franklin D. Roosevelt considered the CCMM's proposals interesting and worthy of consideration but secondary to the more pressing issues of economic recovery and employment (Hoffman, 2003). For this reason, and because of fears of political attacks by the AMA, health care coverage was dropped and not included in Roosevelt's New Deal agenda (Hoffman, 2003).

President Franklin D. Roosevelt's Technical Committee on Medical Care, 1935–1938

Following his decision not to propose or include a medical care program in the 1935 Social Security Act, Roosevelt in 1935 established an informal ad hoc group of federal government experts to study existing governmental health and welfare programs and identify ways to better coordinate them. The hope was that the findings of the group, who were known as the Interdepartmental Committee, would lead to a comprehensive federal health care proposal (Social Security Administration, 2016). This did not come to fruition, but under the auspices of the group, an appointed Technical Committee on Medical Care created a two-part report. The first part of the report was entitled *The Need for a National Health Program*, and argued for comprehensive health care reform in America. Specific recommendations included:

1. An expansion of public health and maternal and child health services under existing titles of the Social Security Act.
2. Federal grants-in-aid to the states for the construction of hospitals and for defraying operating costs during the first three years.
3. Federal grants-in-aid to the states toward the costs of a medical care program for medically needy persons.
4. Federal grants-in-aid to the states toward the costs of a general medical care program.
5. Federal action to develop a program of compensation for wage loss due to temporary and permanent disability.

(Social Security Administration, 2016)

Reception of the report and recommendations was generally enthusiastic. However, the AMA opposed recommendation 4, which was the committee's proposal that the nation begin the development of a national health care system. This aside, the AMA accepted all the other recommendations. However, Roosevelt did not make the recommendations a legislative priority, but decided to defer action. In 1939, Senator Robert Wagner (D-NY) introduced a bill (SB1620) to Congress modeled on the committee's report. The president did not lend strong support to the Wagner bill, and it died in the Senate Finance Committee (Social Security Administration, 2016).

Wagner-Murray-Dingell Bill, 1943

First introduced in 1943, the Wagner-Murray-Dingell bill called for compulsory national health insurance and a payroll tax. The bill was the result of intense lobbying by the committee for the Nation's Health, composed of representatives of organized labor, progressive farmers, and liberal physicians. Opposition to the bill was strong, and opponents launched a scathing attack on the committee, accusing its key policy analyst, I.S. Falk, of being a communist who was aligned with communist organizations hell-bent on world domination, namely the International Labor Organization (ILO). Although the Wagner-Murray-Dingell bill generated extensive national debate, it never passed Congress despite its reintroduction every session for 14 years (Hoffman, 2003).

President Lyndon Johnson and Medicare and Medicaid, 1965

After World War II, a Republican-controlled Congress, the expansion of private health insurance, the growing economy, nearly full employment, and the eradication of most infectious diseases dulled the call for any kind of health reform for nearly 20 years. Indeed, in 1945 and again in 1947 when President Truman called for universal health care, his proposal fell on deaf ears in Congress and was widely condemned by the AMA and the press. Nevertheless, Truman's ideas on health care reform can be seen as the beginning of meaningful health care reform in post-war America (Cohen, 1985).

When health care reform did finally happen in 1965 after some 20 years of the exchange of ideas about a possible national health insurance program, it was significant and partially addressed the nearly 60-year call for a federal government health care program. The reform was the enactment of Medicare and Medicaid in 1965 as Title XVIII and Title XIX of the Social Security Act, respectively (Cohen, 1985). First proposed by a task force convened by President John F. Kennedy in 1961, Medicare and Medicaid came to being as part of President Lyndon Johnson's spate of War on Poverty policies (Cohen, 1985). Medicare extended health coverage to almost all Americans age 65 or over, while Medicaid provided health care services to low-income children deprived of parental support, their caretakers, relatives, the blind, and individuals with a disability. Unlike previous attempts at health care reform, support in Congress was strong for both Medicare and Medicaid (Cohen, 1985).

AIDS/HIV Health Crisis, Discrimination, and Gay Activism, 1981

Over the 50 years since the enactment of Medicare and Medicaid, numerous amendments have been made to both programs to expand coverage to specific groups (see Box 9.1 Timeline). What remained elusive, however, was universal health care for the entire population. Moreover, there was significant discrimination and/or lack of access to health care for a number of groups. Nowhere was this more poignantly illustrated than during the AIDS/HIV crisis of the 1980s.

AIDS/HIV as a health crisis first came to the public's attention on June 5, 1981, when the Centers for Disease Control and Prevention (CDC) published a *Morbidity and Mortality Weekly Report* (*MMWWR*) describing cases of rare lung infections, *Pneumocystis carinii pneumonia* (PCP), among a cluster of previously health gay men in Los Angeles (Curran & Jaffe, 2011). In addition to PCP, the men, two of whom had died by the time of the report's publication, also had other infections that were indicative of a completely compromised immune system that could not protect the body against even minor infections (Curran & Jaffe, 2011; Epstein, 1996). In 1982, the CDC used the term AIDS (acquired immune deficiency syndrome) to describe these collective symptoms, which they estimated had already infected tens of thousands of people. Its rapid spread among gay men and ignorance about its etiology soon had the media erroneously referring to AIDS variously as the gay disease, gay cancer, or the gay plague (Epstein, 1996).

It also became the catalyst for the stigmatization of gay men and others suffering with the disease. The stigmatization manifested itself in a number of ways.

For example, in the years immediately following the CDCs identification of AIDS/HIV as an epidemic, the federal government under the presidency of Ronald Reagan initially failed to launch a single investigation into the etiology of the disease. Furthermore, priority was not given to the CDC's requests for research into a possible cure (Johns, 2015). Just as telling, President Reagan was ominously silent in the early years about the disease, choosing not to address the epidemic in a speech until 1985 and then again in 1987 (Curran & Jaffe, 2011). Indeed, in a 1985 press conference he expressed some trepidation in allowing children with AIDS to continue in school, although he supported their right to do so (Reagan, 1985).

Also, largely silent, save the odd sensationalist headline, were the media, who seemingly abdicated their critical role in educating the public about social problems and helping to create pressure that accelerates a policy response (Curran & Jaffe, 2011). Illustrative of this abdication, between 1981 and 1982, the influential *N.Y. Times* ran a total sum of six articles about AIDS/HIV, none of which appeared on page one. In contrast, the discovery of cyanide-laced capsules in Chicago in October 1982 generated 54 articles in three months (Smith, 2012).

Even more surprising in their stigmatization in the early years of the AIDS epidemic, however, was the medical community, whose practice, in theory, should maintain moral and social neutrality. This was certainly not the case for certain hospitals that isolated AIDS/HIV patients. Other hospitals had AIDS/HIV units in which staff had to manage the wards themselves because of the general fear of contagion on the part of other staff in the hospital. There were also reports of doctors refusing to treat AIDS patients, or would only do so with protective gear. Also, reluctant to be associated with AIDS were foundations, many of whom at least initially refused funding for AIDS research (Epstein, 1996).

Most pointed in their stigmatization, however, were members of the Christian Right and other conservative spokespersons. In their stigmatization, they laid the blame for the AIDS/HIV epidemic squarely at the feet of gay men, suggesting in no uncertain terms that it was their so-called immoral behavior that was the cause of their suffering. In a 1987 *N.Y. Post* column, for example, Pat Buchanan wrote, "There is only one cause of the AIDS crisis—the willful refusal of homosexuals to cease indulging in the immoral, unnatural, unsanitary, and suicidal practice of anal intercourse" (Buchanan, 1987, p. 23).

Evoking God's wrath to explain the AIDS epidemic in much the same way as Puritan John Winthrop did in 1643 when explaining why smallpox had decimated Native Americans (Winthrop, 1897), Jerry Falwell of the Religious Right stated, "Aids is not just God's punishment for homosexuals, it is God's punishment for a society that tolerates homosexuals" (Stewart, 2015).

Compounding the stigmatization was pharmaceutical company price gouging and the blatant discrimination of the health insurance industry. For example, the U.S. Food and Drug Administration (FDA) approved the anti-viral drug azidothymidine (AZT) for the treatment of AIDS in 1987. Later on, the same day of the FDA's approval, it was announced that the pharmaceutical company Burroughs-Wellcome would be granted a monopoly on the drug's patent. The cost of the drug would be somewhere in the region of $10,000 for a single patient annually, making it the costliest drug ever. Not coincidently, after the announcement, Burroughs-Wellcome share price increased 40% (Epstein, 1996). No more helpful was the medical insurance industry, whose coverage contained exclusionary policies for people with an AIDS/HIV diagnosis (Epstein, 1996; Hoffman, 2003).

Finally, the corrosive mix of ignorance and hysteria in the early years of the AIDS/HIV health crisis stoked a public discourse about what should be done to protect the public against AIDS/HIV. In an infamous 1986 op-ed in the *New York Times*, conservative social commentator and *National Review* editor William F. Buckley Jr., made the argument that at some point, public or private interest might be best served by tattooing AIDS-infected persons (Buckley, 1986). Moreover, several states, including California and Kansas, initiated or passed AIDS/HIV quarantine ballot initiatives. Furthermore, there were a number of cases of AIDS/HIV-infected children being prohibited from attending school (Gonsalves & Staely, 2014). The Ray brothers in Arcadia, Florida, and Ryan White in Kokomo, Indiana, were two examples of children barred from attending school because of their AIDS diagnosis that gained national media attention (Gonsalves & Staely, 2014).

It was against this backdrop of stigmatization, government inertia, discrimination, public hysteria, and a fight for their very lives that a grassroots movement of gay men and others with AIDS/HIV and their allies emerged to demand equality of access to health care and health reform. Most prominent and radical among these grassroots movements was the AIDS Coalition to Unleash Power (ACT UP). Founded in 1987 in New York City, ACT UP protesters used confrontation and civil disobedience as their strategies for getting their voices heard. The first action taken by ACT UP was on March 24, 1987, when 250 members arrived on Wall Street in New York City at 7 am and began to wave signs calling attention to the inequitable alliance between the FDA and Burroughs-Wellcome (Epstein, 1996). The protesters sat in the street, stopped traffic, and chanted what became an historic slogan: "Silence = Death." The Wall Street protest was only the beginning of what over the next decade would be an unrelenting push for public recognition and policy change (Epstein, 1996; Hoffman, 2003). ACT UP protesters chained themselves to the desks of drug company executives, poured buckets of fake blood in public places, delayed Wall Street trading, mounted demonstrations that closed tunnels and bridges, interrupted church services, held vigils at hospitals, conducted mock funerals, and tossed cremated ashes of dead bodies onto the White House lawn (Epstein, 1996). They launched a publicity campaign whose centerpiece was a poster that read "Lack of insurance kills people with AIDS: Lack of insurance means lack access to health care, and lack of health care means death" (Hoffman, 2003, p. 81). Additionally, they mounted regular demonstrations at the FDA, the National Institutes of Health (NIH), and the White House (Jason, 2013).

Though often vilified by public officials for their methods (see Box 9.2 Timeline: Selected Examples of ACT UP activism), ACT UP's activism accelerated the development and distribution of AIDS treatment drugs. In doing so, it helped to change the pharmaceutical industry's closed-door research and development process to being inclusive of the insights and research of the activists themselves. It also changed the landscape and future of those diagnosed with the virus from a death sentence to the manageable chronic disease that it is today (Epstein, 1996; Hoffman, 2003).

Box 9.2 Selected Examples of ACT UP Activism, 1987–1999

March 24, 1987: ACT UP holds its first demonstration of Wall Street to protest profiteering of pharmaceutical companies from AIDS drugs, notably Burroughs-Wellcome, the manufacturer of AZT.

October 11, 1987: At the March for Lesbian and Gay Rights in Washington, D.C., ACT UP demands that the Reagan administration fight the spread of HIV/AIDS.

March 24, 1988: On the first anniversary of its founding, ACT UP returns to protest at Wall Street, where it receives its first major media coverage.

October 11, 1988: ACT UP protests the FDA for its slow drug-approval policy. Within a year of the protest, the process is greatly accelerated.

September 14, 1989: ACT UP storms the floor of New York Stock Exchange to protest the price gouging of the pharmaceutical. ACT UP's protest stops trading on the floor of the New York Stock Exchange for the first time in its history.

December 10, 1989: About 4,500 protestors attended the first "Stop the Church" action to protest the Catholic Church's stance on AIDS and abortion.

January 3, 1990: ACT UP interrupts Governor Mario Cuomo's State of the Union Address in Albany. The purpose of the interaction is to bring public attention to his inaction and neglect of the AIDS crisis.

January 8–9, 1990: ACT UP storms the Centers for Disease Control in Atlanta to protest its narrow definition of AIDS. This definition excludes infections that affect women and intravenous drug users.

March 6, 1990: ACT UP/NY's Needle Exchange Committee begins its clean needle exchange program. The exchange collects used needles (dirty) in exchange for new ones (clean) in Manhattan.

May 21, 1990: ACT UP/NY organizes a coordinated national action with other ACT UP chapters to besiege the NIH (National Institutes of Health) in Maryland. Over 1,000 protesters take part, demanding more AIDS treatments. In making this demand they call for a focus on opportunistic infections that kill people, and the end to the underrepresentation of women and people of color in clinical trials.

January 23, 1991: In opposition to President George H.W. Bush's billion-dollar spending on the Gulf War, while claiming there is no money for needed AIDS programs, ACT UP stages a "Day of Desperation" protest, which involves mass protests in all five New York boroughs. The slogan of the protest is "Fight AIDS, not Arabs."

September 1, 1991: ACT UP stages a massive die-in at President Bush's vacation home in Maine. In doing so, ACT UP demands that President Bush declare that the AIDS health crisis can end.

October 11, 1992: ACT UP holds its first political funeral in Washington, D.C. A funeral procession begins at the Capitol and ends with the scattering of the ashes of loved ones on the White House lawn.

January 3, 1994: ACT UP descended on City Hall to tell Mayor Giuliani the AIDS crisis would be Job One on his first day as mayor.

April 25, 1995: Members of ACT UP block the entrance of the Queens-Midtown-Tunnel in protest of Mayor Giuliani's cuts to AIDS services.

December 1995: ACT UP, Housing Works, and *POZ* magazine organize a march of 100 activists outside the White House Conference on AIDS. Inside the conference, an ACT UP member interrupts Clinton's speech, demanding to know why he has not acted as recommended by Bush's AIDS Commission.

June 1996: Members of ACT UP and Housing Works take over the office of New York Senate Majority Leader Joseph Bruno to protest his opposition to restoring funds to the AIDS Drug Assistance Program (ADAP). Within a few weeks, Governor Pataki strikes a deal with Bruno to restore the ADAP funds.

July 1997: ACT UP affinity group takes over Manhattan shareholder office of Glaxo-Wellcome. It does so to protest Glaxo-Wellcome's failure to expand access to its new drug Abacavir, then known as 1592, and its attempt to block generic AIDS drug production in Africa.

October 21, 1997: Two activists interrupt an awards ceremony in New York for former White House aide George Stephanopoulos. The interruption is to protest his support of President Clinton's ban on federal funding for needle exchange.

January 1999: ACT UP/NY and AIDS physician Dr. Alan Berkman convene the first meeting of a broad coalition of AIDS activists and advocates, LGBTQ groups, physicians, and consumer groups. The coalition, which later is named Health GAP (Global Access Project), demands full access to AIDS medications throughout the Global South.

Spring 1999: In what is the first action in the AIDS Drugs for Africa campaign, members of ACT UP/NY and Philadelphia, along with Health GAP, conduct a die-in at the Pharmaceutical Manufacturers of America headquarters in Washington, D.C.

June–July 1999: Members of ACT UP/NY and Health GAP disrupt kick-off events of Vice President Gore's presidential campaign, demanding AIDS Drugs for Africa. Members also denounced Gore's role in the administration's threat of trade sanctions against Nelson Mandela's South Africa if it did not repeal the Medicines Act.

Source: *ACT UP Accomplishments and Partial Chronology* (2009). Retrieved from http://actupny.com/actions/index.php/the-community

Access to Health Care for Everyone and the Affordable Health Care Act of 2010

Like other grassroots movements, which include the women's health movement, Disabled in Action, and the Civil Rights movement, to name just a few, ACT UP called for health care reform to include universal health care for everyone. It was a call that was to reach a crescendo during the latter part of the 20th century and into the first decade of the 21st century. Informing the urgency was the slow but gradual increase in the number of citizens and residents without health care insurance coverage of any kind, a percentage that grew from 12.9% of the population (13 million people) in 1987 to 15.4% of the population in 2010 (48 million people; U.S. Census Bureau, 2013) (see Figure 9.5). Moreover,

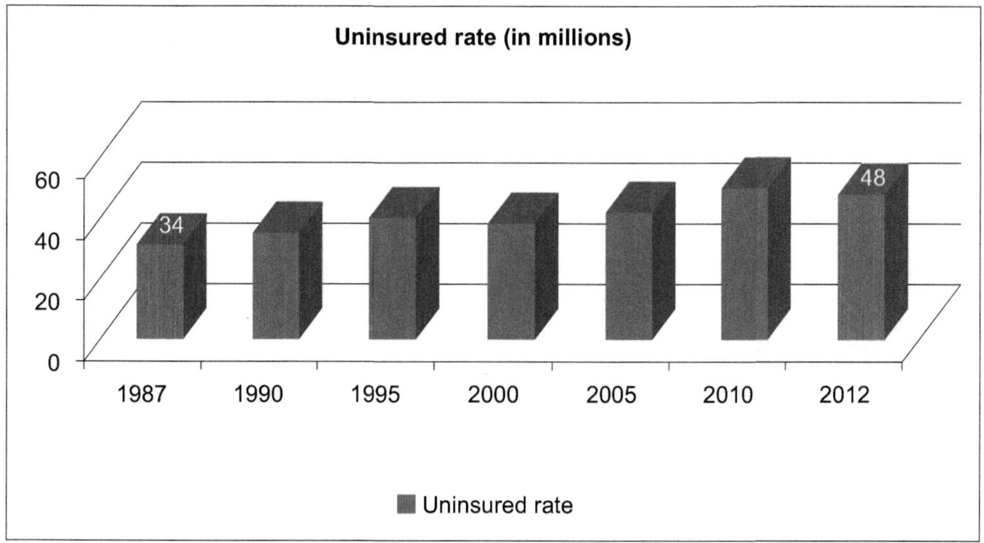

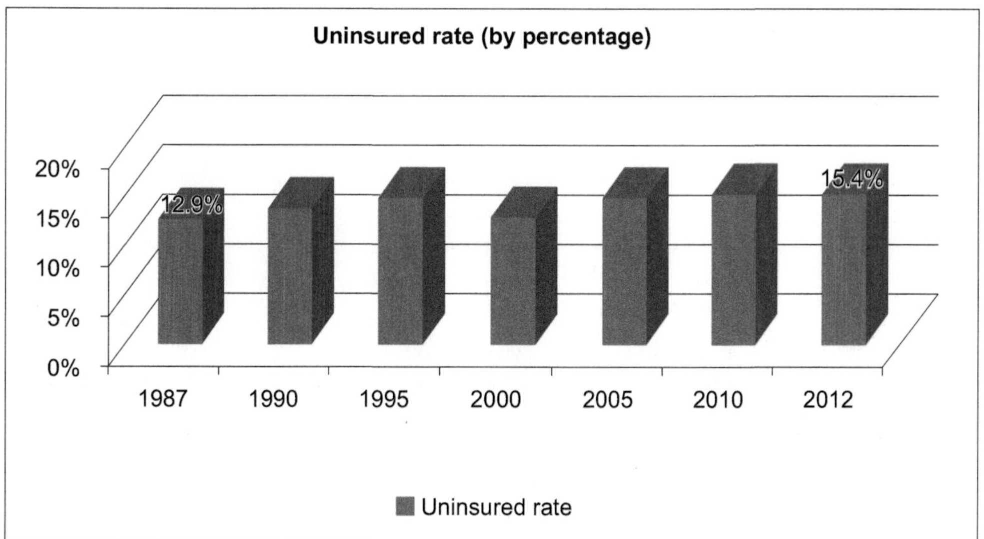

Figure 9.5 Uninsured Rate and Number of Uninsured, 1987–2012
Source: U.S. Census Bureau, Current Population Survey, 1988 to 2013 Annual Social and Economic Supplements

from 1999 through to 2012, there were precipitous declines in private and employee-based health care coverage for citizens and residents (see Figure 9.6; U.S. Census Bureau, 2013), while, as mentioned earlier, there were increases in the number of uninsured as well as the number of people accessing government health insurance programs (see Figure 9.5). By age, the cohort most affected by these trends were people between the ages of 19 and 44 (see Figure 9.7), while by race and ethnicity it was Hispanics, followed by

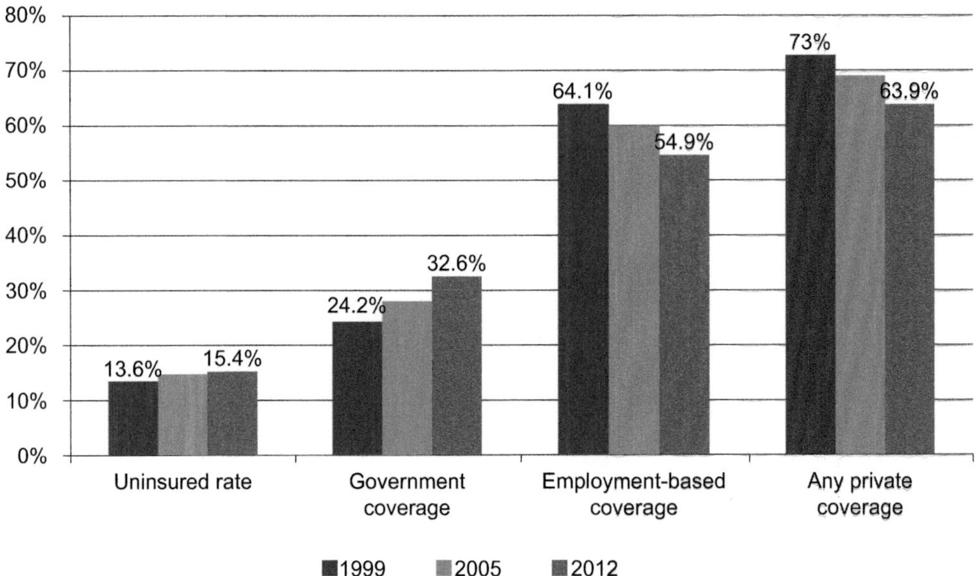

Figure 9.6 People by Type of Health Insurance Coverage, 1999–2012

Source: U.S. Census Bureau, Current Population Survey, 2000 to 2013 Annual Social and Economic Supplements

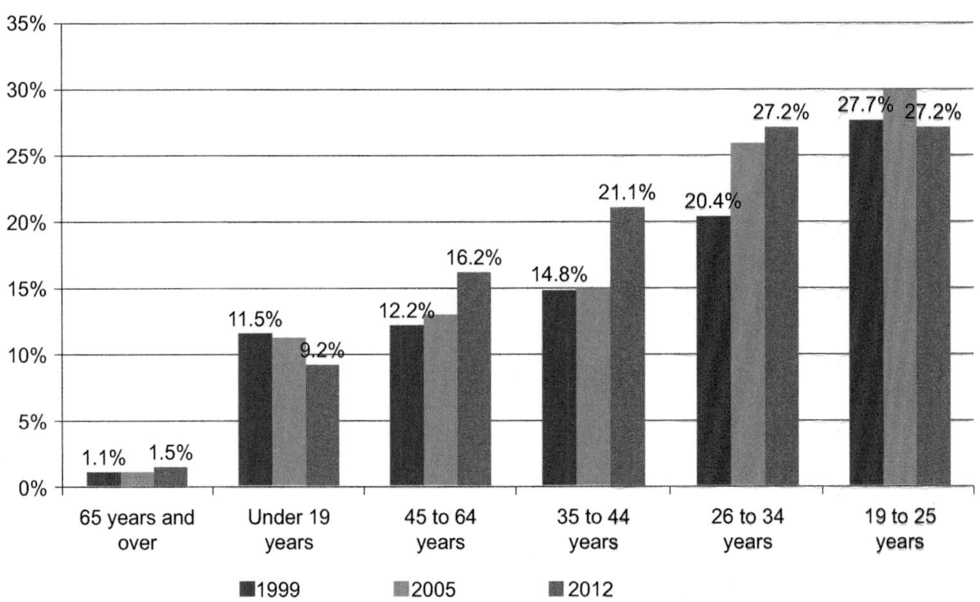

Figure 9.7 Uninsured Rates by Age, 1999–2012

Source: U.S. Census Bureau, Current Population Survey, 2000 to 2013 Annual Social and Economic Supplements

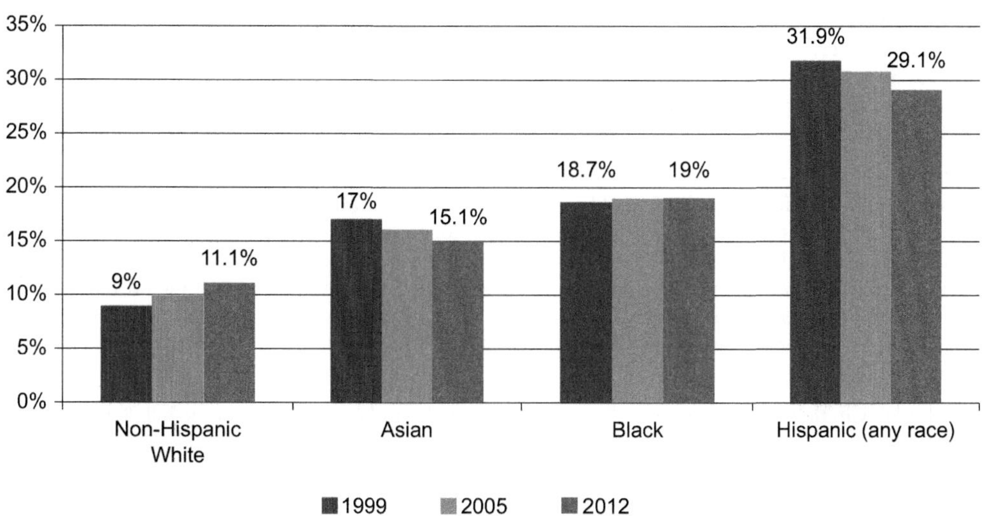

Figure 9.8 Uninsured Rates by Race and Hispanic Origin, 1999–2012
Source: U.S. Census Bureau, Current Population Survey, 2000 to 2013 Annual Social and Economic Supplements

Blacks, Asians, and finally Whites (see Figure 9.8). Added to this was the soaring cost of health care, which among other things was a contributing factor to 17% of the personal bankruptcies in the early 2000s. These personal bankruptcies caused by medical debt only minimally affected the middle class and were far more prevalent among those with income levels closer to the poverty level (Dranove & Millenson, 2006).

These trends reignited the ongoing debate about health reform, more specifically the need for a system that would ensure coverage for all citizens and legal residents, regardless of income or preexisting medical conditions.

On the presidential campaign trail in 2007, both the Democrat nominee, Senator Barack Obama (D-IL), and the Republican nominee, Senator John McCain (R-AZ) tapped into voters' desire for health care reform and proposed plans to reform the health insurance system in the United States (Collins et al., 2008). Befitting their ideological stances, the proposed changes by the candidates were significantly different. Simply put, Senator Obama proposed a health reform plan that would cover everyone, while this was not a goal of Senator McCain's plan (Collins et al., 2008). Senator Obama wanted to institute rules for the individual insurance market, whereas Senator McCain wanted minimum rules. Senator Obama wanted to expand the role of the employer in providing employee health benefits, which Senator McCain wanted to reduce. Senator Obama wanted to expand Medicaid/SCHIP, which again Senator McCain wanted to reduce. Senator Obama wanted to lessen families' exposure to health care costs, while Senator McCain wanted to increase it. Senator Obama wanted to require health care coverage for all, while Senator McCain required it only for children. Senator Obama wanted to have 34 million people covered in the next ten years, while Senator McCain wanted two million covered (Collins et al., 2008). To make clear his rationale for health care reform, two weeks before the presidential election, Senator Obama said, "The American people are too often caught between two extremes—government-run health care with higher taxes or letting the insurance companies operate without rules. . . . I believe both of these extremes are wrong" (Collins et al., 2008).

Upon his election to the presidency in 2008, President Obama made health care reform one of the first orders of business. In March of 2009, he convened a health summit at the White House with doctors, insurers, drug companies, consumer advocates, and lawmakers. The principal message of the summit was that the status quo was not an option and health care reform was going to happen (U.S. Department of Health and Human Services, 2015).

In July of 2009, House Democrats unveiled their 1,000-page plan for reforming the health care system. In November 2009, the House approved its version of health care reform in a 220–215 vote (U.S. Department of Health and Human Services, 2015).

To illustrate the ideological divide on the proposed reform, the bill received only one Republican vote. On December 24, 2009, the Senate approved its version of the health care overhaul in a 60–39 party line vote. To do so, however, Democrats had to break a GOP filibuster. The bill's passage confirmed that it had a majority agreement in both chambers of Congress (U.S. Department of Health and Human Services, 2015).

In January 2010, President Obama made his first State of the Union address in which he told the American people that the health care overhaul would protect every American from the worst practices of the insurance industry. In February 2010, the Democrats in Congress were galvanized around the urgency of health care reform when Anthem Blue Cross of California informed its customers that their premiums would increase by a whopping 39%. In March 2010, House Speaker Nancy Pelosi kept the pressure on Democratic lawmakers to ensure passage of the health care act. On March 21, 2010, the House approved the Senate's version of the health care plan by a vote of 219–212 (U.S. Department of Health and Human Services, 2015).

Consistent with their opposition to it, all of the Republican lawmakers voted against the bill. Republican leader John Boehner asserted that the American people were angry at the speed of health care reform. On March 23, 2010, President Obama signed into law the Patient Protection and Affordable Health Care Act (PPACA) (P.L. 111–148; U.S. Department of Health and Human Services, 2015).

Commonly called the Affordable Care Act or colloquially referred to as Obamacare by its detractors, PPACA and its accompanying amendments in the Health Care and Education Reconciliation Act of 2010 (P.L. 111–52) put into place the most comprehensive overhaul of the United States' health care system since the passage of Medicare and Medicaid in 1965 (U.S. Government Publishing Office, 2015). The primary goals of the PPACA are twofold: first, to improve access to affordable health care for everyone, and second, to protect consumers from abusive insurance company practices. Toward this end, the PPACA requires that most U.S. citizens and legal residents have health insurance. To facilitate this for the uninsured struggling to find affordable health insurance, a new Health Insurance Marketplace in every state offered consumers a choice of private health plans at subsidized rates. In the job market, employers with over 50 full-time employees from 2016 onward were required to provide them with health benefits or face a fine. Regarding insurance companies and the protection of consumers, PPACA created a new Patient's Bill of Rights. These rights put an end to preexisting condition discrimination, which in the past denied coverage or charged a higher premium to people with preexisting health conditions. It also put an end to limits of care, which in the past imposed a dollar limit on the care that could be provided for chronic illnesses such as cancer.

Finally, it put an end to end-of-coverage cancellations, which prevents an insurance company from dropping a consumer's coverage when sick because of a mistake on her or his application. Just as importantly, insurers were now required to cover a number of recommended preventive services, including cancer, diabetes, and blood pressure screening. These preventive services were to be provided by the insurance companies without additional cost sharing such as copays or deductibles. Furthermore, their parents' health insurance company would cover young adults who cannot get insurance benefits through their job until the age of 26 (U.S. Department of Health and Human Services, 2015).

Although these examples are by no means a comprehensive description of the details of the PPACA, they provide a sense of its intent. For a description, see these two websites:

www.gpo.gov/fdsys/pkg/PLAW-111publ148/pdf/PLAW-111publ148.pdf
www.hhs.gov/health care/rights/law/

In passing the PPACA, President Obama built on the legacy of the unsuccessful attempts of former presidents such as Theodore Roosevelt, Harry Truman, John F. Kennedy, and Bill Clinton to expand health care coverage and protections to more citizens and legal residents than at any time in American history. This alone is particularly beneficial for the millions of Americans who because of the high cost of health care had to forego medical treatment. Yet, as was the case with the attempts of former presidents, there has and is bitter conservative and libertarian opposition to the PPACA, even though it stops well short of being universal health care that is in any way comparable to other developed countries.

Illustrative of the opposition, since its passage in 2010, Republican lawmakers in Congress have repeatedly debated the PPACA's implementation and considered bills to repeal, defund, delay, or otherwise amend the act. Indeed, more so than the Senate, the Republican majority House of Representative has voted numerous times to repeal all or parts of the PPACA (Redhead & Kinzer, 2015). Moreover, the law has been challenged in the U.S. Supreme Court twice since its enactment. The first challenge, *National Federation of Independent Business et al. v. Sebelius, Security of Health and Human Services, et al.* came in 2012 before many of the key elements of the act had been fully instituted. In making the challenge, the National Federation of Independent Business argued that Congress did not have the authority to mandate that individuals have health insurance coverage. The Supreme Court rejected this argument in a 5 to 4 vote (*Supreme Court.gov*, 2012). The second challenge, *King et al v. Burwell, Security of Health and Human Service, et al*, came in 2015 from a group of conservative and liberation activists who argued that a strict reading of the statute makes health insurance subsidies available only in a handful of states. On June 25, 2015, the U.S. Supreme Court rejected the challenge in a 6–3 decision (*Supreme Court.gov*, 2015). In doing so it upheld a key part of the PPACA that provides health insurance subsidies to all qualifying Americans or legal residents.

In 2016, Donald Trump was elected to the United States presidency, promising to repeal and replace the PPACA. During President Trump's four years in office, the repeal and replace attempts included executive orders, legislation efforts in Congress, and legal action (see Box 9.1 Timeline for the chronology and details of these attempts).

Despite the relentless ideological and legal attacks, ten years into the PPACA, it has partially delivered on at least one of President Obama's ambitious health care reform goals. That is, increasing the number of citizens and residents of the United States with health care coverage, with the ultimate goal of ensuring that all citizens and residents have health care coverage. Between 2010 and 2016, the coverage rate increased for all racial and ethnic groups. The largest increases were happening after implementing the PPACA Medicaid and marketplace coverage expansions in 2014.

Indeed, in the 12 months between 2013 and the implementation of the PPACA Medicaid and marketplace coverage expansions, the uninsured rate fell from 13.3% to 10.4%. In hard numbers the number of uninsured Americans dropped from 41.8 million to 33 million (Broaddus & Park, 2015). This drop is by the far the largest single-year reduction on record since 1987 (Broaddus & Park, 2015). Moreover, it builds on three years of previously modest gains that probably reflect PPACA provisions permitting young adults to enroll in or remain on their parents' health insurance plan up to the age of 26 (Broaddus & Park, 2015).

While the coverage gains reduced the uninsured rates between most populations of color and their White and Asian counterparts, racial and ethnic disparities persist. Indeed Black, Hispanic, and Native American/Alaska Natives remain more likely than Whites to be uninsured.

Moreover, while insurance rates remain historically high, beginning in 2017 and continuing through 2018, coverage gains halted and began reversing for all groups. Findings from the Commonwealth Fund Biennial Health Insurance Survey, 2020, indicate that there is a looming crisis in health care coverage affordability that is undermining the goals of the PPACA (Collins et al., 2020). Among the survey's highlights was that in the first half of 2020, 43.4% of adults between the ages of 19 to 64 were inadequately insured (Collins et al., 2020). High uninsured rates were reported among people of color, small business workers, people with low incomes, and young adults, and one-quarter of adults in employer plans are underinsured (Collins et al., 2020).

All of this said, in testimony before the House Energy and Subcommittee on Health on September 23, 2020, Aviva Aron-Dine, Vice President of Health Policy for the Center on Budget and Policy Priorities, defended the PPACA. Aron-Dine argued that PPACA and the broader Medicaid program provided a lifeline for millions of Americans during the COVID-19 pandemic and the resulting recession. Indeed, Aron-Dine posited that the nation would have been in a far weaker position if PPACA had been repealed in 2017 (Aron-Dine, 2020).

As we advance, the fate of PPACA is still uncertain, but with the election of Joe Biden as the new president, it has an ardent supporter, who has vowed to protect and build on the PPACA (Biden, n.d.).

Chapter Summary

This chapter identified contemporary health status and health care inequalities in the United States. Using a critical race theory lens, particular attention was paid to the perennial nature of these inequalities for Native Americans and Black Americans by way of an historical examination of their development. Also examined in this chapter using a conflict theory lens was the historic and ongoing quest for health care reform in America. Particular attention was paid to the role of government and grassroots groups in both championing and bringing about health care reform. In doing so, the chapter focused on the AIDS/HIV health crisis of the 1980s and the critical role that the activism of ACT UP played in reversing the discriminatory practices that denied gay men and others with AIDS/HIV fair and equal access to health care. Finally, there was an examination of the Patient Protection and Affordable Care Act, which is arguably the most important health care reform in American history with its demand for health insurance coverage for all Americans.

Retrieval Questions

1. What is health disparity?
2. What is health care inequality?
3. What are some of the human costs of health disparities?
4. What are some of the economic costs of health disparities?
5. What role did European diseases play in Native American health disparities?
6. What was the significance of the Indian Vaccination Act of 1832?
7. What did the Snyder Act of 1921 do?
8. What set of conditions made slaves particularly susceptible to nutrition-related diseases?
9. What did W.E.B. Dubois suggest were the reasons for poor Black health?
10. What was the significance of the Flexner Report? Is a definitive understanding of social class hard to come by in America?
11. What was the significance of the American Association for Labor?
12. What was the significance of Medicare and Medicaid to health care reform?
13. What was the significance of activism during the AIDS/HIV health crisis of the 1980s?
14. What are the primary goals of the PPACA?
15. What groups have been most impacted by COVID-19?

Discussion Questions

1. Identify and discuss some of the social justice issues pertinent to the current health and health care inequalities.
2. As policy practitioners, what responsibility do social workers have to advocate and support health and health care equality?
3. What are some of the potential practice challenges when working with clients that have no form of medical insurance coverage?
4. How might a client's health status affect the social work practice context?
5. How has existing health care and social inequality contributed to the disproportionate impact of COVID-19 infections, hospitalizations, and deaths on Blacks, Native Americans, and Hispanics?

Box 9.1 Health and Health Care Inequality and Reform Timeline, 1800–Present

1832: The first congressional appropriation specifically for Native American health (Center for Disease Control and Prevention [CDC], 2015).

1845: *Types of Mankind*, a book of racial theory essays by Josiah Clark Nott and George Robins Gliddon, is published. Nott and Gliddon argue that although Native Americans once thrived in America, they can no longer compete or co-exist with Whites and in a few generations the last of them will be numbered with the dead. Nott also argued that there were physical and mental differences between Blacks and Whites, which explained the continued disparities between the two groups (Jones, 2006).

1872: American Public Health Association is founded. It is America's first national voluntary organization dedicated to improving public health services. The APHA has four stated goals: to alert people to the importance of sanitary administration; to increase public awareness about sanitary practices; to appoint and promote competent health officials; and to promote science and measures for practical application of hygiene (American Public Health Association (2016).

1892: The U.S. Surgeon General reports that the consumption (tuberculosis) hospitalization rate for Native American soldiers is more than ten times the rate for White soldiers (Jones, 2006).

1906: W.E.B. Dubois publishes *The Health and Physique of Negro America* under the direction of Atlanta University. Dubois rejects the common assertion that the health disparities experienced by Blacks are the result of physical inferiority. Instead, Dubois asserts that the disparity is not racial but rather the result of environmental factors and racism (Centers for Disease Control and Prevention, 2015).

1912: Theodore Roosevelt and his Progressive party endorse social insurance, including health insurance (Kaiser Family Foundation, 2015).

1915: The American Association of Labor Legislation publishes a draft bill proposing compulsory health insurance (Kaiser Family Foundation, 2015).

1920: A catastrophic pellagra epidemic among poor southern sharecroppers points to systemic inequalities. Between 1900 and 1940, pellagra kills more than 100,000 Americans, the overwhelming majority of them women and Blacks. In 1920, public health researchers Joseph Goldberger and Edgar Sydenstricker publish the findings of their ongoing study of pellagra in South Carolina and conclude that sharecroppers are trapped in a cycle of poverty and dependency of sharecropping, which leaves them with a greater exposure and susceptibility to pellagra (Washington, 2006).

1921: The Indian Citizenship Act (P.L. 67–85), also known as the Snyder Act, is signed into law. Among other things, the act authorizes federal funds for health services for Native Americans (Jones, 2006).

1921: Congress passes the Sheppard-Towner Act, which provides matching funds to states for prenatal and child health centers. The act expires in 1929 and is not reauthorized (Kaiser Family Foundation, 2015).

1929: Baylor Hospital in Texas starts a prepaid hospital plan with a local teachers' union. The plan is considered the forerunner of a modern medical insurance program (Kaiser Family Foundation, 2015).

1932: The Department of Health, Education and Welfare establishes the Office of Negro Health (Centers for Disease Control and Prevention, 2015).

1932: The Tuskegee syphilis study of Black men begins (see case study) (Centers for Disease Control and Prevention, 2015).

1935: National Health Survey is conducted under the auspices of the U.S. Public Health Service. The purpose of the survey is to assess the nation's health (Kaiser Family Foundation, 2015).

1935: Electric shock treatment of gay men reported at American Psychological Association (APA) meeting (Cook-Daniels, 2015).

1952: APA includes homosexuality under sociopathic personality disturbance in its first official list of mental disorders (Cook-Daniels, 2015).

1954: Dr. Evelyn Hooker presents a study showing that gay men are as well adjusted psychologically as straight men at an APA meeting (Cook-Daniels, 2015).

1944: In his State of the Union Address, President Franklin Roosevelt outlines an economic bill of rights, including the right to adequate medical care and good health (Kaiser Family Foundation, 2015).

1945: President Truman comes into office strongly committed to a single universal comprehensive health insurance plan that includes all classes of society. The chairman of the House Committee, Senior Republican Senator Taft, refuses to hold hearings on the plan, which he considers to be nothing less than socialism. The AMA similarly denounces the plan, which they posit will make doctors slaves. The plan goes nowhere in Congress (Health Care Timeline, 2015).

1946: The Hill Burton Act (Hospital Survey and Construction Act) is signed into law. The act pays for the construction of hospitals, particularly in rural areas, to close the gap in access to medical care. It also prohibits discrimination on the basis of race, religion, or national origin in the provision of hospital service. It does, however, allow for separate but equal facilities on the grounds of race. Hospitals are required to provide a reasonable amount of charitable care (Centers for Disease Control and Prevention, 2015).

1946: The Center for Disease Control and Prevention is established to investigate all communicable disease and provide assistance to states. It soon grows into a training center for scientists from around the world and a center for epidemiological research. Its many successes include eradicating smallpox and tracking communicable diseases (Centers for Disease Control and Prevention, 1996).

1948: The AMA launches a national campaign against President Truman's national health insurance plan (the Wagner-Murray-Dingell bill). In doing so, the AMA spends over $1.5 million dollars in antireform advertisements, radio spots, letter writing campaigns, and lobbying (Hoffman, 2003).

1956: The Military Medicare program is enacted. The program provides federally funded health insurance for dependents of people in the armed forces (Kaiser Family Foundation, 2015).

1960: The Kerr-Mills Act passes. The act uses federal funds to support state programs to provide medical care to the poor and the elderly. The act is considered a precursor to the Medicaid program (Kaiser Family Foundation, 2015).

1962: *Simpkins v. Moses H. Cone Memorial Hospital* successfully challenges the separate-but-equal practices in hospitals when the U.S. Supreme Court denied the case. The denial of the case upheld a U.S. Court of Appeals ruling that Moses H. Cone Memorial Hospital, a publicly funded facility, had violated the Constitution by denying treatment to Black patients (Centers for Disease Control and Prevention, 2015).

1965: President Lyndon Johnson signs into law the most significant health reform of the century: Medicare and Medicaid. Medicare provides comprehensive health care coverage for people 65 and older, and Medicaid helps states cover long-term care for the poor and disabled (Health Care Timeline, 2015).

1966: To dramatize the problem of racial discrimination in health care, the Rev. Martin Luther King Jr. plans direct action against the City of Chicago hospitals (Centers for Disease Control and Prevention, 2015).

1968: APA moves homosexuality from sociopathic category to sexual deviation (Cook-Daniels, 2015).

1972: Medicare eligibility is extended to include two million individuals under age 65 with long-term disabilities and to individuals with end-stage renal disease (Health Care Financing Review, 2006).

1972: Medicare eligibility for elderly, blind, and disabled residents of a state can be linked to the newly enacted Federal Supplemental Security Income Program (SSI) (Health Care Financing Review, 2006).

1973: APA removes homosexuality from its list of mental illnesses (Cook-Daniels, 2015).

1975: The Indian Health Self-Determination and Education Assistance Act (P.L. 93–638) is passed. The act strengthens tribal sovereignty over health care (Centers for Disease Control and Prevention, 2015).

1982: The Tax Equity and Fiscal Act makes it easier and provides more incentives for health insurance programs to contract with the Medicare program (Centers for Disease Control and Prevention, 2015).

1985: The Emergency Treatment and Labor Act requires Medicare-participating hospitals that operate emergency rooms to provide appropriate medical screenings and stabilizing treatments (Health Care Financing Review, 2006).

1985: The Heckler Report identifies the continued existence of health disparities and clearly establishes that a disparity exists between the majority and minority populations of the United States. These minority populations include Native Americans, Blacks, Hispanics, and Asians/Pacific Islanders. The report declares that despite the explosion of technology to diagnose, treat, and cure disease, minority populations have not shared or benefited from these innovations (Centers for Disease Control and Prevention, 2015).

1987: The Omnibus Budget Reconciliation strengthens existing protections for residents of nursing homes (Health Care Financing Review, 2006).

1987: The Census Bureau begins annual estimate of health insurance coverage in the United States. The first survey in 1987 finds that 13% (31 million people) of the population is uninsured (Kaiser Family Foundation, 2015).

1988: The Medicare Catastrophic Coverage Act (MCCA) expands benefits to include mammography and outpatient drug prescription, and caps patient liability (Health Care Financing Review, 2006).

1988: Mandated coverage changes made to Medicaid. These changes extend coverage for pregnant women and infants to 100%. Moreover, rules are established to prevent spousal impoverishment when caring for wife/husband who is institutionalized (Health Care Financing Review, 2006).

1988: The CDC Office of Minority Health is created (Centers for Disease Control and Prevention, 2015).

1990: The Ryan White Comprehensive AIDS Resources Emergency Act (P.L. 101–381) passes. The act is the largest federally funded program for people in the United States living with AIDS. The goals of the act are to improve the availability of health care for low-income, uninsured, and underinsured victims of AIDS and their families (Hoffman, 2003).

1993: President Bill Clinton proposes the Health Security Act, sending a detailed plan of its proposals to Congress in 1993. The act calls for universal health coverage, competition between insurers, and governmental regulations to control costs. The Health Insurance Association of America and the National Federation of Independent Businesses are firmly opposed to the act, and congressional Democrats are split in their support; all of them block the act's progress (Kaiser Family Foundation, 2015).

1996: As part of comprehensive welfare reform, Aid to Families with Dependent Children entitlement program is replaced by the Temporary Assistance for Needy Families block grant. In doing so, the link to Medicaid is cut and a new low-income group not connected to welfare is added, and enrollment/termination of Medicaid is no longer automatic with receipt of welfare cash assistance (Health Care Financing Review, 2006).

1997: The Balanced Budget Act of 1997 creates the State Children's Health Insurance Program (SCHIP). The program provides health insurance to working families who don't have coverage (Health Care Financing Review, 2006).

1999: The Ticket to Work and Work Incentives Improvements Act expands the availability of Medicare and Medicaid for certain disabled recipients who return to work. It also allows states to offer a buy-in to Medicaid for working age people with a disability (Health Care Financing Review, 2006).

2000: The Benefits Improvement Act increases Medicare payments to providers and managed-care organizations. It also reduces certain Medicare co-payments and improves coverage for preventive services (Health Care Financing Review, 2006).

2003: The Medicare Prescription Drug Improvement and Modernization Act creates a drug prescription drug discount card until 2006 (Health Care Financing Review, 2006).

2003: The Health Equality and Accountability Act (H.R.3459) is introduced to the House, but after 15 actions, including floor amendments, the bill as of this writing is still pending. The purpose of the act is to improve minority health and health care and to eliminate racial and ethnic disparities in health and health care. Among the proposed actions are to strengthen Medicaid and SCHIP coverage for migrant workers and farm workers; provide for health workforce diversity, including career training and support; collect race, ethnicity, and language data to detect ongoing ethnic and racial health care disparities (Congress.gov, 2015).

2006: Massachusetts implements laws to provide health care coverage for nearly all of the state's residents. The laws call for shared responsibility for coverage among consumers, employers, and the state government in financing the expanded program. The laws are a success and within two years, the state's uninsured rate is cut by 50%. Vermont also passes health care reform aiming for universal coverage for all state residents. The law creates a health plan for uninsured residents with a plan of improving overall quality of care (Health Care Timeline, 2015).

2010: President Barack Obama signs the landmark Patient Protection and Affordable Care and Act into law. Among many other items, it is the first health care reform legislation in American history to require all individuals to have health insurance beginning in 2014 (Centers for Disease Control and Prevention, 2015).

2010: The United States Department of Health and Human Services (HHS) publishes its action plan to reduce racial and ethnic health disparities. The HHS Disparities Action Plan in support of the National Stakeholder Strategy aims to accelerate the move toward reducing racial and ethnic health care disparities, a situation that remains significant and has improved little over the past decade (U.S. Department of Health and Human Services, 2010).

2016: Within hours of being sworn into office on January 20, 2017, President Trump signed Executive Order 13765, Minimizing the Economic Burden of the Patient Protection and Affordable Care Act Pending Repeal (Federal Register, 2017b; Jost, 2018). Among the executive order's provisions was not requiring the IRS to ask tax filers to declare whether they were compliant with having medical insurance, which allowed those who were non-compliant to avoid a penalty fine.

2017: In late July of 2017, Republican lawmakers in the Republican-dominated Congress renewed their repeal and replaced the PPACA efforts. Toward this end, Senate Republicans voted on three significant repeals and replace proposals, each one of which failed to garner the necessary votes for passage (Ballotpedia, n.d). The primary reason given by those Republicans who did not vote for the various repeal and replace proposals was a lack of a suitable replacement for the PPACA. After the final defeat, Senate Majority leader Mitch McConnell said it was time to move on from the repeal and replace efforts (Ballotpedia, n.d.; Muchmore, 2019).

2018: On October 12, 2017, Executive Order 13813, Promoting Health Care Choice and Competition across the United States, was signed by President Trump. The order reversed some critical aspects of the PPACA. One of these provisions allowed insurance companies to circumvent PPACA mandates and sell insurance that does not cover mandated conditions and excludes individuals with preexisting conditions (Federal Register, 2017a).

2017: In December 2017, Congress passed the Tax Cuts and Jobs Act, which eliminated the individual mandate penalty of the PPACA (Muchmore, 2019)

2018: On February 26, 2018, 20 Republican states, led by Texas, challenged the constitutionality of PPACA without the individual mandate, filing a lawsuit (*Texas v. the United States*) in Texas to overturn the law entirely (Keith, 2019; Muchmore, 2019; Texas v. United States, 2021).

2018: On April 9, 2018, 17 Democratic states, led by California, challenged and defended the Texas challenge law (Keith, 2019).

2018: On December 14, 2018, Fort Worth U.S. District Judge Reed O'Connor ruled that the individual mandate and penalty are so critical to the PPACA that without them, the PPACA must be struck down (Keith, 2019; Muchmore, 2019).

2019: On January 7, 2019, the *Texas* decision was appealed by the Department of Justice (DOJ) and the Democratic attorneys general from 21 democratic states to the Fifth Circuit Court of Appeal O'Connor's ruling (Keith, 2019).

2019: On December 18, 2019, the Fifth Circuit Court of Appeal in New Orleans partially affirmed the district court decision that declared the PPACA's unconstitutional in a 2–1 ruling but declined to rule on the fate of the remainder of the PPACA laws, asking the lower court to reconsider the question in more detail. However, The democratic attorneys general appealed the decision to the United States Supreme Court (Keith, 2019).

2020: On November 10, 2020, the Supreme Court heard an oral argument over the constitutionality of the individual mandate and the fate of the entire PPACA.

2021: On June 18, 2021, the Supreme Court held in a 7–2 opinion that the states and individuals that brought the lawsuit challenging the PPACA's individual mandate do not have standing to challenge the law (The National Law Review, 2021).

References

American Cancer Society. (2019). *Cancer facts and figures 2019*. Retrieved from www.cancer.org/content/dam/cancer-org/research/cancer-facts-and-statistics/annual-cancer-facts-and-figures/2019/cancer-facts-and-figures-2019.pdf

American College of Obstetricians and Gynecologists. (2011). *Committee opinion. Health care for transgendered individuals*. Retrieved from www.acog.org/Resources-And-Publications/Committee-Opinions/Committee-on-Health-Care-for-Underserved-Women/Health-Care-for-Transgender-Individuals

American Diabetes Association. (2018). *Statistics about diabetes*. Retrieved from www.diabetes.org/resources/statistics/statistics-about-diabetes

American Public Health Association. (2016). *APHA history and timeline*. Retrieved from www.apha.org/news-and-media/newsroom/online-press-kit/apha-history-and-timeline

APM Research Lab. (2020, November 12). *The color of coronavirus: COVID-19 deaths by race and ethnicity in the U.S.* Retrieved from www.apmresearchlab.org/covid/deaths-by-race

Arias, E. (2014). United States life tables, 2010. *Statistics Report*, 63(7). National Center for Health Statistics. Retrieved from www.cdc.gov/nchs/data/nvsr/nvsr63/nvsr63_07.pdf

Aron-Dine, A. (2020). Health care lifeline: The Affordable Care Act and the COVID-19 pandemic: Testimony of Aviva Aron-Dine, Vice President of Health Policy, CBPP, before the House Energy and Commerce Subcommittee on Health. *Center for Budget and Policy Priorities*. Retrieved from www.cbpp.org/health/health-care-lifeline-the-affordable-care-act-and-the-covid-19-pandemic

Artiga, S., Corallo, B., & Phan, O. (2020a, August 17). Racial disparities in COVID-19: Key findings from available data and analysis. *Kaiser Family Foundation*. Retrieved from www.kff.org/report-section/racial-disparities-in-covid-19-key-findings-from-available-data-and-analysis-appendix/

Aritga, S., Orgera, K., & Damico, A. (2020b). Changes in health coverage by race and ethnicity since the ACA, 2010–2018. *Kaiser Family Foundation*. Retrieved from www.kff.org/racial-equity-and-health-policy/issue-brief/changes-in-health-coverage-by-race-and-ethnicity-since-the-aca-2010-2018/

Ballotpedia. (n.d.). *Republican effort to repeal the ACA, July 2017*. Retrieved from https://ballotpedia.org/Republican_effort_to_repeal_the_ACA,_July_2017

Biden, J. (n.d.). Health care. *Joebiden.com*. Retrieved from https://joebiden.com/healthcare/

Boyd, R. T. (1999). *The coming of the spirit of pestilence: Introduced infectious diseases and population decline among Northwest Indians, 1774–1874*. Seattle: University of Washington Press.

Broaddus, M., & Park, E. (2015). Census data show historic gains in 2014: Health reform coverage expansion a major factor. *Center on Budget and Policy Priorities*. Retrieved from www.cbpp.org/research/health/census-data-show-historic-coverage-gains-in-2014

Brondolo, E., Hausmann, L., Jhalani, J., Pencille, M., Atencio-Bacayon, J., Kumar, A., & Schwartz, J. (2011). Dimensions of perceived racism and self-reported health: Examination of racial/ethnic differences and potential mediators. *Annals of Behavioral Medicine*, 14–28.

Brown, N. L. M., & Stentiford, B. M. (Eds.). (2014). *Jim Crow: A historical encyclopedia of the American mosaic*. Santa Barbara, CA: Greenwood.

Buchanan, P. J. (1987, December 2). AIDS and moral bankruptcy. *New York Post*, p. 23.

Buckley, W. F., Jr. (1986). Crucial steps in combating the AIDS epidemic: Identify all the carriers. *New York Times* [Op-ed]. Retrieved from www.nytimes.com/books/00/07/16/specials/buckley-aids.html

Bureau of Labor Statistics. (2019). *Job flexibilities and work schedules-2017-2018 data from the American time use survey*. Retrieved from www.bls.gov/news.release/pdf/flex2.pdf

Bureau of Labor Statistics. (2020). *Labor force statistics from current population survey: Employed persons by detailed industry, sex, race, and Hispanic or Latino ethnicity*. Retrieved from www.bls.gov/cps/cpsaat18.htm

Cancer Disparities Progress Report. (2020). *American Association for Cancer Research*. Retrieved from https://cancerprogressreport.aacr.org/wp-content/uploads/sites/2/2020/09/AACR_CDPR_2020.pdf

Centers for Disease Control and Prevention. (1996). *Historical perspectives history of CDC*. Retrieved from www.cdc.gov/mmwr/preview/mmwrhtml/00042732.htm

Centers for Disease Control and Prevention. (2013a). Education and income: United States, 2009 and 2011. *MMWR* 2013, 62(Suppl. 3), 9–19. Retrieved from www.cdc.gov/mmwr/pdf/other/su6203.pdf

Centers for Disease Control and Prevention. (2013b). Access to healthier food retailers: United States, 2011. *MMWR* 2013, 62(Suppl. 3), 20–26. Retrieved from www.cdc.gov/mmwr/pdf/other/su6203.pdf

Centers for Disease Control and Prevention. (2013c). Unemployment: United States, 2006–2010. *MMWR* 2013, 62(Suppl. 3), 27–32. Retrieved from www.cdc.gov/mmwr/pdf/other/su6203.pdf

Centers for Disease Control and Prevention. (2013d). Residential proximity to major highways: United States, 2010. *MMWR* 2013, 62(Suppl. 3), 46–50. Retrieved from www.cdc.gov/mmwr/pdf/other/su6203.pdf

Centers for Disease Control and Prevention. (2013e). Health insurance coverage: United States, 2008 and 2010. *MMWR* 2013, 62(Suppl. 3), 61–64. Retrieved from www.cdc.gov/mmwr/pdf/other/su6203.pdf

Centers for Disease Control and Prevention. (2015). *Evolution of minority health in America*. Retrieved from www.cdc.gov/minorityhealth/observances/MHMonth/Evolution.html

Centers for Disease Control and Prevention. (2020a, November 17). *Age-adjusted COVID-19-associated hospitalization rates by race and ethnicity*. Retrieved from www.cdc.gov/coronavirus/2019-ncov/covid-data/images/July-28_Race_Ethnicity_COVIDNet.jpg

Centers for Disease Control and Prevention. (2020b, November 12). *COVID data tracker: Demographic trends of COVID-19 cases and deaths in the US reported to CDC*. Retrieved from https://covid.cdc.gov/covid-data-tracker/#demographics

Centers for Disease Control and Prevention. (2020c, November 12). *Health disparities: Race and Hispanic origin*. Retrieved from www.cdc.gov/nchs/nvss/vsrr/covid19/health_disparities.htm

Centers for Disease Control and Prevention. (2020d, June 29). *Adult obesity facts*. Retrieved from www.cdc.gov/obesity/data/adult.html

Centers for Disease Control and Prevention. (2020e, September 8). *Heart disease facts*. Retrieved from www.cdc.gov/heartdisease/facts.htm

Centers for Disease Control and Prevention. (2020f). *National diabetes statistics report 2020: Estimates of diabetes and its burden on the United States*. Retrieved from www.cdc.gov/diabetes/pdfs/data/statistics/national-diabetes-statistics-report.pdf

Cohen, F. S. (1982). *Handbook of federal Indian law*. Charlottesville, VA: Michael Co.

Cohen, W. J. (1985). Reflections on the enactment of Medicare and Medicaid. *Health Care Financing Review*, 3–11.

Collins, S. R., Munira, Z. G., & Aboulafia, G. N. (2020). U.S. health insurance coverage in 2020: A looming crisis in affordability: Findings from the commonwealth fund biennial health insurance survey, 2020. *Commonwealth Fund*. Retrieved from www.commonwealthfund.org/publications/issue-briefs/2020/aug/looming-crisis-health-coverage-2020-biennial

Collins, S. R., Nicholson, J. L., Rustgi, S. D., & Davis, K. (2008). The 2008 presidential candidates' health reform proposal: Choices for America. *The Commonwealth Fund*. Retrieved from www.commonwealthfund.org/publications/fund-reports/2008/oct/the-2008-presidential-candidates-health-reform-proposals-choices-for-america

The Committee on the Costs of Medical Care. (1932). *Medical care for the American people*. Chicago, IL: University of Chicago Press.

Congress.gov. (2015). *H.R. 3459: Healthcare Equality and Accountability Act*. Retrieved from www.congress.gov/bill/108th-congress/house-bill/3459

Cook-Daniels, L. (2015). *Living memory LGBT history timeline: Current elders would have been this old when these events happened*. Transgender Aging Network. Retrieved from www.tandfonline.com/doi/abs/10.1080/15504280802191731

Covey, H. C. (2007). *African American slave medicine: Herbal and non-herbal treatment*. Plymouth, UK: Lexington Books.

Crosby, A. W., Jr. (2003). *The Columbian exchange: Biological and cultural consequences of 1492*. Westport, CT: Praeger Publishers.

Cullen, M. R., Cummins, C., & Fuchs, V. R. (2012). Geographic and racial variation in premature mortality in the U.S.: Analyzing the disparities. *PLoS One*, 7, e32930.

Curran, J. W., & Jaffe, H. W. (2011). AIDS, the early years and CDC's response. *Mortality and Morbidity Weekly Report*, 60(Suppl. 4), 64–69. Retrieved from www.cdc.gov/mmwr/preview/mmwrhtml/su6004a11.htm

Diamond, J. (1977). *Guns, germs, and steel: A short history of everybody for last 13000 years*. London: Jonathan Cape.

Diamond, J. (1997). *Guns, germs, and steel: The fates of human societies*. New York, NY: W.W. Norton.

Dranove, D., & Millenson, M. L. (2006). Medical bankruptcy: Myth versus fact. *Health Affairs*, 25(2), 74–83.

Dublin, L. I., Lotka, A. J., & Spiegelman, M. (1949). *Length of life* (Revised ed., pp. xxv, 370). New York: Ronald Press Co.

Duffy, J. (1951). Smallpox and the Indians in the American Colonies. *Bulletin of the History of Medicine*, 25, 324–341.

Durant, T. J., & Knottinerus, J. D. (1999). *Plantation society and race relations: The origins of inequality*. Westport, CT: Praeger Press.

Epstein, S. (1996). *Impure science: AIDS activism and politics of knowledge*. Berkeley: University of California Press.

Ezzati, M., Friedman, A. B., Kulkarni, S. C., & Murray, C. J. L. (2008). The reversal of fortunes: Trends in county mortality and cross-county mortality disparities in the United States. *Plos Med*, 5, e66.

Federal Register. (2017a). *Executive order 13813, Promoting Health Care Choice and Competition across the United States*. A presidential document ny the executive office of the President on 10/17/2017. Retrieved from www.federalregister.gov/documents/2017/10/17/2017-22677/promoting-healthcare-choice-and-competition-across-the-united-states

Federal Register. (2017b). Minimizing the Economic Burden of the Patient Protection and Affordable Care Act Pending Repeal: A presidential document ny the executive office of the President on 01/24/2017. Retrieved from www.federalregister.gov/documents/2017/01/24/2017-01799/minimizing-the-economic-burden-of-the-patient-protection-and-affordable-care-act-pending-repeal

Fett, S. (2002). *Working curses: Healing, health, and power on southern slave plantations*. Chapel Hill: University of North Carolina Press.

Fisher, W. (1968). Physicians and slavery in the antebellum Southern medical journal. *Journal of the History of Medicine and Allied Sciences*, 45–46.

Fontenot, W. L. (1994). *Secret doctors: Ethnomedicine of African Americans*. Westport, CT: Bergin & Garvey.

Francis, J. M. (2005). *Iberia and the Americas: Culture, politics, and history: A multidisciplinary encyclopedia*. Santa Barbara, CA: ABC-CLIO.

Fuchs, V. R. (2013). How and why U.S. health care differs from that in other OECD countries. *Journal of American Medical Association*, 309, 33–34.

Gamble, V. N., & Stone, D. (2006). U.S. policy on health inequalities: The interplay of politics and research. *Journal of Health, Politics, Policy and Law*, 93(122), 99–108.

Gates, H. L., Jr., Crew, S., & Goodman, C. (2002). *Unchained memories: Readings of from the slave narrative*. Boston, MA: Bullfinch Press.

Gonsalves, G., & Staely, P. (2014). Panic, paranoia, and public health: The AIDS epidemic, lessons for Ebola. *The New England Journal of Medicine*, 18(371), 2348–2349.

Gore, T. B. (2013). A forgotten landmark medical study from 1932 by the Committee on the Cost of Medical Care. *Baylor University Medical Center Proceedings*, 26(2), 142–143.

Gorges, F. (1658). A brief narration of the original undertakings of the advancement of plantations into parts of America. In J. P. Baxter (Ed.), *Sir Ferdinando Gorges and his province of Maine* (Vol. 19, p. 19). Boston, MA: Prince Society Publications.

Griscom, J. H. (1845). *The sanitary conditions of the laboring population of New York: With suggestions for its improvement*. New York, NY: Harper & Brothers.

Hadley, J. N. (1955). Health conditions among Navajo Indians. *Public Health Reports, 70*, 835.

Hales, C. M., Carroll, M. D., Fryar, C. D., & Ogden, C. L. (2020). Prevalence of obesity and severe obesity among adults: United States. 2017–2018. *Center for Disease Control and Prevention*. Retrieved from www.cdc.gov/nchs/products/databriefs/db360.htm

Health Care Financing Review. (2006). *Key milestones in Medicare and Medicaid, selected years: 1965–2003*. Retrieved from www.cms.gov/Research-Statistics-Data-and-Systems/Research/HealthCareFinancingReview/downloads/05-06Winpg1.pdf

Health Care Timeline. (2015). Retrieved from www.annenbergclassroom.org/Files/Documents/Timelines/HealthCare.pdf.

Health Resources & Services Administration. (2020, November 6). *Health center COVID-19 survey*. Retrieved from https://bphc.hrsa.gov/emergency-response/coronavirus-health-center-data

Heck, J. E., Sell, R. L., & Sheinfeld-Gorin, S. (2006). Health care access among individuals involved in same-sex relationships. *American Journal of Public Health, 96*(6), 1111–1118.

Hoffman, B. (2003). Health care reform and social movements in the United States: Public health then and now. *American Journal of Public Health, 93*(1), 75–85.

Hong, S., Walton, E., Tamaki, E., & Sabin, J. (2014). Lifetime prevalence of mental disorders among Asian Americans: Nativity, gender, and socio demographic correlates. *Asian American Journal of Psychology, 5*(4), 353–363.

Humphrey, D. C. (1973). Dissection and discrimination: The social origins of cadavers in America, 1760–1915. *Bulletin of the New York Academy of Medicine, 49*(9), 819–827.

Jacobson, P. H. (1957). An estimate of the expectation of life in the United States in 1850. *The Milbank Quarterly, 35*(2), 197–201.

Jason, L. A. (2013). *Principles of social change*. New York, NY: Oxford University Press.

Johns, A. (2015). *A companion to Ronald Reagan*. Malden, MA: John Wiley & Sons.

Johnson, L. N., & Daniels, O. C. B. (2002). *Breaking the color line in medicine: African Americans in ophthalmology*. Thorofare, NJ: Slack, Inc.

Jones, D. S. (2006). The persistence of American Indian health disparities. *American Journal of Public Health, 96*(12), 2122–2134.

Jost, T. S. (2018). The Affordable Care Act under the Trump administration. *The Commonwealth Fund*. Retrieved from www.commonwealthfund.org/blog/2018/affordable-care-act-under-trump-administration

Kaiser Family Foundation. (2012). *Disparities in health and health care: Five key questions and answers*. Retrieved from http://kff.org/disparities-policy/issue-brief/disparities-in-health-and-health-care-five-key-questions-and-answers/

Kaiser Family Foundation. (2015). *Timeline: History of health reform in the U.S.* Retrieved from https://kaiserfamilyfoundation.files.wordpress.com/2011/03/5-02-13-history-of-health-reform.pdf

Keith, K. (2019). Continued uncertainty as fifth circuit strikes mandate, remands on rest of ACA. *Health Affairs*. Retrieved from www.healthaffairs.org/do/10.1377/hblog20191219.863104/full/

Keith, K. (2020). Supreme Court arguments: Even if mandate fall, rest of Affordable Care Act looks likely to be upheld. *Health Affairs*. Retrieved from www.healthaffairs.org/do/10.1377/hblog20201111.916623/full/

Khazanchi, R., Evans, C. T., & Marcelin, J. R. (2020). Racism, not race, drives inequity across the COVID-19 continuum. *JAMA Network Open*. Retrieved from https://jamanetwork.com/journals/jamanetworkopen/fullarticle/2770954

Kilbourne, A. M., Switzer, G., Hyman, K., Crowley-Matoka, M., & Fine, M. J. (2006). Advancing health disparities research within the health care system: A conceptual framework. *American Journal of Public Health, 96*(12), 2113–2121.

Khazanchi, R., Evans, T. C., & Marcelin, J. R. (2020). Racism, not race, drives inequity across the COVID-19 continuum. *JAMA Network Open*. Retrieved from https://jamanetwork.com/journals/jamanetworkopen/fullarticle/2770954

Kolchin, P. (1993). *American slavery: 1619–1877*. New York: Hill and Yang.

Krug, J. A. (1948). *The Navajo: A long-range program for Navajo rehabilitation*. Washington, DC: U.S. Government Printing Office.

Kwok, J. (2013). Factors that influence the diagnosis of Asian Americans in mental health: An exploration. *Perspectives in Psychiatric Care*, 288–292.

LaVeist, T. A., Gaskin, D. J., & Richard, P. (2009). *The economic burden of health inequalities in the United States: Fact sheet*. Washington, DC: Joint Center for Political and Economic Studies.

Lawrence, J. (2000). The Indian Health Service and the sterilization of Native American women. *The American Indian Quarterly, 24*(3), 400–419.

Leavitt, J. W., & Numbers, R. L. (Eds.). (1997). *Sickness and health in America: Readings in the history of medicine and public health* (3rd ed.). Madison: The University of Wisconsin Press.

Lockley, T. (2012). Like a clap of thunder in a clear sky: Differential mortality during Savannah's yellow fever epidemic 1854. *Social History*, 37(2), 166–188.

Martineau, H. (1838). *Retrospect of western travel* (Vol. 1, p. 140). London, England: Saunders and Otley.

McLaughlin, K. A., Hatzenbuehler, M. L., & Keyes, K. M. (2010). Responses to discrimination and psychiatric disorders among Black, Hispanic, female, and lesbian, gay, and bisexual individuals. *American Journal of Public Health*, 100(8), 1477–1484.

Merrens, R., & Terry, G. D. (1984). Dying in paradise: Malaria, mortality, and the perceptual environment in colonial South Carolina. *Journal of Southern History*, 50(4), 533–550.

Moorman, L. J. (1950). Tuberculosis on the Navajo reservations. *American Review of Tuberculosis*, 61, 589.

Muchmore, S. (2019). Timeline of the Affordable Care Act: Still under siege. *Healthcare Dive*. Retrieved from www.healthcaredive.com/news/timeline-of-the-affordable-care-act-still-under-siege/566964/

Murray, C. J. L., Kulkarni, S. C., Michaud, C., Tomijima, N., Bulzacchelli, M. T., Iandiorio, T. J., & Ezzati, M. (2006). Eight Americas: Investigating mortality disparities across races, counties, and race-counties in the United States. *PLoS Medicine*, 3, e260.

National Institute of Diabetes and Digestive and Kidney Disease. (2014). *Race, ethnicity and kidney disease*. Retrieved from www.niddk.nih.gov/health-information/kidney-disease/race-ethnicity

National Institutes of Health, U.S. Department of Health and Human Services. (n.d.). *NIH health disparities strategic plans and budget fiscal years 2009–2013*. Washington, DC: Author. Retrieved from www.nimhd.nih.gov/docs/2009-2013nih_health_disparities_strategic_plan_and_budget.pdf

The National Law Review (2021, June 21). *The Affordable Care Act survives Supreme Court challenge: What happens next?* Retrieved from https://www.natlawreview.com/article/affordable-care-act-survives-supreme-court-challenge-what-happens-next

Nunn, N., & Qian, N. (2010). The Columbian exchange: A history of disease, food, and ideas. *Journal of Economic Perspectives*, 24(2), 163–188.

Olden, K., & White, S. L. (2005). Health-related disparities: Influences of environmental factors. *Medical Clinics of North America*, 89(4), 721–738.

Pearson, J. D. (2003). Lewis Cass and the politics of disease: The Indian Vaccination Act of 1832. *Wicazo Sa Review*, 18(2), 9–35.

Peterson, C. L., & Rachel, B. (2007). *US health care spending: Comparison with other OECD countries*. Washington, DC: Congressional Research Service Federal Publications.

Pirtle, W. N. L. (2020). Racial capitalism: A fundamental cause of Novel Coronavirus (COVID-19) pandemic inequalities in the United States. *Health, Education Behavior*, 47(4), 504–508.

Postell, W. D. (1951). *The health of slaves on southern plantations*. Baton Rouge: Louisiana State University Press.

Randall, V. R. (2006). *Dying while black*. Dayton, OH: Seven Principles Press.

Reagan, R. (1985). *Action on Aids video transcript*. Against the Odds. Retrieved from http://apps.nlm.nih.gov/againsttheodds/exhibit/video_transcripts.cfm

Redhead, C. S., & Kinzer, J. (2015). *Legislative actions to repeal, defund, or delay the Affordable Care Act*. Congressional Research Service. Retrieved from www.fas.org/sgp/crs/misc/R43289.pd

Rice, M. F., & Jones, W., Jr. (1994). *Public policy and the black hospital: From slavery to segregation and integration*. Westport, CT: Greenwood Press.

Rife, J. P., & Dellapenna, A. J. (2009). *Caring and curing: A history of the Indian Health Service*. Landover, MD: PHS Commissioned Officers Foundation for the Advancement of Public Health.

Robertson, R. G. (2001). *Rotting face: Smallpox and the American Indian*. Caldwell, Idaho: Caxton Press.

Russell, L. M. (2011). *Reducing disparities in life expectancy: What factors matter?* Paper prepared for the workshop on Reducing Disparities in Life Expectancy held by the Roundtable on the Promotion of Health Equity and the Elimination of Health Disparities of the Institute of Medicine. Retrieved from www.iom.edu/~/media/Files/Activity%20Files/SelectPops/HealthDisparities/2011-FEB-24/Commissioned%20Paper%20by%20Lesley%20Russell.pdf.

Savitt, T. L. (1982). The use of blacks for medical experimentation and demonstration in the old south. *The Journal of Southern History*, 48(3), 331–348.

Savitt, T. L. (2006). Abraham Flexner and the Black medical schools. *Journal of the National Medical Association*, 98(9), 1415–1424.

Shattuck, L. C. (1948). *Report of the sanitary commission of Massachusetts, 1850*. Cambridge, MA: Harvard University Press.

Shelton, B. L. (2004). *Legal and historical roots of health care for American Indians and Alaska natives in the United States*. The Henry J. Kaiser Family Foundation. Retrieved from https://kaiserfamilyfoundation.files.wordpress.com/2013/01/legal-and-historical-roots-of-health-care-for-american-indians-and-alaska-natives-in-the-united-states.pdf

Shryock, R. H. (1937). The early American public health movement. *American Journal of Public Health and the Nation's Health, 27*(10), 965–971.

Smedley, B., Stith, A., & Nelson, A. (2003). *Unequal treatment: Confronting racial and ethnic disparities in health care*. Washington, DC: National Academic Press.

Smith, J. (2012). *AIDS and activism part II: Reagan, DeVos and the 1980s crisis*. Grand Rapid Institute for Information Democracy. Retrieved from http://griid.org/2012/11/27/aids-and-activism-part-ii-reagan-devos-and-the-1980s-crisis/.

Social Security Administration. (2016). *Report on the Technical Committee on Medical Care*. Retrieved from www.ssa.gov/history/reports/Interdepartmental.html.

Speiss, A. E., & Speiss, B. D. (1987). New England pandemic of 1616–1622: Cause and archeological implications. *Man in the North East, 34*, 71–83.

Stampp, K. M. (1956). *The peculiar institution: Slavery in the antebellum south*. New York, NY: Vintage.

Stewart, C. (2015). *Proud heritage: People, issues and documents of the LGBT experience*. Santa Barbara, CA: ABC-CLIO.

Substance Abuse and Mental Health Services Administration. (2020). *Double jeopardy: COVID-19 and behavioral health disparities for Black and Latino communities in the U.S.* Retrieved from www.samhsa.gov/sites/default/files/covid19-behavioral-health-disparities-black-latino-communities.pdf

Supreme Court.gov. (2012). *National Federation of Independent Business et al. v. Sebelius, Security of Health and Human Services, et al.* Retrieved from www.supremecourt.gov/opinions/11pdf/11-393c3a2.pdf

Supreme Court.gov. (2015). *King et al. v. Burwell, Secretary of Health and Human Services, et al*. Retrieved from www.supremecourt.gov/opinions/14pdf/14-114_qol1.pdf

Texas v. the United States. (2021). *Constitutional Accountability Center*. Retrieved from www.theusconstitution.org/litigation/texas-v-united-states/

Thornton, R. (1987). *American Indian holocaust and survival: A population history since 1492*. Norman: University of Oklahoma Press.

Trattner, W. I. (1999). *From poor law to welfare state: A history of social welfare in America* (6th ed.). New York, NY: The Free Press.

U.S. Census Bureau. (2013). *Income, poverty, and health insurance coverage: 2012*. Retrieved from www.census.gov/newsroom/releases/pdf/20130917_ip_slides_with_plotpoints.pdf

U.S. Department of Health and Human Services. (2010). *HHS action plan to reduce racial and ethnic health disparities: A nation free of disparities in health and health care*. Retrieved from www.minorityhealth.hhs.gov/npa/files/Plans/HHS/HHS_Plan_complete.pdf

U.S. Department of Health and Human Services. (2015). *The Affordable Health Care Act, section by section*. Retrieved from www.hhs.gov/healthcare/rights/law/

U.S. Department of Health and Human Services. (2020). *Health equity report 2019–2020: Special feature on housing and health inequalities*. Rockville, MD. Retrieved from www.hrsa.gov/sites/default/files/hrsa/health-equity/HRSA-health-equity-report.pdf

U.S. Government Publishing Office. (2015). *Public Law 111–152: Health care and Education Reconciliation Act of 2010*. Retrieved from www.gpo.gov/fdsys/pkg/PLAW-111publ152/content-detail.html

U.S. Public Health Service. (1957). Health services for American Indians. In *Public Health Service Public No. 531* (pp. 90–92). Washington, DC: Government Printing Office.

Washington, H. A. (2006). *Medical Apartheid: The dark history of medical experimentation on Black Americans from colonial times to the present*. New York, NY: Doubleday.

WebMD. (2019). *How race can matter in Type 2 diabetes*. Retrieved from www.webmd.com/diabetes/type-two-diabetes-race

Winthrop, R. C. (1897). *A memoir of Robert C. Winthrop: Prepared for the Massachusetts historical society*. Boston, MA: Little, Brown, and Company.

Wood, W. R., Hunt, W. J., & Williams, R. H. (2011). *Fort Clark and its Indian neighbors: A trading post on the Upper Missouri*. Norman: University of Oklahoma Press.

Woolley, J., & Peters, G. (2015). *Progressive Party Platform 1912*. The American Presidency Project. Retrieved from www.presidency.ucsb.edu/ws/index.php?pid=29617#axzz1ZBVAP3ui

Xavier, J. M. (2000). *The Washington Transgender needs assessment survey: Final report for phase two*. Washington, DC: Administration for HIV/AIDS of the District of Columbia.

CHAPTER 10
Criminal Justice System Inequality

Mass Incarceration in the United States

Over the past 40 years, the United States has become the world's largest jailer, quadrupling its prison and jail populations to 2.3 million, as of 2018 (Sawyer & Wagner, 2020; The Sentencing Project, 2020). Of this number, 1,291,000 are in federal and state prison, 631,000 are in local jails (470,000 of whom are not convicted but are awaiting trial), and 226,000 are in federal prisons and jails (Sawyer & Wagner, 2020). In addition to these numbers, 44,000 are in some form of youth detention, 11,000 in territorial prisons, 42,000 in immigration detention, and 22,000 are involuntarily commitments (Sawyer & Wagner, 2020).

Demographically, the expanse of mass incarceration in the United States has not affected all groups equally (Gramlich, 2020; The Sentencing Project, 2020). More specifically, Black and Hispanic adults (both men and women) with low education levels (less than high school) who live in communities of concentrated disadvantage have been disproportionately affected by America's mass incarceration boom. It is a disproportionality that persists even as imprisonment rates have been declining precipitously across all racial groups—most dramatically for Black males—since 2006 (Carson, 2020; Gramlich, 2020). For example, Black adults represent 12% of the U.S. population, but in 2017 accounted for 33% of the sentenced population in federal and state prisons, nearly triple their share of the U.S. population. Hispanic adults followed at 23% (16% of the population) and Whites at 30% (64% of the population) (Gramlich, 2020).

Also disproportionally affected by mass incarceration is LGBTQ persons and people with disabilities, most especially those of color (National Center for Transgender Equality, 2018; U.S. Commission on Civil Rights, 2019). For example, lesbian, gay, and bisexual persons are three times more likely to be incarcerated than the general public (National Center for Transgender Equality, 2018). And in a 2015 Bureau of Justice Statistics report, prisoners were three times more likely, and jail inmates more than four times more likely, than the general population to have at least one disability (Bronson et al., 2015). Moreover, over half of the prisoners (54%) and jail inmates (53%) with a disability reported a co-occurring chronic condition (Bronson et al., 2015). The U.S. Department of Justice estimates that at least half of incarcerated persons have a mental health diagnosis (U.S. Commission on Civil Rights, 2019).

Racial, ethnic, and LGBTQ youth of color disproportionality is similarly present within the juvenile justice system. On any given day in the United States, 48,000 youth are confined in restrictive, correctional style facilities because of juvenile or criminal justice involvement (Conron & Wilson, 2019; Sawyer, 2019). In 2018, of the 48,000 youth in the juvenile justice system, 16,858 were in detention centers, 10,777 were in long-term secure facilities, and 10,256 were in residential treatment centers. Additionally, 4,535 were in adult prisons and jails; 3,375 were in group homes; and others were in shelters, wilderness camps, boot camps, and diagnostic centers (Sawyer, 2019).

The disproportionality is most pronounced among Black boys and girls and Native American girls (Sawyer, 2019). As an illustration of this, Black youth comprise 14% of the youth population under 18, but in 2017, Black boys and Black girls represented 42% and 35%, respectively, of confinements in juvenile facilities (Sawyer, 2019). And even excluding youth held in Native American county facilities, Native

DOI: 10.4324/9781003023708-10

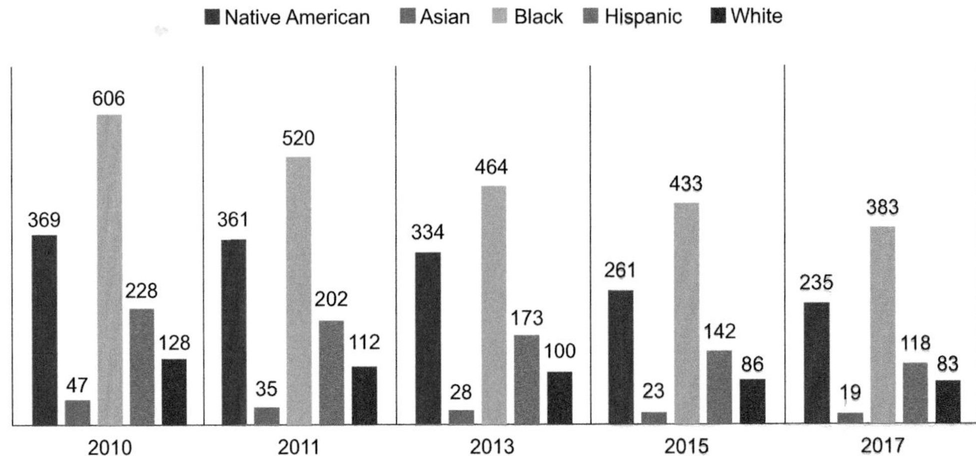

Figure 10.1 Rate of Youth Residing in Juvenile Detention, Correctional, and/or Residential Facilities per 100,000 by Race/Ethnicity, 2010–2017

Source: Sickmund, M., Sladky, T.J., Kang, W., & Puzzanchera, C. (2019). Easy Access to the Census of Juveniles in Residential Placement. Available: www.ojjdp.gov/ojstatbb/ezacjrp/

American girls, who represent less than 1% of the youth population, comprised 3% of the detentions in juvenile facilities, twice that of their male counterparts, at 1.5% (Sawyer, 2019).

Racial disparities are also present in the decisions to transfer youth from juvenile to adult court. In 2017, for example, Black youth accounted for 35% of delinquency cases, but 54% of youth judicially transferred from juvenile court to adult court (Sawyer, 2019). In contrast, White youth accounted for 44% of all delinquency cases, but only 31% of judicial transfers to adult court (Sawyer, 2019). Moreover, at the state level, California sends Hispanic youth to adult facilities by way of a direct file at 3.4 times the rate of White youth. And Native American youth are 1.8 times more likely to receive an adult prison sentence than White youth (Sawyer, 2019).

These disparities exist even as the number of youth in confinement has fallen by 60% since 2000 (Sawyer, 2019). Indeed, such was the level of concern about the racial and ethnic disparities that, in 2018, the Juvenile Justice Reform Act of 2018 was signed into law reauthorizing and substantially amending the Juvenile Justice and Delinquency Prevention Act. The act's primary purpose is to reduce the racial and ethnic disparities in the juvenile justice system (Office of Juvenile Justice and Delinquency Prevention, 2019).

The Effects of Mass Incarceration

In its effect, mass incarceration, along with the policies that inform it, the criminal justice system actions that fuel it, and the racial and ethnic disparities that characterize it, has, as Western and Pettit (2010) so eloquently state, transformed the contours of social inequality for young economically disadvantaged Black and Hispanic men with low levels of education. Joined by the shared experience of economic disadvantage, low levels of education, and incarceration, these already vulnerable men, and increasingly women, have become for all intents and purposes an outcast group whose experiences are almost totally outside of the mainstream population. Of these experiences, incarceration has become an expected marker of adulthood.

For these men, who already have the weakest economic opportunities, spending their early twenties and thirties behind bars further deepens their disadvantage and forestalls any chance of the social mobility that is available to most of the mainstream population (Western & Pettit, 2010). These key years in the life course are when a person is building the human capital so critical to social mobility, including finishing higher education, cultivating marketable skills, gaining on-the-job work experience, and building social networks (Western & Pettit, 2010). In missing these opportunities, these men lose significant ground to their never-incarcerated contemporaries, a loss that over the life course is both cumulative and enduring and whose magnitude is only fully realized upon release (Schmitt & Warner, 2010).

As illustrative of this, one only needs to examine the effects that incarceration and the myriad of civil penalties that attach to a felony conviction have on labor market participation post-release.

Incarceration and the Labor Market

There has been a large volume of research on incarceration and labor market outcomes (Couloute & Kopg, 2018; Geller et al., 2006; Harding et al., 2018; Holzer et al., 2004, 2006, 2007; Raphael, 2007; Western, 2006; Western & Pettit, 2010; Western & Beckett, 1999; Western & Sirois, 2019). The majority of the evidence from this research concludes that incarceration is associated with poor employment outcomes for formerly incarcerated individuals. These outcomes are particularly pronounced for Black and Hispanic—especially women—formerly incarcerated persons, who, even before incarceration, had compromised employment opportunities because of low levels of schooling, work experience, and backgrounds of economic instability (Couloute & Kopg, 2018; Harding et al., 2018; Western & Pettit, 2010).

One of these outcomes is unemployment rates for formerly incarcerated individuals nearly five times higher than the general United States population's unemployment rate. Indeed, it is a rate that is substantially higher than even the worst years of the Great Depression of 1929–1933 (Couloute & Kopg, 2018). These unemployment rates are not altogether surprising given that before incarceration, no racial or ethnic group reached 50% of employment in the formal labor market, with Blacks fairing the worst at the peak of 28% (Couloute & Kopg, 2018; Harding et al., 2018; Looney & Turner, 2018).

These differences are similarly reflected in post-incarceration employment where both Black and White formerly incarcerated experience low levels of employment. However, it is more pronounced for Blacks (particularly Black women) who were below 11% participation in the labor market compared to below 20% for Whites (Couloute & Kopg, 2018; Harding et al., 2018).

Once in the labor market, the formerly incarcerated most often land insecure jobs and in the lowest-paying positions, locating them well below the poverty line (Looney & Turner, 2018). However, there is a racial and gender component to this, with formerly incarcerated White men (87%) more likely to be employed in full-time positions with market-rate salaries. In contrast, Black (33%) and Hispanic (30%) women are most represented in part-time and occasional jobs (Couloute & Kopg, 2018).

An analysis of labor market inequality after incarceration by Western and Sirois (2019) found that when compared to their White counterparts, Blacks and Hispanics are at a disadvantage when reentering the job market after incarceration. The disadvantage is primarily characterized by Whites more than Blacks and Hispanics finding stable, high-paying jobs through social networks that are not present for formerly incarcerated Black and Hispanic persons. In turn, this results in formerly incarcerated Whites in the labor market having higher incomes than their Black and Hispanic counterparts, even when accounting for health, human capital, social background, criminal justice involvement, and job readiness. Indeed, Western and Sirois (2019) posit that this racialized reentry helps explain Blacks' unusual disadvantage at the penal system's nexus and the labor market.

Civil Penalties

In addition to prison time's labor market effects, the formerly incarcerated must also contend with civil penalties (also sometimes referred to as collateral consequences) that attach to a felony conviction. These civil penalties are the intricate web of more than 51,000 local, state, and federal sanctions imposed on a convicted felon post-incarceration (U.S. Commission on Civil Rights, 2019). If civil rights are not restored by way of a pardon at the federal level, these penalties include various actions. These actions include but are not limited to losing the right to serve on a federal jury, serve in the armed forces, be employed in certain occupations, hold public office, and have residency rights if a noncitizen immigrant (Justice.gov, 2015; U.S. Commission on Civil Rights, 2019). At least 70 to 100 million people nationwide are currently or will be affected by civil penalties (collateral consequences) of incarceration, arrest, or conviction (U.S. Commission on Civil Rights, 2019).

Arguably the most severe civil penalties are those for a drug felony conviction, a legacy of America's "get tough on drugs" war. These civil penalties can potentially span a lifetime, making it extraordinarily difficult for formerly incarcerated individuals to move beyond their criminal records and return to at least status quo ante (Lafollette, 2005). These civil penalties are most visible in felony disenfranchisement, and to a lesser extent in the provision of cash and in-kind welfare benefits, public housing, and federal student aid for higher education, where the majority of states are now relaxing or lifting permanent bans on access to these services based on a drug-felony conviction (Quinn, 2019).

Felony Disenfranchisement

Felony disenfranchisement is deeply rooted in the nation's history as a form of punishment principally to prevent Black Americans from voting. Because of the current mass incarceration patterns, felony disenfranchisement is at the highest rate in American history (Manza & Uggen, 2008; Mauer & Chesney-Lind, 2002; Schaefer & Kraska, 2012). As of 2020, depending on the state of residence, a felony conviction can permanently or temporarily disenfranchise a formerly incarcerated person. Currently, 48 states, Maine and Vermont being the exceptions, exercise some form of felony disenfranchisement for a felony conviction (National Conference of State Legislators, 2020; Uggen et al., 2020) (The Sentencing Project, 2015). In 2020, there were an estimated 5.17 million disenfranchised people due to a felony conviction. Moreover, one out of every 44 adults (2.2% of the U.S. voting-eligible population) is disenfranchised because of a current or previous felony conviction (Uggen et al., 2020).

The Black community is particularly hard hit by felony disenfranchisement. One in 16 Black people of voting age is disenfranchised because of a felony conviction, which is 3.7 times greater than that of the non-Black voting age population (Uggen et al., 2020). Indeed, over 6.2% of the adult Black population is disenfranchised compared to 1.7% of the non-Black population (Uggen et al., 2020). Significant in the disenfranchisement rates of Black people is the state of residence. In six states—Alabama, Florida, Kentucky, Mississippi, Virginia, and Wyoming—a little more than one in seven Black people is disenfranchised, a number twice the national average for Black people (Uggen et al., 2020). As of 2020, these are six of the nine states in the union where a post-sentence waiting period or additional action (e.g., a pardon from the governor) is required for franchise restoration (National Conference of State Legislators, 2020).

The Hispanic community is also hard hit by felony disenfranchisement, with a conservative estimate that some 560,000 Hispanics (2% of the eligible voting population) are disenfranchised. Furthermore, there are approximately 1.2 million (a little over one-fifth of the total disenfranchised population) women who are disenfranchised (Uggen et al., 2020).

Welfare Benefits

Section 115 of the Personal Responsibility and Work Opportunity Reconciliation Act (PRWORA) of 1996 permanently disqualifies any individual with a drug-related felony conviction from receiving Temporary Aid to Needy Families (TANF). The only exception to this is if the individual's state of residence has passed legislation opting out of or modifying drug felony disqualification (McCarty et al., 2015).

As of 2019, only ten states, down from 15 in 2015, fully implement PRWORA's drug-felony disqualification requirement. The other states have either passed legislation opting out of the PRWORA's drug felony disqualification requirement or modifying the disqualification to allow individuals with a drug-related felony conviction to receive TANF if they meet specific requirements (Quinn, 2019).

As well as TANF, the PRWORA also permanently disqualifies any individual with a drug-related felony conviction from participating in the Supplemental Nutrition Assistance Program (SNAP). The only exception to this is if the individual's state of residence has passed legislation opting out of or modifying drug felony disqualification (McCarty et al., 2015). As of 2019, only South Carolina has a lifetime ban. Twenty-five states have passed legislation modifying the requirement, and 24 have passed legislation opting out of the requirement (Polkey, 2019).

Housing

For felony convictions in general, the U.S. Department of Housing and Urban Development (HUD) gives local housing authorities a great deal of discretion in deciding whether to provide housing assistance to formerly incarcerated drug offenders. However, if the drug-related felony conviction is for methamphetamine production on the premises of federally assisted housing, no discretion is allowed. In fact, HUD mandates automatic denial of the application, as well as permanent disqualification from participation in the Section 8 voucher program (McCarty et al., 2015).

Higher Education Financial Assistance

A person convicted of any federal or state law involving the possession or sale of drugs for conduct that occurred during a period of enrollment for which a person was receiving federal aid is ineligible to receive federal student grants, loans, or work assistance for higher education. The ineligibility period varies depending on whether the person has committed a first, second, or third offense. An individual can regain eligibility by completing a drug rehabilitation program with certain criteria and passing "two unannounced drug tests," or if the conviction is set aside or reversed (U.S. Commission on Civil Rights, 2019).

Effects of Mass Incarceration on Children and Families

Mass incarceration's social inequalities are not borne by the currently or formerly incarcerated alone; their children and families are also affected. These are children and families for whom financial instability and material hardships were present even before parental incarceration, be it father or mother. For example, in 2017–2018, 26% of Native American children (61,083) under the age of 18 had a parent who had served time or was serving time in jail or prison, followed by 13% of Black children (1,206,132), 7% of Hispanic children (1,177,827), and 6% of White children (2,259,898) (Kids Count Data Center, 2020).

For these children, parental incarceration has several adverse effects on their general well-being. Primary among these effects is that they are less likely to receive economic support from their fathers than similar children whose fathers have not been in prison or jail (Geller et al., 2006, 2011). They are also less likely to be in regular contact with their fathers during incarceration and only sporadically when released (Geller et al., 2006, 2011).

For the family as a whole, parental incarceration diminishes household income. Typically, once a parent is incarcerated, family income drops by at least 22% below its level 12 months before incarceration. Moreover, even in the 12 months after being released, family income remains 15% lower than 12 months before incarceration (Western & Pettit, 2010). Also strained by incarceration are parental relationships, which may be affected by sporadic contact and the tension of financial struggle (Geller et al., 2011).

Finally, for mothers, 68% of whom lived with a minor child or children before incarceration, maintaining or reconnecting with children is often compromised either because of the number of years served or the children's placement in foster care (Glaze & Maruschak, 2008).

The Road to Racial and Ethnic Disparities in Incarceration

Although mass incarceration is a fact of life in the contemporary United States, it has not always been the case and certainly was not characteristic of the nation's history with incarceration (Pager, 2007). Moreover, although Blacks have always been disproportionally incarcerated, historically it was nowhere near the rate it is today and has been for most of the past 35 years. So how did we get to where we are today?

An increasing number of social theorists and academics have located the genesis of mass incarceration in the United States and the resulting racial and ethnic disparities in the late 1960s with the conservative backlash against the civil rights gains and Great Society programs of the President Lyndon Johnson era (Haney-Lopez, 2010). This ideological backlash blamed the civil rights gains of Blacks and Great Society programs for creating a permissive society in which dependency, dysfunction, and crime were rife, most particularly in inner city communities of color. President Nixon declared in his presidential campaign in 1968 that what was needed to redress the dysfunctions was law and order. Toward this end, Nixon argued, "Doubling the conviction rate in this country would do more to cure crime in America than quadrupling the funds for Hubert Humphrey's war on poverty" (Parenti, 1999, p. 8). Once in office, in the wake of urban unrest and protest in the major urban centers of America, President Nixon sought to follow through on his law and order platform in which he linked race and lawlessness. In doing so, he used coded appeals to the racial fears of White America and argued for the need to be tough on crime (Haney-Lopez, 2010; Parenti, 1999). Much as it is today, "tough on crime" was the not-so-subtle code for the need to bring law and order to communities of color, most specifically economically disadvantaged Black and Hispanic urban communities (Haney-Lopez, 2010; Parenti, 1999).

However, President Nixon and his administration had to first contend with the fact that the federal government had little legal authority to deal directly with street crime outside of Washington, D.C. The Nixon administration resolved this dilemma by shifting their law and order focus away from street crime and placing it on drug control, which the federal government did have responsibility for (Nixon, 1971). On June 17, 1971, in a special message to Congress about drug abuse prevention and control, President Nixon declared that drug abuse had assumed the dimensions of a national emergency. It was an emergency, President Nixon argued, that threatened to destroy American families and communities and needed a full-scale coordinated attack from the federal government (Nixon, 1971). To this end, President Nixon asked and got from Congress an amended budget that included an additional $155 million, making a total of $371 million, for a three-pronged "war on drugs" (Nixon, 1971). These three prongs were the rehabilitation of drug users, harsh law enforcement measures that tightened the noose around the necks of drug dealers, and the coordination of a single government agency to halt the supply side of drugs by striking at the producers and traffickers beyond America's borders (Nixon, 1971). One of the consequences of President Nixon's war on drugs was not just the increase in rehabilitation services for drug users but also the increase in drug-related incarceration.

Accompanying these increases was the gradual shift at both the federal and state level from the indeterminate sentencing model, which was rehabilitative in purpose and had prevailed for much of the 20th century, to a determinant model that constrained judicial discretion and whose objective was harsh punishment (Mauer, 2006). The earliest and until very recently still one of the harshest examples of this at the state level was New York's Rockefeller Drug Laws. Adopted in 1973 as part of New York's war on drugs, the law called for a 15-year prison term for anyone convicted of selling two ounces or possessing four ounces of narcotics, regardless of the offender's criminal history (Mauer, 2006).

In short order, the years between 1970 and 1980 saw the prison population of America, which from 1920 to 1970 had remained relatively stable and always fewer than 200,000, gradually increase to 481,616 by 1985 (Justice Policy Institute, 2000; Mauer, 2006; Minor-Harper & Marbrook, 1986; see Figure 10.2).

As dramatic as this increase was, however, it would pale in comparison to the subsequent wars on drugs and crime. These wars were waged first by President Ronald Reagan in the 1980s and then by President Bill Clinton in the 1990s. The declared wars were prompted by a confluence of events, all of which occurred in the years between the mid-1980s and early 1990s. These events included the emergence and proliferation of crack cocaine; high rates of violent, often drug-related crime; and concern about a penal system that

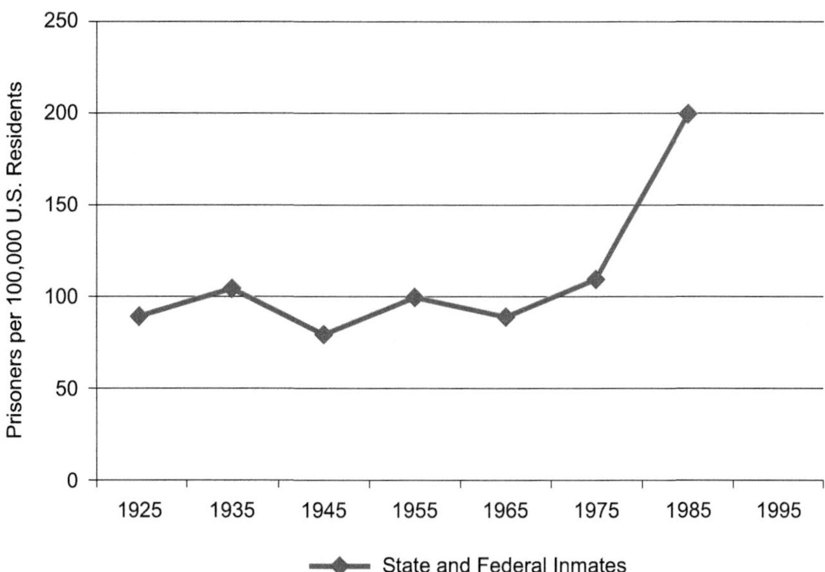

Figure 10.2 Change in Prison Population by Decade, 1920–1985
Source: Bureau of Justice Statistics, National Prisoner Statistics (various years)

was perceived as not properly protecting the public against dangerous criminals (Austin et al., 2000; Levitt, 2004; *Prison Legal News*, 2003). Notable examples of not protecting the public against dangerous criminals were the random murders of Diane Ballasiotes in 1989 and Polly Klass in 1993 by offenders on parole and in a work-release program, respectively. These high-profile examples made headline news nationally and prompted a public outcry (Austin et al., 2000; *People v. Richard Allen Davis*, 2009; *Prison Legal News*, 2003).

Spurred by the public outcry and demand for safer streets and protection against drugs and violent criminals, federal and state lawmakers in the mid to late 1980s and early 1990s began to enact or update a spate of widely supported get-tough-on-drugs and crime statutes (Austin et al., 2000; Mauer, 2006; *People v. Richard Allen Davis*, 2009; *Prison Legal News*, 2003). In 1986, President Ronald Reagan signed into law the Anti-Drug Abuse Act (P.L. 99–570). Among other things, the act created the framework for mandatory minimum sentencing for federal drug trafficking offenses. In 1988, the Anti-Drug Abuse Act of 1988 (P.L. 100–690) was enacted as an amendment to the Anti-Drug Abuse Act of 1986. The Anti-Drug Abuse Act of 1988 made crack cocaine the only drug with a mandatory minimum sentence for a first offence with simple possession. It also made possession of more than five grams of crack cocaine punishable by a minimum five-year sentence (United States Sentencing Commission, 2015).

In 1992, the U.S. Department of Justice released a report entitled "The Case for More Incarceration." In the report, the then-Attorney General William P. Barr made the argument that not only do prisons work but there was also the need for more of them. He further argued that failure to incarcerate cost money because of the high cost of crime not averted when we fail to incarcerate criminals. Indeed, Barr believed and made the argument in the report that much of the violent crime in America was directly attributable to our failure to sentence violent criminals to prison, as well as our failure when we did send them to prison to keep them beyond a fraction of their sentence. This, Barr suggested, was no longer tolerable and that if need be America would have to build more prisons to accommodate a policy for more incarceration. Also in the report, Barr responded to the growing concerns about the high incarceration rates of young Black men, which had not yet reached its zenith. In his response, Barr suggested that one critical fact was being neglected by this concern: "Black Americans living in inner cities, who are victims of violent crime at far higher rates than whites, and persons who live outside the inner cities would enjoy the benefits of increased incarceration disproportionately" (U.S. Department of Justice, 1992, p. 6). Consequently, while increasing incarceration might result in higher numbers of Black men in prison, it would disproportionately benefit the innocent Black victims of their crimes. This, Barr suggested, should be where the concern lay (U.S. Department of Justice, 1992).

In 1993, Washington became the first state to enact a three strikes law, which imposed a sentence of life imprisonment for a third felony conviction (Austin et al., 2000). By 1996, 24 states and Congress had adopted some form of three strikes (Austin et al., 2000). In 1994, and in keeping with his war on crime stance, President Bill Clinton signed into law the Violent Crime Control and Law Enforcement Act of 1994 (P.L. 103–322), which was arguably the most comprehensive and wide-ranging crime bill in American history. The bill committed $8 billion to prison construction, as well as funding for increasing police forces and increasing victims' rights (U.S. Department of Justice Fact Sheet, 1994). The bill, which President Clinton immodestly described as the toughest and smartest in the history of the United States (Public Papers of the President of the United States, 1994), was the catalyst for growing the prison industrial complex and for-profit incarceration. This was a model that first emerged publicly in 1984 when the Corrections Corporation of America (CCA) was awarded a contract to take over a facility in Hamilton County, Tennessee (Cheung, 2002).

In keeping with an era when media stories of warring drug gangs in economically disadvantaged Black and Hispanic communities proliferated, the enforcement of the get tough on drugs and crime policies were disproportionality concentrated on these communities and more specifically on young Black and Hispanic men with low levels of education (Mauer, 2006; Western & Pettit, 2010). In 1993, Senator Daniel Patrick Moynihan predicted this result when he warned that by choosing policies focused on prohibition of drugs "we are choosing to have an intense crime problem concentrated among minorities" (American Sociological Society, 2007). No surprise then, that between the early 1980s and the mid-1990s, the number of Blacks sent to prison grew at a faster rate than the number of Whites (Cahalan, 1986). The net result was that Blacks as a percentage of all people admitted to state and federal prison increased from 39% to 53% (Beck & Mumola, 1999).

In what became a race to incarcerate, the years between 1995 and 2001 saw quite extraordinary increases in the prison and jail population (Mauer, 2006; Western & Pettit, 2010). By 1995, the prison and jail population had reached 1.7 million, which in just ten years had more than doubled the 1985 population (Gillard & Beck, 1995). By 2001, the incarceration rate would reach 2.1 million. These increases were so steep and dramatic that they bore no historical comparison (Beck & Harrison, 2001; Justice Policy Institute, 2000; Mauer, 2006). Moreover, even as the crime rate began to precipitously decline in the early1990s and throughout the 2000s, the two million plus prison and jail population has been maintained and even increased (Beck & Harrison, 2001; Carson, 2015; Gillard & Beck, 1995; Levitt, 2004; Western, 2006).

As of 2014, even with a 1% decline from 2013, the United States still had an estimated 2.3 million people behind bars (Carson, 2015; see also Figure 10.3). Of this number, Black men had the highest imprisonment rate in every age group and were in state or federal facilities 3.8 to 10.5 times more often than White men and 1.4 to 3.1 times more often than Hispanic men (Carson, 2015). Indeed, such is the level of racial disparity in incarceration that in its Black–White ratio it exceeds disparities in unemployment, nonmarital childbearing, infant mortality, and wealth (Muller, 2012, p. 282). Moreover, if current trends continue, one of every three Black males born in 2001 can expect to go prison in their lifetime, as can one in every six Hispanic males, compared to one of every 17 White males (Bonczar, 2003; The Sentencing Project, 2013). Similarly, for women, as of 2001, if current trends continue, 1 in 19 Black women in their lifetime can expect to spend time behind bars, compared to 1 in 45 Hispanic Women and 1 in 118 White women (Bonczar, 2003; see Figures 10.4 and 10.5).

Legal scholar Michelle Alexander (2010) argues that in its wide-ranging impact on Black men, in particular, mass incarceration is the New Jim Crow in an era of supposed color blindness. Much the same as Jim Crow, Alexander posits that mass incarceration has allowed for the modern day control of Black

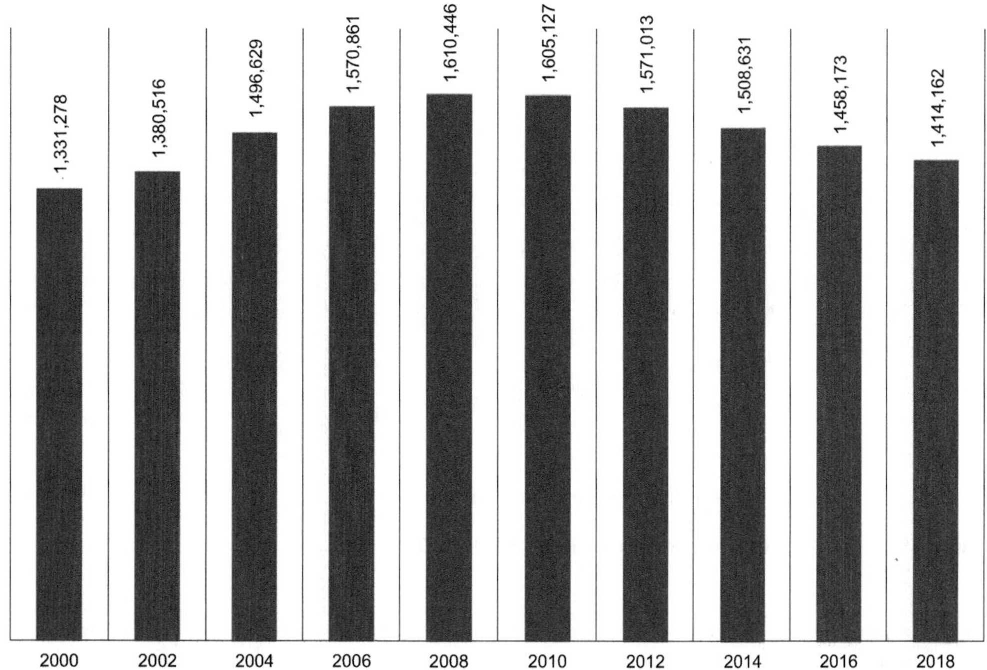

Figure 10.3 U.S. State and Federal Prison Population, 2000–2018

Source: The Sentencing Project (2020). Criminal Justice Facts: U.S. state and federal prison population, 1925–2018. Retrieved from www.sentencingproject.org/criminal-justice-facts/

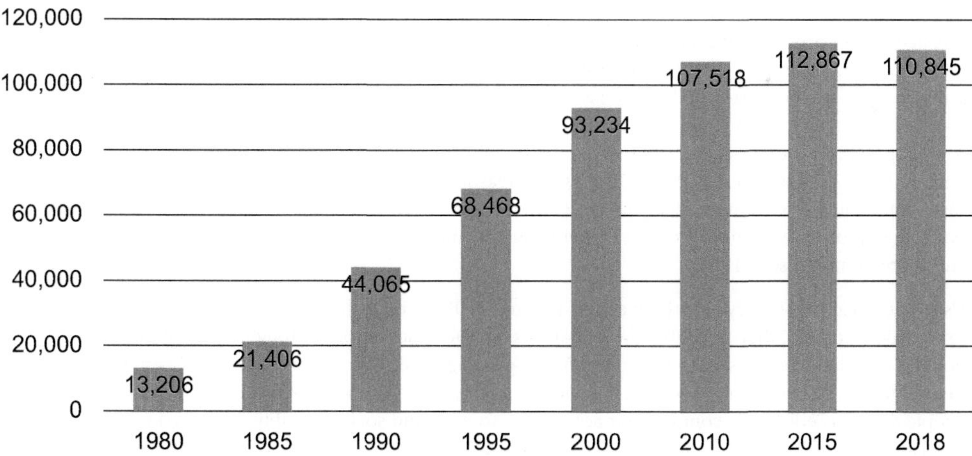

Figure 10.4 Number of Incarcerated Women, 1980–2018

Source: The Sentencing Project. Fact Sheets: Trends in U.S. corrections. Updated August 2020. Retrieved from www.sentencingproject.org/publications/trends-in-u-s-corrections/

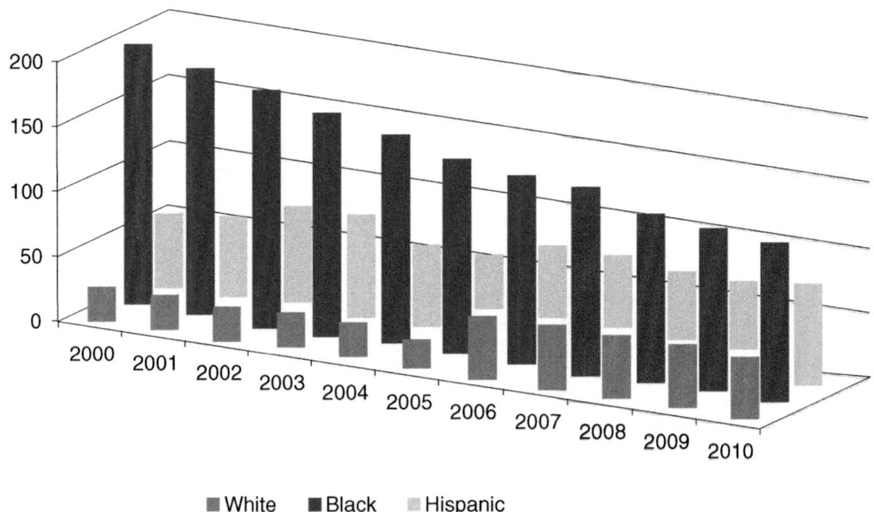

Figure 10.5 Female Incarceration Rate by Race, 2000–2010

men and women in most spheres of their social functioning (Alexander, 2010). As described earlier in the chapter this social control includes the loss of voting rights, and possible access to welfare benefits and funds for higher education, to name just a few ways in which social control is asserted.

Critical Race Theory

Most of the theories of the racial and ethnic disparity in incarceration exist in the realm of differential involvement in the criminal justice system (American Sociological Society, 2007; Mauer, 2011). Simply put, the theories posit that Blacks and Hispanics commit more crimes than Whites and therefore are arrested and incarcerated at higher rates. Indeed, the data do indicate that at every level of the criminal justice system, Blacks and Hispanics are more likely to be arrested than their White counterparts. Once arrested, they are more likely to be processed and convicted. Once convicted, they are more likely to serve a longer prison term even when severity of the offence and criminal history are taken into account (Crow & Johnson, 2008; Durose et al., 2007; Federal Bureau of Investigation, 2009; Kansal, 2005; Mauer, 2011; Spohn, 2000; The Sentencing Project, 2013). The reason Blacks and Hispanics are differentially involved in the criminal justice system has been attributed to a variety of theories, including social isolation; culture of poverty; deviant substructures as represented by gangs; and inequality/deprivation, leading to frustration and aggression (Wilson, 1993).

Using a critical race theory lens, Brewer and Heitzeg (2008) reject the differential involvement explanation. Instead, they posit that the disparities are the function of get-tough-on-drugs and crime policies that have been designed to protect White privilege and its economic and social benefits (p. 625). Central to this disparity are enforcement actions that target and corral large numbers of Black and Hispanic people and thus effectively control their access to resources and social mobility. As argued by Brewer and Heitzeg (2008), using criminal justice policy and law enforcement actions to target and corral large numbers of Blacks is not a new phenomenon; rather, it is the latest in an historically uninterrupted series of legal and political machinations that under the guise of law and order enforce color lines and maintain and protect White privilege and its related benefits, and include the control of Black labor. Historic examples include peonage and convict leasing, both of which are discussed later in this chapter.

As suggested by Brewer and Heitzeg (2008), in today's supposed color-blind meritocracy, get-tough-on-drugs and crime polices and law enforcement actions have none of the racial language of years gone by and are ostensibly race and color neutral. Instead, they have been replaced by a set of codes that describe racialized patterns of alleged crime and actual punishment without ever referring to race. Thus, the dominant narrative shaping the public discourse is not about race, racism, disproportionality, or the lack of resources or opportunity for young Black and Hispanic men and women with low levels of education from economically disadvantaged communities. Rather, it evokes language around fear of crime, criminal gangs, and drug-infested economically disadvantaged urban communities. In doing so, a justification is provided for draconian criminal justice policies and law enforcement actions that disproportionately target young Black and Hispanic men from these communities.

As mentioned earlier, the current tough-on-drugs and crime policies and the racial and ethnic disparities in incarceration are not a new phenomenon for Blacks—they are the latest in the line of policies and practices that have sought to control and diminish Black voting rights and exploit Black labor. These policies and practices, which began in the years immediately following the Civil War, included Black Codes, vagrancy laws, peonage, and convict leasing.

Black Codes, Vagrancy Laws, Peonage, and Convict Leasing

In response to the ratification of the Thirteenth Amendment abolishing slavery in 1865, all the former slave-holding Confederate states and some midwestern states such as Illinois moved quickly to restore the control and economic power of the White majority over the fate of Black Americans. This control was 200 years old and had ensured both White supremacy and the continued supply of free Black labor. To maintain this control after emancipation, all of the southern states, beginning with Mississippi in 1865, enacted a comprehensive body of laws, statutes, and rules most commonly known as Black Codes whose express purpose was to wholly regulate the lives of Black people (Bardolph, 1970). These Black Codes, which only applied to "persons of color" (i.e., anyone with more than one-eighth Negro blood), varied from state to state. Although the codes granted many rights for Blacks that had not been allowed in slavery (e.g., marriage, being a witness in a criminal trial, and the right to sue), they severely restricted others, often leaving Blacks as little more than chattel at the whim of a White employer or the county police or sheriff, who were in charge of ensuring and enforcing Black compliance.

Under the Black Codes, Blacks were denied the right to vote. On specific days of the week they had to prove to the county police or sheriff that they were gainfully employed. Furthermore, they were not allowed to terminate their employment, under the threat of arrest and a fine, before the expiration of the terms of service. If they did, the police and or civil officers were charged with arresting and bringing back to his or her employer any Black who deserted their employment (Blackmon, 2008).

Also contained in all Black Codes were vagrancy laws. These laws stipulated that Blacks who were not gainfully employed and were found congregating together in groups of more than three should be arrested and fined by the sheriff. Any White person willing to pay the fine was entitled to take the person or persons as unpaid labor until the cost of the fine was repaid through labor. This practice, known as peonage, became one of the principal ways Blacks were forced into unpaid labor, more often for terms that were far beyond the debt incurred from their fine (Blackmon, 2008). Other ways in which the Black Codes fed peonage were prohibitions on Blacks keeping or carrying firearms, ammunition, or a bowie knife, committing riots, cruel treatment to animals, disturbance of the peace, foul language, vending intoxicating liquors, practicing as a minister without a license, and making insulting gestures, to name just a few offenses. All of these offenses came with an arrest and fine. Although the responsibility for arrests were those of police officers or civil officers, the Black Codes gave all White citizens the right to act as a police officer for the detection of offenses and the apprehension of offenders, to be handed over to the proper authority. Indeed, so wide ranging and arbitrary were the offenses that Blacks, men in particular, could be arrested and fined for almost anything outside a very narrow band of activities (Blackmon, 2008).

The net result of the Black Codes was the control of Blacks in almost every sphere of life. It also set the precedent by way of its singular focus on Blacks in general and Black men in particular for criminalizing Blackness on the grounds of minor infractions. This in turn became the mechanism for corralling, controlling, and then compelling Blacks to work in a labor economy based on debt or imprisonment, peonage, and convict leasing (Blackmon, 2008).

Peonage and Convict Leasing

Peonage, also called debt slavery or debt servitude, is a system in which an employer compels a worker to pay off a debt with work (Blackmon, 2008; Mancini, 1978). As suggested by Blackmon (2008), in the American South between 1868 and 1921 its practice was slavery by another name and in many cases worse. As noted earlier, it was fueled and supplied by the arbitrary arrests and high fines that indebted tens of thousands of Blacks, who with no means to pay these debts were leased into involuntary servitude until they paid off their debt. They were often leased by farmers and worked long hours at hard labor while receiving no or very little in cash compensation. In reality, few earned enough to pay off what they owed, and were often reduced to a lifetime of servitude. Harsh punishment, including beatings, whippings, and sometimes death were not uncommon.

Although Congress outlawed peonage in 1867, the practice remained for another 50 years as the local police and courts often turned a blind eye to its presence or aided the practice (Daniel, 1972; Freeman, 1999). In the fall, for example, when it was time to pick cotton, large numbers of Black people were arrested in all of the growing cotton counties to ensure a supply of labor. There were similar surges in arrests of Black people in counties in Alabama in the days before labor agents from the coal mines came to pick up whatever county convicts were available. In these surges, local officials often arrested Blacks on false pretenses (Blackmon, 2008).

It was not until 1921 and the Williams and Manning trial in Jasper County, Georgia, for the murders of between four and 12 Blacks in service did peonage come to a halt. John S. Williams was the owner of a farm that used Black debt labor (Daniel, 1972; Freeman, 1999). He was known to be brutal to his charges and had murdered a number of them for minor infractions. One of them, Gus Chapman, escaped from the Williams farm and reported his conditions to the local authorities. After being questioned by the FBI, Williams became concerned about being convicted of the outlawed peonage, so he decided to get rid of any evidence, namely the Blacks in his charge. Williams decided the only way not to be implicated was to kill the evidence. Williams did this by soliciting the help of one of his farmhands, Clyde Manning, and murdering 11 Black charges (Freeman, 1999). Williams and Manning were arrested, charged, and convicted of the murders, for which they were sentenced to life imprisonment. The nationwide publicity of the cruelty of peonage and the treatment of peons effectively ended its practices (Daniel, 1972; Freeman, 1999).

However, the closely related convict leasing, which paralleled peonage in most all respects other than the debt aspect, would have a longer tender and would prove every bit as brutal as peonage. Simply put, convict leasing was a system of penal labor. It was practiced almost exclusively in the southern states and was established by provisional and military governments in the years following the Civil War more as an experiment than a permanent institution. The first convict leasing occurred in Georgia in 1868 when 100 Black convicts were leased to work on the Alabama and Georgia railroads (Blackmon, 2008; Mancini, 1978). Like peonage, the practice of convict leasing was fueled and supplied by Black men and women who had been arrested, charged, convicted, and imprisoned on the most arbitrary of charges (Blackmon, 2008; Mancini, 1978). Leasing convict labor were coal mines, railroads, farm plantations, quarries, farms, lumber camps, and small-town entrepreneurs (Blackmon, 2008).

It its practice, convict leasing was beneficial for everyone involved other than the convicts themselves who served on chain gangs. Like slavery, the convicts were worked hard and brutally treated. Unlike slavery, however, the leasers of convicts had very little personal investment in them and so there was little concern for their welfare. If a convict died or was incapacitated, the leaser could get another one cheaply and easily (Mancini, 1978). In fact, it is estimated that at least 9,000 convict workers were murdered or died of natural causes over the decades of the convict leasing system (Blackmon, 2008).

For the cash-strapped southern states after the Civil War, convict leasing relieved them of the burden of the expenses for thousands of prisoners and soon became a vital source of revenue. For the leasers, it provided a large pool of cheap labor. For the South in general, it permitted the easy exploitation of natural resources, and it helped to attract northern capital. As such, convict leasing, even with its racist practice and poor treatment of convicts, had both a social and economic justification in the South (Mancini, 1978). Indeed, as historian Blackmon (2008) suggested, it was brutal in a social sense, but fiendishly rational in an economical sense.

No surprise, then, that what started as an experiment soon became a permanent structural feature in the South. Over time, a few striking features emerged related to convict leasing. One of them was that the convict leasing population became gradually younger and almost entirely Black. Indeed, by the time convict leasing reached its zenith in 1896, half the convict populations were minors. Moreover, there was a trend toward increased arrests, convictions, and prison terms, as well as longer sentences. In fact, by the end of the 1800s, the southern convict population had increased by tenfold from the end of the Civil War in 1865 (Mancini, 1978).

Although profitable, convict leasing was not without its critics, as many called for its prohibition. The main focus of the call for prohibition was its brutality and exploitation of the primarily Black convict population. Yet, much like the contemporary call for sentencing reform, the demise of convict leasing was not the result of a surge of consternation from the public about its brutality; rather, it was the function of its diminishing returns of the course of the decades it was in place. By the early 20th century it cost more to run and maintain the program than the profit it was making. Also, as Jim Crow became firmly entrenched as the premier all-encompassing mechanism for ensuring White supremacy and access to resources by way of the total control of Black lives, the need for convict labor was superseded and gradually diminished (Mancini, 1978).

As suggested earlier, both peonage and convict leasing and the criminal justice policies that informed them established precedents for using incarceration to subjugate large numbers of Blacks. Once subjugated, much like slavery and Jim Crow, they had few or no rights and were subject to disenfranchisement and economic and social marginalization. Most troubling with these practices, certainly in the case of peonage and convict leasing, is that the Thirteenth Amendment, which ended slavery, ironically allows for involuntary servitude as punishment for a crime when a person has been duly convicted.

Social Work and Criminal Justice Advocacy

From the beginning of its emergence as a distinct profession in the late 19th century, social work has had a deep involvement with the criminal justice field, both at the adult and juvenile level (Maschi & Killian, 2011; Peters, 2011; Reamer, 2004; Roberts & Springer, 2007). For example, paralleling the efforts of the Black child savers who helped to reform the juvenile justice system, social work pioneers such as Julia Lathrop, Jane Addams, Lucy Flower, and Edith and Grace Abbot were instrumental in the establishment of the first juvenile justice court in the United States in 1899 (Maschi & Killian, 2011; Peters, 2011; Ward, 2012).

They were also pivotal in prompting the adult criminal justice system of the early 20th century to adopt a commitment to rehabilitation of adult prisoners. In keeping with this effort, there was also advocacy for humane conditions of confinement for adult prisoners, as well as the establishment of casework services for offenders delivered by either correctional treatment specialists or social workers (Maschi & Killian, 2011).

In the 1940s, 50s, and 60s social workers had an integral role in the development of community-based councils and programs for delinquency prevention, as well as a significant practice presence in probation, correctional facilities, parole service, and the court system (Peters, 2011; Reamer, 2004; Roberts & Springer, 2007; Roberts, 2010).

It is not surprising, then, given this history and social work's core value of social justice advocacy on behalf of the oppressed and vulnerable, that the National Association of Social Workers issued a policy statement recognizing the importance of providing quality social work interventions to the incarcerated population (National Association of Social Workers, 2008). In doing so, it pledged its support for ongoing advocacy to address issues surrounding the disproportionate rates of incarceration of racial and ethnic minorities. It also supports advocacy for safe, humane, and equitable treatment for all incarcerated individuals, educational and vocational opportunities to assist the transition from prison to the community, and research to identify effective alternatives to incarceration.

Additionally, in partnership with other organizations, the NASW has been a consistent voice in advocating for major changes to the criminal justice system; a system that the NASW suggests has failed to distinguish between dangerous criminals and nonviolent men and women in its sentencing practices (Wilson, 2010). The NASW has also commended and supported former Attorney General Eric Holder and the Department of Justice's (DOJ) Smart on Crime initiative. Among other things, the initiative proposed the end of mandatory minimum sentencing for nonviolent drug offenders and prioritizes alternate sentencing, such as drug rehabilitation programs (Wilson, 2010). Along with this support, the NASW has published several social justice briefings, the most recent of which calls for policies and programs that address over-incarceration by diverting low-level drug offenders from prison to treatment-oriented alternatives (National Association of Social Workers, 2013, 2018).

Chapter Summary

Even with crime rates at historically low rates in most of the nation's major cities, America's incarcerated population remains at above two million. This number is not just the largest in the world, but is also unprecedented in American history. Even with wars, economic downturns, and periodic rises in the crime rate, America never incarcerated more than 200,000 people in a single year until President Nixon's politically motivated "war on drugs" in the early 1970s. It was a war that linked criminality and race and set in motion three and half decades of harsh get-tough-on-drugs and crime policies that had conservative and liberal policy makers alike scrambling to be seen as the toughest on crime. The result of these policies was that from the 1980s through to the early 1990s there was a steep climb in the incarcerated population, an increase that could only be partially attributed to the crime rate. Then, and has been the case since the early 1990s through to the present day, the rise and maintenance of the mass incarceration and its racial disparities are almost wholly attributable to the tough drug and crime policies (Schmitt et al., 2010).

Over the past decade, conservative and liberal policy makers alike have begun to retreat from the tough-on-drugs and crime policies, as the cost of mass incarceration has become increasingly prohibitive on the federal, state, and local levels. In 2018, incarcerating individuals in federal prison cost taxpayers $5.8 billion, excluding the cost of things such as health care and solitary confinement. In 2015, it cost taxpayers $43 billion to incarcerate individuals in state prisons (Spengler, 2020). This was almost four times the amount spent in 1982.

Now, after decades of advocacy by grassroots sentencing reform groups and organizations such as the ACLU, the Sentencing Project, Families against Mandatory Minimums, and the Drug Policy Alliance, the conversation is about race-neutral sentencing reform and discontinuing practices such as three strikes and mandatory minimum sentencing. Indeed, since 2000, 28 states have, in some way, amended their mandatory minimum sentencing laws to lessen its severity (Families against Mandatory Minimums, 2013). Of these states, Rhode Island, in 2009, and Montana, in 2017, have gone as far as to repeal all mandatory minimum sentencing laws for drug offenses (Families against Mandatory Minimums, 2017). Previously, drug offenders in Rhode Island received 10- and 20-year sentences, even for possession offenses, along with $10,000 and $25,000 fines (Families against Mandatory Minimums, 2017). In 2009, the New York state legislature enacted comprehensive drug policy reforms that repealed most mandatory minimum sentences for drug offenses. In doing so, it restored a judge's authority to send drug offenders to treatment programs rather than jail (NYCLU, 2009), thus ending the Rockefeller Drug Law, arguably the harshest drug law in the nation (NYCLU, 2009). In 2014, the California state legislature passed the California Fair Sentencing Act, which ensured that people convicted of certain offenses involving crack would no longer receive harsher punishments than people found guilty of the same crimes involving the powder form of the drug (Knafo, 2015).

Relatedly, an increasing number of states and the District of Columbia (D.C.) are beginning to enact policies ending the collateral consequences of convictions. These consequences undermine the ability to participate in the community following a conviction. And as such limits both economic and life opportunities for the formerly incarcerated. One of these consequences, as discussed earlier, is felony disenfranchisement. In 2020, Washington D.C. officials authorized universal suffrage through the passage of the B23–0324, the Restore the Vote Amendment (Council of the District of Columbia, 2020). In doing so, the District of Columbia joined Maine, Vermont, and Puerto Rico in the elimination of felony disenfranchisement (Porter, 2021). In 2020, California's voters overwhelmingly expanded voting rights by approving the Proposition 17 ballot measure. The measure allows voting rights for citizens in the community under parole supervision (LAO, 2020). In doing so, California joined Colorado, New Jersey, Nevada, and New York who had already adopted this policy (Porter, 2021). On August 5, 2020, Iowa Governor Kim Reynolds signed Executive Order 7, restoring the voting rights of thousands of Iowans who had completed their felony sentences (Reynolds, 2020). In signing the order, Reynolds vowed to keep fighting for a state constitutional amendment to make restoring rights a state law (Reynolds, 2020).

Another significant reform effort at the state level in recent years is "ban the box" (also referred to as fair-chance hiring) legislation. Simply put, the legislation provides formerly incarcerated job applicants a fair chance at employment by removing the conviction history question on a job application and delaying the background check inquiry until later in the hiring process (Rodriguez & Mehta, 2015). As of 2018, 35 states, the District of Columbia, and over 150 cities and counties have adopted ban-the-box policies (Alliance, 2020).

The federal government has also been active in reform efforts. In 2010, President Obama signed into law significant criminal justice system reform with the Fair Sentencing Act of 2010 (P.L. 111–220). The act reduced the disparity between the amount of crack cocaine and powder cocaine needed to trigger specific United States federal criminal penalties from a 100:1 weight ratio to an 18:1 weight ratio. It also eliminated the five-year mandatory minimum sentencing for simple possession of crack cocaine (Congress.gov, 2010).

Furthermore, in July 2015, President Obama granted clemency to 46 men and women who had spent years and faced decades in prison for nonviolent drug offenses. The 46 commutations were the most granted by a president in a single day since the Lyndon Johnson administration in the 1960s (Jackson & Korte, 2015).

Finally, and also in July 2015, President Obama asked Attorney General Loretta Lynch to review the overuse of solitary confinement in American prisons. On January 25, 2016, a White House press release announced that as a result of recommendations made in a Department of Justice report, President Obama would have the Bureau of Prisons adopt the report's guiding principles for best practices in federal prisons (The White House, Office of the Press Secretary, 2016). These guiding principles, of which there are more than 50, includes some of the following:

- Inmates should be housed in the least restrictive setting necessary.
- Correctional systems should always be able to clearly articulate the specific reason(s) for an inmate's placement and retention in restrictive housing, which should be supported by objective evidence.
- An inmate's initial and ongoing placement in restrictive housing should be regularly reviewed by a multi-disciplinary committee, including mental health and medical professionals.

(U.S. Department of Justice, 2016)

The guidelines also recommended the end of the practice of placing juveniles in restrictive housing in federal prisons, pursuant to the standards proposed in the Sentence Reform and Corrections Act of 2015 (U.S. Department of Justice, 2016).

In 2016, President Obama signed into law the Comprehensive Addiction and Recovery Act (P.L. 114–198) (see Box 10.1 Criminal Justice Timeline for details). And in 2018, President Trump signed into law the First Step Act—formally known as the Formerly Incarcerated Reenter Society Transformed Safely Transitioning Every Person Act (P.L. 115–391) (James, 2019) (see Box 10.1 Timeline for details).

Another encouraging federal government development for criminal justice reform is H.R.7194—Mandatory Minimum Reform Act of 2020. Sponsored by Representative Maxine Walters, the bill was introduced in the House of Representatives on June 11, 2020. The bill seeks to eliminate mandatory minimum sentences for all drug offenses (H.R.7194, 2020). Only time will tell if the bill becomes law and how the many proposed reforms will play out. Still, it is a step in the right direction; albeit a long-overdue step considering the carnage that has been visited on economically disadvantaged Black and Hispanics because of the war on drugs and crime. Indeed, in July of 2015, in an address at a convention of the NAACP, former President Bill Clinton admitted publicly that his anticrime legislation in 1994 played a significant role in distorting sentencing standards and leading to an era of mass incarceration. He went on to say that the legislation, which he had long considered one of his crowning achievements, went too far by sending even minor criminals to prison for far too long (Baker, 2015).

Retrieval Questions

1. What are some of the factors that contributed to the rise in incarceration rates between 1980 and 2001?
2. How have the racial and ethnic disparities in incarceration transformed social inequality for young, economically disadvantaged Black and Hispanic men with low levels of education?
3. What are some of the labor market effects of incarceration?
4. What are some of the civil penalties that attach to a felony drug conviction?
5. What are some of the effects of incarceration on children and families?
6. What were some of the "war on drugs" and crime policies enacted in the 1990s?
7. What was peonage?
8. What was convict leasing?
9. Since 2000, how many states have passed legislation amending their mandatory minimum sentencing laws?

Discussion Questions

1. Identify and discuss some of the social justice issues pertinent to the current racial and ethnic disparities in incarceration.
2. As policy practitioners, what responsibility do social workers have to advocate and support criminal justice system reform?
3. Identify and discuss some of the potential practice challenges when working with clients who are involved with the criminal justice system.
4. How might the racial and ethnic disparities in incarceration effect the social work practice context?

Box 10.1 Criminal Justice System Timeline, 1629–Present

1629: The Massachusetts Bay Colony establishes the first court in North America (ProQuest, 2011).

1861: While serving as a warden at the Detroit House of Correction and the Elmira Reformatory, Zebulon Brockway implemented the concept of indeterminate sentencing, or parole. Brockway lobbies the New York Prisons Association to abandon time sentences for reformative ones that focus on rewarding inmates with shortened sentences upon evidence of reform. Parole remains an integral part of the criminal justice system. According to the Bureau of Justice Statistics, as of 2011, seven million adults (2.9% of the population) were under some form of adult correctional supervision (ProQuest, 2011).

1920: Pacifist and author Roger Nash Baldwin, feminist lawyer Crystal Eastman, and law professor Walter Nelles create The American Civil Liberties Union (ACLU), a nonprofit, nonpartisan organization. The stated purpose of the ACLU is to defend the constitutional rights and liberties of all Americans. The ACLU was formed as a reaction to the Palmer Raids, when the government, in the form of the FBI, simultaneously arrested thousands of antiwar protesters who J. Edgar Hoover and Attorney General A. Mitchell Palmer suspected of being anarchists and radicals. After being questioned and held without charge without legal representation, the FBI begins deporting non-U.S. citizens (ProQuest, 2011).

1942: President Franklin D. Roosevelt signs Executive Order 9066 (P.L. 503) into law. The order authorizes the evacuation of all persons deemed a threat to national security from the West Coast to relocation centers further inland. At no time did the order use the words "Japanese" or "Japanese American," but the order is primarily directed against them. The order effectively sends 122,000 Japanese-American men, women, and children to internment camps for the duration of World War II. Seventy thousand of those sent to internment are American citizens. The internment camps are fenced, guarded, and located in remote areas in six western states and Arkansas. The government makes no charges against the interns, nor do interns have the right to appeal their incarceration (Executive Order 9066, 1942).

1944: In *Korematsu v. United States*, the U.S. Supreme Court rules that the wartime internment of Japanese-Americans was constitutional (Executive Order 9066, 1942).

1963: In *Gideon v. Wainwright*, the U.S. Supreme Court rules that all defendants accused of crimes have the right to legal representation at the expense of the state (ProQuest, 2011).

1966: In *Miranda v. Arizona*, the Supreme Court rules that all persons accused of a crime must be informed of their constitutional rights, including the right against self-incrimination and the right to an attorney (ProQuest, 2011).

1967: President Lyndon Johnson signs into law the Law Enforcement and Criminal Justice Assistance Act of 1967 (P.L. 90–351), more commonly known as the Omnibus Crime Bill. The act establishes the Law Enforcement Assistance Administration (LEAA). The LEAA, which is later superseded by the Office of Justice Programs, provides research grants to states to develop alternative sanctions for young offenders. It also provides funding to assist local law enforcement to deal with riot control and organized crime. The act also expands the FBI, sets guidelines for obtaining wiretaps, and prohibits the interstate trade of guns (ProQuest, 2011).

1970: President Richard Nixon unveils the "war on drugs," a federal effort to fight drug use and trafficking (ProQuest, 2011).

1972: The National Crime Victimization Survey, administered by the Bureau of Justice Statistics, is established. This survey measures crimes committed against specific victims and includes crimes that were not reported to police (ProQuest, 2011).

1972: In *Furman v. Georgia*, the Supreme Court rules 5–4 on June 29, 1972, that in all cases before the court, the death penalty as administered violated the Eighth and Fourteenth Amendments (ProQuest, 2011).

1976: The Supreme Court reaffirmed the constitutionality of capital punishment for aggravated murder in the July 2, 1976, 7–2 decision in *Gregg v. Georgia* (ProQuest, 2011).

1984: President Reagan signs into law the Comprehensive Crime Control Act Sentencing Reform Act (P.L. 98–473). Among its provisions are increased federal penalties for cultivation, possession, or transfer of marijuana; reinstatement of the federal death penalty; abolishing federal parole; and by way of the Sentencing Reform Act increasing consistency on federal sentencing (United States Sentencing Commission, 2015).

1986: In *Ford v. Wainwright*, 1986, the U.S. Supreme Court holds in a 5–4 vote that the execution of an insane prisoner is an unconstitutional violation of the Eighth Amendment prohibition of cruel and unusual punishment (ProQuest, 2011)

1986: President Reagan signs the Anti-Drug Abuse Act of 1986 (P.L. 99–570) into law (ProQuest, 2011).

1988: President Reagan signs the Anti-Drug Abuse Act of 1988 (P.L. 100–690) into law (ProQuest, 2011).

1989: The first drug court in the U.S. is established in Miami (ProQuest, 2011).

1994: California passes a three-strikes law requiring third-time violent felony offenders to serve 25-years-to-life sentences in prison (ProQuest, 2011).

1994: Congress passes and President Bill Clinton signs into law the Violent Crime Control Act and Law Enforcement Act of 1994 (P.L. 103–322). Originally written by Senator Joe Biden (D-DE), the bipartisan act is the largest and most comprehensive crime bill in the history of the United States. Among its provisions is the congressional appropriation of $9.7 billion for the funding of prisons. It includes new and stiffer penalties for violent and drug trafficking crimes committed by gang members. It authorizations adult prosecution of minors 13 and older charged with certain serious violent crimes, and the enactment of three-strikes mandatory life imprisonment without possibility of parole for federal offenders with three or more convictions for serious violent felonies or drug trafficking crimes (U.S. Department of Justice Fact Sheet, 1994). There are also a number of provisions for victims of sexual, domestic, or other violent acts, as well as the requirement that states enact statutes or regulations requiring sexually violent offenders be registered (U.S. Department of Justice Fact Sheet, 1994).

1994: New Jersey Legislature enacts Megan's Law. The law requires community notification when a sex offender is scheduled to be released (ProQuest, 2011).

1995: The U.S. Sentencing Commission recommends that Congress revisit mandatory minimums, especially the discrepancy between crack and powder cocaine. Congress overrides the recommendation (ProQuest, 2011).

1996: President Clinton signs the Anti-Terrorism and Effective Death Penalty Act (P.L. 104–132) into law. The law adds new federal crimes to the list of those punishable by death (ProQuest, 2011).

2000: California passes Proposition 21, the Gang Violence and Juvenile Crime Prevention Act. The law expands criminal penalties for youths. It also extends the legal definition of gang affiliation, and lowers the age at which youths can be charged and prosecuted as adults to 14 (ProQuest, 2011).

2001: President George W. Bush signs the USA Patriot Act. The act allows law enforcement agencies to use court-approved wiretaps on suspected terrorists, share criminal investigative information with counterterrorism investigators and other government officials, and work with other government agencies with the aim of securing U.S. borders and attacking international money laundering (ProQuest, 2011).

2002: The total U.S. prison population exceeds two million for the first time (ProQuest, 2011).

2008: The Second Chance Act (P.L. 110–199) is introduced by Representative Danny Davis and later signed into law by President George Bush. This legislation, the first of its kind, authorizes $362 million in federal grants to government agencies and nonprofit organizations to provide support strategies and services designed to reduce recidivism by improving outcomes for people returning from prisons, jails, and juvenile facilities (The Justice Center, 2015).

2009: In a 5–4 decision, the Supreme Court rules in the District Attorney's Office for the *Third Judicial District el al. v. Osborne* case that prisoners have no constitutional right to DNA testing that might prove their innocence (ProQuest, 2011).

2010: The Fair Sentencing Act of 2010 (P.L. 111–220) is introduced by Representative Bobby Scott, is adopted, and signed by President Obama. The act reduces the disparity in sentencing for crack and powder cocaine convictions (Congress.gov, 2010).

2010: The Supreme Court rules that investigators may resume questioning a suspect who invokes his Miranda right to a lawyer after the suspect has been out of police custody for 14 days. The 7–2 decision scales back a 1981 Supreme Court decision intended to protect suspects from police badgering to talk and to safeguard the rights established in the 1966 *Miranda v. Arizona* ruling (ProQuest, 2011).

2011: The Supreme Court rules in *Michigan v. Bryant* that statements made to authorities during an emergency can be introduced later as evidence in a criminal trial—even if the person who made the statements dies prior to the trial (ProQuest, 2011).

2011: The Supreme Court rules in *Skinner v. Switzer* that a death row inmate can try to gain access to DNA evidence that might prove his innocence (ProQuest, 2011).

2011: The Supreme Court rules that prisoners have no constitutional right to parole (ProQuest, 2011).

2013: Attorney General Eric Holder launches the Smart on Crime Initiative, which is a comprehensive review of the criminal justice system in order to identify reforms that would ensure federal laws are enforced more fairly and—in an era of reduced budgets—more efficiently. Five goals were identified as a part of this review:

1. To ensure finite resources are devoted to the most important law enforcement priorities.
2. To promote fairer enforcement of the laws and alleviate disparate impacts of the criminal justice system.
3. To ensure just punishments for low-level, nonviolent convictions.
4. To bolster prevention and reentry efforts to deter crime and reduce recidivism.
5. To strengthen protections for vulnerable populations (U.S. Department of Justice, 2013).

2015: The bipartisan Sentencing Reform and Corrections Act of 2015 is introduced in the Senate. The bill's key provision includes the elimination of three-strikes mandatory life provision, reduction (not elimination) of mandatory minimum sentencing for almost all crimes, and limits solitary confinement for juveniles in federal custody, to name but a few (United States Senate Committee on the Judiciary, 2015).

2016: President Obama signed into the law the Comprehensive Addiction and Recovery Act (P.L. 114–198). The act is the first major federal addiction legislation in 40 years. It is a comprehensive and coordinated effort to address the opioid epidemic, and encompasses prevention, treatment, recovery, law enforcement, criminal justice reform, and overdose reversal (P.L. 114–198).

2018: President Trump signed into law the First Step Act—formally known as the Formerly Incarcerated Reenter Society Transformed Safely Transitioning Every Person Act (P.L. 115–391). The key provisions of the bipartisan supported act are to reform federal prisons and sentencing laws in order to reduce recidivism, decrease the federal inmate population, and maintain public safety (James, 2019).

REFERENCES

Alexander, M. (2010). *The New Jim Crow: Mass incarceration in the age of color blindness*. New York, NY: The New Press.

Alliance 2020. (2020). *Ban the box: Fair-chance hiring laws aim to prevent discrimination against applicants*. Retrieved from www.alliance2020.com/resources/ban-the-box/

American Sociological Society. (2007). *Race, ethnicity, and the criminal justice system*. Retrieved from www.asanet.org/images/press/docs/pdf/ASARaceCrime.pdf

Austin, J., Clark, J., Hardyman, P., & Henry, D. A. (2000). *Three strikes and you're out: The implementation and impact of strike laws*. Retrieved from www.ncjrs.gov/pdffiles1/nij/grants/181297.pdf

Baker, P. (2015, July 15). Bill Clinton concedes his crime law jailed too many for too long. *The New York Times*.

Bardolph, R. (1970). *The civil rights record, Black Americans and the law, 1849–1970*. New York, NY: Thomas Y. Crowell Company.

Beck, A. J., & Harrison, P. M. (2001). *Prisoners in 2000: Bulletin*. Washington, DC: Bureau of Justice Statistics. Retrieved from www.bjs.gov/content/pub/pdf/p00.pdf

Beck, A. J., & Mumola, C. J. (1999). *Prisoners in 1998*. Washington, DC: Bureau of Justice Statistics. Retrieved from www.bjs.gov/content/pub/pdf/p98.pdf

Blackmon, D. A. (2008). *Slavery by any other name: The re-enslavement of Black Americans from the Civil War to World War II*. New York, NY: First Anchor Books.

Bonczar, T. P. (2003). *Prevalence of imprisonment in the U.S. population, 1974–2001: Special report*. Washington, DC: Bureau of Justice Statistics. Retrieved from www.bjs.gov/content/pub/pdf/piusp01.pdf

Brewer, R. M., & Heitzeg, N. A. (2008). The racialization of crime and punishment: Criminal justice, colorblind racism, and the political economy of the prison industrial complex. *American Behavioral Scientist*, 51(5), 625–644.

Bronson, J., Maruschak, L. M., & Berzofsky, M. (2015). *Disabilities among prison and jail inmates, 2011–12*. Bureau of Justice Statistics. Retrieved from www.bjs.gov/content/pub/pdf/dpji1112.pdf

Cahalan, M. W. (1986). *Historical corrections statistics in the United States, 1850–1984*. Washington, DC: U.S. Bureau of Justice Statistics. Retrieved from www.bjs.gov/content/pub/pdf/hcsus5084.pdf

Carson, E. A. (2015). *Prisoners in 2014: Bulletin*. Washington, DC: Bureau of Justice Statistics. Retrieved from www.bjs.gov/content/pub/pdf/p14.pdf

Carson, E. A. (2020). *Prisoners in 2019. Bureau of Justice Statistics*. Retrieved from www.bjs.gov/content/pub/pdf/p19.pdf

Cheung, A. (2002). Prison privatization and the use of incarceration. *The Sentencing Project*. Retrieved from www.sentencingproject.org/doc/publications/inc_prisonprivatization.pdf

Congress.gov. (2010, August 3). *Fair Sentencing Act: Public Law 111–220*. Retrieved from www.congress.gov/111/plaws/publ220/PLAW-111publ220.pdf

Conron, K. J., & Wilson, B. D. M. (2019). *The Child welfare and juvenile systems: A research agenda*. UCLA School of Law, Williams Institute. Retrieved from https://williamsinstitute.law.ucla.edu/wp-content/uploads/LGBTQ-YOC-Social-Services-Jul-2019.pdf

Couloute, L., & Kopg, D. (2018). *Out of prison & out of work: Unemployment among formerly incarcerated people*. Prison Policy Initiative. Retrieved from www.prisonpolicy.org/reports/outofwork.html

Council of the District of Columbia. (2020). *B23-0324-Restore the Vote Amendment Act of 2019*. Retrieved from https://lims.dccouncil.us/Legislation/B23-0324

Crow, M., & Johnson, K. (2008). Race, ethnicity, and habitual-offender sentencing. *Criminal Justice Policy Review*, 19, 63–83.

Daniel, P. (1972). *The shadow of slavery: Peonage in the South, 1901–1969*. Urbana: University of Illinois Press.

Durose, M. R., Smith, E. L., & Langan, P. A. (2007). *Contacts between police and the public, 2005*. Washington, DC: U.S. Department of Justice, Bureau of Justice Statistics.

Executive Order 9066. (1942). *General records of the United States government*. Record Group 11: National Archives. Retrieved from www.ourdocuments.gov/doc.php?flash=true&doc=74

Families against Mandatory Minimums. (2013). *Recent state-level reforms to mandatory minimum laws*. Retrieved from http://famm.org/wp-content/uploads/2013/08/FS-List-of-State-Reforms-2.25.pdf

Families against Mandatory Minimums. (2017, May 10). *Recent state-level reforms to mandatory minimum laws*. Retrieved from https://famm.org/wp-

Federal Bureau of Investigation. (2009). *Uniform crime reports. Crime in the United States*. Washington, DC: Author.

Freeman, G. A. (1999). *Lay this body down: The 1921 murders of eleven plantation slaves*. Chicago, IL: Chicago Review Press and Lawrence Hill Books.

Geller, A., Garfinkel, I., & Western, B. (2006). *The effects of incarceration on employment and wages: An analysis of the Fragile Family Survey*. Center for Research on Child Wellbeing, Working Paper # 2006-01-FF. Retrieved from www.saferfoundation.org/files/documents/Princeton-Effect%20of%20Incarceration%20on%20Employment%20and%20Wages.pdf

Geller, A., Garfinkel, I., & Western, B. (2011). Parental incarceration and support for children in fragile families. *Demography*, 48, 25–47.

Gillard, D. K., & Beck, A. J. (1995). *Prison and jail inmates, 1995: Bulletin*. Washington, DC: Bureau of Justice Statistics. Retrieved from www.bjs.gov/content/pub/pdf/PJI95.PDF

Glaze, L., & Maruschak, L. (2008). *Parents in prison and their minor children*. Washington, DC: Bureau of Justice Statistics.

Gramlich, J. (2020). *Fact talks: Black imprisonment rate has fallen by a third since 2006*. Pew Research Center. Retrieved from www.pewresearch.org/fact-tank/2020/05/06/share-of-black-white-hispanic-americans-in-prison-2018-vs-2006/

Haney-Lopez, I. F. (2010). Post-racial racism: Racial stratification and mass incarceration in the age of Obama. *California Law Review*, 98(3), 1023–1073.

Harding, D. J., Bushway, S. D., Morenof, J. D., & Nguyen, A. P. (2018). Imprisonment and labor market outcomes: Evidence from a natural experiment. *American Journal of Sociology*, 124(1), 49–110.

Holzer, H. J., Raphael, S., & Stoll, M. A. (2004). Will employers hire former offenders? Employer preference, background checks and their determinants. In M. Pattillo, D. Weiman, & B. Western (Eds.), *Imprisoning America: The social effects of mass incarceration* (pp. 205–246). New York, NY: Russell Sage Foundation.

Holzer, H. J., Raphael, S., & Stoll, M. A. (2006). Perceived criminality, criminal background checks and the racial hiring practices of employers. *Journal of Law and Economics*, 49, 451–480.

Holzer, H. J., Raphael, S., & Stoll, M. A. (2007). The effects of an applicant's criminal history on employer hiring decisions and screening practices: Evidence from Los Angles. In S. Bushway, M. A. Stoll, & D. F. Weiman (Eds.), *Barriers to reentry? The labor market for released prisoners in post-industrial America* (pp. 117–150). New York, NY: Russell Sage Foundation.

H.R. 7194. (2020, June 11). Mandatory Minimum Reform Act 2020. *Congress.gov*. Retrieved from www.congress.gov/bill/116th-congress/house-

Jackson, D., & Korte, G. (2015, July 14). Obama clemency grants the largest since 60s. *USA Today*.

James, N. (2019). *The First Step Act of 2018: An overview*. Congressional Research Service. Retrieved from https://crsreports.congress.gov/product/pdf/R/R45558

The Justice Center. (2015). *Second Chance Act*. The Council of State Governments. Retrieved from https://csgjusticecenter.org/nrrc/projects/second-chance-act/

Justice.gov. (2015). *Federal statutes imposing collateral consequences upon conviction*. Retrieved from www.justice.gov/sites/default/files/pardon/legacy/2006/11/13/collateral_consequences.pdf

Justice Policy Institute. (2000). *The punishing decade: Prison and jail estimates in the millennium*. Retrieved from www.justicepolicy.org/images/upload/00-05_rep_punishingdecade_ac.pdf

Kansal, T. (2005). *Racial disparity in sentencing: A review of the literature*. Washington, DC: The Sentencing Project.

Kids Count Data Center. (2020). *Children who had a parent who was ever incarcerated by race and ethnicity in the United States*. The Annie E. Casey Foundation. Retrieved from https://datacenter.kidscount.org/data/tables/9734-children-who-had-a-parent-who-was-ever-incarcerated-by-race-and-ethnicity#ranking/1/any/true/1648/1/18995

Knafo, S. (2015, October 14). California takes overdue stand against failed drug laws. *Huffington Post Politics*.

Lafollette, H. (2005). Collateral consequences of punishment: Civil penalties accompanying formal punishment. *Journal of Applied Philosophy*, 22(3), 241–261.

LAO. (2020, November 3). *Ballet: Proposition 17, Restores Right to Vote after Completion of Prison Term: Legislative Constitutional Amendment*. Retrieved from https://lao.ca.gov/ballot/2020/Prop17-110320.pdf

Levitt, S. D. (2004). Understanding why crime fell in the 1990s: Four factors that explain the decline and six that do not. *Journal of Economic Perspectives*, 18(1), 163–190.

Looney, A., & Turner, N. (2018). *Work opportunity before and after incarceration*. The Brookings Institute. Retrieved from www.brookings.edu/wp-content/uploads/2018/03/es_20180314_looneyincarceration_final.pdf

Mancini, M. J. (1978). Race, economics, and the abandonment of convict leasing. *The Journal of Negro History*, 63(4), 339–352.

Manza, J., & Uggen, C. (2008). *Locked out: Felon disenfranchisement and American democracy*. New York, NY: Oxford University Press.

Maschi, T., & Killian, M. L. (2011). The evolution of forensic social work in the United States: Implications for 21st century practice. *Journal of Forensic Social Work*, 1(1), 8–36. doi:10.1080/1936928X.2011.541198

Mauer, M. (2006). *Race to incarcerate*. New York, NY: The New Press.

Mauer, M. (2011). Addressing racial disparities in incarceration. *The Prison Journal*, *91*(3), 87–101.

Mauer, M., & Chesney-Lind, M. (2002). *Invisible punishment: The collateral consequences of mass imprisonment*. New York, NY: New Press.

McCarty, M., Falk, G., Aussenberg, R. A., & Carpenter, D. H. (2015). *Drug testing and crime-related restrictions in TANF, SNAP, and housing assistance*. Congressional Research Service. Retrieved from www.fas.org/sgp/crs/misc/R42394.pdf

Minor-Harper, S., & Marbrook, M. (1986). *State and federal prisoners, 1925–1985: Bulletin*. Bureau of Justice Statistics. Retrieved from www.bjs.gov/content/pub/pdf/sfp2585.pdf

Muller, C. (2012). Northward migration and the rise of racial disparity in American incarceration. *American Journal of Sociology*, *118*(2), 281–326.

National Association of Social Workers. (2008). Social work in the criminal justice system: A revision of existing policy. *Correctional Social Work*. Retrieved from www.socialworkers.org/da/da2008/finalvoting/documents/Correctional%20Social%20Work%20-%202nd%20Round%20Final%20-%20Clean.pdf

National Association of Social Workers. (2013). *A social work perspective on drug policy reform: Public health approach*. Social justice brief. Retrieved from www.naswdc.org/advocacy/DrugReformWP.pdf

National Association of Social Workers. (2018). *Social justice priorities*. Retrieved from www.socialworkers.org/Advocacy/Social-Justice/Social-Justice-Priorities

National Center for Transgender Equality. (2018). *LGBTQ people behind bars: A guide to understanding the issues facing transgender prisoners and their legal rights*. Retrieved from https://transequality.org/sites/default/files/docs/resources/TransgenderPeopleBehindBars.pdf

National Conference of State Legislators. (2020). *Felon voting rights*. Retrieved from www.ncsl.org/research/elections-and-campaigns/felon-voting-rights.aspx

New York Civil Liberties Union. (2009). *Rockefeller drug law reform*. Press Release. Retrieved from www.nyclu.org/issues/racial-justice/rockefeller-drug-law-reform

Nixon, R. (1971). 203: *Special message to the Congress on drug abuse prevention and control*. The American Presidency Project. Retrieved from www.presidency.ucsb.edu/ws/index.php?pid=3048

Office of Juvenile Justice and Delinquency Prevention. (2019). *Racial and ethnic disparities*. Retrieved from https://ojjdp.ojp.gov/programs/racial-and-ethnic-disparities

Pager, D. (2007). *Marked: Race, crime, and finding work in an era of mass incarceration*. Chicago, IL: University of Chicago Press.

Parenti, C. (1999). *Lockdown America: Police and prisons in the age of crisis*. New York, NY: Verso.

People v. Richard Allen Davis, Super. Ct. No. 186000 (2009, June 1). Retrieved from http://murderpedia.org/male.D/images/davis_richard_allen/s056425.pdf

Peters, C. M. (2011). Social work and juvenile probation: Historical tensions and contemporary convergences. *Social Work*, *56*(4), 355–365.

P.L. 114–198. (2016, July 22). Comprehensive Addiction and Recovery Act of 2016. *Congress.gov*. Retrieved from www.congress.gov/114/plaws/publ198/PLAW-114publ198.pdf

Polkey, C. (2019). Most states have ended SNAP ban for convicted felons. *National Conference of State Legislature*. Retrieved from www.ncsl.org/blog/2019/07/30/most-states-have-ended-snap-ban-for-convicted-drug-felons.aspx

Porter, N. D. (2021). Top trends in state criminal justice reform, 2020. *The Sentencing Project*. Retrieved from www.sentencingproject.org/publications/top-trends-in-state-criminal-justice-reform-2020/

Prison Legal News. (2003). $260,000 paid by WA DOC to Ballasiotes family for daughter killed by work release prisoner. Retrieved from www.prisonlegalnews.org/news/2003/dec/15/260000-paid-by-wa-doc-to-ballasiotes-family-for-daughter-killed-by-work-release-prisoner/

ProQuest. (2011). Criminal justice timeline. *Leading Issues Timelines*. Retrieved from www.mrgoslin.com/uploads/9/0/6/3/9063086/criminaljusticetimeline.pdf

Public Papers of the President of the United States. (1994). *William J. Clinton*. Washington, DC: United States Government Printing Office.

Quinn, M. (2019). Criminal justice reform paves the way for welfare reform. *Governing*. Retrieved from www.governing.com/topics/health-human-services/gov-welfare-felons-states-federal-ban-tanf-snap-pennsylvania.htm

Raphael, S. (2007). Early incarceration spells and the transition to adulthood. In S. Danziger & C. Rouse (Eds.), *The price of independence*. New York, NY: Russell Sage Foundation.

Reamer, F. G. (2004). Social work and criminal justice: The uneasy alliance in criminal justice: Retribution vs. restoration. *Journal of Religion & Spirituality in Social Work*, 23(1/2), 213–231.

Reynolds, K. (2020). *Gov. Reynolds signs Executive Order to restore voting rights of felons who have completed their sentence*. Retrieved from https://governor.iowa.gov/press-release/gov-reynolds-signs-executive-order-to-restore-voting-rights-of-felons-who-have#:~:text=Today%2C%20Governor%20Kim%20Reynolds%20signed,have%20completed%20their%20felony%20sentences.&text=When%20someone%20serves%20their%20sentence,right%20to%20vote%20restored%20automatically

Roberts, A. R., & Springer, D. W. (2007). *Social work in juvenile and criminal justice settings* (3rd ed.). Springfield, IL: Charles C Thomas.

Roberts, L. (2010). Mental health courts: An interface between social work and mental health courts. *Columbia Social Work Review*, 1, 36–44.

Rodriguez, M. N., & Mehta, N. (2015). Ban the box: U.S. cities, counties, and states adopt fair hiring policies. *National Employment Law Project*. Retrieved from www.nelp.org/publication/ban-the-box-fair-chance-hiring-state-and-local-guide/

Sawyer, W. (2019). *Youth confinement: The whole pie 2019*. Prison Population Initiative. Retrieved from www.prisonpolicy.org/reports/youth2019.html

Sawyer, W., & Wagner, P. (2020). *Mass incarceration: The whole pie 2020*. Prison Population Initiative. Retrieved from www.prisonpolicy.org/reports/pie2020.html

Schaefer, B. P., & Kraska, P. B. (2012). Felon disenfranchisement: The judiciary role in renegotiating racial divisions. *Race and Justice*, 2(4), 304–321.

Schmitt, J., & Warner, K. (2010). *Ex-offenders and the labor market*. Washington, DC: Center for Economic and Policy Research. Retrieved from www.cepr.net/documents/publications/ex-offenders-2010-11.pdf

Schmitt, J., Warner, K., & Gupta, S. (2010). *The high budgetary cost of incarceration*. Washington, DC: Center for Economic and Policy Research. Retrieved from www.cepr.net/documents/publications/incarceration-2010-06.pdf

The Sentencing Project. (2013). *Report of the sentencing project to the United Nations Human Rights Committee regarding racial disparities in the United States criminal justice system*. Retrieved from http://sentencingproject.org/doc/publications/rd_ICCPR%20Race%20and%20Justice%20Shadow%20Report.pdf

The Sentencing Project. (2015). *Felony disenfranchisement: A primer*. Retrieved from http://sentencingproject.org/doc/publications/fd_Felony%20Disenfranchisement%20Primer.pdf

The Sentencing Project. (2020). *Criminal justice facts*. Retrieved from www.sentencingproject.org/criminal-justice-facts/

Spengler, T. (2020). How much do prisons cost taxpayers? *Gobankingrates.com*. Retrieved from https://www.gobankingrates.com/taxes/filing/wont-believe-much-prison-inmates-costing-year/

Spohn, C. (2000). Thirty years of sentencing reform: The quest for a racially neutral sentencing process. In J. Horney (Ed.), *Criminal justice 2000, Vol. 3 Policies, processes, and decisions of the criminal justice system* (pp. 427–501). Washington, DC: U.S. Department of Justice.

Uggen, C., Larson, R., Shannon, S., & Pulido-Nava, A. (2020). *Locked out 2020: Estimates of people denied voting rights due to a felony conviction. The Sentencing Project*. Retrieved from www.sentencingproject.org/publications/locked-out-2020-estimates-of-people-denied-voting-rights-due-to-a-felony-conviction/

United States Senate Committee on the Judiciary. (2015, October 1). *Senators announce bipartisan Sentence Reform and Corrections Act*. Senate Press Gallery S-325. Retrieved from www.judiciary.senate.gov/meetings/senators-announce-bipartisan-sentencing-reform-and-corrections-act

United States Sentencing Commission. (2015). *Report on cocaine and federal sentencing policy*. Retrieved from www.ussc.gov/report-cocaine-and-federal-sentencing-policy-2

U.S. Commission on Civil Rights. (2019). *Collateral consequences: The crossroads of punishment, redemption, and the effects on communities*. Retrieved from www.usccr.gov/pubs/2019/06-13-Collateral-Consequences.pdf

U.S. Department of Justice. (1992). *The case for more incarceration*. Washington, DC. Retrieved from www.ncjrs.gov/pdffiles1/Digitization/139583NCJRS.pdf

U.S. Department of Justice. (2013). *The Attorney General's Smart on Crime Initiative*. Retrieved from www.justice.gov/ag/attorney-generals-smart-crime-initiative

U.S. Department of Justice. (2016). *Report and recommendations concerning the use of restrictive housing: Final report*. Washington, DC. Retrieved from www.justice.gov/dag/file/815551/download

U.S. Department of Justice Fact Sheet. (1994). *Violent Crime Control and Law Enforcement Act of 1994*. Retrieved from www.ncjrs.gov/txtfiles/billfs.tx

U.S. Senate Committee on the Judiciary. (2015, October 1). *Senators announce bipartisan Sentence Reform and Corrections Act*. Senate Press Gallery S-325. Retrieved from www.judiciary.senate.gov/meetings/senators-announce-bipartisan-sentencing-reform-and-corrections-act

Ward, G. K. (2012). *The Black child-savers: Racial democracy and juvenile justice*. Chicago, IL: The University of Chicago Press.

Western, B. (2006). *Punishment and inequality in America*. New York, NY: Russell Sage Foundation.

Western, B., & Beckett, K. (1999). How unregulated is the U.S. labor market? The penal systems as labor market institution. *American Journal of Sociology, 104*(4), 1030–1060.

Western, B., & Pettit, B. (2010). *Collateral costs: Incarceration's effect on economic mobility*. Washington, DC: The Pew Charitable Trusts.

Western, B., & Sirois, C. (2019). Racialized re-entry: Labor market inequality after incarceration. *Social Forces, 97*(4), 1517–1542.

The White House, Office of the Press Secretary. (2016, January 25). *Fact sheet: The Department of Justice Review of solitary confinement*. [Press Release]. Retrieved from www.whitehouse.gov/the-press-office/2016/01/25/fact-sheet-department-justice-review-solitary-confinement

Wilson, M. (2010). *Criminal justice social work in the United States: Adapting to new challenges*. Washington, DC: NASW Center for Work Studies.

Wilson, W. J. (1993). *The ghetto underclass: Social science perspectives*. London, England: Sage.

CHAPTER 11

Educational Inequality

Educational Inequality in the United States

Since the end of World War II, education has been considered the primary pathway to opportunity and upward mobility in the United States (Duncan & Murnane, 2011). Higher education attainment, for example, is associated with the quality of one's job or career and higher median earnings, a pattern that has been consistent since 2000 (Hirschman & Lee, 2006). To put this in some perspective, in 2019, the median weekly earnings of workers aged 25 years and older with the highest level of education attainment—doctoral and professional degrees—were 2.5 times ($1,883) higher than for workers with a high school diploma ($746) (U.S. Bureau of Labor Statistics, 2020). For workers, 25 years and older, whose highest level of education is either a masters or a bachelor's degree, the weekly earnings are two times ($1,497) and 1.65 times ($1,248), respectively, higher than those with a high school diploma (U.S. Bureau of Labor Statistics, 2020). This higher earnings pattern associated with higher education attainment levels holds for both men and women and across racial/ethnic groups (National Center for Education Statistics, 2015).

K–12 Education

In theory, education in America is consistent with the nation's meritocratic ideals and is provided fairly, equitably, and inclusively, regardless of one's race, ethnicity, gender, class, or ability (Duncan & Murnane, 2011; Johnson & Howard, 2009; Noltemeyer et al., 2012). However, in actuality, at both K–12 and higher education, as gross income and wealth inequality has grown and become an entrenched structural feature of contemporary American life over the past 35 years, so too has inequality of opportunity and access to quality education for scores of America's children and young people (Duncan & Murnane, 2011; Johnson & Howard, 2009; National Center for Education Statistics, 2020a; Noltemeyer et al., 2012). This inequality of opportunity and access to quality education is particularly true for children and young people from low-income households, and Native Americans, Blacks, and Hispanics (Duncan & Murnane, 2011; National Center for Education Statistics, 2020a; Solano & Weyer, 2017). Recent research indicates that the inequality of opportunity and access to quality education begins as early as preschool and reflects the differing level of access between high-income and low-income families to resources that stimulate preschool learning (Garcia & Weiss, 2017; National Center for Education Statistics, 2020a; Nores & Barnett, 2014; Solano & Weyer, 2017). These resources include quality preschool education programs, well-stocked libraries, recreational facilities, and computer access, to name but a few. In the past 35 years, the differing level of access to these resources has been exacerbated by increased residential segregation by income (McArdle & Acevedo, 2017; Nores & Barnett, 2014).

It is hardly surprising then that upon entering kindergarten, children from low-income families, the majority Native American, Black, and Hispanic, have on average weaker all-round academic skills than their high-income counterparts. These weaker academic skills are in the areas of vocabulary, the capacity to learn and adapt to stressful situations, and the ability to sort and organize information and plan ahead (National Scientific Council on the Developing Child, 2014; Reardon, 2011). As found by Duncan and Magnuson

DOI: 10.4324/9781003023708-11

(2011), the skill gaps between children from high-income and low-income families do not appear to grow or narrow appreciably as children progress through school. Rather, it is maintained as children from low-income families, particularly if Native American, Black, or Hispanic, attend schools with high or extremely high levels of poverty (Duncan & Magnuson, 2011; Kewal-Ramani et al., 2007; National Center for Education Statistics, 2020a). Indeed, in 2017, 45% of Black and Hispanic students attend high-poverty schools, followed by Native American/Alaska Native students, 41%, and Pacific Islander students, 24% (National Center for Education Statistics, 2020a). The percentage was much lower for Asian and White students at 15% and 8%, respectively. In contrasts, the percentage of students who attended low-poverty schools in 2017 was much higher for Asian and White students, 39% and 31%, respectively, and much lower for Native American/Alaska Native students, 8%, Hispanic students, 8%, and Black students, 7% (National Center for Education Statistics, 2020a).

Research indicates that high-poverty schools are underresourced and have less stable and less-qualified teaching staff, a higher majority of out-of-field teachers in both English and science, and larger class size than the no poverty and high-income schools (Orfield & Lee, 2005; U.S. Department of Education Office for Civil Rights, 2014a, 2014b). Moreover, students in these schools have less exposure to high-quality curricula, including the full range of math and science courses, than their counterparts in high-income and no poverty schools. They similarly have less opportunity and access to advanced placement classes and gifted programs, as well as important social networks (Johnson, 2003; Orfield & Lee, 2005; U.S. Department of Education Office for Civil Rights, 2014a, 2014b).

It is not surprising, then, that comparing academic achievement as measured by reading and standardized test scores reveals that disparities between high-income and low-income students are large and have been growing. For example, Reardon (2011) found that among children born in the 1950s, 60s, and early 70s, the reading achievement gap between children in high-income families and those in low-income families was about a 0.9 standard deviation. However, for children born in 2000, the gap was at roughly a .25 deviation, or, simply put, 40% larger than the achievement gap several decades earlier. This gap, Reardon suggests, is greater than the concurrent trend in the Black–White achievement gap, which during the 1960s was much larger than the income achievement gap. However, given that the number of children living in low-income homes below the poverty level is significantly higher for Native Americans, Blacks, and Hispanics than for Whites and Asians making such a distinction does not lessen the importance of race and ethnicity in considering education inequality.

Indeed, despite the downward trend in high school dropout rates in the four decades between 1970 and 2012, Black and Hispanic students still continue to have higher dropout rates than White students, 6.4% versus 8% versus 4.2%, respectively (National Center for Education Statistics, 2020b). Moreover, although the National Assessment of Education Progress (NAEP) measures show that there has been an upward trend from 1990 to 2013 in average mathematic scale scores for all students in grades 4, 8, and 12, Black and Hispanic students still continue to trail both Asian and White students. Furthermore, the average mathematic scale scores for students in grade 12 by race and ethnicity in 2005, 2013, and 2015 revealed that Native American, Black, and Hispanic students consistently had lower scale scores than non-Hispanic Whites and Asian students (ChildStats.gov, 2020; see Figure 11.1).

Similarly for reading scores, there has been an upward trend for all students in grades 4 and 8 since 2000, and a fairly stable trend for grade 12 students. As with the mathematic scale scores, however, in 2015, Asian and non-Hispanic White students had higher scale scores than those of Native American, Black, and Hispanic students, a trend that has been consistent across the decade. On both the mathematic and readings scores, Black students consistently score the lowest of all racial and ethnic groups (ChildStats.gov, 2020).

In addition to academic achievement, there are other significant disparities between different groups of students in pre-K–12 education, most notable of these being inequality in school discipline (Harper et al., 2019). In the U.S. Government Accountability Office (2018) analysis of Department of Education national civil rights data for school year 2013–2014, Black students, boys, and students with disabilities were disproportionality disciplined (e.g., suspensions, expulsions) (Government Accountability Office, 2018). Disturbingly, both Black students and students with disabilities were significantly more likely than any other group of students to be arrested and referred to law enforcement, and/or to be restrained and placed in detention in 2011–2012 (U.S. Department of Education Office for Civil Rights, 2014c).

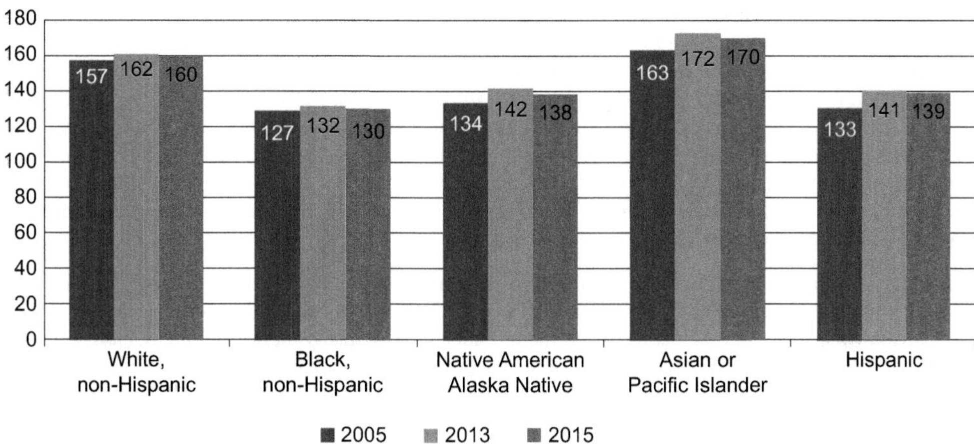

Figure 11.1 Average Mathematics Scale Scores for Students in Grade 12 by Race and Hispanic Origin, 2005, 2013, and 2015

Source: U.S. Department of National Center for Education Statistics. Table 222.10 Average National Assessment of Educational Progress (NAEP) mathematics scale score, by sex, race/ethnicity, and grade: Selected years, 1990 through 2017. Retrieved from https://nces.ed.gov/programs/digest/d17/tables/dt17_222.10.asp?referer=raceindicators

Postsecondary Education

The overall number of undergraduates at colleges and universities in the United States has increased dramatically over the last 20 years. For example, in fall 2018, the total undergraduate enrollment in degree-granting postsecondary institutions was 16.6 million students, an increase of 26% from fall 2000, when enrollment was 13.2 million students (National Center for Education Statistics, 2020c). By 2029, the total undergraduate population will grow to 17 million students (National Center for Education Statistics, 2020c). It is an increase almost exclusively driven by the rising share of undergraduate students who are Black, Hispanic, and/or from low-income families (Fry & Cilluffo, 2019; Libassi, 2018; Smith, 2019). Between 1996 and 2016, the number of undergraduate students from low-income families grew from 12% to 20%, while there was an increase in the number of non-White students from 29% to 47% (Smith, 2019).

While ostensibly encouraging, Fry and Cilluffo (2019) found that the rise has not been occurring uniformly across the postsecondary landscape. Instead, they see disproportionate numbers of Black, Hispanic, and or students from low-income families attending public two-year colleges and the least-selective four-year colleges and universities, including for-profit colleges (Fry & Cilluffo, 2019; Smith, 2019). These postsecondary institutions tend to have fewer resources to help students succeed or offer a quality education (Libassi, 2018). Furthermore, they are underrepresented in engineering, education, mathematics and statistics, and the physical sciences (Libassi, 2018).

Just as troubling are graduation rates that highlight large racial gaps in college completion. For illustration, among students of different racial/ethnic groups who began a bachelor's degree in fall 2010, the six-year graduation rate for first-time, full-time undergraduate students was highest for Asian students (74%). Next was White students (64%), Hispanic students (54%), Black students (40%), and Native American/Alaska Native students (39%) (National Center for Education Statistics, 2019).

While the enrollment growth in Black, Hispanic, and students from low-income families at the less-selective institutions is pronounced, this is certainly not the case for very selective postsecondary institutions. Indeed, there has only been a 3% increase, from 10% to 13% between 1996 and 2016, leaving Black, Hispanic, and students from low-income families significantly underrepresented in these institutions (Libassi, 2018; Smith, 2019).

All in all, then, in their current functioning, K–12 and college/university education is not the great equalizer it promised to be in the first decades after World War II. In fact, it would be more accurate to say that today, education more reflects and reinforces existing social inequality than it challenges it. This phenomenon is not new, however, as education inequality has been rampant in the United States for much of its history (Johnson & Howard, 2009). Indeed, there are fewer areas of American life where social inequality is more keenly felt than in education (Noltemeyer et al., 2012). As is the case today, these inequalities have historically fallen primarily along racial/ethnic, gender, and class lines and have reflected and reinforced existing social inequalities (Reardon, 2011). They have had a profound impact on who has had and not had open opportunity and access to education.

Using intersectionality as an aspect of critical race theory and a conflict theory lens, the rest of this chapter examines the historical development of education inequality in the United States through key social policies and the circumstances that informed them. It focuses particularly on race/ethnicity, class, and gender because of the nation's tragic history of denying countless millions of citizens and residents access to the precious commodity of education based on these differences alone (Johnson & Howard, 2009).

Theoretical Frameworks

Intersectionality and Critical Race Theory

Examining the subject using an intersectionality framework as an aspect of critical race theory (CRT) reveals that educational inequality is one of the mechanisms for maintaining existing racial, ethnic, gender, and class hierarchies in the United States. It does so by way of limiting fair and equal access to quality education along racial, ethnic, gender, and class lines. According to the mythology of meritocracy and institutional objectivity, educational inequality and the resulting academic achievement gaps between subordinated and non-subordinated groups is justified and explained as the result of differing levels of aptitude, commitment to learning, and/or cultural values. For example, for much of United States history, women were portrayed as intellectually inferior to men and thus not suitable for higher education. Consequently, women were denied equal access to higher education, but just as importantly, the existing gender hierarchy was maintained, with men having greater access to society's rewards and privileges. As will be shown later in the chapter, this situation was similarly true for Native Americans, Blacks, Chinese, and Mexicans.

By promulgating the mythology of meritocracy and institutional objectivity, how the intersection of race, ethnicity, gender, and social class affect fair and equal access to quality education and, by extension, society's rewards and privileges is never truly addressed.

Conflict Theory

Seen from a conflict theory perspective, educational inequality is the direct result of a class conflict, in which the elite seeks to monopolize one of the most valuable of society's resources—education. In monopolizing or at least controlling access to education, the elite as represented by corporations and the lawmakers can maintain a subordinated and relatively powerless workforce who has little in the way of bargaining power or opportunity for upward social mobility.

Race, Ethnicity, and Educational Inequality: An Historical Perspective

The ubiquity of education in the United States belies the fact that its widespread availability, be it compulsory public education or college/university, is a relatively recent occurrence in the nation's history. Moreover, at least initially, the goal of widespread education provided by public schools was to indoctrinate, assimilate, socialize, and control the marginalized groups of the day (Freeman, 1978; Johnson & Howard, 2009; Seelau, 2009).

The Native American Experience

Within the sociopolitical context of American expansionism and the plundering of Native American tribal homelands, Native Americans, in particular, were always the ongoing targets of assimilation through education. The efforts began with the Jesuit missionaries in the 17th century and then much more destructively at the height of expansionism in the late 19th century through to the late 20th century with federal government boarding schools (Foley, 1875; Seelau, 2009). Informing the assimilation efforts through education was the prevailing notion of Native American cultural inferiority, as well as the desire to "civilize" Native Americans (Seelau, 2009). To this end, the federal government made provision for assimilation through a series of policies in which education would play a key role.

The Civilization Fund Act of 1819

The earliest and primary federal government policy effort to use education to assimilate children into America's western culture was the Civilization Fund Act of 1819. The stated purpose of the act was to provide against the further decline and extinction of the Native American tribes living on the frontier settlements of the United States. Another stated purpose of the act was to introduce Native Americans to the habits and arts of civilization (Prucha, 2000, p. 33). Native American tribes, the act stipulated, were to be instructed in the methods of agriculture best suited to their situation, and, more importantly, Native American children would be taught reading, writing, and arithmetic and be given Christian religious instruction (Banks, 2012; Prucha, 2000). In support of this stipulation, Congress appropriated an annual sum of $10,000 to encourage benevolent societies to provide this instruction.

Native American Boarding Schools

Initially, Protestant Christian clergy and missionaries provided the instruction in Indian mission schools located on the tribal reservations. However, it was the belief of influential assimilationists such as Colonial Richard Henry Pratt that mission schools on reservations were not sufficiently removed from the influences of tribal life (American Indian Relief Council, 2015; Bergman, 1977; Banks, 2012; Pratt, 1892; Prucha, 2000; Seelau, 2009). Colonial Pratt argued that the only way to completely assimilate Native American children would be through off-reservation boarding schools where they could be fully immersed in the ways of civilized society. Pratt reasoned it was necessary to "kill the Indian in him to save the man" (Pratt, 1892, p. 49). Faithful to his convictions, in 1879 Pratt established the first and most well-known of the federally funded off-reservation boarding schools, the Carlisle Indian School in Carlisle, Pennsylvania. Pratt served as the school's headmaster for 25 years and arguably became the most influential figure of the time in Native American education (American Indian Relief Council, 2015). By 1885, with increased government funding, there were 106 federally funded off-reservation boarding schools across the country.

Taking in children as young as six years old, Carlisle and the other off-reservation boarding schools went about a systematic stripping away of students' cultural identity by first removing all outward signs of tribal life. Upon arrival at the school, for example, the children were stripped of their tribal clothes, the long braids worn by boys were cut, and all children were given a new western name and surname, both Christian (American Indian Relief Council, 2015; Seelau, 2009). Once in the school, the children were prohibited from speaking their native tongue, even to each other. Also, Native American foods were abandoned for western food, and the children were forced to learn the etiquette of eating with knives, forks, and spoons and the proper use of napkins and tablecloths (American Indian Relief Council, 2015; Seelau, 2009). Moreover, the schools limited the duration and frequency of children's visits home to family, arguing it would hinder the assimilation process (American Indian Relief Council, 2015; Bergman, 1977; Seelau, 2009). Conversion to Christianity was required, with most schools developing a curriculum that included religious instruction.

In school, girls learned to cook, clean, sew, and do laundry, while boys learned technical skills or farming. Although there were some academics at the better schools, the need to be as economically self-sufficient as possible meant that students did most of the work in the schools and that academics often languished (American Indian Relief Council, 2015).

Figure 11.2 Pupils at Carlisle Indian Industrial School, Pennsylvania, 1900

Figure 11.3 Pupils at Religious Indian Boarding School

Although promulgated as being in the best interest of Native American children, in truth, the boarding schools were anything but in the best interest of the majority of children. The children were alienated from their families, stripped of their culture, and subject to harsh disciplinary action if found contravening any one of the myriad rules that were present in the schools. Moreover, the schools themselves were often the vectors of diseases, where communal illnesses such as tuberculosis were all too common (American Indian Relief Council, 2015). Indeed, the realization of the often-poor treatment of their children had Native American parents charging the government with ravaging the health and wellness of their children, and often led parents to not return their children to the schools after home visits.

Figure 11.4 Young Boys and Girls at Carlisle Indian Industrial School

The Meriam Report

In 1928, the Institute of Government Research commissioned the *Meriam Report*, a major investigation into Native American affairs. The 847-page report, whose official title was "The Problem of Indian Administration," was scathing about the conditions on reservations and in the off-reservation boarding schools (Prucha, 1984; The Institute for Government Research Studies in Administration, 1928). In its opening about education, the report argued that there was a need for a change in the point of view about Indian education. More specifically, there was a need to move away from the notion that Native American children had to be removed from their homes and culture and placed in segregated schools to be educated (The Institute for Government Research Studies in Administration, 1928). This was particularly true, the report argued, because the education provided by the boarding schools was at best inadequate and typically delivered by instructors whose credentials or lack thereof would not be accepted in good public school systems. The boarding schools were criticized for the poor diet provided, rampant overcrowding, and the lack of adequate medical services, as well as their poor education. Also criticized was the reliance on a uniform curriculum rather than raising teaching standards (Prucha, 1984).

In its recommendations, the *Meriam Report* supported the need for Native American education but rejected the notion that such education should be segregated in separate institutions. Rather, the report noted such education should be provided in an integrated setting (Prucha, 1984; The Institute for Government Research Studies in Administration, 1928). As a result of the report, some corrective actions were put in place, which included President Hoover requesting additional funds to supply adequate food and clothing for pupils and the closure of unpopular reservation boarding. However, with the assimilationist policies almost entirely dependent on off-reservation boarding schools, the boarding schools continued for 50 more years until the passing of the Indian Child Welfare Act of 1978, which granted Native American parents the legal right to deny their children's placement in off-reservation boarding schools (Prucha, 1984). At the time of its discontinuation, student enrollment in the off-reservation boarding schools had peaked at 60,000 (Prucha, 1984).

Unequal access to quality education was not limited to Native Americans in the 19th and early 20th centuries, however. Also profoundly affected were Blacks, Chinese, and Mexicans (Noltemeyer et al., 2012).

Slavery and Education Inequality

As slaves, Africans and their American-born children and descendants were systematically excluded and denied access to even the most rudimentary forms of education, notably the ability to read and write. Afraid that slaves might become emboldened with notions of freedom, most slave masters made little to no effort to ensure that their slaves were literate (Langhorne, 2000). Despite that attitude, the surviving writings of slaves who were literate reveal that the quest for literacy and education was of profound importance and an organizing principle for slaves both before and after emancipation (Williams, 2005). Even while enslaved and socially isolated, slaves devised a myriad of innovative strategies to educate themselves, regarding both literacy and learning about the social events and political happenings of the day (Williams, 2005). These strategies included setting up clandestine schools where slaves would share with each other whatever knowledge they had of reading. Relying heavily on oral and audio systems of information, slaves who had access to White conversations would listen keenly and memorize what was being said, which would be shared later with fellow slaves. This form of eavesdropping fed a grapevine that kept slaves abreast of the happenings of the day (Williams, 2005). As suggested by Williams, access to knowledge, literacy, or otherwise, was one of the areas where slaves and slave owners waged a perpetual struggle.

Whether or not they were aware of the subversive actions of slaves to become literate and knowledgeable, it did not take long for slaveholders and the southern slave states to pass statutes prohibiting the education of slaves. As early as 1740, South Carolina was the first state to pass a statute outlawing the teaching of slaves to read and write or employing a slave to write. It also passed a law prohibiting the assembly of slaves for the purpose of mental instruction, which covered reading, writing, arithmetic, and memorization (Langhorne, 2000; Williams, 2005). Continuing into the 19th century, preventing slaves from being educated would take on even more urgency in the southern slaveholding states, as the growing call for the abolition of slavery threatened the whole institution. The call for abolition was accompanied by the demand for the education of Blacks, which abolitionist groups such as the Quakers answered. It was a demand that brought a swift legislative response from the southern slaveholding states, most of which enacted statutes prohibiting the education of slaves. In the 1830s, Louisiana, North Carolina, and Alabama all passed statutes prohibiting the education of not only slaves but also free Blacks (Langhorne, 2000; Noltemeyer et al., 2012; Williams, 2005). Despite these laws, Blacks continued to resist and in some cases were able to establish Black schools, as in Lexington, Kentucky, in 1830. There were also very rare cases of free Blacks attending college, something that was not common even for Whites, as was the case in 1833 when Oberlin became the first college in America to accept Black students (Noltemeyer et al., 2012).

Although it was the southern slaveholding states that were most threatened by any prospect of Black Americans being educated, they were not the only ones. In the 1830s, in Connecticut, for example, the efforts of the Convention of Colored Men to establish a college of manual labor for Blacks was strongly opposed and prompted the passing of legislation prohibiting the education of Blacks from outside of the state (The Black Law of Connecticut, 1833; Williams, 2005). Similarly, in 1832, when Prudence Crandall, a White Quaker, accepted Black female students into her boarding school for girls in Canterbury, Connecticut, she was prosecuted and convicted, which was later overturned, for violating state statutes on educating Blacks from outside the state. Moreover, her school was vandalized and burned to the ground, forcing Crandall to close permanently (Strane, 1990).

The Freedman's Bureau

The turning point in the quest for equal access to education for Black Americans was the federal government's reconstruction efforts in the aftermath of the Civil War. The most notable of these reconstruction efforts was the establishment of the Bureau of Refugees, Freedmen, and Abandoned Lands, more typically referred to as the Freedman's Bureau, in 1865. Among the bureau's primary functions was to integrate the newly emancipated slaves fully into society. To this end, the bureau provided rations and food, which was in short supply after the war; medical services; legalized marriages, which were not formerly recognized under slavery; and legal services. All of this was done against the backdrop of inadequate funding and virulent and sometimes violent opposition from militia groups within the former slaveholding states.

One of the Freedman's Bureau's lasting and most recognized legacies, however, was the education it provided to millions of newly freed slaves. In conjunction with northern missionaries and aid societies, the bureau spent $3.5 million, which included $1.5 million donated by benevolent organizations and $1 million from Black groups, setting up schools for the newly freed slaves, both children and adults. By the end of 1870, some 4,000 schools were serving 250,000 former slaves (Langhorne, 2000). Indeed, such was the thirst for education among the former slaves that despite the continued hardships they encountered, attendance rates were always anywhere from 79% to 82% (Langhorne, 2000).

However, after the bureau was discontinued in 1872 and the Democratic Party regained political power in the South, the former slaveholding states quickly went about reducing public funds for the education of Black children, along with establishing Black Codes and then Jim Crow legislation that would legally segregate public spaces racially. This legislation would ensure that whatever services were provided to Black Americans, education included, would be inferior to those of their White counterparts (Langhorne, 2000).

Historically Black Colleges and Universities

Despite the Black Codes and Jim Crow, higher education opportunities would be made possible for Blacks by way of the second Morrill Act of 1890. Originally enacted in 1862, the specific purpose of the act, more commonly known as the Land Grant College Act, was to ensure educational opportunities for all classes. To this end, the act provided land to each state, which in turn would sell it and establish an endowment in which the proceeds would be used to build higher learning institutions and colleges in the state. At the time of the 1862 act, the races were separated, and only Mississippi and Kentucky established colleges of higher education for Blacks (Langhorne, 2000). In 1890, this exclusion was rectified when the second act required each state to show that race was not an admission criterion to attend their colleges, or else designate a separate land-grant institution for persons of color. This stipulation helped establish a framework for state-sponsored colleges and ensured the land grant funding for the higher education of Black Americans (Langhorne, 2000). Indeed, a total of 16 historically black institutions and colleges were funded under the program. The colleges served anywhere from 12 to 650 enrolled Black students. Most typically they offered agriculture and industrial training and were the principal means of access to higher education for Black Americans in the South (Lovett, 2011).

The notion of education for Blacks being separate from that of Whites was solidified with the *Plessey v. Ferguson* Supreme Court ruling in 1896, which upheld the constitutionality of separate but equal facilities based on race in public and private institutions such as schools, public transportation, restaurants, and restrooms. Real equality in education, however, would prove elusive for Black Americans both in K–12 and higher education, particularly in the South, where the majority of Blacks resided right up until the mid-20th century. In K–12, Black schools were severely underfunded and underresourced compared with their White counterparts, sometimes having to educate multiple grades together in one room or building and using old books from White schools (Langhorne, 2000).

In many of the Black colleges, with some notable exceptions, the curriculum had to be tailored to the racial sensibilities and expectations of White benefactors. Moreover, as was famously the case with the Tuskegee Institute under the leadership of Booker T. Washington, there was a reticence based on practical considerations to challenge a racial hierarchy in which Black Americans were perceived more as labor than intellectuals (Lovett, 2011). Indeed, Booker T. Washington, a former slave and one of the foremost and influential Black educators of the day, argued that the best way for freed slaves and other Blacks to obtain equality in the United States was by hard work in skilled trades. This perspective was rejected by Black intellectuals such as General Clinton B. Fisk and Princeton-educated W.E.B. Dubois, who argued instead for Blacks to also receive education in the liberal arts to broaden thinking and to assume leadership positions (Lovett, 2011). These two schools of thought would pervade Black colleges and universities throughout the decades, and regardless of the position taken, Black colleges and universities would do more than any other institutions to provide Black Americans with a higher education. Even today, they educate Black professionals at a higher rate than integrated colleges and universities (Lovett, 2011).

Figure 11.5 Segregated School in West Memphis, Arkansas, 1949

Figure 11.6 Segregated School, 1941

The Chinese Experience

In the late 1800s, the experiences of the Chinese regarding equality of access to education on the West Coast paralleled that of Black Americans. Considered racially inferior and an employment threat to the larger White native and immigrant population, the Chinese were the target of restrictive practice policies in all areas of social life. This was the fate of the American-born children of Chinese immigrants who in California wanted to attend public school, which in practice was reserved for White students and was denied to Chinese-American and other children considered to be of color. The denial of public school education for Chinese-American children in California came to a head when the Chinese immigrant parents of eight-year-old American-born Mammie Tape sued the San Francisco School Board in 1884 for denying their child admission to the Spring Valley School. The lawsuit argued that the school board's decision violated the California Political Code, which stated that all schools unless otherwise stated must be open to all students between the ages of six and 21 (Kuo, 1998; Noltemeyer et al., 2012). In the resulting *Tape v. Hurley* ruling in 1885, the California Superior Court ruled for the parents, as did the California Supreme Court, who upheld the lower court decision on appeal (Kuo, 1998; Noltemeyer et al., 2012).

The victory was short lived, as the California State Legislature moved quickly to amend the school laws so that Chinese would be segregated. The amendment ensured that if Chinese-American children were to attend a public school, it would be a segregated public school. To do so, the School Board created a new Chinese Primary School, which had the full legal sanction to practice dejure segregation (Kuo, 1998). It was under these conditions that Chinese-American students, who were previously receiving education outside the public school system in either Chinese language schools or Christian missionary organizations, entered the public school system. Despite several legal challenges, which included *Wong Him v. Callahan* and *Gong Lum v. Rice*, all upheld the segregation of Chinese-American students in the California public school system (Kuo, 1998). It was not until 1947 that the de jure segregation of Chinese-American students in public education was to end officially when the school board's stipulation of segregated schools for Chinese-Americans was repealed (Kuo, 1998).

The Mexican Experience

In the early 1930s, Mexican children in California suffered much the same fate as both Black children and Chinese-American children before them, when they were also denied equal access to public schools attended by Whites. As discussed in Chapter 5, the Anglo-Saxon and Nordic superiority thesis viewed

Figure 11.7 The Sycamore School, Segregated School for Mexican American Children, 1925

Mexican-Americans as culturally inferior to Whites. This perspective was played out in the California public school system, where children of Mexican heritage were placed in segregated non-White schools (Menchaca & Valencia, 1990). Among the justifications offered for this practice were language differences and the children's supposed lack of social etiquette compared with their White counterparts (Donato, 1997). The segregation of Mexican children in the school system in California was to become one of the early battlegrounds for school integration, namely, the *Roberto Alvarez v. the Board of Trustees of the Lemon Grove School District* court case. In this 1931 case, the court ruled that separate school facilities for Mexican or Chicano students were not conducive to their Americanization and prevented them from learning English (Donato, 1997).

Gender and Education Inequality: An Historical Perspective

For much of United States history, hegemonic masculinity and its subordination of women limited and rigidly defined the kinds of educational opportunities women had access to (Noltemeyer et al., 2012). In the colonial era, religious conventions and societal norms dictated that not only was a woman subservient to a man, but also that her rightful and only role in society was that of a faithful guardian of the home, as a daughter, wife, or mother. Consistent with this perspective, educational opportunities for women, such as they were in an era before public schooling for either gender, were limited to basic literacy and all things domestic (Solomon, 1985). Little to no thought was given to the notion that women could be leaders in society or hold significant careers outside of the home. It was a notion that separated men and women into two different spheres: men in the sphere of all things worldly and intellectual and women in the sphere of all things domestic and emotional. This notion would persist for much of the colonial era, denying women the opportunity to attend any of the eight colleges in the Eastern Board colonies, the first of which, Harvard, was founded in the Massachusetts Bay Colony in 1636. Indeed, these colleges, whose primary purpose was to train men for the clergy or leadership positions within the colonial government, would remain for some time the exclusive preserve of rich or well-to-do White men (Aleman & Renn, 2002). Women, for all intents and purposes, were completely excluded.

In the mid-18th century, there was a dramatic shift in the trajectory of women's education with the emergence of Enlightenment thinking in the colonies. Influenced by the European Enlightenment movement and American philosophy, the American Enlightenment fermented new ideas about the world, society, and human potential that were grounded in science, rational thinking, and tolerance and not the religious orthodoxy that dominated many of the northeastern colonies. Among other things, these new ideas created a platform for women to challenge their subjugation and rigidly defined role in society as a domestic goddess. Influential women of the day such as Abigail Adams and Lucy Otis used this platform to call for the direct and full participation of women in all public affairs, including politics and education. They also championed the need for gender equality in leadership (Aleman & Renn, 2002; Kerber, 1976).

The call for leadership roles for women beyond the home was met with significant opposition from both men and women, many of whom saw motherhood as the ultimate role for women in service of a strong nation that needed good citizens (Kerber, 1976). Despite the opposition, the call and the new ideas fermented by the Enlightenment became one of the catalysts for opening opportunities for the higher education of women. Beginning with the founding of the Sarah Pierce Respectable Academy in Litchfield, Connecticut, the years between 1791 and 1850 saw a remarkable proliferation of female-only institutions of higher education (Aleman & Renn, 2002; Solomon, 1985). Initially at least, these institutions, which included seminaries and colleges, were more akin to high school and were not as academically rigorous as their male counterparts. As the education of women became more widespread and uniform, however, the standards gradually began to approximate those of male colleges and seminaries (Aleman & Renn, 2002; Solomon, 1985).

Along with the improvement in the standard of women's higher education, there was also the cautious beginning of coeducation in institutions of higher education when Oberlin College enrolled its first female students in 1837, followed by Antioch College in 1852 (Aleman & Renn, 2002).

By the mid-1800s, a convergence of changing social, religious, political, and economic conditions created unprecedented career opportunities for women. These changing conditions included the Horace

Mann- and Henry Barnard-inspired emergence and growth of common schooling for boys and girls alike, increased opportunities in business for men, the beginnings of the second industrial revolution, and the third spiritual awakening. The growth in common schools, for example, increased the demand for teachers, a demand women would fill without threatening the powerful social norms that still resisted accepting educated women working outside of the home (Aleman & Renn, 2002). Similarly, opening up career opportunities for women outside of the home was the need for increased numbers of missionaries because of the religious fervor awakened in the nation as a result of the third awakening.

As both teachers and missionaries, women for the first time had career paths that did not tie them to home, although teaching had little status and only minimally expanded the edges of women's domestic sphere as the nurturers of children (Solomon, 1985). The demand for teachers, in particular, would increase further after the Civil War, a demand that going into the 20th century would widen the higher education opportunities for women as women's colleges scrambled to prepare women for the workplace. Among the most prominent of these institutions were the "Seven Sister" colleges. Founded in the 1870s, the Seven Sister colleges were Mount Holyoke, Smith, Wellesley, Radcliff, Barnard, Vassar, and Bryn Mawr (Aleman & Renn, 2002; Perkins, 1997). These colleges became well known for producing some of the nation's most successful women, and by the start of the 20th century were widely recognized as the leading institutions of higher education for elite White women, and to a lesser degree elite Black women (Perkins, 1997).

For all their renown, it was not the Seven Sisters colleges that had the biggest influence on broadening the higher education opportunities for women in the 19th and 20th century. What did have the biggest influence was the passage of the Morrill Act of 1862. The act, also known as the Land Grant Act, brought several changes to higher education in the United States, most particularly the development of public education. Before 1862, the majority of colleges were private institutions. Attending these colleges was beyond the financial means of most women and the population in general. Thus college was very much the preserve of the wealthy or well-to-do middle class, be it women or men (Aleman & Renn, 2002). Moreover, even if wealthy, with very few exceptions such as Michigan, Wisconsin, Boston, and Cornell Universities, women remained firmly locked out of attending the private male-only colleges (Aleman & Renn, 2002; Radke-Moss, 2008).

In its intent to broaden educational opportunities in agriculture, the Land Grant Act enabled states to underwrite the building of public colleges that provided higher education that was affordable to all, regardless of social class. As these colleges prospered, for the first time in American history, higher education was made available to new segments of the nation—the working class, Blacks, Native Americans, and immigrants. Although the Morrill Act did not require coeducation, by 1890, every state included women in its land grant charter. Thus, the public colleges created by the Land Grant Act, whether in the West, East, or on the Plains, were all coeducational, which was considered the norm by the end of the century (Radke-Moss, 2008).

Although it became the norm in public institutions of higher education, coeducation was seen as an abomination by many and was acrimoniously debated for many years. Informing this acrimony was the pseudo-scientific musings of the likes of Herbert Spencer and notable books such as Dr. Edward H. Clarke's widely read *Sex in Education; Or a Fair Chance for Girls* (Aleman & Renn, 2002). In 1875, Englishman Herbert Spencer, an avowed adherent to social Darwinism, posited that men and women had specialized roles that were ordained by God and were unique to one's gender. By virtue of their gender, Spencer argued that women were not capable of abstract reasoning, nor could they consider issues of justice but instead were more focused on emotions and caring (Worell, 2002).

Similarly dismissive of women's intellectual capabilities was Dr. Edward H. Clarke, who was a member of the Massachusetts Medical Association, a Fellow of the American Academy of Arts and Science, and a former professor of medicine at Harvard College (Clarke, 1884). In his book *Sex in Education*, Clarke contended that women's brains were less developed than men's brains and as such they could not tolerate the same level of mental stimulation as a man. More importantly, Clarke argued that the brain had an effect on women's reproductive organs, which if overtaxed would interfere with their menstruation cycle. Clarke concluded that because of the difference between men and women, there was the absolute need for a separate system of education for women (Clarke, 1884).

Clarke's book was widely read and tremendously popular. Indeed, it was used as Exhibit A as to why higher education should not be extended to women. Although vigorously opposed and denounced by first-wave feminists and female educators, Clarke's book and the sentiment it expressed caused significant harm that would hang over women's education rights into the latter parts of the 20th century.

As well as Clarke's book, going into the 20th century, anxiety about changing gender roles brought on by the unrelenting call for suffrage and full equality for women would also increase the call to pull back from educating women. Critics argued that education was the cause of the nation's falling birth rates, increasing divorce rates, and the increase in unmarried women, all of which were seen as destabilizing for society (Aleman & Renn, 2002). Despite this criticism and the fact that gender stratification denied women fair and equal access to courses of study in law, medicine, and science, women continued to pursue higher education, reaching its zenith in 1920 when women accounted for 47% of the enrollment in the nation's colleges. This was a number that would fall significantly in subsequent decades as women were pushed back into domesticity until the second wave of feminism in the 1960s (Aleman & Renn, 2002).

The 20th Century and the Growth in Education

High School Graduation

Throughout the first half of the 20th century, common schooling saw each new cohort of American students more likely to graduate high school than the preceding one (Heckman & LaFontaine, 2010). Indeed, high school graduation rates went from 6.4% in 1900 to its peak of 80% in 1970, with stagnation at 77% between 1970 and 2000 (Murnane & Hoffman, 2013). By the late 1960s, so dramatic was the increase in graduation rates in the first five decades of the 20th century that the United States ranked first among countries in the Organization for Economic Co-operation and Development (OECD) on this measurement of educational attainment (Murnane & Hoffman, 2013). The dramatic growth in high school graduation in the 20th century not only helped to increase worker productivity, it also fueled American economic growth in the years between 1940 and 1970 (Heckman & LaFontaine, 2010).

The G.I. Bill

Equally as important in the growth of education in the United States in the first half of the 20th century was the Servicemen's Readjustment Act of 1944 (P.L. 78–346), otherwise known as the G.I. Bill. Arguably no single piece of legislation was as instrumental in increasing college attendance as this bill. Among its many benefits, returning veterans could attend high school, vocational training, or college at the government's expense, with an additional stipend to cover living expenses (Mettler, 2005). Veterans took advantage of these benefits in overwhelming numbers, with over 2.2 million pursuing higher education and 5.5 million attending high school or vocational school (Batten, 2011; Mettler, 2005; Turner & Bound, 2002). By 1950, returning veterans accounted for 47% of college enrollment. These enrollment numbers towered over those of the 1862 and 1890 Morrell Act combined and led to a profound shift in the perception of higher education (Batten, 2011). Indeed, it would be true to say that it democratized higher education on a scope much larger than the 1862 and 1890 acts (Batten, 2011; Mettler, 2005). It also helped to move large numbers of working class White males into the middle class (Mettler, 2005).

However, as with the dramatic rise in high school graduations, the spoils of the increase in higher education opportunities created by the G.I. bill were not equally enjoyed. High school graduation rates, for example, did dramatically increase for Americans across the board, but rates for Native Americans and Blacks were consistently lower than those of Whites, not least because of segregation and inferior resources and schools (Murnane & Hoffman, 2013).

Moreover, there is evidence that while the G.I. Bill was not racially discriminatory in the educational benefits offered, the approximately one million Black veterans, specifically those from the South, had a much more difficult time than their White counterparts in fully utilizing them. Jim Crow legislation was primarily responsible for this difficulty, dictating that Black veterans had to attend racially segregated colleges, high schools, or vocational schools, essentially restricting them to institutions designated as Negro (Batten, 2011; Turner & Bound, 2002). Among the historically Black colleges and universities, most did not offer degrees beyond the baccalaureate, and none offered degrees in engineering or a doctoral program. Moreover, many of the colleges were small, underresourced, and not equipped to meet the enrollment demands of large numbers of veterans, leading to an estimated 22,000 being turned away because of a lack of space (Batten, 2011; Turner & Bound, 2002). Thus, while the G.I. Bill had a substantial impact on the educational attainment of White veterans and Black veterans born outside of the South, for Black veterans born in the South there was little gain in educational attainment. In turn, the educational differences between Black and White men in the South were exacerbated (Turner & Bound, 2002).

The Quest for Educational Equality, 1950–Present

If the first 50 years of the 20th century can be thought of as the growth of education, then the years from 1950 to the present are the quest for an equalizing of educational opportunity for perennially marginalized groups, notably Native Americans, Blacks, Hispanics, and women. These groups were left behind as White males of all social classes were benefiting from the post-war boom in educational and career opportunities.

Brown v. Board of Education, 1954

In the southern states, Jim Crow legislation and the separate-but-equal doctrine willfully denied Black children anything like the resources enjoyed by White school children. In 1932, for example, there were only a handful of Black high schools throughout the South. In stark contrast, every county in the South possessed a high school for White students (Baughman et al., 2001). Schools that were available for Black children were typically at the elementary level, housing multiple grades in a single building. They received nothing like the tax dollars spent on White schools and thus were perpetually underfunded and underresourced. Moreover, while the average annual salary of a White schoolteacher was $833, the average annual salary of a Black schoolteacher was $510 (Baughman et al., 2001). The educational neglect of Black children in the 1930s and earlier reinforced the economic status quo in which 15% of rural adult Blacks had no formal education and 48% had never gone beyond the fifth grade (Baughman et al., 2001).

The inequality inherent in the separate-but-equal doctrine and its effect on Black educational opportunities in the South was of particular concern to the National Association for the Advancement of Colored People (NAACP). In partnership with the Howard University School of Law, the NAACP's chief counsel Charles Hamilton Houston, assisted by his protégé and future Supreme Court Justice Thurgood Marshall, devised a long-range strategy to chip away at the separate-but-equal doctrine by helping local Black plaintiffs bring lawsuits against segregated school systems (National Archives, 2015). The end game was to create a series of legal precedents that would eventually allow for a Supreme Court challenge to the constitutionality of the separate-but-equal doctrine. Beginning in 1935, Houston and Marshall crisscrossed the country researching and mobilizing Black plaintiffs. Between 1938 and 1950, the NAACP set legal precedents in four cases (National Archives, 2015): *Missouri ex. rel. Gains v. Canada*, 1938; *Sipuel v. Oklahoma State Regents*, 1948; *McLaurin v. Oklahoma*, 1950; and *Sweatt v. Painter*, 1950.

In 1951, a class action suit was filed against the Board of Education of the City of Topeka, Kansas, in the District Court for the District of Kansas. The suit called for the school district to reverse its policy of racial segregation. The District Court ruled for the Board of Education, citing the U.S. Supreme Court precedent set in *Plessy v. Ferguson* (National Archives, 2015). In 1952, the U.S. Supreme Court agreed to hear *Brown v. Board of Education*, which consolidated five cases of racial segregation from five jurisdictions around the country. In 1954, the U.S. Supreme Court ruled unanimously that the racial segregation of children in public schools violated the equal protection clause of the Fourteenth Amendment and was therefore unconstitutional, overruling the "separate but equal" principle set forth in the 1896 *Plessy v. Ferguson* case

(National Archives, 2015). In delivering the opinion of the court, Chief Justice Earl Warren made the following statement:

> Segregation of white and colored children in public schools has a detrimental effect upon the colored children. The impact is greater when it has the sanction of law, for the policy of separating the races is usually interpreted as denoting the inferiority of the Negro group.
>
> (*Smithsonian National Museum of American History*, 2015)

Elementary and Secondary Education Act of 1965

BACKGROUND

In the aftermath of the Supreme Court's 1954 *Brown v. Board of Education* ruling, the importance of providing equal educational opportunity for all would take on new urgency. Informing this urgency was the civil rights movement, which, under the leadership of Martin Luther King Jr., called for Black Americans to be afforded their full civil rights as American citizens. Among the issues central to these civil rights was the dismantling of racial segregation in public spaces, voting rights, and fair and equal access to all of society's resources, among them education, health care, and employment (Patterson, 2001). Also informing the urgency for providing equal educational opportunity was the growing awareness of poverty in the United States, which was graphically portrayed in books such as James Conant's *Slums and Suburbs* (1961) and Michael Harrington's *The Other America* (1962). It was a situation that educational policy makers and researchers agreed were causing an educational crisis among poor children. These poor children, liberals argued, had little opportunity to escape their poverty through education because they were stuck in underresourced schools that simply replicated larger societal inequalities (McGuinn & Hess, 2005). Consequently, there was a need for federal involvement to facilitate equal educational opportunities for poor children. Conservatives, in contrast, argued that poor children were the victims of a culture of poverty that undermined educational attainment. What was needed to remedy this problem was not federal involvement but the teaching of middle-class values (McGuinn & Hess, 2005). Despite this ideological rift, there was widespread agreement among educational policy makers and researchers that the federal government should intervene to help bring about the equal educational opportunity for poor children.

In addition to the ideological rift about how best to address the issue of poverty and educational equality, there were states' rights adherents and Roman Catholic school representatives who chafed at the idea of federal government involvement in K–12 educational policy (McGuinn & Hess, 2005). Throughout American history, K–12 education had been the domain of local and state agencies, with almost no federal involvement. Catholics, in particular, were concerned that any federal involvement would focus on public schools, leaving out the private Catholic schools. States' rights adherents, on the other hand, feared that federal involvement would centralize education, thus marginalizing state and local agencies (McGuinn & Hess, 2005). It was a fear states' rights adherents had used to oppose and successfully defeat previous Democrats' proposals for increased federal education spending in the 1940s and 1950s (McGuinn & Hess, 2005).

President Lyndon Johnson, a former schoolteacher, was keenly aware of the impact that poverty and poor schools were having on the educational attainment of poor children. Determined to do something about it, and with a Democratic majority in Congress, President Johnson formed a Commission on Education in 1964, chaired by John W. Gardner. The task of the Commission, known as the Gardner Commission, was to devise a plan for federal education aid (Jennings, 2001). Cognizant of the many potential political obstacles, the Commission proposed linking education aid to President Johnson's popular and well-supported "War on Poverty" policy program. The Commission further recommended that the federal education aid should be targeted to the specific needs of poor children (Jennings, 2001; McGuinn & Hess, 2005).

IMPLEMENTATION

In 1965, President Johnson adopted the approach recommended by the Commission and presented it to Congress as an educational plan linked to the War on Poverty (Jennings, 2001; McGuinn & Hess, 2005). In presenting the bill, President Johnson argued that nothing mattered more to the country than education, which would ensure freedom from ignorance and preserve freedom. President Johnson also reasoned that federal leadership in education was both logical and essential (McGuinn & Hess, 2005). With much cajoling from President Johnson, the bill, the Elementary and Secondary Education Act (ESEA) of 1965, was passed in just three months (Public Law 89–10, 1965). In signing the bill into law, President Johnson stated, "I believe deeply no law I have signed or will ever sign means more to the future of America" (Johnson, 1965).

The ESEA marked the federal government's first significant involvement in K–12 education policy. It also represented the most expansive federal education policy ever passed (McGuinn & Hess, 2005). Developed under the principle of redress, Title I (Improving the Academic Achievement of the Disadvantaged) of the ESEA allocated $1 billion dollars a year to schools with high concentrations of low-income children (Jennings, 2001; Social Welfare History Project, 2015). Title I sought to ensure that all children had a fair, equal, and significant opportunity to obtain a high-quality education (Jennings, 2001; Public Law 89–10, 1965). Title II provided funding for school library resources, textbooks, and other instructional materials. Title III funded the creation of supplementary educational centers and services to stimulate and assist in the provision of vitally needed educational services not available in sufficient quantity or quality. Title IV authorized grants for educational research and training. The purpose of research and training was to identify new and promising teaching methods and curricula. Title V provided grants to strengthen the functioning of state departments of education. Title VI granted monies for general provisions, most notably for school construction, repair, or replacement of equipment. In 1966, an amendment to ESEA included Aid to Handicapped Children, Title VII (Public Law 89–750, 1966). In 1967, further amendments were made to include bilingual education, Title VIII (P.L. 90–247, 1967).

PERFORMANCE

Despite its lofty ideals, the largesse and the political concessions agreed to by President Johnson negatively impacted the effectiveness of the ESEA. The largesse was a result of the political concessions made by President Johnson to allay the fears of states' rights adherents and Catholics. These concessions included an agreement that the federal government would have no direct involvement in the running of schools or devising of curricula, and Title I would include private, parochial schools. The result of the concessions was that the ESEA in practice became a bloated bureaucracy that delivered services to all, rather than just those most in need. Indeed, in the first two years of the ESEA, a staggering 94% of school districts were receiving funding in some form or another (McGuinn & Hess, 2005).

Confirming the poor performance of the ESEA was a 1969 report entitled *Title I of ESEA: Is It Helping Poor Children?* Co-authored by Ruby Martin of the Washington Research Project and Phyllis McClure of the Legal Defense Fund of the NAACP, the report analyzed audits of the ESEA conducted by the U.S. Department of Health, Education and Welfare (Thomas & Brady, 2005). Findings from the analysis indicated the following:

- The intended targets of Title I—poor children—were being the denied the benefits of the act because of improper and illegal use of Title I funds.
- The majority of the Title I programs were poorly planned and executed; thus the needs of educationally deprived children were not being met.
- The state departments responsible for operating and approving Title I programs were not administering the programs in conformity with the law and intent of Congress.
- The United States Office of Education was timid in its administration of Title I, deferring instead to states to enforce the law.
- In many poor communities, poor people and representative community organizations were excluded from the planning and design of Title 1 programs. Moreover, in some communities school officials refused to provide information about Title 1 programs to local residents.

(Martin & McClure, 1969, pp. ii, iii)

REFORM

Not surprisingly, the findings from the Martin and McClure report brought considerable attention to the early shortcomings of Title 1. Of particular concern was the fiscal abuse, and even more so the failure to more precisely meet the congressional intent of serving poor children. To redress the identified shortcomings, Congress amended ESEA four times between 1965 and 1980 (Thomas & Brady, 2005).

Going into the 1980s and a more conservative era, there was a marked ideological shift in the thinking about ESEA. President Ronald Reagan, for example, significantly reduced federal education program funding, and moved toward reducing the federal government's role in public education (Thomas & Brady, 2005). Consequently, support for ESEA waned (Jennings, 2001). In 1981, as part of the Educational Consolidation and Improvement Act, Title I of ESEA was renamed Chapter I. Although Chapter I of ESEA retained its original legislative intent of funding services for educationally disadvantaged children, less federal aid and more relaxed regulatory requirements resulted in significantly fewer eligible students being served (Jennings, 2001; Thomas & Brady, 2005).

In addition, there was the emergence of the standards-and-testing movement that began in the mid-1980s following the release of the report *A Nation at Risk: The Imperative for Educational Reform* (National Commission on Excellence in Education, 1983). Arguably one of the landmark events in American educational history, the publication of the report revealed that American schools were failing. Examples of this failure noted in the report included unacceptably high levels of functional illiteracy among high school students, especially evident among racial and ethnic minorities. Average academic achievement among high school students as measured by standardized tests scores was lower than in 1950. More than 50% of the population of gifted students did not match their tested ability with comparable achievement in school. Furthermore, there were steady declines in science achievement scores and an increase in the need for remedial mathematic courses for entering freshmen in four-year public colleges (National Commission on Excellence in Education, 1983).

Policy reaction to the report was immediate, and by the mid-1980s, 41 states had passed legislation requiring increased academic requirements for high-school graduation (McDonnell & Fuhrman, 1986). Just as importantly, it signaled the beginning of a trend in which successive presidents would make standards and testing a central component of Title I/Chapter 1.

In 1988, Chapter I was amended, requiring states to monitor the academic achievement of their poor children through standardized test scores. As a consequence, for the first time, ESEA funds were linked to the academic achievement of educationally deprived children (Jennings, 2001; Thomas & Brady, 2005). In 1989, President George H.W. Bush and the nation's state governors reached a consensus that Chapter I needed to include higher levels of educational accountability through improved academic standards and more fiscal choice in the allocation of federal aid (Thomas & Brady, 2005, p. 54). In 1994, President Bill Clinton enacted Goals 2000, which provided grants to help states develop academic standards (Rudalevige, 2003). Also in 1994, ESEA was reauthorized with the passage of the Improving America's School Act. Under the act all school districts had to identify schools not making adequate yearly progress (AYP) and take the necessary steps to improve them. Relatedly, as a precondition of receiving Chapter I funds, states would have to demonstrate that the learning goals, academic expectations, and curricular opportunities for Chapter I-eligible students were the same as those for noneligible students (McDonnell, 2005).

Even with the changes in Chapter I, the National Assessment of Education Progress Report of 1998 revealed that little progress had been made in closing the achievement gap of students. For example, 36% of Native American, 43% of Black, 35% of Hispanic, and 25% of Asian/Pacific Islander high school students were reading below a basic level of competency compared with just 17% of White high school students (U.S. Department of Education, 1998). Even more disturbing was the finding that schools with large numbers of racial and ethnic minorities had higher numbers of unqualified teachers in critical subjects such as math and science (Thomas & Brady, 2005).

No Child Left Behind

Concerned that ESEA goals had not been met, Congress called for more accountability and results for the federal funds spent on the ESEA programs. On January 8, 2002, President George W. Bush reauthorized and renamed the ESEA the No Child Left Behind Act (NCLB) of 2002. This rebranding of the ESEA was in many respects the culmination of the standards-and-testing movement's quest for greater accountability in the funding of K–12 education. But by the 2000s, NCLB was as much, and arguably more, the product of the collaboration between civil rights and business groups, as well as both Democrats and Republicans on Capitol Hill and President George W. Bush. These seemingly unlikely allies were united in the goals of improving America's international competitiveness; closing the academic achievement gap between poor and minority students and their more socioeconomically advantaged peers; and providing equality to all American students, regardless of race, ethnicity, or socioeconomic background (Klein, 2015; Thomas & Brady, 2005).

To achieve its stated goals, NCLB instituted federal educational standards for all children. To accomplish this, NCLB mandated the establishment of state standardized testing in reading/language arts, mathematics, and science for all children in grades 3 to 8 and once between grades 10 and 12. The results of this testing had to be reported for students as a whole and for particular subgroups of students, including English-learners, special education students, racial and ethnic minority students, and students from low-income families (Klein, 2015; Thomas & Brady, 2005).

To ensure that schools were effectively preparing students to meet standardized testing goals, NCLB instituted a monitoring mechanism known as the Annual Yearly Progress (AYP) report. Schools that failed to meet their annual achievement targets for two years in a row, either for all students or particular subgroups of students, would be identified as not meeting their AYP and be subject to a number of sanctions. Ranging in their severity, these sanctions included state intervention and school closing, being turned into a charter school, having to allow students to transfer to a better-performing high school, and having to set aside a portion of Chapter I funding for tutoring and school choice.

Another related stipulation of NCLB was that schools had to ensure that their teachers were highly qualified, as defined by having at least a bachelor's degree in areas of teaching and state certification. Moreover, paraprofessionals who assisted in the classroom must have completed at least two years of college, or passed an evaluation demonstrating knowledge of teaching and teaching competence.

Criticism of NCLB

Both at the time of its enactment and even more so today, NCLB has had its critics. Teachers unions have been particularly virulent in both their criticism and opposition to NCLB, which they argue simply focuses on standardized testing rather than taking a more holistic view of academic achievement. The focus on standardized testing and sanctions, teachers unions argue, makes very little allowance for the very real disparities among schools. Indeed, in April of 2015 the largest teachers union launched a $500,000 advertising campaign urging lawmakers to reach a deal to reduce NCLB's focus on standardized testing (Brown, 2015).

Equally vociferous in their opposition to NCLB are those who charge that its mandates intrude too much into education, which has always been the domain of the states. In fact, they argue, the Tenth Amendment stipulates that those powers not delegated to the United States by the Constitution nor prohibited by it to the states, are reserved to the states respectively or to the people (Find Law, 2015). Thus, they contend, education is not a federal responsibility and should remain a state responsibility.

Has NCLB Lived Up to Expectations?

Above and beyond the criticisms, over a decade into NCLB it has not proved to be nearly as effective an educational reform as was hoped. For example, the Center on Education Policy's report on the AYP results for 2011 revealed that 49% of the nation's public schools did not make AYP in 2011, an all-time high and an increase from 39% in 2010 (Usher, 2012). Other notable findings from the report were that in five states, 75% or more of the public schools did not make AYP in 2011. From highest to lowest, these states included Florida, District of Columbia, New Mexico, Massachusetts, South Carolina, and Missouri (Usher, 2012). Finally, none of the four largest states, which together account for one-third of the nation's students, made AYP. Ninety-one percent of Florida's public schools failed to make AYP, followed by 66% in California, 47% in New York, and 28% in Texas (Usher, 2012).

A range of explanations have been forwarded as to why NCLB has not significantly raised academic standards or closed the education achievement gap. Among the most frequently cited are insufficient resources to support the reforms, misunderstanding about the state context of education, and lack of knowledge about the challenges of educating disadvantaged students and the obstacles to meeting NCLB stipulations (Thomas & Brady, 2005, p. 58). In acknowledgment of these difficulties, in 2010, President Obama released his own blueprint for revising NCLB that in exchange for setting high educational standards and putting teacher evaluations based on student outcomes would give states much more control over how to intervene with schools. This control would come in the form of government-granted waivers from NCLB (Klein, 2015). As of 2015, 43 states, the District of Columbia, and Puerto Rico were approved for flexibility waivers to NCLB, so that the majority of the states no longer operate under the NCLB law as written (U.S. Department of Education, 2015).

Every Child Achieves Act of 2015 (P.L. 114–95)

On December 10, 2015, President Obama signed into law the Every Child Achieves Act (GovTrack.us, 2015). Introduced in the Senate on April 30, 2015, the bipartisan bill replaced NCLB, which was seven years past its reauthorization date (Govtrack.us, 2015; Stern, 2015). In its stated objective to ensure that every child achieves educationally, the act expands state and local responsibility for schools, provides grants for charter schools, and reduces the federal test-based accountability of the NCLB Act (GovTrack.us, 2015). Additionally, the act provides federal grants to states and school districts to help improve low-performing schools, as well as reaffirms that states' role in determining education standards (Stern, 2015). Just as importantly for teachers, the act provides federal resources to aid and encourage their professional development. It also allows, but does not require, states to develop and implement teacher evaluation systems (Stern, 2015).

Chapter Summary

Despite the mythology of meritocracy in American education, in practice there are few areas of American life in which inequality has been more keenly felt than in education. This inequality is not a recent occurrence; it has been a structural feature of the United States since the colonial era when women were systematically excluded from equal access to higher levels of education right up until the mid-20th century. In addition to women, Native Americans, Blacks, Hispanics, and Asians/Pacific Islanders have been similarly excluded for much of American history from fair and equal access to educational opportunities. Consequently, even with the more recent policy attempts in the past 50 years to redress the generations of educational inequalities, entrenched structural inequalities continue to hamper the closing of the education achievement gap between poor, Native American, Black, and Hispanic children and their middle or upper-class White and Asian counterparts.

Retrieval Questions

1. Which groups of children are most affected by inequality of opportunity and access to quality education?
2. What did Reardon (2011) find when he looked at previous and current reading achievement gaps between children in high-income families and those in low-income families?
3. What was the purpose of the Civilization Fund Act of 1819?
4. Why was the Freedman's Bureau important to the education of newly freed slaves?
5. Why were the Morrell Act of 1862 and 1890 important?
6. What was the significance of the *Tape v. Hurley* ruling?
7. What was the significance of the *Roberto Alvarez v. the Board of Trustees of the Lemon Grove School District* ruling?
8. What are the Seven Sister colleges?
9. What was the significance of the G.I. Bill for higher education in America?
10. What were two events in the quest for educational inequality in the years between 1950 and the present?

Discussion Questions

1. Identify and discuss some of the social justice issues pertinent to educational inequality.
2. As policy practitioners, how might social workers address educational inequality?
3. What are some of the potential practice challenges when working with clients who have been poorly served by the educational system?
4. How might a client's level of education affect the social work practice context?

Box 11.1 Education Inequality Timeline, 1800–Present

1805: Wealthy businessmen form the New York Public Schools Society to provide education for poor children. Using the Lancastrian model in which one master teaches a class of students in a single room, the schools emphasize qualities that factory owners want of their workers—discipline and obedience (Race Forward, 2013).

1819: Congress enacts the Civilization Fund Act of 1819. Among its many purposes, the act seeks to "civilize" Native American children through westernized education (Prucha, 2000).

1820: Boston English is founded and becomes the first public high school in the United States (Race Forward, 2013).

1827: The state of Massachusetts enacts legislation making all grades of public school available to all pupils free of charge (Race Forward, 2013).

1833: Oberlin College becomes the first college in America to admit Black students (Noltemeyer et al., 2012).

1837: Oberlin College becomes the first coeducational college in America when it admits its first female students, Mary Kellogg, Mary Caroline Rudd, Mary Hosford, and Elizabeth Prall (Noltemeyer et al., 2012; Oberlin College & Conservatory, 2015).

1847: Samuel Gridley Howe convinces Massachusetts's lawmakers to fund the first residential school for idiots, the first of its kind (Trent, 2015).

1851: Massachusetts state legislature passes its first compulsory education law. The purposes of the law are to ensure that children of poor immigrants get civilized, as well as learn obedience and restraint so they make good workers and do not contribute to social disorder (Race Forward, 2013).

1864: Congress makes it illegal for Native Americans to be taught in their native language (Race Forward, 2013).

1879: The first nonreservation Indian boarding school is founded as Carlisle Indian Industrial School (Prucha, 2000).

1896: In *Plessy v. Ferguson*, the U.S Supreme Court rules that Louisiana has the right to require separate but equal railroad cars for Blacks and Whites. The decision adds legal support to southern states' Jim Crow laws racially segregating public schools (Langhorne, 2000).

1905: The U.S. Supreme Court rules that California must extend public education to the children of Chinese immigrants (Race Forward, 2013).

1921: Congress passes the Snyder Act. The act authorizes federal funding for the benefit, care, and assistance for Native Americans throughout the United States. Education is included in the care (American Indian Higher Education Consortium, 2015).

1928: The *Meriam Report* reveals that Native American students in off-reservation Indian boarding schools live in extremely poor conditions and receive little in the way of effective education. The report questions the necessity of off-reservation education for Native American children (The Institute for Government Research Studies in Administration, 1928).

1944: Congress enacts the Servicemen's Readjustment Act of 1944 (P.L. 78–346), more commonly known as the G.I. Bill. Among other things, the act provides millions of working-class men with college scholarships (Mettler, 2005).

1954: In the *Brown v. Board of Education of Topeka*, the Supreme Court rules unanimously that segregated schools are inherently unequal and must be abolished (National Archives, 2015).

1957: A federal court orders the integration of Little Rock Arkansas public schools. In defiance of the court order, Governor Orval Faubus uses the National Guard to physically stop Black students from enrolling at all-White Central High School. In response, President Eisenhower sends federal troops to enforce the federal court order (Race Forward, 2013).

1958: To strengthen national defense and encourage science education in America in the wake of Russia's successful launching of Sputnik I, the world's first artificial satellite, President Dwight Eisenhower signs into law the National Defense Education Act (P.L. 85–864). The NDEA provides funding to United States education institutions at all levels (P.L. 85–864, 1958).

1964: President Lyndon Johnson signs into law the Civil Rights Act of 1964 (P.L. 89–10). Among its many stipulations, the act authorized the Commissioner of Education to arrange for support for institutions of higher education and school districts to provide in-service programs for assisting instructional staff in dealing with problems caused by desegregation (P.L. 88–352, 1964).

1965: On the heels of the Civil Rights Act of 1964, President Lyndon Johnson signs into law the Elementary and Secondary Education Act (P.L. 89–10). The ESEA represents the federal government's first significant involvement in K–12 education policy. It also represents the most expansive federal education policy ever passed (McGuinn & Hess, 2005; Public Law 89–10, 1965).

1965: In May 1965, President Lyndon B. Johnson and Mr. Shriver establish the Head Start program, an eight-week summer program for children from low-income communities entering public school in the fall. In its first summer, the program serves over 500,000 children across the nation. It provides the children with preschool classes. In 1969, the program becomes permanent and is transferred from the Office of Economic to the Office of Child Development in the Department of Health Education and Welfare (Office of Head Start, 2015).

1966: The first amendments are made to the Elementary and Secondary Act of 1965 (P.L. 89–750). Among other things, the amendments provide grants to meet the needs of educationally deprived Native American children on reservations served by the Department of the Interior. The amendments also provide the first federal grant program for the education of children and youth with disabilities at the local school level. Also established were the Bureau of Education of the Handicapped (BEH) and the National Advisory Council (now called the National Council on Disability; Public Law 89–750, 1966).

1968: The first tribal college, Navajo Community College, is founded. The college is renamed Dine College in 1997 (American Indian Higher Education Consortium, 2015).

1972: Title XI of the Educational Amendments prohibits the exclusion of any person from participation in an educational program or the denial of benefits based on gender. More specifically, Title XI requires that both genders have equal opportunities to participate in sports and enjoy the benefits of competitive athletics (National Women's Law Center, 2012).

1974: In the *Milliken v. Bradley* case, the U.S. Supreme Court rules that schools may not be desegregated across school districts. The ruling effectively legally segregated students of color in inner-city districts away from White students in wealthier suburban districts (Race Forward, 2013).

1975: President Richard Nixon signs the Indian Self-Determination Act into law (P.L. 93–638). The act gives tribal governments more authority over education, health, and social services (American Indian Higher Education Consortium, 2015).

1975: President Richard Nixon signs into law the Education for All Handicapped Children Act (P.L. 94–142). The goal of the act is to ensure that all handicapped children have a free education designed to meet their special needs (P.L. 94–142, 1975).

1984: Congress passes the Education of the Handicapped Act Amendments (P.L. 98–199). The law adds the Architectural Barrier amendment and clarifies participation of handicapped children in private schools (African American Voices in Congress, 2015).

1996: In *United States v. Virginia*, the Supreme Court rules that the all-male Virginia Military School must lift its ban on women if it is to continue to receive public funding (Strum, 2002).

2002: The No Child Left Behind Act of 2001 (P.L. 107–110) is signed into law. The act requires states to develop assessments in basic skills to be given to all students in grades 3–8 and once in grades 10–12, if those states are to receive federal funding for schools. The act does not mandate a national achievement standard; standards are instead set by each individual state (P.L. 107–110, 2002).

2009: President Obama signs into law the American Reinvestment and Recovery Act of 2009. The fiscal stimulus bill provides more than $90 billion for education, approximately half of which is for school modernization and repair, and prevents teachers' layoffs. Also included is the Race to the Top initiative, a $4.35 billion program designed to create reform in K–12 education (Hayes & Boyle, 2020).

2010: President Obama releases his blueprint for revising the Elementary and Secondary Education Act (ESEA). The blueprint challenges the nation to embrace education standards that would put America on a path to global leadership. It provides incentives for states to adopt academic standards that prepare students to succeed in college and the workplace, and creates accountability systems that measure student growth toward meeting the goal that all children graduate and succeed in college (African American Voices in Congress, 2015).

2015: On December 9, the U.S. votes 85–12 to approve the Every Student Succeeds Act, which President Obama signs into law on December 10. This latest edition of the Elementary and Secondary Education Act (ESEA) replaces No Child Left Behind, and in doing so, allows more state control in evaluating school quality (American Educational History, 2020).

2017: The U.S. Supreme Court rule in the *Endrew v. Douglas Count School District* case that schools must offer an individualized education program reasonably calculated to enable a child to make progress commensurate with the child's circumstances (American Educational History, 2020).

2017: On February 28, President Trump issues Executive Order 13779—White House Initiative to Promote Excellence and Innovation at Historically Black Colleges and Universities. The order seeks to strengthen HBCUs through enhanced planning and development collaboration with the private sector, participation in federal programs, and upgrading infrastructure (Govinfo.gov, 2017).

2017: On April 6, President Trump issues a presidential Executive Order on Enforcing Statutory Prohibitions on Federal Control of Education. The order restores the proper division of power under the Constitution between the federal government and the states to prohibit federal interference with state and local control over education (Whitehouse.gov., 2017).

References

African American Voices in Congress. (2015). *Timeline: Education policy*. Retrieved from www.avoiceonline.org/edpol/timeline.html

Aleman, A. M. M., & Renn, K. A. (2002). *Women in higher education: An encyclopedia*. Santa Barbara, CA: ABC-CLIO, Inc.

American Educational History. (2020). *A hypertext timeline*. Retrieved from www.eds-resources.com/educationhistorytimeline.html

American Indian Higher Education Consortium. (2015). *A timeline of the tribal college movement and AIHEC*. Retrieved from www.aihec.org/who-we-are/about.cfm

American Indian Relief Council. (2015). *History and culture: Boarding schools*. Retrieved from www.nrcprograms.org/site/PageServer?pagename=airc_hist_boardingschools

Banks, J. A. (2012). *The encyclopedia of diversity in education*. Thousand Oaks, CA: Sage.

Batten, D. D. (2011). The G.I. Bill, higher education and American society. *Grove City College of Law and Public Policy*, 2, 14–30.

Baughman, J. S., Bondi, V., Layman, R., McConnell, T., & Tomkins, V. (2001). The 1930s: Education overview. In *American Decades* (Vol. 4). Detroit, MI: Gale. Retrieved from http://ic.galegroup.com/ic/uhic/ReferenceDetailsPage/ReferenceDetailsWindow?query=&prodId=UHIC&displayGroupName=Reference&limiter=&disableHighlighting=true&displayGroups=&sortBy=&zid=&search_within_results=&action=2&catId=&activityType=&documentId=GALE%7CCX3468301121&source=Bookmark&u=sand55832&jsid=55d9d90c4bad282ee2debc3c18227fed

Bergman, R. (1977). The human cost of removing Indian children from their families. In S. Unger (Ed.), *The destruction of American Indian families* (pp. 34–36). New York, NY: Association of American Indian Affairs.

The Black Law of Connecticut 1833. (2007). *Citizens all: African Americans in Connecticut, 1700–1850*. Retrieved from http://cmi2.yale.edu/citizens_all/stories/module4/page3.html

Brown, E. (2015, April 6). Nation's largest teachers union launches campaign as Congress debates No Child Left Behind. *The Washington Post*. Retrieved from www.washingtonpost.com/news/local/wp/2015/04/06/nations-largest-teachers-union-launches-ad-campaign-as-congress-debates-no-child-left-behind/

ChildStats.gov. (2020). *America's children in brief: Key national indicators of well-being, 2020*. Retrieved from www.childstats.gov/americaschildren/ed_fig.asp

Clarke, E. H. (1884). *Sex in education, or a fair chance for girls*. Boston, MA: Houghton, Mifflin.

Conant, J. B. (1961). *Slums and suburbs: A commentary on schools in metropolitan areas*. New York, NY: McGraw Hill.

Donato, R. (1997). *The other struggle for equal schools: Mexican Americans during the civil rights era*. Albany: The State University of New York Press.

Duncan, G. J., & Magnuson, K. (2011). The nature and impact of early education achievement skills. In G. J. Duncan & R. J. Murnane (Eds.), *Whither opportunity? Rising inequality, schools, and children's life chances* (pp. 47–70). New York, NY: Russell Sage Foundation.

Duncan, G. J., & Murnane, R. J. (2011). Introduction: The American dream, then and now. In G. J. Duncan & R. J. Murnane (Eds.), *Whither opportunity? Rising inequality, schools, and children's life chances* (pp. 3–24). New York, NY: Russell Sage Foundation.

Find Law. (2015). *Criticism of No Child Left Behind*. Retrieved from http://education.findlaw.com/curriculum-standards-school-funding/criticism-of-no-child-left-behind.html

Foley, H. (1875). *Records of the English province of the society of Jesus: Historic facts illustrative of the labors and sufferings of its members in the sixteenth and seventeenth centuries*. London, England: Burns and Oates. Retrieved from https://archive.org/stream/recordsofenglish00fole#page/n7/mode/2up

Freeman, B. R. (1978). *Public education in the United States: From revolution to reform*. New York, NY: Holt, Rinehart and Winston.

Fry, R., & Cilluffo, A. (2019). *A rising share of undergraduates are from poor families, especially at less selective colleges*. Pew Research Center. Retrieved from www.pewsocialtrends.org/2019/05/22/a-rising-share-of-undergraduates-are-from-poor-families-especially-at-less-selective-colleges/

Garcia, E., & Weiss, E. (2017). *Education inequalities at the starting gate: Gaps, trends, and strategies to address them*. Retrieved from www.epi.org/publication/education-inequalities-at-the-school-starting-gate/

Government Accountability Office. (2018). *K-12 Education: Discipline disparities for black students, boys, and student with disabilities*. Retrieved from www.gao.gov/products/GAO-18-258

Govinfo.gov. (2017). *Executive Order 13779:White House Initiative to Promote Excellence and Innovation at Historically Black College and Universities*. Retrieved from www.govinfo.gov/content/pkg/DCPD-201700149/html/DCPD-201700149.htm

GovTrack.us. (2015). S: 1177: Every Child Achieves Act of 2015. *Govtrack.us*. Retrieved from www.govtrack.us/congress/bills/114/s1177

Harper, K., Ryberg, R., & Temkin, D. (2019). Black students and students with disabilities remain more likely to receive out-of-school suspensions, despite overall declines. *Child Trends*. Retrieved from www.childtrends.org/publications/black-students-disabilities-out-of-school-suspensions

Harrington, M. (1962). *The other America: Poverty in the United States*. New York, NY: Touchstone.

Hayes, A., & Boyle. M. J. (2020). What is the American Reinvestment and Recovery Act (ARRA)? *Investopedia*. Retrieved from www.investopedia.com/terms/a/american-recovery-and-reinvestment-act.asp

Heckman, J. J., & LaFontaine, P. A. (2010). The American high school graduation: Trends and levels. *Review of Economics and Statistics*, 92(2), 244–262.

Hirschman, C., & Lee, J. C. (2006). Race and ethnic inequality in educational attainment in the United States. In M. Rutter & M. Tienda (Eds.), *Ethnicity and causal mechanics* (pp. 107–138). Cambridge, UK: Cambridge University Press.

The Institute for Government Research Studies in Administration. (1928). *The problem of Indian administration*. Baltimore, MD: The Lord Baltimore Press. Retrieved from www.alaskool.org/native_ed/research_reports/IndianAdmin/Indian_Admin_Problms.html

Jennings, J. F. (2001). Title 1: Its legislative history and promise. In G. D. Bowman, S. C. Springfield, & R. E. Slavin (Eds.), *Title 1: Compensatory education at a crossroads* (pp. 1–23). Mahaw, NJ: Erlbaum.

Johnson, E., & Howard, T. C. (2009). Issues of difference contributing to U.S. education inequality. In D. B. Holsinger & W. J. Jacob (Eds.), *Inequality in education: Comparative and international perspectives* (pp. 444–460). Hong Kong, China: Comparative Education Research Center, Springer.

Johnson, L. B. (1965). Johnson's remarks on signing the Elementary and Secondary Education Act. *LBJ Presidential Library*. Retrieved from www.lbjlibrary.org/lyndon-baines-johnson/timeline/johnsons-remarks-on-signing-the-elementary-and-secondary-education-act

Johnson, T. (2003). *Reporting on race, education and No Child Left Behind: A guide for reporters*. Oakland, CA: Applied Research Center. Retrieved from http://cleweb.org/sites/cleweb.org/files/assets/wecksteinaccountability2003.pdf

Kerber, L. (1976). The Republican mother: Women and the enlightenment: An American perspective. *American Quarterly*, 28(2), 187–205.

Kewal-Ramani, A., Gilbertson, L., Fox, M., & Provasnik, S. (2007). *Status and trends in the education of racial and ethnic minorities* (NCES 2007–039). National Center for Education Statistics, Institute of Education Sciences, U.S. Department of Education. Washington, DC.

Klein, A. (2015). No Child Left Behind: An overview. *Education Week*. Retrieved from www.edweek.org/ew/section/multimedia/no-child-left-behind-overview-definition-summary.html

Kuo, J. (1998). Excluded, segregated and forgotten: A historical view of the discrimination of Chinese Americans in public schools. *Asian American Law Journal*, 5(7), 182–211.

Langhorne, M. (2000). The African American community: Circumventing the compulsory education system. *Beverly Hill Bar Association Journal*, 12(31), 13–17.

Libassi, C. J. (2018). *The neglected college race gap: Racial disparities among college completers*. Center for American Progress. Retrieved from www.americanprogress.org/issues/education-postsecondary/reports/2018/05/23/451186/neglected-college-race-gap-racial-disparities-among-college-completers/

Lovett, B. L. (2011). *America's historically black colleges and universities: A narrative history from the nineteenth century into the twenty-first century*. Macon, GA: Mercer University Press.

Martin, R., & McClure, P. (1969). *Title I of ESEA: Is it helping poor children?* Washington, DC: Washington Research Project of the Southern Center of Studies in Public Policy and the NAACP Legal Defense and Education Fund.

McArdle, N., & Acevedo, D. (2017). *Consequences of segregation for a children's opportunity and wellbeing*. Joint Center for Housing Studies of Harvard University. Retrieved from https://jchs.harvard.edu/sites/jchs.harvard.edu/files/a_shared_future_consequences_of_segregation_for_children.pdf

McDonnell, L. M. (2005). No Child Left Behind and the federal role in education: Evolution or revolution? *Peabody Journal of Education*, 80(2), 19–38.

McDonnell, L. M., & Fuhrman, S. (1986). The political context of reform. In V. D. Mueller & M. P. McKeown (Eds.), *The fiscal, legal, and political aspects of state reform of elementary and secondary education* (pp. 43–64). Cambridge, MA: Ballinger.

McGuinn, P., & Hess, F. (2005). Freedom from ignorance? The great society and evolution of the Elementary and Secondary Education Act of 1965. In S. Milkis & J. Mileur (Eds.), *The Great Society and the high tide of liberalism* (pp. 17–42). Amherst: University of Massachusetts Press.

Menchaca, M., & Valencia, R. R. (1990). Anglo-Saxon ideologies in the 1920s–1930s: The impact of segregation on Mexican students in California. *Anthropology and Education Quarterly*, 21(3), 222–249.

Mettler, S. (2005). *Solders to citizens: The G.I. Bill and the making of the greatest generation*. Oxford, England: Oxford University Press.

Murnane, R. J., & Hoffman, S. (2013). Graduation on the rise. *Education Next*, 13(4), 59–65.

National Archives. (2015). *Timeline of events leading to the Brown v. Board of Education decision*. Retrieved from www.archives.gov/education/lessons/brown-v-board/timeline.html

National Center for Education Statistics. (2015). *Annual earnings of young adults*. Retrieved from https://nces.ed.gov/programs/coe/pdf/coe_cba.pd

National Center for Education Statistics. (2019). *Indicator 23: Postsecondary graduation rates*. Retrieved from https://nces.ed.gov/programs/raceindicators/indicator_red.asp

National Center for Education Statistics. (2020a). *Concentration of public school students eligible for free or reduced-price lunch*. Retrieved from https://nces.ed.gov/programs/coe/indicator_clb.asp#:~:text=In%20fall%202017%2C%20the%20percentages,Asian%20students%20(15%20percent)%2C

National Center for Education Statistics. (2020b). *Status dropout rates*. Retrieved from https://nces.ed.gov/programs/coe/indicator_coj.asp

National Center for Education Statistics. (2020c). *Undergraduate enrollment*. Retrieved from https://nces.ed.gov/programs/coe/indicator_cha.asp

National Commission on Excellence in Education. (1983). *A nation at risk: The imperative of educational reform*. Retrieved from http://datacenter.spps.org/uploads/sotw_a_nation_at_risk_1983.pdf

National Scientific Council on the Developing Child. (2014). *Excessive stress disrupts the architecture of the developing brain: Working paper No. 3*. Updated edition. Retrieved from www.developingchild.harvard.edus

National Women's Law Center. (2012). *Title XI 40 years and counting: Fact sheet*. Retrieved from www.nwlc.org/sites/default/files/pdfs/nwlcathletics_titleixfactsheet.pdf

Noltemeyer, A. L., Mujic, J., & McLoughlin, C. S. (2012). The history of inequality in education. In A. L. Noltemeyer, J. Mujic, & C. S. McLoughlin (Eds.), *Disproportionality in education and special education* (pp. 3–21). Springfield, IL: Charles C Thomas.

Nores, M., & Barnett, S. W. (2014). *Access to high quality early care and education: Readiness and opportunity gaps in America*. Ceelo Policy Report. Retrieved from http://ceelo.org/wpcontent/uploads/2014/05/ceelo_policy_report_access_quality_ece.pdf

Oberlin College and Conservatory. (2015). *Women's history month: Famous women in Oberlin history*. Retrieved from https://new.oberlin.edu/events-activities/womens-history/oberlin-women.dot

Office of Head Start. (2015). *History of Head Start*. Retrieved from www.acf.hhs.gov/programs/ohs/about/history-of-head-start

Orfield, G., & Lee, C. (2005). *Why segregation matters: Poverty and educational inequality: The Civil Rights Project*. Cambridge, MA: Harvard University Press.

Patterson, J. T. (2001). *Brown v. Board of Education: A civil rights milestone and its troubled legacy*. New York, NY: Oxford University Press.

Perkins, L. (1997). The African American elite: The early history of African American women in Seven Sisters colleges, 1880–1960. *Harvard Educational Review*, 67(4), 718–757.

Pratt, R. H. (1892). *The advantages of mingling Indians with Whites*. In Official Report of the Nineteenth Annual Conference of Charities and Corrections (pp. 46–59). Reprinted in *Americanizing the American Indians: Writings by the friends of the Indian, 1880–1900*. (1973). F. P. Prucha (Ed.). Cambridge, MA: Harvard University Press.

Prucha, F. P. (1984). *The great father: The United States government and the American Indians*. Lincoln: University of Nebraska Press.

Prucha, F. P. (2000). *Documents of United States Indian policy* (3rd ed.). Lincoln: University of Nebraska Press.

Public Law 85–864. (1958). *Government Printing Office*. Retrieved from www.gpo.gov/fdsys/pkg/STATUTE-72/pdf/STATUTE-72-Pg1580.pdf

Public Law 88–352. (1964). *Government Printing Office*. Retrieved from www.gpo.gov/fdsys/pkg/STATUTE-78/pdf/STATUTE-78-Pg241.pdf

Public Law 89–10. (1965). Elementary and Secondary Act of 1965. *Government Printing Office*. Retrieved from www.gpo.gov/fdsys/pkg/STATUTE-79/pdf/STATUTE-79-Pg27.pdf

Public Law 89–750. (1966). *Title I Amendments to the Elementary and Secondary Act of 1965*. Retrieved from http://uscode.house.gov/statutes/pl/89/750.pdf

Public Law 90–247. (1967). Title I Amendments to the Elementary and Secondary Act of 1965, and related amendments. *Government Printing Office*. Retrieved from www.gpo.gov/fdsys/pkg/STATUTE-81/pdf/STATUTE-81-Pg783.pdf

Public Law 94–142. (1975). *Government Printing Office*. Retrieved from www.gpo.gov/fdsys/pkg/STATUTE-89/pdf/STATUTE-89-Pg773.pdf

Public Law 107–110 (2002). *Government Printing Office*. Retrieved from www.gpo.gov/fdsys/pkg/PLAW-107publ110/html/PLAW-107publ110.htm

Race Forward. (2013). *Historical timeline of public education in the U.S.* Retrieved from www.raceforward.org/research/reports/historical-timeline-public-education-us

Radke-Moss, G. A. (2008). *Bright epoch: Women and co-education in the American west*. Lincoln: University of Nebraska Press.

Reardon, S. F. (2011). The widening achievement gap between rich and poor: New evidence and possible explanations. In G. J. Duncan & R. J. Murnane (Eds.), *Whither opportunity? Rising inequality, schools, and children's life chances* (pp. 91–116). New York, NY: Russell Sage Foundation.

Rudalevige, A. (2003). The politics of No Child Left Behind. *Education Next*, 63–69.

Seelau, R. (2009). Regaining control over the children: Reversing the legacy of assimilative polices in education, child welfare, and juvenile justice that targeted Native American youth. *American Indian Law Review*, 37(1), 63–109.

Smith, A. A. (2019). Study finds more low-income students attending college. *Inside Higher Ed*. Retrieved from www.insidehighered.com/news/2019/05/23/pew-study-finds-more-poor-students-attending-college

Smithsonian National Museum of American History. (2015). *Separate is not equal: Brown v. Board of Education*. Retrieved from http://americanhistory.si.edu/brown/history/5-decision/detail/slip-opinion.html

Social Welfare History Project. (2015). *Elementary and Secondary Education Act of 1965*. Retrieved from www.socialwelfarehistory.com/programs/education/elementary-and-secondary-education-act-of-1965/

Solano, I. S., & Weyer, M. (2017). Closing the opportunity gap in early education. *National Conference of State Legislators*. Retrieved from www.ncsl.org/research/education/closing-the-opportunity-gap-in-early-childhood-education.aspx

Solomon, B. M. (1985). *In the company of educated women*. New Haven, CT: Yale University Press.

Stern, B. H. (2015). Senate passes the every child act to replace No Child Left Behind. *The National Law Review*. Retrieved from www.natlawreview.com/article/senate-passes-every-child-achieves-act-to-replace-no-child-left-behind

Strane, S. (1990). *A whole-souled woman: Prudence Crandall and the education of Black women*. New York, NY: W.W. Norton.

Strum, P. (2002). *Women in the barracks: The VMI case and equal rights*. Lawrence: University of Kansas Press.

Thomas, J. Y., & Brady, K. P. (2005). The Elementary and Secondary Education Act at 40: Equity, accountability, and the evolving federal role in public education. *Review of Research in Education*, 29(51), 51–67.

Trent, J. W., Jr. (2015). Samuel Gridley Howe, romantic, reformer. *Disability Museum History*. Retrieved from www.disabilitymuseum.org/dhm/edu/essay.html?id=41

Turner, S., & Bound, J. (2002). *Closing the gap or widening the divide: The effects of the G.I. bill and World War II on the educational outcomes of Black Americans*. Population Studies Center Research Report No. 02–515. Institute for Social Research, Ann Arbor: University of Michigan.

U.S. Bureau of Labor Statistics. (2020). *Learn more, earn more: Education leads to higher wages, lower unemployment*. Retrieved from www.bls.gov/careeroutlook/2020/data-on-display/education-pays.htm

U.S. Department of Education. (1998). *National assessment of progress*. Washington, DC: Author.

U.S. Department of Education. (2015, November 9). *ESEA flexibility (including DC and PR)*. Retrieved from www2.ed.gov/policy/elsec/guid/esea-flexibility/index.html

U.S. Department of Education Office for Civil Rights. (2014a, March). *Data snapshot: Teacher equity* (Issue Brief No. 4). Retrieved from www2.ed.gov/about/offices/list/ocr/docs/crdc-teacher-equity-snapshot.pdf

U.S. Department of Education Office for Civil Rights. (2014b, March). *Data snapshot: College and career readiness* (Issue Brief No. 3). Retrieved from www2.ed.gov/about/offices/list/ocr/docs/crdc-college-and-career-readiness-snapshot.pdf

U.S. Department of Education Office for Civil Rights. (2014c, March). *Data snapshot: School discipline* (Issue Brief No. 1). Retrieved from www2.ed.gov/about/offices/list/ocr/docs/crdc-discipline-snapshot.pdf

Usher, A. (2012). AYP results for 2010-11-May 12 update. *Center on Educational Policy*. Retrieved from www.cep-dc.org/displayDocument.cfm?DocumentID=403

Whitehouse.gov. (2017). *Presidential Executive Order on Enforcing Statutory Prohibitions on Federal Control of Education*. Retrieved from www.whitehouse.gov/presidential-actions/presidential-executive-order-enforcing-statutory-prohibitions-federal-control-education/

Williams, H. A. (2005). *Self-taught: African American education in slavery and freedom*. Chapel Hill: The University of North Carolina Press.

Worell, J. (2002). *Encyclopedia of women and gender: Sex similarities and differences* (Vol. 1). San Diego, CA: Academic Press.

CHAPTER 12
Child Welfare Inequality

Foster Care Disproportionality

Protecting children from maltreatment, abuse, and neglect is the primary mission of the child welfare system in the United States, principally through preventive services and foster care. At least, in theory, the child welfare system's mission is bias free and protects all children regardless of race, ethnicity, gender, social class, ability, sexual orientation, and immigration status (Sedlak & Broadhurst, 1996; Sedlak et al., 2010). There is overwhelming statistical evidence, however, that in actual practice, the child welfare system reflects an inequitable social order that is anything but bias free (Chipungu & Bent-Goodley, 2004; Cooper, 2013; Ellis, 2019; McRoy, 2005; Sedlak & Broadhurst, 1996). This inequitable social order is especially true in foster care, where even when controlling for poverty and other risk factors related to child maltreatment, abuse, and neglect, Native American/Alaska Native and Black children are still disproportionately represented in removals from the home and placement in foster care when compared with their representation in the general population of children (Anna E. Casey Foundation, 2018a; Child Trends Data Bank, 2019; Child Welfare Information Gateway, 2020, 2016; Cooper, 2013; Curtis & Denby, 2011; Hill, 2006; MST Services, 2019; National Indian Child Welfare Association, 2019; McRoy, 2005; Padilla & Summers, 2011; Puzzanchera & Taylor, 2020; Sedlak et al., 2010; U.S. Census Bureau, 2009).

Also disproportionality represented in the foster care system is LGBQ/GNCT youth. These youth are primarily of color (Irvine & Canfield, 2016). As an illustration of the disproportionality, LGBQ youth are seven times more likely than straight youth to be placed in a group or foster home (Irvine & Canfield, 2016). Similarly, GNCT youth are five times more likely than their gender-conforming counterparts to be placed in a group or foster home. The two most common reasons for LGBQ/GNCT youth coming into contact with the child welfare system and placement in a group or foster home are high rates of physical abuse and conflict with parents (Irvine & Canfield, 2016). Indeed, LGBQ youth are twice as likely to have experienced physical abuse than their straight counterparts. GNCT youth are even more likely to have suffered physical abuse, at three times the rate of their gender-conforming counterparts (Irvine & Canfield, 2016).

Although the degree of racial and ethnic disproportionality in foster care placement varies significantly across the country, it is nevertheless present at some level in virtually every state (Ganasarajah & Siegel, 2017).

Illustrative of the racial and ethnic disproportionality in foster care, in 2017, non-Hispanic Whites were 52% of the overall population under 18, but only 44% of the foster care population (Child Trends Data Bank, 2019. Conversely, Blacks were 14% of the overall population under 18 but composed nearly a quarter of the foster care population (23%), and similarly, Native American/Alaska Native children were 1% of the overall population under 18 but represented 2% of the foster care population (Child Trends Data Bank, 2019). It is also significant that while not disproportionately represented nationally, at 21% and 25%, respectively, the number of Hispanic children in foster care has grown over the past decade. Moreover, in 17 states, Hispanic children were disproportionately represented in foster care (Child Trends Data Bank, 2019).

Also notable is that while the number of Black and Native American/Alaska Native children coming into foster care has decreased over the past decade, they nevertheless remain the primary racial and ethnic

DOI: 10.4324/9781003023708-12

groups affected by disproportionality in foster care (Child Trends Data Bank, 2019). Evidence of this disproportionality has been available for public view since the Adoption and Safe Families Act (P.L. 105–89) of 1997 required child welfare agencies to submit tracking and demographic data regarding children in foster care to the Adoption and Foster Care Analysis and Reporting System (Padilla & Summers, 2011). This evidence reveals just how extensive racial and ethnic disproportionality has been in foster care over the past decade and a half. As a result, racial and ethnic disproportionality in foster care has attracted significant public, academic, legal, and political attention. Indeed, racial and ethnic disproportionality in foster care is the object of numerous advocacy efforts, including from powerful foundations, such as the Center for the Study of Social Policy, who fight to reduce it (Bartholet, 2009; Raimon & Weber, 2015). Several states are also in the process of taking policy action (Breidenbach et al., 2011; National Conference of State Legislators, 2020a), and many journal articles and books have been published (Child Welfare Information Gateway, 2020, 2016; Cooper, 2013). The topic was the subject of a U.S. House of Representatives hearing in 2008 (U.S. Government Printing Office, 2008).

The Road to Foster Care Disproportionality

Of particular concern in all of the efforts of advocacy groups is the large shadow that racial and ethnic disproportionality in foster care cast over children and families. The road to disproportionality for Black, Native American, and Hispanic families compared with White and Asian families, most particularly when low income and headed by a single parent, begins with the greater likelihood of being reported for alleged maltreatment, abuse, or neglect of a child or children (Ards et al., 2003; Cooper, 2013; Ellis, 2019; Fluke, MST Services, 2019; Fluke et al., 2003; Gryzlak et al., 2005; Lane et al., 2002; Lu et al., 2004; Lyle, 2003; McRoy, 2005). Once reported, there is a greater likelihood of the allegation being investigated and substantiated (Ards et al., 2003; Baird, 2005; Barth, 2005; Cooper, 2013; Ellis, 2019; Fluke et al., 2003; MST Services, 2019; Sabol et al., 2004; U.S. Department of Health and Human Services, 2005). Once substantiated, there is a greater likelihood of the children being removed from their families and placed in foster care (Barth, 2005; Cooper, 2013; Ellis, 2019; Goerge & Lee, 2005; Lu et al., 2004; Needell et al., 2003; U.S. Department of Health and Human Services, 2005; Wulczyn et al., 2005). Following placement, Black children, particularly if infants or adolescents, are less likely than White children to be reunified with parents or adopted, and therefore on average have longer lengths of stay in foster care than their White counterparts (Ellis, 2019; Hill, 2006; MST Services, 2019; Stoltzfus, 2005; Wulczyn, 2003, 2004).

The Effects of Foster Care Placement

Arguably most troubling about the racial and ethnic disproportionality in foster care is its residual effects on what is an already vulnerable population (Bruskas, 2008). Above and beyond the trauma of removal from biological parents, there is ample evidence that a considerable number of children who have been in foster care struggle with a host of problems throughout the life course (Osgood et al., 2010; Vig et al., 2005). Manifestations of these problems, which more often than not have their origins in the experiences of living in unstable environments prior to foster care placement, include children in foster care having poor developmental, mental health, and education outcomes (Casey Family Programs, 2005; Children's Administration Research, 2004; Pears et al., 2010). Moreover, going into adulthood they have high rates of homelessness (Park et al., 2004), criminal justice involvement, and physical health problems. All in all, then, foster care might not be the origin of the life course problems experienced by those who have been in foster care, but it does in many instances exacerbate them.

Theoretical Frameworks

Although there is consensus on the prevalence of racial and ethnic disproportionality in foster care, there are two opposing perspectives on its causes: the racial justification movement and the racial disproportionality movement. The racial justification movement posits that mere disproportionality of racial and ethnic minority children in foster care is not itself evidence of discrimination or bias (Cooper, 2013). Rather, they postulate that exposure to the primary risk factor for maltreatment and subsequent child welfare services, namely poverty, is disproportionally experienced by racial and ethnic minorities, most particularly Native American, Black, and Hispanic families. For example, Native American and Hispanic families with children have higher poverty rates than their White counterparts. Relatedly, Black children are more than three times as likely to live in poverty as Whites, and 14 times more likely to live in neighborhoods of concentrated childhood poverty (Annie E. Casey Foundation, 2018b; Chipungu & Bent-Goodley, 2004; Drake & Rank, 2009). Thus, the sheer numbers of racial and ethnic minority families who are poor relative to White families result in a real difference in the underlying incidence of maltreatment, abuse, and or neglect, most particularly for Blacks (Bartholet, 2009). As such, the racial and ethnic disproportionality in foster care is rational, and the risk of harm to children in removal and foster care outweighs the risk of harm of maltreatment if left at home (Bartholet, 2009; Cooper, 2013, p. 2013). Adding credence to this argument are the findings of the latest National Incidence Study of Child Abuse and Neglect—(NIS-4). For the first time in 35 years, these findings revealed racial differences in maltreatment rates, with Black children experiencing maltreatment at higher rates than White children in several categories (Sedlak et al., 2010).

Informed by critical race theory, the racial disproportionality movement, on the other hand, characterizes disproportionality as a vestige of slavery and institutional and structural racism (Cooper, 2013). From this perspective, Americans share a common and historical cultural heritage in which racism plays a central role. In this central role, racism is what Crenshaw (1988) describes as the ideological and political pillar upholding White privileges and worldviews. These privileges and worldviews are deeply ingrained in all of America's institutions and structures and are transmitted by tacit understandings that knowingly or otherwise provide the public rationale to legitimize racism (Crenshaw, 1988). In the child welfare system, these privileges and worldviews unconsciously pervade all decision making. Within the decision-making process in child welfare, White middle-class values pathologize non-White family functioning, most particularly if poor (Chipungu & Bent-Goodley, 2004; Cooper, 2013; Roberts, 2012). These values legitimize disproportionality through a narrative that focuses not on the strengths of families of color in the midst of poverty and structural racism, but rather on the supposed dysfunction associated with poverty. In doing so, Roberts (2012) argues, poor mothers of color, particularly if Black, are blamed for their disadvantaged position. This blame is reflected in poor Black mothers, in particular, being the disproportionate focus of investigations by the child welfare system. In collaboration with the criminal justice and welfare systems, the child welfare system labels these mothers as undeserving and seeks to monitor, regulate, and punish them for their supposed failings to meet White middle-class standards of motherhood.

For example, Roberts (2012) highlights how the convergence of the welfare reform and "war on poverty" policies of the 1990s saw not just an attack on the morality of Black single mothers, but also the institution of coercive welfare regulations, accompanied by more punitive forms of law enforcement and child protection. The net result of these policy and practice actions was a dramatic decrease in the welfare rolls. There was also an unprecedented spike in the incarceration rates for poor Black women and a significant increase in the foster care population, peaking at 567,000 in 1998 and remaining at over half million until 2007 when it stabilized at 400,000 (Child Trends Data Bank, 2014). As of September 30, 2018, there were an estimated 437,283 children in foster care.

This matrix of domination, Roberts suggest, preserves U.S. race, gender, and class inequality in a neoliberal age (2012, p. 1476). In doing so, racial and ethnic disproportionality in child welfare and its precursors are seen as right and proper, obscuring the need for social change (Roberts, 2012).

Child Welfare and Its Historical Development

Some historical background is necessary to contextualize the current racial and ethnic disproportionality in child welfare. Ironically, given the current circumstances, for most of the historical development of the U.S. child welfare system, Black families and children were largely excluded from its services right up until the 1950s. What has remained consistent is that while ostensibly protecting vulnerable children, the child welfare system has equally served as a mechanism for ensuring conformity by families and children to patterns of behavior prescribed by the larger society, absent consideration of social and environmental factors.

1601–1800

From the colonial period until the mid- to late-19th century, the notion of childhood as we know it today was nonexistent. Children had no legal rights and in a rural-agrarian time when infant mortality was high and a family-based economy was the order of the day, if children survived past the age of five or six they were expected to contribute labor to the home. When very young, children were responsible for chores around the house and caring for siblings. As they grew older and stronger, boys were taught to work with the farm, construction, or trade tools, while girls took on the responsibility for the domestic chores needed to keep the family fed and clothed. These domestic duties included the backbreaking chore of churning milk into butter (McGowan, 2005). In this period before the advent of formal schooling, labor in and for the home taught children the skills they would need as adults. Child labor was not thought of as problematic or exploitative and was in fact supported by churches and the local government. Indeed, preachers warned that the devil makes work for idle hands, and some of the colonies enacted laws mandating that children work (McGowan, 2005).

Although a valuable labor source, there was very little consideration of the needs of children, either individually or collectively. However, as early as the days of the colonial poor laws there was a recognition that two categories of children needed special attention from public officials—orphans and children of paupers (McGowan, 2005). Informing the special attention of public officials was the doctrine of *parens patriae*, that is, the ruler's power to protect minors. This power justified the official intervention into the sacrosanct parent–child relationship, either to enforce parental responsibility or to provide substitute care (Otto & Melton, 1995). In all cases, the actions taken on behalf of children served two functions. The first was to protect children from maltreatment, abuse, and neglect. The second, and equally important, was to be a potent instrument of social control that would ensure conformity to prescribed patterns of acceptable behavior. As early as 1642, Massachusetts enacted a law that gave local magistrates authority to remove children from parents who did not, in the parlance of the day, "train up their children properly" (Myers, 2007, p. 450). In the same vein, children of the unworthy poor were separated from their parents and apprenticed or placed in an institution so they might be saved from developing the slothful ways of their parents (Costin, 1985). In the 18th century, Virginia expanded its court's jurisdiction over children beyond the context of poverty when it allowed for separating children from parents who were not providing them with good breeding, with neglecting their formal education, being unchristian, and being idle (Rendleman, 1971).

1800–1920

In the absence of a child welfare system, social provisions for orphaned children or children of paupers were provided primarily in one of two ways: the almshouse/poorhouse or apprenticeship (McGowan, 2005). In addition to these public provisions there were, in some cases, private orphanages. In the main, there were no child welfare specific organizations. However, dramatic social changes in the 19th century were to change how children were viewed and what society's responsibility was to be to ensure their protection (McGowan, 2005). Primary among these changes were two waves of mass immigration, urbanization, the growth of philanthropy, the industrial revolution, and the emergence of the progressive movement toward the end of the 19th century. Mass immigration to the United States from northern Europe beginning in the 1830s brought an unprecedented number of largely poor German and Irish migrants to America's growing urban centers (Trattner, 1999). In turn, a large pool of needy children was created, as well as a labor pool for the factories that were beginning to dominate the urban landscape. The second wave of mass immigration from eastern and southern Europe beginning in the 1880s brought an even larger pool of migrants from Italy, Russia, and the Baltics. Like the first wave, these immigrants were largely poor, non-English speaking, and not Protestant. Much the same as with the first wave of migrants, a large pool of needy children was created (Trattner, 1999).

In response to the first wave of needy migrant children in the 1830s, there was a rise of institutional care in the form of orphanages. These orphanages were established under a variety of auspices—public, voluntary, and sectarian (McGowan, 2005). Their primary function was to provide care for children whose parents were not able to care for them properly. The rise of the orphanage was in large part a response to reports from philanthropic organizations for the poor that highlighted the deplorable conditions under which children were being cared for in almshouses. The backlash caused by these reports precipitated the move toward orphanages, which were deemed to be more humane and would enable poor immigrant children to be indoctrinated into being good citizens that would not upset the social order. Consistent with the racism of the day, excluded from these early orphanages were free Black dependent children. Instead, Black institutions served Black dependent children. The first institution to do so was the Philadelphia Association for the Care of Colored Children, established by the Society of Friends (Quakers) in 1822 (McGowan, 2005).

In most states, there were separate colored orphan asylums that cared for dependent Black children. Much like their White counterparts, the purpose of colored orphan asylums was to provide and maintain a home for dependent colored children. In the colored orphan asylums, children were instructed and assisted in ways that best equipped them for life. However, because of their perceived connection with the abolitionist movement they were frequently the target of racist mobs; the most infamous example of this being the 1863 draft riot in New York, which saw White mobs burn the New York Colored Asylum to the ground (Barbour et al., 1995).

Orphanages were not, however, enough to meet the needs of the growing number of children made destitute by the demands that urbanization and industrialization placed on poor and working-class immigrant families in the second half of the 19th century. In their demands, family dislocation became a common occurrence, and if not gainfully employed in the dangerous and exploitative factories, children were left to their own devices (Schene, 1998). In the nation's major urban centers, it was not uncommon to see large numbers of homeless children, ragged, hungry, and roaming the streets. Indeed, child vagrancy was an ongoing problem that many felt threatened the social order (Schene, 1998). The horrendous conditions under which destitute children were living became the catalyst for a well-meaning if fragmented move toward saving children. Central to the child-saving movement was the view that children should be a protected class of people, separate from adults, and as such they should have the opportunity to live in the best conditions possible, be protected from exploitation in the workplace, and not be treated as adults if prosecuted for a crime (Platt, 1969).

In 1853, a young minister named Charles Loring Brace founded the Children's Aid Society of New York with the express purpose of child saving. By the end of the 19th century, there would be children's aids societies established across the country (McGowan, 2005; Schene, 1998). Concerned with the level of child vagrancy and delinquency in New York, Brace believed that the way to change the future of these children was to remove them from the streets and place them with morally and spiritually upright families. To this end, Brace proposed sending these children by train to live and work with families in rural farm communities in the southern and midwestern regions of the country. Not only would the children be an extra pair of hands on the farms, but also in turn they would reap the benefit of living in a stable home environment where they would have the opportunity to grow into productive citizens (Trammell, 2009).

Between 1854 and the early 1900s, what became known as the orphan trains movement sent an estimated 120,000 to 200,000 destitute or temporarily placed children, aged six to 18, to foster homes in 45 states across the country as well as Canada and Mexico. The sending child welfare agencies included the Children's Aid Society, Children's Village, New York Foundling, and the Grand-Windham Home for Children. The receiving foster families for the children were required to sign a contract agreeing to care for the children as a member of the family. Depending on the age of the child, the contracts contained formal indenture agreements and clauses to terminate custody if a trial period was not successful (Trammell, 2009).

As one might expect, such a large undertaking in so-called child saving was not without criticism. Among the criticisms was the hasty nature of placements without properly vetting receiving families. There was also insufficient follow-up with placements (Trammell, 2009). Just as troubling was the accusation from the western states that the orphan trains were simply dumping undesirable children onto them. Catholic and Jewish religious organizations accused the movement of placing a substantial number of Catholic and

Jewish children in Protestant homes to change their religious practices. Another troubling accusation was that not all the children on trains were indeed orphans, with a significant number being children who had only been temporarily placed in foster care by parents (Trammell, 2009). There were also numerous stories of children being exploited and mistreated by host families (Trammell, 2009). Indeed, the orphan train movement was the subject of several lawsuits by parents wanting their children returned to the city. They were also the target of lawsuits from host families and receiving states that among other things argued that they had lost money because of unsatisfactory outcomes. As the western states grew more urbanized and started to have child welfare problems of their own, they passed legislation prohibiting the importation of children from other states, effectively putting an end to the orphan train movement in 1929 (Trammell, 2009).

In retrospect, the orphan train movement has been lauded as a bold experiment that proved a better alternative to the grim realities of life on the streets for destitute children. Although certainly true for some children, it is also true that rather than address the cause of the destitution, the orphan train movement simply chose to remove poor immigrant children. They did this even when it was against the wishes of parents, who themselves were in many cases erroneously portrayed as unfit by the middle-class standards of the day. Regardless of the criticism, the orphan train movement established foster care as one formalized alternative for protecting children (Myers, 2007).

Another critical development in the child-saving movement was the establishment in New York of the first Society for the Prevention of Cruelty to Children (SPCC) in 1875. The SPCC was the first agency in the world completely devoted to the protection of children (Myers, 2007). Before its formation, no laws effectively protected children from maltreatment, nor were children accorded rights. Indeed, other than in the most extreme cases, the abuse of children was tolerated (Myers, 2007; Schene, 1998). However, the catalyst for change was to come in the form of Mary Ellen Wilson in 1874. Mary Ellen Wilson was a nine-year-old orphan who lived with her guardian in one of the worst tenements in New York's Hell's Kitchen. She was routinely beaten and neglected by her guardian. When Mary Ellen's situation came to the attention of religious missionary to the poor Etta Wheeler, she reported it to the police. The police, however, refused to intervene. Appalled by the police inaction and concerned about the safety of Mary Ellen, Wheeler sought the advice of the influential founder of the American Society for the Prevention of Cruelty to Animals, Henry Bergh. Bergh, in turn, asked his lawyer, Elbridge Gerry, to explore legal means to rescue Mary Ellen, which they were able to do (Myers, 2007; Schene, 1998). However, they were perturbed that there were no government agencies or organizations responsible for protecting children from maltreatment, abuse, and or neglect. To this end, Berg and Gerry recruited respected philanthropist John D. Wright and formally pledged themselves to the establishment of organized child protection. Out of this pledge, the New York Society for the Prevention of Cruelty to Children was founded in 1875. John D. Wright became its first president, with Berg and Gerry as vice presidents (NYSPCC, 2015).

The idea for child protection societies spread quickly, and by 1922 there were 300 nongovernmental child protection societies established across the country (Myers, 2007; Schene, 1998). These agencies, the forerunners of today's child protective services, were a pragmatic mixture of religious, humane concern, and private and public partnerships that for the most part were able to work past any political, sectarian, and economic differences (Costin, 1985; NYSPCC, 2015; Myers, 2007). The SPCCs investigated reports of alleged child abuse and neglect, filed complaints in court against alleged perpetrators, and assisted the courts in prosecution hearings. In most jurisdictions, SPCCs were granted law enforcement powers to remove children from the home pending an investigation (Costin, 1985; Myers, 2077; Schene, 1998). Although there was some variation, generally speaking, the mission and focus of the SPCCs were removals rather than family preservation. Overwhelmingly, the families investigated were poor and immigrant and were judged by the White, Protestant, middle-class values and mores of the day (Schiff, 1997). Indeed, in its initial punitive emphasis, the SPCCs were dismissive of parents, who were often deemed unworthy of parenthood. In its first 14 years of existence, the NYSPCC alone had investigated some 70,000 complaints of maltreatment involving 209,000 children. Of these 209,000 cases, prosecutions were pursued in 24,500 cases, resulting in some 24,000 convictions and the removal of 36,300 children (Schiff, 1997, pp. 413–414).

As a result of the emergent progressive movement in the late 19th century, there was a new understanding of poverty that moved beyond individual culpability and lax morals to look at environmental factors and the role that laws and policies could play in ending destitution. There was also an increased focus on the need to protect children in all spheres of life, as well as to strengthen families so they could better care for children. The result of this shift saw several progressive reforms. These reforms included the establishment of the juvenile justice system in 1909 (Platt, 1969), state enactment of the mother's pension in 1911 (Skocpol, 1995, see Chapter 6), and the federal government's enactment of the Children's Bureau in 1913. There was also the passing of child labor laws in the 1920s, and the enactment of the Sheppard-Towner Maternity and Infancy Protection Act of 1921. Furthermore, the SPCCs shifted their focus away from child removals to family preservation (Myers, 2007; Schiff, 1997).

1920–1950

Between 1920 and 1950, the child protective functions of the SPPCSs were gradually assumed by governmental agencies at the state, county, and local level. Although uneven, the governmental acceptance of child protective functions marked the beginning of the modern child welfare system. At the federal level, the passage of the Social Security Act of 1935 established Aid to Dependent Children, whose cash assistance enabled poor mothers to retain custody of their children. Moreover, Title IV-B of the Social Security (Child Welfare Services) offered states federal funding if they established preventive and protective services for vulnerable children (Social Service Administration, 2015). In the main, though, states used the federal funds provided by Title IV-B not to provide preventive services, but rather to fund foster care services (Schene, 1998).

1950–Present

Up until the 1950s, child welfare services, including both protection and foster care, had excluded Black children and families who were forced instead to rely on extended family networks, churches, and the few available inferior and overcrowded colored orphanage asylums (Hill, 2006; Roberts, 2001). However, some significant social events in the 1950s and 1960s were to see the child welfare system gradually shift within 25 years from an almost exclusively White serving institution to one in which Black and Native American children would be disproportionately represented (Hill, 2006; Smith & Devore, 2004). The social events that were the catalyst for this shift were the second great migration of Blacks from the rural Jim Crow South to major urban centers in the country's Midwest and Northeast in the late 1940s and 1950s, the civil rights movement from the late 1950s through to the end of the 1960s, and the White flight from the major urban centers to the newly developing suburbs (Boustan, 2010; McRoy, 2005; Roediger, 2006). Just as importantly, among the 1962 amendments to the Social Security Act was a stipulation that state child welfare plans make a satisfactory showing that by 1975 services would be available to all children regardless of race, ethnicity, and or socioeconomic status (Cohen & Ball, 1962).

In addition to these social events, beginning in 1962, child abuse would enter the nation's consciousness and prompt the exponential growth in the child welfare field. This growth would see the child welfare field go from what McGowan described (2005) as a relatively small, self-contained local service system with limited staff, resources, and reach to a robust, well-resourced state service system underpinned by federal policy. Critical to the beginning of this process was the publication of the article "The Battered Child Syndrome" in 1962 by pediatrician Dr. Henry Kempe and colleagues (Kempe et al., 1962). In this groundbreaking article, Dr. Kempe and colleagues drew on data from their nationwide survey of hospitals where young children had been treated because of serious physical abuse, generally from a parent or foster parent. Findings from their data analysis revealed that serious physical abuse was a frequent cause of minor injury, permanent disability, and/or death. Also troubling was that the physical abuse, which Kempe called battered child syndrome (BCS), too often went unrecognized by radiologists, orthopedists, pediatricians, and social service workers, who erroneously attributed symptoms to failure to thrive, a metabolic disorder, or an infection. Kempe suggested that even when recognized or diagnosed, physicians because of their reluctance to bring the case to the attention of the proper authority inadequately handled BCS. Kempe posited that the parents or guardians who caused these injuries to children were not confined to those with mental illnesses or borderline socioeconomic status; they were just as likely to be educated and from a stable financial and social background. Kempe concluded by recommending that BCS should be considered in any child exhibiting evidence of possible trauma or neglect (i.e., bone fracture, subdural hematoma, multiple soft tissue issue, poor skin hygiene, and malnutrition) or when there was a clear contradiction between clinic findings and parent reporting (Kempe et al., 1962, p. 17).

Kempe et al.'s seminal article not only led to a Nobel Prize nomination for being the first in the medical community to identify and recognize BCS, but more importantly it captured the media's attention and became a newsworthy topic that had the public enthralled. What followed the increased attention to child abuse was a cascade of articles and personal testimonies elucidating the damage caused by the abuse of children at the hand of parents and guardians. In 1962, amendments to the Social Security Act identified child protective services as a part of all child welfare services (Cohen & Ball, 1962; Myers, 2008).

Also in 1962, prompted by increased reports of physical child abuse, the Children's Bureau held a meeting in Washington, D.C., to examine how it might assist states in addressing the problem of child abuse (Children's Bureau Centennial, 2015). The recommendations made in the meeting were the genesis of the introduction of the first mandated state child abuse reporting laws, the first being enacted in 1963 (Children's Bureau Centennial, 2015; Myers, 2008). By 1967, all 50 states had enacted a mandated child abuse reporting law (Myers, 2008).

What followed the nationwide institution of state child abusing laws was an enormous increase in child abusing reporting and exponential growth in the foster care population from the late 1960s through the 1970s (Myers, 2008). Indeed, by the latter part of the 1970s, the foster care population had risen from 272,000 in 1962 to 503,000 in 1977, with Native American and Black children now being disproportionately represented (Johnson, 2014). As posited by Pelton (1989), the enormous increase in child abuse reporting and the foster care population had less to do with an actual increase in child abuse than with child abuse and neglect definitions that from state to state were so broad that they unnecessarily brought hundreds of thousands of suspect families to the attention of child protective agencies. These families were primarily poor and increasingly of color. Just as problematic, Pelton (1989) suggested, was that once these families became known to protective agencies and the child welfare system, the system had little in the way of resources for supportive services, and foster care placements became the default position of child welfare agencies.

In 1974, the federal government, who up until that point had played only a cursory role, assumed a leadership role in child protection and by extension child welfare with the enactment of the Child Abuse Prevention and Treatment Act of 1974 (P.L. 93–247). The act would change the trajectory of child welfare, making protecting children a federal responsibility rather than a state or local one for the first time in United States history. The act authorized federal funds to improve and standardized state response to the physical/sexual abuse or neglect of children. It was deemed necessary, because although each state had a mandatory child abuse reporting system, they varied in quality and comprehensiveness. To this end, the act created the National Center on Child Abuse and Neglect for training staff and established a clearinghouse on the prevention and treatment of abuse and neglect (Public Law 93–247, 1974).

In a parallel development, Native American and Black family advocates were raising concerns about the disproportionate representation of their children in foster care. However, just as problematic for both Native American and Black family advocates was that their children were too often being placed in homes that were not culturally compatible. This situation was particularly true for the 35% of Native American children who were in foster care, most with non-Native American families. Black children appeared to fare slightly better, although the concern was enough that in 1972, the National Association of Black Social Workers (NABSW) issued a position statement on transracial adoption (NABSW, 1972). In the statement, the NABSW argued that one's racial and ethnic identity was critical to their healthy development, most particularly for Blacks, who for so long had been denied their cultural identity. When Black children are placed in White foster homes, the NABSW suggested, they lose the opportunity to develop their cultural identity. For this reason, the NABSW was vehement in its opposition to both placing Black children in White foster homes and/or having them adopted by White families (NABSW, 1972).

Legislatively, however, it was the issue of Native American children in foster care that gained traction. In states such as Alaska and South Dakota, Native American children composed between 15% and 18% of the population under 18, but accounted for over 50% of the population in foster care. Native American civil rights groups argued that many of these children were cared for by relatives, but were nevertheless removed because relatives were not considered suitable. As a redress to the many years of large numbers of Native American children in foster care with non-Native American homes, Congress passed the Indian Child Welfare Act (ICWA) of 1978 (P.L. 95–608). The ICWA strengthened the role played by tribal governments in determining the custody of Indian children so that tribal governments were granted jurisdiction over Indian child custody proceedings and placements. Furthermore, the ICWA specified that preference should be given to Native American placements with extended family, rather than to Indian foster homes. The ICWA also authorized grants to allow tribes and Indian organizations to deliver preventive services, but they have not been funded (P.L. 95–608).

Although no specific legislation was enacted to keep Black foster children with Black families or kinship care, in 1979, a Supreme Court ruling in *Miller v. Youakim* would have a direct bearing on the foster care placement of Black children. The ruling stated that children living in a relative's home are entitled to the same level of foster care payments as children living in nonkinship foster care (*Miller v. Youakim*, 1979). In doing so, kinship foster care would become a much-used placement option for Black children. This was especially true during the 1980s when the emergence of crack cocaine and HIV/AIDS caused a surge in foster care placements in urban minority communities and an accompanying request from overburdened child welfare agencies for relatives to become foster parents to fill the demand for caregivers (Geen, 2003). Simply put, kinship care is an arrangement in which relatives raise their kin within the child welfare system (Geen, 2003), an arrangement that saw as many as half of the Black children in foster care during the 1980s being placed with a relative, most typically a grandparent. In theory, at least, kinship care would appear to offer the least disruptive alternative for the children. The evidence indicates, however, that despite the often disadvantaged economic status, kinship caregivers often received fewer services and benefits and lower financial assistance than nonrelated caregivers (Alstein & McRoy, 2000). That said, there is also evidence that children in kinship care experience fewer foster home replacements and greater levels of placement stability, thus the longer average stays in foster care (Geen, 2003).

In the wake of mounting criticism of the rising number of children in foster care without a real plan for permanency, the 1980s saw a concerted legislative effort to stem the tide of placements and preserve families (McGowan, 2005). In 1980, Congress enacted the Adoption Assistance and Child Welfare Act of 1980 (P.L. 96–272). The act mandated states to establish programs and make procedural reforms to move children out of foster care and reunite them with their families, or else have them adopted promptly. Toward this end, the act required individual case planning reviews and with it introduced the notion of permanency planning as a federal child welfare policy. As a carrot and stick for agencies, the act authorized federal funding for social services for families, but also set a conditional ceiling on foster care reimbursement (McGowan, 2005).

However, even with the leveling off of foster care placements immediately following the enactment of the Adoption Assistance and Child Welfare Act of 1980, child abuse and neglect continued to rise, with the number exceeding one million. To put this in context, in 1974, the number of reported cases was 60,000 (Myers, 2008). Much of the reason for this, it was speculated, were the three biggest social crises of the 1980s—poverty, drugs, and homelessness. From 1984 onward, these social crises saw a slow but steady increase in the foster care placements, with kinship placements, most particularly for Black children, becoming a much larger share of foster care placements (Pelton, 1989). Eighty-six percent of the increase in foster care placement occurred in just 11 states, with New York and California accounting for 65% of these placements (Pelton, 1989).

Despite the increase in foster care placements, going into the 1990s, there continued to be congressional support for family preservation. To this end, Congress passed the Family Preservation and Support Service Act of 1993 (P.L. 103–66), which increased funding for family support to prevent maltreatment. The tide was turning, however, for family preservation as conservative lawmakers grew increasingly discontented as the number of child abuse and neglect reports continued to grow (two million by 1990) and foster care placements steadily increased (Weisman, 1994). In what was in keeping with a general attack on poor mothers, conservative politicians and commentators took aim at family preservation with an intent to end foster care drift; a situation where foster children remain out of the natural family home without a clear plan of either returning home or finding some other permanent home (Hartley, 1984). To this end, in 1994, Newt Gingrich included four pro-adoption provisions in the Republican Contract with America, including one that called for the reduction of time that foster children waited for permanency. What followed was a deluge of articles questioning preserving families that were clearly dysfunctional and a danger to children. In her article "The Ideology of Family Preservation" commentator Heather McDonald posed the question "Can a single welfare mother who has been beating her children, or failing to feed and bathe them, be turned into a reasonable parent at public expense?" (1994, p. 45). As if to make McDonald's point, Gelles' *The Book of David: How Preserving Families Can Cost Children's Lives* (1996) used the true story of the murder of infant David Edwards at the hands of his mother to make the case that society's priority must be protecting children rather than preserving families. Newspapers were also not immune to blaming family preservation for endangering children, with numerous articles highlighting any tragic death of a child by the hand of a parent who was known to the child welfare system (Roberts, 2001).

The sentiments expressed by the likes of McDonald and Gelles, though blaming and not necessarily representative, certainly captured the conservative and increasingly neoliberal concern about family preservation, most particularly kinship care, which many were beginning to believe rewarded parents for the abuse of their children. There was also the very real concern that family preservation had been allowed to supersede the best of interest of the child. Consequently, children lingered in care for years without a permanent plan. Moreover, there was the real possibility that children could still be hurt in the home. Indeed, the belief was that it was the best of interest of the child and not the reasonable efforts credo that informed family preservation that needed to be the predominate focus of child welfare (McGowan, 2005). Notably absent in this call was any examination of root causes or studies such as the National Incidence Study of Child Abuse and Neglect, the third of which in 1996 found that children of all races and ethnicities were equally as likely to suffer abuse and neglect (Sedlak & Broadhurst, 1996).

Adoption and Safe Families Act of 1997

As evidence of the shift in thinking about family preservation, in 1994, Congress enacted the Multiethnic Placement Act of 1994 (P.L. 103–82), which prohibited child welfare agencies from denying or delaying adoptive placement on the grounds of race. More profoundly, in 1997, President Clinton signed into law, with bipartisan support, the Adoption and Safe Families Act (ASFA) of 1997 (P.L. 105–89). The act, considered the most sweeping change in foster care and adoption history, shifted child welfare thinking away from family preservation as a principal goal to an emphasis on child safety first (Spar & Shuman, 2004). It was a shift that one of the acts co-sponsors, Republican Senator John H. Chafee of Rhode Island, articulated on signing. Chafee said, "We will not continue the current system of always putting the needs and rights of the biological parents first. . . . It's time we recognize that some families simply cannot and should not be kept together" (Seelye, 1997, p. 1). The two stated goals of ASFA are (1) to ensure that consideration of children's safety is paramount in child welfare decisions, so that children are not returned to unsafe homes, and (2) to ensure that necessary legal procedures occur expeditiously, so that children who cannot return home may be placed for adoption or another permanent arrangement quickly (Spar & Shuman, 2004, p. 1). Following is a summary of the provisions contained in the act.

Child Safety

- Reasonable efforts to preserve families, unless court finds that a parent has subjected the child to aggravated circumstances.
- Criminal background checks for all prospective foster parents or adoptive parents, with a denial of approval for a felony conviction for child or spousal abuse.

Timeframe Provisions

- Reasonable efforts to promote adoption within 30 days if the court finds that efforts to preserve or reunify a family are not required.

- Permanency hearing for child to occur within 12 months of the date the child is determined to have entered care and changed the name to "permanency" hearing.
- Termination of parental rights (TPR) must be pursued if child has been in care for 15 of the most recent 22 months (known as the 15 of 22 provision). The only exception to this provision is if a TPR is not in the best interest of the child. Examples of this include a child who is an unaccompanied refugee minor, adoption is not appropriate permanency goal for the child, or there are no grounds for a TPR.

Eligibility for Adoption and Medical Assistance

- Under Title IV-E, states may receive open-ended federal entitlement funds for part of the costs of operating adoption assistance programs for special needs children.
- Children who are eligible for federal adoption assistance are also deemed eligible for Medicaid.

Reauthorization and Renaming of Family Preservation Program

- The family preservation program was renamed Promoting Safe and Stable Families, which along with the existing family preservation and community based-family support added to new programs: time-limited family reunification and adoption promotion and support services.

State Accountability for Performance

- State outcome measures regarding timely reunification and adoption of children to be recorded in state registry.

Adoption Incentive Program

- Establishment of a new program of incentive payments to states to increase their number of foster child adoptions, with additional incentives for the adoption of older children and children with special needs.

How Has ASFA Changed Child Welfare?

Because of the variability from state to state, defining how successful ASFA has been since its enactment is difficult to assess. There are, however, some general findings that can provide some idea of how ASFA has changed the child welfare landscape. For example, as intended, ASFA has shifted child welfare agency culture toward a focus on permanence and the timely decision making required to accomplish it (Golden & Macomber, 2009; Phagan-Hansel, 2018). This shift in culture is most evident in the heightened attention to adoption. Relatedly, ASFAs financial incentives for reaching adoption goals appears to work, as the number of adoptions has increased steadily from 38,221 in 1998 to 60,000 by 2017, a 57% increase (Phagan-Hansel, 2018). The increase in adoptions has seen a decrease in the number of children who stay in foster care for long periods. In 1998, the average stay in foster care was 32.8 months. By 2017, the average stay was down to 20.1 months (Phagan-Hansel, 2018).

The converse to the former shift is there has been less innovation and focus on reunification, which has posed a particular challenge to parents with a mental illness or who are incarcerated. Indeed, the report "Rebuilding Families, Reclaiming Lives" blames ASFA timelines (15 of the last 22 months) for unintentionally expediting the permanent separation of children from incarcerated parents (Allard & Lu, 2006). The report goes on to suggest that too many children are at risk of being permanently separated from mothers whose worst crime is drug addiction. This situation has particular resonance for Black and Hispanic mothers who are more likely than any other group of mothers to be incarcerated for nonviolent drug offenses.

The effect of maternal incarceration is most keenly felt by Black children, 6.7% of whom had a parent behind bars, followed by Hispanic children at 2.4%, and then White children, 0.9% (Glaze & Maruschak,

2008). Although the ASFA legislation made no provisions for considering drug addiction or incarceration when seeking to achieve permanency for a child in foster care, several states, New York being a notable example, have extended timelines in an effort to not unduly penalize parents who have a substance abuse issue or are incarcerated.

For both its initial supporters and many detractors, ASFA remains a divisive and contentious child welfare policy. Supporters of putting the best interest of the child before family preservation as a principal goal decry what they see as the myriad of loopholes and exceptions that potentially undermine the intent of ASFA. As argued by Bartholet (1999), having exceptions to filing a TPR leaves far too much room for those in the child welfare system who are committed to family preservation to evade the true intent of ASFA. These exceptions include not filing a TPR if the child is in a kinship placement, the state did not supply the parents of the child services promptly, or it is not in the best interest of the child.

Similarly critical, but for different reasons, are those who see ASFA as a federally mandated attack on poor families of color, most particularly Black families and Black single mothers. As argued by Roberts (2001), child welfare and policies such as ASFA unfairly target poor Black mothers who are blamed for the systemic inequalities that keep them disadvantaged. In the blaming, the narrative is that they are unfit mothers who are a danger not just to their children but also to society. Hence, punitive policy actions and reforms, which include ASFA, welfare reform (see Chapter 6), and the war on drugs (see Chapter 10), have all over the past decade and a half disproportionately affected poor Black mothers. ASFA, in particular, White (2006) posits, uses the pretext of advancing child welfare but in actuality promotes destruction of Black familial bonds and represents a serious threat to Black communities.

Family First Prevention Service Act of 2018 (P.L. 115–123)

On February 9, 2018, President Trump signed into law the bipartisan Family First Preservation Service Act. The act reforms the federal child welfare financing streams, Title IV-E, and Title IV-B of the Social Security Act to provide services to families at risk of entering the child welfare system (Torres & Mathur, 2018). The act's primary intent is to prevent children from entering foster care by allowing federal reimbursement for mental health services, substance abuse training, and parenting skill training. Among the many family preservation provisions of the act through Title IV-E and Title IV-B are eliminating time limits for family reunification and states maintaining a prevention plan for children to remain safe. The act also seeks to curtail congregate or group home care for children (National Conference of State Legislators, 2020b). For the details of the act, use the following link: https://campaignforchildren.org/resources/fact-sheet/fact-sheet-family-first-prevention-services-act/

It is too early to assess whether or not the act will put child welfare-involved families first and eliminate the foster care disproportionality experienced by Black, Native American/Alaska, and Hispanic families.

Chapter Summary

As with the other social systems discussed in this book, child welfare both currently and historically continues to reflect society's existing social inequalities, most particularly as it pertains to the treatment of marginalized families. Under the guise of protecting children from maltreatment, abuse, and neglect, marginalized families, whether the poor immigrant families of the 1800s or the poor Native American, Black, and Hispanic families in the 2000s, have been blamed and punished for their marginality by the removal of their children. Although there have been occasional attempts at family preservation and helping to strengthen rather than sanction poor families, the default position of child welfare has more typically been one of punishment for lack of adherence to middle- and upper-class norms with little consideration of the structural impediments imposed by poverty. Thus, rather than address existing societal inequalities, the status quo is maintained by way of punitive child welfare policies and actions that under the guise of the best interest of the child promote parental culpability, social regulation, and sanction. Nowhere is this more evident than in the Adoption and Safe Families Act of 1997, whose incentives and rigid timelines are heavily weighted against family preservation in favor of family dissolution and adoption.

Retrieval Questions

1. Which groups of children are most affected by foster care disproportionality?
2. What are some of the residual effects of foster care placement on already vulnerable populations?
3. What does the racial justification movement posit about the reason for foster care disproportionality?
4. What does the racial disproportionality movement posit about the reason for foster care disproportionality?
5. What was the state of children's rights for much of American history?
6. What did the doctrine of *parens patriae* state?
7. What is the significance of Charles Loring Brace to child welfare?
8. What is the significance of the Society for the Prevention of Cruelty of Children to child welfare?
9. What significant contribution did Dr. Henry Kempe make to child welfare?
10. Why was the Child Abuse Prevention and Treatment Act of 1974 significant?
11. What was significant about the Indian Child Welfare Act (ICWA) of 1978?
12. How did the *Miller v. Youakim* ruling affect foster care?

Discussion Questions

1. Identify and discuss some of the social justice issues pertinent to the Adoption and Safe Families Act of 1997.
2. As policy practitioners, identify and discuss how social workers might address foster care disproportionality.
3. Identify and discuss some of the potential practice challenges you might face when working with parents who are involved with child welfare in light of ASFA's rigid timelines.

Box 12.1 Child Welfare Events and Significant Legislation Timeline, 1854–Present

1854: First orphan train heads west (Children's Bureau Timeline, 2015).

1875: The first Society for the Prevention of Cruelty of Children (SPCC) is established in New York. The SPCC was the first agency in the world completely devoted to protection of children (Myers, 2007).

1899: First juvenile court system in the world is established in Cook County, Illinois (Children's Bureau Timeline, 2015).

1909: White House Conference on the Care of Dependent Children is held. The conference brings together 200 leaders in child welfare issues to discuss the negative effects of institutional care on dependent and neglected children (Children's Bureau Timeline, 2015).

1912: The Children's Bureau is founded. It is the first federal agency to focus exclusively on improving the lives of children and families. Julia Lathrop is appointed the first head of the bureau, becoming the first woman to head a federal government agency (Children's Bureau Timeline, 2015).

1919: White House Conference on Child Welfare Standards is held. As a result of the conference, new minimum standards for the health, education, and work for American children are established (Children's Bureau Timeline, 2015).

1930: White House Conference on Child Health and Protection is held. The 3,000 conference attendees produce a 19-point Children's Charter, addressing all children's needs as regard to education, health, welfare, and protection (Children's Bureau Timeline, 2015).

1935: Social Security Act of 1935 includes limited funds under Title IV for child welfare services (Child Welfare League of America, 2015).

1938: The Fair Labor Standards Act is passed. The act mandates a minimum age of 16 for general full-time employment and 18 for dangerous occupations (Children's Bureau Timeline, 2015).

1940: White House Conference on Children in a Democracy is held. The 700 attendees discuss and examine the well-being of children in a democracy. Of particular focus are poverty and equal opportunity (Children's Bureau Timeline, 2015).

1958: Title IV amendments require states to match federal child welfare funds if they choose to draw down funding (CWLA, 2015).

1961: President John F. Kennedy signs into law the Juvenile Delinquency and Youth Offenses Control Act (P.L. 87–274). The act provides federal assistance for projects that demonstrate or develop techniques and practices leading to solutions to control the nations delinquency control problems (P.L. 87–274, 1961).

1961: Aid to Families with Dependent Children (AFDC) Title V amendments allow states to use funds for foster care expenses if the child comes from an AFDC-eligible family and the court decides it is in the child's best interest to be removed from the home (Child Welfare League of America, 2015).

1967: Child welfare funding under Title V becomes Title IV-B, Child Welfare Services (Child Welfare League of America, 2015).

1970: White House Conference on Children and Youth is held. The elimination of racism and poverty are among the concerns discussed by the conference's 5,000 participants (Children's Bureau Timeline, 2015).

1974: The Child Abuse Prevention and Treatment Act is signed into law. The act authorized federal funds to improve and standardized state response to the physical/sexual abuse or neglect of children (Child Welfare League of America, 2015).

1978: Indian Child Welfare Act (P.L. 95–608) is signed into law. The act strengthens the role played by tribal governments in determining the custody of Indian children (Public Law 95–608, 1978).

1980: The Adoption Assistance and Child Welfare Amendments (P.L. 96–272) of 1980 is enacted. The act establishes a new Title IV-E Foster Care and Adoption Assistance entitlement program (Child Welfare League of America, 2015, 2015; Public Law 96–272, 1980).

1984: Child Abuse Amendments of 1984 (P.L. 98–457) is signed into law. The amendments seek to extend and improve provisions of laws relating to child abuse and neglect and adoption (Child Welfare Information Gateway, 2015; Public Law 98–457, 1984).

1985: Title IV-E is amended to include a new independent living program to help youth aging out of the foster care system (Child Welfare League of America, 2015).

1992: Child Abuse, Domestic Violence, Adoption, and Family Services Act of 1992 (P.L. 102–295) is signed into law. Among other provisions, the act provides federal funding to states in support of prevention, assessment, investigation, prosecution, and treatment activities (Children's Bureau Timeline, 2015; Public Law 102–295, 1992).

1993: Title IV-B is amended to create a new Family Preservation and Family Support program (Child Welfare League of America, 2015).

1994: Multiethnic Placement Act is enacted. The act prohibits child welfare agencies from denying or delaying adoptive placement on the grounds of race (Child Welfare League of America, 2015).

1996: Multiethnic Placement Act of 1994 is amended to omit any language specific to the consideration of race in placement decisions (Child Welfare League of America, 2015).

1997: Adoption and Safe Families Act is enacted. It creates timelines for moving children to permanency, as well as providing adoption incentive bonuses for states (Child Welfare League of America, 2015).

1999: The Foster Care Independence Act of 1999 (P.L. 106–169) is enacted. Authorized under Title IV-B, the act reforms and expands the independent living program (Child Welfare Information Gateway, 2015; Public Law 106–169, 1999).

1999: The Child Abuse Prevention and Enforcement Act of 2000 (P.L. 106–169) is enacted. The act seeks to reduce incidence of child abuse and neglect (Child Welfare Information Gateway, 2015; Public Law 106–169, 1999).

2003: The Keeping Children and Families Safe Act of 2003 (P.L. 108–36) is enacted. The act reauthorizes the Child Abuse Prevention and Treatment Act (CAPTA) and improves the Adoption Opportunities Act, the Abandoned Infants Assistance Act, and the Family Violence Prevention and Services Act (Child Welfare Information Gateway, 2015; Public Law 108–36, 2003).

2006: Safe and Timely Interstate Placement of Foster Children Act of 2006 (P.L. 109–239) is enacted. The act improves protections for children and holds states accountable for the safe and timely placement of children across state lines, and for other purposes (Child Welfare Information Gateway, 2015; Public Law 109–239, 2006).

2008: Fostering Connections to Success and Increasing Adoptions Act is signed into law. The act amends parts B and E of Title IV of the Social Security Act in order to support relative caregivers and improve outcomes for children and youth in foster care. The act also provided funds for tribal foster care, as well as improved incentives for adoption (Child Welfare League of America, 2015).

2018: On February 9, 2018, President Trump signed into law the bipartisan Family First Preservation Service Act. The act reforms the federal child welfare financing streams, Title IV-E, and Title IV-B of the Social Security Act to provide services to families at risk of entering the child welfare system (Torres & Mathur, 2018).

References

Allard, P. E., & Lu, L. D. (2006). *Rebuilding families and reclaiming lives: State obligation to children in foster care and their incarcerated parents*. New York, NY: Brennan Center for Justice, New York University Law School.

Alstein, H., & McRoy, R. (2000). *Does family preservation serve a child's best interest?* Washington, DC: Georgetown University Press.

Anne E. Casey Foundation. (2018a). *Kids Count Data Center: Children in foster care by race and Hispanic origin in the United States*. Retrieved from https://datacenter.kidscount.org/data/tables/6246-children-in-foster-care-by-race-and-hispanic-origin#detailed/1/any/false/871,870,573,869,36,868,867,133,38,35/2638,2601,2600,2598,2603,2597,2602,1353/12992,12993

Anne E. Casey Foundation. (2018b). Kids of color more likely to live in high-poverty neighborhood now than during the great recession. Retrieved from www.aecf.org/blog/kids-of-color-more-likely-to-live-in-high-poverty-neighborhoods-now/

Ards, S., Myers, S., Malkis, A., Sugrue, E., & Zhou, L. (2003). Racial disproportionality in reported and substantiated child abuse and neglect: An examination of systemic bias. *Children and Youth Services Review*, 25(5/6), 375–392.

Baird, C. (2005). The effect of risk assessments and their relationship to maltreatment recurrence across races. In D. Derezotes, J. Poertner, & M. Testa (Eds.), *Race matters in child welfare: The overrepresentation of African American children in the system* (pp. 131–146). Washington, DC: Child Welfare League of America.

Barbour, H., Densmore, C., Moger, E. H., Sorel, N. C., Van Wagner, A. D., & Worrall, A. J. (1995). *Quaker crosscurrents: Three hundred years of Friends in the New York yearly meetings*. Syracuse, NY: Syracuse University Press.

Barth, R. (2005). Child welfare and race: Models of disproportionality. In D. Derezotes, J. Poertner, & M. Testa (Eds.), *Race matters in child welfare: The overrepresentation of African American children in the system* (pp. 25–46). Washington, DC: Child Welfare League of America.

Bartholet, E. (1999). *Nobody's children: Abuse and neglect, foster drift, and the adoption alternative*. Boston, MA: Beacon Press.

Bartholet, E. (2009). The racial disproportionality movement in child welfare: False facts and dangerous directions. *Arizona Law Review*, 51(871), 873–932.

Boustan, L. P. (2010). Was postwar suburbanization "white flight"? Evidence from the black migration. *The Quarterly Journal of Economics*, 125(1), 417–443.

Breidenbach, R., Rollins, T., & Olson, J. (2011). *Disproportionality in child protective services: Updated results of statewide reform efforts*. Texas Department of Family and Protective Services. Retrieved from www.dfps.state.tx.us/documents/Child_Protection/pdf/2011-08-01_Disproportionality.pdf

Bruskas, D. (2008). Children in foster care: A vulnerable population at risk. *Journal of Child and Adult Psychiatric Nursing*, 21(2), 70–77.

Casey Family Programs. (2005). *Findings from the Northwest Foster care alumni study*. Retrieved from www.casey.org/media/AlumniStudies_NW_Report_FR.pdf

Children's Administration Research. (2004). *Foster youth transition to independence study: Final report: 2004*. Seattle, WA: Department of Social and Health Services. Retrieved from www.dshs.wa.gov/sites/default/files/CA/pub/documents/FYTfinal2004.pdf

Children's Bureau Centennial. (2015). *Children's Bureau timeline*. Retrieved from https://cb100.acf.hhs.gov/childrens-bureau-timeline

Children's Bureau Timeline. (2015). *Children's Bureau centennial*. Retrieved from https://cb100.acf.hhs.gov/childrens-bureau-timeline

Child Trends Data Bank. (2014). *Foster care: Indictors on children and youth*. Retrieved from www.childtrends.org/wp-content/uploads/2014/07/12_Foster_Care.pdf

Child Trends Data Bank. (2019). *Foster care*. Retrieved from www.childtrends.org/indicators/foster-care

Child Welfare Information Gateway. (2015). *Timeline of major federal legislation concerned with child protection, child welfare, and adoption*. Washington, DC: Children's Bureau, Administration for Children and Families, U.S. Department of Health and Human Services.

Child Welfare Information Gateway. (2016). *Racial disproportionality and disparity in child welfare*. Washington, DC: U.S. Department of Health and Human Services, Administration for Children and Families, Children's Bureau. Retrieved from www.childwelfare.gov/pubPDFs/racial_disproportionality.pdf

Child Welfare Information Gateway. (2020). *Foster care statistics 2018*.Washighton, DC: U.S. Department of Health and Human Services, Administration for Children and Families, Children's Bureau. Retrieved from www.childwelfare.gov/pubs/factsheets/foster/

Child Welfare League of America. (2015). *Timeline of major child welfare legislation*. Retrieved from www.cwla.org/wp-content/uploads/2014/05/TimelineOfMajorChildWelfareLegislation.pdf

Chipungu, S. S., & Bent-Goodley, T. B. (2004). Meeting the challenges of contemporary foster care. *Children, Families and Foster Care*, 14(1), 75–93.

Cohen, W. J., & Ball, R. M. (1962). Public welfare amendments of 1962 and proposals for health insurance for the aged. *Bulletin*, 3–22. Retrieved from www.socialsecurity.gov/policy/docs/ssb/v25n10/v25n10p3.pdf

Cooper, T. A. (2013). Racial bias in American foster care: The national debate. *Marquette Law Review*, 97(2), 217–277.

Costin, L. B. (1985). The historical context of child welfare. In J. Laird & A. Hartman (Eds.), *A handbook of child welfare* (pp. 34–60). New York, NY: Free Press.

Crenshaw, K. W. (1988). Race, reform and retrenchment: Transformation and legitimation in antidiscrimination law. *Harvard Law Review*, 101(7), 1331–1387.

Curtis, C. M., & Denby, R. W. (2011). African American children in the child welfare system: Requiem or reform? *Journal of Public Child Welfare*, 5(1), 111–137.

Drake, B., & Rank, M. (2009). The racial divide among American children in poverty: Reassessing the importance of neighborhood. *Children and Youth Services Review*, 31, 1264–1271.

Ellis, K. (2019). *Race and poverty bias in the child welfare: Strategies for child welfare practitioners*. American Bar Association. Retrieved from www.americanbar.org/groups/public_interest/child_law/resources/child_law_practiceonline/january-december-2019/race-and-poverty-bias-in-the-child-welfare-system-strategies-f/

Fluke, J., Yuan, Y., Hedderson, J., & Curtis, P. (2003). Disproportionate representation of race and ethnicity in child maltreatment: Investigation and victimization. *Children and Youth Services Review*, 25(5/6), 359–373.

Ganasarajah, S., & Siegel, G. (2017). Disproportionality rates for children of color in foster care, 2015. *National Council of Juvenile and Family Court Judges*. Retrieved from www.ncjfcj.org/wp-content/uploads/2017/09/NCJFCJ-Disproportionality-TAB-2015_0.pdf

Geen, R. (Ed.). (2003). *Kinship care: Making the most of a valuable resource*. Washington, DC: Urban Institute.

Gelles. R. J. (1996). *The book of David: How preserving families can cost children's lives*. New York, NY: Basic Books.

Gingrich, N. (1994). *A contract with America*. Evanston, IL: McDougal Littell.

Glaze, L. E., & Maruschak, L. M. (2008). *Parents in prison and their minor children*. U.S. Bureau of Justice Statistics. Retrieved from www.bjs.gov/content/pub/pdf/pptmc.pdf

Goerge, R., & Lee, B. (2005). The entry of children from the welfare system into foster care: Differences by race. In D. Derezotes, J. Poertner, & M. Testa (Eds.), *Race matters in child welfare: The overrepresentation of African American children in the system* (pp. 173–186). Washington, DC: Child Welfare League of America.

Golden, O., & Macomber, J. (2009). The Adoption and Safe Families Act. In *A look back at the Adoption and Safe Families Act* (pp. 8–34). Washington, DC: Center for the Study of Social Policy and Urban Institute.

Gryzlak, B., Wells, S., & Johnson, M. (2005). The role of race in child protective services screening decisions. In D. Derezotes, J. Poertner, & M. Testa (Eds.), *Race matters in child welfare: The overrepresentation of African American children in the system* (pp. 63–96). Washington, DC: Child Welfare League of America.

Hartley, E. K. (1984). Government leadership to protect children from foster care drift. *Child Abuse and Neglect*, 8(3), 337–342.

Hill, R. B. (2006). Synthesis of research on disproportionality in child welfare: An update. *CSSP-Casey Alliance for Racial Equity*. Retrieved from www.cssp.org/reform/child-welfare/other-resources/synthesis-of-research-on-disproportionality-robert-hill.pdf

Irvine, A., & Canfield, A. (2016). The overrepresentation of lesbian, gay, bisexual, questioning, gender non-conforming and transgender youth within the child welfare to the juvenile justice crossover population. *Journal of Gender, Social Policy & the Law*, 24(2), 243–261.

Johnson, R. (2014). *Historical statistics on adoption in the United States, plus statistics on child population and welfare*. Retrieved from www.johnstonsarchive.net/policy/adoptionstats.html

Kempe, C. H., Silverman, F. N., Steel, B. F., Droegemueller, W., & Silver, H. K. (1962). The battered child syndrome. *Journal of the American Medical Association*, 181, 17–24.

Lane, W., Rubin, D., Monteith, R., & Christian, C. (2002). Racial differences in the evaluation of pediatric fractures for physical abuse. *Journal of the American Medical Association*, 288(13), 1603–1609.

Lu, Y. E., Landsverk, J., Ellis-MacLeod, E., Newton, R., Ganger, W., & Johnson, I. (2004). Race, ethnicity and case outcomes in child protective services. *Children and Youth Services Review*, 26(5), 447–461.

Lyle, C. G. (2003). *Structured decision making, race, and racial disparity in Ramsey County maltreatment reporting*. St. Paul, MN: Ramsey County Community Human Services Department, Office of Performance Measurement & Evaluation.

McDonald, H. (1994). The ideology of family preservation. *National Affairs*, 115, 46–60.

McGowan, B. G. (2005). Historical evolution of child welfare services. In G. P. Mallon & P. M. Hess (Eds.), *Child welfare for the 21st century: A handbook for practices, policies, and programs* (pp. 10–46). New York, NY: Columbia University Press.

McRoy, R. G. (2005). Overrepresentation of children and youth of color in foster care. In G. P. Mallon & P. McCartt Hess (Eds.), *Child welfare for the 21st century: A handbook of practices, policies, and programs* (pp. 623–634). New York, NY: Columbia University Press.

Miller v. Youakim. (1979). Miller v. Youakim, 44 U.S. 125. Retrieved from https://supreme.justia.com/cases/federal/us/440/125/

MST Services. (2019). *Is racial bias still a problem in child welfare*. Retrieved from https://info.mstservices.com/blog/racial-bias-problem-child-welfare

Myers, J. E. B. (2007). A short history of child protection in America. *Family Law Quarterly*, 449–463.

Myers, J. E. B. (2008). A short history of child protection in America. *Family Law Quarterly*, 449–463.

National Association of Black Social Workers. (1972). *National Association of Black Social Workers position statement on transracial adoptions*. New York, NY: Author. Retrieved from http://c.ymcdn.com/sites/nabsw.org/resource/

collection/E1582D77-E4CD-4104-996A-D42D08F9CA7D/NABSW_Trans-Racial_Adoption_1972_Position_(b).pdf

National Conference of State Legislators. (2020a). *Disproportionality and disparity in child welfare*. Retrieved from www.ncsl.org/research/human-services/disproportionality-and-disparity-in-child-welfare.aspx

National Conference of State Legislators. (2020b). *Family First Prevention Service Act*. Retrieved from www.ncsl.org/research/human-services/family-first-prevention-services-act-ffpsa.aspx

National Indian Child Welfare Association. (2019). *2019 Report on disproportionality of placement of Indian children*. Retrieved from www.nicwa.org/wp-content/uploads/2019/08/Disproportionality-Table-2019.pdf

Needell, B., Brookhart, A., & Lee, S. (2003). Black children and foster care placement in California. *Children and Youth Services Review*, 25(5/6), 393–408.

New York Society for the Prevention of Cruelty to Children. (2015). *History of the NYSPCC*. Retrieved from www.nyspcc.org/about-the-new-york-society-for-the-prevention-of-cruelty-to-children/history/

Osgood, D. W., Foster, E. M., & Courtney, M. E. (2010). Vulnerable populations and the transition to adulthood. *Future for Children*, 20, 209–229.

Otto, R. K., & Melton, G. B. (1995). Trends in legislation and case law on child abuse and neglect. In R. T. Ammermund & M. Herson (Eds.), *Children at risk: An evaluation of factors contributing to child abuse and neglect* (pp. 55–83). New York, NY: Plenum.

Padilla, J., & Summers, A. (2011). *Disproportionality rates for children of color in foster care*. National Council of Juvenile and Family Court Judges. Reno, NV: University of Nevada. Retrieved from www.ncjfcj.org/sites/default/files/Disproportionality%20TAB1_0.pdf

Park, J. M., Metraux, S., & Culhane, D. P. (2004). Child welfare involvement among homeless children. *Child Welfare*, 83, 423–437.

Pears, K. C., Bruce, J., Fisher, P. A., & Kim, H. K. (2010). Indiscriminate friendliness in maltreated foster children. *Child Development*, 15, 64–75.

Pelton, L. (1989). *For reasons of poverty: A critical analysis of the public child welfare systems in the United States*. New York, NY: Prager.

Phagan-Hansel, K. (2018). One million adoptions later: Adoption and Safe Families Act at 20. *The Imprint Youth & Family News*. Retrieved from https://imprintnews.org/adoption/one-million-adoptions-later-adoption-safe-families-act-at-20/32582

Platt, A. (1969). The rise of the child saving movement: A study in social policy and correctional reform. *Annals of the American Academy of Political and Social Science*, 381, 21–38.

Public Law 87–274. (1961). Retrieved from www.gpo.gov/fdsys/pkg/STATUTE-75/pdf/STATUTE-75-Pg572.pdf

Public Law 93–247. (1974). *Government Printing Office*. Retrieved from http://uscode.house.gov/statutes/pl/93/247.pdf

Public Law 95–608. (1978). *Government Printing Office*. Retrieved from www.ssa.gov/OP_Home/comp2/F095-608.html

Public Law 96–272. (1980). Retrieved from http://uscode.house.gov/statutes/pl/96/272.pdf

Public Law 98–457. (1984). Retrieved from www.brockport.edu/library/help/socpol/pl9845a.pdf

Public Law 102–295. (1992). Retrieved from www.brockport.edu/library/help/socpol/pl1022a.pdf

Public Law 106–169. (1999). H.R. 3443 (106th): Foster Care Independence Act of 1999. Retrieved from www.govtrack.us/congress/bills/106/hr3443

Public Law 108–36. (2003). *Government Printing Office*. Retrieved from www.acf.hhs.gov/sites/default/files/cb/capta2003.pdf

Public Law 109–239. (2006). *Government Printing Office*. Retrieved from www.hunter.cuny.edu/socwork/nrcfcpp/downloads/PL109-239.pdf

Puzzanchera, C., & Taylor, M. (2020). Disproportionality rates for children of color in foster care dashboard. *National Council of Juvenile and Family Court Judges*. Retrieved from http://ncjj.org/AFCARS/Disproportionality_Dashboard.aspx

Raimon, M. L., & Weber, K. (2015). Better outcomes for older youth of color in foster care. *The Center for the Study of Social Policy*. Retrieved from https://cssp.org/wp-content/uploads/2019/04/Better-Outcomes-for-Older-Youth-of-Color-in-Foster-Care.pdf

Rendleman, D. R. (1971). Parens patriae: From chancery to juvenile court. *South Carolina Law Review*, 23, 205–259.

Roberts, D. E. (2001). *Shattered bonds: The color of child welfare*. New York, NY: Basic Civitas Books.

Roberts, D. E. (2012). Prison, foster care, and the systemic punishment of Black mothers. *UCLA Law Review*, 1476–1499.

Roediger, D. R. (2006). *Working toward whiteness: How America's immigrants became white: The strange journey from Ellis Island to the suburbs*. New York, NY: Basic Books.

Sabol, W., Coulton, C., & Pouousky, E. (2004). Measuring child maltreatment risk in communities: A life table approach. *Child Abuse & Neglect*, 28, 967–983.

Schene, P. A. (1998). Past, present, and the future roles of child protective services. *The Future of Children*, 8(1), 23–38.

Schiff, C. (1997). Child custody and the ideal motherhood in the late nineteenth-century New York. *Georgetown Journal of Fighting Poverty*, 4, 403–420.

Sedlak, A. J., & Broadhurst, D. D. (1996). *Third National Incidence Study of Child Abuse and Neglect (NIS-3)*. Washington, DC: U.S. Department of Health and Human Services.

Sedlak, A. J., McPherson, K., & Das, B. (2010). *Supplementary analyses of race differences in child maltreatment rates in the NIS-4*. Washington, DC: U.S. Department of Health and Human Services. Retrieved from www.acf.hhs.gov/sites/default/files/opre/nis4_supp_analysis_race_diff_mar2010.pdf

Seelye, K. Q. (1997, November 17). Clinton to approve sweeping shift in adoption. *New York Times*. Retrieved from www.nytimes.com/1997/11/17/us/clinton-to-approve-sweeping-shift-in-adoption.html

Skocpol, T. (1995). *Protecting soldiers and mothers: The political origins of social policy in the United States*. Cambridge, MA: Harvard University Press.

Smith, C., & Devore, W. (2004). African American children in the child welfare and kinship system: From exclusion to over-inclusion. *Children and Youth Service Review*, 26(5), 427–446.

Social Service Administration. (2015). *Compilation of the social security laws*. Retrieved from www.ssa.gov/OP_Home/ssact/title04/0400.htm

Spar, K., & Shuman, M. (2004). *Child welfare: Implementation of the Adoption and Safe Families Act (P.L. 105–89)*. Congressional Research Services. Retrieved from http://greenbook.waysandmeans.house.gov/sites/greenbook.waysandmeans.house.gov/files/2012/RL30759_gb.pdf

Stoltzfus, E. (2005). *Race/ethnicity and child welfare*. Washington, DC: Congressional Research Services. Retrieved from http://66.227.70.18/programs/culture/memo050825race.pdf

Torres, K., & Mathur, R. (2018). Fact sheet: Family first prevention act. *First Focus Campaign for Children*. Retrieved from https://campaignforchildren.org/resources/fact-sheet/fact-sheet-family-first-prevention-services-act/

Trammell, R. S. (2009). Orphan trains myths and legal realities. *The Modern American*, 3–13. Retrieved from www.wcl.american.edu/modernamerican/documents/Trammell.pdf

Trattner, W. I. (1999). *From poor law to welfare state: A history of social welfare in America* (6th ed.). New York, NY: The Free Press.

U.S. Census Bureau. (2009). *S0901. Children characteristics from the 2008 America Community Survey data set*. Retrieved from http://factfinder.census.gov/faces/tableservices/jsf/pages/productview.xhtml?src=bkmk

U.S. Department of Health and Human Services. (2005). *Child maltreatment, 2003*. Washington, DC: U.S. Government Printing Office.

U.S. Government Printing Office. (2008). *Hearing on racial disproportionality in foster care.tz* Subcommittee on Income Security and Family Support of the Committee on Ways and Means U.S. House of Representatives. Retrieved from www.gpo.gov/fdsys/pkg/CHRG-110hhrg48117/html/CHRG-110hhrg48117.htm

Vig, S., Chinitz, S., & Shulman, L. (2005). Young children in foster care: Multiple vulnerabilities and complex service needs. *Infants & Young Children*, 18(2), 147–160.

Weisman, M. L. (1994). When parents are not in the best interest of the child. *The Atlantic Online*. Retrieved from www.theatlantic.com/past/docs/issues/96apr/orphan/weisorp.htm

White, C. (2006). Federally mandated destruction of the Black family: The adoption and safe families. *Northwestern Journal of Law and Social Policy*, 1(12), 303–337.

Wulczyn, F. (2003). Closing the gap: Are changing exit patterns reducing the time African American children spend in foster care relative to Caucasian children? *Children and Youth Service Review*, 25, 431–462.

Wulczyn, F. (2004). Family reunification. *The Future of Children*, 14(1), 95–114.

Wulczyn, F., Barth, R., Yuan, Y., Jones-Harden, B., & Landsverk, J. (2005). *Beyond common sense: Child welfare, child well-being and the evidence for policy reform*. New Brunswick, NJ: Aldine Transaction.

Index

9780367903091